Introduction to
CORRECTIONS

I dedicate this book to the late Dr. Harold Williamson. From one TDC boss to another, you were a man for all seasons. Thank you for the guidance during your last few years with us.

I dedicate this text to the Eastham UC. Through thick and thin, I could always count on you.

I dedicate this text to my brother, Sgt. Guy Hanser, with the Texas Department of Criminal Justice — Institutional Division. I am proud of you and the work that you do.

Lastly but most importantly, I also dedicate this text to all the men and women who work, have worked, and will eventually work in the field of corrections, whether institutional or community-based. Your dedication to public safety and fair-minded actions under stressful circumstances is appreciated. All of us are depending on you.

Introduction to
CORRECTIONS

ROBERT D. HANSER
University of Louisiana at Monroe

Los Angeles | London | New Delhi
Singapore | Washington DC

Los Angeles | London | New Delhi
Singapore | Washington DC

FOR INFORMATION:

SAGE Publications, Inc.
2455 Teller Road
Thousand Oaks, California 91320
E-mail: order@sagepub.com

SAGE Publications Ltd.
1 Oliver's Yard
55 City Road
London EC1Y 1SP
United Kingdom

SAGE Publications India Pvt. Ltd.
B 1/I 1 Mohan Cooperative Industrial Area
Mathura Road, New Delhi 110 044
India

SAGE Publications Asia-Pacific Pte. Ltd.
3 Church Street
#10-04 Samsung Hub
Singapore 049483

Acquisitions Editor: Jerry Westby
Editorial Assistant: MaryAnn Vail
Assistant Editor: Rachael Leblond
Production Editor: Laura Stewart
Copy Editor: Melinda Masson
Typesetter: C&M Digitals (P) Ltd.
Proofreader: Stefanie Storholt
Indexer: Michael Ferreira
Cover Designer: Karine Hovsepian
Marketing Manager: Terra Schultz
Permissions Editor: Karen Ehrmann

Printed in Canada

Library of Congress Cataloging-in-Publication Data

Hanser, Robert D.
Introduction to corrections / Robert D. Hanser.

p. cm.
Includes bibliographical references and index.

ISBN 978-1-4129-7566-7 (pbk.)

1. Corrections. 2. Corrections—United States. I. Title.

HV8665.H36 2013
364.6—dc23   2012017344

This book is printed on acid-free paper.

12 13 14 15 16 10 9 8 7 6 5 4 3 2 1

MIX
Paper from
responsible sources
FSC® C011825
FSC
www.fsc.org

Brief Table of Contents

Table of Contents

Preface

This text is intended to provide the reader with a view of corrections that is both practitioner-driven and grounded in modern research and theoretical origins. Though this text does integrate research and theory within its pages, its specific strength is the practicality and realism provided in describing and explaining today's world of corrections. This single aspect of the text, along with its insightful portrayal of prison logic, subcultural issues in prison, and the emphasis on persons who work within the field, both institutional and community-based, is what sets this text apart from others in the correctional textbook market.

Video Link
Watch a video of the author as he introduces this text.

While this text does integrate the world of the practitioner with theoretical aspects, it is important to note that this is not a theory text. Rather, this text illustrates how the day-to-day practitioner conducts business in the field of corrections, including both institutional and community settings. At the same time, theoretical applications are made explicit to demonstrate to the student that contemporary punishment, incarceration, and supervision schemes are grounded in theories that are often otherwise overlooked. Indeed, this text shows that theory and the practical world do not have to be disjointed and disconnected from one another. Rather, each can serve to augment the other, and, in this text, each aspect provides the student with additional facets of *how* correctional practice is implemented (reflecting the world of the practitioner) and *why* it is implemented in that manner (rooted in theoretical perspectives).

This text is intended to serve as a stand-alone text for undergraduate students in introductory courses on correction, correctional systems, and/or correctional practices. A special effort is made to tie the readings to practical uses that the majority of our students will encounter in the world of work. This includes discussions on qualifications of specific types of officers, stressors confronted in daily correctional work, examples of tools and instruments that are used in the field, and so forth. The organization of the book follows a logical flow through the system, including the historical development of punishment and corrections; jail facilities and operations, pretrial release, and diversion; the use of probation and intermediate sanctions; legal issues; theoretical underpinnings; correctional facility design and layout; inmate and officer subcultures; specialized offenders such as women, offenders with mental challenges, and juveniles; correctional administration; education and work programming; substance abuse treatment; religious and recreational programming; parole and reintegration; the death penalty; and evaluation and best practices in corrections. In short, this text covers the full array of topics related to nearly any aspect of corrections, on an introductory level, of course.

In addition, the role of technology has been highlighted throughout this text. Indeed, each chapter has a specific *Technology & Equipment* section that highlights some type of development in technology or equipment that is used within the field of corrections. These sections, along with other areas of focus within other chapters throughout the text, provide the student with an idea of how the correctional industry has developed and continues to develop and adapt to the changing demands that exist when working with the offender population. The role of technology in security processes, assessment/classification/case management, intermediate sanctions, drug testing, medical procedures, and other correctional processes is highlighted throughout this text. This again provides a practitioner focus as the student becomes familiar with the tools and equipment used by people who work in this segment of the criminal justice system. Further, this allows the student to see how corrections has evolved into a profession that uses state-of-the-art technology applications.

Finally, this text is also unique in one other critical aspect. The data, figures, tables, and various programs showcased in this text are predominantly drawn from federal government documents and briefings. Thus, the data and programs selected are solid and tend to be of better quality than one might typically use. Federal research by the National Institute of Corrections abounds that examines many issues in corrections, and the right to public domain of much of this material has allowed the author to integrate it within the pages of this text. This provides for rich data and examples that are guaranteed to aid in student learning. Further, the sources have been subjected to rigorous scrutiny and consideration, ensuring that all information is valid and up to date.

APPROACH AND STRUCTURE OF THE TEXT

Significantly and perhaps uniquely, this text not only connects the practical world of corrections to the theoretical, but it also connects treatment and security aspects in the field of corrections to show the dichotomous connection between these two types of approaches in offender management. Further, the practical aspects of this text are reinforced with specific exercises that are included where students themselves apply and synthesize the various concepts found throughout the chapters. In providing this content, this text consists of 19 chapters that cover all the basic aspects of correctional systems and practices. These chapters are summarized as follows:

Chapter 1: Early History and Evolution of Punishment and Corrections

This chapter of the text serves as an introduction to and overview of the historical development of corrections in Europe and the United States. This includes a brief overview of the philosophical underpinnings of punishment and how they apply to the use of various forms of incarceration as well as alternative sanctions in the community. Included in this chapter is history of the development of sanctions as well as an overview of many classic figures in the history of corrections, to include Charles Montesquieu, Cesare Beccaria, William Penn, and John Howard, among others.

Chapter 2: The Development of Prisons in the United States

This chapter provides a detailed discussion of prisons in the United States. From the earliest prison used in the original 13 colonies to modern-day maximum-security facilities, the development of prisons and prison systems at both the state and federal levels is discussed. The Pennsylvania system, the Auburn system, southern penology, the reformatory era, and the use of the Big Houses are all discussed. Different models of correctional operation are provided as well as a brief overview of modern-day prison facilities.

Chapter 3: Ideological and Theoretical Underpinnings to Corrections

This chapter revisits the purpose of corrections as a process whereby practitioners from a variety of agencies and programs use tools, techniques, and facilities to engage in organized security and treatment functions intended to correct criminal tendencies among the offender population. It is with this purpose in mind that a variety of philosophical underpinnings are presented, including retribution, incapacitation, deterrence, rehabilitation, restorative justice, and reintegration. Discussion regarding the use of incarceration as a primary tool of punishment is provided; community-based sanctions are given extensive coverage; the death penalty is presented as the most serious sanction available, and its utility and effectiveness are put to serious question in this chapter. Lastly, types of sentencing models as well as disparities in both prison and death penalty sentences are highlighted. In discussing the issue of disparity, the distinction between disparity and discrimination is made clear.

Chapter 4: Correctional Law and Legal Liabilities

This chapter demonstrates how, during recent correctional history in America, there has been a constant interplay between state-level correctional systems and the federal courts. Amidst this evolution of correctional operations in America, the interpretation of constitutional standards has been the central feature of this change as well as the Supreme Court's interpretation of its own role in ensuring that those standards are met. The distinctions between federal suits and state suits are clarified. Lastly, a brief overview of injunctions and other forms of court-oriented remediation is presented. These actions are what ultimately led to the sweeping changes that we have seen in the field of corrections.

Chapter 5: Jail and Detention Facilities

Jail facilities are presented as complicated facilities that are not usually appreciated for the vital role that they play within the criminal justice system. The different types of tasks, such as the holding of persons prior to their court date, providing a series of unique sentencing variations, and the incarceration of persons who are technically part of the larger prison system, are all considered. The problems and challenges for jail facilities can be quite varied, and this creates a demanding situation for jail staff and administrators. Overall, jails have been given short shrift in the world of corrections, but they are one feature of corrections that will be given much more attention in times to come.

Chapter 6: Probation

The evolution of probation beginning with recognizance and suspended sentences through modern-day uses is presented. This chapter also includes a variety of different types of probation administrative models that include not only the qualifications of officers but the supervisory strategies and responsibilities of offenders. Presentence investigation reports as well as revocation and legal procedures are also included.

Chapter 7: Intermediate Sanctions

This chapter provides an overview of several types of intermediate sanctions that are used around the country. The use of community partnerships is again emphasized. Various intermediate sanctions, such as community service, the payment of fines, intensive supervision, GPS monitoring, home detention, and day reporting centers, are discussed. Together with community involvement, agency collaboration, and solid case management processes, intermediate sanctions are shown to be a key interlocking supervision mechanism that improves the overall goal of public safety.

Chapter 8: Correctional Facilities

This chapter demonstrates that the physical features of a prison require forethought that occurs before the ground is even broken at the construction site. Issues related to the location of the prison facility, the types of custody levels and security, the function of the facility, logistical support for the facility, and institutional services (such as laundry, kitchen, and religious services) are all important considerations. Technological developments and improvements in security, including cell block and electric fence construction, are presented.

Chapter 9: Classification and Custody Levels

Effective classification is presented as an essential aspect of both security needs and the needs of the inmate. This chapter discusses Alexander Maconochie's impact on correctional classification processes through his mark system. It shows as well that classification processes are important for both security and treatment purposes.

Chapter 10: Prison Subculture and Prison Gang Influence

This chapter provides a glimpse of the "behind the scenes" aspects of the prison environment. The notion of a prison subculture, complete with norms and standards that are counter to those of the outside world, is presented. The effects of professionalism within the correctional officer ranks, the diversity of correctional staff, and the difference in this generation of inmates all have led to changes in the inmate subculture in modern times. Gangs have emerged as a major force in state prison systems. From this chapter, it is clear that prison gangs have networks that extend beyond the prison walls.

Chapter 11: Female Offenders in Correctional Systems

Female offenders, though a small proportion of the correctional population, are rapidly growing in number. The need for improved services and programming for female offenders is discussed in this chapter. The importance of mother-child programming is presented as critical to female offender reformation. Legal issues specific to female offenders are discussed, and guiding principles to improve female offender reentry are provided.

Chapter 12: Specialized Inmate Populations

In this section, we include a discussion on the supervisory strategies used for a special offender population, which includes sex offenders, substance abusers, mentally ill offenders, and mentally retarded offenders. This growing population in the community offers special concerns for community safety and strategies to supervise. This section addresses some of these issues as well as providing suggestions for effective supervisory strategies.

Chapter 13: Juvenile Correctional Systems

In this chapter, a very brief overview of both institutional and community-based supervision strategies used for juvenile offenders is presented. These include detention, probation, residential programs, juvenile aftercare, and even adult prisons when youth are tried as adults. Legal developments in juvenile justice are discussed. Additional topics include types of abuse and neglect of youth, the juvenile court system, the role of juvenile records, child protective services, and youth gangs.

Chapter 14: Correctional Administration

This chapter provides an overview of the organizational structure of both the federal and state prison systems in the United States. Styles of management and the delegation of responsibility are discussed. The rise of women in the field of corrections is presented. Private prison management is included in this chapter along with the conclusion that such programs can be quite successful. Lastly, emergency response issues along with emergency response management are discussed in this chapter.

Chapter 15: Prison Education, Work, and Basic Services and Programming

This chapter provides an extensive overview of many of the typical programs offered to inmates within the prison environment. Educational, vocational, drug treatment, medical, recreational, food service, and religious programs are all presented. Prison programming is shown to be effective in inmate management and also to produce positive benefits for offender reentry. Thus, prison education, work, and other forms of programming have public safety benefits.

Chapter 16: Therapeutic, Recreational, and Religious Programming

In this chapter, students are provided an extensive overview of many of the typical programs offered to inmates within the prison environment. Programs discussed include drug treatment, recreational, and religious services. Like the programming presented in Chapter 15, these types of programs are effective tools for inmate behavior management, and they produce positive outcomes in offender reentry initiatives. These programs are also linked to lowered rates of recidivism among offenders upon release and, therefore, also provide public safety benefits to society beyond the confines of the prison walls.

Chapter 17: Parole and Reintegration

This chapter provides an overview of the evolution of parole to its modern-day usage. Early historical figures attributed to the development of parole, such as Sir Walter Crofton and Alexander Maconochie, are noted. This chapter also includes a variety of different types of parole administrative models that include not only the qualifications of officers but the supervisory strategies and responsibilities of offenders. The use of prerelease planning and mechanisms, along with the parole board and revocation, is also included. The controversial nature of parole and other early-release mechanisms is discussed.

Chapter 18: The Death Penalty

This chapter provides students with an understanding of the reasons and justifications that are commonly touted for implementation of the death penalty as well as typical criticisms that are leveled toward the use of this sanction. Further, the means by which the death penalty is implemented, as well as the types of offenses and offenders likely to receive the death penalty, are also presented. Disparities in the use of the death penalty are examined.

Chapter 19: Program Evaluation, Evidence-Based Practices, and Future Trends in Corrections

This chapter illustrates the importance of evaluative research and distinguishes between process and outcome measures. The use of the assessment-evaluative cycle in corrections is discussed. Evidence-based practices are presented as a measure of both agency effectiveness and willingness to excel in service delivery. A variety of future trends in correctional practice are presented during the last few pages of this chapter.

PEDAGOGICAL AIDS AND ANCILLARIES

A number of pedagogical aids have been included in each chapter of this text. Their primary goal is to facilitate student learning and to aid the student in synthesizing the learning goal and applying it to the modern world of corrections. Through these added features, specific theories are identified and linked to a specific point in the correctional setting. Also, cross-national perspectives are provided within each chapter to acquaint the student with applications that exist in other nations around the globe. In addition, this text has a number of ancillaries that accompany it, all as a means of further improving student learning. The pedagogical features and ancillaries associated with this text are listed below:

- *Chapter learning objectives*: At the beginning of each chapter is a set of learning objectives. These learning objectives serve as cues for the student and also provide for easy assessment of learning for the instructor. These points are germane to the chapter and prompt the student as to the information that will be covered. They also let the student know what is critical to the text readings.

- *Focus Topics*: Many chapters include Focus Topic boxes that provide additional insight regarding specific points in the chapter. The Focus Topics typically help to add depth and detail to a particular subject that is considered important or interesting, from a learning perspective. The inclusion of these boxes has been done with care and consideration to ensure that the material does indeed reinforce the learning objectives at the beginning of each chapter.

- *Applied Theory inserts*: Within most chapters, Applied Theory inserts are included. These inserts provide clear and focused application of a specific theory to a particular issue or set of issues in community corrections. This is an important feature because many textbooks fail to navigate the disconnection that seems to exist between the world of theory and the world of the practitioner. These inserts bridge the two worlds and also highlight issues specific to the chapter from a theoretical perspective.

- *Technology & Equipment inserts*: Also within most chapters is an insert that showcases some type of technological development in the field of corrections or some type of tool or equipment germane to work in the field. This provides the student with an additional glimpse of the practitioner's world through the examination of the working tools of the trade. This also provides the student with an awareness of the many developments that have occurred and continue to occur within the field of corrections.

- *Corrections and the Law inserts*: In each chapter, students will find legal inserts that explain, in detail, some type of important legal issue or Supreme Court ruling that is associated with the topic of the chapter. This again shows the student how the field of corrections is constantly changing and also provides the student with additional insight regarding the legal concerns and considerations experienced by many correctional administrators.

- *Key Terms*: At the end of each chapter is a list of key terms. These key terms help to augment information relevant to the chapter learning objectives. The terms are in bold throughout the text and are included in the glossary.

- *Discussion Questions*: At the end of each chapter is a list of 5 to 7 discussion questions. These discussion questions usually ask students about chapter content that is germane to the learning objectives found at the beginning of each chapter. In this way, they serve the function of reinforcing specific knowledge that is applicable to the learning objectives and further clarify for the student the main points and concepts included therein.

- *"What Would You Do?" exercises*: At the close of each chapter, these exercises present some sort of modern-day correctional scenario that the student must address. In each case, a problem is presented to students, and they must explain what they would do to resolve the issue or solve the problem. This feature provides an opportunity for students to apply and synthesize the material from the chapter and ensures that higher-order learning of the material takes place.

- *Applied Exercise features*: These assignments require the student to perform some type of activity that integrates the material in the text with the hands-on world of the practitioner. In some cases, these assignments require that the student interview practitioners in the field, while in other cases students may need to utilize specific tools or instruments when addressing an issue in corrections. In each case, the student is required to demonstrate understanding of a particular aspect of the chapter readings and must also demonstrate competence in using the information, techniques, or processes that he or she has learned from the chapter. These exercises often also require the student to incorporate information from prior chapters or other exercises in the text, thereby building upon the prior base of knowledge that the student has accumulated throughout the text.

- *Cross-National Perspective segments*: Within each chapter, these additions provide a brief examination of a related topic in corrections as it applies to a country other than the United States. In addition to a brief write-up on the subject, students are provided website information to read further on the cross-national topic, and they are also encouraged to consider the implications of the cross-national perspective through critical thinking questions at the end of the segment.

- *Text glossary*: A glossary of key terms is included at the end of the text. These key terms are necessary to ensure that students understand the basics of corrections. Definitions are provided in simple but thorough language.

To enhance this text and to assist in the use of this book, a variety of different ancillaries have been created. Each of these is briefly described below.

- *The interactive features of this text*. This text is one of several by SAGE that strive to give the text its own sense of life through the use of various media and online resources that enhance the reading of the text, particularly online.

- *Instructor Teaching Site* . A variety of instructor's materials are available at www.sagepub.com/ hanserintro. For each chapter, this includes a complete set of test questions, PowerPoint slides, discussion questions, sample syllabi, SAGE journal articles and links to video, audio, reference, and web resources.

- *Student Study Site*. The open-access student study site, available at www.sagepub.com/hanserintro, provides access to several study tools including eFlashcards and web quizzes, as well as links to the SAGE journal articles, video clips, audio clips, reference articles, state rankings documents, and web resources mentioned within the text.

Acknowledgments

At this time, I would like to first thank the Executive Editor Jerry Westby. Jerry's continued support and faith in this project have been an inspiration and are greatly appreciated, as are those efforts and the support of Denise Simon, who has been instrumental in assisting with the organization of the text and development of the overall product. These individuals were able to maintain a three-way dialogue between the authors, editors, and reviewers, which resulted in this text being a top-notch product, both in content and in delivery.

I would like to extend special gratitude to all of the correctional practitioners who carry out the daily tasks of our correctional system, whether institutional or community-based. These individuals deserve the highest praise as they work in a field that is demanding and undervalued—I thank you all for the contributions that you make to our society.

I would also like to thank Secretary LeBlanc of the Louisiana Department of Public Safety and Corrections as well as Ms. Pam Laborde, Communications Director for the Louisiana DPS&C, and all those who allowed me to interview and showcase various elements of that state's correctional system. In addition, Warden Burl Cain and Assistant Warden Cathy Fontenot deserve thanks and gratitude for allowing the filming and photo shots at Louisiana State Penitentiary Angola.

In addition, I would like to thank Mr. Billy McConnell and Mr. Clay McConnell, Warden Keith Deville, and other personnel and staff of LaSalle Southwest Corrections. Their support for this text and willingness to interview, allow filming, and photo shots at Richwood Correctional Center added a very unique, useful, and educational element to the text.

I am also grateful to the many reviewers who spent time reading the document and making a considerable number of recommendations that helped to shape the final product (see below). Every effort was made to incorporate those ideas. Their suggestions and insights helped to improve the final product that you see here, a product that, in truth, is a reflection of all those who were involved throughout its development.

Gaylene Armstrong, Sam Houston State University

Kelly Asmussen, Peru State College, Nebraska

Jack Atherton, Northwestern State University, Louisiana

Jeri Barnett, Virginia Western Community College

Debra Baskin, Cal State Los Angeles/Rio Hondo College

Lindsey Bergeron, Nova Southeastern University

Ashley G. Blackburn, University of North Texas

Kristie Blevins, University of North Carolina Charlotte

Michael Botts, Arkansas State University

Pauline Brennan, University of Nebraska, Omaha

Mark Brown, University of South Carolina

Brenda Chappell, University of Central Oklahoma

Roger Cunningham, Eastern Illinois University

Marie Griffin, Arizona State University

Jennifer Grimes, Indiana State University, Terre Haute

Ricky S. Gutierrez, California State University, Sacramento

Zachary Hamilton, Washington State University

Howard Henderson, Sam Houston State University

Pati Hendrickson, Tarleton State University

Carly Hilinski, Grand Valley State University, Michigan

Robert Homant, University of Detroit

Rob Huckabee, Indiana State University

Martha Hurley, The Citadel

Polly Johnson, Austin Community College

David Keys, New Mexico University

Janine Kremling, California State University, San Bernardino

Jessie Krienert, Illinois State University

Margaret Leigey, Cal State University Chico

Richard Lemke, University of West Georgia

Cathy Levey, Goodwin College, Connecticut

Robert McCabe, Old Dominion University

Danielle McDonald, Northern Kentucky University

Michael Montgomery, Tennessee State University

Alfredo Montalvo, Emporia State University

Robert Morris, University of Texas at Dallas

Robert Peetz, Midland College

O. Elmer Polk, University of Texas at Dallas

Karla Pope, Mississippi Gulf Coast Community College

Magnus Seng, Loyola University-Chicago

Diane Sjuts, Metropolitan State Community College

Quanda Stevenson, University of Alabama

Sheryl Van Horne, Widener University

Lindsey Vigesaa, Nova Southeastern University

Brenda Vose, University of North Florida

Arnold Waggoner, Rose State College

Ted Wallman, University of North Florida

About the Author

Robert D. Hanser is an associate professor and head of the Department of Criminal Justice at the University of Louisiana at Monroe. Rob has also administered a regional training academy in northeastern Louisiana (North Delta Regional Training Academy) that provides training to correctional officers, jailers, and law enforcement throughout a 12-parish region in Louisiana. He is also the program director of the Blue Walters Substance Abuse Treatment Program at Richwood Correctional Center, a prison-based substance abuse treatment program in Louisiana. Further, Rob is the lead facilitator for the 4th Judicial District's Batterer Intervention Program (BIP) and serves on the Board of Directors for the Louisiana Coalition Against Domestic Violence. He likewise serves as the board president for Freedmen, Inc., a faith-based organization that provides reentry services for offenders in Louisiana. Lastly, he is the board president and CEO of North Delta Human Services Authority (NDHSA), which is a nonprofit organization that provides contract therapeutic services for the 4th Judicial District Adult Drug Court and DWI Court in Northeast Louisiana. He has dual licensure as a professional counselor in Texas and Louisiana, is a certified anger resolution therapist, and has a specialty license in addictions counseling.

chapter 1

Early History and Evolution of Punishment and Corrections

LEARNING OBJECTIVES:

1. Discuss the similarities and differences between punishment and corrections.

2. Identify various forms of punishments used in ancient and medieval times.

3. Identify early historical developments in the use of punishment and corrections.

4. Discuss how religion has played a part in the development of corrections in the United States.

5. Identify key persons who shaped the field of corrections.

6. Discuss some of the justifications behind the use of punishment and corrections.

INTRODUCTION

Defining Corrections: A Variety of Possibilities

In this text, **corrections** will be defined as a process whereby practitioners from a variety of agencies and programs use tools, techniques, and facilities to engage in organized security and treatment functions intended to correct criminal tendencies among the offender population. This definition underscores the fact that corrections is a process that includes the day-to-day activities of the practitioners who are involved in that process. Corrections is not a collection of agencies, organizations, facilities, or physical structures; rather the agencies and organizations consist of the practitioners under their employ and/or in their service, and the facilities or physical structures are the tools of the practitioner. The common denominator between the disparate components of the correctional system is the purpose behind the system. It is this inherent purpose that, on the one hand, includes the simple use of punishment while, on the other hand, consisting of much more than the mere application of a punitive sanction. We now turn our attention to ancient developments in law and punishment, which, grounded in the desire to modify criminal behavior, served as the precursor to correctional systems and practices as we know them today.

THE NOTION OF PUNISHMENT AND CORRECTIONS THROUGHOUT HISTORY

As might be determined by the title of this section, there has been a long-standing connection between the concepts of punishment and correction. It is as if our criminal justice system considers these two concepts as being one in the same. However, as we will find, these two terms are not always synonymous with one another. Rather, the purpose that underlies each is probably a better guide in distinguishing one from the other, not identifying their similarities. It is the application of penalties that has the longest history, and it is with this in mind that punishment is first discussed with additional clarification provided in defining the more modern term of *corrections*.

Official punishments tended to have two key objectives throughout early history. First was the intent to provide a consequence for a given behavior that was not desired. Though the offenses and the sanctions may have varied, there was always the desire to ensure that persons committing infractions were given some sort of negative consequence for their misdeed. Second, there was often the intent to provide some sort of compensation and/or atonement to the victim or to society for the wrongs that had been done. In most early societies, the compensation was often made to the victim or the victim's family. In such cases, this may have even required effort on the part of the aggrieved party to ensure that the offender was held accountable. As societies evolved, the official government tended to take the role of moderator, dispute handler, and collector of compensation. It was at this point that the individual victim and/or the victim's family became less involved in the process.

When applying punishments, it was hoped that the consequence would prevent the offender from committing future acts that were unwanted. Though one would consider it a good outcome if offenders are prevented from committing further crimes, this is not necessarily an act of *correction* regarding the offender's behavior. Though this may seem like an argument grounded in semantics, it is actually relevant since it sets the very groundwork for what we consider to be corrections. This very premise has served as the basis for how and why correctional systems have operated throughout the nation and throughout the world. Essentially, the common logic rests upon the notion that if we punish someone effectively, he or she will not do the crime again, and is therefore corrected. Naturally, this is not always the final outcome of the punishment process. In fact, research has found cases where exposure to prison actually increases the likelihood of future criminal behavior (Fletcher, 1999; Golub, 1990). Likewise, some research has demonstrated higher rates of violent crime when the death penalty is applied, seemingly in reaction to or correlated with the use of the death penalty (Bowers & Pierce, 1980). This observation is referred to as the **brutalization hypothesis**, the contention of which is that the use of harsh punishments sensitizes people to violence and essentially *teaches* them to use violence rather than acting as a deterrent (Bowers & Pierce, 1980).

Some might argue on behalf of a **theory of disablement**, whereby the offender is either temporarily or permanently isolated or maimed as a means of preventing a type of crime in the future. Removal of an offender through either short-term consequences—a stint in jail or prison—or long-term consequences—such as banishment in early societies and life imprisonment in modern societies—might also be considered a form of disablement. In such cases, the intent is to provide a consequence, but the emphasis is not necessarily one of *correction*. While offenders might indeed correct their future behavior, the primary objective of this perspective is to simply remove their ability to inflict crime in the future. As we will see later in this chapter and other chapters, the distinction between corrections and punishment may be quite blurred.

EARLY CODES OF LAW

Early codes of law were designed to guide human behavior and to distinguish that which was legal from that which was not. Many of these laws were, among other things, grounded in mores and social norms common to persons in the region in which the laws were enacted. These laws often also stated the forms of punishment that would occur should a person run errant of a given edict. Because laws reflected the cultural and social norms of a given people and because laws tended to include punishments, it could then be said that the types of punishment used by a society might give an outside observer a glimpse of that society's true understanding of criminal behavior as well as its sense of compassion or lack thereof.

Babylonian and Sumerian Codes

The earliest known written code of punishment was the **Code of Hammurabi**. Hammurabi (1728–1686 B.C.) was the ruler of Babylon sometime around 1700 B.C., which dates back nearly 3,800 years before our time (Roth, 2011). This code included the widely touted "eye for an eye" mentality that is even popular today among many people in the United States. However, the actual saying, "an eye for an eye, a tooth for a tooth ... and a life for a life," is derived from the later Mosaic Code, not the Code of Hammurabi. Rather, the Code of Hammurabi used the term **lex talionis**, which referred to the Babylonian law of equal retaliation (Roth, 2011). This legal basis reflected the instinctive desire for humans who have been harmed to seek revenge. Hammurabi's Code included a number of corporal punishments, many of which were harsh. But, this code also provided a sense of uniformity in punishments, thereby organizing the justice process in Babylon. Before the advent of this code, offenders in Babylon usually faced barbaric and capricious punishments that were often extracted by the hands of victims and/or their families (Stohr, Walsh, & Hemmens, 2009).

Video Link 1.1
Watch a video about the Code of Hammurabi.

The Code of Hammurabi served to codify the natural inclination of victims to seek revenge upon the person causing the harm, but these laws also illustrated the need to restrain personal revenge from turning into a cycle of back-and-forth warfare between mutually aggrieved parties. Indeed, this often happened between families, resulting in fierce and bitter family feuds. In the process, **blood feuds** would continue (perhaps for generations) and further generate the injustice that revenge was supposed to assuage (Johnson, Wolfe, & Jones, 2008). Thus, over time, laws would regulate the process involved in achieving justice as well as the severity of punishment that would be considered commensurate to the injustice that had been committed. Both the process and the outcome of punishment would ultimately be taken from the hands of the victim's family and would transfer to authority vested in the state. We will expound on this a bit later in this chapter, but for now, we turn our attention to other means by which crime was identified and the punitive reactions that were typically connected to those crimes.

PHOTO 1.1

The Code of Hammurabi is one of the most ancient attempts to codify criminal acts and their corresponding punishments.

Journal Article Link 1.1
Read more about blood feuds and modernity.

Roman Law and Punishment and Their Impact on Early English Punishment

Punishments in the Roman Empire were severe and tended to be terminal. Imprisonment was simply a means of holding the accused until those in power had decided the offender's fate. Even those condemned to penal servitude had to be kept in some place of holding throughout the night. However, it would seem that very little has been recorded regarding the custody of persons in servitude. From what is known, it would appear that most places of confinement were simply cages. Otherwise, there are recorded accounts of quarries (deep holes used for mining/excavating stone) that were also used to hold offenders (Gramsci, 1996). From what can be determined, one place of confinement in Rome that was well known was the Mamertine Prison, which was actually a sprawling system of underground tunnels and dungeons that were built under the sewer system of Rome sometime around 64 B.C. and was the place where the Christian Apostles Paul and Peter were incarcerated (Gramsci, 1996).

Rome and other societies during this period considered convicted offenders to have the legal status of a slave. It is important to understand that during this time, according to Roman law, these sentences also entailed a complete loss of citizenship (Gramsci, 1996; Johnson et al., 2008). Again, we will see in modern times where these same types of issues emerge by way of disenfranchisement. In today's society, extensive disenfranchisement is thought to essentially marginalize groups of citizens, particularly when the right to vote and conduct other business is restricted. However, in the times of the Roman Empire, marginalization of the offender population would have been an understatement; such individuals were treated as if they were essentially dead to society (Gramsci, 1996; Johnson et al., 2008). This was essentially a form of civil death, whereby the offender's property would be excised by the government and the marriage (if any) between the offender and his or her spouse was declared void, providing the status of widow to the spouse. The widow was afforded the legal right to remarry, and, in most cases, these women did so when an eligible suitor emerged (Gramsci, 1996). For all practical and legal purposes, the offender in penal servitude was dead to society, to be forgotten or placed forever in the past.

The use of harsh punishments was something that would continue throughout Europe and was adopted in England, the country that serves as the basis for the U.S. legal system. Just like the Romans, throughout English history there was an equal overreliance on the use of the death penalty. Indeed, during the 1700s, roughly 220 crimes qualified for the death penalty. Such sanctions ranged from the use of the gallows to having offenders boiled to death. Thus, it is clear that the use of barbaric forms of death continued from Rome to England. It would not be until the 1800s that a change in this approach would take place.

EARLY HISTORICAL ROLE OF RELIGION, PUNISHMENT, AND CORRECTIONS

Perhaps the most well-known premodern historical period of punishment is the Middle Ages of Western Europe. The Middle Ages was a time of chaos in Europe where plague, pestilence, fear, ignorance, and superstition prevailed. Further, through these dark times in Europe, the common citizenry, consisting largely of peasants who could neither read nor write, placed their faith in religious leaders who, in comparison, were well educated and literate. In particular, it was of course the Christian church that was influential and, more specifically, the Catholic Church that maintained primary power throughout the European continent.

The Church, at this time, was co-opted with the justice system; that is, an offender would need to pay two debts (one secular and one religious) developed within the process of paying one's penalty. In the process, redemption was seen as being more in line with religious processes whereas fulfilling one's punishment met only secular requirements. However, it was the saving of one's soul and assurance of one's place in the afterlife that was considered the higher-order concern, at least according to the clergy.

While one might stand at trial for charges by the state, it was the trial by ordeal that emerged as the Church's equivalent to a legal proceeding (Johnson et al., 2008). In addition, even secular courts sometimes adopted these practices when they were unable to determine guilt or innocence, this essentially being an appeal to divine intervention when determining guilt or innocence (Johnson et al., 2008). The **trial by ordeal** consisted of very dangerous and/or impossible tests to prove the guilt or innocence of the accused. For instance, the ordeal of hot water required that the accused thrust a hand or an arm into a kettle of scalding hot boiling water (Johnson et al., 2008). If after three days of binding the arm, the offender emerged unscathed, he or she was considered innocent. Another option was the ordeal by hot iron, which required the accused to carry a red-hot bar of iron with his or her bare hands before dropping it to the

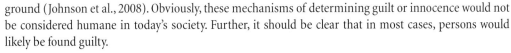
ground (Johnson et al., 2008). Obviously, these mechanisms of determining guilt or innocence would not be considered humane in today's society. Further, it should be clear that in most cases, persons would likely be found guilty.

Of note would be the general reason provided by the Church for its use of punishments. It would seem that the Church response to aberrant (or sinful) behavior was, at least in ideology, based on the desire to save the soul of the wayward offender. Indeed, even when persons were burned at the stake, the prevailing belief was that such burning would free their souls for redemption and ascension to Heaven. The goal, in essence, was to purify the soul as it was released from the body. This was especially true of persons who were convicted of witchcraft and who were believed to have consorted with spirits and/or were believed to be possessed by evil spirits.

Sanctuary

While the Church may have had a role in the application of punishments throughout history, it also provided some unique avenues by which the unjustly accused might avoid unwarranted punishment. One example would be the granting of sanctuary to accused offenders.

The provision of sanctuary dates back to the time of Moses. During this time, many nations had a city or a designated building, such as a temple or a church, where accused offenders could stay, free from attack, until such time that their innocence could be established (presuming that they were, in fact, innocent). Until the late 1200s, a criminal could obtain sanctuary for up to 40 days. Upon the expiration

PHOTO 1.2

Churches such as the one shown here may have been one source of temporary sanctuary for many offenders. Such practices occurred during a time when the separation of church and state had not yet emerged.

of this 40-day period, the accused was expected to surrender or confess his or her guilt. At that point, the offender would be given safe passage out of the nation. This amounted to a form of banishment for the offender. By the mid-17th century, the practice of sanctuary was eliminated in England.

In Europe, the use of sanctuary began during the 4th century and consisted of a place—usually a church—where the king's soldiers were forbidden to enter for purposes of taking an accused criminal into custody (Cromwell, Carmin, & Alarid, 2002). In such cases, **sanctuary** was provided until some form of negotiation could be arranged or until the accused was ultimately smuggled out of the area. If, while in sanctuary, accused offenders confessed to their crimes, they were typically granted abjuration (Cromwell et al., 2002). Abjuration required that the offenders promise to leave England with the understanding that any return to England without explicit permission from the Crown would lead to immediate punishment (Cromwell et al., 2002).

This form of leniency lasted for well over a thousand years in European history and was apparently quite common in England. Even if the accused offenders did not confess to their crimes as a means of seeking abjuration, they could still be granted sanctuary. Over time, however, specific rules were placed upon the use of this form of leniency. For instance, during the 13th century, felons who sought sanctuary could stay up to 40 days or, before the expiration of that time, could agree to leave the kingdom. If they remained past the 40 days, "they risked being forced out of sanctuary through starvation" (Sahagun, 2007, p. 1). Eventually, sanctuary lost its appeal in Europe, and, "in the 15th century, several parliamentary petitions sought to restrict the right of sanctuary in England. In the next century, King Henry VIII reduced the number of sanctuaries by about half" (Sahagun, 2007, p. 1). From roughly 1750 onward, countries throughout Europe began to abolish sanctuary provisions as secular courts gained power over ecclesiastical courts. The process of eliminating sanctuary was a long and protracted one that took nearly 100 years before sanctuary ultimately disappeared as an option of leniency for accused offenders (Sahagun, 2007).

EARLY SECULAR HISTORY OF PUNISHMENT AND CORRECTIONS

The issue of law and the origin of law was one of debate during medieval times. Over time, secular rulers (often royalty and nobility) became less subservient to the Church and gained sufficient power to resist some of the controls placed upon them by the ecclesiastical courts. As such, much of the royalty, nobility, merchant class, and scholarly community advocated separation between government rule (at this time the king or queen) and the Church. Though this was an ultimately successful process, many did die as a result of their views.

The earlier views of law and punishment held by the Romans had greatly impacted the rest of Western Europe during medieval times. During the time that the Roman Empire fell into decline, the beginning of the modern national state began to emerge. The result was the rapid decline of a European culture that had once been based on Roman culture and the Christian church's teachings. Prior to this, Western Europe and England enjoyed a common heritage of Roman law, the Latin language, and Christianity. But by the year 1000 A.D., all that remained was a minority of literate and educated persons who, in most cases, were connected with the Church; remember again that the clergy, in particular, tended to be well educated.

Because of this, there was a large population of commoners (the vast majority of Europeans at that time) who could not read or write and were unskilled laborers. This surplus population of uneducated and unskilled persons created a weak and ineffectual underclass who, without work on plantation manors provided by the educated and literate nobility, would likely starve. The need for labor was fulfilled by giving peasants a small plot of land to work in which they raised crops for their own purposes while working the fields of the manor lord. In essence, the common populace was little more than slaves, and the only step down in status would have been something akin to slave status. Thus, rationale again emerged that criminal offenders held status as slaves of the state. From this arose the rebirth of penal servitude and the use of the civil death as means of retaliation for offenses against the Crown. As with the Roman Empire, kingdoms of the Middle Ages also had prisoners serve as oarsmen on galleys or work in sulfur mines, in addition to other forms of hard labor. Further, the use of harsh punishments was a mainstay, including lashings, whippings, and other forms of physical punishment (see Table 1.1).

It was at this time that criminal behavior became widely recognized as an offense against the state. Indeed, by 1350 A.D., the royalty (consisting of kings, queens, and the like) had established themselves as the absolute power, and they became less tolerant of external factors that undermined their own rule; this meant that the Church continued to lose authority throughout Europe. Ultimately, all forms of revenue obtained from fines went to the state (or the Crown), and the state administered all punishments. This also led to the development of crime being perceived as an act in violation of a king or queen's authority. This meant that harsh punishments deterred those who might challenge the ruler's position, thereby solidifying the secular approach to punishment and corrections (Johnson et al., 2008).

Public Wrongs

Public wrongs are crimes against society or a social group and tended to include sacrilege as well as other crimes against religion, treason, witchcraft, incest, sex offenses of any sort, and even violations of hunting rules (Johnson et al., 2008). Among early societies, religious offenses were considered the most dangerous since these crimes exposed both the offender and the rest of the group to the potential anger and wrath of that culture's deity or set of deities. For such crimes, the offender might have been stoned to death or killed in some other barbaric manner. In later medieval times, the act of heresy was also considered a public crime as well as a public sin. This was perhaps one of the most common forms of public religious crimes that occurred during the Middle Ages.

Witchcraft was commonly thought to entail genuine magical powers that would be used by the witch for personal revenge or personal gain; the use of such magic was considered bad for a social group because it drew evil spirits in the direction of the community. For Christian belief systems, the witch was considered an enemy of God who was in league with Satan. The key basis for the fear of witches is drawn from a number of scriptures in the Christian Bible. As an example, consider the following passage in Leviticus 20:27 (King James Version):

> A man also or woman that hath a familiar spirit, or that is a wizard, shall surely be put to death: they shall stone them with stones: their blood shall be upon them.

Journal Article Link 1.2
Read about witchcraft accusations in contemporary Ghana.

The book of Leviticus made up part of the "Law of Moses," which was the primary history of the Jewish people. The books consisting of the Law of Moses were written in the 6th century B.C., most likely during a time when the Jewish population was in exile while King Merodach, an enemy of the Jews, reigned throughout Babylon. The Jewish disdain for witches would impact all of Europe (and the Americas) for years to come.

Indeed, the fear of witchcraft would continue for several hundred years, reaching its height of hysteria in the 1500s. Suspicion of witchcraft and the use of mass executions became commonplace during this time. For instance, authorities in Geneva, Switzerland, burned 500 accused witches at the stake in 1515 (Linder, 2005). Nine years later in Como, Italy, a spreading spiral of witchcraft charges led to as many as 1,000 executions (Linder, 2005). During the years between 1273 and 1660, Europe would execute thousands of suspected witches, the majority of them women. The total number of persons executed due to witchcraft charges may have exceeded 100,000 (Linder, 2005).

Treason, another common public crime, involved the aiding and abetting of the enemy during a time of war. In England during the 1400s, the crime of treason became commonplace among the nobility due to a series of wars known as the Wars of the Roses, which took place between two competing royal families (the Yorks and the Lancasters). Throughout this ongoing struggle, nearly every feudal noble had, at one point or another, ended up on the side of a king who had been defeated (temporarily) in battle. Once in this position, many of these nobles were quickly tried for treason, found guilty, and executed.

Private Wrongs and Retaliation

In ancient times, resorting to private revenge was the only avenue of redress for victims who suffered a **private wrong**. These types of wrongs might have included physical injury, damage to a person's property, or theft. In such cases and in many areas of Europe, there was no official authority present; the victim was on his or her own to gain any justice that could be obtained. There was also additional incentive to retaliate against perpetrators, for if the victim was able to gain revenge this was likely to deter the perpetrator from committing future crimes against the victim. However, it is not surprising that in these cases, the original perpetrator may have fought back against the retaliatory strike from the victim, regardless of whoever was wrong or right. This would then lead to a continual tit-for-tat situation that might ultimately develop into a perpetual conflict.

Thus, as groups of people became more advanced, the responsibility for determining punishment shifted from the individual and/or family to the entire social group. From this developed the blood feud, which operated under the notion that acts against one individual were viewed as acts against the victim's entire kinship group, thereby requiring the victim's family, tribe, or community to aid in gaining revenge (Silverman, 2001). Examples of this in different parts of Europe abound. In Germany, kindred groups were formed by blood relationships (Johnson et al., 2008). The basic relationship for purposes of vengeance was the tie of consanguinity, but this was sometimes modified to include other family relatives. As an example, a widow whose husband was murdered might first expect help from her husband's kinsmen (such as a son, a father, or brothers) to obtain revenge. If that request did not result in suitable vengeance, she might still appeal to her own kindred (Johnson et al., 2008).

There developed a complex set of rules that governed who would be entitled (or required) to seek vengeance. These rules got so complicated that there are recorded accounts where the accused slayer had difficulty determining who should be given the intended compensation (Johnson et al., 2008). Regardless of the complexity of these rules and even though this process was barbaric, the use of these restrictive rules tended to limit the scope of violence that might ensue as well as the seriousness of that violence. The existence of these blood feuds existed between the 5th and 11th centuries of the Middle Ages when European society was primarily composed of feuding families and tribes (Johnson et al., 2008).

Retaliation Through Humiliation

During early parts of European history, retaliation also occurred through the use of humiliation. Humiliation, or shame, has been and continues to be a widely used means of public notification of wrongdoing; there is a desire to make offenders pay for the crimes they have committed through embarrassment, and to hopefully deter them from future criminal behavior. A number of punishments were utilized, some of which might even be considered corporal in nature (such as the ducking stool as well as the stocks and pillories), but they are included in this section because the distinctive factor lies more in their intended outcome: to humiliate and embarrass the offender. For punishments based on humiliation, the primary goal was to simply embarrass and ridicule the offender. This is more of a retaliatory function than anything else. While it might indeed have had a deterrent effect on the offender, this was not the primary purpose of the punishment (Johnson et al., 2008).

Audio Link 1.3
Listen to research on the deterrent effect of the death penalty.

One early punishment was the **gag**, which was a device that would constrain persons who were known to constantly scold others (usually their spouse) or were guilty of habitually and abusively finding fault with others, being unjustly critical, or lying about other persons (Silverman, 2001). An even more serious form of retaliatory punishment was the use of the bridle. The **bridle** was an iron cage that fit over the head and included a metal plate in the front. The plate usually had spikes, which were constructed so as to fit into the mouth of the offender; this made movement with the tongue painful and thereby reduced the likelihood that the offender would talk (Silverman, 2001).

The **ducking stool** was a punishment that used a chair suspended over a body of water. In most cases, the chair hung from the end of a free-moving arm. The offender was strapped into the chair, which was located near a riverbank. The chair would be swung over the river by the use of the free-moving arm and would be plunged into the water while the offender was restrained therein. This was a punishment typically reserved for women. In particular, women who were known to nag on others or use profane

or abusive language were given this punishment. Women who gossiped were also given this punishment. This punishment was sometimes used with brawlers, slanderers, prostitutes, wife abusers, shop owners who sold bad foodstuffs, and married couples who were given to loud and public arguments (Johnson et al., 2008). In this later case, the husband and the wife (in Old England, cohabitation of couples rarely existed) were tied back-to-back, and they were ducked into the water together (Johnson et al., 2008).

It should be pointed out that the practice of ducking offenders was a bit more serious than this description, so far, would indicate. This is because, in most cases, this punishment would be administered during the winter months when the water was extremely cold; this alone was a miserable experience. In addition, some offenders drowned to death through this practice. Further, there was a strong sense of shame attached to this punishment, and the offender would be labeled among other community members.

Another common punishment in the Middle Ages was the stocks and pillories. **Stocks** consisted of wooden frames that were built in the outdoors, usually in a village or town square. A set of stocks

PHOTO 1.3

The ducking stool was one of many punishments used in early America for what were considered fairly minor crimes. In some cases, persons subjected to this punishment drowned to death or froze if the practice was conducted during the winter months.

TABLE 1.1   Types of Punishment in Early Correctional History

Name of Punishment	Purpose	Description
Trial by ordeal	Determine guilt or innocence	Very dangerous and/or impossible tests to prove the guilt or innocence of the accused
Gag	Humiliation	A device that would constrain persons who were known to constantly scold others
Ducking stool	Humiliation and deterrence	Punishment that used a chair suspended over a body of water
Stocks	Humiliation	Wooden frames that were built in the outdoors, usually in a village or town square
Pillory	Humiliation	Similar to the stock except the pillory consisted of a single large bored hole where the offender's neck would rest
Branding	Humiliation and warn public	Usually on thumb with a letter denoting the offense
Whipping	Deterrence	Lashing the body of criminal offenders among a public audience
Capital punishment	Deterrence	Putting the offender to death among a public audience
Banishment and transportation	Deterrence	Exile from society
Hulk imprisonment	Retribution and incapacitation	Offenders kept in unsanitary decommissioned naval vessels
Indentured servitude	Retribution and incapacitation	Offender subjected to virtual slavery

consisted of a thick piece of lumber that had two or more holes bored into it. The holes were round and wide enough so that an offender's wrists would fit through. The board was cut into halves, and a hinge was used so that the halves could be opened and then closed. Specifically, the boards would be opened, the offender would be forced to rest his or her wrists into the half-circle of the bottom half of the wooden board, and then the top half would be closed over his or her wrists, with a lock being used on the side opposite the hinge to keep the offender trapped, hands and wrists restrained by the board. The stock was usually constructed atop a beam or post set into the ground so that the offender, with both wrists restrained by the stock, would have to stand (rather than sit) in the prone position, sometimes for days and, in extreme cases, perhaps weeks.

The **pillory** was similar to the stock except the pillory consisted of a single large bored hole where the offender's neck would rest. When shut and locked, the offender was restrained with his or her head immobilized and body stooped over. The device was specifically set atop a post at a height where most adult offenders could not fully stand up straight, adding to the discomfort of the experience. As with a set of stocks, the offender would be required to stand in this stooped position, head secured between a cutout plank of lumber, for several days and nights. In many cases, the offender might be required to be constrained by a combination of these devices, known as a stocks and pillory, where both the offender's head and hands were immobilized and while the offender would stand in a stooped position.

It was at this point that the use of branding became more commonplace. **Branding** was used to make criminal offenders, slaves, and prisoners of war easily identifiable. Offenders were usually branded on their thumb with a letter denoting their offense—for instance, the letter *M* for murder or *T* for theft. Harkening back to the connection between crime and sin, consider that even as late as the 1700s, the use of branding for humiliation occurred with the crime of adultery. In New Hampshire, a specific statute (1701) held that offenders guilty of adultery would be made to wear a discernable letter *A* on their upper-garment clothing, usually in red, but always in some color that contrasted with the color of the clothing. The requirement to wear this letter might last for years or even life, with the message being that the offender not only committed the crime but should be judged for the crime indefinitely. It is therefore obvious that the use of branding was grounded in the desire to humiliate the offender.

Wergild Compensation

Because blood feuds and the pursuit of revenge could start a generations-long vendetta, a widely used solution emerged as an alternative. This was a system of fining or compensation, otherwise known as wergild among many of the Germanic tribes where this process was known to be used on a widespread basis. **Wergild** was usually a form of payment that was made by the offender or his or her family for a wrongful death that had been inflicted by the offender. Wergild was used even for the crime of homicide, other forms of negligent death, and any variety of lesser crimes. This legal tool was important within early German society since it prevented the need for blood feuds yet, at the same time, honored the victim or the victim's family. Monies received as wergild were most often allocated to the victim's family or clan (Johnson et al., 2008).

Corporal Punishment

Up to the 1700s, corporal punishment tended to be the most frequently used punishment. This punishment was often administered in a public forum to add to the deterrent effect, thereby setting an example to others of what might happen if they were caught in the commission of a similar crime. Naturally, these types of punishment also included purposes of retribution. The most widely used form of corporal punishment was **whipping**, which dates back to the Romans, the Greeks, and even the Egyptians as a sanction for both judicial and educational discipline.

The use of corporal punishment varied somewhat, and the purpose behind the use of whipping varied. For instance, in ancient Sparta, young males who were preparing for manhood would subject themselves to whipping as a means of building willpower and proving strength. In the Roman Empire, whipping was used as punishment and could range in the number of lashes. A sentence of 100 lashes was, for most offenders, a virtual death sentence as the whipping was quite brutal across the back and shoulders, usually drawing blood and removing pieces of flesh.

During the 1500s, the use of whipping was particularly publicized throughout Europe, turning into a spectacle for large public audiences. This form of entertainment largely appealed to the lower socioeconomic classes of the day, and, as one might expect, offenders subjected to these types of punishments were typically of lower socioeconomic standing. Additionally, it was not uncommon for this type of punishment to be inflicted upon sailors in navies throughout many nations, including the United States. The use of flogging among U.S. sailors continued throughout the 1700s but diminished over time (Morgan, 2004).

The use of the whip as an instrument of punishment has evolved throughout history. Among the ancient Romans, there existed three different types of whips: the *ferula*, which was a simple whip made from a leather strap; the *scutica*, which was made of twisted parchment thongs; and the *flagrum*, which was a whip that had multiple leather lashes that ended in sharp metal points (Morgan, 2004). Later developments in the whip resulted in the widespread use of scourges, which had several thongs fastened to a handle, similar to the flagrum, but was made from different types of material ranging from leather, to rope, and even to woven hair. Lastly, the cat-o'-nine-tails developed and was used extensively in the British Royal Navy until the late 1800s (Morgan, 2004). The cat-o'-nine-tails was most often made of wound rope to create a nine-tailed whipping instrument.

Capital Punishment

This section will be brief due to more extensive coverage of the death penalty in Chapter 18. Historically speaking, the types of death penalties imposed are many and varied. Some examples include being buried alive (used in Western civilization as well as ancient China), being boiled in oil, being thrown to wild beasts (particularly used by the Romans), being impaled by a wooden stake, being drowned, being shot to death, beheading (especially with the guillotine), and hanging, as well as lethal gas and lethal injection. By far, the most frequently used form of execution is hanging, which has been used throughout numerous points in history.

During the medieval period, the offender's execution was often preceded by a period of torture. This torture might include drawing and quartering, which required that the offender be dragged on a wooden frame to the place of execution; hanged by the neck for a short time until almost dead; disemboweled, with the body divided into four parts; and beheaded. Other forms of mutilation were also completed against the offender. This naturally elongated the death process and was designed to do this so that a public spectacle could be made.

Banishment

Banishment was considered an effective alternative to capital punishment because the offender was removed from society and, in cases where there might be some doubt as to the level of guilt, the populace could feel assuaged by the fact that the offender's life had been spared. Throughout history, **banishment** came in two versions, depending on the country in question and the time period involved. First, banishment could be permanent and, in some cases, temporary. Second, banishment could mean simple exile from the country or, in many cases, exile to and/or enslavement in a penal colony.

Video Link 1.2
Learn more about the banishment of offenders.

Yet, at the same time, there was an overreliance on the death penalty. During the period between 1100 and 1700 England's criminal code was nicknamed the "Bloody Code," and though the rich and powerful may have been supportive of the harsh penalties, there was an undercurrent of commoner discontent with the capricious and continuous use of the death penalty. Further, the mid-1700s saw the emergence of numerous scholars and enlightened thinkers who advocated for reform. Their voice, the voice of various religious groups such as the Quakers, and the voice of downtrodden commoners affected the otherwise hasty tendency of the nobility and royalty to resort to the death penalty. Thus, banishment proved a very useful alternative that became used with increasing regularity in lieu of the death penalty.

In reaction, the 1600s and 1700s saw the implementation of banishment on a widespread scale. The development of English colonies in the Americas opened up new opportunities for banishment that could also rid England of her criminal problems on a more permanent basis. Thus, criminals were sent to the American colonies under reprieve and through stays of execution. Thus, the convicts had their lives spared, but this form of mercy was generally only implemented to solve a labor shortage that existed within the American colonies. Essentially, the convicts were shipped to the Americas to work as indentured servants under hard labor.

TRANSPORTING OFFENDERS

Transportation became a nearly ideal solution to the punishment of criminal offenders because it resolved all of the drawbacks associated with other types of punishment. The costs were minimal, it was difficult (if not impossible) for offenders to return to England, and offenders could become sources of labor for the new colonies. Johnson et al. (2008) notes that of those offenders who had been subjected to transportation, the majority were male, unskilled, and from the lower classes, and had probably resorted to crime due to adverse economic conditions.

Indentured Servitude

Audio Link 1.4
Listen to a clip about indentured servitude.

The use of indentured servants included both free persons and offenders. Generally speaking, free persons who indentured themselves had better treatment due to the fact that they had some say in their initial agreement to working requirements prior to being transported to the American colonies. Such persons came of their own accord in hope of making a new life in the New World. Most of these persons were poor with few options in England. Though this meant that their lot was one of desperation, they were still not typically subjected to some of the more harsh treatment that offenders were administered when indentured into servitude.

It should be understood that, for all practical purposes, indentured status was essentially a form of slavery, albeit one that had a fixed term of service. During the time that persons were indentured, they were owned by their employer and could be subjected to nearly any penalty except death. It is estimated that nearly half of all persons who came to the Americas during the 1600s and 1700s were indentured servants (Johnson et al., 2008). The conditions by which convicts were shipped were barbaric. They were chained below deck in cramped, damp, and disease-infested conditions.

The selling of convicts was similar to a modern-day cattle auction, and convicts were purchased for all types of uses, including agricultural, retail, and industrial forms of work. Though women consisted of only a fifth of those indentured in the New World, they were considered less valuable due to their inability to perform much of the heavy labor that male indentured servants could perform. Thus, many found themselves serving their period of servitude as mistresses and consorts of their owners. If these women became pregnant, whether due to sexual activity with other servants or with their owners, their term of service was extended by a year to compensate for the work lost as they completed the term of their pregnancy. Lastly, these offenders were considered the private property of the owner and were often treated with rough discipline.

PHOTO 1.5

The hulk prison ship was usually a vessel that was old and squalid inside. Little if any lighting was provided, and women, children, and men would be imprisoned together. The conditions were filthy, and rodents commonly lived among the offenders trapped therein.

Hulks and Floating Prisons

When the American revolution began in 1776, there was an abrupt halt to the transporting of convicts to those colonies. Due to the fact that transportation to the American colonies was not feasible, England began to look for new ideas regarding the housing of prisoners. One idea was to house offenders in hulks, which were broken-down and decommissioned war vessels of the British Royal Navy. These vessels were anchored in the River Thames and were used to house offenders, thereby being prisons on the water. The

TECHNOLOGY AND EQUIPMENT 1.1

The Evolution of the Cat-o'-Nine-Tails

The evolution of the cat-o'-nine-tails is one that dates back in history. Ancient Egyptian hieroglyphics show various authorities to use single whips and even multipronged whips when commanding slaves and/or laborers around 1400 B.C. In addition, whips were used by Egyptian and later Roman charioteers. This means that the single whip has a long history, and, throughout history, the use of multipronged whips has existed as well.

For the most part, whips tended to be used through the ages with one to three prongs. Even as late as 1637, it was most common to see whips having no more than three lashes. In the late 1600s there is public record of a whip with six lashes being used to punish a religious enemy of King James II of England. This enemy, by the name of Titus Oates, received numerous lashes between Newgate and Tyburn Gate in the city of London. It is from this point that the cat-o'-nine-tails emerged in history, being used as a tool of discipline by the British Army and Royal Navy.

During the early 1800s, the British Royal Navy used a cat-o'-nine-tails that had a handle made of rope about 2 feet long and about an inch in diameter. This instrument of punishment was frequently covered or wrapped in a red baize cloth. The tails of this nine-pronged whip were made of cord or hemp material that was about one fourth of an inch in diameter and around 2 feet long. The tails were usually knotted three times each at approximately half-inch to 2-inch intervals. The first knot is 2 inches from the end of each strand. A faintly discernible strand of red cotton usually ran through each tail. This strand was sometimes visible and served as an example of the Admiralty's marking of rope to prevent theft. In some cases, a cat-o'-nine-tails might be made to have a wooden handle, to give additional gripping strength. In addition, steel balls or barbs of wire were sometimes added to the tips of each tail to maximize the potential injury inflicted.

The cat-o'-nine-tails was often made fresh for each flogging and was sometimes made by the ship's boatswain's mate (a sea-tested sailor with seniority among the enlisted ranks). In many cases, it was the boatswain's mate who might administer the lashes, and, when the captain was particularly angered by the infraction of the sailor who had committed an infraction, a left-handed boatswain might be requested to provide half of the lashes so as to inflict an extra-painful crisscross effect with the scarring. Usually, no more than 12 lashes were administered at sea where the entire crew would be gathered to witness the event.

In later years, the cat-o'-nine-tails was also used with adult male convicts in prisons. One article in the *New York Times*, released in 1896, confirmed the use of the cat-o'-nine-tails with male prisoners. In addition, a memorandum was distributed as late as 1951 among facilities in England. This memorandum specifically instructed prison administrators to use only a cat-o'-nine-tails from the national stock at Wandsworth prison. These instruments were to be tested before being used on inmates for discipline. Incidentally, this testing was to ensure that an appropriate amount of pain would be inflicted for the offender—much different from today, where the concern would be that the punishment might be too harsh.

Transportation served as an intermediate punishment between death and lesser sanctions such as whipping or the use of the stocks and pillories. The passage of the Transportation Act of 1718 in England heralded an unprecedented era whereby banishment through transportation was utilized.

Hulks Act, as it was called, was passed in England as a temporary measure to house offenders on these large men-of-war (Duncan, 1999). This law was passed by England with the expectation that England would ultimately defeat the American colonies and the colonies would again be available for transportation. Naturally, it became clear that the colonies would maintain their independence, and this resulted in an extended period of time where hulks were used as prisons. During the time when hulks were most widely used (1800s), there were over 10 such vessels that held over 5,000 offenders (Branch-Johnson, 1957).

Conditions aboard these decommissioned ships were deplorable. The smell of urine and feces, human bodies, and vermin filled the air. Overcrowding, poor ventilation, and a diet lacking appropriate nourishment left offenders in a constant state of ill health. Punishments for infractions were severe, and, as one might expect, there were no medical services. Further, all types of offenders were kept together aboard these vessels, including men, women, and vagrant youth. In many cases, there was no proactive effort to separate these offenders one from another. This then allowed for victimization of women and youth aboard these vessels by other stronger and predatory offenders.

Video Link 1.3
Watch a video about hulks.

During the late 1700s there was a push to identify other areas to which offenders could be transported. A variety of locations had been considered, including areas of West Africa and even South America. However, it was the continent of Australia that was ultimately selected. The reason for this selection had to do with the fact that Australia had potential as an area of agricultural production, was too distant for offenders to return to England, and had a very distinct need for settlers. The economic benefits of expanding to the Pacific region were valued by the British Empire, and Australia held greater promise than other areas of the world.

THE ENLIGHTENMENT AND CORRECTIONAL REFORM

As demonstrated earlier in this chapter, the roots of punishment tend to be ingrained in a desire for revenge. From this intent emerged a number of ghastly tortures and punishments. With the beginning of the 1700s, a new mind-set began to develop throughout Europe. Indeed, the developments that occurred throughout the early to late 1700s are very important to any student of corrections. It was during this period, referred to as the Age of Enlightenment, that many of the most famous philosophers of modern Western history found their place and left their mark (Carlson, Roth, & Travisono, 2008). Among the areas of thought that reached their minds and consciences was the issue related to the human condition, its frailty from perfection, and the reaction to that imperfection. This is when thinkers and reformers such as William Penn, Charles Montesquieu, Francois Voltaire, Cesare Beccaria, John Howard, and Jeremy Bentham became known as leading thinkers of punishment as well as advocates of humane treatment for prisoners (see Table 1.2).

William Penn, the Quakers, and the Great Law

William Penn (1644–1718) was the founder of the state of Pennsylvania and was also a leader of the religious Quakers. He was an advocate of religious freedom as well as individual rights (Carlson et al., 2008). He was also instrumental in spreading the notion that criminal offenders were worthy of humane treatment. The Quaker movement in penal reform did not just exist in America, but it also took hold in Italy and England. In the process, it was the work of the Quakers that would influence other great thinkers like Cesare Beccaria, John Howard, and Jeremy Bentham, all of whom would achieve prominence sometime after the death of William Penn.

TABLE 1.2   Major Correctional Thinkers in Early History

Name	Period Lived	Known For
William Penn	1644–1718	The Great Law and Quaker reform
Charles Montesquieu	1689–1755	French philosopher who wrote *Persian Letters* on criminal law abuses in Europe
Francois Voltaire	1694–1778	Wrote critically of the French government and was imprisoned in the Bastille
Cesare Beccaria	1738–1794	Wrote treatise An Essay on Crimes and Punishments, was an anti–death penalty activist, and is the father of classical criminology
John Howard	1726–1790	Sheriff of Bedfordshire in England, advocated prison reform, wrote State of Prisons treatise for British Parliament
Jeremy Bentham	1748–1832	Believed behavior could be determined through scientific principles, created pleasure-pain hypothesis (aka hedonistic calculus)

The Quakers followed a body of laws, called the **Great Law**, which was more humane in approach than the typical English response to crime. The laws of English origin, referred to as the Anglican Code, predominated throughout the American colonies and were harsh in orientation. Because the Quakers were a religious group, the Great Law was also religious in nature and reflected some of the traditional combinations of criminal and sinful behavior. Regardless of this, there is no doubt that this law and the punishments that it authorized were less extreme than the Anglican Code.

According to the Great Law, hard labor was a more effective punishment than the death penalty. With the revisions by the Quakers, only premeditated murder was punishable by death in America. In addition, religious crimes were stricken, and only secular issues of criminal law were addressed. Under the Great Law, a "house of corrections" was established with most punishments consisting of hard labor. This became a new trend in American corrections, where hard labor was viewed as part of the actual punishment for serious crimes rather than simply being something that was done prior to the actual punishment given to the offender (Johnston, 2009). This was also the first time that offenders received a loss of liberty (albeit while completing hard labor) as a punishment, in and of itself. This same concept would later be adopted by a future scholar held in high regard: Cesare Beccaria.

PHOTO 1.6

William Penn is both a historical and a humane figure in the field of corrections. A member of the Quakers, a religious group involved in social issues, he was among the first reform-minded thinkers in the United States to advocate for humane prison conditions.

Charles Montesquieu, Francois Voltaire, and Cesare Beccaria

Montesquieu and Voltaire were French philosophers who were very influential during the Age of Enlightenment, and they were particularly concerned with what would be considered human rights in today's society. **Charles Montesquieu** (1689–1755) wrote an essay titled *Persian Letters*, which was instrumental in illustrating the abuses of the criminal law in both France and Europe. *Persian Letters* was a collection of fictional letters from two Persian noblemen who visited Paris for their first time. The letters, supposedly written by these two noblemen, reflected the thoughts of these two characters on European laws and customs as compared to Persian laws and customs. The entire collection of letters was bound into a single work that was a satire of the French government.

PHOTO 1.7

Cesare Beccaria was a leading thinker on crime and punishment during the early history of corrections. He is considered the father of classical criminology and was also a well-known advocate of humane forms of punishment for offenders.

At about the same time, **Francois Voltaire** (1694–1778) became involved with a number of trials that challenged traditional ideas of legalized torture, criminal responsibility, and justice. Voltaire, who had studied law from 1711 to 1713, was intrigued with inequities in government and among the well-to-do. Like his friend Montesquieu, Voltaire wrote critically of the French government. In fact, he was imprisoned in the Bastille (a fortified prison) for 11 months for writing a scathing satire of the French government. In 1726, Voltaire's wit, public behavior, and critical writing offended much of the nobility in France, and he was essentially given two options; he could be imprisoned or agree to exile. Voltaire chose exile and lived in England from 1726 to 1729. While in England, Voltaire became acquainted with John Locke, another great thinker on crime, punishment, and reform.

These two philosophers helped to pave the way for one of the most influential criminal law reformers of Western Europe. **Cesare Beccaria** (1738–1794) was very famous for his thoughts and writings on criminal laws, punishments, and corrections. Beccaria was an Italian philosopher who, in 1764, wrote a brief treatise titled *An Essay on Crimes and Punishments* (1764). This treatise was the first argument ever made in public writing against the death penalty among scholars and philosophers. The text was considered a seminal work and was eventually translated into French, English, and a number of other languages.

Beccaria condemned the death penalty on two grounds, first due to the notion that the state does not actually possess any kind of spiritual or legal right to take lives. Second, the death penalty was neither useful nor necessary as a form of punishment. Beccaria also contended that punishment should be viewed as having a preventive rather than a retributive function. He also believed that it was the certainty of punishment (not the severity) that achieved a preventative effect, and that in order to be effective, punishment should be prompt. Many of these tenets comport with classical criminological views on crime and punishment.

Due to Beccaria's beliefs and contentions, he was held out as the father of classical criminology, which was instrumental in shifting views on crime and punishment toward a more humanistic means of response. Among other things, Beccaria advocated for proportionality between the crime that was committed by an offender and the specific sanction that was given. Since not all crimes are equal, the use of progressively greater sanctions became an instrumental component in achieving this proportionality. **Classical criminology**, in addition to proportionality, emphasized that punishments must be useful, purposeful, and reasonable. Rather than employing barbaric public displays (itself being a deterrent approach) designed to frighten people into obedience through deterrence, reformers called for more moderate correctional responses. Beccaria, in advocating this shift in offender processing, contended that humans were hedonistic—seeking pleasure while wishing to avoid pain—and that this required an appropriate amount of punishment to counterbalance the rewards derived from criminal behavior.

Further, Beccaria advocated for the more routine use of prisons as a means of incapacitating offenders and denying them their liberty. This was perhaps the first time that the notion of denying offenders their liberty from free movement was seen as a valid punishment, in its own right. This is important because up until this time, the denial of liberty was not viewed as an option among the range of punishments and, when it did occur, it was simply a consequence of the offender's wait for punishment that was more gruesome, such as torture or execution.

Lastly, it can be seen that many of the tenets of classical criminology mesh with Beccaria's ideas in his treatise *An Essay on Crimes and Punishments*. Further, his classical criminological view on crime, the causal factors associated with crime, and the nature of offenders serve as the underpinnings for the suggestions that he provides in his world-renowned treatise. These same tenets are used as primary bases for many of the criminal justice responses that we see today. It is interesting that many of his points regarding the use of punishment (the use of speedy trials, liberty as a form of punishment, the greatest good for the greatest number, etc.) are concepts that we still use today as a means of justification for the laws and customs that are inherent to our justice system. This is a testament to the influence of Beccaria on our modern-day sense of justice and also his importance to the history of corrections.

John Howard: The Making of the Penitentiary

John Howard (1726–1790) was a man of means who inherited a sizable estate at Cardington near to Bedford (in England). He ran the Cardington estate in a progressive manner and with careful attention to the conditions of the homes and education of the citizens who were under his stead. In 1773, the public position as Sheriff of Bedfordshire became vacant, and Howard was given the appointment. Among his duties as Sheriff was that of prison inspector. While conducting his inspections, Howard was appalled by the unsanitary conditions that he found. Further, he was dismayed and shocked by the lack of justice in a system where offenders paid their gaolers (an Old English spelling for jailers) and were kept jailed for nonpayment even if they were found to be innocent of their alleged crime.

Howard traveled throughout England and elsewhere throughout Europe, examining prison conditions in a wide variety of settings. He was particularly moved by the conditions that he found on the English hulks and was an advocate for improvements in the conditions of these and other facilities. Howard was impressed with many of the institutions in France and Italy. In 1777, he used those institutions as examples from which he drafted his *State of Prisons* treatise to be presented to Parliament.

APPLIED THEORY 1.1

Classical School of Criminology, Behavioral Psychology, and Corrections

Beyond Cesare Beccaria, another noteworthy figure associated with classical criminology was Jeremy Bentham. In addition to his notion of hedonistic calculus, Bentham is known for advocating that punishments should be swift, severe, and certain. This has been widely touted by classical criminologists and even by many modern-day criminologists who have leanings toward classical and/or rational choice theories on crime. Essentially, Bentham believed that a delay in the amount of time between the crime and the punishment impaired the likely deterrent value of the punishment in the future. Likewise, Bentham held that punishments must be severe enough in consequence as to deter persons from engaging in criminal behavior. Lastly, Bentham noted that the punishment must be ensured; otherwise offenders will simply become cleverer at hiding their crimes once they know that the punishment can be avoided.

Current research actually supports some aspects of classical criminology while refuting other points. In particular, it has been found that the certainty of the punishment does indeed lower the likelihood of recidivism. Likewise, the less time between the crime and the punishment, the less likely offenders will reoffend in the future. However, it has not been found to be true that the severity of the punishment is successful in reducing crime. In fact, there has been substantial historical research on the death penalty that seems to indicate that general deterrence is not achieved with the death penalty, even though it is the most severe punishment that can be given.

In addition, many behavioral psychologists note that if punishment is to be effective, certain considerations must be taken into account. These considerations, summarized by Davis and Palladino (2002, pp. 262–263), are presented below:

1. The punishment should be delivered immediately after the undesirable behavior occurs
(similar to the "swiftness" requirement of classical criminologists).

2. The punishment should be strong enough to make a real difference to that particular organism. *This is similar to the "severity" requirement of classical criminologists, but this point also illustrates that "severity" may be perceived differently from one person to another.*

3. The punishment should be administered after each and every undesired response. *This is similar to the "certainty" requirement of classical criminologists.*

4. The punishment must be applied uniformly with no chance of undermining or escaping the punishment. *When considering our justice system, it is clear that this consideration is undermined by the plea-bargaining process.*

5. If excessive punishment occurs and/or is not proportional to the aberrant behavior committed, the likelihood of aggressive responding increases. *In a similar vein and as noted earlier, excessive prison sentences simply increase crime, including violent crime.*

6. To ensure that positive changes are permanent, provide an alternative behavior that can gain reinforcement for the person. *In other words, reintegrative efforts to instill positive behaviors and activities must be supplemented for those behaviors and activities that are criminal in nature.*

From the above points, it should be clear that there is a great deal of similarity between classical criminologists and behavioral psychologists on the dynamics associated with the use of punishment. This is important because it demonstrates that both criminological and psychological theories can provide a clear basis as to how correctional practices should be implemented. In addition, the second consideration above demonstrates the need for severity, but it illustrates a point often overlooked; severity of a punishment is in the eye of the beholder. For instance, some offenders would prefer to simply "do flat time" in prison rather than complete the various requirements of community supervision. This is particularly true for offenders who have become habituated to prison life. In these cases, the goal should be to acclimate the offender not to prison life, but to community life as a responsible and productive citizen.

SOURCE: Excerpted from Davis, S. F. & Palladino, J. J. (2002). *Psychology* (3rd Ed.). Upper Saddle River, NJ: Prentice Hall.

Jeremy Bentham: Hedonistic Calculus

Jeremy Bentham (1748–1832) was the leading reformer of the criminal law in England during the late 1700s and early 1800s, and his work reflected the vast changes in criminological and penological thinking that was taking place at that time. Born roughly 10 years after Beccaria, Bentham was strongly influenced by Beccaria's work. In particular, Bentham was a leading advocate for the use of graduated penalties as a means of more closely connecting the punishment with the crime. Naturally, this was consistent with Beccaria's ideas that punishments should be proportional to the crimes committed.

Bentham believed that a person's behavior could be determined through scientific principles. He believed that behavior could be shaped by the outcomes that it produced. This led to expected outcomes that influenced future behavior. Bentham, like Beccaria, believed that human behavior was rational and that the shaping of this rational behavior was due to an inherent human desire to maximize a sense of pleasure and to minimize experiences that were painful or unpleasant. Indeed, Bentham contended that the primary motivation for intelligent and rational people was to optimize the likelihood of obtaining pleasurable experiences while minimizing the likelihood of obtaining painful or unpleasant experiences. This is sometimes called the pleasure-pain principle and is more officially referred to as **hedonistic calculus**. Bentham's views are reflected in his reforms of the criminal law in England. Bentham, just like Beccaria, believed that punishment could act as a deterrent and that punishment's main purpose, therefore, should be to deter future criminal behavior.

The Walnut Street Jail in America

In 1790, the establishment of the first true correctional facility in America occurred. This facility was called the **Walnut Street Jail** and was America's first attempt to actually incarcerate inmates with the purpose of reforming them. This occurred when the Pennsylvania legislature officially allocated one wing of the jail as an official penitentiary where convicted felons were provided educational opportunities, religious services, basic medical attention, and access to productive work activity. These innovations and acts of humane treatment were well ahead of their time, and it is because of these distinctions (and the official declaration by the Pennsylvania legislature) that the Walnut Street Jail is commonly considered the first penitentiary in America (Carlson et al., 2008). Further, it is important to note that this description of services mirrors the definition of corrections that was provided to students earlier in this chapter. Thus, it is perhaps accurate to say that the Walnut Street Jail was also the first attempt at correction in the United States (Carlson et al., 2008).

However, it is very important that students read the following point very carefully: *The Walnut Street Jail was not the first prison in America; rather it was the first penitentiary*. The difference is that a penitentiary, by definition, is intended to have the offender seek penitence and reform, whereas a prison simply holds an offender in custody for a prolonged period of time. Aside from technical aspects of the definition of a penitentiary, it is important to note that there was, in actuality, another prison that had been established in Connecticut prior to the addition of the penitentiary wing of the Walnut Street Jail. Though this prison was crude in construction, its remnants can be found even today in Granby, Connecticut. This prison, **Old Newgate Prison**, was established in 1773 and was the very first prison structure in America. More on this first prison will be presented in Chapter 2, but it is mentioned here to ensure historical accuracy since very few corrections textbooks even mention this prison within their pages. This is an oddity in corrections texts, and the failure of authors to mention this prison is an oversight of an important detail in American corrections.

During the same year that Old Newgate Prison was established, the construction of the Walnut Street Jail was first authorized. The Walnut Street Jail was constructed to replace a another jail in Philadelphia, the High Street Jail, which had been constructed in 1718. The High Street Jail had consisted of two buildings, one for criminals and the other for debtors, runaway apprentices, and the idle poor. This reflects a truly different era in criminal justice history where debt and the inability to do one's agreed-upon workload was considered punishable by criminal law. In some cases, indentured servants might also be kept in jail, but only until their "masters" had them released; money was lost keeping them in jail with each day that they did not perform labor. Thus, servants and slaves did not spend much time (if any) in jail but were instead quickly returned to be put to work.

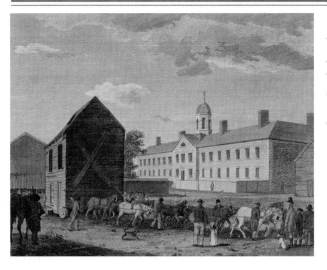

PHOTO 1.9

The Walnut Street Jail, pictured here, was America's first attempt to actually incarcerate inmates with the purpose of reforming them.

In January 1776, the first American Penitentiary Act was passed, and this marked the beginning of reform (Carlson et al., 2008). However, the American Revolutionary War delayed progress until 1790, when the Quakers and other prison reform advocates were able to gain legislative attention. During this time, due to the influence of the Quakers, the Pennsylvania legislature declared a wing of the Walnut Street Jail to be a penitentiary that would house convicted felons except those who were sentenced with a death penalty. Thus, while jails and workhouses had existed in America and Europe, this was the first facility to be specifically set aside for offenders under the auspices of corrections. There was also some degree of legislative influence to have counties from throughout Pennsylvania transport their prisoners with long-term sentences to the Walnut Street Jail (Carlson et al., 2008). This has been advocated as being the first trend toward the centralization of a prison system to the authority of the state rather than individual counties, as jails are organized. Thus, the Walnut Street Jail also heralded in the era where prisons would be a state-level function, not one presiding at the county level.

CONCLUSION

Corrections is a term that has origins in the need and/or desire to punish those who commit an aberrant behavior that is proscribed by society. Indeed, the terms *punishment* and *corrections* have shared common meanings throughout history. While this may be the case, this text provides a unique definition of corrections that describes the purpose of corrections and the activities of practitioners in the field. This text presents the term *corrections* as a process whereby practitioners from a variety of agencies and programs use tools, techniques, and facilities to engage in organized security and treatment functions intended to correct criminal tendencies among the offender population. This is provided as a more refined and improved definition of the term when compared with other textbooks on corrections.

In ancient times, the ability of an aggrieved party to gain retribution for a crime required some form of retaliation. In most cases, individuals or groups only achieved retribution if they were able to personally extract it from the offender. Later, over time, rulers of various groups organized processes of achieving retribution, thereby reducing the likelihood that conflicts between individuals and groups would escalate. Different types of compensation, such as wergilds and dooms, were implemented, which produced a variety of rules and customs when determining how crime victims should be compensated.

Regardless of the type of customs that existed in various areas of Europe, the use of physically humiliating punishments and crippling punishments was still widespread. When examining the history of punishment and corrections, it is clear that early punishments were quite barbaric when compared with today's forms of punishment. The use of corporal and capital punishments was common, and prisoners were seen as slaves of the state. Early laws regarding offenders and prisoners were rigid and stern. Much of the basis for these laws and for the harsh punishments revolved around the notion of deterrence; the thinking was that more severe punishments would deter others from crime.

The rise of the age of reason and the writings of a variety of scholars and philosophers helped shape the use of simple punishments from barbaric cruelty to corrective mechanisms intended to reduce problematic behaviors. Further, a distinct sense of rationality was used in administering punishments with new concepts being introduced. One of the premiere figures who advocated the use of reason was Cesare Beccaria. It was Beccaria who advocated for proportionality between the crime committed and the punishment that is received. Beccaria also contended that it was the certainty of punishment, not the severity, that would be more likely to deter crime. These novel concepts, as well as the contention that offenders should be treated humanely, marked the age of reason and the emergence of prison reform in Europe and the United States. It was during this time that the notion of corrections developed a true identity—one that was distinct from the simple infliction of pain and punishment.

END-OF-CHAPTER DISCUSSION QUESTIONS

1. Identify punishment and identify corrections. Explain how each differs from the other, and explain why they are often confused with one another.

2. Explain how punishment has progressed from ancient and medieval times to current-day practices. Are there still similarities in thought, and, if so, what are they?

3. What is the difference between public wrongs and private wrongs? Give an example of each in your response.

4. What role has religion played in the development of corrections in the United States? Provide an explanation of this role and key figures who were involved.

5. Identify key thinkers and persons of influence who have impacted the field of corrections. For each, be sure to highlight their particular contribution(s) to the field.

6. Provide a discussion of the theoretical/philosophical justifications associated with punishment and corrections.

7. What is the significance of Old Newgate Prison? What distinguishes this structure from the penitentiary wing added to the Walnut Street Jail?

8. Explain how the classical school of criminology, behavioral psychology, and the field of corrections can be interrelated in reforming offender behavior.

KEY TERMS

Banishment	Francois Voltaire	Public wrongs
Blood feuds	Gag	Sanctuary
Branding	Great Law	Stocks
Bridle	Hedonistic calculus	Theory of disablement
Brutalization hypothesis	Hulks Act	Treason
Cesare Beccaria	Jeremy Bentham	Trial by ordeal
Charles Montesquieu	John Howard	Walnut Street Jail
Classical criminology	Lex talionis	Wergild
Code of Hammurabi	Old Newgate Prison	Whipping
Corrections	Pillory	William Penn
Ducking stool	Private wrongs	Witchcraft

APPLICATION EXERCISE 1.1

Student Debate

Many people in society believe that incarcerated offenders should be made to work as a means of paying for their crime and supporting their stay while in prison. This, in and of itself, is not a problematic notion. However, inmates must be given humane working conditions, and, as a result, there are limits to the type of work they do and the circumstances under which it is done.

The ancient Romans essentially considered the inmate to be civilly dead and to also be a slave of the state. Though modern-day thinking with prison management does not advocate for inmates to hold such an arbitrary classification, some might say that such a legal classification is appropriate for offenders.

For this exercise, have half of the students in the classroom (or the online forum) provide tangible and logical reasons for why inmates should be treated as slaves of the state. Have the other half of the room or forum argue against categorizing inmates as slaves of the state.

Students should keep in mind some of the counterintuitive findings when punishment is too severe, and they should also keep in mind the thoughts of Cesare Beccaria and other philosophers on corrections. Both teams of students should come up with at least three substantial points to argue on whichever side they have been assigned.

"WHAT WOULD YOU DO?"

You are a judge in Old England, the year is 1798, and the Crown has given you some very explicit instructions for this week. It appears that there is no room onboard the hulks that float in the River Thames, and, with the traitorous rebellion of the American colonies in the New World, there is nowhere that exists to transport criminals for banishment. With this in mind, the Crown is desperate to reduce criminal acts and has recently decided that the best means to do this is by setting some very strong and severe examples to the public. Thus, you have been told that you must use one of two sentences today: provide the death penalty for anyone found guilty of any crime that is eligible for the death penalty or find those persons innocent of their charges and thereby make invalid the need for any punishment whatsoever. In other words, you must either rule innocence or give offenders in your court the death penalty.

This is also during a time when England's criminal code has been given the nickname of "Bloody Code" among the commoners of the British Empire. You are well aware that there is serious discontent among the peasantry in your area with this code and that the Crown has previously approached the extensive use of the gallows with trepidation; such circumstances can breed riots and, in very extreme times, rebellion. On the other hand, you know that many of the wealthy in the area are typically supportive of harsh penalties against the working poor (such penalties discourage theft of their own property). You sit at your bench, waiting to make your determination regarding three offenders who are accused of different crimes. All of the crimes for which they are accused will entail the use of the death penalty. These three offenders and their circumstances are noted as follows:

Offender 1: Mr. Drake Dravies, a brigand and a buccaneer who deflowered a 10-year-old girl, against her will, and attempted to kill her but was caught before doing so. *You know for a fact that this man committed this crime.*

Offender 2: Ms. Eliza Goodberry, a single spinster maid who worked in the fish market. She was found guilty of being a witch and consorting with demons. It is rumored that she gave secret birth to a demon child. *You know for a fact that this woman did not commit this crime, and you know that she is not, in actuality, a witch.*

Offender 3: Mr. John McGraw, a general laborer who stole food in the open market (and almost got away with it) to feed his family. Labor shortages and tough economic times have left him with few other options. *You know for a fact that this man committed this crime, and you also know that it is true that he committed this crime simply to feed his family.*

You must make a decision; either you must declare all three innocent of the crimes, as charged, or you must give all three the death penalty by hanging at the gallows. There is no option to try these persons for these crimes at a later date.

What do you do?

CROSS-NATIONAL PERSPECTIVE 1.1

Penal Slavery in Western Europe and East Asia

The use of penal slavery was extensive in ancient Rome, though the actual economic benefits for this type of labor were minimal. For the most part, penal slavery in Rome was restricted to those offenders who had been given a life sentence. In such cases, these offenders suffered a civil death and no longer existed in society; they were thereby permanent slaves of the state. A strong distinction was drawn between these offenders and those who did not have a life sentence. Among those offenders not serving life, penal servitude was exacted. Though this was similar in most respects to penal slavery, there was a time limit in which the sentence was considered served.

In many East Asian countries, penal slaves were a source of both public and private slaves. Prisoners provided the bulk of the enslaved population in Vietnam even though slavery was not an important industry in that country. In Korea, which is thought to have one of the most advanced slave systems in East Asia, penal slavery was used but was not the primary source of slaves. In Japan, around the 6th century A.D., the two primary sources of slaves were prisoners of war and the familial relatives of convicted criminals as well as the offenders themselves. However, it was the nation of China that truly used penal slavery on a widespread basis.

The enslavement of family members related to condemned offenders was, in actuality, the primary and perhaps the only source from which penal slaves were drawn. Due to a strong rank system whereby family honor subsumed individual identity, if a family were disgraced by the acts of a criminal, it was the entire family that could be held accountable for the crime(s) committed. Prior to the Han Dynasty, there was a tendency to execute criminal offenders and imprison their family members, but over time Chinese royalty imprisoned all persons.

Because most if not all slaves were penal slaves in China, the common view of slaves became one of being criminal and therefore unworthy of fair treatment. The status of criminal opened the door for mutilation, torture, and abuse, all of which were condoned by Chinese law, just as was found in much of old Europe. However, China was unusual in one routine practice in its penal slavery policy; many penal slaves ended up becoming property of private owners. Usually given as gifts to the affluent and/or powerful, they were often acquired by unscrupulous government officials and/or military officers. It is in this manner that many of the elite private citizens in China had slaves of various sorts.

It would appear that many of the ancient punishments, such as flogging, and the use of different forms of the death penalty, were used by cultures in the East and the West. Further, most cultures in either area of the world refrained from using jails for anything other than holding an offender in custody until punishment could be administered. The use of prisons as a form of punishment, in and of itself, was not common in either area of the world. However, the use of criminal offenders as cheap and exploitable labor seems to be common in both areas of the world. A primary distinction between East and West revolved around the strong family honor system, which, in the grand scheme of things, generated a much larger penal slave population that included a large number of women as well as men in Imperial China. This, and the existence of slaves among private Chinese social elites, demonstrates how cultural differences can impact the means by which punishments such as penal servitude are implemented.

Question 1: What are two key distinctions between penal slavery in Rome and penal slavery in Imperial China? Why did these differences exist?

Question 2: For what purpose were jails used in both the Eastern and the Western parts of the world? Was there widespread use of prisons as we know them today?

SOURCE: Patterson, O. (1982). *Slavery and social death: A comparative study*. Cambridge, MA: Harvard University Press.

STUDENT STUDY SITE

Visit the Student Study Site at **www.sagepub.com/hanserintro** to access links to the videos, audio clips, SAGE journal articles, state rankings, and reference materials noted in this chapter, as well as additional study tools including eFlashcards, web quizzes, and more.

chapter 2

The Development of Prisons in the United States

LEARNING OBJECTIVES:

1. Discuss the development of the first few prisons in the United States.

2. Distinguish between the Philadelphia and Auburn prison systems.

3. Identify differences in region and era regarding prison operations in American corrections.

4. Explain how state and federal prisons differ and identify the Big Four in American corrections.

5. Identify case law that was important in shaping penology in the United States.

INTRODUCTION: PUNISHMENT DURING EARLY AMERICAN HISTORY

As pointed out in Chapter 1, the population in the early American colonies tended to view crime more as an act of sin than as a social problem. In most cases, criminal offenders were viewed as sinners who should seek redemption. Further, the punishments that the American colonies used had been carried over from England. As we have seen, these punishments were harsh and tended to be physical in nature. But, with the close of the American Revolution, there was a social shift in correctional thinking. During this time, new ideas emerged, and, as we have seen, new thinkers on correctional practice began to change perceptions in America.

With the exception of William Penn, the penal reformists presented in Chapter 1 all came from Europe and did the majority of their work on that continent. Indeed, each of these persons (Montesquieu, Voltaire, Beccaria, Howard, and Bentham) was not influential until after Penn's death in 1718. In fact, Beccaria, Howard, and Bentham were not born until after William Penn had passed away, while Montesquieu and Voltaire were in their mid- to late 20s at this time. The reason that this is important is twofold. First, it is important for students to understand the historical chronological development of correctional thought. Second, this demonstrates that while the American colonies experienced reform in the early 1700s, this reform was lost when the Great Law in Pennsylvania was overturned upon Penn's death in 1718. From the time of Penn's demise until about 1787, penal reform and new thought on corrections largely occurred in Europe, leaving America in a social and philosophical vacuum (Johnson, Wolfe, & Jones, 2008).

This digression in correctional thought continued throughout the 1700s and culminated with what is, today, a little known detail in American penological history. The Old Newgate Prison, located in Connecticut, was the first official prison in the United States. The structure of this prison reflects the lack of concern for reforming offenders, which developed during this era. Old Newgate Prison was crude in design and, in actuality, served two purposes; it was both a chartered copper mine and used as a colonial prison from 1773 until 1827. This prison housed inmates underground and was designed to punish the offenders while they were under hard labor. This underground prison is reminiscent of the old Roman prisons that utilized limestone quarries to contain prisoners who would toil the day away as they served their sentences. Due to the desire to strengthen security of the facility (there had been successful escape attempts from this prison), a brick-and-mortar structure was built around the entry to the mine that consisted of an exterior walled compound and observation/guard towers. Thus, this facility truly was a prison, albeit a crude one. However, it was not built for correctional purposes; its purpose was solely punishment.

Students are encouraged to read Focus Topic 2.1: Escape From Old Newgate Prison, for a very interesting tale and historical account of the development and use of this prison. As noted in Chapter 1, this prison is hardly mentioned in most texts on American corrections; this should not be the case since this was, in actuality, a very significant development in American penological history. Further, Old Newgate Prison demonstrates how the development of prison construction and correctional thought occurred over the span of years with many lessons that were hard learned. Thus, the history of this prison is a critical beginning juncture in American penology and also demonstrates how modifications to prison structure became increasingly important when administering a system designed to keep offenders in custody. As we will see in future chapters, the concern with secure custody plagued correctional professionals throughout subsequent eras of prison development, with custody of the offender being the primary mandate of secure facilities.

PHOTO 2.1

Contrary to popular thought, Old Newgate Prison (pictured here), located in Connecticut, was the first official prison in the United States.

While the Old Newgate Prison was in full operation in Connecticut, advocates of prison reform in Pennsylvania were gaining momentum after several decades of apparent dormancy. A little over 60 years elapsed from William Penn's death when, in the late 1780s, an American medical doctor and political activist by the name of **Benjamin Rush** became influential in the push for prison reform (Carlson, Roth, & Travisono, 2008). Rush was an opponent of public punishment and

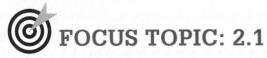

FOCUS TOPIC: 2.1

Escape From Old Newgate Prison

Just a couple of years before the first shots of the American Revolution were fired, the Connecticut General Assembly decided that what the colony needed most was a good, heavy-duty gaol. In the legislators' wisdom, any new prison would have to meet certain specifications. It would have to be fairly close to Hartford; absolutely escape-proof; self-supporting (i.e., inmates would have to be "profitably employed"); and—most important of all, then as now—cheap to build and maintain.

Near "Turkey Hills," in the region of northern Simsbury (now East Granby), there were some abandoned copper mines that had been sporadically dug with disappointing results since early in the century. It was thought that these mines might be suitable as a makeshift prison. The legislature immediately appointed a three-member study commission to "view and explore the copper mines at Simsbury . . . and consider whether they may be beneficially applied to the purpose of confining, securing and profitably employing such criminals and delinquents as may be committed to them." So, off went the commissioners into the Turkey Hills.

When they filed their report with the assembly a few months later, it was obvious that the study group had been mighty impressed with the prison potential of a many-shafted mine that ran deep under a mountain called, appropriately enough, Copper Hill. Only 18 miles from Hartford, the mine boasted at least one cavern, 20 feet below ground, large enough to accommodate a "lodging room" 16 feet square. There were also lots of connecting tunnels where prisoners could be gainfully employed by being made to pick away at the veins of copper ore located there.

Better yet, according to the report, the only access to the mine from outside came from two air shafts: one 25 and the other 70 feet deep, the latter leading to "a fine spring of water." Still better was the £37 total estimated cost of mine-to-gaol conversion: £17 for the underground room, and £20 for the "doors" to cover the outside access holes. By October 1773, the government had obtained a lease from the landowner at Copper Hill, carpenters had built the lodging room, and workmen had fitted a heavy iron door into the 25-foot air shaft, 6 feet beneath the surface. In the same month, also, the General Assembly designated the place as "a public gaol or workhouse, for the use of this Colony"; named it "Newgate Prison," after London's dismal house of detention; and appointed a "Master" (or "Keeper") and three "Overseers" to administer the gaol.

Only men (never women) who had been convicted of the most dastardly crimes known to the colony—burglary, robbery, counterfeiting or passing funny money, and horse-stealing—were eligible for a one-way trip down the 25-foot hole in the ground into the state's dank, dark prison-without-walls. Chosen for the dubious honor of being Newgate's first prisoner was one John Hinson, a 20-year-old man about whom—considering his historic, "groundbreaking" status—surprisingly little is known. Convicted for some unrecorded crime and remanded to Newgate by the Superior Court on December 22, 1773, Hinson spent exactly 18 days in the "escape-proof" gaol, before departing quietly for parts unknown, apparently during the early morning hours of January 9, 1774. Although no one saw him leave, obviously, there was some evidence that he had used the 70-foot well shaft to climb out of the mine, a difficult but not impossible feat, given Hinson's youth, diminutive size (5 feet, 6 inches), and compelling motivation.

Since there was no wall or enclosure of any kind around Newgate's grounds at the time, it was a simple matter, so the story ran, for someone to walk up to the deep but coverless well shaft, drop a rope down, and pull the prisoner out of the underground gaol. Since the natural barriers were so forbidding, the argument continued, no man could have escaped without some sort of "outside" help. Therefore, concluded the Overseers, Hinson must have had assistance in his climb to freedom and subsequent disappearance.

As a consequence of the successful escape of John Hinson and, three months later, three more Newgate prisoners, the Connecticut General Assembly reluctantly came to the conclusion that two holes and an underground mine do not necessarily a prison make. So they ordered a series of modifications that included, in 1802, the erection of a high stone wall around the prison.

Finally, in September 1827, after almost 54 years of operation, during which well over 800 prisoners were committed to its clammy subterranean dungeons, Newgate Prison was abandoned, and the remaining inmates were transferred to the new state prison at Wethersfield. Significantly enough, the last escape attempt occurred on the night before the move to Wethersfield, when a prisoner fell back into the well—and drowned—as he tried to emulate old John Hinson, of sainted memory. Coming when it did, at the bitter end of the facility's long, dark history, the death was a tragic, but somehow fitting, reminder of Newgate's most enduring legend.

SOURCE: Philips, D.E. *Legendary Connecticut: Traditional Tales from the Nutmeg State*. Willimantic: Curbstone Press. Copyright © 1992 by Joseph L. Steinberg. Reprinted by permission of Northwestern University Press.

also held that punishment should be used to reform the offender rather than existing as a mechanism of humiliation and/or revenge. In 1787, Rush, Quakers, and other reformers met together in what was then the first official prison reform group, the **Philadelphia Society for Alleviating the Miseries of Public Prisons** (which was later named the Pennsylvania Prison Society) to consider potential changes in penal codes among the colonies (Carlson et al., 2008). This group, in addition to the Quakers, was active in the ultimate development of the penitentiary wing within the Walnut Street Jail, which was established in 1790 (Carlson et al., 2008).

While the Walnut Street Jail marked a clear victory for prison reformers, the jail (and its corresponding penitentiary wing) eventually encountered serious problems with overcrowding, time management, and organization, as well as challenges with the maintenance of the physical facilities. Over time, frequent inmate disturbances and violence led to high staff turnover, and, by 1835, the Walnut Street Jail was closed. This icon of reform stayed in operation only eight years longer than the Old Newgate Prison.

THE PENNSYLVANIA SYSTEM

During the 1820s two models of prison operation emerged; these were the Pennsylvania and Auburn systems (Carlson et al., 2008). These two systems came into vogue as the Old Newgate Prison was closed and once it became fairly clear that the Walnut Street Jail was not a panacea for prison and/or correctional concerns. With the approved allocation of Western State Penitentiary and Eastern State Penitentiary, the beginning of the Pennsylvania system was set into motion. The site for Western Penitentiary was just outside of Pittsburgh, while Eastern Penitentiary was located near Philadelphia in an area referred to as Cherry Hill. Throughout history and particularly in most introductory textbooks on corrections, much more attention is given to Eastern Penitentiary than to Western Penitentiary. This may seem odd since Western Penitentiary was actually built first. However, early historical circumstances surrounding each prison facility can explain why this occurred.

In 1826, almost three years prior to the building of Eastern Penitentiary, the doors of **Western Penitentiary** were open for the reception of inmates. Western Penitentiary opened with solitary cells for 200 inmates following the original ideal of the Philadelphia Society for Alleviating the Miseries of Public Prisons to have solitary confinement without labor (Stanko, Gillespie, & Crews, 2004). However, doubts immediately arose as to whether this would truly have reformative benefits among offenders and if it would be economical. Advocates of Western Penitentiary contended that solitary confinement would be economical because offenders would be likely to repent more quickly, resulting in a reduced need for facilities (Sellin, 1970).

Video Link 2.1
Take a video tour of the Eastern Penitentiary.

Although Western Penitentiary operated in this manner from 1826 to 1829 (when Eastern Penitentiary opened), the Pennsylvania legislature made inmate labor a requirement as a means of offsetting the costs of solitary confinement that quickly exceeded the early estimates of penitentiary planners. Stanko et al. (2004) note that the cells of Western Penitentiary were too small and dark to allow inmates to work adequately. Though attempts were made to remodel the prison structure, the process was costly and very difficult considering the brick-and-mortar construction of the facility. In 1833, the cell blocks were demolished, and Western Penitentiary was rebuilt to better accommodate inmates and to provide sufficient space whereby labor could be completed within the solitary cells (Stanko et al., 2004). While this occurred, construction of Eastern Penitentiary continued, but planners were careful to learn from the mistakes of Western Penitentiary. It is because of this that Eastern Penitentiary has drawn most of the attention when historians and prison buffs talk about the Pennsylvania system of corrections.

In 1829 **Eastern Penitentiary** was opened and designed on a separate confinement system of housing inmates, similar to Western Penitentiary. This system was designed so that inmates could reside in their cells indefinitely. Aside from unforeseen emergencies,

PHOTO 2.2

Western Penitentiary, located outside of Pittsburgh, Pennsylvania, first opened with approximately 200 solitary cells for inmates in 1826.

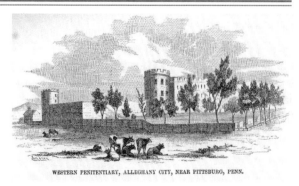

WESTERN PENITENTIARY, ALLEGHANY CITY, NEAR PITTSBURG, PENN.

special circumstances, or medical issues, inmates spent 24 hours a day in their cells. Inmates in Eastern Penitentiary ate, slept, and worked within the confines of their cells. These inmates also received moral instruction in their cells and were provided the Holy Bible as their only reading source. Inmates at Eastern Penitentiary had very little contact with other human beings and were expected to keep silent. They had interactions with only a few human beings, including the warden, guards, the prison chaplain, and persons who visited the prison from time to time to see its progress.

Eastern Penitentiary was sometimes referred to as the Cherry Hill facility because it had been built on the grounds of a cherry tree orchard. This facility, when originally built, had seven wings that resembled spokes in a wheel that extended out from a central section of the structure. The original structure had 252 cells, and each cell block had a single passage running down the center with 21 cells on either side. Each of the cells was much more spacious than those of Western Penitentiary, with dimensions being 12-foot width by 7-foot length and an overall height of 16 feet to the ceiling. The conditions within Eastern Penitentiary were quite humane and well ahead of their time. Indeed, Johnston (2009, p. 1) notes,

Journal Article Link 2.1
Read little known facts about the Eastern Penitentiary.

> Each prisoner was to be provided with a cell from which they would rarely leave and each cell had to be large enough to be a workplace and have attached a small individual exercise yard. Cutting edge technology of the 1820s and 1830s was used to install conveniences unmatched in other public buildings: central heating (before the U.S. Capitol); a flush toilet in each cell (long before the White House was provided with such conveniences); shower baths (apparently the first in the country).

It is clear that the physical conditions of this facility were sanitary even by today's standards. Further, the conditions of day-to-day treatment were also similar to what one might find in some prisons today. Inmates were allowed one hour of exercise recreation per day. For those inmates who had cells on the ground floor, individual walled exercise yards were connected to their cells. Those inmates who were kept on the second floor of the cell block were allocated an extra cell used for recreation and exercise. This same type of recreational system is still used today in many correctional systems that have inmates who are in administrative segregation or under similar classification statuses. Though inmates in modern facilities may be escorted to their recreation space (minimizing the need for extra cells), the basic concept used today for recreation is still similar to that used in Eastern Penitentiary.

Advocates of the Pennsylvania system believed that solitary confinement was, in and of itself, sufficient punishment for offenders since human beings are social creatures and the inmate would be restricted from social activities. This was a novel point in providing a rationale for this approach to confinement since it essentially noted that the loss of liberty, including social liberty, was a pain of imprisonment that alone equated to a punishment serious enough to be commensurate with a criminal act. As with Western Penitentiary, it was thought that solitary confinement would save expenses since offenders would reform more rapidly and would need less time in individual confinement than if they were not kept separate. This reduced amount of time was supposed to lower the costs of housing inmates, in the longest of terms (Sellin, 1970). Just like Western Penitentiary, this was ultimately found to be false.

Ultimately, the Pennsylvania system of separate confinement drew substantial controversy. This system of confinement could not keep up with the rising number of offenders who were incarcerated. Further, reports of abusive treatment of inmates at the hands of custodial staff began to emerge. Rumors and allegations continued so that, in less than a decade, an appointed body of inspectors had been tasked to examine the developments within the penitentiary. The result of these inspections found that inmates were having emotional breakdowns, with various forms of mental illness emerging due to the extreme isolation. Prison suicide attempts became commonplace within the facility, which, by religious Quaker standards, meant that those inmates would not have their souls redeemed—an obvious failure at reform, both in the material world and in the spiritual world that the Quakers believed in.

As a means of keeping inmates in check, custodial staff had resorted to physical punishments, which naturally undermined the point and purpose of the Pennsylvania system's orientation to corrections. Further, crowding continued in Pennsylvania as well as other states, and, over time, the use of individual confinement was eliminated. Though Pennsylvania would continue to adamantly attempt this form of correctional management throughout the early 1800s, the start of the Civil War would necessitate more space and also made funds less available, the result being that the practice of individual confinement was largely abandoned by that time in history. Such was the demise of the Pennsylvania system of penitentiary management.

FOCUS TOPIC: 2.2

Prisoner Number One at Eastern Penitentiary

In 1830, Charles Williams, prisoner number one of Eastern State Penitentiary, contemplated his situation with a sense of somber and solemn reflection. He did this undisturbed, due to the excruciating silence that seemed to permeate most of his incarceration. On occasion, he could hear keys jingling, and he might hear the sound of footsteps as guards brought his food or other necessities. On some occasions, he could hear the noise of construction as the facility was not yet fully finished and would not be fully functional for years to come. Otherwise, there was no other sound or connection to the outside world, with silence being the most common experience throughout most of the daylight hours and throughout the entire night.

To be sure, Charles had all of his most basic needs met while here at Eastern Penitentiary. He had his own private cell that was centrally heated and even had running water. He had a flushing toilet, a skylight, and a small adjacent walled private recreation yard for his own personal use. In his high-pitched and sky-lit cell, Charles had only natural light, the Bible, and his assigned work (he was involved in basic weaving) to keep him busy throughout the day. He was not allowed interaction with the guards or other inmates, and his food was brought to him via a slot in the door. In addition, he was to not leave his cell for anything other than recreation in his own walled yard, and—even then—he was required to wear a special mask that prevented communication with other guards or inmates while he entered the yard.

Charles was a farmer by trade. He had been caught and convicted of burglary and had been found to have stolen a $20 watch, a $3 gold seal, and a gold key. For his crime, he was sentenced to two years of confinement with hard labor. He had served seven months of his sentence (being brought to Eastern Penitentiary on October 23, 1829), and already he felt as if he had been incarcerated for an eternity. He reflected daily (and quite constantly) on his crime. However, he had no idea what Eastern State Penitentiary would be like. As it turned out, it was quite numbing to Charles's sense of mental development, and he sometimes felt as if he did not even exist. Charles remembered his first glimpse of the tall, foreboding exterior of the then unfinished prison as his locked carriage approached the structure. It was an intimidating sight, and Charles, being only 18 at the time of his sentencing, did indeed feel remorseful. He remembered when Warden Samuel R. Wood received him and explained that he would be overseeing his stay at Eastern Penitentiary. The warden was very direct and matter-of-fact and exhibited a mean-spirited temperament. Charles found the warden to be reflective of his entire experience while serving in prison cell number one at Eastern. He likewise had determined that he did not want to spend any more of his life in such confinement.

Charles considered the fact that he still had 18 months of his sentence. He could hear the further construction of the penitentiary (it would be under construction for years to come) and knew that other inmates would soon follow his stay. However, he was not the least bit curious about the future of Cherry Hill. He was indeed repentant, but not necessarily for the reasons that early Quaker advocates might have hoped when they advocated for Eastern State Penitentiary. Rather than looking to divine inspiration as a source of redemption from future solitary incarceration, he simply decided that he would never again be in a position where he could be accused of, guilty of, or caught in the commission of a crime. He just wanted to go back to simple farming and leave Cherry Hill (Eastern Penitentiary) out of his mind and life for the remainder of his years. In the meantime, he had another 17 months to go, an eternity for most 18-year-olds

SOURCE: Author.

THE AUBURN SYSTEM

In 1816, just 11 years before Old Newgate Prison closed in 1827, 19 years before the Walnut Street Jail closed in 1835, 10 years prior to the opening of Western Penitentiary in 1826, and 13 years prior to the opening of Eastern Penitentiary in 1829, the state of New York opened the Auburn Prison (see Table 2.1). The means by which New York operated its prison grounds were different than the modes of operation in Pennsylvania. This alternative system was termed the **Auburn system** or congregate system, which was a harsh program in which inmates were kept in solitary confinement during the evening but were permitted to work together during the day. Throughout all of their activities, inmates were expected to stay silent and were not allowed to communicate with one another by any means whatsoever. Initially, this type of prison operation was implemented in Auburn, New York, and Ossining, New York. Ossining would later be known as Sing Sing Prison. The Auburn system of prison management was a significant turning point in American penology since it redefined much of the point and purpose of a prison facility.

TABLE 2.1   Timeline for the Opening and Closure of Early American Prisons

Prison	Year Opened	Year Closed
Old Newgate Prison	1773	1827
Walnut Street Jail	1790	1835
Auburn Prison	1816	Still Open. Renamed: Auburn Correctional Facility
Western Penitentiary	1826	Closed in 2005 and Reopened in 2007. Renamed: State Correctional Institution Pittsburgh
Eastern Penitentiary	1829	1971

Auburn designs tended to have much smaller cells than the Pennsylvania system, due to the fact that inmates were allowed out of their cells on a daily basis so that they could go to work. Auburn facilities were designed as industry facilities that had some type of factory within them. The economic emphasis throughout the Auburn system was one that became popular among other states and spread throughout the nation. In addition to the overall economic model and concept, there was strict enforcement that ensured obedience to prison employees and institutional regulations. Chains, whippings and beatings, solitary confinement, and limited food rations became tools to shape behavior within the prison (Carlson & Garrett, 2008).

PHOTO 2.3

Auburn Prison, in the state of New York, was first opened in 1816. Today it is still in operation but has been renamed Auburn Correctional Facility.

In 1821, **Elam Lynds** was made warden at Auburn, and he was the primary organizer behind the development of the Auburn system. Warden Lynds contended that all inmates should be treated equally, and he also believed that a busy and strict regimen was the best way to run a prison. The prison schedule consisted of a number of activities that included lockstep marching and very rigid discipline. It is at this time that the classic white-and-black striped uniforms appeared, these uniforms being the product of the Auburn system. All inmates were expected to work, read the Bible, and pray each day. The idea was that through hard work, religious instruction, penitence, and obedience, the inmate would change from criminal behavior to law-abiding behavior (Carlson & Garrett, 2008).

The Auburn system of prison operation initially had economic success due to several factors. First, the proceeds generated from inmate labor aided in offsetting the costs of housing the inmates. Second, the use of the congregate system allowed more productive work to take place—work that often required group effort. Third, the construction of the cell blocks in the Auburn system was different than that of the Pennsylvania system, whose cell blocks occupied the outside wall of the prison building, with a long hall in the middle. In the Auburn system, as a means of saving money, the cells were built back-to-back, five tiers high in the shell of a building. The use of this design allowed for more inmates to be contained within the cell block and also cost less to build and maintain. Thus, the use of inmate labor, the inclusion of congregate supervision, and changes in facility construction all worked to make the Auburn system much more economically viable than the Pennsylvania system.

In addition to the operation of the prison itself, there were other innovations of the Auburn system that ensured its profitability. One of these was the use of inmate labor for profit through a contract labor system, which eventually became a mainstay feature of the Auburn system. The **contract labor system** utilized inmate labor through state-negotiated contracts with private manufacturers, who provided the prison with raw materials so that prison labor could refine the materials for the manufacturer (Roth, 2011). Items such as footwear, carpets, furniture, and clothing were produced through this system.

TWO AMERICAN PROTOTYPES IN CONFLICT

Both the Pennsylvania system and the Auburn system of prison construction and management had achieved attention in Europe by the late 1830s and were seen as unique models of prison management that were distinctly American in thought and innovation (Carlson et al., 2008). It was not long, however, until questions regarding the superiority of one system over the other began to emerge. Both the Pennsylvania system and the Auburn system had potential benefits and drawbacks. While Pennsylvania advocates criticized the Auburn system on several points, they particularly noted that it was not feasible to enforce silence when inmates would eat, work, and exercise together. Further, keeping inmates quiet when around one another was, in itself, a constant challenge that required constant discipline, as evidenced by the reliance on harsh punishments in the Auburn system. On the other hand, Auburn advocates criticized the Pennsylvania system by noting that prolonged periods of isolation created cruel and harmful conditions for the inmates that bred mental health problems and produced high rates of suicide.

Ultimately, the Auburn system was the model that states adopted due to the economic advantages that were quickly realized. In addition, the political climate of the time favored an emphasis on separation, obedience, labor, and silence since sentiments toward crime and criminals were less forgiving during this era. Maintaining a daily routine of hard work was the key to reform. Idleness, according to many advocates of this more stern system, provided convicts with time to teach one another how to commit future crimes. Thus, it was important to keep convicts busy so that they did not have the time or energy to dwell on the commission of criminal activity.

THE SOUTHERN SYSTEM OF PENOLOGY: PRE–CIVIL WAR

The climate and philosophy of southern penology has been captured on the silver screen in several classic prison movies such as *Cool Hand Luke* and *Brubaker*. Indeed, more modern films such as *O Brother, Where Art Thou?* portray southern penology in a manner that is similar to its predecessors. When examining southern penology, it is important to understand the different cultural and economic characteristics of the region, particularly when comparing this type of prison system with the Pennsylvania and New York systems. From a historical, social, and cultural standpoint, students should keep in mind that the slave era took place during the early to mid-1800s (up until 1864 or so), and this also impacted the manner in which corrections was handled in the South.

Prior to the Civil War, separate laws were required of slaves and free men who turned criminal. These laws were referred to as **Black Codes** and included harsher punishments for crimes than were given to White offenders (Browne, 2010). What is notable is that black slaves were not usually given prison sentences because this interfered with the ability of plantation owners to get labor out of the slave, a commodity desperately needed in the plantation system (Browne, 2010; Roth, 2011). Thus, during the pre–Civil War era, prisons typically had populations that included mostly White inmates with only a few free Blacks (Browne, 2010).

The 1850s saw the widespread leasing of inmates to private contractors to complete work outside of the prison facility. Often this included construction

PHOTO 2.4

These types of antebellum plantation homes were usually associated with plantation slavery. Rather than being put in prison, most African American slaves who committed crimes were kept on plantations and leased out for work due to the demand for labor in the South.

CORRECTIONS AND THE LAW 2.1

Ruffin v. Commonwealth *(1871)*

In 1871, the Virginia State Supreme Court noted that inmates were the "slave of the state" while serving their sentence. This case, known as *Ruffin v. Commonwealth* (62, Va. 790, 1871), established what has often been touted as the hands-off doctrine, whereby courts consistently left matters inside prisons to those persons tasked with their operation. Essentially, the courts (including the Supreme Court) stayed out of prison business during this period.

The reason for this approach is understandable. In the year 1871, the Civil War had come to a close just a few years prior, and it was not surprising that prior Confederate states like Virginia would consider inmates to be slaves of the state. However, this same legal principle was equally maintained in both the Northern and Southern regions of the United States. Much of this also had to do with the fact that, despite the end of the Civil War, issues related to state sovereignty were still a sensitive issue, and judges did not want to be enmeshed in legal issues that might aggravate an already tenuous situation. With this in mind, most judges refused to intervene on the grounds that their function was limited to freeing those inmates who had been illegally confined, which did not include meddling with the means by which prison administrators operated their facilities.

Thus, prisons operated in a virtual social vacuum, and wardens did not have to be concerned with public sentiments or any type of legal reprisal from inmates or their families. The legal stance of the courts all but ensured that prisons would operate in an unconstitutional manner since there was no incentive to do otherwise and since there was no punishment involved for the mistreatment of inmates. This would remain the case until the "hands-on era" took place alongside the civil rights movement, which ushered in sweeping social changes throughout the nation. The official turning point in which the hands-off doctrine began to eclipse was *Holt v. Sarver* (1969).

There is one last point that should be added. The ruling in *Ruffin v. Commonwealth* reflects a mentality regarding prisoners that harkens back to ancient Rome. As we have seen in this chapter, the Romans viewed criminals in custody as having a "civil death" while in custody. The rights afforded in *Ruffin* are similar, the presumption being that inmates are devoid of any rights or legal standing. It would appear that the legal status of offenders had not changed much throughout the centuries, allowing atrocities and cruel behavior to go unchecked as inmates were held as the invisible slaves of society.

---

on canals, roads, and bridges (Ayers, 1984; Browne, 2010). In all cases, the emphasis on labor and economic gain was prevalent throughout the South, especially since this region of the United States had an economy based on agriculture. Given the plantation-driven economy of the southern United States, it should be no surprise to find that the Auburn system of prison operation was used (Browne, 2010).

Similar to prison facilities in the North, these agriculturally based facilities had industrial shops that produced a variety of products that could be sold on the open market. However, the ability for these facilities to be truly self-sufficient was impractical. This led to the development of a convict lease system in many southern states (McShane, 1996a, 1996b; Roth, 2011). This lease system often contracted with private companies who would send skilled persons to supervise the work of the inmates within prison shops (Browne, 2010; McShane, 1996a, 1996b). This allowed for the use of inmate labor with more complicated (and more lucrative) forms of manufacture, all under the direction of a skilled expert who had incentive to maximize the labor outcome. Because company contractors had a strong profit motive, they would lower overhead by feeding and clothing the inmates as cheaply as possible, using guards to assist in the labor if they were willing to work at substandard wages, and working inmates from dusk until dawn.

THE SOUTHERN SYSTEM OF PENOLOGY: POST–CIVIL WAR

After the Civil War, the economy was in ruin, and the social climate was chaotic throughout the southern United States. In a time when things were very uncertain, there were few resources of any sort, and there were few ideas as to how the inmate population should be dealt with. Because there were not sufficient prison resources, the lease system continued to be implemented and expanded. It is interesting to point out that after the Civil War, over 90% of all leased inmates were in the South (McShane, 1996a, 1996b; Roth, 2011). This was largely due to the political and economic characteristics of the region as well as the termination of slavery that occurred with the South's defeat.

The lease system gained continued favor throughout the South for several reasons. After the Civil War, large numbers of emancipated African Americans began to be arrested as criminals and soon accounted for 90% of those incarcerated (McShane, 1996a, 1996b). Much of the reason for this was that most recently freed African Americans had not had access to paid employment, owned no property, and generally started out with no resources from which to support themselves. Indeed, many chose to simply remain on the plantation from which they had been enslaved, and many of those who stayed toiled to simply have some sort of place to stay. Basically, nearly the entire African American population was poverty-stricken due to their impoverished status as slaves. Without the benefit of years of wealth accumulation, most started from ground zero in the process of building their lives and the lives of their children (Browne, 2010).

Another issue that ensured that the leasing system would continue was the change from a slave-driven agricultural economy to an economy that was industrialized. Dangerous work, such as mining, building railroads, and the production of chemical compounds like turpentine, was assigned to convict labor forces. Further, convicts were worked under conditions that could not be attempted with free laborers. According to Silverman (2001), in many work camps, inmates would be awoken at 4:30 a.m. and work well into nightfall with only a 40-minute dinner being allowed throughout the interim.

Since the majority of the law-abiding citizenry had no concern for the welfare of convicts and tended to not be sympathetic to the inhumane working conditions that occurred, this proved to be a lucrative and workable arrangement for businesses and state systems. With this in mind, it is perhaps accurate to say that southern penology took a step backward in correctional advancement and did so in a manner that maximized profit at the expense of long-term reform and crime reduction. Because the system was profitable, there was no incentive to eliminate abuses within the prison system; incentive existed instead to further the cause of making money under inhumane practices.

The Chain Gang and the South

Chain gangs were a common feature within the southern penal system. This type of labor arrangement was primarily used by counties and states to build railroads and levees, and to maintain county roads and state highways (Carroll, 1996). Most jurisdictions viewed this type of labor as a way to make money and also reduce overhead in housing inmates. Indeed, the shackles were never removed from inmates on many chain gangs, and the men would usually sleep chained together in cages (Carroll, 1996). This eliminated the need for expensive prison beds and housing. As a means of squeezing maximum profit from the process, armed guards were routinely used. Whipping and other harsh practices were implemented (again, similar to the Auburn system) to discipline inmates who were not compliant (Carroll, 1996).

Convicts sentenced to work on the chain gang pulled work shifts of 10 to 12 hours a day in the inclement weather and good weather alike (Carroll, 1996; Roth, 2006). In addition, the overseers of this system were poorly paid and were often illiterate. This meant that, in a manner of speaking, the guard staff became dependent upon this system where, lacking any true job skills, they would settle for the substandard wage given as they furthered the cause of a system that exploited even them, though to a lesser extent when compared with the convict. Given these circumstances and the limited skills of the guard staff, the use of brute force and clumsy tactics of inmate control prevailed.

Southern Prison Farms

As the southern states slowly began to abolish the leasing system in the early 1900s, they began to create large prison farms that were reminiscent of the old plantations of the South (Roth, 2006). These farms operated to maximize profits and reduce the costs associated with incarceration of the inmate population. The method of treatment was not much of an improvement for these offenders than was the treatment they had received while on the chain gang. During the 1930s, major southern penal farms such as Angola in Louisiana and Cummins in Arkansas developed a sense of notoriety (Roth, 2006).

However, it was the Parchman Farm of Mississippi that developed into the prototype farm and was the envy of other states throughout the South. In Mississippi, penal farms were divided into autonomous

Audio Link 2.1
Hear about working on a chain gang.

Reference Link 2.1
Read about plantation prisons in the South.

field camps for purposes of crop rotation, accountability, self-sufficiency, and the disbursement of laborers. By 1917, Mississippi had 13 such farms that were profitably producing cotton and their own food for self-consumption (Roth, 2006). Labor on these farms began at sunrise, and continued for six days out of the week. The inmates were marched into the fields under the supervision of an unarmed sergeant and unarmed assistants, with several armed "trusty guards" on duty. These trusty guards were themselves inmates who were highly trusted by the staff and had aligned themselves with the staff and the correctional system. These types of prison farms remained profitable in Mississippi well into the 1940s (Roth, 2006).

PHOTO 2.5

Louisiana State Penitentiary Angola is a sprawling farm-like state prison that was built on the grounds of a plantation in the old South. This prison is now modern and sophisticated in the programming that is offered.

When the Great Depression occurred and when cotton prices lowered, the system became much less profitable. By the 1950s, the decline in profitability led to the pardoning and early release of more inmates, including the trusty inmates who maintained control over the institution. As conditions worsened and weakened, the civil rights movement began to take shape, and the emphasis of the prison on profit rather than reform came under greater scrutiny (McShane, 1996a, 1996b). Ultimately, the Parchman Farm and other institutions in Mississippi were not self-sustainable, and, amidst increasing inmate unrest on the inside and public concern on the outside, the system eventually was dismantled (Roth, 2006).

THE WESTERN SYSTEM OF PENOLOGY

As crime rose in the Wild West, settlers responded by building crude jails in the towns that lay scattered across the desert terrain. These jails were not very secure and typically did resemble how they are often portrayed on American television (Carlson & Garrett, 2008). For the most part, they were simply used as holding cells, and plans or long-term housing simply did not exist. During the years when most western states were still simply territories that had not achieved statehood, inmates were usually held in territorial facilities or in federal military facilities (Johnson et al., 2008).

PHOTO 2.6

Yuma prison, pictured here, is reflective of the southwestern style of penology.

As the need for space became more and more clear, most western states found it more economical and easier to simply contract with other states and with the federal government to take custody of their inmates (Carlson & Garrett, 2008). The western states paid a certain set cost each year and simply shipped their offenders elsewhere; given the social landscape at the time, this was perhaps the most viable of options that the western states could choose. According to Carlson and Garrett (2008), western states were paying approximately 50 cents per day, per inmate, for other states to maintain custody of their offenders. This allowed western states to avoid the costs of building and maintaining large prisons and/or plantations. As time went on, state governments in the West developed, and the region became more settled. Once this occurred, western states began to build their own prisons. These prisons were designed along the lines of the Auburn system with an emphasis on labor.

APPLIED THEORY 2.1

The Subculture of Violence Theory and Corrections

As presented by Wolfgang and Ferracuti (1967), the *subculture of violence theory* has been used to explain violence (particularly homicide) in a number of contexts and for a variety of different social groups. In their effort to explain why some groups are more prone to violence, Wolfgang and Ferracuti utilized elements of social learning theory in their work, contending that the development of favorable attitudes and norms toward violence generally involved some type of learned behavior. According to Wolfgang and Ferracuti, the subculture of violence simply suggests that there is a very clear theme of violence in the lifestyle of subculture members. In laying out their thesis, Wolfgang and Ferracuti proposed a series of tenets or key themes to explaining violent subcultures. A select set of these tenets, and their potential application to the field of corrections, is presented below:

1. **The constant state of vigilance and willingness to engage in violence demonstrates how violence permeates that culture and its sense of identity.** In this case, the number of incidents where a member engages in violence and the seriousness of that violence can serve as a social barometer of the member's assimilation within the subculture. In such circumstances, the overt use of violence and the use of serious violence (especially homicide) indicate the level of commitment that a member has to that subculture. Obviously, this has very clear implications for modern-day correctional systems that contend with prison gang problems, in which members may be required to commit some act of lethal violence as a requirement for membership and/or to gain an elevated status or rank within the gang.

Wolfgang and Ferracuti (1967) also make a very interesting point to note that among members of a given subculture, one would be able to recognize quantitative differences on psychological instruments and psychometric scales between members who are more prone to violence and those who are not as committed to a belief system grounded in violence. These differences would likely include the differential perception and processing of violent stimuli (including perceived aggressive intent where there is none), levels of compassion and/or remorse for violent acts, and/or differences in cognitive problem-solving skills. This is an important point to consider because this demonstrates how mental health professionals (i.e., psychologists, social workers, and counselors) can play a critical role in the correctional process. As is clear in this chapter, the medical model left a lasting legacy whereby mental health interventions became part-and-parcel to the correctional process.

2. **Nonviolence is considered a counternorm.** Peaceful approaches to the resolution of conflict are not respected between and among members: For members who do not act in kind to situations that require a violent response, their acceptance by others in the subculture will decrease. In short, cowardice and weakness bring dishonor on the group and on the individual member. In cases where the requirement for violence is considered a particularly strong expectation, members who fail to meet their obligation may themselves be killed by others in the subculture. This is particularly true within some organized crime groups and is also true among some street gangs and prison gangs. Because these values are learned out on the street as they are in prison, this type of thinking is doubly reinforced. However, survival in the violent prison environment can be contingent on adhering to this precept. Thus, inmates who wish to maintain the protection of gang membership while serving time will have to be willing to engage in violence.

3. **The various mechanisms of learning inherent to differential association theory and social learning theory apply to violent subcultures; violence is a learned behavior that is reinforced through shared identity and associations that favor violent acts.** This tenet explains how norms and values are shaped within the group as a whole and also explain how norms may vary from group to group both in the type and in the lethality of violence as a product of differential associations and differential forms of reinforcement. This holds clear implications for correctional administrators because it is likely that unchecked violence will beget additional violence. Even more interesting is the thought that the use of violence among security staff may magnify the effects of social learning upon many inmates who are subjected to this treatment and who observe it routinely.

4. **Within subcultures, the use of violence may not be perceived as wrong behavior and, as a result, is not likely to generate feelings of guilt or remorse among members.** This is a very important aspect of this theory and, in actuality, tends to reflect the emotional framework of psychopaths and/or offenders diagnosed with antisocial personality disorder. These groups of offenders tend to have a greater propensity to violence than do other offenders, and, in many cases, their autonomic nervous systems do not seem to process anxiety, fear, and even guilt or remorse as do other persons in the general population. These offenders will also tend to have psychological and personality characteristics that are quantifiable via psychometric tests, including such characteristics as levels of compassion or remorse (among others). This demonstrates again that the field of psychology provides a number of contributions for correctional systems that process offenders with offenders who are prone toward violence.

THE AGE OF THE REFORMATORY IN AMERICA

In 1870, prison reformers met in Cincinnati and ultimately established the National Prison Association (NPA). This organization was responsible for many changes in prison operations during the late 1800s that were listed in its Declaration of Principles (Wooldredge, 1996). This declaration advocated for a philosophy of reformation rather than the mere use of punishment, progressive classification of inmates, the use of indeterminate sentences, and the cultivation of the inmate's sense of self-respect—perhaps synonymous with self-efficacy in today's manner of speaking. These innovations were progressive at the time and, as we will see in later chapters, proved to be themes in the evolution of corrections. It is important to emphasize that this meeting and the recommendations that emanated from it were actually quite remarkable for the time period in which this occurred. This time period occurred only a handful of years after the Civil War and occurred while the cattle drives and Old West tales had not yet become legend.

As it would turn out, the NPA would survive for well over a hundred years and would become what is now known as the American Correctional Association (ACA). The ACA is the premiere professional organization for correctional workers in the United States today (Wooldredge, 1996). With this in mind, it can be seen that the reformers of the NPA were the shapers of future thinking in corrections. Thus the contributions of the NPA were pivotal to developing modern corrections as we know it, and the use of reformatories represented that organization's initial step to implement a true process of correctional reform (Wooldredge, 1996).

The first reformatory was named **Elmira Reformatory**, and was opened in July 1876 when the facility's first inmates arrived from Auburn Prison. Ironically, the site of the Elmira Reformatory had, at one time, been a prisoner-of-war camp for captured Confederate soldiers during the days of the Civil War (Brockway, 1969; Wooldredge, 1996). There had been a vile history associated with that camp, and thousands of southern soldiers died in the squalid, harsh, and brutal environment. However, the use of Elmira in 1876 was one of reform (thus the word *reformatory*), and this ushered in a new era in the field of penology. The NPA sought to establish a facility that was a product of the lessons learned in both the Auburn and Pennsylvania systems. Because of this, Elmira did not use strict corporal punishment, striped uniforms, or lockstep marching, which had been advocated in years past among prison administrators (Wooldredge, 1996).

Video Link 2.2
Watch a video about the history of the Elmira Reformatory.

The warden of Elmira Reformatory was a man by the name of **Zebulon Brockway**, who started his career in corrections as a prison guard in a state prison in Connecticut (Brockway, 1969). He would remain the warden at Elmira for over 24 years, residing from 1876 to 1900. Brockway contended that imprisonment was designed to reform inmates, and he advocated for individualized plans of reform. The idea of individualized treatment planning is something that is carried out, even today. Brockway particularly rejected the use of pointless harsh labor, a regime of silence, religious and moral lectures, and brutality to gain strict and overly rigid obedience (Brockway, 1969).

During his term as warden, Brockway embarked on perhaps the most ambitious attempts to have the Declaration of Principles (established by the NPA in 1870) implemented within a correctional facility (Wooldredge, 1996). Judges, working within the framework of these principles and also adopting an indeterminate sentencing approach, would sentence first-time offenders with modified indeterminate sentences. When serving these sentences, the reform of the offender was monitored, and, if successfully reformed, the offender was released prior to the expiration of the sentence. If the offender did not demonstrate sufficient proof of reform, he simply served the maximum term.

The Elmira Reformatory used a system of classification that had been produced due to Brockway's admiration of the work of Alexander Maconochie, a captain in the British Royal Navy, which in 1837 was placed in command over the English penal colony in at Norfolk Island. While serving in this command, Maconochie proposed a system where the duration of the sentence was determined by the inmate's work habits and righteous conduct. Called a **mark system** because "marks" were provided to the convict for each day of successful toil, this system was quite well organized and thought out (Brockway, 1969).

Under this plan, convicts were given marks and were moved through phases of supervision until they finally earned full release. Because of this, Maconochie's system is considered indeterminate in nature, with convicts progressing through five specific phases of classification. **Indeterminate sentences** include a range of years that will be potentially served by the offender. The offender is released during some point in the range of years that are assigned by the sentencing judge. Both the minimum and maximum times can be modified by a number of factors such as offender behavior and offender work ethic. The indeterminate sentence stands in contrast to the use of **determinate sentences**, which consist of fixed periods of incarceration imposed on the offender with no later flexibility in the term that is served. Brockway was a strong advocate of the indeterminate concept and believed that it was critical to turning punishment into a corrective and reformative tool. The ideas and innovations with Elmira Reformatory spread throughout the nation between the years of 1877 and 1913, with reformatories being built in 17 states (Silverman, 2001). However, these institutions were actually no more successful at molding inmates into law-abiding and productive citizens than were prisons. By 1910, the reformatory movement began to decline as, to the dismay of correctional reformers, it became clear that these facilities were not more effective than other approaches.

THE INDUSTRIAL ERA

The manufacture of handmade crafts among inmates kept in isolation at Eastern Penitentiary turned out to be the origin of prison industries that would follow throughout the nation. Over time, as the factory production system was brought into the prison environment, these factories produced profits, and this convinced prison administrators that prison industries were the most practical solution when operating a facility. The industrial prison was the product of the profits that states made during the early years of prison and plantation maintenance. By the time that the 1860s arrived, the system of absolute silence had been largely discarded due to the need for the inmates to communicate with one another when working.

The concept of the industrial prison was generated by attention to the early profits generated by state prisons. During the 1800s many free world laborers began to take issue with the unfair competition with the free prison labor that was utilized by prison industrial programs. The emergence of the labor union movement and the abuses of the contract lease systems of prison labor led to the slow demise of prison industrial programs. The true ending of large-system prison industries was the enactment of two pieces of federal legislation that controlled prison products. This legislation was enacted into law and consisted of the Hawes-Cooper Act, which was passed in 1929, and the Ashurst-Sumners Act, which was passed in 1935. The **Hawes-Cooper Act** required that prison products be subject to the laws of states to which those products are shipped. The **Ashurst-Sumners Act** required that all prison-manufactured products shipped out of a state be stamped with the prison name, and, with an amendment in 1940, prison products were banned from being shipped via interstate lines.

PRISON FARMING SYSTEMS FROM 1900 AND AFTER WORLD WAR II

The prison farm concept was one that, while having its primary genesis in Mississippi, actually extended throughout a number of southern states. The use of these types of prison operations lasted until well after the Second World War. As was noted earlier, these types of prison systems were profit driven and were based on agricultural production. Even though their particular market was agricultural, much of their operation was similar in approach to industrial prisons; the key difference was simply in the product that was manufactured. Two systems, in particular, capture the essence of southern prison farming: Arkansas and Texas.

The Arkansas System: Worst of the Worst

Video Link 2.3
Learn more about the Arkansas prison system.

The conditions within the Arkansas prison system are thought to be the worst of all those among the southern prison farm era. The Arkansas prison farm system actually only consisted of two prison plantations, the Cummins Farm, which consisted of approximately 16,000 acres of territory, and the Tucker Farm, consisting of about 4,500 acres of territory. Each of these facilities produced rice, cotton, vegetables, and livestock. What made this prison system so particularly terrible was the corruption, brutality, and completely inhumane means of operation that existed.

The Arkansas prison system, similar to the Mississippi prison system, had inmates who were in charge of other inmates. In Arkansas, these inmates were referred to as **trusties** and were at the top of the

TECHNOLOGY AND EQUIPMENT 2.1

The Tucker Telephone

The "Tucker Telephone" was a torture device invented in Arkansas and regularly used at the Tucker State Prison Farm (now the Tucker Unit of the Arkansas Department of Correction) in Jefferson County. It was likely used on inmates until the 1970s.

The Tucker Telephone consisted of an old-fashioned crank telephone wired in sequence with two batteries. Electrodes coming from it were attached to a prisoner's big toe and genitals. The electrical components of the phone were modified so that cranking the telephone sent an electric shock through the prisoner's body. The device was reputedly constructed in the 1960s by, depending upon the source, a former trusty in the prison, a prison superintendent, or an inmate doctor; it was administered as a form of punishment, usually in the prison hospital. In prison parlance, a "long-distance call" was a series of electric shocks in a row.

The name Tucker Prison evoked scenes of sadism and brutality prior to the prison reform initiatives put forward by Governor Winthrop Rockefeller. According to a February 20, 1967, *Newsweek* report, inmates were punished with beatings, whippings, torture with pliers, and needles put under their fingernails, in addition to the use of the Tucker Telephone. Much of the abuse was carried out by guards and the prison trusties who reported to them. The 1980 movie *Brubaker*, loosely inspired by events within the Arkansas prison system, depicts an inmate named Abraham being tortured with the Tucker Telephone.

Devices similar to the Tucker Telephone have been employed up to the present day. A Tucker Telephone was allegedly used in a Chicago violent crime unit managed by Lieutenant Jon Burge to torture suspects during the 1980s. During the Vietnam War, some American GIs reportedly converted their field phones into torture devices, and something like the Tucker Telephone was used by American interrogators to torture Iraqi prisoners at Abu Ghraib prison.

SOURCE: Reprinted by permission of the *Encyclopedia of Arkansas History and Culture*.

inmate hierarchy. Civilian employees in each of the prisons in Arkansas were scarce, meaning that trusties were responsible for most of the day-to-day order on the farm. The trusties served as guards over the other inmates and carried weapons on the farm. They also controlled and operated critical services such as food and medical services. Trusties had their own dormitory to themselves, more freedom than other inmates, and the best food, and they were free to extort other inmates for money, goods, or services. As one might expect, extortion happened quite frequently.

The overall supervisor of this system was the superintendent whose primary role was to ensure that the prison farm operated at a profit. This meant that the superintendent tended to provide all authority to the trusties, so long as they made the superintendent a profit. The control of desperate, underfed, exhausted, and often ill inmates was maintained through a process of constant punishment. Some of these punishments were nothing less than the use of torture. Punishments included whipping; having one's fingers, nose, ears, or genitals pinched with pliers; and even having needles inserted under the inmate's fingernails. One of the most infamous forms of torture used was the "Tucker Telephone." This device is discussed in greater detail in "Technology and Equipment: The Tucker Telephone."

The Texas System

The first penitentiary in Texas was established in the city of Huntsville in 1849. This facility was based on the Auburn system, and, common to other prisons based on that system, the schedule of that facility revolved around the completion of labor and the maintenance of fiscal solvency. In other words, the inmates were expected to produce sufficient goods to be self-sufficient. Because of the strong desire to have a prison system that supported itself and because of the challenges that were encountered, there were several eras in Texas prison operation as the state sought to find the most workable remedy.

During the period of 1876 and 1883, a contract lease system was established with private contractors. Though the contract lease system was used for quite some time, it proved to not be an effective system, and

Journal Article Link 2.2
Read more about
contract leasing.

Texas eventually quit using this type of arrangement. While the contract lease system slowly dissipated, the use of plantation farms became more common. Indeed, around 1880 the Texas prison system began to buy thousands of acres of farmland around Huntsville and other areas of the state. Eventually, the agricultural initiative in Texas prisons would prove to be a very large undertaking that, while not completely self-sufficient, did offset a large portion of the expenses associated with running the prison. However, the treatment of inmates was as brutal as the conditions in the Arkansas prison system.

While the Texas prison system had more staff (especially guards) than did Arkansas during the early 1900s, the use of trusty inmates, termed *building tenders*, was widespread throughout the system. **Building tenders** were inmates who were chosen for their strength or intelligence to supervise the inmate population, particularly in the dormitories and cell blocks. Just was with the Arkansas system, these inmates were given complete power over the other inmates, and they carried weapons (but not firearms) to enforce their rule. Building tenders were given status, power, and numerous rewards and benefits. Building tenders maintained their superior position among the inmate population through fear, intimidation, and physical force.

The building tender system was organized along different levels of authority and status among the inmates. The **head building tenders** were given control of cell blocks and/or dormitories, and they were held responsible for behavior that occurred within those facilities. These were the highest-ranking inmates in the system. The **rank-and-file building tenders** were assistants to the head building tenders and helped to ensure that order was maintained. **Turnkeys** were inmates who were tasked with opening and closing interior locked gates and doors of the prison. Inmates with the title of bookkeeper kept various prison records. Other inmates that held some degree of importance were called **runners and strikers**, and these inmates kept the cell block clean, dispensed supplies, and provided the building tenders with additional muscle during times when the general inmate population became unruly (Crouch & Marquart, 1989).

As noted earlier, Texas prisons were designed along a farm or plantation model and this meant that the majority of the inmates did agricultural work. Indeed, all inmates spent at least the first six months of their sentence on the *hoe line*, which consisted of squads of inmates who stood in rows in the fields and used their hands and/or hand tools to work the ground, plant crops, or collect the harvest. Some inmates would, over time, be rewarded with work assignments raising livestock or poultry or operating machinery. In other cases, inmates might be given the ability to learn a trade such as electrical work, plumbing, or carpentry or other such forms of skilled labor. It was also common to use these skilled inmates to build and/or maintain prison buildings as well as other structures. In fact, many of the original buildings of the College of Criminal Justice at Sam Houston State University (located in Huntsville, Texas) were built through the use of inmate labor.

Court Intervention: The Downfall of the Prison Farm System

There were many court cases, the vast majority of them federal, that ultimately dismantled the prison farm system in southern states. The reason for this was not the constitutionality of prison farms, per se, but had more to do with the brutal means by which they were run; in short, the operational methods used on these prison farms were unconstitutional. An early case in the state of Arkansas, *Holt v. Sarver I* (1969), assessed the operation of prison farms in that state. Aside from the fact that this was the first of a series of federal court cases to rule on various southern prison farms, this court implemented a unique concept in determining the constitutionality of prison conditions. In this case, the federal court under Judge J. Smith Henley utilized a standard that it dubbed the totality of the conditions to determine whether the Arkansas system was constitutional.

In considering the level of proof in the totality of the conditions, Judge Henley made it clear that individually, certain conditions, though far from ideal, do not necessarily rise to a constitutional level. But, the court noted, when taken together, the totality of these cumulative circumstances did constitute cruel and unusual punishment in violation of the Eighth Amendment. In describing the circumstances, the court noted the following:

> For the ordinary convict a sentence to the Arkansas Penitentiary today amounts to a banishment from civilized society to a dark and evil world completely alien to the free world, a world that is administered by criminals under rules and customs completely foreign to free world culture ... A convict ... has no assurance whatever that he will not be killed, injured, or

sexually assaulted … However constitutionally tolerable the Arkansas system may have been in former years, it simply will not do today … (*Holt v. Sarver II*, 1970, p. 381)

This judgment made the Arkansas prison system the first in the nation to be ruled unconstitutional. This case actually consisted of two separate court rulings, one titled *Holt v. Sarver I* **(1969)** and the other *Holt v. Sarver II* **(1970)**, demonstrating that the resolution of problems in the Arkansas prison system was a drawn-out and tenuous process. A judgment and decree was entered on February 18, 1970, determining that the confinement of human beings at the Cummins and Tucker prisons constituted cruel and inhuman punishment, as prohibited by the Eighth Amendment. In addition, Judge Henley was one of the first to rule on the racial segregation of inmates, holding that such institutional practices violated the Equal Protection Clause of the Fourteenth Amendment. Judge Henley then ordered the State Correction Board of Arkansas to generate a plan of action to remedy the constitutional violations.

Shortly after the ruling handed down to the state of Arkansas, a similar ruling followed in Mississippi in 1971. In this case, inmates of the Parchman Farm in the state of Mississippi filed a class action lawsuit that sought relief from unconstitutional conditions. This case was filed in the U.S. District Court for the Northern District of Mississippi and was known as *Gates v. Collier* **(1972)**. The result of this case was a finding that the confinement conditions at the prison farm were in violation of the constitution. The judge, William Colbert Keady, found that the Mississippi system practiced racial discrimination; provided inadequate physical facilities, medical facilities, protection of inmates, and training to trustees; and made use of excessive disciplinary rules, punishment without adequate procedure, and unconstitutional censure of mail.

Practices at the Parchman Farm were found to violate the Sixth, Eighth, and Fourteenth Amendments. An injunctive order was issued against the Mississippi prison farm system providing immediate, intermediate, and long-range relief. This case essentially ended the prison farm operations that made Mississippi prison farming so profitable.

A few years later, yet another case examining prison farm conditions in a southern state made prison case law history. This case was *Ruiz v. Estelle* (1980), and it forever changed the prison culture of the state. *Ruiz v. Estelle* started as a lawsuit initially filed by David Ruiz, an inmate who continually wrote writs and letters of complaint regarding the conditions within the Texas prison system. For years, these writs seemed ineffectual and were, according to some accounts, a source of mockery for Ruiz while serving in the Texas prison system. However, these complaints eventually caught the attention of a federal judge by the name of William Wayne Justice, who was reform-minded. Judge Justice took Ruiz's petition and combined it with six other petitions, making it a class action lawsuit against the Texas Department of Corrections.

The *Ruiz* case brought about the most widespread change to any correctional system that has been seen in all of U.S. penal history. Judge Justice found numerous violations of minimal constitutional safeguards and ultimately placed the prison system under federal court supervision. The mandates set by Judge Justice, through legal injunctions, forced the Texas Department of Corrections to improve standards of security by hiring noninmate staff, which eliminated the building tender system. Further orders related to overcrowding, standards of health care, access to courts, the use of custodial discipline, and other areas were all leveled against the state prison system.

THE PROGRESSIVE ERA

From 1900 to 1920, numerous reforms took place across the United States, and this led to some dubbing this period the Age of Reform. For prison operations, the Age of Reform reflected an era of change and attention to humane treatment of inmates. During this time, a particularly influential group, known at the Progressives, cast attention on social problems throughout the nation and sought to improve the welfare of the underprivileged. The Progressives tended to come from upper-class areas, and this meant that they had some degree of influence. At heart, these activists believed that civic-minded people could apply scientific knowledge and breakthroughs to solve social problems, including criminal behavior.

According to Morris and Rothman (2000), the **Progressive Era** was a period of extraordinary urban and industrial growth, and it was also one of unprecedented social problems. Among a variety of agendas for reform was the need to improve conditions in prisons throughout the United States.

The Progressives were early advocates of individualized treatment planning. In their work within prisons, Progressives held great hope for the emerging principles of behavioral science. The members of this group remained steadfast in the belief that understanding deviant behavior lay with social and psychological causes, and they also contended that social and psychological treatment programs were the key to offender reform. Due to this line of thought and the influence of the Progressives, the field of penology eventually included psychologists, social workers, and psychiatrists just as much as lawyers and security staff.

THE ERA OF THE "BIG HOUSE"

The Big House era lasted from the early 1900s to just before the emergence of the Civil Rights Era. During this period of time, inmate populations nearly tripled from about 50,000 nationwide during the early 1900s to over 150,000 in the 1950s (Cox, 2009). This growth in the prison population, over the span of more than 50 years, would not have been unusual in today's world given that prison populations continue to grow at the same time that free-world populations continue to grow. However, it is important to understand that prior to the late 1800s and/or early 1900s, the use of prisons was not necessarily commonplace. Indeed, many prisons had not even been built until the early 1800s, and their use was somewhat sparing, usually with only one or two facilities existing in most states. Prior to this period, leasing strategies and the use of deplorable facilities had been commonplace.

PHOTO 2.7

The Big House was typically a large stone structure with brick walls, guard towers, and checkpoints throughout the facility. The key architectural feature of Big House prisons was the use of concrete and steel. Many were several stories in height.

Big House prisons were typically large stone structures with brick walls, guard towers, and checkpoints throughout the facility. The key architectural feature to Big House prisons was the use of concrete and steel. The cell blocks sometimes had up to six levels, making the entire structure large and foreboding. The interior of each cell block often was extremely hot and humid during the summer months and cold and chilly during the winter months. In addition, these structures magnified noise levels, creating echoes throughout as steel doors and keys clanged open and shut, announcements were made, and machinery operated within the facility.

Inmates in the Big House

The Big House era is where much of the stereotypical ideals and values emerged within the inmate subculture. This subculture, known as the **convict code**, was an inmate-driven set of beliefs that inmates aspired to live by, at least in theory. The convict code was the ideal standard by which an inmate could do time and have respect within the inmate subculture (Cox, 2009; Stojkovic, 1996). This could espouse loyalty between inmates when facing staff or others in authority as well as the following:

1. Do not be a snitch.

2. Show no emotional weakness or softness.

3. Maintain cohesion against the guards.

4. Maintain a masculine form of dignity.

Video Link 2.4
Watch a video about the convict code.

For the most part, the pervasive influence of this code helped those inmates who were physically strong or influential. This code was more closely followed by the career criminal than the first-time incarcerated. Further, almost all inmates claimed adherence to this code, but many could not actually maintain it effectively. Despite this, the convict code was the means by which inmates in the Big House would evaluate one another (Cox, 2009; Stojkovic, 1996). In addition to the general edicts of the convict code, the inmate subculture tended to hold manipulative persons in high regard. This, in addition to sheer physical prowess, was a pivotal way for inmates to gain respect among their peers. Those inmates who were able to trick or dupe others and/or beat the prison system were considered smart and streetwise.

Guards in the Big House

In many of the Big House facilities, prison guards operated in a world where the convict code often applied to them just as much as it did to the inmate. Indeed, the hostile environment where the inmate's code eschewed cooperation between the inmates and prison staff created a culture of hostility between the two (Cox, 2009). Further, the convict code required that inmates remain loyal to one another, stay out of one another's business, and refrain from letting guards know what may be occurring among the inmate ranks. This ensured continued and organized resistance to guards and made the life of the guard all the more difficult (Cox, 2009; Stojkovic, 1996).

Further, guards were expected to have control of their cell blocks. They were, in many cases, held responsible if inmates were unruly and/or did not mind. In fact, if inmates acted up on the cell block, the general consensus was that the guard may be "weak" and unable to exert control or influence over the inmates in his stead. This put guards in a precarious position because they had to maintain control, on the one hand, but they also found it prudent to not have constant inmate outbursts and/or signs of resistance on the other (this showing a lack of fear and respect). While guards could enforce the rules rigidly, this could have drawbacks since inmates might eventually refuse to cooperate and since this also made the guard easy to predict. Because guards were usually evaluated on their ability to control the inmate population, they sometimes found ways to gain inmate cooperation as a means of maintaining the cell block. A loud, rebellious, and dirty cell block tended to leave the impression that he could not control the inmates under his supervision, and this would result in his having less favor with the administration of the prison (Cox, 2009; Stojkovic, 1996).

While guards could (and did) use disciplinary methods of physical punishment to control inmates, this often was not the most effective means to control large numbers of inmates, particularly since the inmate population grossly outnumbered the number of guards on a given shift (Cox, 2009; Stojkovic, 1996). Because of this, guards often resorted to methodical means of exacting punishment and using leverage and manipulation to keep inmate behavior under control. In some cases, the guard might overlook minor rule violations and/or allow privileges for certain inmates who had status or influence and/or did not cause problems for the guard. By restricting unruly inmates from similar privileges, the inmates would learn to behave when certain guards were on duty, provided that the incentives provided or withheld by the guard were valued by the inmate population (Cox, 2009; Stojkovic, 1996).

A process of corrupt favoritism (Silverman, 2001) emerged whereby guards granted special privileges to certain inmates if they gave assistance in maintaining order. While this obviously violated the convict code and was similar to arrangements in the past where privileged inmates provided assistance in controlling other less fortunate inmates, this ended up being a common practice in many institutions. Typically, those inmates who received these privileges were themselves those who had power within the inmate subculture, and it was as if it was their right to break the convict code since they possessed the means to do so with impunity.

Aside from inmate concerns, guards were usually not treated well by their own supervisory staff. Guards could be disciplined for failing to salute prison staff who had rank, just as if they were in the military (Silverman, 2001). During this period of prison history, guards typically lived on the premises, and their barracks were routinely inspected just like the military as well. These inspections were to ensure compliance with cleanliness standards and were also to ensure that guards did not have contraband that they might trade with inmates. In general, the life circumstances for Big House guards were oppressive and dreary (Cox, 2009; Stojkovic, 1996). The world of the guard was little better than that for the inmate in many regards, and it is because of this that the saying "you do your time; and I will do my time, 8 hours at a time" became a maxim from guards to inmates—the point being that neither group had an enviable set of circumstances when compared to outside society.

Reference Link 2.2
Read about the prison code as part of the Big House culture.

THE MEDICAL MODEL

During the 1930s there emerged another perspective regarding inmate treatment and the likelihood for reform. The medical model developed in tandem with the rise of the behavioral sciences in the field of corrections (Carlson et al., 2008). The **medical model** can be described as correctional treatment that utilizes a type of mental health approach incorporating fields such as psychology and biology; criminality is viewed as the result of internal deficiencies that can be treated. The key to the medical model is understanding that it is rehabilitative in nature.

The medical model was officially implemented in 1929 when the U.S. Congress authorized the Federal Bureau of Prisons, a brand-new organization at that time, to open correctional institutions that would use standardized processes of classification and treatment regimens within their programming. One early proponent of the medical model and its clinical approach to rehabilitation was **Sanford Bates,** who was the first director of the Bureau of Prisons and had also served as a past president of the American Correctional Association (students will recall that this was originally named the National Prison Association in 1870).

Though the medical model was introduced to the new Bureau of Prisons in 1929, it was largely an approach that did not take hold in other areas of the nation until after World War II (Carlson et al., 2008). Following the war, the medical model was increasingly incorporated into many state programs. Indeed, the late 1940s fed into what was considered to be an era of rehabilitation, and, in many cases, rehabilitation become the cited basis for many correctional programs. This was particularly true in the states of California, Illinois, New Jersey, and New York, where both classification processes and treatment interventions were implemented and refined. Further, public sentiments were also supportive of treatment efforts at this time, and this helped to fuel a movement toward this approach (Carlson et al., 2008).

PHOTO 2.8

Assistant Attorney General Willebrandt hired Sanford Bates, a well-respected name in the field of corrections, as Superintendent of Prisons in 1929. He helped lay the groundwork for the formation of the Federal Bureau of Prisons.

During this period, many correctional officials were encouraged and even compelled to follow a rehabilitation model due to the strength of the movement from both public support and legislative action (Carlson et al., 2008). This model consisted of three components: diagnosis, evaluation, and treatment. These three components of correctional service began to impact both the lives of inmates and the standards of behavior among guards. New facilities were built in the Bureau of Prisons and in numerous states that were designed for diagnostic and classification purposes.

At the heart of the medical model was the classification process; everything in the medical model that followed hinged on the accuracy and effectiveness of the classification process. The developers of these classification processes believed that such systematic approaches would improve treatment outcomes and overall recidivism among offenders. However, as Carlson et al. (2008) note, "although classification was one of the greatest concepts invented during this period, it became at best a management process rather than a reliable tool to aid in rehabilitation" (p. 13). This, unfortunately, emerged as the truth across the nation, and classification ultimately became a systematic process for housing and to aid institutional and community-based professionals in managing the inmate population rather than changing the inmates' actual behavior. To be clear, while classification did help to separate out those inmates who might be amenable to treatment from those who were not, it did not lay the basis for any assurance that inmates would be less likely to reoffend in the future.

Further, the support for the medical model among rank-and-file security as well as some administrators was not near as strong as was held among the public. Wardens and superintendents had a difficult time accepting the change due to the loss of power and authority in maintaining inmates. Carlson et al. (2008) point out that despite the friction that this might have caused between veteran wardens and new movements throughout the correctional industry, "wardens had to adapt, or they would face the wrath of the central authorities attempting to gain a foothold in the new correctional leadership hierarchy" (p. 13). Thus, the medical model was embraced by some administrators and forced upon others; this led to a longtime schism between "soft-line" treatment professionals and "hard-line" security professionals that would continue throughout the decades that followed.

THE REINTEGRATION MODEL

The **reintegration model** evolved during the last few years that the medical model was still in vogue. The term *reintegration* was used to identify programs that looked to the external environment for causes of crime and the means by which criminality could be reduced. The reintegration model held the community as the basic etiological factor for criminal behavior. According to the reintegration model, criminal offending was the product of the local community that excluded, failed to provide for, or discriminated against the offender (Hanser, 2010). This model was commonly used during the 1960s and 1970s in reaction to the failures of the medical model and as an alternative to a punitive approach that was gaining momentum. The reintegration model overlapped with the medical model and was, in some instances, presented as an extension of the medical model due to its treatment emphasis.

During this same period of the 1970s, crime was increasing, and public concern became an issue with publicly elected officials. Further, these high crime rates were primarily perceived as being the result of high recidivism rates among offenders. Because of this, strong skepticism of both the medical model and the reintegration model became commonplace. However, one of the sharpest and most distinctive blows to both of these models "was a rather infamous negative report produced in the early 1970s by a researcher studying rehabilitation programs across the country" (Carlson et al., 2008, p. 16). This report was the work of Robert Martinson, who had conducted a thorough analysis of research programs on behalf of the New York State Governor's Special Committee on Criminal Offenders.

Martinson (1974) examined a number of various programs that included educational and vocational assistance, mental health treatment, medical treatment, and early release. In his report, often referred to as the **Martinson Report**, he noted that "with few and isolated exceptions, the rehabilitative efforts that have been reported so far have had no appreciable effect on recidivism" (Martinson, 1974, p. 22). Martinson's work was widely disseminated and used as ammunition for persons opposed to treatment, whether individual- or community-based. Thus, skepticism of rehabilitation and/or reintegration was brought to its pinnacle as practitioners cited (often in an inaccurate manner) the work of Robert Martinson. By this time, official support for the medical model or the reintegration model had, for all practical purposes, vanished from the world of corrections.

THE CRIME CONTROL MODEL

Starting around 1975 and lasting throughout the late 1900s, a more punitive ideology began to emerge. Throughout the '80s and '90s, crime control had become a very serious and well-touted topic among politicos and ideologues. Changes in sentencing laws occurred during this time, with the War on Drugs burgeoning the prison population beyond proportions that had ever been seen before. During this time, many states abolished parole (Hanser, 2010). Further, the use of enhanced sentences, mandatory minimum sentences, and three-strikes sentences further lengthened the time for various sentences and further increased the population of the prison in states across the nation. The primary approach throughout the 1980s and early 1990s was to incapacitate offenders from committing future crime through vigorous incarceration. Prison building increased at rates that had never before been witnessed in correctional history.

The **crime control model** emerged during a "get tough" era on crime. The use of longer sentences, more frequent use of the death penalty, and an increased use of intensive supervised probation all were indicative of this era's approach to crime. The use of determinate sentencing laws took the discretion from many judges so that, like it or not, sentences were awarded at a set level regardless of the circumstances associated with the charge. Increasingly, states and the federal government are realizing that the approach of the crime control era may have been a bit too ambitious, particularly since states cannot afford, in this current state of economic crisis, to pay the bills for the long-term incarceration that has been invoked under this approach.

Journal Article Link 2.3
Read more about "get tough" crime control policies.

THE MODERN-DAY FEDERAL SYSTEM: INMATE CHARACTERISTICS AND WORKING CONDITIONS

The Federal Bureau of Prisons (BOP) was initially established by Congress in 1930 and has since that time become a highly centralized organization with over 33,000 employees who supervise more than

209,000 inmates. The federal system has over a hundred facilities that include maximum-security prisons, "supermax" facilities, detention centers, prison camps, and even halfway houses. The variety of correctional services provided by this system is much greater than most state systems provide (Federal Bureau of Prisons, 2010).

Since the War on Drugs that occurred during the 1980s, the proportion of drug offenders has remained high, constituting 51.4% of the BOP population (Federal Bureau of Prisons, 2010). However, unlike state prisoners, most federal offenders are not violent, and their drug crimes are also not usually associated with violence. Indeed, the federal inmate tends to be a bit more intelligent than many of the state inmates, in terms of their lifestyle and success with crime commission but also on standardized test comparisons examining intellectual level of ability. Also interesting is that roughly 26% of all federal inmates are citizens of other countries (Federal Bureau of Prisons, 2010). As an indicator of the types of crimes and the types of criminals that tend to be included in the federal system, consider that 54% of federal inmates are classified as being either a low- or minimum-security risk, with the average time served for BOP inmates being around 6.5 years in length (Federal Bureau of Prisons, 2010).

MODERN-DAY STATE SYSTEMS: INMATE CHARACTERISTICS AND WORKING CONDITIONS

There is quite a bit of variety among state correctional systems, in terms of both their operation and the inmates that they house. Aside from the fact that individual states can vary in size and demographics compared to one another, the size of prisons within one state can have a great degree of variability. Indeed, the Louisiana State Penitentiary (Angola) houses over 5,000 inmates (more than the entire state of North Dakota) while other prisons in other states may house fewer than 1,000 inmates. There is a wide variety of types of facilities that may be included in a state system, just as with the federal system described previously.

Audio Link 2.2
Listen to an inmate's
account of prison life.

Generally speaking, the proportion of inmates incarcerated for violent crimes at the state level tends to be much greater than in the federal system. Also, state budgets tend to not be as large as the federal budget, so funding is often an issue that keeps state systems from operating as effectively as the BOP. This also means that working conditions, salaries, and training among state prison staff tend to vary, though the American Correctional Association has been very influential in professionalizing the field of corrections throughout numerous states. All in all, state corrections tends to be the most common form of corrections, but, despite advances, these systems do not fare as well as the BOP. Even with this in mind, working for one state prison system can be quite different from working for another, in terms of salary, training, opportunities, and so forth.

State Crime Rankings 2.1
Prisoners in State
Correctional Institutions
(2009)

It is also important to note that the majority of inmates are housed in state prison systems. Among these, most are in custody among the 10 largest prison systems, with the top four states—California, Texas, Florida, and New York—having unique characteristics. Because of this, we will take a brief look at these state systems and will refer to them as the "Big Four" in corrections, a term that was originally coined by Clear and Cole (2002).

THE EMERGENCE OF THE "BIG FOUR" IN CORRECTIONS

This term, the **"Big Four" in corrections**, is an apt description of the four largest state correctional systems in the United States (Clear, Cole, & Reisig, 2008). California is the largest system with 171,275 inmates, neck-in-neck with Texas, which has 171,249 inmates (Bureau of Justice Statistics, 2010). The third largest prison system is Florida with 103,915 inmates, followed by the state of New York, which had 58,687 inmates at the close of 2009 (Bureau of Justice Statistics, 2010). These four systems are, quite naturally, referred to as the Big Four due to the fact that they are the top four systems according to inmate count. Even though this is the case, we will not discuss each state individually. Rather, students should understand that the Big Four in corrections are important for a number of reasons that go beyond their mere head count.

First, these four states have large overall free-world populations as well as prison populations. This means that each of these states has a large population that is individually likely to be more representative of the overall U.S. population than would be the case for numerous other states. When taken in total, these four states should be considered somewhat representative of the overall U.S. population. Because they are representative, this means that research conducted from samples taken from these four states will, collectively, be likely to yield results that generalize to the rest of the United States.

Second, each of these states has had to grapple with immigration issues and the constant ingress and egress of legal and illegal persons within its borders. This is a unique characteristic that is not shared by a majority of the states. While other states may also struggle with this issue, the Big Four do so on a large-scale basis. This makes a difference because of the type of crime problems that are encountered (i.e., more drug trafficking, smuggling issues, and organized crime activity), as well as the factors that are associated with those problems (more drug use, cultural clashes, and more complicated crime problems). Further, the continued flow of personnel within these states' borders ensures that law enforcement and corrections will have populations that include a large proportion of international inmates/prisoners.

Third, each of these states possesses a truly diverse array of racial and cultural groups. The history of each of the Big Four reflects exchanges between various cultures. In all four states, the Latino population is well represented, as is the African American population. Further, the Asian American population is concentrated in California and New York but also has sufficient representation in Texas and Florida. Other racial and cultural groups are likewise represented in each of these four states, partially due to routine immigration and also due to the unique histories of all four states.

Fourth and lastly, each of these four states tends to have a fairly robust economy. The market conditions in all four states are active and vibrant due to the location of each state (each has extensive coastlines) and due to a sufficient number of urban areas within its borders. The fact that these four states tend to have more stable economies (at least throughout most of their history) impacts how well they are able to fund their correctional programs. This can make a considerable difference in the overall approach to a correctional agency's response in processing the offender population.

Audio Link 2.3
Hear more about the population increase in California's state prison.

Audio Link 2.4
Learn more about controversial immigration laws.

CONCLUSION

As with the prior chapter, quite a bit of history has been covered within this chapter. Starting with the early American colonies, this chapter progresses all the way up to the modern world of corrections. Not only is there a great span of time that is covered, but this period in history is when there was perhaps more activity in the field of corrections than at any other point in human history. In addition, it is in the United States where the birth of the modern prison occurred. Therefore, the depth of coverage in this chapter is likely to be greater than that provided in the previous chapter, which covered more ancient times of penological development.

One of the key points in this chapter to understand is that, at the outset, prison development in America began with two competing mind-sets: the Pennsylvania and Auburn systems of prison operation. Numerous dichotomies and disagreements in philosophy as to the rightful goal of prisons would emerge as the Pennsylvania system and the Auburn system competed. Though both of these orientations were operational outlooks on prisons, it is the Pennsylvania system that is touted as being the first true correctional system. The intent of the Pennsylvania system was strictly to reform offenders. On the other hand, the primary motive behind the Auburn system had a business-model perspective; prisons should be self-sufficient or as close to self-sufficient as possible. Ultimately, the money-making option agreed with the capitalist notions of the United States, and the Auburn system gave way to the penal farm, particularly in the southern United States.

The profit motive ultimately drove southern states to implement the farming prison while the northeastern areas of the nation adopted the use of prison industries. In both cases, inmates were leased out to private businesses that could make a profit off of inmate labor. This again highlighted the impact of the Auburn system. In the South, the use of prison farms became reminiscent of the old plantation era prior to the Civil War, and, in fact, some prisons were built right on the grounds of prior plantations. The traditions in the South along with racial discrimination and disparity, as well as poor economic circumstances, served to replicate many of the injustices that occurred in the prior slave era, just under a different guise.

The Big House era emerged from the prison industry model, but, unlike the prison industry or the prison farming approach, inmates in the Big House were not put through grueling labor, and they were not subjected to the same level of rule setting as inmates in the past. Amidst this, an inmate subculture emerged that ran counter to the prison guard. The Big House ultimately became what the media (especially Hollywood) would portray as the true prison. The use of manipulation was a respected skill in this environment, for the inmates and the guards. Toward the later end of the Big House era, a public rise in civil rights interests extended into prison environments, and, as society changed, so too did prison systems.

Eventually, the Big House era, the prison industry model, and the prison farm model gave way to the state and federal systems that we now have in place. In 1930, the Federal Bureau of Prisons was established and has emerged as a premiere correctional agency. State prison systems have gone through a process of transformation. Amidst this, four state prison systems have emerged as the largest and most influential in the nation. These four states consist of California, Florida, New York, and Texas, and they collectively include over half of the entire inmate population across the country. Because of this, any research or other generalization made about corrections in the United States should, at least for the most part, include each of these states as an object of interest.

END-OF-CHAPTER DISCUSSION QUESTIONS

1. Why is Old Newgate Prison important to correctional history in the United States?

2. What are some key differences between the Philadelphia and Auburn prison systems?

3. How did different regions differ in their approaches to prison operations? Compare at least two regions.

4. What are some key distinctions between state and federal prison systems?

5. What is meant by the Big Four in American corrections, and why is this important?

6. Identify and discuss at least two Supreme Court cases that shaped penology in the United States.

7. Provide a brief overview of the models of correctional thought presented in this chapter.

8. Explain how the subculture of violence theory applies to offender behavior in the field of corrections.

KEY TERMS

Ashurst-Sumners Act

Auburn system

Benjamin Rush

"Big Four" in corrections

Big House prisons

Black Codes

Building tenders

Contract labor system

Convict code

Crime control model

Determinate sentences

Eastern Penitentiary

Elam Lynds

Elmira Reformatory

Gates v. Collier (1972)

Hawes-Cooper Act

Head building tenders

Holt v. Sarver I (1969)

Holt v. Sarver II (1970)

Indeterminate sentences

Mark system

Martinson Report

Medical Model

Philadelphia Society for Alleviating the Miseries of Public Prisons

Progressive Era

Rank-and-file building tenders

Reintegration model

Runners and strikers

Sanford Bates

Trusties

Turnkeys

Western Penitentiary

Zebulon Brockway

APPLICATION EXERCISE 2.1

Consider the cases of *Holt v. Sarver I* (1969), *Gates v. Collier* (1972), and *Ruiz v. Estelle* (1980). In each case, a federal court system declared a state prison system unconstitutional. Each of these cases dealt specifically with southern prison farm systems. Divide students in your classroom and/or in your online discussion forum into two assigned groups, Group 1 and Group 2. Provide each with the respective assignments below:

Group 1: Argue on behalf of federal intervention in state prison systems. In particular, note that without federal intervention, state prison systems would not have changed their mode of operation. Also, provide arguments as to how these states violated the Constitution. Cite specific amendments and specific prison system practices.

Group 2: Argue against federal intervention in state prison systems. This group should note that states are supposed to have sovereignty over their own affairs, including those within the executive branch of state government. Also, note that the federal prison system is not hampered by the same financial constraints that states have to face; in theory, federal dollars can be unlimited, but not state dollars. Lastly, explain whether citizens in the states that were regulated really desired prison reform if they felt that conditions in their prison systems were appropriate for offenders who were "doing time" for crimes committed.

The instructor should regulate the debate and encourage students to find specific examples from the text and/or their own independent research.

"WHAT WOULD YOU DO?"

You are a warden in the Texas Department of Corrections, and the year is 1983. During the past few years, the Texas prison system has been sent into a state of turmoil due to the outcome of a recent lawsuit filed by inmate Ruiz and six other inmates. In essence, an injunction has been placed against the Texas prison system, and a wide variety of aspects have been found to be unconstitutional. William Wayne Justice, the federal judge whose ruling has led to these changes, is not liked by nearly any prison guard or staff member in the entire prison system. In fact, while the state of Texas has to come into compliance, by law, there is a wide degree of passive resistance from employees throughout the system.

You are skeptical of the new changes and wonder if the federal court really understands what it has done. The Texas system has traditionally been hailed as a system that is secure and that works. Now, with the building tender system dismantled (a requirement of the *Ruiz* stipulations), there is a virtual power vacuum among the inmates. Though some new guards have been hired, there are not enough, and they simply do not have the leverage necessary to ensure inmate compliance. Further, the system now costs more money than ever, and the farms are not producing near the crop output that they once did.

Conditions in the field and inside the building of your prison are poor as the morale among your correctional staff is the lowest that you have ever seen it. On the other hand, inmates push the boundaries on every rule, making custodial staff seem ineffectual. To further aggravate the situation, a few prison gangs have emerged and seem to be creating a power base among the inmate subculture. Your prison never had problems with gang inmates until now. Currently, the activity is building up, and the gangs are becoming violent within your facility.

You know that there are pockets of officers on your farm who have been keeping things under control, but they have been using force and the "old school" means of maintaining compliance among the "hard head" inmates. They have been doing this, somewhat covertly, in various field areas and even sometimes in various areas of the prison itself. The word among your inmate informants is that inmates are leaving those "bosses" alone. You think to yourself, "The word *boss* is used for guards in the system, so I wonder why that word became the norm some years ago." Then you think to yourself, "What they are doing is not according to policy and may not be legal; however, their areas of the farm are the only areas that seem to run without problems," and you ponder this issue. You have noted that certain areas of the farm run really well, despite *Ruiz,* and you suspect that in most of those areas, heavy-handed discipline is likely used by the staff assigned there. Those staff members have always been very loyal to you, as the warden, and you hear that they consider it their job to protect the administration from being implicated in their operations. In fact, you have reason to believe that many ranking officers throughout your prison farm know of these occurrences but turn a blind eye; some are rumored to even provide some degree of support.

You know that this is in violation of the stipulations, but you do not have any inmate complaints whatsoever. If these officers are stopped, how well will the farm operate? Also, if they are stopped, how will this affect morale for the remaining staff? Likewise, how will the inmate population react once they know that these guards have been disciplined? And lastly, will you discipline these guards? If not, how will you implement change among the prison staff?

You think this over as you see a long line of inmates coming in during sunset from their work in the fields. Two "field bosses" are riding state-issue horses and maintaining security over the inmates who are returning from their day's work. You think to yourself, "How on Earth will I be able to keep this all together in times like these?"

What do you do?

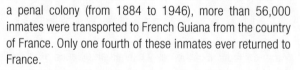

CROSS-NATIONAL PERSPECTIVE 2.1

Early Prisons in France

Though the French are commonly touted as having been supporters of humane treatment of prisoners during the time that the American colonies were first forming their own concepts regarding prisons, there are some notable exceptions to this. Perhaps the most well known is the Bastille, which some have indicated may be the most famous prison in history. The Bastille was originally built as a fortress in the late 1300s but was later used as a prison. The Bastille (French for "little bastion") was originally called the Chastel Saint Antoine. The Bastille was a four-story stone structure that had eight closely spaced towers connected by a 15-foot-thick stone wall. The entire structure was surrounded by a moat. Eventually, this structure was made a state prison. During its early years, the Bastille was a state prison for the upper class, consisting mostly of nobles who had been charged with treason. In addition, political prisoners and religious prisoners were held within its walls. By the late 1700s, however, this facility was housing inmates who had committed typical crimes.

Yet another infamous French prison was actually not in the country of France. Rather, this facility was in South America in an area called French Guiana. The area called Devil's Island actually included structures on two other nearby islands as well as facilities on the mainland area nearby

the islands. This area became a penal colony when Napoleon III began to settle the area with political prisoners. During the period that this area existed as a penal colony (from 1884 to 1946), more than 56,000 inmates were transported to French Guiana from the country of France. Only one fourth of these inmates ever returned to France.

On the mainland, atrocities took place in timber camps where inmates were forced to work in water up to their waists—water that was infested with malaria and mosquitoes. In addition, these men would often be forced to urinate and defecate in the same water where they worked, the entire surroundings being filled with stench and disease-producing conditions. As one might suspect, these inmates were underfed and worked long constant hours. The conditions at Devil's Island were so terrible that men often attempted to swim from the island prisons even though the surrounding waters were piranha infested. There are hundreds of accounts where inmates were eaten by the piranhas while attempting to escape.

As noted, the area on the mainland near Devil's Island as well as two islands close by consisted of the entire penal colony. The colony had numerous work camps dispersed throughout the territory. The deadliest camp was Camp Kourou, where 4,000 inmates died during a three-year span in the early years of operation. This camp was known as the administrative regulating camp. Whenever the entire penal colony region's population became greater than it could support, inmates were sent to Kourou for labor. The labor was backbreaking, and most inmates died. During the years that Camp Kourou was in operation (from 1907 to 1946), it was found that the length of the road that inmates had been working on had never progressed beyond the point of 25 kilometers. It was obvious that Kourou was intended to be a last-stop point of no return. The atrocities of Devil's Island and the surrounding penal colonies ended only when the French closed the entire facility in 1946.

From the descriptions above, it is clear that the prisons in France could be quite different from one another. French prison conditions, in many respects, were not actually much better than those in America. However, the nation of France did produce some of the most influential thinkers on penology and corrections. As we have seen in our past readings, it is the deplorable condition of French prisons that led these philosophers and criminologists to become outspoken against the French system of incarceration.

Question 1: In your opinion, how do the two French prisons noted above compare with early American prisons?

Question 2: The use of transporting inmates continued well past the period that the English had engaged in the practice, all the way up to 1946. How do you think that French correctional systems were affected when transportation ceased?

SOURCE: Charriere, H. (2001). *Papillon*. New York: Harper Perennial.

STUDENT STUDY SITE

chapter 3

Ideological and Theoretical Underpinnings to Corrections

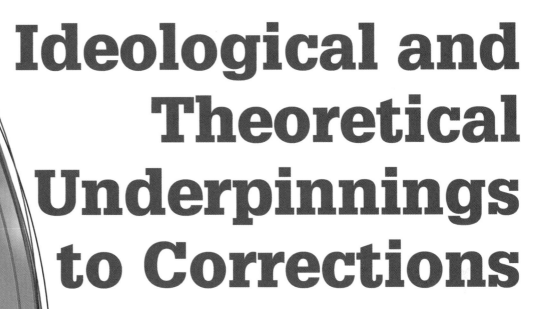

LEARNING OBJECTIVES:

1. Identify and discuss the philosophical underpinnings associated with correctional processes.

2. Identify and discuss different types of sanctions used in correctional operations.

3. Evaluate the outcomes of different sentencing schemes.

4. Apply criminological theories to different correctional processes.

5. Integrate philosophical underpinnings, types of sanctions, sentencing schemes, and criminological theories to develop a multifaceted understanding of corrections.

INTRODUCTION

This chapter focuses on the reasons for providing correctional services in today's society. In providing the reasons for implementing correctional programs, it is important to understand two key aspects related to corrections. First, it is perhaps important to understand the historical developments related to punishment and corrections. Both Chapters 1 and 2 have provided information that is necessary to understand how our current views on correctional practices have evolved. Understanding the history of corrections helps us to make sense of our current correctional system. This is true for legal precedent that shapes correctional policies as well as philosophical and/or political motives behind our use of correctional resources. Thus, it is the rich history of corrections that has shaped it into what we know today.

The second aspect related to corrections is the need for a clear definition of the term *corrections*. As demonstrated in Chapter 1, the term *corrections* can have many different meanings to many different practitioners, scholars, and researchers around the world. Nevertheless, it is important to be able to define the term in a clear and succinct manner so that one can correctly connect it with the means by which correctional practices are implemented and the reasons for implementing them. This is important since it is what will provide clarity in purpose, which, in turn, should lead to clarity in action.

THE PURPOSE OF CORRECTIONS: REVISITED

As pointed out, the ability to define corrections is important in determining the underlying purpose to the practice of corrections. As noted in Chapter 1, *corrections* is defined as a process whereby practitioners from a variety of agencies and programs use tools, techniques, and facilities to engage in organized security and treatment functions intended to correct criminal tendencies among the offender population. As determined, the term *corrections* describes the day-to-day activities of those practitioners who are involved in a similar purpose: to modify human behavior from criminal to prosocial. To add further clarity, facilities or physical structures are merely the tools of the practitioner, and the agencies involved in corrections are simply the groupings of practitioners who are involved in the behavior modification process. From the readings in Chapters 1 and 2, it should be clear to the student that, throughout the ages, the processing of offenders has gone from the mere punitive application of penalties to the intent to change human behavior. Over time, the use of physical punishments has been discouraged, and the notion of generating a self-sufficient system of corrections has now disappeared.

As an additional observation that relates the past historical accounts of corrections in Chapters 1 and 2, it is interesting to see that while the Auburn system was originally popular throughout the early history of the United States, modern correctional practice espouses motivations that are more in line with what the Pennsylvania system might have advocated. Though today's correctional systems do not maintain all inmates in a single cell (many use dormitories), and though inmates may communicate with one another freely, the main purpose to most correctional practices is, at least in theory, to reduce criminal behavior through the process of reform, incapacitation, or the aging-out of the criminal offender. It is with this in mind that we proceed with this chapter.

PHILOSOPHICAL UNDERPINNINGS

Within the field of corrections itself, four goals or philosophical orientations of punishment are generally recognized. These are retribution, deterrence, incapacitation, and treatment (rehabilitation). Two of these orientations focus on the offender (treatment and specific deterrence) while the other orientations (general deterrence, retribution, and incapacitation) are thought to generally focus more on the crime that was committed. The intent of this section of the chapter is to present philosophical bases related to the correctional process. In doing this, it is useful to first provide a quick and general overview of the four primary philosophical bases of punishment (see Table 3.1). The philosophical bases of punishment and corrections were touched upon in Chapter 1 but are now provided in more detail and with the purpose of elucidating the true purposes and rationales behind the correctional process.

Retribution

Retribution is often referred to as the "eye for an eye" mentality, and simply implies that offenders committing a crime should be punished in a like fashion or in a manner that is commensurate with the severity of the crime that they have committed. In other words, retribution implies proportionality of punishments to the seriousness of the crimes committed. As discussed in Chapter 1, retribution is the justification for punishment by the concept of *lex talionis*. It is a "just desserts" model that demands that punishments match the degree of harm that criminals have inflicted on their victims (Stohr, Walsh, & Hemmens, 2009). In other words, offenders should be given the punishment that they justly deserve; those who commit minor crimes deserve minor sentences, and those who commit serious crimes deserve more severe punishments (Stohr et al., 2009). This model of punishment is grounded in the idea that, regardless of any secondary purpose that punishment might be intended to serve, it is simply right to punish offenders because justice demands it. In essence, society has an ethical duty and obligation to enforce the prescribed punishment, or the sentencing process is based on lies and exceptions.

It is important that students not equate retribution with the mere use of primitive revenge; retribution has many distinctions from such a simplistic understanding. Retribution is constrained revenge that is tempered with proportionality and is enacted by a neutral party. This neutral party is required to stay within the bounds of laws that mandate offenders with certain rights, despite the fact that they are to be punished. As we have seen from Chapters 1 and 2, the use of this formalized method of punishment emerged out of the chaotic times where blood feuds and retaliation for private wrongs abounded. Retribution was grounded in the notion that the offender (or the offender's family) must pay for the crime committed. The need to keep feuds from escalating between aggrieved families and those that housed members who had committed crimes against the aggrieved was important among the ruling class. Thus, retribution was designed to be based along a rational process of progressive sanctions, separating this from mere retaliation.

In addition, when we hold offenders accountable for their actions, we make the statement that we (as a society) believe that offenders are free moral agents who have self-will. It is the responsibility of the offender, not society, to pay for the crime that has been committed. Once this payment (whatever the sanction might be) has been made, there is no further need for punishment. While this type of approach works well in justifying punishment of offenders who are culpable and cognizant of their crime, this type of approach is not appropriate for offenders who have mental deficiencies and/or mitigating circumstances that remove fault from the offender. It is in these cases where retribution loses its logical application within the punishment or correctional process.

Incapacitation

Incapacitation simply deprives offenders of their liberty and removes them from society with the intent of ensuring that society cannot be further victimized by these offenders during their term of incarceration. The widespread use of incapacitation techniques during the 1990s is purported by some experts to be the cause for the drop in crime that was witnessed after the year 2000. Though incapacitation has not been proven to be the cause of this drop in crime, the argument does seem to possess some potential validity.

Video Link 3.1
Watch a video about selective incapacitation.

Regardless, it has become increasingly clear that the use of mass incarceration efforts simply cannot be afforded by most state budgets. This has led to more increased use of community corrections techniques and to techniques of selective incapacitation.

Selective incapacitation is implemented by identifying inmates who are of particular concern to public safety and by providing those specific offenders with much longer sentences than would be given to other inmates. The idea is to improve the use of incapacitation through more accurate identification of those offenders who present the worst risks to society. This then maximizes the use of prison space and likely creates the best reduction in crime, dollar for dollar, since monies are not spent housing less dangerous inmates.

Deterrence

Deterrence is the prevention of crime by the threat of punishment (Stohr et al., 2009). Deterrence includes general and specific deterrence. **General deterrence** is intended to cause vicarious learning whereby observers see that offenders are punished for a given crime, and themselves are discouraged from committing a like-mannered crime due to fear of punishment. **Specific deterrence** is simply the infliction of a punishment upon a specific offender in the hope that that particular offender will be discouraged from committing future crimes. For specific deterrence to be effective, it is necessary that a punished offender make a conscious connection between an intended criminal act and the punishment suffered as a result of similar acts committed in the past.

PHOTO 3.2

Jail inmates share a laugh in squalid "Tent City" where over 1,000 inmates serve their sentence. It is hoped that placing offenders in such noxious circumstances will deter them from further criminal behavior. There is no actual empirical proof that this is the case. These women have not committed violent crimes; their crimes range from petty theft to drug use to prostitution.

Stohr et al. (2009) note that the effect of punishment on future behavior also must account for the contrast effect, a notion that distinguishes between the circumstances of the possible punishment and the life experience of the person who is likely to get punished. Stohr et al. (2009) explain as follows:

> For people with little or nothing to lose, an arrest may be perceived as little more than an inconvenient occupational hazard, an opportunity for a little rest and recreation, and a chance to renew old friendships, but for those who enjoy a loving family and the security of a valued career, the prospect of incarceration is a nightmarish contrast. Like so many other things in life, deterrence works least for those who need it the most. (p. 10)

Thus, it appears that deterrence has as much to do with *who* is being deterred as it does with *how* deterrence is being implemented. However, research on deterrence has generally been mixed, even during the mid-1990s to about 2006 (Kohen & Jolly, 2006), when the use of increased incarceration was touted to be the primary cause for lowered crime rates. It is still seemingly impossible to determine whether a deterrent effect, or simply an incapacitation effect, was being observed.

Rehabilitation

Rehabilitation implies that an offender should be provided the means to fulfill a constructive level of functioning in society, with an implicit expectation that such offenders will be deterred from reoffending due to their having worthwhile stakes in legitimate society—stakes that they will not wish to lose as a consequence of criminal offending. Vocational training, educational attainment, and/or therapeutic interventions are used to improve the offender's stakes in prosocial behavior. The primary purpose of rehabilitation is aimed solely at the recovery of the offender, regardless of the crime that was committed. In other words, if it is deemed that offenders are treatable and if, as it turns out, they can be successfully treated to refrain from future criminal behavior, rehabilitation is considered a success, and concern over the severity of the past crime is not considered important. With this approach, it is feasible that offenders with lesser crimes may end up serving more time behind bars than a person with a more serious crime if it is determined that they are not amenable to rehabilitative efforts.

Video Link 3.2
Learn more about the rehabilitation of veterans.

TABLE 3.1 Philosophical Underpinnings in Corrections

Philosophical Underpinning	Premise
Retribution	Implies that offenders committing a crime should be punished in a like fashion or in a manner that is commensurate with the severity of the crime.
Incapacitation	Deprives offenders of their liberty and removes them from society with the intent of ensuring that society cannot be further victimized.
Deterrence (General and Specific)	General deterrence occurs when observers see that offenders are punished for a given crime, and are themselves discouraged from committing crime. Specific deterrence is punishment upon a specific offender in the hope that the offender will be discouraged from committing future crimes.
Rehabilitation	Offenders will be deterred from reoffending due to their having worthwhile stakes in legitimate society.
Restorative Justice	Interventions that focus on restoring the health of the community, repairing the harm done, meeting victims' needs, and emphasizing that the offender can and must contribute to those repairs.
Reintegration	Focused on the reentry of the offender into society.

The rehabilitative approach is based on the notion that offenders are provided treatment rather than punishment. Punitive techniques are completely alien to the rehabilitative model; the goal is to cure the offenders of their criminal behavior much as would be done with a medical or mental health issue. As a result, sentencing schemes under a rehabilitation orientation would be *indeterminate*, a term that will be discussed in more detail later in this chapter. Indeterminate sentences have no specific amount of time provided upon which offenders are released from custody. Rather, a minimum and maximum amount of time is awarded, and, based on offenders' treatment progress, they are released prior to the maximum duration of their sentence once rehabilitative efforts have been determined a success.

Audio Link 3.2
Hear about rehabilitation of drug offenders.

Restorative Justice

Restorative justice is a term for interventions that focus on restoring the health of the community, repairing the harm done, meeting victims' needs, and emphasizing that the offender can and must contribute to those repairs. This definition was adapted from restorative justice advocate Thomas Quinn during his interview with the National Institute of Justice in 1998. More specifically, restorative justice considers the victims, communities, and offenders (in that order) as participants in the justice process. These participants are placed in active roles to work together to do the following:

Journal Article Link 3.1
Read more about victims' roles in restorative justice.

- Empower victims in their search for closure.
- Impress upon offenders the real human impact of their behavior.
- Promote restitution to victims and communities.

Dialogue and negotiation are central to restorative justice, and problem solving for the future is seen as more important than simply establishing blame for past behavior. Another key factor to this type of correctional processing is that the victim is included in the process. Indeed, the victim is given priority consideration in the process, yet, at the same time, the process is correctional in nature as offenders must face the person whom they victimized, and the offenders must be accountable for the crimes that they committed against the victim.

Video Link 3.3
Watch how restorative justice principles are applied.

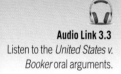

PHOTO 3.3

This group photo is a collection of various victim-offender dialogue (VOD) facilitators in the state of Louisiana. The author of this text is part of this group, which facilitates VOD in that state.

Reintegration

Reintegration is focused on the reentry of the offender into society. The ultimate goal of reintegration programs is to connect offenders to legitimate areas of society in a manner that is gainful and productive. When used inside correctional institutions, this approach emphasizes continued contact between offenders and their families, their friends, and even the community. This approach is set against the backdrop realization that the overwhelming majority of offenders will ultimately return to society. While reintegration efforts do emphasize offender accountability, the use of reintegration processes is focused on ensuring that the offender has a maximal set of circumstances that, at least initially, diminish the need or desire to engage in crime by cultivating the connections that the offender has to legitimate society. Reintegration efforts are intended to reduce recidivism among offenders. During the past few years, there has been an upsurge in national interest in offender reentry programs, which, inherently, are all reintegrative in nature.

TYPES OF SANCTIONS

Audio Link 3.3
Listen to the *United States v. Booker* oral arguments.

It is through the use of intermediate (graduated) sanctions, various types of probation, incarceration, and the death penalty that various types of punishments (also known as sanctions) are meted out. While the public perhaps identifies prison with the final outcome for criminal offenders, the reality is that few offenders go to prison. Rather, the overwhelming majority are placed on probation or on some type of community supervision. Indeed, prisons and jails tend to hold only one fifth to one fourth of the entire offender population. However, chronic offenders and those who commit serious crimes tend to be given some period of incarceration.

Problems in determining the appropriate sentence for offenders are noted in the literature and have even been the focus of at least one influential Supreme Court ruling. In 2005, the U.S. Supreme Court held in *United States v. Booker* that federal judges no longer were required to follow the sentencing guidelines that had been in effect since 1987. The Court held that federal judges now must only consider these guidelines with certain other sentencing criteria when deciding a defendant's punishment. Because of this ruling, and because of the trend toward alternative sanctions, it is speculated that sentencing will be more indeterminate in nature during the next few years (Debro, 2007). This also is consistent with much of the push for reintegrative efforts that has been observed throughout the nation.

The Continuum of Sanctions

The continuum of sanctions refers to a broad array of sentencing and punishment options that range from simple fines to incarceration and ultimately end with the death penalty. Between each of these visible points in the sentencing/sanctioning process (fines, incarceration, and the death penalty) is a variety of options that are used throughout the United States. The reason for this variety of sanctions is manifold. Perhaps chief among these reasons is the desire to calibrate the sanction in a manner that is commensurate with the type of criminal behavior.

When using the term *calibrate*, it is meant that sanctions can be selected in such a manner that allows us to, through an additive process, weight the seriousness of the sanction, as well as the number of sanctions that are given, so that the punishment effect is as proportional to the crime as can be arranged. The desire to establish proportionality naturally harkens back to the thinking of classical criminologists, and this should not be surprising. Classical criminologists appealed to the use of reason in applying punishments, and that is precisely what a continuum seeks to achieve as well: a reasonable, commensurate, and gradual progression of sanctions that can be consistently additive in nature so as to be logically proportional to the frequency and seriousness of the criminal behavior in question (Bosworth, 2010; Lilly, Cullen, & Ball, 2007).

In addition to the desire for proportionality, there is another reason for the use of varied sanctions, particularly intermediate sanctions: the desire to save beds in prisons. As noted earlier in this chapter, there is a push for reintegration efforts in the federal government and in many states throughout the nation. The reason for this has to do with both a shift in ideologies and, more specifically, the rising costs of imprisonment. In fact, at the time of this writing, the increased costs of imprisonment occur amidst a national and international economic crisis that has negatively impacted numerous state budgets throughout the United States. Thus, many states are even more cash-strapped than usual, making the use of alternatives in sentencing all the more appealing.

Another rationale for this continuum is associated with treatment purposes. While we have noted that rehabilitation efforts are typically not contingent on the sentence that is imposed, the fact that indeterminate sentences tend to be used with a rehabilitation orientation demonstrates the need for incentives to exist so that offenders will change their behavior. Without an indeterminate sentence, offenders might not find their efforts toward reform to have any substantive reward; thus early release provides a strong incentive that encourages offenders to actively work toward behavior change. The use of alternative sanctions follows this same logic, where lesser sanctions can be given to those offenders who show progress in treatment, and more serious sanctions can be administered to offenders who prove to be dangerous or a nuisance to a given facility.

From this point, we move to a description of some of the more common versions of sanctions. In providing these descriptions, we will progress from the least severe to the most severe types of sanctions that are usually encountered. The sanctions that follow are not provided as an all-encompassing list of sanctions that are used but simply are intended to provide the student with an understanding of the types of sanctions used and the means by which they are categorized. We begin with sanctions that involve fines or monetary penalties and progress to the ultimate form of punishment: the death penalty.

Monetary

Most monetary sanctions come by the way of fines. Most offenders convicted of a criminal offense are assessed a fine as a punishment for committing the offense. A **fine** can be defined as a monetary penalty imposed by a judge or magistrate as a punishment for being convicted of an offense. In most cases the fine is a certain dollar amount established either by the judge or according to a set schedule dependent upon the offense committed. The logic behind the fine is that it will deter the offender from committing another offense in the future for fear of being fined. In most jurisdictions the fines are assessed and paid in monthly payments to the receiving agency.

Journal Article Link 3.2
Read about how race and ethnicity affect monetary sanctions.

Probation and Intermediate Sanctions

The use of probation and other community-based sanctions accounts for all the varied types of sentencing punishments available short of a jail or prison sentence. When on probation, offenders will report to a probation officer (in most cases) on a scheduled routine that varies with the seriousness of their crime and their expected risk of recidivism. Additional community-based sanctions, tacked on to a probation sentence, further allow for the calibration of the sentence with respect to the crime that was committed and the offender who is on supervision. Intermediate sanctions are a range of sentencing options that fall between incarceration and probation, and are designed to allow for the crafting of sentences that respond to the offender and/or the offense, with the intended outcome of the case being a primary consideration. The purpose of intermediate sanctions is to make available a continuum of sanctions scaled around one or more sanctioning goals. Such a continuum permits the court or corrections authority to tailor sanctions that are meaningful with respect both to their purposes and to the kinds of offenders that come before them.

Incarceration

Imprisonment is the most visible penalty to the public eye in the United States (Bosworth, 2010). Less than 30% of all offenders under supervision are in prisons or jails, but this type of sentence still draws public interest due to its ominous nature. This punishment remains the most commonly used for serious offenders. It is thought by some that imprisonment has a deterrent effect on offenders (Bosworth, 2010). But other researchers have noted that, in many respects, the likelihood of recidivism increases once an offender is incarcerated. Thus, the effectiveness of incarceration to change potential criminal behavior is questionable. Because of this, it is recommended that incarceration be viewed as best suited for meeting the goals of incapacitation (and perhaps retribution) rather than rehabilitation, deterrence, or crime reduction.

Incarceration Options

Among incarceration options, the jail facility is considered the first stage of incarceration for the offender. Jail facilities come in a variety of sizes and designs, but all are generally intended to hold offenders for sentences that are short. Aside from those persons who are held for only brief periods (such as immediately after an arrest), jails tend to hold offenders who are sentenced to a year or less of incarceration. In most cases, jail facilities are the first point at which an offender is officially classified as being in the correctional component of the criminal justice system. In simple terms, a jail is a confinement facility, usually operated and controlled by county-level law enforcement, that is designed to hold persons charged with a crime who are either awaiting adjudication or serving a short sentence of one year or less after the point of adjudication. Similarly, the Bureau of Justice Statistics (2008) defines jails as "locally-operated correctional facilities that confine persons before or after adjudication. Inmates sentenced to jails usually have a sentence of a year or less, but jails also incarcerate persons in a wide variety of other categories." Thus, there is some degree of variance in the means by which jails are utilized, but they tend to be short-term facilities in most cases.

On the other extreme, consider the use of the supermax prison. The supermax prison is perhaps the epitome of incarceration-based sentences. There are some prison administrators who contend that supermax facilities have a general deterrent effect. However, this is unlikely because inmates in supermax facilities do not facilitate bonds with persons in the prison or outside of the prison. Further, the disruptive inmates who will be kept in supermax facilities are least likely to care about the consequences of their actions and/or their ability to bond with other people. Deterrence as a philosophical orientation targets those inmates who would otherwise engage in antisocial behavior, if but for the deterring mechanism. However, the inmates typically channeled into the supermax facility are those who have not been deterred when incarcerated in less secure environments, such as the minimum-, medium-, and maximum-security facilities. Thus, these inmates are unlikely to be among those who would commit crimes were it not for the penalty of incarceration; they are impervious to the threat of incarceration and the deprivations that this sanction entails. Thus, supermax facilities act as simple holding spaces for the most incorrigible of inmates, being devoid of any deterrent and/or therapeutic value.

Video Link 3.4
Learn more about conditions inside a supermax prison.

Because much of this text involves coverage of the prison environment, further discussion related to specific aspects of incarceration schemes will not be provided at this time. However, it is sufficient to say that incarceration, while accounting for no more than 30% of the entire correctional population, tends to draw substantial public attention, including the media. Further, the offenders who are kept incarcerated are among those who are either repetitive or violent, or both. Therefore, the correctional process within institutions is one that deals with harder-core offenders than might be encountered among community supervision personnel.

Death Penalty

Of all penalties that can be implemented, it is the death penalty that is of course the most severe. It is this penalty that has historically been the most controversial, both on a philosophical level and on a practical level. In other words, scholars, advocates, and practitioners have long debated the merit of this sanction in terms of the philosophical "rightness" of this punishment, and they have just as passionately argued over the means by which it is implemented. The fact that the death penalty has been abandoned in numerous U.S. states speaks to the fact that the death penalty is a controversial sanction that has created a deep schism between those who are in favor of the sanction and those who are not. Further evidence of the controversial nature of this penalty can be found amongst a variety of death penalty cases that have been heard by the Supreme Court. For now, the death penalty is still considered a constitutional sentence, but this truth exists against a backdrop of precedence that has considerably limited its use and application.

TECHNOLOGY AND EQUIPMENT 3.1

Methods of Administering the Death Penalty

In Chapters 1 and 2, it is clear that punishments were barbaric and quite painful. Further, the use of the death penalty was widespread and was administered in a torturous manner. Capital punishments that involved burning the offender at the stake, drawing and quartering the offender, and the guillotine all seem cruel and also seem like ancient practices. However, since the late 1800s it seems that the United States has been searching for more humane means of executing offenders. The innovations that have emerged have presented challenges and, in many cases, seem somewhat barbaric in their own right. Lethal injection, which is the most modern of innovations in administering the death penalty, seems to be the most humane method available, and, as we will see in Chapter 15, it is the most commonly used method among the 50 states. For now, we turn our attention to five specific means of administering the death penalty that have been part and parcel to American corrections: hanging, electrocution, firing squad, gas chamber, and lethal injection.

Hanging

Until the 1890s, hanging was the primary method of execution used in the United States. Hanging is still used in Delaware and Washington, although both have lethal injection as an alternative method of execution. For execution by this method, the inmate may be weighed the day before the execution, and a rehearsal is done using a sandbag of the same weight as the prisoner. This is to determine the length of "drop" necessary to ensure a quick death. If the rope is too long, the inmate could be decapitated, and if it is too short, the strangulation could take as long as 45 minutes. The rope, which should be 0.75 to 1.25 inches in diameter, must be boiled and stretched to eliminate spring or coiling. Immediately before the execution, the prisoner's hands and legs are secured, he or she is blindfolded, and the noose is placed around the neck, with the knot behind the left ear. The execution takes place when a trapdoor is opened and the prisoner falls through. The prisoner's weight should cause a rapid fracture and dislocation of the neck. However, instantaneous death rarely occurs (Weisberg, 1991).

Electrocution

Seeking a more humane method of execution than hanging, New York built the first electric chair in 1888. Soon, other states adopted this execution method. Today, electrocution is not used as the sole method of execution in any state. Electrocution was the sole method in Nebraska until the state Supreme Court ruled the method unconstitutional in February 2008. For execution by the electric chair, the person is usually shaved and strapped to a chair with belts that cross his chest, groin, legs, and arms. A metal skullcap-shaped electrode is attached to the scalp and forehead over a sponge moistened with saline. The sponge must not be too wet or the saline short-circuits the electric current, and not too dry as it would then have a very high resistance. An additional electrode is moistened with conductive jelly (Electro-Creme) and attached to a portion of the prisoner's leg that has been shaved to reduce resistance to electricity. The prisoner is then blindfolded (Weisberg, 1991). After the execution team has withdrawn to the observation room, the warden signals the executioner, who pulls a handle to connect the power supply. A jolt of between 500 and 2,000 volts, which lasts for about 30 seconds, is given. The current surges and is then turned off, at which time the body is seen to relax. The doctors wait a few seconds for the body to cool down and then check to see if the inmate's heart is still beating. If it is, another jolt is applied. This process continues until the prisoner is dead.

Firing Squad

Firing squad still remains a method of execution in Idaho, although lethal injection as an alternative method is allowed. For execution by this method, the inmate is typically bound to a chair with leather straps across his waist and head, in front of an oval-shaped canvas wall. The chair is surrounded by sandbags to absorb the inmate's blood. A black hood is pulled over the inmate's head. A doctor locates the inmate's heart with a stethoscope and pins a circular white cloth target over it. Standing in an enclosure 20 feet away, five shooters are armed with .30 caliber rifles loaded with single rounds. One of the shooters is given blank rounds (Weisberg, 1991). The offender dies as a result of blood loss caused by rupture of the heart or a large blood vessel, or tearing of the lungs. The person shot loses consciousness when shock causes a fall in the supply of blood to the brain. If the shooters miss the heart, by accident or intention, the prisoner bleeds to death slowly (Weisberg, 1991).

Gas Chamber

In 1924, the use of cyanide gas was introduced as Nevada sought a more humane way of executing its inmates. Today, five states authorize lethal gas as a method of execution, but all have lethal injection as an alternative method. For execution by this method, the condemned person is strapped to a chair in an airtight chamber. Below the chair rests a pail of sulfuric acid. A long stethoscope is typically affixed to the inmate so that a doctor outside the chamber can pronounce death. Once everyone has left the chamber, the room is sealed. The executioner flicks a lever that releases crystals of sodium cyanide into the pail. This causes a chemical reaction that releases hydrogen cyanide gas (Weisberg, 1991). The inmate dies from hypoxia, the cutting off of oxygen to the brain (Weisberg, 1991). At postmortem, an exhaust fan sucks the poison air out of the chamber, and the corpse is sprayed with ammonia to neutralize any remaining traces of cyanide.

Lethal Injection

In 1977, Oklahoma became the first state to adopt lethal injection as a means of execution, though it would be five more years until an actual execution by lethal injection would occur. Today, 35 of the 36 states that have the death penalty use this method. When this method is used, the condemned person is usually bound to a gurney, and a member of the execution team positions several heart monitors on the skin. Two needles (one is a backup) are then inserted into usable veins, usually in the inmate's arms. Long tubes connect the needle through a hole in a cement block wall to several intravenous drips. The first is a harmless saline solution that is started immediately. Then, at the warden's signal, a curtain is raised exposing the inmate to the witnesses in an adjoining room. Then, the inmate is injected with sodium thiopental—an anesthetic, which puts the inmate to sleep. Next flows Pavulon or pancuronium bromide, which paralyzes the entire muscle system and stops the inmate's breathing. Finally, the flow of potassium chloride stops the heart. Death results from anesthetic overdose and respiratory and cardiac arrest while the condemned person is unconscious (Ecenbarger, 1994; Weisberg, 1991).

SOURCE: Excerpted from *Descriptions of Execution Methods*, Death Penalty Information Center.

PHOTO 3.4

An inmate on death row walks in the corridor at the Ellis Unit in Huntsville, Texas. Texas has more than 500 inmates on death row.

Issues related to the use of the death penalty will be discussed in detail in Chapter 18; therefore those details will not be included in this section. Rather, the correctional philosophies and the rationale for the death penalty will be briefly presented in this current chapter to demonstrate how philosophy, ideology, and theory are all related in providing justification for and argument against the implementation of this sanction. As noted in Chapter 1, the death penalty was perhaps one of the most commonly used sanctions in the ancient world, aside from banishment. It was with the advent of the prison and/or prison-like facilities that other options besides death or exile were developed.

While the early history of corrections included a wide range of physically torturous sanctions, the use of intermediate sanctions and prisons for long-term custody was almost nonexistent. This is important because the lack of these correctional features limited the options available among social groups when seeking punishments against offenders and when a desire emerged to reform an offender. With the continuum of sanctions that is used in today's society, the options that exist for processing offenders have greatly increased, and this has resulted in even more scrutiny being cast on the use of the death penalty.

SENTENCING MODELS

Sentencing involves a two-stage decision-making process. After the offender is convicted of a crime, the initial decision is made as to whether probation should or should not be granted. The chief probation officer or his or her designee will typically make this decision based on the presentence investigation (PSI). The presentence investigation report is a thorough file that includes a wide range of background information on the offender. This file will typically include demographic, vocational, educational, and personal information on the offender as well as records on his or her prior offending patterns and the probation department's recommendation as to the appropriate type of sentencing for the offender.

If incarceration is chosen, the second decision involves determining the length of the sentence. For many judges, deciding the length of the sentence (when they are required to do so) is not an easy task. There are frustrations in sentencing that tend to be related to the need to consider the possibility for rehabilitation, the need to protect society, the need to fulfill the demand of retribution, and the implementation of deterrence strategies. The most important factor in deciding on a sanction is the seriousness of the crime. Sentencing on the basis of seriousness is one key way that courts attempt to arrive at consistent sentences. Once the seriousness of the crime has been determined, the next factor to consider is the prior record of the offender. The worse the prior record, the more likely the offender will receive a lengthy sentence. The last few issues considered in the sentencing process are mitigating and aggravating factors. **Mitigating factors** do not exonerate offenders but do make their commission of the crime more understandable and also help to reduce the level of culpability that the offenders might have had. **Aggravating circumstances**, on the other hand, magnify the offensive nature of the crime and tend to result in longer sentences. Each of these factors can impact the outcome of the sentence. It is with this in mind that we turn our attention to the two types of sentencing: indeterminate and determinate sentencing.

Indeterminate Sentences

Indeterminate sentencing is sentencing that includes a range of years that will be potentially served by the offender. The offender is released during some point in the range of years that are assigned by the sentencing judge. Both the minimum and maximum times can be modified by a number of factors such as offender behavior and offender work ethic. Under the most liberal of approaches using indeterminate sentences, judges will assign custody of the offender to the department of corrections, and the release of the offender is completely dependent on the agency's determination that the offender is ready to function appropriately in society. This type of sentence is typically associated with treatment-based programming and community supervision objectives. In such cases, indeterminate sentencing provides correctional officials a good deal of control over the amount of time that an offender will serve.

Penal codes with indeterminate sentencing stipulate minimum and maximum sentences that must be served in prison (2 to 10 years, 3 to 5 years, and so forth). At the time of sentencing, the judge will explain to the offender the time frame that the offender may potentially be in prison. The offender is also informed of any potential eligibility for parole once the minimum amount of time has been served. However, the actual release date is determined by the parole board, not the judge. Note that this particular sentence is different from the determinate *discretionary* sentence that will be described in the following subsection. The difference is that while the determinate *discretionary* sentence has a range of time to be served, the specific sentence to be served within that range is decided by the judge at the point of initial sentencing. Once this specific amount of time has been decided, there is no further modification to the sentence, regardless of the offender's progress within the institution.

Reference Link 3.2
Read about indeterminate sentencing.

Determinate Sentences

Determinate sentencing consists of fixed periods of incarceration with no later flexibility in the term that is served. This type of sentencing is grounded in notions of retribution, just desserts, and incapacitation. These types of sentences came into vogue due to disappointments with the use of rehabilitation and to increased support for retribution. When offenders are given a determinate sentence, they are imprisoned for a specific period of time (e.g., 5 years, 10 years, 20 years). Once that time has expired, the inmate is released from prison.

It should be pointed out that in many states inmates may be given "good time" if they maintain good behavior while in the correctional facility (Weisburd & Chayet, 1996). Generally, this entails a willingness to work in the prison, engage in educational and therapeutic programs, and participate in other prosocial activities. Good time earned is taken off the total sentence that inmates must serve, thereby allowing them to be released early from prison. While this does add some degree of variability to the total time that offenders serve in the institution, the actual sentence given to the inmates is not connected to their level of participation in treatment or to the likelihood of parole or early release (Weisburd & Chayet, 1996).

One variant of the determinate sentence is the determinate presumptive sentence. The **determinate presumptive sentence** specifies the exact length of the sentence to be served by the inmate. Judges are required to impose these sentences, unless there are aggravating or mitigating circumstances, in which case they may lengthen or shorten the sentences within narrow boundaries and with written justification. This type of sentence is perhaps more realistic than a pure determinate sentencing model because it accounts for the variety of circumstances that are different from one case to another. In fact, very few criminal cases are exactly alike even when the charge is the same. The circumstances associated with each type of criminal case (e.g., theft) tend to vary, with different motivations, different outcomes, and different issues, and this may make the crime seem more or less severe in nature, especially on a human level (Carter, 1996).

To further demonstrate the potential complexity of sentencing schemes, consider also the determinate discretionary sentence. The **determinate discretionary sentence** (discussed briefly in the prior subsection) sets a stated range of time that must be served. This range of time (e.g., 3 to 5 years) is not subject to modification by judges who impose a sentence under this model (Carter, 1996). However, the judge is able to use his or her own discretion in determining the exact sentence so long as it falls within the 3- to 5-year range that has been predetermined by legislative bodies. Thus, the sentence is, in fact, determinate in nature with parameters being set at a minimum of 3 years and a maximum of 5 years, but it is also discretionary since it allows the judge to select the exact time that will be served. Note that this sentence is different from the indeterminate sentence that was presented in the prior subsection. The difference is that while the indeterminate sentence often has a range of time to be served, the eventual date of release for the offender is decided by correctional officials who work with the offender and determine his or her progress toward and suitability for reintegration into society. Thus, the exact amount of time served depends on an offender's progress within the correctional treatment regimen.

Mandatory Minimum Sentences

Mandatory minimum sentences require that some minimum length of incarceration be served by offenders who commit certain specified crimes, such as drug-related crimes. In these cases, judges are extremely limited in their consideration of the offender's background or circumstances, and the use of community-based sanctions is out of the question. One type of mandatory minimum sentence is the "three strikes and you're out" law. These laws require that judges award a long-term prison sentence (in some cases life in prison) to offenders who have three felony convictions. This has resulted in the growth of prison populations around the nation and has also resulted in a graying of the prison population in the United States. As more and more inmates serve lengthy mandatory minimum sentences, the proportion of inmates who are elderly continues

PHOTO 3.6

Johnny Lee Wilson, convicted of murder, stands handcuffed in the hallway of the Jefferson City Correctional Center in Missouri.

to climb. Since elderly inmates are more costly to house than younger inmates (due to medical care and other related costs), this has proven to be a serious drain on many state-level prison systems.

Indeed, this issue has been given considerable attention in recent years, with Texas, California, Florida, New York, and Louisiana all experiencing a rise in per-capita elderly inmates that are incarcerated. The states just mentioned either have the largest prison population or have the highest rates of incarceration around the United States. In all cases, the costs that are associated with the elderly inmate are exponentially higher than those associated with the average inmate. This has led to other issues that begin to emerge for administrators, such as the possibility of early release of inmates who are expected to die, the implementation of human caregiver programs such as hospice, and accountability to the public. It is this accountability that places prison administrators in a dilemma since public safety is the primary concern for all custodial programs. Thus, in one generation, mandatory minimum, three strikes, habitual offender, and other enhanced sentences have created a new crisis that looms on the correctional horizon of the United States. This outcome is likely to affect sentencing patterns in the future, which, in turn, will impact the state of corrections in the future.

Sentencing Disparities

The term *disparity* should be held distinct from the better known term *discrimination*. **Disparity** refers to inconsistencies in sentencing and/or sanctions that result from the decision-making process. This typically results when the criminal justice system provides an unequal response toward one group as compared with the response given to other groups. Distinct from this is **discrimination**, which focuses on attributes of offenders when providing a given sentence. This usually results in a differential response toward a group without providing any legally legitimate reference to reasons for that differential response. According to Neubauer (2002), the most commonly cited forms of disparity in sentencing involve geography and judicial attitudes. We now proceed with a discussion of these two types of disparity and will further explore how disparities impact corrections throughout the United States.

Geographical disparity in sentencing patterns has been tied to various areas of the United States and reflects the cultural and historical development of correctional thought in those regions. Neubauer (2002) notes that geographical differences in justice are the product of a variety of factors such as the amount of crime, the types of crime affecting a given area, the effectiveness of police enforcement, and media attention given to criminal activity in the region. Overall, it is clear that the South imposes more harsh sentences than other areas of the nation, and the western part of the United States seems to follow suit. Interestingly, executions are concentrated in these regions as well. When one considers our discussion in Chapter 2 regarding southern penology as well as the development of corrections in the West, this observation may not be too surprising.

Lastly, a discussion regarding disparity in sentencing would not be complete without at least some reference to observed disparity in death penalty sentences. While this chapter will not focus on the death penalty, per se, the use of this sentence and problems regarding racial disparity in its application help to illustrate why disparity in sentencing is an important issue to the field of corrections. This also helps to illustrate a philosophical or ideological influence on the sentencing process that is at least perceived to be true by many in the public arena.

More extensive discussion regarding the death penalty and disparity in its application will be provided in Chapter 18, but the simple point to this current discussion is to highlight that disparity in sentencing may underlie other alleged reasons for sentencing outcomes that are observed. This then may undermine punishment schemes that are intended to rehabilitate offenders and/or deter all offenders. Rather, the cultural impact and/or influence from individuals of influence in the justice system may obscure and impair the intended outcome of various sentencing and punishment schemes. In regard to rehabilitation, this can create additional distrust of helping professionals from a given group that has been marginalized. From a deterrence viewpoint, these factors may only deter one group while giving the impression that criminal activity will be tolerated among other groups. It is clear that these impressions undermine the correctional process and, as a result, add further complication to the correctional process as a whole.

Video Link 3.5
Watch a video about three strikes legislation.

Journal Article Link 3.3
Read about racial and ethnic disparities in girls' sentencing.

United States v. Booker *on Determinate Sentencing*

In January 2005 the U.S. Supreme Court held in *United States v. Booker* that federal judges no longer are required to follow the sentencing guidelines that had been in effect since 1987. Specifically, the Court ruled in *Booker* that the U.S. sentencing guidelines were unconstitutional in that particular case and, more importantly, that this could only be remedied by making the guidelines voluntary for federal judges. This was important because up until this time, the sentencing guidelines had not been officially challenged, even if judges gave sentences (due to aggravating circumstances) that went beyond the guidelines.

In the *Booker* case, a federal judge had added extra time to the offender's sentence due to additional facts that were based on a preponderance of the evidence (the standard used in a civil trial). In examining the circumstance, the High Court held that federal judges now must only consider these guidelines with certain other sentencing criteria when deciding a defendant's punishment. However, the Court did note that, should a sentence beyond the guidelines be given by a judge, a separate sentencing hearing must be held before a jury, thereby placing such enhancements under the scrutiny of the defendant's peers. Because of this ruling, and because of the trend toward community supervision, alternative sanctions, and offender reintegration, it is speculated that sentencing will become more indeterminate in nature.

Debro (2007) discusses the *Booker* case and several other Supreme Court cases and notes that it is likely that American judicial practices may gradually extend more sentencing discretion to judges. In support of this notion, Debro (2007) points toward the fact that "between 2004 and 2006, 22 states enacted some form of sentencing reform. The United States Sentencing Commission also has recommended changes to federal sentencing guidelines" (p. 506). In these cases, there has been a clear intent to reduce disparities in sentencing and to increase judge-based discretion. This is a bit ironic because, in the past, the use of discretion was precisely what led to disparate outcomes.

Whether this is for the better or for the worse is not completely clear, but it has historically been the case that the criminal justice system operates on a spectrum with punitive philosophies at one end and reformative philosophies on the other. The previous 10 to 15 years have been reflective of a crime control model of criminal justice that has had an emphasis on mandatory minimums for sentencing as well as purely determinate sentencing schemes. Historically speaking, the timing may begin to swing toward less restrictive prison sentencing that may lead to more use of community corrections.

SOURCE: Debro, J. (2007). The future of sentencing. In P. M. Carlson & J. S. Garrett (Eds.), *Prison and jail administration: Practice and theory* (pp. 503–510). Boston: Jones & Bartlett.

CRIMINOLOGICAL THEORIES AND CORRECTIONS

If a correctional program is to be effective it must have a clear theoretical and philosophical grounding. Numerous criminological theories exist that are used to explain why crime occurs and how one might predict crime. The ability to predict crime allows us to find those factors that lead to crime and therefore give us guidance on what should be done to prevent crime. Further, if we are able to explain why crime occurs, we can better determine those factors that must be addressed to correct aberrant tendencies toward criminal behavior. Thus, appropriate grounding in theoretical underpinnings to criminal behavior can improve any correctional effort. However, theoretical applications may not always be quite so clear in the day-to-day practice of corrections.

The specific theoretical applications to institutional corrections may not be clear to many students. Thus, a discussion on some of the more common theories of criminal behavior is presented so that students can connect philosophies on correctional intervention, the use of different sentencing characteristics, and theories on criminal behavior as a means of understanding the many different bases to the field. Further, the philosophical underpinnings behind punishment are important to understand since this will often shape official reactions to criminal offending. Both sociological and psychological theories are important for this process and are, therefore, included within the pages that follow.

Individual Traits

According to some theorists, criminal behavior can be directly connected to specific personality characteristics that offenders tend to possess. **Individual personality traits** that are associated with criminal behavior include defiance, self-assertiveness, extroversion, impulsivity, narcissism, mental instability, a tendency toward hostility, a lack of concern for others, resentment, and a distrust of authority. These traits are, quite naturally, psychological in nature, and, presuming that these characteristics are the root causal factor behind an offender's criminal behavior, correctional interventions along the line of the medical model would be most appropriate. In such circumstances, criminal behavior would be treated as a form of pathology and would be treated with a correctional scheme that integrates mental health interventions (Lilly et al., 2007).

Classical Theory and Behavioral Psychology

Students will recall from Chapter 1 that classical criminologists contend that punishment must be proportional, purposeful, and reasonable. Beccaria, in advocating this shift in offender processing, contended that humans were hedonistic—seeking pleasure while wishing to avoid pain—and that this required an appropriate amount of punishment to counterbalance the rewards derived from criminal behavior. It will become clear in subsequent pages that this emphasis on proportional rewards and punishments dovetails well with behavioral psychology's views on the use of reinforcements (rewards) and punishments.

Though our correctional system today is much more complicated than in times past, classical criminology serves as the basic underlying theoretical foundation of our criminal justice system in the United States, including the correctional components. It is indeed presumed that offenders can (and do) learn from their transgressions through a variety of reinforcement and punishment schedules that corrections may provide.

Operant Conditioning

One primary theoretical orientation used in nearly all treatment programs associated with correctional treatment is operant conditioning. This form of behavioral modification is based on the notion that certain environmental consequences occur that strengthen the likelihood of a given behavior, and other consequences tend to lessen the likelihood that a given behavior is repeated. We now turn our attention to those consequences that impact human behavior, for better or worse.

Reinforcers and Punishments

Those consequences that strengthen a given behavior are called reinforcers. Reinforcers can be both positive and negative, with **positive reinforcers** being a reward for a desired behavior (Davis & Palladino, 2002). An example might be if we provided a certificate of achievement for offenders who completed a life skills program. Negative reinforcers are unpleasant stimuli that are removed when a desired behavior occurs (Davis & Palladino, 2002). An example might be if we agreed to remove the requirement of wearing electronic monitoring devices when offenders successfully maintained their scheduled meetings and appointments for one full year without any lapse in attendance.

Consequences that weaken a given behavior are known as punishments. Punishments, as odd as this may sound, can be either positive or negative. A **positive punishment** is one where a stimulus is applied to the offender when the offender commits an undesired behavior (Davis & Palladino, 2002). For instance, we might require offenders to pay an additional late fee if they are late in paying their restitution to the victim of their crime. A **negative punishment** is the removal of a valued stimulus when the offender commits an undesired behavior (Davis & Palladino, 2002). An example might be when we remove offenders' ability to leave their domicile for recreational or personal purposes (i.e., place them on house arrest) if they miss any of their scheduled appointments or meetings.

The key in distinguishing between reinforcers and punishments to keep in mind is that reinforcers are intended to *increase* the likelihood of a *desired* behavior whereas punishments are intended to *decrease* the likelihood of an *undesired* behavior. In operant conditioning, the term *positive* refers to the addition of a stimulus rather than the notion that something is good or beneficial. Likewise, the term *negative* refers to the removal of a stimulus rather than being used to denote something that is bad or harmful. For further information on these points, students should refer to Applied Theory 3.1, "Classical Criminology, Behavioral Psychology, and Corrections."

APPLIED THEORY 3.1

Classical Criminology, Behavioral Psychology, and Corrections

In addition to Cesare Beccaria, another noteworthy figure associated with classical criminology was Jeremy Bentham. Bentham is known for advocating that punishments should be swift, severe, and certain. This has been widely touted by classical criminologists and even by many modern-day criminologists who have leanings toward classical and/or rational choice theories on crime. Essentially, Bentham believed that a delay in the amount of time between the crime and the punishment impaired the likely deterrent value of the punishment in the future. Likewise, Bentham held that punishments must be severe enough in consequence as to deter persons from engaging in criminal behavior. Lastly, Bentham noted that the punishment must be assured; otherwise offenders will simply become cleverer at hiding their crimes once they know that the punishment can be avoided.

Current research actually supports some aspects of classical criminology, while refuting other points. In particular, it has been found that the certainty of the punishment does indeed lower the likelihood of recidivism. Likewise, the less time between the crime and the punishment, the less likely offenders will be to reoffend in the future. However, it has not been found to be true that the severity of the punishment is successful in reducing crime. In fact, there has been substantial historical research on the death penalty that seems to indicate that general deterrence is not achieved with the death penalty, even though it is the most severe punishment that can be given.

Further, research on the use of prisons has shown that prisons may actually *increase* the likelihood of future recidivism for many offenders. Obviously, this is counterproductive to the desire of the criminal justice system. While some offenders are simply too dangerous to be released into the community, others who are not so dangerous will ultimately be returned. Among those, the goal of any sanction should be to reduce the likelihood that they will commit crime—not increase that likelihood. The research of Smith, Goggin, and Gendreau (2002) provides evidence that the prison environment may simply increase the likelihood of recidivism among many offenders. Smith et al. (2002) conducted a meta-analysis of various recidivism studies and concluded that prisons could indeed be considered "schools of crime" (p. 21). Further, they found that the longer the term of imprisonment, the more likely offenders were to recidivate. Thus, severity of the punishment does not reduce crime and, in actuality, increases the likelihood of future crime. Other studies substantiate this research.

This alone presents a valid argument against the unnecessary use of prisons, particularly when community corrections can provide effective supervision and sanctions without the reliance on prison facilities. Community corrections sanctions can be swifter in implementation, and they are much more certain in their application. For example, many offenders may be given a certain number of years in prison but will later be released early, reducing the certainty (and severity) that they will be held to serve their intended punishment. Further, the plea-bargaining system in the United States provides an opportunity for the convicted to avoid incarceration entirely, even when a prison sentence would typically be given for the crime that the offender committed. It is then clear that the use of such pleas detracts from the certainty of the sentence.

In addition, overcrowding may delay the time during which an offender is placed in prison, with law enforcement jail facilities holding the offender during the interim. Further, offenders are able to avoid the assumption of responsibility for their crimes when they are simply given a sentence and allowed to serve their time without being accountable to the victim and/or society. Community corrections sentencing, on the other hand, has a number of additional conditions and programs that often require that the offender make restitution, provide services, and/or pay fines to victims and/or the community (examples of these conditions will be presented in later chapters). Thus, the flexibility of this type of sanctioning provides an element of certainty that offenders will be held accountable, and these types of sanctions can be administered quite quickly.

In addition, many behavioral psychologists note that if punishment is to be effective, certain considerations must be taken into account. These considerations, summarized by Davis and Palladino (2002, pp. 262–263), are presented below:

1. The punishment should be delivered immediately after the undesirable behavior occurs (similar to the "swiftness" requirement of classical criminologists).

2. The punishment should be strong enough to make a real difference to that particular organism. *This is similar to the "severity" requirement of classical criminologists, but this point also illustrates that "severity" may be perceived differently from one person to another.*

3. The punishment should be administered after each and every undesired response. *This is similar to the "certainty" requirement of classical criminologists.*

4. The punishment must be applied uniformly with no chance of undermining or escaping the punishment. *When considering our justice system, it is clear*

that this consideration is undermined by the plea-bargaining process.

5. If excessive punishment occurs and/or is not proportional to the aberrant behavior committed, the likelihood of aggressive responding increases. *In a similar vein and as noted earlier, excessive prison sentences simply increase crime, including violent crime.*

6. To ensure that positive changes are permanent, provide an alternative behavior that can gain reinforcement for the person. *In other words, the use of reintegrative efforts to instill positive behaviors and activities must be supplemented for those behaviors and activities that are criminal in nature.*

From the presentation above, it can be seen that there is a great deal of similarity between classical criminologists and behavioral psychologists on the dynamics associated with the use of punishment. In addition, the second consideration above demonstrates the need for severity, but it illustrates a point often overlooked: Severity of a punishment is in the eye of the beholder. For instance, some offenders would prefer to simply "do flat time" in prison rather than complete the various requirements of community supervision. This is particularly true for offenders who have become habituated to prison life. In these cases, the goal should be not to acclimate offenders to prison life, but instead to acclimate offenders to community life as responsible and productive citizens. Corrections encourages this outcome and utilizes a range of sanctions that can be calibrated to be more or less "severe" as needed by the individual offender. In other words, corrections utilizes techniques from behavioral psychology/classical criminology in a manner that individualizes punishment for the offender. It is for this reason that prison should be utilized only for those offenders who are simply not receptive to change and/or the assumption of responsibility for their crimes.

SOURCES: Davis, S. F., & Palladino, J. J. (2002). *Psychology* (3rd ed.). Upper Saddle River, NJ: Prentice Hall; Smith, P., Goggin, C., & Gendreau, P. (2002). *The effects of prison sentences on recidivism: General effects and individual differences.* Saint John, Canada: Centre for Criminal Justice Studies, University of New Brunswick.

Social Learning

Social learning theory and differential association theory are presented together because they have a common history and because many of the basic precepts are similar (Ronald Akers's social learning theory being spawned from Edwin Sutherland's differential association theory). As with differential association theory, **social learning theory** contends that offenders learn to engage in crime through exposure to and adoption of definitions that are favorable to the commission of crime (Lilly et al., 2007). While both theories contend that exposure to normative definitions that are favorable to crime commission can influence others to commit crime (through vicarious learning and/or reinforcement for repeating similar acts), social learning explicitly articulates the manner by which such definitions are learned by criminals. Differential association, on the other hand, does not clarify this point, and this is the primary distinction between the two theories.

Audio Link 3.4
Learn more about social learning theory.

Anomie/Strain

The next theory to be examined is **strain theory/institutional anomie**. This theory denotes that when individuals cannot obtain success goals (money, status, and so forth), they will tend to experience a sense of pressure often called *strain*. Under certain conditions, they are likely to respond to this strain by engaging in criminal behavior. Merton (1938) and Messner and Rosenfeld (2001) note that this is often aggravated in American society by the continued emphasis on material (monetary) success and the corresponding lack of emphasis on the means by which such material accumulation is obtained. In other words, these authors contend that society in the United States emphasizes winning the game (of life) much more than how the game (of life) is played.

Labeling and Social Reaction

Another theoretical application that is relevant to the correctional process is **labeling theory**. This theory contends that individuals become stabilized in criminal roles when they are labeled as criminals, are stigmatized, develop criminal identities, are sent to prison, and are excluded from conventional roles (Cullen & Agnew, 2006). In essence, the label of "criminal offender" or "convict" simply stands in the way of the offender reintegrating back into society. Such labels impair the offender's ability to obtain employment, housing, and/or other necessary goods or services to achieve success. Naturally, these forms of tracking and labeling often result from the need to ensure public safety (as with pedophiles) and thus are simply a necessary aspect of the punishment, incapacitation, and public safety objectives of many community corrections programs. However, it may be that these functions can be achieved in a manner that aids public safety while at the same time does not prevent the offender from achieving reintegration.

Audio Link 3.5
Listen to examples of labeling theory during reintegration.

PHOTO 3.7

State Crime Rankings 3.1
Offenders in State Sex Offender Registries (2010)

Journal Article Link 3.4
Read about how labeling theory is used to explain the relationship between custody levels and misconduct.

The desire to allow for public information of an offender's past errors (due to a need to achieve public safety) without undo blockage of the offender's ability to reintegrate has been directly addressed by labeling theory scholars. One particular labeling theorist, John Braithwaite, provided a particularly insightful addition to the labeling theory literature that is specifically suited for the field of community supervision. In his work *Crime, Shame, and Reintegration*, Braithwaite (1989) holds that crime is higher when shaming is stigmatizing and criminal activity is lower when shaming effects serve a reintegrative purpose.

According to Braithwaite (1989), the negative effects of stigmatization are most pronounced among offenders who have few prosocial bonds to conventional society (such as family, religious institutions, and civic activities). This would place young males who are unmarried and unemployed at the greatest risk of being thrust further into criminality due to shaming effects. Due to their lack of resources, connections, and general social capital, these offenders find themselves further removed from effective participation in legitimate society. Over time, these offenders will find that it is much easier to join criminal subcultures where tangible reinforcements for their activities can be found. Thus, a cycle is created where a given segment of the offender population is further encouraged to repeat criminal activity simply due to the fact that other options have essentially been knifed away from them.

Conflict Criminology

According to **conflict theory**, the concepts of inequality and power are the central issues underlying crime and its control. This theory is derived from the work of Karl Marx (Lilly et al., 2007). Conflict criminologists note that capitalism perpetuates a system that benefits the rich. In the process, the poor are denied access to economic opportunities and are therefore prevented from improving their social standing. Thus, the wide economic gap between the social classes is increased and perpetuated with each successive generation. In a similar vein, the state—which includes the criminal law and the criminal justice system—operates to protect social arrangements that benefit those profiting from capitalism (Lilly et al., 2007). In general, the injurious acts committed by the poor and powerless are defined as crime, but the injurious acts committed by the rich and powerful are not brought within the reach of the criminal law. One can see this in sentencing practices that tend to mete our harsher terms to those groups who lack wealth and the ability to hire expensive defense attorneys, and that tend to assign comparatively light sentences to those who are wealthy. Thus, critical criminologists point at the social system itself as the chief cause of America's growing prison population.

CONCLUSION

This chapter began with a review of the purpose of corrections as a process whereby practitioners from a variety of agencies and programs use tools, techniques, and facilities to engage in organized security and treatment functions intended to correct criminal tendencies among the offender population. It is with this purpose in mind that a variety of philosophical underpinnings were presented, including retribution, incapacitation, deterrence, rehabilitation, restorative justice, and reintegration. As can be seen, each of these philosophical approaches has held sway throughout the history of corrections at one time or another. However, it is clear from the definition of corrections, as provided in this text, that the ultimate and modern philosophy of corrections is one that likely includes elements of rehabilitation, restorative justice, and reintegration more than it does retribution, incapacitation, and deterrence.

Though modern corrections is considered more reintegrative in nature, the reality cannot be ignored: Prisons are not effective instruments of rehabilitation or reintegration. Research demonstrates that incarceration is not likely to lower recidivism and, in some cases, may actually increase recidivism. Thus, other philosophical uses of prisons such as incapacitation and deterrence continue to proliferate among correctional agencies. However, one criminal offense is not always equal to another, and this has necessitated the need for a continuum of sanctions. This continuum provides for a number of punishments (sanctions) that have varying levels of severity. Monetary fines are perhaps the least serious of sanctions, followed by a very wide range of intermediate community-based sanctions. Community-based sanctions are given extensive coverage due to their variability in administration and their effectiveness in calibrating the punishment to the criminal offense and the criminal offender. Discussion regarding the use of incarceration as a primary tool of punishment was provided with explanation for the different types of custody arrangements when using incarceration with serious offenders. Lastly, the death penalty was presented as the most serious sanction available; its utility and effectiveness were put to serious question in this chapter.

Next, types of sentencing models were presented, which included indeterminate, determinate, and mandatory minimum sentences. The reasons for using these types of sentences were provided as well as the pitfalls to each one. While intentions may be good, the outcomes of each of these types of sentencing schemes have not necessarily been effective in achieving the desired goal in their application. Further still, despite the use of complicated sentencing approaches and philosophical approaches to administering punishments, it is clear that sentencing disparities exist throughout America. Disparities were noted to be especially problematic in the southern and western parts of the United States. Further, when discussing disparity in punishments, it was found that this existed both with prison sentences and with the application of the death penalty. In discussion of the issue of disparity, the distinction between disparity and discrimination was made clear.

Lastly, a number of criminological theories were presented with an emphasis on their application to the field of corrections. An understanding of the theoretical bases of the criminal justice discipline in general and the correctional system in particular will aid in the correctional process. Indeed, if we are able to explain why different types of crime occur, we can then determine those factors that should be addressed to eliminate the likelihood of criminal behavior. This means that an understanding of the theoretical underpinnings to criminal behavior can improve any correctional effort. Though a diverse number of theories were presented, each provides its own vantage on how and why crime exists, and each provides a framework from which correctional agents can approach the task of providing organized security and treatment functions intended to correct criminal tendencies among the offender population and, in the process, of enhancing public safety.

END-OF-CHAPTER DISCUSSION QUESTIONS

1. Compare and contrast the two philosophical orientations of *incapacitation* and *deterrence*. In your opinion, which one is the better approach to correctional practice?

2. Compare and contrast the two philosophical orientations of *rehabilitation* and *retribution*. In your opinion, which one is the better approach to correctional practice?

3. Provide a topical overview of the different types of informal sanctions discussed in this chapter. Also, explain what is meant by the "continuum of sanctions" when talking about informal sanctions.

4. Compare and contrast the terms *disparity* and *discrimination*. Which one do you think is most appropriate to explaining the overwhelming proportion of minority inmates behind bars?

5. Compare and contrast indeterminate and determinate sentencing. What are the pros and cons of each?

6. Discuss restorative justice and explain how it is unique from many other perspectives on the resolution of crime.

7. According to the chapter, in what ways are classical criminology and operant conditioning similar to one another in their orientations on shaping human behavior?

KEY TERMS

Aggravating circumstances

Conflict theory

Determinate discretionary sentence

Determinate presumptive sentence

Discrimination

Disparity

Fine

General deterrence

Incapacitation

Individual personality traits

Labeling theory

Mandatory minimum

Mitigating factors

Negative punishment

Positive punishment

Positive reinforcers

Retribution

Rehabilitation

Reintegration

Restorative justice

Retribution

Selective incapacitation

Social learning theory

Specific deterrence

Strain theory/institutional anomie

United States v. Booker (2005)

APPLIED EXERCISE 3.1

Match the following modern-day programs with their appropriate philosophical underpinning, sentencing scheme, or theoretical orientation.

Program	*Ideology or Philosophy of Origin*
1. You are sentenced to 10 years in prison and must serve no less than 80% (8 years) without the benefit of early release or parole.	A. Restorative justice
2. Laws that select specific types of offenders and provide enhanced penalties to ensure that they are effectively removed from society (habitual offender laws, 3-strikes laws, etc.).	B. General deterrence
3. Punishing an offender in public so other observers will refrain from criminal behavior.	C. Negative punishment
4. Providing the offender an opportunity to restore damages done to the victim and minimizing stigma/shame for the offender.	D. Treatment
5. Removal of visitation privileges because an offender commits the undesired criminal behavior of child abuse.	E. Indeterminate sentencing
6. Exacting a fine for undesired behavior.	F. Mandatory minimum
7. Treats crime similar to a mental health issue or along the medical model perspective.	G. Determinate sentencing
8. Providing substance abusers with certificates of graduation when completing an addiction treatment program.	H. Positive reinforcement
9. Sentencing has no flexibility in terms.	I. Positive punishment
10. Sentencing with variable terms, affected by the context of the crime and later behavior of offenders while serving their sentence.	J. Incapacitation

You are the judge in a small-town court. In this town, everybody knows each other, and things are usually fairly informal. Your position and title carries a great deal of respect throughout the town, and, because of this, you take your role with the community very seriously. You have recently had a case appear on your docket that is very troubling. A mentally challenged man, 19 years old, is in the county jail; he bludgeoned another man to death with a ball-peen hammer, hitting the victim repeatedly across the head to the point that the deceased victim was barely recognizable. The defendant, Lenny Gratzowskowitz, was in a fit of fury during the crime and continued pounding the skull of the deceased well beyond the point of death.

The police who arrested Lenny were careful to ensure their behavior was well within ethical boundaries, and the agency ensured that legal representation was present before asking any questions. In fact, many of the police officers (including the chief of police) know Lenny on a semipersonal basis because of the tight-knit nature of the town. Generally, Lenny is not problematic, and he has never been known to be violent. However, throughout his history, from childhood on up, he has been subjected to ridicule and embarrassment by a handful of town residents who are of a fairly unsavory disposition.

In fact, the victim, Butch Wurstenberger, had been a childhood bully in grade school, and he had terrorized Lenny on numerous occasions. Now, as an adult, Butch was known to be an abrupt and sarcastic man, but not violent. Both Butch and Lenny had obtained jobs with a general contractor to complete construction of a Walmart Supercenter that was slated for a grand opening during the upcoming year. Each had worked in the construction field; Butch had become known for his skill with foundation work and drywall setting and his experience with industrial air-conditioning and refrigeration systems. Lenny had been hired due to his routine dependability on other job sites and his willingness to work, regardless of the circumstances.

Once both arrived on the job site, Butch heckled Lenny on a few but sparing occasions. Most other members of the work crew were from out of town and were not aware of the history between Butch and Lenny. None of the other work crew members noticed any serious problems between Butch and Lenny— that is, not until they reported to work one morning to find that both Butch and Lenny had arrived at the work scene early, and one of them (Butch) was dead while the other (Lenny) was bloody from the act of violence that he had committed.

Consider this situation and determine which philosophical orientation you would use when sentencing Lenny. Select only *one* of the following philosophical orientations: retribution, deterrence, incapacitation, treatment, restorative justice, or reintegration. Consider why you selected that orientation and why each of the other orientations might not be as appropriate as the one that you would select if deciding upon Lenny's case. Write this down as an essay that answers the following question:

What would you do?

CROSS-NATIONAL PERSPECTIVE 3.1

The Philosophy of Corrections in Thailand

Corrections in Thailand has typically been oriented toward the goals of retribution and deterrence. This has historically been true in Thailand, and has caused problems in providing the appropriate sentence in many cases because the mandatory minimum punishments are somewhat severe. Further, as with the United States, the desire for consistency in sentencing has been expressed while there is a hesitance to impair discretion among the courts. Guidelines and best practices exist, but they are not compulsory. Obviously, one can see that the issues confronting Thailand's sentencing process are similar to those in the United States.

Currently, there are five primary categories of sentencing options employed by judges in Thailand: (1) the death penalty, (2) imprisonment, (3) confinement, (4) monetary fines, and (5) forfeiture of property. These categories of sentencing reflect the combined influences of the French,

Italian, Indian, and Japanese penal codes. As was discussed earlier in this chapter with sentencing in the United States, sentencing in Thailand has come under a great deal of scrutiny. In particular, the purposes of punishment, the use of discretion, and noted problems with disparity have impacted Thai corrections since the 1970s.

The strong emphasis on deterrence can still be seen today in the sentencing schemes that are utilized. Thai penalties are stiff, and, in response to crimes that are considered widespread or particularly problematic, the punishments get stiffer on a graduated level. Amidst this, it is not Thai policy to simply lock up offenders as a means of detaining them from further crime. Rather, the stated goal continues to be the deterrence of future crime among other persons who might consider criminal activity; this is a general deterrence philosophy.

Similar to the United States, Thailand has cracked down on drug use, with particular attention given to opium and the use of amphetamines. The typical sentence given to drug offenders (both traffickers and users) has been incarceration. The rationale for this sentence is, again, based on retribution for the crime(s) committed and general deterrence among the general public. The specific deterrence element (deterring that specific offender) is one goal as well, but it is considered secondary. As we have seen in the United States, the extensive use of prisons in a campaign against drugs has fueled a large growth in the Thai prison population. Thus, the main challenge facing the Thai correctional system is overcrowding due to aggressive sentencing policies related to drug use.

It is important to note that the constitution of Thailand protects the human rights of inmates, including the ability to access legal assistance. Thus, it is likely that Thai prisons do provide a humane environment, regardless of how stiff the sentence may be. Interestingly, the high number of offenders who have been incarcerated has led to the development of specialized treatment programming during the past few years. The treatment regimen entails a holistic combination of medical treatment, educational services, vocational training, and religious programming. This significantly departs from the traditional emphasis on retribution and deterrence and demonstrates an awareness among Thai officials that those two philosophical approaches do not always work to reduce recidivism. Thus, the Thai Department of Corrections has assumed responsibility for providing rehabilitation programs to inmates in an effort to do more about the drug problem than locking people up and throwing away the key.

Question 1: What are some similarities that were mentioned between correctional approaches in Thailand and in the United States?

Question 2: What key type of criminal activity is similar in both countries? How might this knowledge help professionals to improve treatment programs related to substance abuse and drug offending?

For a closer look at correctional treatment in Thailand, drug offense sentencing, and the response to those incarcerated in the Thai antidrug campaign, see the following source:

SOURCE: Kuratanavej, S. (2009). *Crime prevention: Current issues in correctional treatment and effective countermeasures.* Retrieved from http://www.unafei.or.jp/english/pdf/PDF_rms/no57/57-26.pdf

STUDENT STUDY SITE

Visit the Student Study Site at **www.sagepub.com/hanserintro** to access links to the videos, audio clips, SAGE journal articles, state rankings, and reference materials noted in this chapter, as well as additional study tools including eFlashcards, web quizzes, and more.

chapter 4

Correctional Law and Legal Liabilities

LEARNING OBJECTIVES:

1. Identify and discuss court cases associated with the different eras in corrections.

2. Identify and discuss legal liabilities associated with correctional staff.

3. Evaluate the current relationship between corrections and judicial oversight.

4. Apply legal principles to challenges in the field of corrections.

5. Integrate legal knowledge with historical information related to correctional thought.

INTRODUCTION

From our previous three chapters, it is clear that the field of corrections has gone through many transformations throughout the ages. But, as Chapter 3 demonstrates, some of these changes took place due to courthouse intervention into prison operations. The period when the hands-off doctrine ended marked the beginning of case law that has permanently impacted correctional operations in the United States. An understanding of this case law and its impact on corrections is critical to both the practitioner and the student. It is with this in mind that this chapter is presented, allowing students to develop an understanding of the legal issues associated with correctional processes and practices.

Prison Tour Video Link 4.1
Watch two wardens describe laws and their impacts on prisons.

THE ROLE OF THE U.S. SUPREME COURT

During the early history of corrections in the United States, the courts were not generally involved in prison operations. This is generally because, as we have seen in our prior chapters, inmates were seen as slaves of the state. With such a philosophy, the need for concern regarding prisoners' rights seemed alien to most people at the time. As a result of the culture and the times, there was little reason for the Supreme Court to be involved with inmate issues, and, at that time, inmates would not have considered the possibility of suing the Court; such options did not exist (Branham & Hamden, 2009).

In addition, there was a general belief that the public and even the courts should not be concerned about the goings-on inside the prison. Since inmates were considered slaves of the state and since prisons were not intended to be pleasant places of existence, it was thought that prison operations were best left in the hands of those who operated them (Branham & Hamden, 2009). There was no need to meddle, and, essentially, the "no news is good news" mentality prevailed with the public and the Court in regard to prison operations.

Video Link 4.1
Watch a video about the U.S. Supreme Court.

PHOTO 4.1

The Justices of the Supreme Court are, starting with the back row and going left to right, Sonia Sotomayor, Stephen G. Breyer, Samuel A. Alito, and Elena Kagan. In the front row, going left to right are Clarence Thomas, Antonin Scalia, Chief Justice John G. Roberts, Anthony Kennedy, and Ruth Bader Ginsburg.

THE HANDS-OFF DOCTRINE

The period of time during which the Supreme Court and the lower courts avoided intervening in prison operations is generally known as the **hands-off doctrine**, and was based on two primary premises. First was the premise that, under the separation of powers inherent in the U.S. Constitution, the judicial branch was not justified to interfere with prisons, which were operated by the executive branch. The second premise was, simply put, that judges should leave prison administration to the prison experts. With these two premises in place, states tended to operate their prisons with impunity; they were free to do as they pleased with no fear of outside scrutiny (Branham & Hamden, 2009).

As we have seen in prior chapters, courts did eventually begin to intervene in prison operations during the early to mid-1900s. This was, in part, due to reform-minded persons who were publicly active in educating the public in regard to inmate issues. As public sentiments changed to views that were more rehabilitative in nature, prisons began to catch the eye of the courts more routinely. Further, the civil rights movement of the 1960s highlighted the abuses that occurred in prisons as well as the complete lack of legal protections for inmates. As civil rights issues became center stage, civil rights issues in prisons also drew more attention from both the public and the courts.

THE HANDS-ON DOCTRINE AND
THE BEGINNING OF JUDICIAL INVOLVEMENT

Perhaps the clear beginning of the end for the hands-off doctrine occurred in the 1941 Supreme Court case, *Ex parte Hull.* In times before this case, it was common for prison officials to screen inmate mail, including legal mail. As a result, prison staff were known to misplace petitions and even deny the inmate the opportunity to mail them. In *Hull,* the Supreme Court held that no state or its officers could legally interfere with a prisoner's right to apply to a federal court for writs of habeas corpus. The term *habeas corpus* refers to a challenge of the legality of confinement and is a Latin term that literally means "you have the body," and a writ of habeas corpus is a court order requiring that an arrested person be brought forward to determine the legality of his or her arrest. In *Hull,* the Supreme Court ruled that inmates had the right to unrestricted access to federal courts to challenge the legality of their confinement (Branham & Hamden, 2009; Stohr, Walsh, and Hemmens, 2009). This was important because writs of habeas corpus were the primary mechanism that inmates had to challenge unlawful incarceration. Without the ability to use this avenue of redress, inmates were powerless to make legal challenges to their confinement.

One case truly opened the door for inmate civil litigation. This case, **Cooper v. Pate (1964)**, validated and made clear the right of inmates to sue prison systems and prison staff. In this case, the Court ruled that state prison inmates could sue state officials in federal courts under the Civil Rights Act of 1871. This act was initially enacted to protect southern African Americans from state officials (such as judges) who were often members of the subversive group, the Ku Klux Klan. This act is now codified and known as 42 U.S.C. Section 1983, or simply Section 1983 in day-to-day conversation among legal experts and/or practitioners. This act holds that "every person who under color of law of any statute, ordinance, regulation, custom, or usage of any state or territory, subjects or causes to be subject, any citizen of the United States or other person within the jurisdiction thereof to the deprivation of any rights, privileges, or immunities secured by the Constitution and laws, shall be liable to the party injured in an action at law" (Branham & Hamden, 2009).

Because it had been determined that the Court was responsible for protecting against misuses of power that was possessed by those vested with state authority, it became clear that the Court was within its purview to rule regarding any number of issues related to civil rights of the inmate. Further, it was determined that officials "clothed with the authority of state law" did include prison staff and security personnel. Therefore, state prison personnel who violated an inmate's constitutional rights while performing their duties under state law could be held liable for their actions in federal court. The clarity provided in *Pate* and the route of litigation opened for inmates essentially created what some have called the hands-on doctrine of correctional case law, which we now consider in the following subsection.

THE EMERGENCE OF INMATE RIGHTS

As noted earlier, much of the public concern with the rights of inmates dovetailed with the civil rights movement during the 1960s. During this time, the NAACP (National Association for the Advancement of Colored People) Legal Defense and Educational Fund and the National Prison Project of the American Civil Liberties Union began to advocate for the rights of inmates. At the same time, legal protections for inmates were given substantial public and political attention. In determining inmate rights, the balance between human treatment and the need to maintain public safety remained an issue amongst the courts. Many courts used contradictory rulings to navigate the myriad complications that emerged from balancing these two overarching concerns.

Audio Link 4.1
Listen to the *Turner v. Safely* oral arguments.

The difficulty in setting this balance led to further involvement by the Supreme Court in the landmark case of **Turner v. Safley (1987).** In this case, the Court ruled on a Missouri ban against correspondence sent among inmates in different institutions within the state's jurisdiction (Del Carmen, Ritter, & Witt, 2005). The Court upheld the ban, noting that such forms of regulations are valid if they are "reasonably related to legitimate penological interests." Further, the Court enunciated four key elements of what are known as the **rational basis test.** These four elements are as follows:

1. There must be a rational and clear connection between the regulation and the reason that is given for that regulation's existence.

2. Inmates must be given alternative means to practice a given right that has been restricted, when feasible.

3. The means by which prison staff and inmates are affected must be kept as minimal as realistically possible.

4. When less restrictive alternative means of impeding upon an inmate's rights are available, prison personnel must utilize those alternative means.

This rational basis test has provided a good degree of clarity in resolving the conflict between inmate rights and the need for institutional and public safety. It is within these guidelines that the rights of inmates have emerged but, at the same time, been held in check sufficiently to allow correctional agencies to maintain security. Thus, inmate rights became a permanent fixture in the U.S. correctional system, but these rights were tempered with some degree of feasible pragmatism.

Access to Courts and Attorneys

In tandem with the newfound rights of inmates was a corresponding recognition that such rights were not usable unless inmates were afforded access to the courts. The primary case that deals with inmate access to the courts is **Johnson v. Avery (1969)**. In this case, the Supreme Court held that prison authorities cannot prohibit inmates from aiding other inmates in preparing legal documents unless they also provide alternatives by which inmates may access the courts. In addition, and more importantly, the Court further made it clear that, as a result, prison systems have an obligation to provide some form of documented access to the courts, to attorneys, or to some sort of legitimate legal aid (Anderson, Mangels, & Dyson, 2010).

Video Link 4.2
Watch how a jailhouse lawyer teaches law school students.

PHOTO 4.2

This photo provides a view of a law library that has been created for inmates in a large regional jail. Many times when inmates sue state agencies, they may use resources such as the law library.

Law Libraries

The primary case that addresses the issue of law libraries is **Bounds v. Smith (1977)**. In this case, the Court held that even when prison policies allow jailhouse lawyers to provide assistance to other inmates, prison systems must still provide inmates with either adequate law libraries or adequate legal assistance from persons trained in the law (Anderson et al., 2010). As with *Johnson v. Avery*, the opinion of the Court in *Bounds v. Smith* was far from specific in explaining what would constitute legal services and materials. However, most lower courts, in interpreting the ruling by the Supreme Court, have concluded that the requirements in *Bounds* are satisfied when states provide inmates with adequate law libraries and access to materials with some quasi-professional help (Del Carmen et al., 2005).

While the specific requirements under *Bounds* are not necessarily clear, it would appear that, at a minimum, most courts currently require either an adequate law library or assistance from persons who have some sort of verifiable legal training. When determining whether the inmates of a prison have the appropriate assistance for filing court documents, courts generally consider the following four factors:

1. The number of inmates entitled to legal assistance.

2. The types of claims these inmates are entitled to bring.

3. The number of persons rendering assistance.

4. The training and credentials of those who provide legal assistance.

Although *Bounds* still remains the primary case regarding inmate right to access to the court, another case, *Lewis v. Casey* (1996), has since narrowed the scope of inmates' rights to court access in a manner that provides prison officials with much more leeway when establishing legal assistance that is likely to be constitutionally permissible. In *Lewis*, the Court held that any inmate who alleges a violation of *Bounds* must show that shortcomings in the prison's library or services for assistance caused an actual harm or injury in that these shortcomings are directly attributable to the inmate's inability to pursue legitimate legal claims.

Journal Article Link 4.1
Read about strategies used to comply with prisoners' rights to court access.

APPLIED THEORY 4.1

Peacemaking Criminology and Suffering Begets Suffering

Peacemaking criminology contends that crime is suffering and the ending of crime is only possible with the ending of suffering (Quinney, 1991). This means, then, that peacemaking criminologists would contend that punitive reactions to criminal behavior are not likely to end crime. Indeed, because punitive reactions entail a degree of suffering, many peacemaking criminologists would perhaps contend that crime is likely to *increase* rather than decrease in occurrence. This notion holds many interesting implications for the field of corrections. Indeed, because it is the field of corrections that is tasked with providing the long-term application of sanctions upon offenders, the type of sanction and rationale for that sanction becomes a central concern in reducing future crime among offenders.

As we have seen in prior chapters, classical criminologists such as Cesare Beccaria made note that punishments should be proportional to the crime. This is an important observation because Beccaria's contention was not just philosophical in nature; rather, it was pragmatic as well. Beccaria had observed that, when sufficiently provoked, people have strong reactions to unpleasant stimuli. Thus, whether or not an offender's punishment is deserved, those punishments that are too severe will simply elicit provocation from the offender rather than reformation. In other words, overly severe punishments are likely to make future behavior of the offender worse, not better.

In addition to Beccaria's views on harsh punishment and the impact on future behavior, other researchers have concluded that excessive punishment will likely increase aberrant behavior, especially violent behavior (Davis & Palladino, 2002). Naturally, this can be detrimental to society. Further, of all the crimes that we would least like to see repeated, it is violent crime. If excessive punishment runs the risk of increasing this type of crime, then this is truly something that should be avoided.

One other interesting point that should be added, in regard to the death penalty in particular, is the brutalizing effect that may occur after the use of this most serious of sanctions. The brutalizing effect results in an increase in the number of murders due to the fact that the death penalty itself helps to reinforce the use of violence (Bowers & Pierce, 1980). Thus, it may well be that the use of this sanction further transmits the seeds of violence beyond that one offender and onward to many others in society. This may, in part, explain why many of the states in the southern and western parts of the United States tend to have higher-than-average crime rates; they also tend to have harsher-than-average prison terms and are more prone to use the death penalty.

Thus, peacemaking criminology may have some interesting insights for corrections. In order for us to lower crime, it may well be that we must seek to end the suffering and blight that breeds environments that are ripe for such behavior. In addition, it may be that correctional systems will have to moderate their use of punitive measures in a manner that emphasizes positive change, rather than rigid, strict, and/or harsh techniques. As we have seen, this has, in fact, occurred within the field of corrections. As state systems have had to adopt more humane standards, the amount of suffering (particularly for suffering's sake) has been reduced among inmates. Likewise, the current emphasis on offender reentry programs is based on research that shows lower recidivism rates for those who are on community supervision when compared to those incarcerated for long periods of time. Perhaps, then, peacemaking criminology has some insights for administrators and policymakers, as well as society as a whole.

FIRST AMENDMENT CASES IN CORRECTIONS

The First Amendment states that "Congress shall make no law respecting an establishment of religion, or prohibiting the free exercise of religion thereof; or abridging the freedom of speech, or of the press; or the right of the people peaceably to assemble, and to petition the government for a redress of grievances." This amendment essentially safeguards the very right to speak, communicate, and act freely. Given the strict confines of the prison setting, it is no surprise that this amendment was the legal basis behind numerous forms of inmate redress. Generally, case law has revolved around inmate access to publications, mail censoring processes, correspondence with family, and religious practices within the institution (see Table 4.1).

Turner v. Safley, having set the rational basis test, was also a case that involved prison staff's basis for censoring different types of mail among inmates. When considering mail and other forms of written communications, prison staff may censure and otherwise engage in oversight so long as there is a legitimate penological interest. Some of the reasons that might be provided include the following:

1. Safety and security of the institution.

2. Rehabilitative concerns.

3. Prison order.

Prison Tour Video Link 4.2
Watch a warden discuss religion in prison.

TABLE 4.1   First Amendment Prison Law Cases From the Supreme Court

First Amendment issues include inmate rights to freedom of speech and freedom of religion. Cases below are organized in chronological order.	
Court Case	*Ruling*
Fulwood v. Clemmer (1962)	The Muslim faith is a valid religion that requires prison officials to allow Muslim inmates to engage in their respective religious activities.
Gittlemacker v. Prasse (1970)	Inmates must be allowed to practice their religion, but states are not required to provide a clergy member in such cases.
Cruz v. Beto (1972)	Inmates must be given reasonable opportunities to exercise their religious beliefs.
Procunier v. Martinez (1974)	Prison officials may censor inmate mail only to the extent necessary to ensure security of the institution.
Kahane v. Carlson (1975)	Jewish inmates have a right to their kosher diet, as a bona fide part of their religion. If this cannot be provided, prison officials must show why such a diet cannot be provided.
Theriault v. Carlson (1977)	Bogus or fake religious sects that are not genuinely practiced with sincerity are not protected under the First Amendment.
Turner v. Safley (1987)	A prison regulation that impinges on inmates' constitutional rights is valid if it is reasonably related to legitimate penological interests.
O'Lone v. Estate of Shabazz (1987)	Prison policies that in effect prevent inmates from exercising freedom of religion are constitutional because they are reasonably related to legitimate penological interests.
Beard v. Banks (2006)	Prisons may implement policies that restrict access to magazines, publications, and photographs for inmates who are classified as higher risk to the safety and security of the institution.

Courts tend to defer to the judgment of prison administrators when considering First Amendment issues, as it is considered that they are the best suited in determining security and safety needs.

When considering religion, the Court has made at least two significant determinations. In **Cruz v. Beto (1972)**, the Court ruled that inmates must be given reasonable opportunities to exercise their religious beliefs (see Table 4.1). In this case, Cruz was a member of the Buddhist faith and was an inmate in the Texas Department of Corrections. He had been placed in solitary confinement and, during that time, was not allowed access to religious services for his faith while other inmates of other religions (i.e., Catholic, Jewish, and Protestant faiths) who were in solitary confinement were given such benefits. The Court held that inmates with unconventional beliefs must be afforded reasonable opportunities to exercise their religious beliefs, especially if this is afforded to inmates of other faiths (Anderson et al., 2010; Branham & Hamden, 2009).

In another case, **O'Lone v. Estate of Shabazz (1987)**, the Court held that the free exercise rights of a Muslim inmate were not violated when prison officials would not adjust the time of his work schedule (see Table 4.1). The reason for this ruling was that the prison system's justification for avoiding alterations in the work schedule was grounded in security and logistic concerns, which, according to the Court, were sufficient and legitimate penological interests. Since this ruling, various religious minorities among the inmate population have gained ground in securing the means for practicing their religions. As an example, lower court decisions have supported specialized dietary requirements for different religious faiths, to assemble for services, to contact religious leaders of the inmate's respective faith, and even to wear a beard if one's religion legitimately calls for it. While district courts in the federal system have generated these rulings, the Supreme Court has not (Del Carmen et al., 2005).

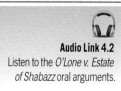

Audio Link 4.2
Listen to the *O'Lone v. Estate of Shabazz* oral arguments.

When considering religion, the right to practice has been recently strengthened through the **Religious Land Use and Institutionalized Persons Act of 2000.** This act prohibits the government from substantially burdening an inmate's religious exercise. To do so requires the demonstration of a compelling governmental need, but only if the burden is the least restrictive alternative to further those legitimate interests. Specifically, Section 3 contends that governments cannot impose a "substantial burden on a person residing in or confined to an institution" including inmates, of course. Thus, the issue of religion has been under consideration for over 30 years, and it seems that, just as the American cultural and religious landscape has become more diverse in society, so too has the world of corrections and correctional religious services.

PHOTO 4.3

Muslims attend Juma, Friday's group prayer, in a gathering room reserved for prisoner activities at a state prison in Virginia.

Reference Link 4.1
Read about prisoners' rights to practice religious beliefs in prison.

FOURTH AMENDMENT CASES IN CORRECTIONS

According to the Fourth Amendment, "the right of the people to be secure in their persons, houses, papers, and effects, against unreasonable searches and seizures, shall not be violated, and no Warrants shall issue, but upon probable cause, supported by Oath or affirmation, and particularly describing the place to be searched, and the persons or things to be seized." In prison settings, the Fourth Amendment has limited applicability because, for the most part, inmates do not have a legitimate expectation of privacy while serving their sentence. Indeed, the fact that they are incarcerated limits such an expectation given that prison officials must assume responsibility for their safety and security while in custody. Students should understand that inmates have no expectation of privacy when in the institution (whether in a cell or in a dorm-like setting), nor do they have such an expectation upon their person. Whenever prison staff determine appropriate, inmates are subject to search without any justification being necessary beyond a security rationale (see Table 4.2).

For offenders who are on probation and/or parole, however, the issue can be a bit more complicated. In such circumstances, police officers and other external enforcement officials need to adhere to Fourth Amendment considerations when dealing with probationers and parolees. However, community

TABLE 4.2 Fourth Amendment Prison Law Cases From the Supreme Court

Fourth Amendment issues address unreasonable searches and seizures of persons and their things. In prisons, this tends to involve invasive searches of inmates and/or their property that inmates believe should be protected.	
Court Case	*Ruling*
Lanza v. New York (1962)	Verbal and written conversations in jail (and prison) visitation rooms do not enjoy any Fourth Amendment privacy safeguards.
United States v. Hitchcock (1972)	Searches of inmate cells and dormitories are not subject to Fourth Amendment considerations. Prison staff may conduct searches of inmate living quarters as the need arises.
Bell v. Wolfish (1979)	The use of body cavity searches of inmates after contact visits is permissible. Prison staff may search inmates' quarters in their absence. Double bunking does not deprive inmates of their liberty without due process of law.
Hudson v. Palmer (1984)	A prison cell may be searched without a warrant and without probable cause. Prison cells are not protected by the Fourth Amendment.

supervision staff (e.g., probation and parole officers) are not under those same restrictions, particularly if the inmate is on their own caseload. In such circumstances, police have been known to work in partnership with community supervision personnel to avoid Fourth Amendment restrictions; such partnerships exist throughout the nation and have been found to be constitutionally permissible.

One area that has generated substantial litigation is that of cross-gendered searches of the person. However, when correctional staff of the opposite gender conduct a search, there is no constitutional violation. So long as the search is conducted according to policy, in a professional manner, and without sexual connotations, the inmate will have no standing for a grievance. Though this is the case, it is generally considered prudent for prison administrators to consider an inmate's privacy as much as is reasonable, such as in showers and dressing rooms. Though personal searches are not considered problematic, the use of opposite-gendered strip searches is usually prohibited by most courts. Thus, prison and jail systems with inmates of both genders will find it wise to have staff of both genders readily available as well.

Searches of the person are conducted at varying levels of intrusiveness. Some consist of the simple pat search of the outer clothing, others require strip searching of the inmate who is nude, and the most invasive form of search is the body cavity search. Policies should clearly demonstrate the need for more invasive searches, connecting them to a legitimate institutional need. Thus, the more invasive the procedure, the more clear the evidence must be that a legitimate institutional interest was at stake, and the more important it is that the search be documented and justified (Branham & Hamden, 2009).

Video Link 4.3
Watch a discussion of the U.S Supreme Court's decision in *Florence v. Board of Chosen Freeholders*.

EIGHTH AMENDMENT CASES IN CORRECTIONS

The Eighth Amendment states that "excessive bail shall not be required, nor excessive fines imposed, nor cruel and unusual punishments inflicted." For the most part, this amendment is cited in most cases involving excessive use of force or other physical injuries where inmates file suit (see Table 4.3). But, in addition to such overt acts where civil rights are in question, inmates use this amendment as the basis for a number of other issues, such as the conditions of confinement, medical care, and other minimal standards of living. In general, when determining if acts or conditions are violations under the Eighth Amendment, the courts have utilized three basic considerations:

1. Whether the treatment shocks the general conscience of a civilized society.

2. Whether the treatment is cruel beyond necessity.

3. Whether the treatment is within the scope of legitimate penological interests.

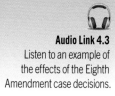

Audio Link 4.3
Listen to an example of the effects of the Eighth Amendment case decisions.

To further aid in determining claims against prison conditions under the Eighth Amendment, federal courts have implemented a standard that takes into account various factors. This standard, which was born out of Supreme Court case law, is known as the totality of circumstances in general precedent by the Court. The totality of circumstances has been modified in prison law to consist of the **totality of the conditions**, to determine if conditions in an institution are in violation of the Eighth Amendment. In numerous cases, the Court has made a point to effect positive change in prison operations throughout the nation. In doing so, the Court laid out three principles that should be implemented when mandating change. The three principles, as articulated in *Hutto v. Finney* (1978), provide the following:

1. Courts should consider the totality of the conditions of confinement.

2. Courts should make a point to specify each individual factor that contributed to this totality of conditions that were found to be unconstitutional, with clear orders for remediation and changes.

3. When and where possible, courts should articulate the minimal standards necessary for an institution to remedy the constitutional violation.

As noted just previously, inmates also use the Eighth Amendment as the legal basis to challenge force used against them. For instance, in *Hudson v. McMillian* (1992), the Supreme Court ruled that inmates do not need to suffer a severe physical injury in order to file an Eighth Amendment claim—as long as the use of force or abusive treatment involved the "wanton and unnecessary infliction of pain," or if the force was used "maliciously or sadistically for the very purpose of causing pain." Naturally, such forms of treatment serve no legitimate penological interest and simply aggravate criminogenic mind-sets among the offender population.

There is one other legal area that falls under Eighth Amendment consideration; that is the death penalty. While the death penalty has been held as constitutional since the ruling of **Gregg v. Georgia (1976)**, the specific means by which that penalty is administered is still subject to potential legal challenge (see Table 4.3). Though legal as a form of punishment, there is an expectation that the application of this penalty not be arbitrary or capricious in nature. Further, as with *Hudson v. McMillian*, the imposition of the death penalty must not consist of the unnecessary infliction of pain or be malicious or sadistic in nature. As we saw in Chapter 1, the death penalty has been implemented through a variety of cruel and barbaric means, while Chapter 3 made it clear that this punishment has gone through an evolutionary process throughout the years of its use in the United States. Much of this change is the result of legal challenges that have been presented to the use of this penalty.

Journal Article Link 4.2
Read about the Eighth Amendment death penalty restriction for juveniles.

TABLE 4.3   Eighth Amendment Prison Law Cases From the Supreme Court

Eighth Amendment issues address whether treatment of inmates entails cruel or unusual punishment.	
Court Case	*Ruling*
Ruiz v. Estelle (1980)	The conditions in the prison system of Texas were found to be unconstitutional.
Estelle v. Gamble (1976)	Deliberate indifference to inmate medical needs constitutes cruel and unusual punishment and is therefore unconstitutional.
Gregg v. Georgia (1976)	Death penalty statutes that contain sufficient safeguards against arbitrary and capricious imposition are constitutional.
Rhodes v. Chapman (1981)	Double celling of inmates does not, unto itself, constitute cruel and unusual punishment.
Whitley v. Albers (1986)	The shooting of an inmate, without prior verbal warning, to suppress a prison riot does not violate that inmate's right against cruel or unusual punishment.
Wilson v. Seiter (1991)	Deliberate indifference is required for liability to be attached to condition of confinement cases. This means that a culpable state of mind on the part of prison administrators must be demonstrated.
Overton v. Bazzetta (2003)	Prison staff may restrict prison visitations so long as their actions are related to legitimate penological interests.
Hill v. McDonough (2006)	Methods of implementing the death penalty are subject to suit under Section 1983 litigation.

FOURTEENTH AMENDMENT
CASES IN CORRECTIONS

According to the Fourteenth Amendment, "all persons born or naturalized in the United States, and subject to the jurisdiction thereof, are citizens of the United States and of the state wherein they reside. No state shall make or enforce any law which shall abridge the privileges or immunities of citizens without due process of law, nor deny to any person within its jurisdiction the equal protection of the laws." The primary application of the Fourteenth Amendment to prison law issues has to do with procedural due process issues and issues related to equal protection (see Table 4.4). The Fourteenth Amendment often comes into play when inmates file suit regarding parole release, intraprison transfers, and disciplinary hearings. The other aspect of the Fourteenth Amendment that is relevant to prison law is equal protection. Inmates using this aspect of the Fourteenth Amendment may file suit regarding equal protection pertaining to issues based on race, gender, or religious discrimination (Anderson et al., 2010).

The case of **Wolff v. McDonnell (1974)** provided guidelines for minimal due process rights that should be afforded inmates facing disciplinary proceedings (see Table 4.4). The Court held that when a prisoner faces serious disciplinary action resulting in the loss of good time or some form of housing custody change, the procedures used should provide the following:

1. The inmate must be given 24-hour written notice of the charges.

2. There must be a written statement by the fact finders as to the evidence relied on and reasons for the disciplinary action.

3. The inmate should be allowed to call witnesses and present documentary evidence in his or her defense so long as this does not jeopardize institutional safety and security.

4. Counsel substitute must be permitted when the inmate is illiterate or when the complexity of the issues makes it unlikely that the inmate will be able to collect and present the evidence for an adequate comprehension of the case.

5. The prison disciplinary board must be impartial.

While the above conditions must be provided, the Court has made it clear that disciplinary hearings do not rise to the standard of a true courthouse proceeding, but are designed to provide some measure of protection against arbitrariness.

In **Baxter v. Palmigiano (1976)**, the distinction between prison disciplinary proceedings and genuine courtroom affairs was directly addressed (Anderson et al., 2010). The Court noted that inmates do not have the right to either retained or appointed counsel for disciplinary hearings that are not part of an actual criminal prosecution (see Table 4.4). Further, inmates are not entitled to confront and cross-examine witnesses at all times. In addition, and unlike courtroom proceedings, an inmate's decision to remain silent when faced with disciplinary proceedings can be used as adverse evidence of the inmate's guilt by disciplinary decision makers. Thus, disciplinary hearings simply require fundamental fairness and nondiscriminatory application; they are not to be confused with regular court proceedings.

Audio Link 4.4
Listen to the *Baxter v. Palmigiano* oral arguments.

TABLE 4.4   Fourteenth Amendment Prison Law Cases From the Supreme Court

The Fourteenth Amendment addresses due process of law and equal protection under the law.	
Court Case	*Ruling*
Wolff v. McDonnell (1974)	Inmates are entitled to due process in prison disciplinary proceedings that can result in the loss of good time credits or in punitive segregation.
Baxter v. Palmigiano (1976)	Inmates are not entitled to counsel or cross-examination in prison disciplinary hearings. In addition, silence by inmates in a disciplinary proceeding may be used as adverse evidence against them.
Vitek v. Jones (1980)	Inmates are entitled to due process in involuntary transfers from prison to a mental hospital.
Superintendent, Walpole v. Hill (1985)	Disciplinary board findings that result in loss of good time credits must be supported by a "modicum" of evidence to satisfy due process requirements.

SOURCE: Del Carmen, R. V., Ritter, S. E., & Witt, B. A. (2005). *Briefs of leading cases in corrections* (4th ed.). Anderson Publishing.

THE PRISON LITIGATION REFORM
ACT OF 1995

According to Carlson and Garrett (2008), the **Prison Litigation Reform Act of 1995** (PLRA) contains these provisions:

1. Limit inmates' ability to file lawsuits.

2. Require inmates to exhaust all available administrative remedies prior to filing suits.

3. Require the payment of full filing fees in some instances.

4. Impose harsh sanctions, including the loss of good time credit for filing frivolous or malicious lawsuits.

5. Require that any damages awarded to inmates be used to satisfy pending restitution orders.

PHOTO 4.4

It is from the local or federal courthouse that legal suits are filed. The courthouse has the role of determining inmate rights as well as the rights of offenders on probation or on parole.

Further, the PLRA puts a limit on the relief that an inmate may secure from the courts, the restriction being that courts may only require of prison systems a minimum of modification so as to most expediently and in a Spartan manner address a noted deficiency. Even with this, courts must keep their requirements narrow in focus, and they must consider the potential impact that their ruling may have on overall institutional and public safety. Further, oversight from federal judges regarding prison operations was given an expiration of two years unless another successful hearing proves that constitutional violations continue to persist within that prison facility or system. Thus, the PLRA has provided state governments with a mechanism by which they can limit the effects of suits regarding prison conditions. This is good news for state prison systems that were, in their earlier history, under the constant scrutiny of federal courts, as was discussed in Chapter 2. Figure 5.1 demonstrates the impact that the PLRA has had on the overall number of state inmates who have filed petitions in U.S. district courts.

It is noteworthy that the PLRA has been challenged in court, but the U.S. Supreme Court has continued to support and uphold the provisions of this act. For example, in *Booth v. Churner* (2001), the Court ruled that inmates must exhaust all of their available administrative processes for a grievance before filing suit, even if those provisions do not allow for monetary damages. This is an important point because, up until this time, inmates would sometimes utilize legal remedies to simply gain monetary compensation rather than using available tools within the prison to rectify wrongs.

FIGURE 5.1: The Effect of the PLRA on Petitions Filed by State Inmates from 1990 to 2006

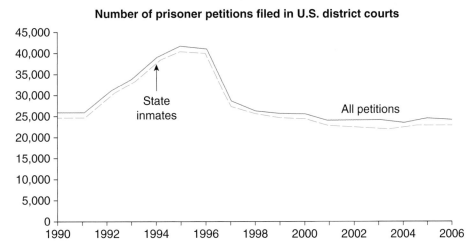

SOURCE: U.S. Department of Justice. (2009). *Civil rights complaints in U.S. district courts, 1990–2006.* Washington, DC: Author.

Journal Article Link 4.3
Read about how the PLRA reduced the amount of prisoner litigation.

Further, some inmates have been determined to have filed three or more lawsuits that have been dismissed as frivolous. In addition, the waiver of legal fees and court costs has been made more difficult under the PLRA. Therefore, the PLRA has been a boon for prison administrators. But, the PLRA and its general stance on inmate litigation are reflective of another more recent trend; it appears that the Supreme Court is again turning back to a more conservative approach with prison rulings. In fact, it appears that the Court is leaning more toward a "one hand on, one hand off" doctrine regarding intervention in prison operations. More conservative rulings are handed down form the Court, and this reflects an eclipse of the hands-off doctrine in American corrections.

A RESTRAINED HANDS-ON PERSPECTIVE AND COURT DEFERENCE TO PRISONS

In changing to a more restrictive interpretation of inmate rights, two cases, *Bell v. Wolfish* (1979) and *Rhodes v. Chapman* (1981), served as major turning points. These cases reflect an attempt of the Court to balance institutional operations with the need to protect inmates' constitutional rights from oppressive government actions. In *Bell v. Wolfish*, the Court noted,

Audio Link 4.5
Listen to the *Rhodes v. Chapman* oral arguments.

> Maintaining institutional security and preserving internal order and discipline are essential guides that may require limitation or retractions of the retained constitutional rights of both convicted prisoners and pretrial detainees.... Prison officials must be free to take appropriate action to ensure safety of inmates and correctional personnel and to prevent escape or unauthorized entry. (p. 1878)

Thus, it is clear that the Court has been receptive to the challenges that face prison staff and administrators. However, in the case of *Rhodes v. Chapman* (1981), the Court, in addressing the totality of conditions regarding prison facilities, noted very clearly that "the constitution does not mandate comfortable prisons," nor should prisons aspire to reach such an ideal standard of living.

PHOTO 4.5

The balanced scales are a common symbol of balanced justice in the United States. When considering the totality of the circumstances, it is the role of the court to come to reasonable rulings that are balanced, equitable, and within the bounds of the rule of law.

From 1980 onward, the Court has taken a more balanced approach to inmate litigation. This balanced approach is known as the **one hand on, one hand off doctrine**. This doctrine contends that while incarcerated, (1) inmates do not forfeit their constitutional rights, (2) inmate rights are not as broad and encompassing as are free persons', and (3) prison officials need to maintain order, security, and discipline in their facilities.

Over time, the Supreme Court has become even more conservative regarding inmates' rights and meddling into the affairs of prison operations. The very passage of the PLRA demonstrates that the pendulum has swung from a balanced approach to Court deference to prison officials. Court cases that have upheld various provisions of the PLRA further demonstrate that not only does the Court tend to again defer to prison officials in the operation of their facilities, but it also tends to restrict the amount of prisoner complaints that it will hear.

STATE AND FEDERAL LEGAL LIABILITIES

The means by which liability may ensue can be many. First, liability can attach at both the state and the federal levels of government. Second, this liability, though most often civil, can be criminal as well. In most cases, the sources of liability are, in actuality, typically not restricted to community supervision officers but often serve as the bases of liability for any officer of the state. Nevertheless, just as with other practitioners

CORRECTIONS AND THE LAW 4.1

Estelle v. Gamble, Farmer v. Brennan, and the Legal Concept of Deliberate Indifference

In *Estelle v. Gamble* (1976), it was found that deliberate indifference to an inmate's medical needs constitutes cruel and unusual punishment, a violation of the Eighth Amendment. In this case, inmate J. W. Gamble alleged that the Texas prison system had provided him with inadequate medical care and that prison officials were "deliberately indifferent" to his medical needs. This case occurred during the time that Texas and other states were feeling the pains of federal oversight, as discussed Chapter 3.

But *Estelle v. Gamble* is considered important because, in that case, the Court defined the fluid term *deliberate indifference* by stating that "deliberate indifference to serious medical needs or prisoners constitutes the unnecessary and wanton infliction of pain," which, in essence, means that prison officials go out of their way to ensure that pain will occur. Other cases since *Estelle v. Gamble* have equated deliberate indifference with having a culpable state of mind. Thus, this standard was used widely in a number of civil cases as precedent for determining standards of care and treatment in prisons among administrators who may not be forthcoming with their activities or their failures to act in good faith.

But, as the historical development of corrections resulted in an evolutionary metamorphosis, so too did the legal developments. This was true with the concept of deliberate indifference, which between the time of *Estelle v. Gamble* and the mid-1990s had become a common catchphrase among prison law experts. In 1994, a most curious ruling came about that would take this term and significantly limit its far-reaching impact in corrections.

In **Farmer v. Brennan** (1994), it was found that a prison official is not liable under the Eighth Amendment for injury inflicted on an inmate by another inmate unless it can be determined that the prison official knew of the excessive risk of harm to that inmate and that the official chose to disregard that harm. What is important about this case is that the Court made it clear that liability does not attach to prison officials by the reasonable person standard.

The *reasonable person standard* is a common term used by the Supreme Court when creating criteria for determinations that do not have a clear and specific answer. Often, this is used in discretionary circumstances and simply means that when determining whether an action was or was not prudent, the Court considers what a reasonable and everyday person might consider appropriate. This is a means of determining whether a person should, or truly should not, have known how to respond in a given situation. While this is not an ideal standard, it does allow the Court to consider all of the circumstances and to make decisions that are practical and realistic.

The *Farmer* case is significant because it sets a limit to the notion of deliberate indifference that was so important in the case of *Estelle v. Gamble*. The *Farmer* case essentially defines the standard of liability in inmate-on-inmate assaults. In this case, inmate Farmer was a transsexual who had been transferred from federal prison to state prison. Inmate Farmer had feminine traits and had even undergone surgical enhancements to appear as a woman. Given his appearance, it was obvious that he would face sexual assault, and ultimately he was assaulted. However, the Supreme Court noted that it is not sufficient that the prison official "should have known that harm was inevitable because the risk was so obvious that a reasonable person should have noticed it." Rather, the official must have "knowingly disregarded an excessive risk of harm." This decision makes it difficult for inmates to hold prison officials liable during inmate-on-inmate altercations because it is extremely difficult to prove that officials actually *knew* that a danger existed and that they then deliberately disregarded that danger. Thus, *Farmer* breaks from the generally sympathetic attitudes of the Court that have been noted in other deliberate indifference cases such as *Estelle v. Gamble*. Ironically, this ruling also dovetails with the general trend noted among the courts regarding interference with prison operations. Thus, it is clear that the Court has had a general perceptual shift in regard to the field of corrections, as reflected in its rulings of various issues.

who act under "color of law" (a term we will expound upon later in this chapter), community supervision officers typically incur potential liability due to their role as agents of the state (*state* being used in a general sense to cover local, state, and federal government). In addition, the types of liability may actually apply in a variety of forms and from multiple sources. For instance, civil and even criminal liability can emerge, and a correctional officer can be subject to both state and federal levels of civil liability, depending upon the circumstances. For purposes of this chapter, we will first begin with state-level forms of liability and then progress our way toward federal levels of liability as well (students should also see Table 4.5 for additional details).

TABLE 4.5   Comparing State and Federal Lawsuits Against Community Supervision Officers

State Tort Cases	*Federal Section 1983 Cases*
Based on state law.	Based on federal law.
Plaintiff seeks money for damages.	Plaintiff seeks money for damages and/or policy change.
Usually based on decided cases.	Law was passed in 1871.
Usually tried in state court.	Usually tried in federal court.
Public officials and private persons can be sued.	Only public officials can be sued.
Basis for liability is injury to person or property of another in violation of a duty imposed by state law.	Basis for liability is violation of a constitutional right or of a right secured by federal law.
Good faith defense usually means the officer acted in the honest belief that the action taken was appropriate under the circumstances.	Good faith defense means the officer did not violate a clearly established constitutional or federal right of which a reasonable person should have known.

Adapted from: Del Carmen, R. V., Barnhill, M. B., Bonham, G., Hignite, L., & Jermstad, T. (2001). *Civil liabilities and other legal issues for probation/parole officers and supervisors.* Washington, DC: National Institute of Corrections.

PHOTO 4.6

A state employee prepares to take the stand and provide testimony. In cases where employees of agencies must go to court, they are "sworn in" prior to the question-and-answer process that occurs in a court proceeding.

State Levels of Liability

Civil liability under state law often is referred to as "tort" law. A **tort** is a legal injury in which the action of one person causes injury to the person or property of another as the result of a violation of one's duty that has been established by law (Del Carmen et al., 2001). Torts can be either deliberate or accidental in nature. A deliberate tort is considered intentional and refer to acts that are intended to have a certain outcome or to cause some form of harm to the aggrieved. On the other hand, an accidental tort would generally be one that is committed out of negligence with the intent of harm being non-existent.

Intentional Torts

According to *Black's Law Dictionary*, an **intentional tort** is one in which the actor, whether expressed or implied, was judged to have possessed intent or purpose to injury. This means that an intentional tort has numerous components, all of which must be proven by a plaintiff if the suit is to prevail. The components of an intentional tort that must be proven are as follows:

- An act was committed by the defendant.
- The act was deliberate and can be shown to be such due to the fact that the defendant had to have known of the potential consequences of the act.
- The resulting harm was actually caused by the act.
- Clear damages can be shown to have resulted from the act.

A hypothetical example might be a scenario where a Correctional Officer X conducts a search of an inmate's cell. While in the cell, the correctional officer assaults the inmate and says, "I can reach out and touch you anytime, and if you say anything about it, I will see to it that you get written up and lose your good time." The inmate is injured, has to go to the infirmary for internal injuries, and decides to disclose the source of his injuries. In this case, the correctional officer has obviously committed an intentional tort. The assault was committed by Correctional Officer X (the defendant in this case), the assault was obviously on purpose and Correctional Officer X was clearly cognizant of his actions, and clear damages in the way of physical injuries occurred as a direct result of the assault.

In regard to nonphysical torts, several specific types of offenses or damages might occur. These include defamation, acts that cause harm to a person's emotional well-being, or malicious prosecution, among other things. Because this area of liability is so broad, it is necessary to address many of these concepts, specifically, to ensure that the student has a clear understanding of each potential source of liability. Though the following discussion will not be exhaustive, it will highlight the more common areas of liability that correctional officers may face.

First, **defamation** is an invasion of a person's interest through his or her reputation. In order for this to occur, some form of slander or libel must have occurred against the aggrieved individual. Many people use the term *slander* loosely but often are unclear about its meaning, though they may not realize it when they use this term. To be clear, **slander** is any oral communication provided to another party (aside from the aggrieved person) that lowers the reputation of the person discussed and where people in the community would find such facts to actually be damaging to that person's reputation. **Libel**, on the other hand, is the written version of slander.

The next category, infliction of **emotional distress**, refers to acts (either intentional or negligent) that lead to emotional distress of the client. Emotional distress can occur due to words or gestures, and of course the conduct of the community supervision officer may constitute sufficient grounds for liability. For instance, tactics that bully or abuse an inmate would fall within this category. Even words alone can attach liability, depending on the circumstances and context, such as a situation where the correctional officer causes verbal insult to the inmate while in front of other inmates. However, one simple incident, though not likely to be in adherence to agency policy, typically does not incur liability unless the situation can be shown to be "extreme" and "outrageous" (Del Carmen, Barnhill, Bonham, Hignite, & Jermstad, 2001).

The last area of nonphysical tort that will be discussed is malicious prosecution. **Malicious prosecution** occurs when a criminal accusation is made by someone who has no probable cause and who generates such actions for improper reasons. In such cases, the accused must be, as a matter of material fact, innocent of the charges that were made. Take, for instance, a scenario where Correctional Officer X is talking with a female inmate in the facility. The female inmate is attractive, and Correctional Officer X knows that before serving prison time, the female inmate was an exotic dancer and an active prostitute. Correctional Officer X propositions her and notes that he will bring various forms of contraband to the facility in exchange for sex. If the female inmate does not consent to sexual relations, Correctional Officer X threatens to write up the female inmate for soliciting an officer (the implication being that Correctional Officer X will tell the judge that the female inmate propositioned *him* for contraband in exchange for sexual favors). The female inmate refuses to comply with the request, and Correctional Officer X files criminal charges against her soliciting an officer. Unbeknownst to Correctional Officer X, Internal Affairs has held this officer under suspicion for some time and conducted inquiries among inmates and staff prior to this incident. Corroboration between multiple witnesses eventually found that the female inmate was innocent of the charges and, in turn, Internal Affairs charged Correctional Officer X with malicious prosecution. Correctional Officer X lost his job, and the female inmate sued the prison system, later settling out of court.

Negligence Torts

The next primary category of state tort includes acts of negligence. In the vast majority of cases, negligence suits do not actually win, particularly if the officer adheres to agency policy. Most agencies do have sufficient policy safeguards to ensure that an adequate good faith attempt is made at public safety, and, presuming that the officer follows policy, liability is not likely to be incurred. Nevertheless, this area of concern can be troublesome since it is never pleasant to be faced with the prospect of a suit. This can (and does) add stress for the officer, with lawsuits being yet another contributor to the high rate of burnout that occurs among community supervision officers.

It is important to have a clear understanding of what negligence is, and is not. For purposes of this text, **negligence** is defined as doing what a reasonably prudent person would not have done in similar circumstances, or failing to do what a reasonably prudent person would have done in similar circumstances. The following minimal conditions are typically required to establish a case of negligence:

1. A legal duty is owed to the aggrieved person (in prisons, such a duty exists between custodial staff and inmates).

2. A breach of that duty must have occurred whether by the failure to act or by the commission of action that was not professionally sufficient to fulfill that duty.

3. The aggrieved can demonstrate that an injury did occur.

4. The person with the duty owed to the aggrieved person committed the act (or lack of action) that was the proximate cause of the injury.

Liability Under Section 1983 Federal Lawsuits

This avenue for civil redress is one of the most frequently used by persons seeking damages from the government. Though there is substantial history associated with this particular form of liability, this text will delve right into the substantive issues associated with Section 1983 liabilities. Essentially, there are two simple requirements that must exist in order for liability to be imparted to a person so charged:

1. The person charged (the defendant) acted under color of state law.

2. The person charged violated a right secured by the constitution or by federal law.

Both of these requirements need some bit of explanation. First, the term *color of state law* must be clarified. This term simply means that the actor committed his or her behavior while under the authority of some form of government. In this case, the term *state* is meant to imply government in general, regardless of the level of the government (e.g., local, state, or federal) that is associated with the agency. Thus, local jailers, state correctional officers, and community supervision officers all act under the color of state law when they are performing their duties in the employment of their respective agencies. This liability does not, however, apply during their off-time "normal" lives. In further clarifying this concept, Del Carmen et al. (2001) note that anything that correctional officers do in the performance of their regular duties and during the usual hours of employment is considered as falling under the color of state law. In contrast, whatever these same people do as private citizens during their off-hours falls outside and beyond the color of state law.

In regard to Section 1983 itself, it is important to point out that violations of an inmate's rights do not necessarily automatically become a constitutional or federal issue. Rather, as Del Carmen et al. (2001) put it, "the violation must be of constitutional proportion" (p. 34). Though there is some degree of ambiguity in determining what exactly is (and is not) an issue of constitutional proportion, it does underscore the fact that most cases that will incur federal liability must be serious—perhaps even "unusually serious" according to Del Carmen et al.—if it is likely to be considered sufficient grounds for a Section 1983 suit. Simple words, threats, gestures, and even actual pushes and/or shoves do not automatically constitute a civil rights violation.

FORMS OF IMMUNITY AND TYPES OF DEFENSES

One key protection for correctional staff, as agents of the state, is their potential immunity from tort suits. *Official immunity* is a term that refers to being legally shielded from suit. Official immunity is granted to those professions that must be allowed to, at least in the majority of circumstances, actively pursue their duties without undue fear or intimidation. Otherwise, law enforcement, correctional, and judicial professionals simply could not fulfill their duty correctly. However, official immunity comes in a number of different forms, reflecting the different levels of responsibility and liability associated with different functions in the justice system. For purposes of this text, students need only to discern between *absolute immunity* and *qualified immunity*.

Absolute immunity exists for those persons who work in positions that require unimpaired decision making. Judges and prosecutors have this type of immunity since their jobs require that they make very important decisions regarding the livelihood of persons in their courts; these decisions must be made free of intimidation or potential recrimination, and therefore these court actors enjoy absolute immunity when carrying out their responsibilities (Del Carmen et al., 2001). For correctional officers and community supervision officers, protection through immunity is typically referred to as qualified immunity. **Qualified immunity** requires that the community supervision officer demonstrate three key aspects prior to invoking this form of defense against suit: (1) The community supervision officer must show that he or she was performing a discretionary act, not one that was mandatory by agency policy; (2) the correctional officer must have been acting in good faith—that is, holding the sincere belief that his or her action was correct under the circumstances; and (3) the correctional officer must have acted within the scope of his or her designated authority. Thus, most correctional officers do not enjoy the same level of immunity as do their colleagues in the judicial arena since they have to demonstrate the grounds for their possession of immunity (Del Carmen et al., 2001).

Journal Article Link 4.4
Read more about about qualified immunity in private prisons.

Beyond the initial forms of liability protection (i.e., qualified immunity and the public duty doctrine) afforded correctional officers, there are some defenses that officers can raise on their own behalf. First among these is the good faith defense. The **good faith defense** essentially buffers a correctional officer from liability in Section 1983 cases (not state tort cases) unless the officer violated some clearly established constitutional or federal statutory right that a reasonable person would have known to exist.

From the previous discussion of both state tort and Section 1983 forms of suit, it is clear that the issue of *good faith* is important. The notion that the officer acted in good faith (with the sincere belief that his or her action was appropriate) is important to establishing qualified immunity against state tort suits. The term *good faith* is the same, but its applications to both types of lawsuit (state tort and Section 1983) are different. Because students often find the differences in state tort law and federal protections under Section 1983 a bit confusing, and because the terminology regarding good faith defenses is similar in appearance but different in actual application, students are encouraged to examine Table 4.5 for further clarity in classifying each type of legal redress and its particular parameters.

INDEMNIFICATION AND REPRESENTATION

When correctional officers are faced with lawsuits (whether state or federal), the issue of legal representation is an automatic concern. This issue, as well as that of indemnification (payment for court costs), varies greatly from state to state. As a general rule, most states around the nation are willing to provide assistance in civil cases, but this is not nearly as true when the charges are criminal in nature. While it is typical for states to cover financial costs associated with civil proceedings, many do not necessarily do this automatically, and this makes it likely, from time to time, that officers face such instances without any financial assistance from their place of employment—a scary thought indeed.

Most states cover an officer's act or omission to act in civil cases, provided that it is determined that the incident occurred within the scope of the officer's employment (Del Carmen et al., 2001). In some cases, this may also require a good faith element where it can be reasonably shown that the officer did act in good faith within the scope of his or her duty. In most cases where good faith is established, the officer will be represented by the state's attorney general. However, the attorneys general in all states have a wide degree of discretion before agreeing to defend an officer faced with a civil suit. If it should turn out that the AG (as the attorney general's office may be called from time to time) does not agree to defend the officer, that individual will have to retain private counsel at his or her own expense.

Once the issue of representation is resolved, the last issue of concern tends to revolve around the payment of legal costs. Most typically, when state tort cases are involved, both the plaintiff (in this case the offender) and the defendant (the community supervision officer) would pay their own attorney's fees, and this would remain the arrangement regardless of the case outcome. Thus, even if the correctional worker is found innocent of the allegations that the offender has construed, he or she will still be likely to have to pay his or her own courts costs if the case is a state tort case. To remedy these concerns, officers may, in some cases, opt to purchase their own professional liability insurance, but they will typically be required to pay the premium themselves and, in several cases, may not even have the ability to purchase such insurance since companies may not be operating in the state to underwrite the policy.

TYPES OF DAMAGES

Lastly, most all civil cases (particularly tort cases) seek to obtain monetary damages. The amount can vary greatly, depending on the type of injury, the type of tort that is found (i.e., gross or willful negligence), and the severity of that injury. Most often, these financial awards come in the way of **compensatory damages**, which are payments for the actual losses suffered by a plaintiff (typically the offender). In some cases, **punitive damages** may also be awarded, but these monetary awards would be reserved for an offender who was harmed in a malicious or willful manner by agency staff; however, these damages are often added to emphasize the seriousness of the injury and/or to serve as a warning to other parties who might observe the case's outcome. The types of award for civil rights cases under Section 1983 suits can also vary greatly and often are similar to those under tort law.

However, it is common for Section 1983 cases to also result in other types of remedies that go beyond financial awards. These remedies are typically geared toward agencies rather than individual officers, though both financial damages and additional awards can be made. One such nonmonetary award that is occasionally granted is the **declaratory judgment**, which is a judicial determination of the legal rights of the person bringing suit (Neubauer, 2002). An example might include a suit where an inmate sues for violation of certain due process safeguards in disciplinary proceedings. A court may award a declaratory judgment against the agency to ensure that future inmates in custody are afforded the appropriate safeguards established by prior Supreme Court case law.

COMPLIANCE WITH JUDICIAL ORDERS

Video Link 4.4
View a recent example of compliance with judicial orders.

Inmates in state and federal prison have increasingly petitioned the courts for relief under a variety of statutes. Virtually every function and service of the correctional process has been examined by the courts. Aspects of prison life such as the use of force, indifference to medical needs, cruel and unusual punishment, food services, overcrowding, religious practice, psychological services, the right to treatment, and conditions of confinement have all produced case law under the Supreme Court. Thus, prison systems were forced to come into compliance with judicial orders during the hands-on era, which impacted every aspect of their operation (Carp & Stidham, 1990). Students will recall from Chapter 3 that different prison systems operated in a manner that was contrary to what progressive-minded prison advocates would prefer. As such, the involvement of the courts in prison operations can be viewed as an example of how the U.S. judicial system is affected by the norms and mores of our society, being reflected in case law and court rulings—rulings that ultimately extended into the prison world, which had, until that time, been separate and distinct from mainstream society.

PHOTO 4.7

Judges have the ability to issue injunctions that order correctional systems to correct a noted deficiency or set of deficiencies.

Injunctions and Court-Imposed Remedies

In addition to the typical award of damages against a correctional agency or correctional staff, courts may also employ injunctions against an agency. An **injunction** is a court order that requires an agency to take some form of action(s) or to refrain from a particular action or set of actions (Neubauer, 2002). Though the PLRA has narrowed the scope of federal court interference and has limited the time frame from which judges can impose their edicts on a prison system or

TECHNOLOGY AND EQUIPMENT 4.1

The Use of Video Cameras in Prisons to Protect Staff From Inmate Lawsuits

Video cameras in prison are not necessarily common, depending on the type of prison that is considered. However, they are a very useful tool, from the standpoint of both security and liability. One means by which various forms of cameras are used is conducting "forced cell moves," which are necessary when inmates are unruly or dangerous in their cell and must therefore be removed from that cell. In such instances, a team of five correctional officers will "suit up" with riot gear (padding, helmets, and a riot shield for the lead officer) and go into the cell to extract the inmate.

When conducting forced cell moves, officers are trained so that the lead officer will enter quickly, using the shield to wedge the inmate into a prone position. Other officers will work to get all four limbs (both arms and both legs) secured. Each officer will have a specific arm or leg that he or she holds and places into a restraining position. All the while, behind this forced cell extraction team, an officer can be found, with a supervisor, operating a camcorder or another such videotaping device. The entire incident is filmed and provides footage so that, if the inmate should falsely allege that officers used excessive force, evidence to the contrary can be presented.

In addition to such portable uses, the inclusion of fixed video cameras can greatly enhance security in the institution, and this will, in turn, make the institution safer for staff and other inmates. The experts at VideoSurveillance. com note the benefits of surveillance as follows:

1. **Improved visual coverage**—Many prisons and correctional facilities are expansive, consisting of a variety of different areas, all of which require close monitoring. While guards and officers can't be everywhere at once, security cameras can provide continuous coverage of an entire facility.

2. **Monitor inmate activity**—The constant presence of surveillance cameras helps officers to spot suspicious inmate activity, and can prevent prison incidents from getting out of hand.

3. **Provide visual evidence**—Archived surveillance footage is an extremely valuable resource for investigations of prison incidents.

4. **Reduce the frequency of assaults**—In prisons and correctional facilities, tension is high, and fights are inevitable. Security cameras work to deter such behavior and also help in analyzing incidents of violence.

5. **Monitor officer behavior**—Instances where guards and correctional officers act out of line toward inmates are caught on camera. Such footage is used in investigations and can help to prevent further misconduct.

6. **Enhanced search capabilities**—Digital surveillance technology allows video footage to be archived and stored on digital video recorders and hard drives rather than bulky cassette tapes. Searching footage is significantly easier and more efficient in digital format.

Liability for the agency is likewise minimized in many of the instances above. For instance, liability for inmate safety can be minimized if agencies can demonstrate that cameras are used to watch over the inmates so that officers can ensure their safety from assault in the recreation yards and other high-traffic areas. In addition, inappropriate officer behavior can be severely curtailed by the ability to detect such behavior. Further, the ability to detect and prevent drug smuggling is an important feature, especially during visitation periods when family and friends will visit the inmate. In such cases, families or friends may smuggle contraband into the facility. The ability to keep such information assists in conducting investigations against persons who bring contraband into the prison. As should be apparent, video cameras and surveillance equipment have many potential applications in a prison system.

facility, injunctions remain an effective remedy, particularly when federal civil rights or federal statutes are violated.

If the plaintiff inmate is successful in court (which is rare, but does happen on occasion), judges may issue injunctions that order correctional systems to correct a noted deficiency or set of deficiencies. But, in these cases, prison officials must be given the time and opportunity to rectify conditions that are deemed unconstitutional. For the inmate population, this is very important because inmates are likely to be in the facility for a long period, and, even though the court ruling may have been provided, they will be required to live in the institution for years afterward. Thus, ensuring that administrators do make the required changes and that they are given the realistic ability to make these changes is directly important to the inmate population.

In the past, injunctions or court orders have required a variety of changes. First, they have mandated the abolition of certain prison regulations and state statutes relating to discipline, censorship, and court access. Second, these orders required improvements in institutions or in the services provided, including training for correctional staff, sanitation conditions, quality of food, and other aspects previously discussed in this chapter and in prior chapters. Third, jails, prisons, and/or sections of such facilities have been ordered closed when found to house inmates under conditions determined to be in violation of Eighth Amendment requirements. Thus, injunctions have had widespread impact upon prison systems.

Consent Decrees

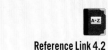

Reference Link 4.2
Read about the consent decree that resulted from the 1980 New Mexico Riot.

As an alternative option to going to trial, inmate plaintiffs may have conditions remedied in a much more expedient fashion if they agree to settle with the agency in developing a suitable consent decree. Essentially, a **consent decree** is an injunction, but with the defendant and the agency (Carp & Stidham, 1990). A consent decree, therefore, involves both parties agreeing to work out the terms of a stated settlement that is given official weight by the court. The benefit to this remedy is that time and expense is spared, and the uncertainty of a trial is eliminated. This also allows for a mutually agreeable solution rather than forcing the prison system into compliance.

CONCLUSION

This chapter demonstrates how during recent correctional history in America, there has been a constant interplay between state-level correctional systems and the federal courts. This interplay has been marked in controversy, challenges, and conflict between state priorities regarding crime and prison operations and the need to adhere to constitutional standards. Amidst this evolution of prison operations in America, it is the interpretation of those Constitutional standards that has been the central feature of this change as well as the Supreme Court's interpretation of its own role in ensuring that those standards, as interpreted, are met.

The legal history of corrections in the United States reflects the norms and mores of our society in relation to crime, punishment, and prison operations. The hands-off era reflected common public understanding regarding prisons; inmates were slaves of the state and entitled to nothing in particular. Thus, the need for intervention, whether by the mainstream public or the Supreme Court, seemed to be unnecessary to all but the most ardent of reform-minded persons.

Conversely, the hands-on era that occurred during the civil rights movement reflected the sentiments of a court that was in tune with social changes occurring throughout society. The sweeping changes that were mandated by the courts upon state prison systems reflected the norms and mores of the time, which were reform-minded. The hands-on era was tumultuous for many state prison systems, and the result created larger expenses for the taxpaying public, yet, at the same time, the ethics, integrity, and general social conscience of the corrections field were improved. It is due to these changes that the corrections field became professionalized.

In addition, legal issues that face both administrators and line staff are important to know and understand. The distinctions between federal suits and state suits is important since each will consist of different standards that must be met. Staff must understand where their liability begins and where it ends when working in the field of corrections. Individual knowledge of the parameters associated with liability aids correctional agencies as a whole since such knowledge can act as a preventative mechanism against inmate suits filed against correctional staff. The individual knowledge of staff regarding legal issues ensures that agencies, as a whole, are in compliance.

Lastly, a brief overview of injunctions and other forms of court-oriented remediation is presented. These actions are what ultimately led to the sweeping changes that we have seen in this and preceding chapters. However, the courts have now adopted a more neutral stance in intervening in prison operations. The passage of the PLRA has also been instrumental in limiting the role of the courts and reflects a growing sentiment toward a "middle ground" approach to handling inmate claims and standards in prison operations. It now appears that the field of corrections has matured into a professionalized and widely recognized discipline that has come into a new and more balanced means of operation.

END-OF-CHAPTER DISCUSSION QUESTIONS

1. What was the "hands-off doctrine," and how were prisons run during this era?

2. What was the importance of *Ex parte Hull,* and how did it change corrections?

3. Give a brief overview of *Turner v. Safley* and explain how it defined a variety of aspects related to correctional decision making.

4. Identify and discuss legal liabilities associated with correctional staff.

5. How would you describe the current relationship between corrections and judicial oversight? Is it now balanced, or are prisons systems still under close scrutiny?

6. Compare and contrast state tort cases and federal Section 1983 cases.

7. Discuss injunctions and consent decrees. What are their purpose when leveled against a correctional system?

8. Refer to Applied Theory 4.1. In what way is peacemaking criminology related to the reduction of recidivism and lower crime rates?

KEY TERM

Absolute immunity	Good faith defense	Punitive damages
Baxter v. Palmigiano (1976)	Hands-off doctrine	Rational basis test
Bell v. Wolfish (1979)	Hudson v. Palmer (1984)	Qualified immunity
Bounds v. Smith (1977)	Injunction	Rational basis test
Compensatory damages	Intentional tort	Religious Land Use and Institutionalized Persons Act of 2000
Consent decree	Johnson v. Avery (1969)	
Cooper v. Pate (1964)	Libel	Ruiz v. Estelle (1980)
Cruz v. Beto (1972)	Malicious prosecution	Slander
Declaratory judgment	Negligence	Slight negligence
Defamation	O'Lone v. Estate of Shabazz (1987)	Tort
Emotional distress		Totality of conditions
Estelle v. Gamble (1976)	One hand on, one hand off doctrine	Turner v. Safley (1987)
Ex parte Hull	Prison Litigation Reform Act of 1995	Vitek v. Jones (1980)
Farmer v. Brennan (1994)		Wilson v. Seiter (1991)
Gregg v. Georgia (1976)	Procunier v. Martinez (1974)	Wolff v. McDonnell (1974)

APPLIED EXERCISE 4.1

For this exercise, the instructor should organize several students (perhaps up to 12 students per group) into a mock jury, with one student designated as the foreman. Students must consider the following case, which is the same case that will be introduced in the "What Would You Do?" exercise that follows (but that version of the case will have a twist not encountered in this applied exercise). Students must identify specific legal criteria to determine liability involved with Officer Jimmy Joe, Officer Hackworth, Officer Guillory, Officer Killroy, Officer Ortega, Sergeant Smith, and Nurse Hatchett. Use information from your chapter regarding personal liability issues among correctional workers as your basis in providing your response.

The defendant, Jimmy Joe, a correctional officer at the Charles C. Broderick Maximum Security Facility, has claimed that he was unable to observe any of the events that are alleged by inmate Baker. Jimmy Joe's incident report notes that he was upstairs conducting a security check of the cell block; his documentation for that day does corroborate with his story, according to date and time of the activity.

Inmate Baker alleges that Jimmy Joe watched as he was beaten, in the foyer of the dayroom, by Officers Hackworth, Guillory, and Killroy. Inmate Baker also insists that when he was removed from the cell block and taken to the infirmary, Officer Ortega operated the video camera that recorded his escort. While recording, inmate Baker contends that Ortega deliberately moved the angle of the camera during key times when the officers "accidentally" bumped inmate Baker into infirmary doors and wall corners . . . All the while, Nurse Hatchett, who inmate Baker alleges was working in tandem with the officers, would ask the officers to have inmate Baker moved to another room, thereby repeating the haphazard escorting process. Throughout his visit to the infirmary, Baker was handcuffed behind his back as officers Guillory and Killroy escorted him from room to room.

Inmate Baker also contends that nurse Hatchett was deliberately rough with him when administering bandages. These allegations were not captured on video camera, and, as inmate Baker contends, there are some periods where the camera appears to be pointed off center for a few seconds.

Officer Ortega claims that he has not been trained with the video camera and that this was his first time recording an escort after a use-of-force incident. An investigation of official prison records indicates that what Officer Ortega says is true.

Sergeant John Smith arrived on the scene with Officer Ortega, and it was Sergeant Smith who instructed Ortega to grab the camera and simply make his best good faith effort to record the incident. Institutional policy precludes sergeants from using the camera when supervising infirmary escorts. According to Sergeant Smith's incident report, Officer Ortega was the only officer available at the time, and Smith had to make a quick discretionary call; he chose to not delay in responding and to aid Ortega with verbal instruction when using the camera while on the scene and as the situation permitted.

Officer Ortega and Sergeant Smith arrived on the scene, with the camera, to see inmate Baker in cuffs and restrained on the floor by Officers Guillory and Killroy. Officer Hackworth had administered the cuffs and appeared to be on standby, waiting to aid in the escort once the supervisor and the camera appeared. All of these actions were consistent with institutional policy, including the restraining techniques used by Guillory and Killroy.

Inmate Baker contends that prior to their arrival, Officers Hackworth, Guillory, and Killroy had trapped him in a nonvisible portion of the dayroom, and they had repeatedly assaulted him. He also noted that Officer Jimmy Joe was near the scene the entire time and that he refused to render aid. Rather, he watched from a corner view as Baker was beaten for 10 minutes by Hackworth.

Officers Guillory, Killroy, and Hackworth contend that inmate Baker had been acting aggressively when they tried to allow him off the cell block to go to commissary. Officer Hackworth, noting that the cell door had been closed and also noting that the dayroom was clear of other inmates, instructed the junior officers to temporarily place inmate Baker in the dayroom to contain the situation. Officer Hackworth claims that his intent was to either defuse the situation or, if that did not work, escort Baker to his cell once staff in the picket (an area from which the cell doors are opened) were able to get his cell back open.

Officer Hackworth's incident report claims that inmate Baker began to yell and, because he had a strong dislike for Guillory, took a swing at Officer Guillory with his right arm. When inmate Baker did this, all three officers moved to restrain inmate Baker. Inmate Baker is a known weightlifter in the prison and has a past history of violence. Officers Hackworth, Guillory, and Killroy all contend that inmate Baker resisted with great force and fury . . . and all three officers found it difficult to restrain him. In the process, inmate Baker received several welts and bruises from bumping into walls (while trying to get distance from the officers) and from fighting after being restrained on the concrete. He also had three chipped teeth from landing, face first, against the concrete when placed in an arm-restraining hold. No other serious injuries were sustained.

Once the incident was over, Officer Hackworth said to Jimmy Joe, "Quick, call a supervisor, we have an inmate down, and we need him escorted to the infirmary."

Now, as you sit on the jury, you must decide whose version of the story is true. Should any or all of these officers be found guilty of cruel and unusual punishment, as per the Eighth Amendment? Are there any areas of potential liability for the officers in the altercation, Officer Jimmy Joe, Nurse Hatchett, Officer Ortega, Sergeant Smith, or the correctional agency? Be sure to provide specific details in regard to your response.

"WHAT WOULD YOU DO?"

Jimmy Joe, a corrections officer at the Charles C. Broderick Maximum Security Facility, remembers the situation all too clearly. Inmate Baker had always been a difficult inmate, and he was a tough number. While serving time at Broderick Maximum, inmate Baker had shanked two inmates on one occasion, and he had done the same with a correctional officer on another occasion. So, it was not like everyone did not know that inmate Baker was dangerous.

Even though inmate Baker was dangerous and had been a serious problem for many of the guards working at Broderick Maximum, Jimmy Joe was not really interested in getting "revenge" on Baker. However, Officer Hackworth could not ever get it out of his mind. For some reason, he had a constant fixation on inmate Baker and would often mention that no inmate should be allowed to assault an officer and live to talk about it. For a long time Baker did not think much of Hackworth's comments—he was just another frustrated prison guard blowing off steam about the hardhead inmates on the cell block.

But one day, a hot summer day, inmate Baker was hollering because he wanted off the cell block to go to commissary, and two officers instead told him no, not until they were ready to allow inmates to leave for the commissary line. On that particular day, the commissary was running late, but other inmates had told Baker that this was not true; instead he thought that the officers were lying to him as a means of "messing with his head." In fact, one inmate explained to Baker, "Man, it's like they're tryin' that guard crap again, you know, mentally punkin' you out." The inmate then added, "Ya know, they're always doing that crap with only you, all because they know you won't take it. They want you to stud up, man—what you gonna do?"

The excessive summer heat of the prison, located in the Deep South of the United States, was working on Baker, his overall mood and demeanor had become quite sour, and, as the officers stood there, Baker said, "Look, you two little girls better get out of my way, and you'd better quit runnin' game on me." At this same time, Officer Hackworth walked onto the cell block; he had arrived to assist in moving an inmate to another cell block but overheard Baker's voice and comment and, instead, decided to walk over to where Baker and the two officers were located. Jimmy Joe was the officer in charge of the cell block and, seeing Hackworth head in that direction, kept an eye on everyone.

The dayroom was nearly empty in the cell block because most of the inmates were either at work or out on the recreation yard. Hackworth told the officers near Baker that he would be right back. Hackworth then walked up to Jimmy Joe, who was a very new officer still on his six-month probationary period, and said, "Look, you need to get them inmates out of that dayroom. If this gets sloppy, we don't want them hangin' around here making up crap that they think they have seen. Tell them that TV time is over and they gotta get on the rec yard" followed with "if you ain't man enough to run them out, then let me know, and I will get their butts out of here myself."

Jimmy Joe ordered the inmates to go to the rec yard, which they did without much grumbling. They did look at Hackworth in a strange manner, almost as if they knew what was going on, and they looked at Baker in a sympathetic manner. Hackworth then told Jimmy Joe, "Look, Bub, you stay here and just man your post. If someone is about to come on the cell block, let us know."

Then "the Hack," as everyone referred to him, went back down the cell block and told the other two officers that maybe they should go ahead and let Baker approach the outer door of the cell block, just so he would be ready for the commissary call when it happened. Baker then said, "Yeah, man, let me up front so I will be ready. You know it ain't even closed—y'all are just making this difficult." Hackworth walked with the two officers and inmate Baker, and, as they approached the front of the cell block, the door to the dayroom was on their right. Hackworth said, "Hey Baker, look, we don't want no problems, so if you want, feel free to go into the dayroom and watch the TV until you hear the commissary call. We will leave the door open so you can come as soon as the call is sounded"

Baker began to think that maybe, perhaps, the commissary line was not ready and, since he had no TV in his own cell, liked the idea of watching one of the channels while waiting for the commissary line. He went in, sat down on a bench facing the TV, and was switching the channels when Hackworth entered with the two other officers. From an angle of a sort, Jimmy Joe could barely make out their position. Hackworth then said, "Hey, Baker, next time you pick up that channel changer, you need to ask to do so—that is a prison regulation, and you just broke that regulation" followed with "and it looks like you are being resistant and assaultive, so I am going to have to put you on the ground."

What happened next was a blur. Hackworth and the two other officers basically tackled inmate Baker and began punching him repeatedly. They made a point to do this in an area of the dayroom foyer that was not clearly visible to Jimmy Joe. Inmate Baker tried to scream, but Hackworth shoved a bandanna in his mouth, cursed at him, and continued with the pounding. Once the incident was over, the officers said to Jimmy Joe, "Quick, call a supervisor, we have an inmate down, and we need him escorted to the infirmary."

Now, here it is about 15 months later. *Jimmy Joe, Hackworth, the two other officers, and inmate Baker are all together in the federal district court. Baker filed a Section 1983 lawsuit that has actually made it to court. A jury sits across from Jimmy Joe—a jury of real people who do not seem to give any clue as to how they feel about the case in front of them.*

At the time of the incident, Hackworth and the other two officers wrote in their paperwork that the incident started because inmate Baker had tried to assault one of the officers. Hackworth claimed that the use of force was necessary to contain the inmate and to ensure officer safety. It is now Jimmy Joe on the stand, and he is being asked whether Baker initiated the assault. In his paperwork, Jimmy Joe had indicated that he did not see or hear anything but had been doing his rounds on the cell block. If Jimmy Joe changes his testimony, he will of course end up in trouble and will be labeled a "snitch" among coworkers. In essence, he would be better off quitting his job. If he stays with his story, he knows that he is lying, and he also does not know what the jury might believe.

If you were Jimmy Joe, **what would you do?**

CROSS-NATIONAL PERSPECTIVE 4.1

Human Rights in Prisons and the Story of Abu Ghraib

As can be seen throughout the previous chapters and throughout the case law in this chapter, human rights and standards of decency have been a constant concern in corrections. This is only quite natural since the treatment of people who are being punished can lead and has led to a number of heinous outcomes. Even in the past 50 years, Supreme Court cases have illustrated the need to monitor human rights issues in prisons, though the case law falling under their purview is referred to as civil rights, which are derived from the Constitution. Nevertheless, whether we refer to these rights as civil rights or human rights, they share the same fundamental concept of holding value for human lives, regardless of their transgressions. This is particularly true for those persons within the custody of the government.

Every day, around the nation, there continues to exist a variety of lawsuits that result in settlements among state and especially county correctional agencies. Consider, for example, a recent settlement in Orange County, California, for $3.75 million that was awarded to a jail detainee who had been severely beaten by other inmates. This settlement, just reached in 2009, is reminiscent of the issue noted in Corrections and the Law 4.1 that dealt with deliberate indifference to an inmate's likelihood of being assaulted. However, in the case that was settled in Orange County, jail deputies were cited for a failure to render aid when the inmate was attacked by other inmates. In this case, the jail staff were found liable.

Though incidents like this may appear to be isolated, they do occur, and, because of this, training on civil liabilities such as those discussed in this chapter is very important. Naturally, the implementation and emphasis on ethical behavior should also be woven into agency training. This is an important point for many reasons, but one reason should be particularly showcased. This is the notion that many practitioners seem to have an attitude of "yeah, yeah, yeah, I know, I know, we are not supposed to do this, or we are not supposed to do that—I already know all that." This attitude toward ethics training is common among jaded practitioners; but ethical and professional behavior, in addition to adherence to agency policy, is perhaps the best safeguard against civil suits. Thus, these issues are intertwined and are equally important to practitioners whether they be entry level, executive level, or otherwise.

If you doubt this, consider the media-catching incidents at Abu Ghraib. In 2004, accounts of physical, psychological, and sexual abuse came to light in this American military prison in Iraq. These acts of torture, all committed amidst the fervor of the conflict in Iraq, the antiterrorism initiative, and other factors, were committed by U.S. Army military police personnel as well as other officials. An article in the *New York Times*, released in 2005, reported testimony that indicated the following types of torture and/or techniques of degradation had taken place:

1. Urinating on detainees.

2. Jumping on detainees' leg (a limb already wounded by gunfire) with such force that it could not thereafter heal properly.

3. Pounding detainees with collapsible metal batons.

4. Pouring phosphoric acid on detainees.

5. Sodomization of detainees with batons and other instruments.

6. Tying ropes to the detainees' legs or penises and dragging them across the floor.

In addition, many of the prison staff forced Iraqi prisoners to stand in various humiliating poses and engage in acts that were embarrassing. While engaged in these activities, numerous photos were taken of both the Iraqi prisoners and the U.S. military personnel engaged in these atrocities. These photos were ultimately disseminated throughout the mass media and were seen by millions of people in the United States and around the world. The entire affair was exposed as an international incident and drew sharp criticism toward the United States and its military. Naturally, investigations were conducted into the incidents at Abu Ghraib, and this resulted in numerous military and civilian personnel being disciplined within their organizations and in criminal charges for many of the personnel. A number of military and civilian personnel involved in these atrocities were given prison sentences for their acts of abuse and torture.

Many scholars and other experts have written and spoken about the acts at Abu Ghraib as a means of explaining and analyzing the circumstances. A variety of explanations have been given as to how American military personnel could be involved in such an embarrassing and dishonorable set of events. Regardless of the reasons, it is clear that training and emphasis on ethical and professional behavior is something that is still needed among personnel. Thus, an awareness and fundamental appreciation for the human rights or civil rights of inmates is critical, even for criminal offenders or enemies of the state.

Question 1: What factors do you think helped to exacerbate the likelihood of unethical behavior among military correctional personnel in Abu Ghraib?

Question 2: In your opinion, if ethical and professional behavior is simply common sense, and if "everyone already knows right from wrong," why does unethical behavior continue to persist in prisons?

STUDENT STUDY SITE

Visit the Student Study Site at **www.sagepub.com/hanserintro** to access links to the videos, audio clips, SAGE journal articles, state rankings, and reference materials noted in this chapter, as well as additional study tools including eFlashcards, web quizzes, and more.

chapter 5

Jail and Detention Facilities

LEARNING OBJECTIVES:

1. Compare issues for large metropolitan jails to those for small rural jails.

2. Identify characteristics of the jail inmate population.

3. Discuss challenges with jail staff, staff motivation, and training.

4. Identify special types of sentencing options in jails.

5. Identify special needs inmates within the jail environment.

INTRODUCTION

Jails are a unique aspect of the correctional system because they fulfill many different functions. The multiplicity of functions and the rapid processing of offenders within their confines separate them out from the prison facility. Indeed, it is common for the jail population at any typical facility to change in composition quite quickly throughout the year, whereas the prison population will remain more stable from year to year. Jails have a very long history within the field of corrections, though their actual original purpose was not to correct at all. Nowadays, jails perform a number of functions that go well beyond the mere housing of inmates.

JAILS IN THE PAST

As with many aspects of the American criminal justice system, the use and operation of jail facilities owe their origin to England. During early American history, jails were informal and were used to detain persons awaiting trial. Eventually, as there was less reliance on corporal punishments, jails began to be used more frequently to house offenders (Giever, 2006). Jails eventually became a form of punishment, in and of themselves, considered suitable for minor offenders.

Jails in England were referred to as **gaols**, during the Middle Ages. One of the earliest examples of a jail used for confinement purposes was the **Tower of London**, which was constructed after 1066 A.D. under the reign of King William I of England (Giever, 2006). Following this time period, various other gaols were constructed and used to house a variety of offenders. Eventually, gaols were constructed in every shire (the equivalent of a modern-day county), and the local shire gaols were placed under the care of the shire reeve, the early-day version of today's sheriff (Giever, 2006).

As we have seen in previous chapters, the 17th century saw the development of houses of corrections in England and later in the United States (Giever, 2006). These early types of facilities also performed the functions of jails, and during the 18th century jails and prisons were included under the same roof, such as the Walnut Street Jail, which also included a prison wing at that location (Carlson, Roth, & Travisono, 2008). Thus, from the earliest of times, offenders were housed simultaneously together or, at the least, near one another, regardless of whether they were held for a short-term period or sentenced for long-term confinement.

The first jail built in the United States was constructed in Jamestown, the first true settlement in the United States. Inmates were housed in the jail as early as 1608, according to official records (Johnson, Wolfe, & Jones, 2008; Roth, 2011). Early jails had no specific architecture or design. However, most were located within close proximity of the stocks and pillory. These facilities also did not usually utilize individual cells. Rather, inmates were housed in groups, often with a mix of serious and minor offenders in each room (Carlson et al., 2008; Giever, 2006).

During this time, jail inmates were required to provide their own amenities. This could be done by having family and friends provide needed items or by purchasing them from jailers (Giever, 2006). Obviously, this system led to a high level of corruption as jailers tended to exploit inmates who were in need. The practice of collecting monetary compensation from inmates for services became known as the "fee system," and there is even record that some jails charged inmates for their very room and board (Giever, 2006). This system was generally successful in supplementing the jailer's meager salary and was often able to be maintained by offenders since most were in early colonial jails while waiting trial or corporal punishment (Giever, 2006). Nevertheless, some were kept in jail for exceedingly lengthy amounts of time (i.e., years) during which these inmates would have little recourse if family or friends were not available to provide aid. In such cases, survival was bleak and meager, with these inmates completely at the mercy of their jail caretakers.

THE MODERN JAIL

In today's justice system, jail facilities are typically the first point at which an offender is officially classified as being in the correctional component of the criminal justice system. However, this is a bit deceptive since most persons are only being detained after they have been arrested. This detainment, or detention, occurs at a local detention facility that is typically administered by the county and operated by the sheriff's office. This detention facility is typically what is thought of when we use the term *jail*. In simple terms, a **jail** is a confinement facility, usually operated and controlled by county-level law enforcement, that is designed to hold persons charged with a crime who are either awaiting adjudication or serving a short sentence of one year or less after the point of adjudication. Similarly, the Bureau of Justice Statistics defines jails as "locally-operated correctional facilities that confine persons before or after adjudication. Inmates sentenced to jail usually have a sentence of a year or less, but jails also incarcerate persons in a wide variety of other categories" (Sabol & Minton, 2008). This is important because this means that there is quite a bit of flow in and out of a jail facility for two reasons. First, persons who are arrested are automatically held within the jail facility, but many are released within two to three days due to the placement of bond and/ or a judge releasing them on their own recognizance. Second, offenders who serve jail terms do so for one year or less as longer sentences are most often reserved for persons serving true prison sentences. Thus, even among those serving a jail sentence, the turnover tends to be rapid because most sentences are only for a few months to one year.

Recent findings by Minton (2011) regarding jail operations and jail populations in the United States indicated the following:

- The total rated capacity of local jails at midyear 2010 reached 866,974 beds, up from an estimated 677,787 beds at midyear 2000.

- At midyear 2010, jail jurisdictions (173) with an average daily jail population of 1,000 or more inmates accounted for about 6% of all jail jurisdictions and about 49.6% of the jail inmate population.

- At midyear 2010, the jail incarceration rate declined to 242 inmates per 100,000 U.S. residents, the lowest rate since 2003.

Further, Table 5.1 demonstrates that jail jurisdictions around the nation tend to hold lower numbers of inmates. Indeed, the number of jurisdictions that held 50 or fewer inmates decreased between 1999 and 2005, with a corresponding decrease in every single category of inmate total count except fewer than 50 inmates and holding 100 to 249 inmates (Minton, 2011). This does mean that there is a trend for jails to have fewer inmates per jurisdiction, which demonstrates lower per-capita growth in the total number of inmates housed. As Table 5.1 demonstrates, the largest percentage growth is in the category of fewer than 50 inmates. Thus, the trend is for jurisdictions to have smaller inmate populations.

Rural Jails

Rural jails are often challenged with tight budgets and limited training for staff. The author of this text has himself visited numerous rural jails and has trained staff of rural jails on several occasions. It is clear that county-level governments tasked with operating jails do so amidst a number of competing problems, both financial and political. Unlike most urban area jail staff, Wallenstein and Kerle (2008) note that few jail staff in rural areas receive official police or corrections training, and, in jurisdictions where such training is offered, the sheriff is hard-pressed to allow officers to attend the training due to limited numbers of security staff (Kerle, 1982).

The author of this text operates a regional training facility and has witnessed this problem firsthand. As a result, the regional training facility frequently has instructors travel to the jail facility itself to train persons, though this still impacts county budgets since staff members must be paid while attending the training (an additional expenditure), and they must stay late for work or arrive prior to their work shift. Thus, training issues for rural jails are a serious concern that, in the absence of training providers who are able to be flexible, provides a daunting challenge to sheriff agencies and county governments.

In addition, the conditions in rural jails are often substandard, and this is again exacerbated by the lack of funds that tends to be common among most rural jurisdictions. Kerle (1982) notes that one third of all jails in the United States have no physician services, and less than 40 percent have regular nonemergency medical services. Further still, dental services are often limited to simple tooth extractions for jail inmates with no other type of dental service being offered. Kerle's observations in 1982 are, of course, somewhat dated, but still seem to remain true today. Simply put, rural jails cannot provide the services that larger and better-funded jails can provide.

Video Link 5.1
Watch an account of the jail experience.

Audio Link 5.1
Listen to the affects of bail on jail populations.

Journal Article Link 5.1
Read about the complex differences beyond rural and urban characteristics of jails.

TABLE 5.1   Inmates Confined in Local Jails (Midyear, 2010)

Inmates confined in local jails at midyear, by size of jurisdiction, 2009 and 2010						
	Number of inmates			Percentage change	Percentage of all inmates	
Jurisdiction size[a]	2009	2010	Difference		2009	2010
Total[b]	767,434	748,728	−18,706	−2.4%	100.0%	100.0%
Fewer than 50 inmates	22,046	22,806	760	3.4%	2.9%	3.0%
50 to 99	37,838	37,460	−378	−1.0	4.9	5.0
100 to 249	86,279	88,750	2,471	2.9	11.2	11.9
250 to 499	108,462	106,826	−1,636	−1.5	14.1	14.3
500 to 999	123,442	121,704	−1,738	−1.4	16.1	16.3
1.000 or more[b]	389,368	371,181	−18,187	−4.7	50.7	49.6

NOTE: Detail may not add to total due to rounding.

[a]Based on the average daily population during the 12-month period ending June 30, 2009. Average daily population is the sum of all inmates in jail each day for a year.

[b]Based on revised data from selected jail jurisdictions for the number of inmates confined at midyear 2009. See *Methodology* for a description of revised data.

SOURCE: Minton, T. D. (2011). *Jail inmates at midyear 2010.* Washington, DC: Bureau of Justice Statistics.

Because of these challenges, there is incentive to use alternatives to jail incarceration in many jurisdictions. Some proponents have advocated for placing jail operations under state-level government, to be managed by the state's correctional department (Wallenstein & Kerle, 2008). This may be one means of streamlining jail operations, but, as we will see with state prison systems, this is no panacea. In fact, many state prison systems are overcrowded, making it unlikely that states will be any better at managing jail facilities than are persons at the county level of government.

Even more interesting is that, in some states, there is incentive for rural departments to embrace the jail operation industry. In these cases, facilities tend to house state-level inmates due to the fact that many states have burgeoning prison populations. In these state prison systems, there is simply no room to warehouse offenders, and, because of this, the state will pay county-level jails to keep state-level inmates housed. This can generate substantial revenue for the jail, and, as a result, sheriffs may actively solicit the state for additional inmates—all as a means of raising funding from the fees charged to the state (Giever, 2006; Wallenstein & Kerle, 2008). This leads to a bit of a paradoxical situation for state jails where, instead of a desire to limit inmates, the jail administration will seek to remain full to capacity as much as possible.

In a 2001 survey of small jail facilities, the National Institute of Corrections found that the most pressing issues confronting small jails include the following:

- A lack of qualified candidates for hiring, inadequate funding for personnel and/or operations, staff turnover, contraband control, inadequate funding for the physical facility, difficulty managing special inmates, and crowding.

- Issues of greater concern in direct supervision jails compared to nondirect facilities include a lack of qualified candidates for hiring, inadequate funding for personnel/operations, crowding, and outdated technology/equipment.

- Small jails reported that they are most likely to need more space for the following functional areas: records storage, general storage, disciplinary cells, and inmate property storage.

Metropolitan Jail Systems

Jails in large metropolitan areas have numerous challenges that impact their operation. First off, these facilities tend to have large populations that are diverse and present with a variety of issues. Second, there is a tendency for offenders who live rough-and-tumble lifestyles to process in and out of the jail facility. Indeed, the average daily population data used to mark the number of persons in jail do not adequately portray the important role of the jail and its expanded importance to the correctional and judicial arms of the justice system. While the population of jail facilities may be around 800,000 persons nationally on any given day, "between 10 and 15 million persons pass through the jail systems during a calendar year" (Wallenstein, 1999, p. 49). This statistic suggests that jail facilities around the nation essentially process roughly 10 times the number of persons than is reflected in a count taken on any given day of the year (Wallenstein, 1999).

In many cases, particularly in urban jail facilities, a similar group of offenders may recycle in and out of the jail facility, perhaps going through intake and exit from jail at a variety of points throughout the year. Because these inmates recycle through the jail facility, this provides a number of challenges and difficulties for jail staff who must contend with this constantly changing offender population. This also means that jail facilities have a substantial impact on the public safety of communities that surround them. It would then appear that jail administrators have a very big responsibility, both to the jail staff and to the community at large. The jail agency, therefore, is pushed and pulled by the ingress and egress of inmates as well as the demands of and concern for the community.

Urban jails also book a large number of persons with mental disturbances, this often being comorbid with drug and alcohol problems. It is for this reason that large jail facilities tend to have mental health personnel and substance abuse specialists on staff and available 24 hours a day to diagnose and manage the array of problems that these offenders may present (Kerle, 1999). Such services are often only routinely available in larger jail facilities, however, while smaller jails in rural areas may have no such staff at all. Even with larger jail facilities, these staff may be so overworked as to hardly be available during times not considered peak hours for intake. Further, the risk of suicide is greater in jail facilities than in prisons, particularly during the first 48 hours and especially if the person is under the influence of alcohol or drugs. The booking officer and other staff must be quick to screen for potential suicide in all circumstances, noting mental health, substance abuse, or other factors that might exacerbate its likelihood. As noted earlier, jails may commonly house persons who cycle in and out of their confines. The reason for this is that the majority of criminal activity is committed by a small group. These offenders, roughly 10% of the total offender population, commit well over half of all the crime in a local jurisdiction. While much of this crime may be petty, these repeat offenders tend to cycle in and out of jail between charges, with long-term prison not occurring due to the low priority of the criminal activity. Further, these offenders tend to know each other (Giever, 2006). Indeed, many are drug users who may sell, share, and/or use drugs with one another. Others may be partners in criminal activity, and, even more disturbing, some may be mutual members of a street gang. The point is that there tend to be interconnections between members of the criminogenic population due to chance meetings that occur on the streets or their periodic contact while in prison. Thus, in many larger jurisdictions, this offender population tends to maintain contact, both in and out of jail, revolving back and forth from the community to the jail and back again.

Among these petty and small-time offenders may be the homeless; this is especially true in urban areas. The homeless are particularly a problem for larger jurisdictions, with most all beat cops knowing these individuals by name—so often is the contact between police and homeless individuals. Many homeless may have substance abuse issues, problems with trauma and anxiety, or other metal health disturbances. All of these factors are further worsened by an unstable lifestyle that consists of poor nutrition, inadequate health maintenance, and substance abuse. Further still, communicable diseases may be more common among these individuals due to poor personal maintenance and risky lifestyle choices. This is particularly true for female offenders who may resort to prostitution to pay for either their drug habit or their basic needs. In such cases, these offenders are likely to be "regulars" for police officers in those jurisdictions and for jail staff who will book these nuisance offenders multiple times throughout the course of a year. In fact, it is even common among the homeless population for offenses to coincide with colder months of the year, with such persons committing petty crimes so that they may spend the winter indoors within the jail facility rather than outside on the streets during the cold of winter.

Table 5.2 provides an overview of the 50 largest jail jurisdictions in the United States. This table demonstrates that, with the exception of a handful of major jail systems (e.g., New York City; Dade County,

Audio Link 5.2
Listen to a clip about what the conditions are like in a large jail.

Video Link 5.2
Watch as officers respond to a jail inmate in mental distress.

Audio Link 5.3
Listen to how inmates with mental health issues pose challenges to jail administrators and staff.

TABLE 5.2 The 50 Largest Jail Jurisdictions

The 50 largest local jail jurisdictions, by number of inmates held, average daily population, and rated capacity, midyear 2008–2010

Jurisdiction	Number of inmates[a]			Average daily Population[b]			Rated capacity[c]			Percent of capacity occupied[d]		
	2008	2009	2010	2008	2009	2010	2008	2009	2010	2008	2009	2010
Los Angeles County, CA	19,533	19,869	16,862	19,836	19,437	18,036	22,349	22,477	18,112	87.4	88.4	93.1
New York City, NY	13,804	13,130	12,745	13,849	13,365	13,049	19,554	19,636	19,404	70.6	66.9	65.7
Harris County, TX	10,063	11,360	10,264	10,000	11,361	10,242	9,391	9,391	9,391	107.2	121.0	109.3
Cook County, IL	9,984	9,737	9,777	9,900	9,383	9,586	10,158	10,607	10,607	98.3	91.8	92.2
Philadelphia City, PA	8,824	9,436	8,325	8,811	9,359	8,804	8,685	8,685	8,685	101.6	108.6	95.9
Maricopa County, AZ	9,536	8,745	7,549	9,265	9,215	8,055	9,395	9,395	9,395	101.5	93.1	80.4
Dallas County, TX	6,252	6,222	6,909	6,385	6,039	6,865	7,665	8,097	7,805	81.6	76.8	88.5
Miami-Dade County, FL	7,082	5,992	5,653	7,050	6,051	5,770	5,845	5,845	6,035	121.2	102.5	93.7
Shelby County, TN	5,925	5,961	5,560	5,765	5,943	5,766	6,675	6,669	6,912	88.8	89.4	80.4
San Bernardino County, CA	5,596	5,923	5,720	5,593	5,591	5,755	5,970	5,914	5,984	93.7	100.2	95.6
Orange County, CA	6,216	5,990	4,847	6,000	6,255	5,134	5,078	5,063	5,063	122.4	118.3	95.7
San Diego County, CA[e]	5,435	5,215	4,863	5,363	5,263	4,848	4,972	4,664	4,692	109.3	111.8	103.6
Broward County, FL	5,509	4,915	4,631	5,500	4,981	4,583	5,722	5,504	5,144	96.3	89.3	90.0
Alameda County, CA	4,345	4,405	4,132	4,371	4,444	4,305	4,243	4,673	4,673	102.4	94.3	88.4
Sacramento County, CA	4,592	4,796	3,972	4,563	4,700	4,199	5,075	5,075	4,318	90.5	94.5	92.0
Bexar County, TX	4,256	4,191	4,242	4,062	4,236	4,169	4,596	4,596	4,596	92.6	91.2	92.3
Jacksonville City, FL	3,799	3,950	3,837	3,606	3,728	3,835	3,137	3,137	3,137	121.1	125.9	122.3
Baltimore City, MD	4,265	3,957	3,595	4,010	3,997	3,701	3,683	3,683	3,683	115.8	107.4	97.6
Orange County, FL	4,665	3,721	3,591	4,294	4,206	3,604	4,721	4,721	4,721	98.8	78.8	76.1
Santa Clara County, CA	4,644	4,244	3,776	4,660	4,498	3,587	3,825	3,825	3,825	121.9	111.0	98.7
Dekalb County, GA	3,365	3,304	3,516	2,906	3,404	3,560	3,636	3,636	3,636	92.5	90.9	96.7
Davidson County, TN[e]	3,934	3,748	3,636	3,528	3,567	3,551	3,679	4,010	4,010	106.9	93.5	90.7
Orleans Parish, LA	2,370	3,473	3,505	2,613	2,750	3,522	2,633	3,514	3,514	90.0	98.8	99.7
Riverside County, CA	3,597	3,675	3,342	3,530	3,472	3,410	3,132	3,132	3,132	114.8	117.3	106.7
Hillsborough County, FL	3,857	3,503	3,296	3,985	3,658	3,340	4,190	4,190	4,190	92.1	83.6	78.7
Tarrant County, TX	3,574	3,151	3,135	3,500	3,432	3,248	3,386	3,386	3,386	105.6	93.1	92.6
Allegheny County, PA[e]	3,219	3,196	3,342	3,246	3,103	3,233	3,371	3,713	3,727	95.5	86.1	89.7
Pinellas County, FL	3,463	3,233	3,220	3,559	3,145	3,225	4,155	4,151	/	83.3	77.9	/
Gwinnett County, GA	3,415	3,289	3,233	3,311	3,361	3,198	3,419	3,492	4,196	99.9	94.2	77.0
Clark County, NV[f]	3,121	3,109	3,311	3,115	3,101	3,158	2,957	2,984	2,984	105.5	104.2	111.0
District of Columbia[g]	3,046	3,364	3,071	3,012	3,030	3,102	3,825	3,522	3,250	79.6	95.5	94.5
Palm Beach County, FL	2,987	2,973	3,059	2,900	2,825	2,901	3,359	3,366	3,165	88.9	88.3	96.7
Milwaukee County, WI	3,025	2,884	2,525	3,037	2,963	2,710	3,000	2,974	2,835	100.8	97.0	89.1
Travis County, TX	2,533	2,459	2,722	2,662	2,434	2,691	3,137	3,008	3,659	80.7	81.7	74.4
Bernalillo County, NM	2,589	2,724	2,688	2,607	2,636	2,689	2,236	2,236	2,236	115.8	121.8	120.2
Kern County, CA	2,368	2,291	2,364	2,372	2,405	2,483	2,698	2,698	2,698	87.8	84.9	87.6
Cobb County, GA	2,467	2,369	2,373	2,579	2,440	2,369	2,559	2,559	3,451	96.4	92.6	68.8
King County, WA	2,517	2,437	2,328	2,657	2,426	2,343	3,154	3,154	3,154	79.8	77.3	73.8
York County, PA	2,235	2,238	2,264	2,211	2,262	2,284	2,446	2446	2,497	91.4	91.5	90.7
Suffolk County, MA[h]	2,494	2,399	2,934	2,455	2,463	2,280	2,990	2,644	2,644	83.4	90.7	111.0

Jurisdiction	Number of inmates[a]			Average daily Population[b]			Rated capacity[c]			Percent of capacity occupied[d]		
	2008	2009	2010	2008	2009	2010	2008	2009	2010	2008	2009	2010
Mecklenburg County, NC	2,647	2,285	2,258	2,610	2,496	2,274	2,668	2,668	2,988	99.2	85.6	75.6
Fulton County, FL	2,821	3,026	2,271	2,789	2,970	2,269	3,115	2,949	2,652	90.6	102.6	85.6
Polk County, FL	2,369	2,293	2,214	2,456	2,315	2,268	1,808	1,808	1,808	131.0	126.8	122.5
Salt Lake County, UT	2,021	2,022	2,238	1,995	2,100	2,196	2,000	2,088	2,098	101.1	96.8	106.7
Essex County, NJ	2,389	2,365	2,136	2,260	2,300	2,151	2,434	2,434	2,434	98.2	9 7.2	87.8
Denver County, CO	2,299	2,217	2,085	2,380	2,248	2,101	1,792	1,792	2,377	128.3	123.7	87.7
Oklahoma County, Ok	2,263	2,133	2,100	2,150	2,145	2,100	2,635	2,635	2,635	85.9	80.9	79.7
Marion County, IN[e]	2,336	2,541	2,303	2,344	2,485	2,096	2,656	2,656	2,599	88.0	95.7	88.6
Clayton County, GA	1,997	1,991	1,966	1,958	1,900	2,080	2,146	2,162	2,162	93.1	92.1	90.9
Franklin County, OH	2,544	2,313	2,194	2,457	2,251	2,041	2,541	2,541	2,541	100.1	91.0	86.3

NOTE: Jurisdictions are ordered by their average daily population in 2010.

/Not reported.

[a]Number of inmates held in jail facilities on the last weekday in June. Based on revised data from selected jail jurisdictions for the number of inmates confined at midyear 2008 and 2009. See *Methodology* for a description of revised data.

[b]Based on the average daily population for the year ending June 30. Average daily population is the sum of all inmates in jail each day for a year, divided by the number of days in the year. Based on revised data for selected jail jurisdictions in 2009.

[c]Number of beds or inmates assigned by a rating official to facilities within each jurisdiction.

[d]Number of inmates at midyear divided by the rated capacity and multiplied by 100

[e]Includes privately operated facilities

[f]Confined population total for Clark County, NV, excludes inmates held in contract facilities.

[g]Includes the Central Detention Facility (D.C. Jail), Correctional Treatment Facility (Contract Adult Detention Center), and contractual bed space at four halfway houses. The maximum physical capacity is fixed at the Central Detention Facility and Correctional Treatment Facility, and new capacity has not been constructed since 2003. The Central Detention Facility capacity is capped by D.C. Statute at 2,164, and the contracted bed space varies annually per budget and operational requirements.

[h]Data for 2008 and 2009 exclude inmates held in the pre-trial facility. In 2010, inmates held in the pre-trial facility are included.

SOURCE: Minton, T. D. (2011). *Jail inmates at midyear 2010.* Washington, DC: Bureau of Justice Statistics.

Florida; Shelby County, Tennessee), most large jail systems operate at 90% percent capacity or more. Some of these systems operate with capacities over 100% of what they were intended to hold. Thus, jail systems in large metropolitan areas tend to have large offender populations that push the limit of what dedicated facilities can handle.

The large number of offenders in larger metropolitan areas, coupled with the various issues prevalent among the offender population (e.g., substance abuse, mental health issues, medical issues), requires that these facilities provide more comprehensive services. While larger jail systems may have more staff and the ability to provide more extensive services than jail systems located in rural regions of the United States, it seems that these services are provided just enough to meet the demand; more money from city tax dollars simply corresponds with the need for more extensive services. Thus, large jail systems often find themselves strapped, despite their larger revenue base in the community, due to the corresponding needs of offenders who are drawn from this larger population base in the metropolitan area.

Podular Direct-Supervision Jails

During the 1980s, a new kind of jail was under construction in the United States. The two key components of this new type of jail, the **podular jail**, included rounded or "podular" architecture for living units and a "direct," as opposed to indirect, form of supervision of inmates by security staff. In short, security staff would be present in the living units at all times. It was thought that this architectural design would complement the staff's ability to supervise the inmate population while negating the ability of predatory inmates to control a cell block or dormitory. Other important facets of this type of jail was the provision of more goods and services in these units (e.g., more access to telephone privileges, visiting booths, and library facilities) and a more enriched dialogue between staff and inmates. This, in turn, enhances the staff's knowledge of individual inmates—their personalities, issues, and challenges. Such knowledge improves both security and the day-to-day operational aspects of the jail.

As would be expected, the role of the jail officer needed to adapt to this different paradigm of institutional design and operation. Zupan (1991) identified seven critical areas of new-generation jail officer behavior that included the following:

1. Proactive leadership and conflict resolution skills.

2. Building a respectful relationship with inmates.

3. Uniform and predictable enforcement of the rules.

4. Active observation of all inmate behavior within the living space.

5. Attending to inmate requests with respect and dignity.

6. Disciplining inmates in a fair and consistent manner.

7. Having an organized and open supervisory style.

Though many of these principles may seem commonsense in nature, the effects of the day-to-day challenges of jail operations, coupled with the difficulties in dealing with the jail offender population, require that agencies provide training in these areas (Zupan, 1991). This training must be reinforced by leadership in the jail and must also be reinforced with future in-service training for officers. Over time, an organizational culture within the jail will develop that will reflect these principles, if they are reinforced sufficiently.

Though podular direct-supervision jails or prisons are not necessarily a panacea for all the challenges associated with jail operation, they are a significant improvement over more traditional jail designs. When operated effectively and when they have the most critical design components, they tend to be less costly, primarily due to the fact that fewer lawsuits occur and fewer prevail than at jail facilities using other designs (Stohr, Walsh, & Hemmens, 2008). This is naturally due to the fact that the open nature of the design prevents most incidents from escalating into grounds for a lawsuit.

Reference Link 5.1
Read about new generation jails and see an architectural design of one.

Community Jails, Intermediate Sanctions, and Reentry Programs for Jails

Other innovations in jail operations include the development of community jails as well as reentry programs (Stohr et al., 2008). Community jails are devised so that programming provided on the outside (i.e., in the community) does not end at the jail facility. Rather, the programming is continued on a continuum that extends beyond incarceration and well into the community. This is an important concept because it addresses the fact that many jail inmates return to the jail facility, primarily because many of their needs are not met. Once in the community, inmates with special needs and/or a lack of resources simply resort back to criminal behavior, and the already full jail system once again must absorb the offenders into the burgeoning population. Thus, regardless of whether the inmates are in or out of the facility, their needs are addressed and services are provided so that they

PHOTO 5.1

Caddo Parish Correctional Center (seen here) houses a jail reentry program that operates on the premise that inmates who receive reentry programming will be less likely to lead a life of crime in the future.

can reintegrate into the community with greater success. This then lowers crime in the longest of terms since recidivism is lowered.

Further, as we will see in Chapter 7, there is a wide range of intermediate sanctions that can be used with offenders, including jail offenders (see Table 5.3). These intermediate sanctions will be covered in much more depth in Chapter 7, but, for now, students should know that some jails include weekend programs, electronic monitoring, home detention, day reporting, and community service, among others. This means that a stint in jail, for some offenders, may actually be a stint that is part-time in jail and part-time in the community. This blurring of the sentence and the type of confinement serves many purposes, such as the easing of overcrowding as well as a means for jail offenders to keep their employment so as to afford fines and fees while they are in jail.

Jail reentry programs are somewhat similar in nature but focus more on the fact that, ultimately, the inmate is likely to be on some form of community supervision. Thus, jail reentry programs tend to be interlaced with probation and parole agencies as a means of integrating the supervisory functions of both the jail and the community supervision agencies. Amidst this, the continued care of the offender's specific needs is addressed (similar to community jails). One study found that effective interventions to improve reentry include everything from referral to counseling to drug treatment, depending on the needs of the offender. However, community safety must remain paramount, especially if agencies hope to have support from community members in the surrounding areas. Because reentry is a complicated process that requires a team approach among many different agencies and personnel, it requires that jail staff and

TABLE 5.3   Confinement Status of Jail Inmates

Persons under jail supervision, by confinement status and type of program, midyear 2000 and 2006–2010						
Confinement status and type of program	Number of persons under jail supervision					
	2000	2006	2007	2008	2009	2010
Total[a]	687,033	826,041	848,419	858,388	837,647	809,360
Held in jail[a]	621,149	765,819	780,174	785,536	767,434	748,728
Supervised outside of a jail facility[b]	65,884	60,222	68,245	72,852	70,213	60,632
Weedend programs[c]	14,523	11,421	10,473	12,325	11,212	9,871
Electronic Monitoring	10,782	10,999	13,121	13,539	11,834	12,319
Home detention[d]	332	807	512	498	738	736
Day reporting	3,969	4,841	6,163	5,758	6,492	5,552
Community service	13,592	14,667	15,327	18,475	17,738	14,646
Other pretrial supervision	6,279	6,409	11,148	12,452	12,439	9,375
Other word programs[d]	8,011	8,319	7,369	5,808	5,912	4,351
Treatment programs[f]	5,714	1,486	2,276	2,259	2,082	1,799
Other	2,682	1,273	1,857	1,739	1,766	1,983

[a]Based on revised data from selected jail jurisdictions for the number of inmates confined at midyear 2008 and 2009. See *Methodology* for a description of revised data.

[b]Excludes persons supervised by a probation or parole agency.

[c]Programs that allow offenders to serve their sentences of confinement on weekends only (i.e., Friday to Sunday).

[d]Includes only persons without electronic monitoring.

[e]Includes persons in work release programs, work gangs, and other alternative work programs.

[f]Includes persons under drug, alcohol, mental health, and other medical treatment.

SOURCE: Minton, T. D. (2011). *Jail inmates at midyear 2010*. Washington, DC: Bureau of Justice Statistics.

administrators prioritize the needs that they target and the interventions that will be applied while also considering the network of community agencies that will provide these services. In fact, Hanser (2010) notes that this requires a collaborative process between custodial staff (jail security and treatment staff) and members of surrounding agencies, while at the same time including members of the community in the process. Such collaborative efforts can educate the community on the process of reentry, builds rapport between the community and the jail facility, and enhances the supervision of offenders since more eyes will be upon them within the community. Incidentally, this also provides the offenders with enriched support, thereby increasing the likelihood for motivated offenders to rebuild their future lives.

JAILS AS SHORT-TERM INSTITUTIONS

According to Kerle (1999), **short-term jails** are facilities that hold sentenced inmates for no more than one year. A jail, particularly a short-term jail, is an institution where both pretrial and sentenced inmates are confined. A lockup is often a police-operated facility where individuals who have been arrested are held for 24 to 72 hours, depending on the circumstances and the jurisdiction. Once a maximum of 72 hours has elapsed, the inmate held in the lockup is transferred to the local jail where he or she is admitted. Lockups exist in most all larger cities because they make the arrest and booking process more convenient and less complicated. Once inmates are in the lockup, other personnel transport them to the jail. Lockups are often housed at the police station itself, and they are the true "holding cell" type of facility, used for no other purpose.

Kerle (1999) notes that lockups should actually be used sparingly, if at all. Much of this has to do with the fact that most police agencies cannot sufficiently man and operate such a facility. Also, it is during the first 24 to 48 hours that inmates are most vulnerable to mental health issues, potential medical complications, and suicide. Since most lockups are not well staffed and the stay of these offenders is very short-term in nature, Kerle (1999) points to the International Association of Chiefs of Police (IACP), which encourages police agencies to refrain from using lockups as much as is feasible.

PHOTO 5.2

The sally port is used as a location where inmates can be transported into the bay area with the front gate closed behind them. This then allows for the second door or gate to open, admitting the inmates into the facility without having any point of potential escape since the outer door/gate is closed and locked.

The Booking Area

The most important area in short-term and long-term jail facilities is where intakes occur, usually called the booking area (Kerle, 1999). There are greater risks in the booking area than in other areas of the jail due to the fact that so many offenders and suspected offenders enter and exit the jail from this point. It is important that staff in booking areas keep very good records related to the intake of an inmate. Indeed, if the appropriate arrest or commitment papers are not possessed, then the suspected offender cannot be legally confined. Because it is the responsibility of booking officers to ensure that these records are maintained, their job as the entry point in the jail custodial process becomes even more serious (Kerle, 1999).

Most all booking areas have what is commonly referred to as a "sally port" that is adjacent to the booking area. The sally-port is a secure area where vehicles can enter, with the area being closed after the transport vehicle has entered the compound. A **sally port** allows security staff to bring vehicles close to the admissions area in a secure fashion. In many small jails, a sally port may not exist, and, in such cases, additional care in the processing of inmates is required in order to make sure that security is provided (Kerle, 1999).

Most offenders who are arrested and brought into the booking area are under the influence of drugs or alcohol, or they may present with some type of other factor that impairs their functioning. The stress level of those being booked is likely to be heightened, and this means that they are likely to be more problematic. Some of these individuals will present with aggressive responses and may be assaultive. It is commonly observed that jail altercations occur in the booking area rather than in other areas of the jail.

Jails also book a large number of persons with mental disturbances, this often occurring in tandem with drug and alcohol problems. Because of this, the booking officer must be able to identify unusual behavior, perhaps being trained through in-service processes to observe sudden shifts in mood or personality, hallucinations, intense anxiety, paranoia, delusion, and loss of memory (Kerle, 1999). Further, as noted above, the risk of suicide is greater in jail facilities than in prisons, particularly during the first 48 hours and especially if the person is under the influence of alcohol or drugs. The booking officer and other staff must be quick to screen for potential suicide in all circumstances, noting mental health, substance abuse, or other factors that might exacerbate its likelihood.

Due to the challenges associated with the booking process and the types of offenders that will be seen, it is important to have some kind of holding cell located near the booking area. Holding cells can be useful for detoxifying short-term inmates. The use of holding cells allows staff to book inmates without having distractions from other inmates while completing the admission process (Kerle, 1999). In short, holding cells tend to alleviate much of the chaos associated with booking. While the use of a holding cell may seem to be common sense, many smaller jails cannot afford the luxury of jail space that is not specifically used to house an inmate for a period longer than 72 hours, an indication of how cash-strapped many of these agencies tend to be (Kerle, 1999).

Issues With Booking Female Inmates

In the past few years, there has been a rise in the number (and proportion) of females who are housed in jails. Because female offenders, just like male offenders, may stay anywhere from a day to a year in the jail facility, it is important that staff are trained on issues related to female confinement. In this instance, it is certainly a benefit to have female employees available to assist in processing these offenders. However, the job of "jailer" tends to be male dominated, and this means that in some jails female officers may not be present during one or several shifts (Kerle, 1999).

Male officers who work in the booking area should be provided with additional training to ensure sensitivity to female issues. This also has advantages from a legal perspective, since male officers should use good professional discretion when processing female offenders. Given that inappropriate staff-on-inmate relations have been identified in recent years as an area of concern, it is important that male staff make a point to safeguard themselves from allegations.

Lastly, Kerle (1999) notes that booking forms and documents should be inclusive enough to contain questions about physical and sexual abuse, as a sign that jail administrators recognize these issues as serious. This provides documentation that can be important should later allegations result in grievances or courtroom lawsuits. Aside from legal concerns, it is also useful for jail staff to develop an awareness of their own impact upon the situation, both in how they may serve to heighten stress and generate hostility among entering inmates.

Information Technology and Integration

Unfortunately, there has been very little integration of systems between agencies and even within the police agency in regard to jail data. In many agencies, police officers and jailers of the same agency do not engage in routine information exchange. While this does tend to be true among agencies, it is not because high-quality information technology products do not exist. For instance, the SmartJAIL system, developed by CTS America, provides all the information needed to manage data and processes for jails of any size or complexity. SmartJAIL tracks and manages all aspects of an inmate's stay in a correctional facility. SmartJAIL is integrated with a name index and initial arrest reports (within the records management system)

Video Link 5.3
Watch as officers process new jail admissions.

Journal Article Link 5.2
Read about a screening instrument that identifies depression and anxiety disorders in female detainees.

to help speed up the booking process by using information already collected in these other programs. The system supports cell assignments, and tracks inmate movements, activities, and events. SmartJAIL also accounts for personal property, mug shots, visitors, and inmate accounts, and includes historical bookings. SmartJAIL is equipped to do the following:

- **Jail Booking:** Tracks inmate booking, including mug shots, medical screening information, inmate property items, and all events involving the inmate.

- **Inmate Visitation:** Tracks the date and time of each visit made to an inmate.

- **Inmate Transportation and Movement:** Tracks the movement of inmates by displaying all scheduled inmate movements, allowing time for the arrangement of transportation and scheduling.

- **Jail Management Configuration:** Maintains lists for use by other jail management modules, including bed and cell locations, vehicles for transport, destinations, judges, and gain-time calculations.

- **Jail Log:** Enables officers to keep an electronic duty log to report activities or information to other officers.

- **Jail Incidents:** Records incidents requiring use of force, disciplinary action, or institutional charges against an inmate.

- **Jail Medical:** Records medical visits made by an inmate, including the initial medical screening. Historical records are maintained for easy review of an inmate's health.

- **Jail Commissary:** Tracks inmate banking and purchasing at the commissary.

- **Jail Search:** Provides administrators an easy, fast way to locate inmate records based on extensive search criteria.

- **Jail Administrative Reports:** Provides administrators easy access to dozens of the most commonly used reports in the system, including billing reports and statistical reports required by the federal government.

- **Mobile Inmate Tracking:** Designed for handheld devices, this module checks inmates in and out of a facility by scanning inmate ID tags and providing accurate historical tracking records.

From the above description, it is clear that automated systems exist that hold a large amount of information. Whether this information is utilized to its fullest potential is debatable. The lack of communication between agencies and even within agencies limits the use of much of the information that is stored. Over time, it is expected that jail systems will increasingly share data, both with other jail facilities and with police agencies whose officers may come into contact with jailed offenders who are subject to eventual release. This last application of information exchange can be particularly valuable when combating gang offenders who tend to cycle in and out from the community to the jail and back again.

JAILS AS LONG-TERM FACILITIES

Since the 1990s, an increasing number of larger jails have been required to house inmates who serve sentences that exceed the typical one-year term. Understandably, jail facilities and the staff at those facilities have had difficulty maintaining these types of populations. Most jails are simply not designed or constructed to house inmates on a long-term basis. These facilities often lack the space for programming and education, as well as full recreational facilities that would be necessary for long-term populations. The use of jails for long-term inmates can be traced to the following three broad reasons:

1. The use of longer jail sentences has resulted in the more extensive use of jails in many jurisdictions.

2. Many local and regional jurisdictions have been required to house inmates who have been sentenced to state prisons. This is because many state prisons have been so crowded that they have been unable to accept the newly sentenced offenders.

3. Some local jurisdictions have leased out beds to other jurisdictions, such as state correctional systems. These contractual agreements have created income for local sheriffs who oversee these jail facilities. This has created a situation where some sheriffs actively solicit state correctional systems for inmates to fill their beds—sometimes even soliciting systems outside of their own state, when feasible.

As crowding in state prisons became a longer-term problem, many jails began to hold sentenced inmates for anywhere from two to five years in duration (Wallenstein & Kerle, 2008). In 2004, jail facilities held roughly 5% of all state and federal inmates (roughly 74,000 inmates). The southern area of the United States held the largest number of sentenced inmates in local jails (roughly 60,000 inmates). Table 5.4 contains data regarding jail facilities that house long-term inmates. Note that the states of Louisiana, Tennessee, and Kentucky utilize this approach with great frequency. Indeed, nearly half of all state inmates are in local jail facilities in Louisiana.

TABLE 5.4 State and Federal Prisoners Held in Local Jails

Total population of state and federal inmates held in local jails:		
2003	73,440	
2004	74,445	
During the above years, approximately 5% of all U.S. inmates were housed in local jails.		
Total population of state and federal inmates held in local jails throughout the southern region of the United States (region with greatest use of jails for state inmates):		
2003	60,810	
2004	62,966	
Percentage of state inmate population housed in local jails (those having 20% or more):		
2004	Louisiana	47.3%
2004	Kentucky	28.5%
2004	Tennessee	25.4%
2004	Mississippi	22.0%
2004	West Virginia	21.3%

SOURCE: Harrison, P., & Beck, A. (2005). *Prisoners in 2004*. Washington, DC: Bureau of Justice Statistics.

State Rankings Link 5.1
Percent of State Prisoners Held in Local Jails in 2009.

Local Jails That House State Inmates

Many of the excess jail inmates in recent years have been the legal responsibility of various state correctional facilities. However, many state correctional administrators allowed these state inmates to be held in jails to relieve prison overcrowding. Some states had more problems with overcrowding than did others. We discuss two states that exemplify differences in overcrowding and the means by which jails provided relief to these burgeoning systems. We will focus on the prison systems of Texas and New York.

PHOTO 5.3

Correctional health care is an important area of service delivery in institutions. These professionals deal with a variety of issues that are complicated by the criminogenic lifestyles of most inmates who are their patients.

In Texas, thousands of state inmates were placed into county-level jails. Much of the reason for this had to do with a significant legal development related to the Supreme Court ruling in *Ruiz v. Estelle*

(1980). In this ruling (which students should recall from Chapter 2), the Texas prison system was found to be in violation of the Eighth Amendment prohibition against cruel and unusual punishments due to inadequate, unhealthy, and abusive prison practices in operation. One of the key issues in this case addressed the overcrowded facilities that existed in that system. Ultimately, this case resulted in population capacity limitations being imposed on various facilities throughout the system. This resulted in approximately 21,000 state offenders being detained in jails since the state prison system was unable to accommodate these inmates.

Later lawsuits between county jails and the state prison system resulted in the state being forced to meet its statutory obligation (see *County of Nueces, Texas, v. Texas Board of Corrections*, 1989) to house inmates. If unable to meet this obligation, the plaintiffs for the county jails contended that the state of Texas would need to, at a minimum, reimburse county governments for the expense of housing such inmates. The Fifth Circuit federal court agreed, and the state was forced to pay counties a specified daily amount for each state-level inmate held within county jail facilities. This total amount ultimately added up to well over $100 million in compensation, a hefty sum by any account (Wallenstein & Kerle, 2008).

In New York, the situation was similar to that in Texas. The state prison system in New York, unable to accommodate all of the inmates assigned to its charge, left some inmates in local jails. In the later part of the 1980s, a collective lawsuit from the state sheriff's association successfully sued the state prison system. State courts ruled that the state prison system would be required to accept all state inmates within 10 days of readiness. According to Wallenstein and Kerle (2008), by the end of 2002, only 320 state inmates were kept in county jails throughout New York. By 2005 the total number had further dropped to only 11 inmates (Wallenstein & Kerle, 2008). This demonstrates that, when given incentive, state governments can and will find the means to meet their obligation to incarcerate inmates, or, at the very least, they are able to refrain from exploiting county-level jail systems in the process.

Jails as Overflow Facilities: For a Fee

In many states, sheriffs have begun to see the operation of jail facilities as a potential money-making endeavor. This is true in states like Louisiana, where inmates from the Department of Corrections are routinely assigned to jail facilities, operated by local sheriffs, for a set fee that is paid to the sheriffs' agency. In many cases, for rural regions, this may be a primary source of revenue and may also provide several jobs in the area that would otherwise not exist. Some critics of this type of operation note that this creates a sort of dependency on the state inmate population. On the other hand, proponents note that this type of system helps to keep costs down, eliminates the need for reduced sentences among offenders who should be kept locked up, and also disseminates revenue to areas of the state that are cash-strapped. So long as the local population does not object, it would seem that such forms of operation are win-win for both local and state government.

Going even further, some jail systems have taken inmates from states outside of where they are actually located. For instance, the Spokane County Jail in Washington State agreed to take inmates, for an agreed-upon fee, from the District of Columbia Department of Corrections (Washington, DC). In another instance, Texas jails in Denton County contracted with the state of Oregon's prison system to house inmates. In this case, Denton County added stipulations that Oregon inmates would have to return to Oregon for their release and also that all accepted inmates would need to have at least two years remaining on their sentence. Denton County also later set up similar contracts with the U.S. Immigration and Naturalization Service (since 2003 called U.S. Citizenship and Immigration Services) to hold federal detainees. Thus, it is clear that jail systems have been used as money-making ventures with such partnerships consisting of jurisdictions that may span very different regions of the nation.

Jail Overcrowding and the Matrix Classification System

In many of the larger jail systems, issues related to overcrowding have led to lawsuits and legal concerns that plague jail administrators. This has prompted officials in various jurisdictions to build even more jail facilities and to add onto those that already exist. Often, this results in the need to generate revenue to finance this construction, which often is obtained through the use of bonds. In many cases, bonds must be passed by the voting community, and this means that, in addition to everything else, the jail becomes a political issue whereby sheriff's offices attempt to get bond referendums passed for the construction of more jail space. In some instances, voters are not receptive to the needs of the sheriff's agency and then fail to elect for such bonds.

Wallenstein and Kerle (2008) point to this occurring in Multnomah County, Oregon. They note that in the 1980s, voters had twice rejected potential bonds to build more jail space as well as rehabilitation-related projects. During this time, the federal court had placed the county facility under federal court order due to the crowding issues that existed. In 1986, the federal court allowed the sheriff to release inmates prematurely as a means of keeping jail populations within the limits of the facility's capacity.

Multnomah County developed what is now known as the matrix system, which was designed to release inmates early from the jail when the facility's population exceeds the capacity of the structure. This system is designed to first release the least dangerous offenders, determined via a computerized scoring system. With this system, an individual who was booked into the jail was scored on the basis of the charges and failure to appear after being served a warrant. The matrix system was used to the control the population in custody without placing the community at additional risk of harm. Specifically, this system was designed to meet the following goals:

- Remain an objective tool of assessment.

- Allow for the use of additional information related to potential danger, if it can be measured objectively.

- Have all functions fully automated.

- Identify dangerous inmates and prevent their release.

Wallenstein and Kerle (2008) note that from the beginning of Multnomah County's use of the matrix, over 10,000 inmates have been released to reduce crowding. Assessment and classification programs such as the matrix have become more and more important in many jail and prison facilities. When combined with the housing of long-term inmates, the overcrowding issue in jails becomes much more difficult in prisons, particularly since jails hold both convicted offenders and persons being detained until they see a judge.

JAIL POPULATIONS AND CHARACTERISTICS

According to data provided by the Bureau of Justice Statistics, roughly 714,000 persons are held in jails throughout the year (Harrison & Beck, 2005). However, this number does not truly reflect how integral the jail is to the American criminal justice system, as a whole. In terms of the total number of persons processed within jails throughout the year, it is estimated that anywhere from 10 million to 15 million persons enter and exit jail facilities in the United States. When compared with an overall prison population of approximately 1.4 million, it seems that jails process approximately 10 times the amount of inmates than do prisons throughout a given year.

Most individuals who are booked in jails remain for short periods of time that range from just a few hours to several months. The majority of infractions that entail contact with jails include misdemeanor crimes, substance abuse issues, domestic crimes, and public safety issues. In addition, it is common for persons involved in the illicit sex industry (i.e., prostitutes and their customers), as well as persons who fail to appear for court hearings, to routinely land in jail. Thus, jails consist of a changing population of offenders who have a variety of legal infractions, leading to a diverse array of offenders, legally speaking. Students are encouraged to examine Table 5.5 for additional information regarding offenders in jail facilities.

HEALTH CARE IN JAILS

One of the largest health care systems that exist within the United States can be found in jails. Nearly every person who enters a jail receives some sort of basic screening and evaluation. This is necessary to maintain constitutional requirements, risk avoidance, and institutional safety concerns. Indeed, offenders in jails have a number of health care problems. According to a 2002 study of jail inmates conducted by the Bureau of Justice Statistics, more than a third of all jail inmates, or approximately 229,000 inmates, reported some sort of medical problem that was more serious than a cold or the flu

TABLE 5.5   Characteristics of Jail Inmates

Estimated percentages of local jail inmates, by selected characteristic and ratio estimates, 2010		
Characteristic	*Estimate*	*Standard error*
Sex		
Male	87.7%	0.10%
Female	12.3	0.10
Race/Hispanic origin		
White[a]	44.3%	0.41%
Black/African American[a]	37.8	0.39
Hispanic/Latino	15.8	0.30
Other[a,b]	1.3	0.17
Two or more races[a]	0.6	0.03
Conviction status[c]		
Convicted	38.9%	0.42%
Unconvicted	61.1%	0.42%

NOTE: Detail may not sum to total due to rounding.

[a]Excludes persons of Hispanic or Latino origin.

[b]Includes American Indians, Alaska Natives, Asians, Native Hawaiians, and other Pacific Islanders.

[c]Includes juveniles who were tried or awaiting trial as adults.

SOURCE: Minton, T.D. (2011). *Jail inmates at midyear 2010.* Washington, DC: Bureau of Justice Statistics.

PHOTO 5.4

In today's correctional environment, women are commonly employed in institutional settings, including jails.

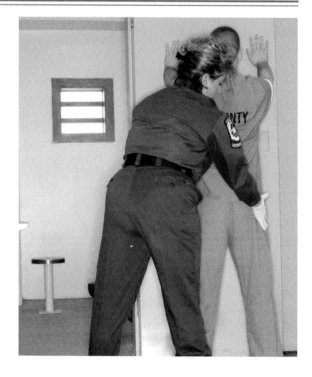

(Maruschak, 2006). Most medical problems tend to precede the offender's placement into the jail system and include problems such as HIV/AIDS, hepatitis, sexually transmitted diseases, tuberculosis, heart disease and diabetes, women's issues, and disorders related to aging. This is not to mention issues related to substance abuse that affect many of the inmates encountered in jails.

Other issues related to the health and well-being of jail inmates include diet and exercise, special needs prisoners (i.e., mentally ill, disabled, or some other special characteristic), sexual assault issues, and/or pregnancy. This places numerous and varied demands upon jail staff and the resources within jails. Because of this, jail staff have learned to cooperate as a means of providing service delivery, meaning that medical staff and security must work in tandem with one another.

As one might expect, the elderly are much more prone to some medical problems than are the young population of inmates. According to the 2002 Bureau of Justice Statistics study, approximately 61% of those over 45 reported a medical problem when in jail (Stohr et al., 2008). "With the exception of asthma and HIV, which tended to be more prevalent among younger inmates, the older inmates were much more likely" to have medical problems, which makes older inmates more costly to house than younger inmates (Stohr et al., 2008, p. 501). Thus, when and where feasible, it is often in the best interest of the jail administrator to have nondangerous elderly offenders released as soon as possible due to their exorbitant medical costs. Naturally, this should not be done at the expense of public safety; but in those cases where the elderly offender is kept for nuisance crimes and other such petty issues, it is likely that jail facilities will process these offenders out as soon as is reasonable.

Like older inmates, women were also much more likely to report medical problems (53% for female inmates as opposed to 35% for male inmates). Female inmates indicated a cancer rate that was nearly 8 times that of male inmates, with the most common form of cancer for women being cervical. Indeed, for every medical problem documented in the study, female inmates reported more prevalence than male offenders, except for paralysis and tuberculosis (Stohr et al., 2008). Thus, female inmates tend to have more health care concerns than do male inmates. This means that housing these inmates presents a plethora of issues in the way of security procedures, specialized needs, and health care considerations.

In many respects, jails have not been given the attention that they deserve. This is particularly true in regard to the training of staff. The National Institute of Corrections has, in recent years, published numerous manuals and videos and has also provided a variety of training programs for jail staff and leadership. This has been in response to the realization that jails have traditionally been overlooked until this recent decade. Indeed, the training of jail staff has a fairly short history, having started only 50 years ago with the Federal Bureau of Prisons (BOP). Formal training began in the BOP when federal agencies became concerned that states were not adequately training their jail staff. At this time, the BOP established a training school for sheriffs and jailers in 1948.

The existence of formal training standards varies quite considerably from state to state. Most of the short-term jails tend to use on-the-job training. This can create many problems since such training tends to be unorganized, with gaps in the required knowledge that staff must have to be truly competent. Since many new staff must learn through a process of trial and error, the incidence of lawsuits tends to rise, and, even worse, the likelihood that inmate plaintiffs prevail in court against the agency also correspondingly increases. This is one of the primary reasons that many police agencies choose to refrain from operating a jail facility; the legal liability and responsibility offset the value of the convenience.

Language, Ethnic Diversity, and the Selection of Staff

Inmates processed in jail intake units reflect the cultural and linguistic diversity that exists throughout the United States. Because of this, it is important that staff have linguistic skills and that they are knowledgeable about different cultures, particularly those likely to be in the jail facility in their area. The need that staff be able to work with a diverse array of inmates has developed a corresponding need for a diverse staff. Indeed, this can extend into the multinational realm as well as the multicultural realm. Consider, for example, that in California jails may house a substantial number of Asian offenders as well as Latino offenders. In some areas of the northeastern United States, the need for Jamaican, Russian, or Ukrainian staff may exist. Thus, jail administrators face the need to develop a workforce that reflects the composition of the offender population in their area.

PHOTO 5.5

The author is a trainer at a regional academy for jailers and police officers. Hanser is seen here providing instruction to a corrections academy at North Delta Regional Training Academy.

Challenges Faced by Female Staff

Female staff face a number of challenges that are not as often encountered among male staff. In many jails, women are not afforded the same respect as men, both by the inmates and by their fellow officers. Much of this may have to do with the inmate subculture, the organizational culture of the agency, and other factors that impact a female officer's professional development in law enforcement. Likewise, since so many of the inmates are male, female officers find themselves a minority among both the inmates and the officers. Thus, many female officers are utilized with female inmates, when and where possible, to alleviate concerns with searches and maintenance security as well as medical issues common to female offenders.

Other Employee Issues

There are approximately 300,000 jail staff around the country. Typically, these staff are underpaid in relation to other law enforcement officers and/or correctional officers in state (rather than local) facilities. Many of these employees take these jobs on a temporary basis while waiting for openings in other areas of their sheriff's agency. However, many of these employees have only limited education and/or skill development and do not fare as well in the competition for better positions and, therefore, find themselves in their position for longer periods of time. However, some truly do find the work rewarding and/or develop a set

Video Link 5.4
Learn more about the responsibilities of jail staff.

Journal Article Link 5.3
Read about predictors of job satisfaction for jail officers.

PHOTO 5.6

Jail deputies pictured here are commissioned peace officers who maintain the facility. Their job requires that they work with offenders who often process into the jail from their own local/regional area. Because of this, they are usually very much aware of inmates' criminal tendencies, both in the jail facility and out in the community.

of specialized skills within the jail that make them invaluable to the jail's operation. For these individuals, working in the jail becomes as lucrative as (and perhaps even more lucrative than) working in other positions in the agency. One example is training officers in jail settings who, over time, can become quite sought out among other agencies and can command a high wage for their knowledge and expertise.

For the most part, jailers do not seem to have an effective career track that is sufficiently rewarding in many jurisdictions. Turnover is very high, with many jails reporting a complete change in staff every few years. This has generated a serious concern regarding the quality of employees in many jails as well as the quality of their training. As a means of improving the quality of training for jailers throughout the nation, the National Institute of Corrections Jails Division has implemented programs to increase the number of trainers for jail staff to ensure that there are enough opportunities for training among employees of various agencies. While this is an admirable approach, the true long-term answer to this problem is an increase in pay and career incentives for these employees—thereby translating to justification for better requirements.

EVOLVING PROFESSIONALISM

Prison Tour Video Link 5.1
Watch the author discuss ongoing training and technology.

One of the most direct means of increasing professionalism in the jailer's career track is to utilize what Stohr et al. (2008) refer to as coequal staffing. In this type of staffing, programs provide comparable pay and benefits to those who work in the jail and those who work in routine law enforcement positions. In some jurisdictions, agencies have created two career tracks—one for law enforcement and the other for jailers—with equal pay. There is some evidence that this approach has had a phenomenal effect on the professional operation of jails (they are better staffed) and on the morale of those assigned to them (Stohr et al., 2008).

As our jails become more professionalized, the requirements for training and higher entry standards become more important. In fact, some states now require that jail officers be certified through some type of official academy training. Even though this is the case, in many places that require such training, it still tends to fall shorter than the number of hours required in traditional law enforcement

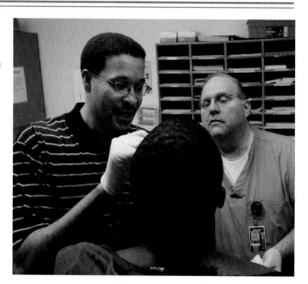

PHOTO 5.7

Given the possibility of contracting communicable diseases and/or viruses, jail staff must wear protective gear just as do their counterparts in the medical profession.

positions. Silverman (2001) notes that the reluctance of local jurisdictions to meet their training obligation has served as the impetus behind the American Jail Association's monthly training bulletins, which consist of video and web-based training segments. Lastly, refresher training is critical and is offered in many jurisdictions. Among the topics, the use of CPR, fire safety, aerosol pepper spray and taser proficiency, riot-control techniques, and human relations skills are examples of the diverse areas in which jailers must develop expertise.

As it turns out, and as noted above, the author of this text is the head administrator of a regional training academy that trains both jailers and law enforcement cadets. Requirements of the Peace Officer Standards and Training (POST) are used to guide agencies and training facilities in a number of states toward ensuring that jail officers have the requisite skills needed to perform their job assignment(s). Ensuring that jailers receive training that is top-quality, serious, professional, and well developed improves the jail systems in the area while also providing a clear message to jailers in training: Your job is important, and we take it seriously. The result is that the jailers take their job seriously as well, and employee morale tends to be much higher in local agencies throughout the region.

SPECIALIZED TYPES OF JAIL SENTENCES

Extended confinement of persons who, by legal standards, are presumed innocent until proven guilty, such as with pretrial detention of the nonadjudicated offender, creates a serious custody problem for jails that prisons are not forced to contend with. The defendant who is truly innocent, but is required to spend long periods of time in jail confinement, will eventually develop a sense of resentment toward the criminal justice system. Further, this simply does not smack of fundamental fairness and instead creates a situation where innocent persons feel victimized, even though that is not the intent. Thus, the use of specialized jail sentences can create "middle road" forms of custody that can help to mitigate these negative effects.

Weekend Confinement

Weekend confinement is used to lessen the negative impact of short-term incarceration and to allow those in custody to maintain their employment. Jurisdictions using **weekend confinement** have implemented methods of confinement that are restricted to the weekends or other times when the person in custody is off from work. In some respects, this can be likened to serving a sentence on an installment plan, whereby other aspects of life that keep the person functional in society are not impaired, yet, at the same time, the offender is required to pay for his or her crime through a series of small stints in jail. This type of weekend confinement typically is assigned to misdemeanants and usually requires that they check in on Friday evening and leave on Sunday at a specified time. This type of sentence, through the addition of stints throughout a number of months, adds up credit toward confinement until the total sentence is served. These types of sentences are used with minimum-security facilities and with offenders who have committed minor or petty crimes.

Reference Link 5.2
Read more about weekend confinement.

Community Work Orders

Sentencing judges occasionally order misdemeanants to complete a period of service to the community as a substitute for or to augment a sentence. In such cases, the offender volunteers his or her services to a community agency for a certain number of hours per week over a specified period of time. The total number of hours, often assessed at the legal minimum wage, is determined by the amount of a fine that might have been given for the offender's crime or another similar crime. This sentence is also typically referred to as community service and is usually given as part of a suspended sentence or of probation.

Community service is the work that individuals conduct in hopes of repaying their debt to society after being found at fault for committing a criminal or deviant offense. In most cases community service is ordered by the sentencing judge and supervised by the community supervision officer. Most judges prefer that offenders sentenced to complete community service do so at a not-for-profit agency within their local jurisdiction. Types of community service range from your typical trash pickups to caring for animals at an animal shelter or participating in menial labor at the local public facilities. Community service serves a dual purpose, both to rehabilitate and to punish offenders. In terms of rehabilitation, community service affords offenders a time to participate in something constructive, all the while providing them with an opportunity to build sweat equity in something that is beneficial to the community. Community service is punitive in that offenders are forced to give up their own time to work off their criminal debt without being paid.

At latest count, most U.S. states had some form of community service at either the juvenile or the adult offender level. Most offenders placed on probation are required to complete some specified amount of community service inclusive of various other conditions of probation. Though statutorily prescribed amounts of community service may be ordered, the amounts typically given out are very subjective, dependent upon the appropriate amount as determined by the presiding judge.

The amount of community service ranges, and in most cases offenders must find time to complete their hours within the confines of their normal workweek. For those offenders without employment, officers often require that they complete as many as 40 hours of community service per week until they have completed assignment. In certain jurisdictions offenders are allowed to work off some of their fines by completing additional hours of community service. Most cases call for the subjective determination of the value of the hours-to-community service ratio by the directors of such agencies. The standard has been that the offenders are provided at least minimum-wage credit for each hour of community service. Due to the low cost of overhead in funding community work order programs, coupled with the added use of much needed labor in communities, community work order options will continue to be well utilized by most larger jail systems.

Shock Incarceration/Split Sentences

For certain offenders the mere subjection to a loss of freedom is all that is needed to get their lives in order. As a result, the mechanism used for its stunning value is shock incarceration. **Shock incarceration** is short-term incarceration followed by a specified term of community supervision in hopes of deterring the offender from recidivating. Because the brief stint of incarceration is meant to provide a sense of punitive reality to the offender, most shock incarceration programs are designed for juvenile offenders and those who have never been incarcerated before. Given the basic tenets of shock incarceration it is mostly used in the form of mixed sentencing. In this case offenders are given a short term of confinement and then placed on community supervision to complete their term of probation or parole. In split sentencing, more commonly known as shock incarceration, offenders are sentenced to a term of confinement only to be released after a set time and ordered to serve the remainder of their time on probation. The logic behind such action is that the offender will develop a natural dislike of incarceration and will seek to abstain from criminal behavior in hopes of avoiding such unpleasant incarceration. It is believed that shock incarceration was developed in 1965. Vito and Allen (1981) held that shock incarceration should be viewed as a viable intermediate sanction because it (1) allows offenders the opportunity to realistically reintegrate into the community, (2) allows offenders to continue positive connections with existing family, (3) decreases the amount of time offenders spend in prison, (4) decreases prison populations, and (5) decreases the amount of funding spent on prisons. Research has demonstrated that at least three quarters of all shock incarceration programs show some sense of effectiveness.

SPECIAL ISSUES IN JAILS

As if the various categories of offenders and their movement into and out of the jail facility were not enough to complicate the job of jail staff and administrators, jail offenders also have a host of other issues with which jail systems must contend. Indeed, many jail inmates have problems with illiteracy, substance abuse, mental illness and stability, general medical conditions, and communicable diseases, as well as suicide ideation. Because many of these issues go untreated in the community, the jail becomes the dumping ground for these offenders. Thus, jails must service a diverse offender population with specialized problems and specialized needs. We now turn our attention to some of these specialized needs that emerge in the jail setting.

Substance-Abusing Offenders in Jails

Throughout the literature it is commonly noted that substance abuse issues are rampant within the jail population. This observation is true regardless of the region of the United States and/or the time of year at which one considers this point. Simply put, substance abuse is a major problem that confronts jails, and this problem impacts the day-to-day operation of jails, in terms of both security and programming. According to the Bureau of Justice Statistics 2002 study, fully 68% of all jail inmates report substance abuse or dependence problems (Karberg & James, 2005, p. 1). In fact, half of convicted inmates reported being under the influence of drugs or alcohol at the time they committed their offense, while another

APPLIED THEORY 5.1

Labeling Theory and the First-time Jail Inmate

According to labeling theory, individuals are more prone to commit future acts of crime if they are stigmatized by previous acts of deviance that are labeled unusual and are stigmatizing. Whether an act is stigmatizing depends on two points. First, the actions of those around the person will determine the social repercussions for that individual. If family, friends, society, and the criminal justice system respond in a manner that escalates the circumstances, it is likely that the experience will be stigmatizing. Likewise, if the experience lasts for a prolonged period of time, this, too, will likely make it stigmatizing.

In many cases, a person's initial stay at a jail will be short-term. While this may not, on the face of it, seem overly serious, this can, in actuality, be quite problematic for a person who has never been incarcerated. The entire experience is alien, and there is a very distinct sense of the unknown. One's safety is in the hands of others, and there are few options of recourse, at least for the short term. However, this experience, for most persons charged with a crime, is short-term and, while potentially traumatic, does subside once they leave the facility.

However, the experience does not end at this point. Rather, there are issues associated with postjail paperwork, bond payments, potential time missed at work, discussions with family, and a variety of other experiences that continue to remind the person of the experience and also serve as additional consequences for going to jail. In addition, the person now has a criminal record, which will also follow him or her for life.

It is at this point that labeling can have its most damaging impact. Often, this can serve as a key point at which individuals may decide that, since things have already taken a turn for the worse, there is less harm if they continue to dabble in those activities that are questionable. This can particularly be true if these are, say, vice crimes like prostitution, small-time drug use, or drinking and driving. Further, because these persons will have this record on them, they are more vulnerable to detection should they do this behavior again. Thus a cycle can develop where they may be more prone to engage in deviant behavior, and, because they have been detected once, they are at increased odds of getting detected. This then results in another jail stint, and so forth. Along the way, this is normalized by friends, family, and associates as part of this person's common behavior, and, with time, this becomes a facet of the person's everyday identity. At this point, the jail experience has resulted in the successful labeling of the individual as a criminal, and the identity ultimately becomes internalized and accepted by that individual him- or herself.

16% indicated that they engaged in criminal behavior as a means of supporting their drug habit. Female offenders indicated drug use at the time of their offense more frequently than did males, and Caucasian offenders were more likely to indicate drug usage at the time of their offense than were other racial categories of offenders (Karberg & James, 2005).

The drugs of choice for abusers and users vary and include, by prevalence of use, marijuana, cocaine or crack, hallucinogens, stimulants, and inhalants. As would be expected, those who indicated substance abuse problems were also more likely to have a criminal record. In addition, homelessness is very common among substance abusers who end up in jail. In fact, as noted above, it is not uncommon for many addicts who live on the streets to deliberately commit crimes during the winter months as a means of having a warm place to stay during the coldest periods of the year.

It is interesting to note that roughly 63% of offenders with a substance abuse or use problem have been in treatment at some time prior to their jail stint (Karberg & James, 2005). Most of these programs were self-help in nature, such as Alcoholics Anonymous or Narcotics Anonymous. However, nearly half of these offenders who had received prior treatment did so within a detoxification program or a residential treatment facility. Treatment within the jail itself for drug abuse is somewhat unusual, unfortunately. Much of this has to do with the fact that offenders tend to move in and out of the jail facility much more quickly than in a prison facility; thus, there is little time between implementation of treatment and the offender's departure from the facility. Treatment programs are usually focused on jail inmates who have a substance abuse problem and have longer-term sentences, but, even in these cases, detoxification tends to be the primary approach to treatment, coupled with the support group interventions of Alcoholics Anonymous and/or Narcotics Anonymous.

Detoxification is designed for persons dependent on narcotic drugs (e.g., heroin, opium) and is typically found in inpatient settings with programs that last for 7 to 21 days. The rationale for using detoxification as a treatment approach is grounded in two basic principles (Hanson, Venturelli, & Flechenstein, 2011; Myers & Salt, 2000). The first is a conception of "addiction" as drug craving accompanied by physical dependence that motivates continued usage, resulting in a tolerance to the drug's effects, and a syndrome of identifiable physical and psychological symptoms when the drug is abruptly withdrawn. The second is that the negative aspects of the abstinence syndrome discourage many addicts from attempting withdrawal, which makes them more likely to continue using drugs. The main objective of chemical detoxification is the elimination of physiological dependence through a medically supervised procedure.

While many detoxification programs address only the addict's physical dependence, some provide individual or group counseling in an attempt to address the problems associated with drug abuse. Many detoxification programs use medical drugs to ease the process of overcoming the physical symptoms of dependence that make the detoxification process so painful for the addicted substance abuser. For drug offenders in jails and in prisons, the mechanism of detoxification varies by the client's major drug of addiction. For opiate users, methadone or clonidine is preferred. For cocaine users, desipramine has been used to ease the withdrawal symptoms. Almost all narcotic addicts and many cocaine users have been in a chemical detoxification program at least once (Inciardi, Rivers, & McBride, 2008). However, studies show that in the absence of supportive psychotherapeutic services and community follow-up care, nearly all are certain to suffer from relapse (Ashford, Sales, & Reid, 2002).

In all detoxification programs, inmate success depends upon following established protocols for drug administration and withdrawal. In a recent assessment of research literature on the effectiveness of detoxification, there appear to be promising rates of program completion. Yet many clinicians note that mere detoxification from a substance is not drug abuse "treatment" and does not help people stay off drugs. Detoxification in no way ensures that relapse will not occur, and thus it is important for any program to have much more than a simple detoxification process. In essence, detoxification should be viewed as an initial step, after the intake process, of a comprehensive treatment process.

Because jails are not typically long-term facilities, they will not usually offer much more than detoxification programs. However, this does not address the needs of those inmates who are kept on a long-term basis. In such cases, the services for these inmates should be on par with those for inmates who are kept long-term in prisons. While some of the larger jail systems in the United States might offer more comprehensive services, most do not. Thus, offenders who are kept on a long-term basis in a jail facility (e.g., state prison inmates who are housed in local jails on a long-term basis) find themselves without suitable intervention services.

Mental Health Issues in Jails

Jails in this country are full of the mentally ill, and, in many cases, these offenders are homeless. Data from the Bureau of Justice Statistics indicate that roughly 64% of all jail inmates have a mental health problem (James & Glaze, 2001). This contrasts with mental health problems in prisons where only 10.6% of these inmates present with mental illnesses. Further still, for nearly every manifestation of mental illness, more jail inmates than state or federal inmates are likely to exhibit symptoms, particularly in regard to hallucinations and delusions. Jail inmates tend to have mental health problems with specific diagnoses that include mania (approximately 54%), major depression (30%), and psychotic disorders (24%), according to Stohr et al. (2008). The specific identification of a mental illness for each inmate is based on the specific criteria used among mental health practitioners, a tome known as the *Diagnostic and Statistical Manual of Mental Disorders* (DSM-IV-TR). The DSM-IV-TR is a manual used by clinicians that provides the specific criteria and symptoms to be considered when qualifying an inmate with a diagnosis and is the accepted standard among members of the American Psychiatric Association.

A host of problems can be associated with mental illnesses in jail systems including homelessness, greater criminal engagement, prior abuse, and substance use. Among the findings from James and Glaze (2001) was that those with a mental illness designation were almost twice as likely as other inmates to have been homeless prior to being placed in jail. In addition, inmates with mental illnesses tend to have more incidents of incarceration than do those who have no record of mental illness. Roughly 3 times as many jail inmates with a mental health problem have a history of physical or sexual abuse than do those without such a problem (James & Glaze, 2001; Stohr et al., 2008). Likewise, nearly 75% of inmates with a mental health issue also have a substance abuse problem. Thus, those inmates with mental health problems tend to have a multiplicity of other issues that affect them as well. Naturally, these issues affect the inmate's behavior and thus place a drain on the time and effort of jail staff.

One study in particular demonstrates how, for mentally ill jail inmates, there is a confluence of factors that aggravate their circumstances. McNeil, Binder, and Robinson (2005) found in their study in San Francisco County that jail inmates with mental illness were prone to have multiple issues that seemed to dovetail with their mental illness. They found that mental illness, substance abuse, and prior jail incarcerations were connected life events (Stohr et al., 2008). In addition, among those inmates who were mentally ill and/or had substance abuse or dependence issues, homelessness was a much more common phenomenon. Thus, the mentally ill inmate presents with a number of challenges for jail staff—challenges that are not easily separated from each other. While it is not clear if the mental illness itself spawned these other issues or if these issues served to increase the likelihood of mental illness, it is clear that these offenders are in need of help that extends well beyond the intended scope of most jail facilities.

Communicable Diseases in Jails

Bloodborne and airborne pathogens are now a common part of operations within most jail facilities (Carlson & Garrett, 1999). Communicable diseases found in jails include hepatitis A, hepatitis B, hepatitis C, HIV/AIDS, tuberculosis, measles, and rubella (Carlson & Garrett, 1999). To ensure that both staff and inmates are sufficiently protected, jails must have a written exposure plan that includes the following: engineering of physical facilities that helps to isolate identified pathogens, work practices that control the spread of pathogens, availability of personal protective equipment, routine staff training, the availability of appropriate vaccines, and detailed records of training provided and vaccines available (Carlson & Garrett, 1999).

Journal Article Link 5.4
Read more about disease in jails.

Further, most guidelines require that written protocols for responding to spills, occupational exposures, and other possible means of transmission be kept and disseminated among staff. In addition, confidential counseling for employees due to occupational exposure to a communicable disease must be made available. Concerns regarding jail security and the prevention of communicable diseases are integral to most jail facilities as these diseases affect inmates, staff, and the outside community simultaneously. Though these procedures are becoming more commonplace, there are still some areas of operation with communicable diseases that seem to need improvement in many jail systems.

Data from the National Commission on Correctional Health Care (NCCHC, 2002) suggest that many jails are not adequately addressing three communicable diseases: human immunodeficiency virus/acquired immunodeficiency syndrome (HIV/AIDS), syphilis, and tuberculosis (TB). Although rudimentary HIV/AIDS education programs are becoming more widespread in jails, few jail systems have implemented comprehensive HIV/AIDS prevention programs in all of their facilities. Most jail systems provide HIV/AIDS antibody testing only when inmates ask to be tested or have signs and symptoms of HIV/AIDS. Testing is not aggressively "marketed" in most jail systems (Carlson & Garrett, 1999).

Very few jail systems routinely screen inmates for syphilis. Despite the availability of fairly inexpensive diagnostic and treatment modalities for syphilis, a national survey conducted by the Centers for Disease Control and Prevention (CDC) found that fewer than one half of all jails (46%–47%) offer routine laboratory testing for the disease as a matter of policy (NCCHC, 2002). Even jails that report aggressive screening policies actually screen less than half of inmates (48%). As a result, on average, less than a quarter of jail inmates undergo laboratory testing for syphilis while incarcerated. In jails that offer testing only to patients with suggestive symptoms or signs, only 2%–7% of inmates are tested. Continuity of care for inmates released with syphilis and other sexually transmitted diseases (STDs) is also inadequate (NCCHC, 2002).

Although more jails screen for TB than for STDs, too few conduct TB screening. According to a 1997 survey conducted for the National Institute of Justice (NIJ) and CDC, more about one half of jails routinely screen at intake for TB. In part, however, because of short inmate stays in jail, TB skin test results—which require 48–72 hours before they indicate infection—may not be read. Ninety-eight percent of state and federal prison systems and 85% of jails report that they isolate inmates with suspected or confirmed TB disease in negative pressure rooms (NCCHC, 2002). Some facilities, however, do not test the rooms to ensure that they are working properly, or they use the rooms even when they are known to be out of order. Directly observed therapy for latent TB infection (watching patients swallow each dose of medication) is the reported policy for all patients in 85% of jails (NCCHC, 2002).

Jail Suicide

Data regarding jail suicide for this section have been drawn from a 2002 study on jail issues, conducted by the Bureau of Justice Statistics and authored by Karberg and James in 2005. As indicated from the data presented in this study, those incarcerated in jails often enter while intoxicated, and many will have some sort of mental disability. Further, their booking in the jail may be their first experience with the incarceration process and may, therefore, be one of the lowest points in their life. In such circumstances, jail inmates are at heightened risk of suicidal ideation and to attempt suicide (Hanser, 2002).

In comparison to prisons, inmates in jails are much more likely to commit suicide. In fact, the rate of suicide in jails is 3 times that in prisons. However, during the past several years, jail and prison deaths due to suicide have declined, with jail suicide rates decreasing by a dramatic two thirds of what it was in the 1980s (Stohr et al., 2008). In the early 1980s, jail suicide was the primary cause of death for inmates, but, by 2002, illness had replaced suicide as the primary cause of death for jail inmates.

Suicide rates in jails vary by type of inmate and the size of the jail. White male inmates under the age of 18 and over 35, as well as those with a more violent history of commitment, are more likely to commit suicide than are other groups of offenders. Further, a study by Winter (2003) found that during a 10-year period, jail suicide data in one Midwestern state indicated that those who committed suicide were typically younger, were arrested for some type of violent offense, tended to lack a history of mental illness (contrary to popular opinion), and did not necessarily display classic signs of suicidal ideation, but they were more likely to be under the influence of drugs or alcohol. These findings are interesting because they demonstrate that staff may not be able to use simply observation techniques to know who is truly at risk of suicide. These results also point toward the impact that drugs and alcohol have on the occurrence of jail suicides.

Moreover, according to Karberg and James (2005), the suicide rate at large urban jails, where fewer Caucasian inmates (per capita) tend to be held, tended to be about half that of jails in rural jurisdictions. In a similar manner, Tartaro and Ruddell (2006) found that inmates in smaller jails (those with fewer than 100 inmates) were 2 to 5 times more likely to have attempted and completed suicides than those in larger jails. This is important because it demonstrates that jails that are smaller and tend to have less funding and poorer staff training are the ones where suicide tends to occur more frequently and where the outcome is usually a completion of the suicidal action. Thus, the jurisdictions where the risk is greatest tend to also be those where the ability to respond adequately is most compromised.

Further, these researchers also found that crowded jails and those with "special needs and long-term inmates" were also more likely to have a higher number of suicide attempts (Stohr et al., 2008; Tartaro & Ruddell, 2006, p. 81). This is also another very important finding because it demonstrates, as one would suspect, that specialized offenders with a variety of issues (e.g., mental disorders, physical disabilities, the elderly, female offenders) have heightened risks of suicidal ideation and that these individuals are more likely to complete their suicidal act. An emphasis on inmates who have special circumstances is important in jails, due to the welfare of the inmate but also due to liability considerations. Likewise, jails that operate as long-term facilities, especially those that house long-term inmates, should heed these research findings and must ensure that documentation of policies and responses is maintained.

Stohr et al. (2008) note that the shock of incarceration may be one explanation for the higher jail suicide rates, when compared to prisons. However, this does not seem to fit well with data that show persons in their mid-30s and older or in small jails to be more at risk. One thing is clear from prior research: Jail inmates are most at risk of suicide during the first 48 to 72 hours of being locked up, and the likelihood of suicide goes down dramatically for men after 9 days of incarceration and for women after 4 days. Thus, it is important to be especially attentive to this issue during the first few days that an inmate is in custody.

Lastly, it may well be that larger jail facilities that have greater resources may be better able to provide training and resources for staff. As an example, younger and less experienced offenders who are apprehensive of being housed with older offenders who may victimize them can often be segregated in larger jails where such options are available. In smaller jail facilities, space may not exist for such protective considerations. In such cases, inmates who are in fear of victimization, and who are already at a low point in their life, would likely be at an increased risk of suicide ideation. Thus, the ability to alleviate some of the anxiety is also likely to reduce the likelihood for ideation and suicide completion.

CONCLUSION

Jail facilities are perhaps the most complicated of facilities within the field of corrections. In addition, jail facilities are perhaps not appreciated for the vital role that they play within the criminal justice system. The volume of persons processed in jail facilities, in and of itself, is sufficient to warrant a closer examination of the jail facility. In addition, jails perform many different types of tasks, such as the holding of persons prior to their court date and providing a series of unique sentencing variations, as well as the incarceration of persons who are technically part of the larger prison system.

Jails and jail staff must attend to a variety of offenders who present with a number of issues. The range of problems and challenges can be quite varied, and this then creates a demanding situation for jail staff and administrators. The variety of offender typologies, needs, and issues presents staff with problems that are not easily rectified, and, correspondingly, there is a need for staff to be well trained and well equipped. Unfortunately, jails frequently do not have sufficient funding to ensure that staff are adequately trained or equipped for the challenges that confront them. This is especially true with small rural jails where funds and expertise are limited. Overall, it appears that jails have been given short shrift in the world of corrections but that, as the state of affairs has emerged, the jail facility is one feature of corrections that will be given much more attention in times to come.

END-OF-CHAPTER DISCUSSION QUESTIONS

1. Compare issues for large metropolitan jails to those for small rural jails.
2. Provide a discussion regarding the demographics and characteristics of the jail inmate population.
3. Discuss some of the challenges associated with training and motivating jail staff.
4. What are some special types of sentencing options in jails?
5. What is "booking," and why is this area of the jail so important?
6. Discuss the dynamics of suicide within the jail facility.
7. How have communicable diseases impacted jail operations during recent years?
8. Explain how a first-time jail experience can result in labeling a person and thereby potentially increasing his or her likelihood of continuing in a life of crime.

KEY TERMS

Community service

Detoxification

Gaols

Jail

Jail reentry programs

Podular jail

Rural jail

Sally port

Shock incarceration

Short-term jail

Tower of London

Weekend confinement

APPLIED EXERCISE 5.1

For this exercise, students will need to determine how they would informally address the issue of sexually transmitted diseases (STDs) and other sex-related illnesses in their institution.

You are the assistant warden of a large metropolitan jail in your city. Your jail contends with a constant ingress and egress of inmates who tend to be drawn from population groups that are traditionally high-risk for various STDs as well as HIV/AIDS. Your jail system naturally has an identifiable policy, and, like the staff of many large jail systems, the members of your staff are trained on these types of illnesses, diseases, and viruses. Occasional in-service training is also provided to staff, when and where time and resources permit.

Recently, the city of Sodom, where your jail facility is located, has experienced an outbreak of herpes that has reached epidemic proportions. In addition, your county, the county of Gomorrah, was identified last year as having the highest incidence of HIV/AIDS in the state. Thus, issues related to STDs, HIV, and AIDS are serious in your jurisdiction.

Recently, in response to community concerns regarding public health, the mayor of Sodom met with the chief of police of Sodom and the sheriff of Gomorrah County to discuss the issue. It was decided that a very quick and aggressive crackdown on vice crime would be instituted in areas targeted with high levels of prostitution, other illicit sex industry activity, and intravenous drug use. Police officers and sheriff's deputies were mobilized for this major enforcement activity. Amidst this, the mayor, police chief, and sheriff implemented plans for increased jail space in facilities throughout the city and the county; it was understood that this major enforcement effort would result in a larger number of persons jailed in the area. Thus, resources for containing this population have been sufficient.

However, staff in the jail facilities—and your facility is the largest in the system—tend to be very stern and unsympathetic to the plight of those inmates who are being locked up for various types of criminal behavior that correlate with the spread of STDs and HIV/AIDS. While there is no specific requirement that they be particularly empathetic, the deliberate heckling of these inmates and the calloused approach that seems to predominate does not help the situation. This attitude is exacerbated by local TV and printed news media that have showcased the public health hazards, essentially dramatizing the situation to epic proportions. In fact, the media have been critical of law enforcement and the mayor's office for being a bit slow and ineffective in their response. Thus, many jail employees feel as if their agency is considered lax on this problem.

Your concern, as the assistant warden, is centered on the increased number of accidents, altercations, and general upheaval within your facility. The warden of the facility (your boss) has explained that lawsuits are likely to emerge in the near future. The city and the county both have their legal budgets stretched way beyond what allocations would typically allow. So, the warden asks you to implement some type of intervention program that will ameliorate the problems that are occurring between staff and STD-positive inmates.

The issue, it seems, has to do with the informal culture of members of the jail staff and their perceptions of the problem as well as their role in addressing that problem. It seems that, in their rough handling of these offenders, they are actually aggravating the long-term problem for the city and the county. While, at their day-to-day level of operations, the consequences of their actions do not seem to be serious, they will likely develop into some very costly problems in the future. Further still, their behavior will not aid the process of trying to get these offenders to change their sex and drug-using behaviors. It is important to the warden that something be done to change this informal culture and, if that is not possible, that some type of documentation exist to at least address this issue since the warden is quite convinced that it will be relevant in civil court in the next few months.

TO THE STUDENT: The task before you is to design some type of intervention method to reach and change the behavior of staff who seem to be calloused and antagonistic toward offenders who have STDs or HIV/AIDS within your facility. This must go beyond simply making a policy statement or providing a training segment since both of these types of programs already exist in your jail system. While you may add to the policy and the training segment, explain what else you might do to address this issue, both formally and informally.

"WHAT WOULD YOU DO?"

Here you are again, the assistant warden of the largest jail facility in the city of Sodom, located in the county of Gomorrah. Recently, you have found that many of the offenders who have been locked up due to a crackdown on vice crime, sex industry offenses, and intravenous drug use are offenders who were, at the time of arrest, on some type of drugs and/or alcohol. Amidst these persons, numerous "johns" and other typically noncriminal persons have been arrested and jailed in the process of implementing the crackdown. Needless to say, many of these persons are not used to being incarcerated, and, as it turns out, they seem to have a difficult time with the experience. This is coupled with the fact that many of these current inmates suffer from high levels of guilt and embarrassment, not to mention problems with their employer and/or spouse. While many are able to get out quickly through the bail/bonds offices in the area, many stay in the facility for several days.

An unexpected outcome is that, among these persons, several suicide attempts have been made. In fact, two attempts have been successful while the other four serious attempts were detected in time to prevent their successful completion. One of the decedents who just recently committed suicide was from a very affluent family, and it is thought that the family may sue the jail facility. The sheriff has met with members of the family to attempt to mitigate some of their concerns and complaints regarding the incident, but it is not yet clear how the situation may unfold.

Your facility does have a suicide policy that requires routine use of additional supervision of inmates at risk of suicide, the use of suicide contracts, and additional services. However, the sheriff, the mayor, and the chief of police all believe that much can be done if staff are given training on how to provide informal crisis prevention skills for new inmates, particularly those determined to be at heightened risk via jail intake protocols. The warden of the jail has talked with you and noted that she has set aside money from the budget so that you can develop and implement some type of crisis-response training for jail staff. You have also been given an additional administrative staff member to help with this process.

You are essentially required to develop some type of crisis response methodology for jail staff with those inmates who are found to be at increased risk of jail suicide. You must first determine who is at increased risk, and then you must identify what might be done among jail staff to minimize this risk.

You are given 30 days to implement this program. **What would you do?**

CROSS-NATIONAL PERSPECTIVE 5.1

A Jail Facility in Canada: Central East Correctional Centre, Ontario, Canada

The Central East Correctional Centre (CECC) is a correctional/detention center in the city of Kawartha Lakes. It is operated under the jurisdiction of the Ministry of Community Safety and Correctional Services of Ontario. People convicted of crimes with custodial sentences of less than two years are housed in this jail, along with a large population of inmates who have been detained prior to trial. The inmates detained prior to trial have been deemed by the courts to be a flight risk, or too dangerous to be at large.

The CECC is a 1,184-bed multipurpose correctional facility, consisting of six pods of 192 beds each for male accommodation (1,152), and a separate 32-bed female unit. It houses inmates in a maximum-security setting who are serving sentences of up to two years less a day, as well as those on remand awaiting court proceedings. The CECC was built on approximately 35 hectares of land and is approximately 10 acres under roof. The institution includes areas for rehabilitation, programming, and an infirmary and separate buildings for an industrial work program. This facility, constructed in 2002, ran a cost of approximately 84 million Canadian dollars. For their money, the Ontario correctional authorities received a facility that includes the following:

1. All inmate-occupied areas are surrounded by a 16-foot fence, topped with 300 meters of razor ribbon. All doors, windows, locks, and perimeter walls are built to maximum-security standards.

2. The most advanced security technology available includes 21 different security systems. Closed-circuit television is designed to enhance sight lines for correctional officers and allows for the simultaneous viewing of several indoor and outdoor areas. The six video court suites will reduce the need for offender transportation to and from court for short court appearances.

3. The design is unique in Canada and features six interconnected octagonal "pods." Each pod contains six living units, an enclosed exercise yard, and dedicated program and visiting areas. Meals and health care services are brought to the living units to reduce inmate movement throughout the facility.

4. Living units have 16 cells, each accommodating two offenders. This design features clear and unobstructed sight lines between correctional officers and inmate living areas and a small number of inmates per housing unit.

5. Core support services include a medical infirmary, a 40-bed segregation unit, a meal preparation facility, a separate inmate industries building, and administrative office space.

6. The separate female unit is inaccessible to male inmates and accommodates 32 female offenders. Also included are separate programming areas, recreation yard, medical and segregation units, and an admissions and discharge area for female offenders.

Question 1: If you had to rate your impression of this facility's security (with 1 being the lowest rating and 10 being the highest), from what you have read above, what would be your rating? Provide a brief explanation for your answer.

Question 2: When considering the description of the Central East Correctional Centre in Ontario, Canada, would you consider the facility structure sufficient to address the various special issues pertaining to jails, as discussed in this chapter? Briefly explain why or why not.

Sources: Bondfield Construction. (2009). *Correctional and police facilities*. Retrieved from http://www.bondfield.com/correctional/centralontario.html.

City of Kawartha Lakes Police Services. (2009). *Central East Correctional Centre*. Retrieved from http://www.kawarthalakespolice.com/cecc.html.

STUDENT STUDY SITE

Visit the Student Study Site at **www.sagepub.com/hanserintro** to access links to the videos, audio clips, SAGE journal articles, state rankings, and reference materials noted in this chapter, as well as additional study tools including eFlashcards, web quizzes, and more.

chapter 6

Probation

LEARNING OBJECTIVES:

1. Discuss how probation impacts the jail and prison systems of a jurisdiction.

2. Compare different means by which probation agencies are organized.

3. Identify the qualifications and characteristics of most probation officers.

4. Apply knowledge of probation to determine decisions regarding release, incarceration, or revocation of offenders.

5. Discuss the importance of the presentence investigation report.

State Rankings Link 6.1
Adults on State Probation
in 2009.

INTRODUCTION

Probation, as implemented by county and state jurisdictions around the country, is the most common sanction administered in the United States. For this reason, if nothing else, attention to this sanction should be given. However, probation is specifically important to corrections because it is, by its very nature, an option that facilitates the process of correcting offenders. In addition, probation impacts the jail and prison systems through revocation processes and by acting as a filtering process as offenders are inputted into the jail and prison systems. Since such resources are scarce, probation alleviates overcrowding problems at the front end of the criminal justice system.

Thus, probation is a sanction that serves as an important tool for jurisdictions that operate local jails, and, ultimately, this sanction can act as a preventative tool to prison overcrowding, particularly with offenders who are not serious risks to public safety. It is with this in mind that we will examine the use of probation, considering that this sanction greatly impacts the inmate flow within correctional institutions. This is particularly true within the jail setting, and it is therefore appropriate that our discussion of probation occurs just after our discussion of jail facilities and the issues that impact jail systems. Now that you, the reader, have a better understanding of jail facilities and the issues inherent to their operation, the following discussion related to probation and jail population flow should become much clearer.

PROBATION WHEN THE JAIL IS FULL

In many cases, probation sentences are meted out at the county level of government. This is, as it turns out, the same level of government that tends to administer jail facilities. Thus, probation is typically administered by the same courthouse that oversees the jail facility in a given jurisdiction. As a result, these two justice functions—probation and jailing—tend to work in tandem with one another. Even though this is the case, this is not to imply that coordination and communication between jail administrators and probation administrators is optimal; in many cases these two functions operate in a manner that is disjointed, despite the fact that the same courthouse may impact both probation and jail agencies.

While jails and probation agencies may (or may not) have a collaborative relationship, it is undeniable that the district attorney (the office that prosecutes criminals) will have a close working relationship with the local sheriff or sheriffs in the region as well as city police chiefs who collectively oversee law enforcement activities. These activities result in the flow of criminals before the courthouse and ultimately require that a judge sentence an offender to one of three likely options: community supervision (usually probation), a jail sentence (sometimes with additional community supervision requirements), or a prison sentence (if incarceration is to exceed a year in duration).

Because the majority of offenders tend to commit crimes that are petty, nonserious, or nonviolent, this means that they will tend to qualify for jail or probation. Those offenders who do commit serious crimes will, naturally, be sentenced to prison and then are therefore the concern of state prison system authorities. However, the bulk of the offender population will remain at the county level, and it is in this manner that the jail population develops. In many instances, the jail facility will fill quite quickly with the volume of offenders who commit crimes, particularly in large urban areas of the nation. Thus, the use of probation becomes a critical tool to monitor and mitigate the flow of inmates into the jail.

Probation is thus a control valve mechanism that mitigates the flow of inmates sent directly to the jailhouse. Without the use of probation sanctions, jails would simply collapse in their operation because the current jail facility structure throughout the United States could not even come close to containing the total offender population in correctional systems across the United States. Further, this problem is exacerbated by circumstances where state prison systems are full and when jail facilities are required to keep inmates who, legally speaking, should be housed within a state prison facility. This demonstrates how the jail facility can feel pressure from inmate flow from the front end and the back end of its operational system.

A BRIEF HISTORY OF PROBATION

Probation, as it turns out, is a uniquely American invention (see Focus Topic 6.1). At its inception, probation was used as an alternative to incarceration, and it was unique to the United States. **John Augustus,** a cobbler and philanthropist of Boston, is often recognized as the father of modern probation. During the time that John Augustus provided his innovative contribution to the field of community corrections, the temperance movement against alcohol consumption was in full swing. Augustus, aware of many of the issues associated with alcoholism, made an active effort to rehabilitate prior alcoholics who were processed through the police court in Boston.

While acting as a volunteer of the court, Augustus observed a man being charged for drunkenness who would have, in all likelihood, ended up in the Boston House of Correction if it were not for Augustus's intervention. Augustus placed bail for the man, personally guaranteeing the man's return to court at the prescribed time. Augustus helped the man to find a job and provided him with the guidance and support that was necessary so that the defendant was able to become a functioning and productive member within the community. When the court ordered the return of the offender three weeks later, the judge noticed a very substantial improvement in the offender's behavior. The judge was so impressed by the initial outcome that he granted leniency in sentencing (Augustus, 1852; Barnes & Teeters, 1959). From this point in 1841 until his death in 1859, Augustus continued to bail out numerous offenders, providing voluntary supervision and guidance until they were subsequently sentenced by the court. During his 18 years of activity, Augustus "bailed on probation" 1,152 male offenders and 794 female offenders (Barnes & Teeters, 1959, p. 554). His rationale centered on his belief that "the object of the law is to reform criminals and to prevent crime and not to punish maliciously or from a spirit of revenge" (Dressler, 1962, p. 17).

This quote by Dressler (1962) is important because it is consistent with this text's definition of corrections, as a process whereby practitioners from a variety of agencies and programs use tools, techniques, and facilities to engage in organized security and treatment functions intended to correct criminal tendencies among the offender population. In other words, corrections, as used in this text, is intended to do more than simply *punish* the offender but instead seeks to *reform* the offender. This is just as true with the use of probation as it would be with any other form of correctional sanction.

While probation may act as a valve that mitigates the flow of inmates into the jailhouse, this is not and should not be the primary purpose of this sanction. Rather, consistent with the earlier presented definition of corrections, probation should place primary emphasis on correcting criminal human behavior. Issues related to jail logistics and other such concerns should be secondary. The fact that this was the original intent when administering probation is clear from Dressler's (1962) passage since Augustus was primarily concerned with the malicious treatment of offenders and the desire for revenge that could easily cloud society's vision. This line of thought is further supported by Lindner (2006) who notes that Augustus, though sometimes criticized for his work, sought only to offer reform to those persons who were capable of such potential. Lindner (2006) further notes that Augustus did his work with no concern as to his own personal gain, financial or otherwise. Thus, it was rehabilitation that Augustus ultimately sought to achieve, regardless of whether jails or houses of correction were beyond population capacity (in fact, crowding was commonplace during his time in history).

PHOTO 6.1

John Augustus was a volunteer of the court in the Boston area during the mid-1800s. He is regarded as the father of modern probation.

Reference Link 6.1
Read more about John Augustus.

THE ADMINISTRATION OF PROBATION

Earlier in this chapter, it was noted that in many cases, probation is administered through the same jurisdiction that also oversees the jailhouse. While this is, in many cases, true, there are other means by which probation is administered. Indeed, the specific means by which probation operates can vary if it is not the county level of government that oversees the probation sanctioning process. Correctional systems, including community

FOCUS TOPIC: 6.1

Historical Developments in Probation

1841   John Augustus becomes the "father of probation."

1869   First official probation program developed in Massachusetts (the home of probation).

1901   New York creates the first statute officially establishing adult probation services.

1925   Federal probation is authorized by Congress.

1927   Forty-nine states implement juvenile probation (all but Wyoming).

1943   Presentence investigation reports formally created by federal probation system.

1956   Mississippi is the 50th state to formally establish adult probation.

1965   The birth of "shock probation" occurs in the state of Ohio.

1979   Various risk/needs assessments are developed by the state of Wisconsin.

1983   Intensive supervised probation has its birth in Georgia.

To be sure, Augustus was aware that jail and prison conditions were barbaric in many cases. Yet this still was not his primary reason for implementing his intervention. Rather, he selected his candidates with due care and caution, offering aid to those who tended to be first-time offenders. He also looked to their character, demeanor, past experiences, and potential future influences when making his decisions. Thus, whether you use the word *reform, rehabilitate,* or *reintegrate,* it is clear that the initial early intent of probation was to provide society with people who were more productive after sentencing than they had been prior to sentencing. This intent stood on its own merit and sense of purpose, regardless of jail or prison conditions that might have existed, thereby establishing the original mission of community corrections as a whole.

PHOTO 6.2

This building contains offices of numerous probation officers.

Audio Link 6.1

Listen to an account of probation reform.

supervision components, can vary greatly from state to state. Thus, a bit more discussion on the organizational aspects of probation administration is provided since this greatly impacts the operations of probation services within a given jurisdiction.

The Probation Agency

When examining the means of operation within a probation agency, one key characteristic to consider is the degree of centralization that exists within that agency. Indeed, adult probation in one state may be administered by a single, central state agency, by a variety of local agencies, or by a given combination of the two. When considering local levels of administration, agencies may operate at the county or even municipal level. However, these supposedly smaller jurisdictions should not be underestimated. Consider, for example, the probation departments in New York City where felony and misdemeanor caseloads are larger than those of many entire state systems.

Generally, probation systems can be separated into six categories, with states having more than one system in operation simultaneously (Allen & Sawhney, 2010; Hanser, 2010). The six categories of operation are as follows:

1. Juvenile: Includes separate probation services for juveniles that are administered through county or municipal governments, or on a statewide basis.
2. Municipal: Independent probation agencies that are administered through lower courts or through the municipality itself.

3. County: The probation agency is governed by laws and/or guidelines established by the state that empowers a county to operate its own probation agency.

4. State: One agency administers a centralized probation system that provides services throughout the state.

5. State combined P&P: Probation and parole services are administered together on a statewide basis by a single agency.

6. Federal: Probation is administered nationally as a branch of the courts.

Consider, further, that in many cases the administration of probation may be determined by the seriousness of the offense. For instance, felony offenses may be supervised by state-level personnel while misdemeanor cases may be supervised by local governmental probation agencies. For instance, in Michigan, adult felony probation is administered through the state department of corrections while adult misdemeanor probation is administered through the local district courts.

Further still, juvenile probation adds a whole new dimension of organizational considerations. Indeed, over half of all juvenile probation agencies are administered at the local level. To illustrate, juvenile probation may be provided through a separate agency or through a subdepartment of the large adult probation system. In over a dozen states, juvenile probation services are split, with the juvenile court administering services in urban jurisdictions and the state administering such services in rural areas. Lastly, some states have a statewide office of juvenile probation that is located in that state's executive branch (Allen & Sawhney, 2010; Hanser, 2010).

The Presentence Investigation

The **presentence investigation report** is the file that includes a wide range of background information on the offender. This file will typically include demographic, vocational, educational, and personal information on the offender as well as records on his or her prior offending patterns and the probation department's recommendation as to the appropriate type of sentencing and supervision for the offender in question. In many respects, the presentence investigation (PSI) report is the initial point of assessment, and it will often be utilized when the offender is first brought into a prison facility. In other words, the PSI report is not just used in probation sentences; it also is used when offenders are imprisoned. Because the PSI report is a centerpiece component of the probation process and because it even comes into play when offenders are in prison, it is important that students understand this important report.

PHOTO 6.3

During the completion of the PSI report, the probation officer will often make several inquiries of the offender during a face-to-face interview.

The primary purpose of the PSI report is to provide the court with the necessary information from which a sentencing decision can be derived. The PSI is conducted after a defendant is found guilty of a charge (whether by pleading or by court finding) but prior to the point of sentencing. During this point betwixt conviction and sentencing, the probation officer will complete the PSI report, which will include extensive information pertaining to the offender. This information, along with a sentencing recommendation, will aid the judge, who must ultimately fashion a sentence as well as any corollary obligations attached to that sentence.

Likewise, the PSI report tends to serve as a basic foundation for supervision and treatment planning throughout the future of the offender's sentence, both when on probation and later if the offender is incarcerated. It is quite often the case that this document will serve as a reference point for placing the offender in a variety of programs. This may be true when the offender is on supervision and may serve as a guidepost for jail and detention facilities as well. The PSI report will contain sundry amounts of information about an offender's background, including education, social and medical history, and work experience. "A probation file may also consist of other reports written by counselors, psychologists, and case workers. Therefore, a large amount of personal and confidential information is maintained by the probation officer which should not be disclosed arbitrarily" (Michigan Department of Corrections, Michigan Presentence Investigation, 2003, p. 33).

Among other things, the PSI report will contain information related to the character and behavior of the offender. This then means that the probation officer's impressions of the offender can greatly impact the outcome of the PSI. The PSI is typically conducted through an interview with the offender. Because the PSI report information is largely obtained from the interview process, it is naturally important that probation officers have good interviewing skills. This cannot be overstated given the fact that probation officers are in contact with persons on a routine basis where they must collect and record information. Further, the probation officer will often conduct interviews with family members, employers, and so forth to validate the information received by the offender. It is of course important that the PSI report contain reliable information that is relevant to the defendant's character, attitude, and activities. Thus, the presentence investigator must make a point to seek reliable sources, to verify information, and to corroborate all information with as many objective and/or external sources as is reasonably possible. The written report should include the full police report related to the criminal incident, the defendant's version of the incident, the victim's input related to the offense, and a complete background on the offender.

While procedures do vary from region to region, a sentencing phase will be conducted at some point during the processing of a criminal conviction. At this point, the defense counsel can have an impact on the overall process for the offender. Defense counsel will usually challenge any inaccurate, incomplete, or misleading information that may end up in the PSI report. This last function of the defense counsel is actually quite critical since the PSI report will be used to classify the offender if he or she should be incarcerated and will also be used in future decisions regarding supervision issues within the community. Thus, verification of the PSI report's validity is crucial to the welfare of the defendant and keeps from creating scenarios that make an already bad situation worse.

From the standpoint of the probation officer, the two most important sections of the PSI report are the evaluation and the recommendation. There is typically a high degree of agreement between the probation officer's recommendations and the judge's decision when sentencing, and this means that the PSI report is very important in, at least partially, determining the offender's sentencing fate. Proof that the PSI report plays an important role in both the sentencing phase and subsequent outcomes can be found when one considers that, if a defendant can afford such services, his or her defense counsel may purchase private services to construct a supplemental PSI report to be considered by the court.

Granting Probation

According to Neubauer (2007), the public perceives the judge as the principal decision maker in criminal court. But, in actuality, the judge often is not the primary decision maker in regard to an offender's sentencing and/or the granting of probation. This is not to say that the judge does not have ultimate authority over the court, nor does it mean to imply that judges have a diminished sense of importance when presiding over their court. Rather, Neubauer demonstrates the collaborative nature of the various courtroom actors when processing offender caseloads. Throughout this process, judges will often voluntarily defer to the judgment of other members of the court, namely prosecutors, defense attorneys, victim's rights groups, and the probation agency.

PHOTO 6.4

The judge of the court is the final authority on rulings related to probation sentencing and conditions. The judge will usually work closely with probation officers who see offenders from his or her court of jurisdiction.

During a typical day in criminal court, judges may accept bail recommendations offered by the district attorney, plea agreements that are struck by the defense and the prosecution, and even sentences recommended by a probation officer (though there is of course some debate as to the actual weight given to the probation officer's recommendation, at least in some courts). The main point is that though judges do of course retain their power over the courtroom, they often share influence over the adjudication process with a variety of courtroom actors (Neubauer, 2007). This is an informal process that often takes place amongst courtroom actors who, when working together over time, know each other in both a professional and a semipersonal sense (Neubauer, 2007).

Further, there are some challenges that can emerge when judges do not allow the input of other courtroom actors. For instance, jail overcrowding may be worsened if the judge is not receptive to the input of the sheriff and/or the police chief who will administer the local county or city jail. In addition, probation officer caseloads can become too burdensome to ensure public safety concerns if the judge does not consider the recommendations of the chief probation officer.

When defense attorneys and their defendants seek to have probation considered as a sentencing option, it may behoove the offender's defense counsel to consider the specific judge who presides over the court as well as the dynamics of a given courtroom. Because of this, in larger court jurisdictions a technique of judge selection may be common (Neubauer, 2007). Through a process of implementing motions of continuances and motions for a change of judge, defense attorneys may maneuver to have their case heard by a judge who is expected to be the most receptive to the offender's plight. Though judges do strive to remain within common guidelines in decisions and rulings, the fact of the matter is that they do tend to differ in terms of the sentences that are given, including the granting of probation and/or the conditions attached to a probation sentence (Neubauer, 2007). An understanding of these tendencies can aid the defense in achieving a more favorable outcome for the offender.

Conditions of Probation

As one can tell, the dynamics of sentencing in the courtroom can allow for some degree of leeway in the final decision-making process. Further illustrating the fluid nature of this process, consider that the setting of conditions during probation can be, at least in part, agreed upon prior to the judge's actual formal sentencing. Though the bargaining process may of course impact the final outcome of the probationer's sentence, the length of probation, and the conditions of that probation, the judge is always free to require additional conditions as he or she sees fit. The conditions that may be required are quite lengthy, but some of the more commonly required conditions are noted in Figure 6.1.

Many of the conditions listed in Figure 6.1 may be statutorily authorized by state legislators as a means of validating their application to probation sentences. This is reflective of the fact that most legislators desire some degree of uniformity and consistency in the supervision requirements and process

Journal Article Link 6.1
Read about the association between sentences and probation recommendations.

Audio Link 6.2
Listen to a judge's mandate to probationers.

FIGURE 6.1 Terms of Probation

1. Refrain from associating with certain types of people (particularly those with a conviction) or frequenting certain locations known to draw criminal elements.

2. Remain sober and drug free; restrictions include using or being in possession of alcohol or drugs.

3. Obey restrictions on firearm ownership and/or possession.

4. Obey requirement to pay fines, restitution, and family support that may be due.

5. Be willing to submit to drug tests as directed by the probation officer and/or representatives of the probation agency.

6. Maintain legitimate and steady employment.

7. Refrain from obtaining employment in certain types of vocations (e.g., an embezzler would be restricted from becoming a bookkeeper, or a computer hacker would be restricted from working with automated systems).

8. Maintain a legal and legitimate residence with the requirement that the probation officer is notified of any change in residence prior to making such a change.

9. Obey the requirement that permission be requested to travel outside of the jurisdiction of the probation agency and/or to another state.

10. Refrain from engaging in further criminal activity.

(Del Carmen, Barnhill, Bonham, Hignite, & Jermstad, 2001; Hanser, 2010). Some states have only a few such requirements while others have an extensive list that clearly requires judges and probationers to structure probation sentences according to a certain prescribed template of conditions. Further, and related to the use of discretionary conditions imposed by judges, some legislators may also clearly note that judges are to be given deference in assigning specialized conditions on certain types of offenders; this is especially true with sex offenders and/or substance abuse offenders (these offenders, the terms and conditions of their supervision, and therapeutic programming will be discussed in later chapters of this text).

The American Probation and Parole Association (APPA, 2011) notes that offenders on probation should be expected to lead a law-abiding life, but also states that the type of supervision (i.e., intensive as opposed to nonintensive, lengthy versus short-term) depends on the circumstances related to the individual offender and the resources available for that offender. The APPA further notes that other conditions should be left to the purview of the probation officer who should primarily be responsible for setting conditions that are consistent with the circumstances of each case. Generally speaking, the APPA notes that aside from providing deterrent conditions to the commission of future recidivism, conditions should by and large be minimal. Further still, Del Carmen et al. (2001) note that in general, "a special condition of probation or parole is invalid only if it has all three of the following characteristics: (1) has no relationship to the crime, (2) relates to conduct that is not in itself criminal, and (3) forbids or requires conduct that is not reasonably related to the future criminality of the offender or does not serve the statutory ends of probation or parole" (p. 77). Thus, it is clear that if put to the test, judges do have a great deal of discretion and latitude when assigning conditions to an offender on probation. So long as the condition has some relation to the crime or to the ability of the agency to monitor for potential future recidivism, then the condition is almost certain to be considered valid if it is later challenged.

Audio Link 6.3
Learn about the challenges of probation for sex offenders.

PROBATION OFFICERS

No chapter on the probation process would be complete without a thorough discussion of the nature of the job and function of probation personnel. The job of a probation officer is quite stressful and challenging, and at the same time, it does not pay near as well as many other professions. Further still, the qualifications for probation officers tend to be fairly high, at least in relation to the demands and pay that are associated with the position. This is truly an unfortunate paradox within the criminal justice system since it is the probation officer who supervises the lion's share of offenders in the correctional system.

Because of the stress involved with probation work, there is a great deal of turnover in the field. Naturally, this can also have negative effects on the correctional system since personnel with expertise are even harder to keep. This can impact the service delivery that agencies are able to provide, and, in some respects, this is likely to affect outcomes among offenders on community supervision. Indeed, it may be likely that the prognosis for recidivism can be impacted (at least in part) by the longevity of the probation officer and his or her demeanor on the job.

Thus, the content of this chapter is more than a simple orientation to work in the field of probation. This chapter also presents an aspect of the field that is critical for students and other persons in society to understand. Indeed, it is society that should perhaps show a display of gratitude for these personnel since it is they, just as well as police personnel, who are largely responsible for keeping society safe from known criminals. Interestingly, most probation agencies pay lower salaries than do police agencies in their same region. This tends to be true in terms of starting, midcareer, and managerial salaries.

Video Link 6.1
Watch a video about probation and parole officers.

PHOTO 6.5

Work in the field of probation often requires that officers work together, both in the office and in the field.

Demographics of Probation Officers: Gender

One interesting aspect of probation work is the fact that the majority of probation staff tends to be female, with

CORRECTIONS AND THE LAW 6.1

Gagnon v. Scarpelli (1973)

Gagnon v. Scarpelli, 411 U.S. 778 (1973), was the second substantive ruling by the U.S. Supreme Court related to the rights of offenders who violate the terms and/or conditions of their probation or parole agreement. The prior ruling, *Morrissey v. Brewer*, 408 U.S. 471 (1972), occurred a year prior to the ruling in *Gagnon*, but was specific to parole. Because this chapter addresses the sanction of probation, emphasis is on the *Gagnon* ruling, but students should understand that *Gagnon* was based upon a similar ruling in *Morrissey* that addressed the rights of parolees who face the possibility of revocation.

The case involved Gerald Scarpelli, a man serving a probation sentence in the state of Wisconsin for armed robbery. While the judge sentenced Scarpelli to 15 years of imprisonment, the judge suspended Scarpelli's sentence and ordered him to serve 7 years of probation. After the probation sentence began, Scarpelli was arrested for burglary in Illinois. Scarpelli's probation was revoked by the Wisconsin Department of Public Welfare subsequent to his confession to police that he was involved in the burglary. The confession in question was later challenged by Scarpelli as being made under duress. After the revocation proceedings, Scarpelli was incarcerated.

After serving three years of imprisonment, Scarpelli challenged the revocation of his probation on the basis that he should have been provided a hearing. The state of Washington, noting the legitimacy of the rationale of the revocation, contended that no such right to a hearing existed and, therefore, the revocation of Scarpelli's probation was constitutional.

The Supreme Court held, in an 8-1 decision, that a probationer's sentence can only be revoked after a preliminary revocation hearing and final revocation hearing. Justice Lewis Powell, in delivering the opinion of the Court, held that Scarpelli was indeed entitled to a hearing regarding his probation status. The Court also noted that, on a case-by-case basis, the use of legal counsel may be required, depending on whether the offender is being tried for a new offense where information from the probation revocation proceeding may be used as evidence in later criminal proceedings.

When considering the right to a revocation proceeding, the Court determined that the probation sentence of an individual cannot be revoked without a hearing. If a probationer commits a violation of his or her probation, that probation sentence can be revoked only after holding a final violation hearing. The Court explained:

> When the view of the probationer or parolee's conduct differs in this fundamental way from the latter's own view, due process requires that the difference be resolved before revocation becomes final. Both the probationer or parolee and the State have interests in the accurate finding of fact and the informed use of discretion—the probationer or parolee to insure that his liberty is not unjustifiably taken away and the State to make certain that it is neither unnecessarily interrupting a successful effort at rehabilitation nor imprudently prejudicing the safety of the community.

In noting the need for legal counsel when a probationer is arrested and given new charges within the period of probation, the Court indicated that counsel should be provided on a case-by-case basis. Justice Powell wrote for the majority and clarified:

> The differences between a criminal trial and a revocation hearing do not dispose altogether of the argument that under a case-by-case approach there may be cases in which a lawyer would be useful but in which none would be appointed because an arguable defense would be uncovered only by a lawyer. Without denying that there is some force in this argument, we think it a sufficient answer that we deal here, not with the right of an accused to counsel in a criminal prosecution, but with the more limited due process right of one who is a probationer or parolee only because he has been convicted of a crime.

exact proportions of female and male officers being dependent on the area of the United States. This is substantially different from fields such as law enforcement, where male officers tend to predominate; women tend to consist of less than 15% of the entire policing community (Shusta, Levine, Wong, & Harris, 2005). This is, in actuality, perhaps partly due to the nature of probation as compared to law enforcement. Indeed, even among police officers, women have been found to be highly effective in defusing conflict situations and/or providing less contact-prone means of response. The National Center for Women and Policing (2003) notes that female police officers tend to be inherently more suited to facilitate cooperation and trust in stressful contact situations and that they are less prone to use excessive force. Likewise, there tend to be fewer citizen complaints against female officers. Though these observations are related to female

PHOTO 6.6

Fieldwork is an important aspect of probation supervision. This requires that officers talk with the offender and others who know the offender in areas outside of the office.

police officers, these same characteristics would seem to be well suited to probation work given the fact that probation has a reintegrative and supportive role with offenders on the officer's caseload.

Demographics of Probation Officers: Race

On the other hand, probation officers also tend to be Caucasian. This can be an important issue when one considers the fact that there is a disproportionate amount of minority representation on most client caseloads. Given that there is such a lack of minority representation among probation officers, it is likely that diversity-related training is all the more necessary and important in cultivating a rapport between community supervision personnel and those on community supervision. There is an abundance of literature that has examined issues related to therapist-client interactions when the two are of different racial and/or ethnic groups. Generally, the prognosis in mental health research does not tend to be as good as when there is a degree of matching or when specific training and consideration are given for racial or cross-cultural issues. Since community corrections has a reformative element, it is not unreasonable to presume that such observations could also be equally true among probation officers and their probationers.

Demographics of Probation Officers: Education

Lastly, most probation officers have a college degree. This does mean that this group is, as a whole, a bit more educated than much of the general workforce. It may perhaps be true that this can mitigate some of the cross-cultural differences, and this also may help to mitigate job dissatisfaction and stress since higher-educated persons tend to, on the whole, be motivated by more than external reward. Though this is obviously not always the case, less emphasis on money does tend to correlate with better-educated workforce members. Somewhat supporting this is the fact that several studies have found that probation work in general tends to be more enriching and challenging, requiring more of an emphasis on problem-solving skills that are likely to mesh well with high-functioning and educated persons. From this, it is clear that probation work is becoming more professionalized and has been likened to an art where probation officers must be skilled at matching security and treatment issues with the particular offender's needs (Bureau of Labor Statistics, 2011). This, as well as the helping aspects of the profession (despite the supervisory components of the profession), is likely to appeal to educated females who seek a professional track in their lives.

Tasks and Nature of Work for Probation Officers

Probation officers, quite naturally, supervise offenders who are placed on some form of probation and tend to spend more time monitoring the activities of these offenders than anything else. Probation officers most frequently maintain this supervision through personal contact with the offender, the offender's family, and the offender's employer. In addition to making contact with the offender through a combination of field visits and/or officer interviews, probation officers make routine contact with the offender's therapist(s), often having therapeutic reports either faxed or delivered to their office. These reports, providing the clinician's insight as to the offender's emotional progress and/or mental health, can be very important to the probation officer's assessment of the offender's progress.

Presentence Investigation Reports

One other function of the probation officer ties in with the local court. In many cases, the probation officer will be tasked with investigating the background of the offender and writing *presentence investigation reports* (described above). While doing this, probation officers may review sentencing recommendations with the offender and even (perhaps) with the offender's family. Note that this is aside from any other arrangements that might be made throughout the plea-bargaining process between the offender's counsel

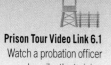

Prison Tour Video Link 6.1
Watch a probation officer describe the training and education needed to become a probation officer.

Reference Link 6.2
Read about the importance of presentence investigation reports.

and the prosecutor's office. In some cases, probation officers may also be required to testify in court as to their findings and recommendations. They also will attend hearings for offenders on their caseload and will often update the court on the offenders' efforts at rehabilitation and compliance with the terms of their sentences.

Working Conditions

The daily working conditions for probation officers can be quite safe when in the office, but can also be fairly dangerous when conducting field visits. Some of the offenders on a probationer's caseload may themselves be more dangerous than their arrest record or actual conviction may indicate. Further, these offenders may still (in violation of their probation) continue to maintain contact with other associates who are more prone to violence than is the probationer. In many instances, the probation officer may have to conduct fieldwork in high-crime areas.

This point should not be taken lightly, and it is unlikely that the average person can understand the true contextual feeling that is associated with such an experience when conducting casework. Often, members of the community may display negative nonverbal behavior toward the probation officer and may be evasive if the officer should happen to ask questions about the offender in their own neighborhood. In fact, in most cases, persons living next to the probationer may not disclose anything because they are also at cross-purposes with the law. In addition, family members are not always happy to have the probation officer visit the home and, while complying with the requirement, may openly resent the intrusion. Lastly, from time to time, the probation officer may make unannounced visits only to find the probationer in the company of unsavory sorts and/or in acts that are criminal in nature (e.g., drinking, trafficking drugs, or discussing various criminal opportunities). All of these issues can lead to some dangerous occurrences. This is even truer when one considers that most probation officers do not carry a firearm. The issue of firearm protection is a controversial one and will be discussed later in this chapter. However, it is safe to say at this point that there is a safety concern when meeting probationers on their own turf.

Travel

In addition, the travel may be quite extensive if the probation officer works in a large rural area of the nation. Some jurisdictions can be quite large, requiring substantial time on the road to reach probationers. The road time that may be involved can further exacerbate the stress since these same officers will be likely to have numerous court-imposed deadlines, PSI reports, and other paperwork to complete, creating an even heavier caseload. Though probation officers are thought to generally work a 40-hour week, the reality is that they may work much more than this, especially during crime-prone seasons of the year. Add to this the fact that most probationers are technically on call 24 hours a day to supervise and assist offenders and/or agency concerns, and it becomes clear that work in probation is not a "cookie-cutter" style of employment from day to day.

Probation Officers in the Role of Law Enforcers and Brokers of Services

Probation officers tend to approach their jobs from different vantage points, much of this having to do with their own perceptions of their particular role in the community corrections process. Daniel Glaser (1964) conducted seminal research on the orientation by which community supervision officers approach their job. Though Glaser focused on parole officers, his contentions apply equally well to probation officers. Thus, Glaser's work will be utilized in this chapter to provide a general framework for probation officers and the informal roles that they play when supervising their caseloads. Basically speaking, Glaser contended that officers tend to operate at differing points along two spectrums: offender control (law enforcers) and offender assistance (brokers of services). These two spectrums work in seeming contradiction with one another, as they each tend to put officers at cross-purposes when trying to balance their job as reformer and public safety officer. This means that four basic categories emerge that describe the officer's general tendency when supervising offenders.

Paternal officers use a great degree of both control and assistance techniques (Glaser, 1964). They protect both the offender and the community by providing the offender with assistance, as well as praising and blaming. This type of officer can seem sporadic at times. These officers are ambivalent to the concerns of the offender or the community; this is just a job that they do. Indeed, these officers may be perceived as being noncommittal by taking the community's side in one case and the offender's in another. These

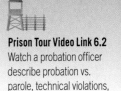

Prison Tour Video Link 6.2
Watch a probation officer describe probation vs. parole, technical violations, and why programs are used.

PHOTO 6.7

Probation officers routinely work in general probation as well as with specialized programs, such as drug courts. Probation Officer Barbara Watts of the 4th Judicial Court, (pictured here), stands outside the main office where probationers wait to meet with their supervision officers. Ms. Watts works with misdemeanor court probationers who have been convicted of a variety of offenses from drug violations to domestic battering.

officers tend not to have a high degree of formal training or secondary education, but they tend to be very experienced and thus are able to weather the difficulties associated with burnout within the field of probation.

Punitive officers (pure law enforcers) see themselves as needing to use threats and punishment in order to get compliance from the offender. These officers will place the highest emphasis on control and protection of the public against offenders, and they will also be suspicious of offenders on their caseload. This suspiciousness is not necessarily wrong or unethical, however, as this is part and parcel of the supervision of offenders, but these officers may in fact never be content with the offender's behavior until they find some reason to award some form of punitive sanction. In other words, the view is that those on the caseload are doing wrong, but they are just not getting caught. Naturally, human relations between this officer and his or her caseload are usually fairly impaired and sterile.

The **welfare worker** (pure broker of services) will view the offender more as a client rather than as a supervisee on the caseload. These individuals believe that, ultimately, the best way they can enhance the security and safety of the community is by reforming the offender so that further crime will not occur. These officers will attempt to achieve objectivity that is similar to a therapist and will thus avoid judging the client. These officers will be most inclined to consider the needs of their offender-clients and their potential capacity for change. These officers view their job more as a therapeutic service than as a punitive service, though this does not mean that they will not supervise the behavior of their caseload. Rather, the purpose of their supervision is more likened to the follow-up screening that a therapist might provide to a client to ensure that he or she is continuing on the directed trajectory that is consistent with prior treatment goals.

The **passive agent** tends to view his or her job as just that, a job. These officers tend to do as little as possible, and they do not have passion for their job. Unlike the punitive officer and the welfare officer, they simply do not care about the outcome of their work so long as they avoid any difficulties. These individuals are often in the job simply due to the benefits that it may have as well as the freedom from continual supervision that this type of job affords.

In reality, it is not likely that officers would best be served using one consistent type of approach rather than using each orientation when appropriate. Thus, the community supervision process can be greatly impacted by the approach taken by the community supervision officer. Further, agencies can transmit a certain tendency toward any of these orientations through policies, procedures, informal organizational culture, or even daily memos. The tone set by the agency is likely to have an effect on the officer's morale and subsequently his or her approach to the supervision process.

On the other hand, some agencies may be very clear about their expectations of community supervision officers. In this case, if the agency has a strict law-and-order flavor, the officer may be best served by utilizing the approach of a punitive officer to ensure that he or she is a good fit with agency expectations. In another agency, the emphasis might be on a combined restorative/community justice model coupled with community policing efforts designed to reintegrate the offender. In an agency such as this, the officer may find that a welfare worker approach is the best fit for that agency and that community. Thus, the culture of the community service organization will have a strong impact upon the officer's orientation, and, if the officer's personal or professional views are in conflict with the organizational structure, the likelihood

Video Link 6.2
Watch a video about the community model.

of effective community supervision is impaired. This is important because it again comes back to the stress encountered among most community supervision workers.

Education, Training, and Qualifications for Probation Officers

The field of community corrections in general and probation in particular has undergone a shift toward increased professionalization. Organizations such as the APPA and the American Correctional Association (ACA) have been instrumental in developing the field of community corrections into a professionalized form of service delivery. This has led to a number of onsite training conferences, correspondence, and online in-service training opportunities. While many states do not necessarily certify their probation officers, some states do have various forms of certification that credential the skills of qualified professionals.

Qualifications

At the point of recruitment, some basic background qualifications are listed in the *Occupational Outlook Handbook* (Bureau of Labor Statistics, 2012). The background qualifications for probation officers vary by state, but generally a bachelor's degree in criminal justice, social work, or a related field is required for initial consideration. Though this was not always the case in times past (some states allowed for less education when combined with experience), this is increasingly becoming the norm in most all states. Some employers may even require previous experience in corrections, casework, or a treatment-related field, or a master's degree in criminal justice, social work, psychology, or a related discipline.

Journal Article Link 6.2
Read about the training and education qualifications for probation officers.

Entry-level probation officers should be in good physical and emotional condition. Most agencies require applicants to be at least 21 years old and, for federal employment, not older than 37 (Bureau of Labor Statistics, 2011). In many jurisdictions, persons who have been convicted of a felony may not be eligible for employment in this occupation (Bureau of Labor Statistics, 2011). Familiarity with the use of computers is typically expected given the increasing use of computer technology in probation and parole work (Bureau of Labor Statistics, 2011). Probation officers should have strong writing skills because they are required to prepare many reports. In addition, a graduate degree in a related field such as criminal justice, social work, counseling, or psychology can aid an employee if advancing into supervisory positions within the agency (Bureau of Labor Statistics, 2011).

According to the *Occupational Outlook Handbook*, applicants are also usually administered a written, oral, psychological, and physical examination. Given the concern with job stress that is inherent in this field of work, it is no surprise that changes in screening mechanisms have been observed during the hiring phase (Bureau of Labor Statistics, 2011). Indeed, hiring and selection procedures may include psychological interviews and personality assessments to identify those most able to handle the stress and psychological challenges of probation and parole work (Bureau of Labor Statistics, 2011). This demonstrates that agencies are aware of the unique challenges with this type of work and wish to identify those persons hearty enough to withstand the pressures that are inherent therein. This is of course a wise and prudent move on the part of agencies from a liability standpoint, a public safety standpoint, and an employee-agency relations standpoint. Effective recruitment and selection at the forefront can prevent a host of problems that would likely be encountered by supervisors and agency leaders in the future.

Training

Beyond recruitment and selection considerations, probation officers are also required to complete a training program sponsored by their particular state of employment. In some states, this may be similar to a police academy method of training. Typically, this training follows with some type of on-the-job training and mentoring between senior community supervision officers and those just graduating from the academy. When local agency field offices provide a well-structured period of follow-up on-the-job training along with effective professional mentoring, probation officers will generally be more prepared for the challenges associated with their new function.

During this period of mentoring, many agencies will have new probation officers work as trainees or on a probationary period for up to one year before being given a permanent position. This allows the agency to further assess the fit between the new hire, the agency, and the line of work required. This is again a prudent move that can prevent many long-term problems likely to occur during later stages of that person's employment. In addition, many agencies will have several levels of probation officer rankings, which can provide additional compensation as well as recognition of competency in the field. Indeed, agencies that do not have varying levels of staff classification should seriously consider adopting such a program, regardless of whether the compensation is greatly adjusted, since there is an inherent and intrinsic reward associated with the mere acknowledgment of the employee's expertise by the organization. This can go a long way in motivating and retaining experienced staff within the agency.

Caseload Management

The job of a probation officer is stressful, placing numerous and diverse demands upon the professional working in such a role. Indeed, the workload can be difficult to quantify since much of the time that is allocated to various functions may not always be easy to truly understand or operationalize. Nevertheless, the need to quantify expectations has resulted in an analysis of community supervision caseloads, the main issues involved with such a formal analysis being both the number of offenders and the type of offenders on one's caseload. It should be clear that, if community supervision officers are stretched too thin among the various offenders being supervised, the safety of the public is then compromised. Thus it is that the workload of a probation officer is directly linked to the safety and security of the public.

During the past two decades, the APPA has attempted to identify the ideal caseload for community supervision officers. The first official attempt to address this issue occurred in the early 1990s when a paper issued by the APPA recommended that probation and parole agencies examine staffing needs and caseload size within their own organizations (American Probation and Parole Association, 1991; Burrell, 2006). Though this seemed to be a reasonable recommendation, it has been much harder to implement than might initially have been imagined. The quest for determining the ideal caseload size has been an elusive one that has been complicated by multiple factors that are difficult to resolve and/or include into any specific equation.

When considering prior attempts to reduce caseloads, a consensus model has slowly emerged throughout the nation (Burrell, 2006). This is the result of input from experienced and thoughtful practitioners in the field of community supervision (Burrell, 2006). Though not necessarily ideal for all agencies, these generally agreed-upon recommendations provide a baseline from which other agencies can operate, comparing and modifying their own operations against the backdrop of the consensus that has emerged. Table 6.1 provides the recommended maximum number of offenders per type of offender category. Classifying offenders on these relevant criteria is critical since it ensures that offenders are correctly matched with the level of supervision necessary to optimize their potential for completing their community supervision requirements (Burrell, 2006; Hanser, 2007).

Hanser (2007) has provided a strong argument for the implementation of valid, reliable assessment instruments, demonstrating that such tools are the critical first step in providing effective supervision of offenders. This allows agencies to allocate resources most accurately and effectively by eliminating the likelihood of false positives and false negatives (Burrell, 2006; Hanser, 2007). This likewise allows these agencies to maximize public safety (Hanser, 2007). In essence, the "evidence suggests that staff resources and services should be targeted at intensive and moderate-to high risk cases, for this is where the greatest effect will be had. Minimal contacts and services should be provided to low risk cases" (Burrell, 2006, p. 7). However, the reality is that this reallocation of staff would simply shift supervision staff to higher-risk offenders and away from those who are low risk (Burrell, 2006). It is in this manner that community supervision caseloads can be structured to optimize overall public safety while at the same time supporting the reintegrative aspects that serve as the basis of any correctional system that truly seeks to correct human behavior that is criminal.

TABLE 6.1   Recommended Caseload Sizes When Considering Type of Offender Case

Adult Caseload Standards	
Case Type	Cases-to-Staff Ratio
Intensive	20:1
Moderate to High Risk	50:1
Low Risk	200:1
Administrative	No limit? 1,000?
Juvenile Caseload Standards	
Case Type	Cases-to-Staff Ratio
Intensive	15:1
Moderate to High Risk	30:1
Low Risk	100:1
Administrative	Not recommended

SOURCE: Burrell, B. (2006). *Caseload standards for probation and parole.* Washington, DC: National Institute of Corrections.

TECHNOLOGY AND EQUIPMENT 6.1

The Use of GPS Tracking and Home Confinement

Global positioning systems (GPS) use a series of satellites to monitor and locate offenders. The Florida Department of Corrections first initiated this program to track probationers in real time at any point during the day or night (Champion, 2002). This system is far superior to any other program of supervision because it ensures that probation officers have near-instantaneous notification of an offender's violation of his or her community supervision. With this system, supervision officers can track an offender within a computer system and can even tell which street the offender is on within any part of the country. Further, these programs can be programmed to detect areas of inclusion or exclusion within the limits of offender travel. This means that if an offender enters a certain area that is restricted, the supervision officer is instantly notified (Champion, 2002).

Community supervision programs utilize military-type technology to keep track of offenders. GPS devices use 24 military satellites to determine the exact location of a coordinate. By using the satellite monitoring and remote tracking, offenders can be tracked to their exact location. GPS tracking used with offenders is joined with an ankle or wrist device that sends a signal to a tracking device that houses a microtransmitter and antenna, which send a signal to the GPS. The tracking device is capable of being placed in an offender's bag, and the offender must remain within 100 feet of the receiver. After receiving the signal, a continuous report is sent to a computer, which tracks the whereabouts of the tracked offender. The GPS tracking device for offenders allows supervising officers to place location restrictions on the offenders so that certain places are off-limits. For example, sex offenders may be excluded from being within the vicinity of a schoolyard or church. If the offender enters a prohibited area, an alarm will sound. On the flip side, officers are allowed to program the offender's schedule for work and religious services and regular day-to-day whereabouts so that it can be easier to detect and verify where and when the offender does what he or she is supposed to. In some cases the system can send notification via pager or telephone that the offender is near the victim or any other excluded location. The advantage of such a program is that the offender's whereabouts are known in a more real-time manner.

Given all of the new advances that GPS technology has provided for community corrections, there are obvious disadvantages such as expense and loss of signal. Just as with any other satellite device, GPS offender tracking devices often lose their signal during bad weather or when in an area densely populated with trees. Of the disadvantages the most noted one is the monetary concerns. Due to the extensive nature of the parties involved, GPS tracking is very expensive, and, in this day of drastic budget cutbacks in community corrections, many agencies are not willing to provide funding for such contemporary and often unnecessary devices. Some have suggested that a way to cut back on the operational costs of GPS devices is that agencies should request the offenders' whereabouts every 30 minutes or so as opposed to every minute. Others have suggested that GPS devices be reserved for the most serious offenders within the community such as child molesters and rapists. Across the country approximately 150,000 offenders are being supervised by electronic monitoring devices.

PROBATION REVOCATION

This discussion is intended to present the use of revocation as a sanction and a component of the probation process in circumstances where offenders are not able to complete their initially given probation sentence. Previous research demonstrates that roughly 4 in 10 probationers fail to complete the initial requirements of their probation (Glaze & Bonczar, 2006). However, some areas of the nation are more prone to revocation than others. Certain counties and/or communities may be more criminogenic in nature and will therefore tend to have more offending as well as more serious offenders processed through the local justice system. In such areas, it should not be surprising that probation departments will generate higher rates of revocation proceedings.

Generally, revocation proceedings are handled in three stages. First, the **preliminary hearing** examines the facts of the arrest to determine if probable cause exists for a violation. Second, the **hearing stage**

State Rankings Link 6.2
Percent of Adults on Probation Traced by Global Positioning Systems in 2009.

Video Link 6.3
Watch a discussion about the probation revocation process.

allows the probation agency to present evidence of the violation while the offender is given the opportunity to refute the evidence provided. Though the agency (or the local government) is not obligated to provide an attorney, the offender does have the right to obtain legal representation, if he or she should desire. Third, the **sentencing stage** is when a judge requires either that the offender be incarcerated or, as in many cases where the violation is minor, that the offender continue his or her probation sentence but under more restrictive terms.

Lastly, it is not uncommon for offenders to have some sort of hearing or proceeding throughout their term of probation. The longer the period of probation, the more likely this is to happen. Nevertheless, many do eventually finish their probation terms. For those offenders who do complete the terms of their probation (eventually meeting all of the requirements), termination of the sentence then occurs. These offenders are free in society without any further obligation to report to the justice system. It is at this last point that their experience with community corrections ends, presuming that they lead a conviction-free life throughout the remainder of their days.

Court Decisions on Revocation

Audio Link 6.4
Hear the arguments of the United States Supreme Court in *Gagnon v. Scarpelli.*

Essentially, there are two primary cases that established due process rights for probationers. The first case to emerge was *Morrissey v. Brewer* (1972), which, in actuality, dealt with revocation proceedings for parolees, not probationers. However, this case was followed by another Supreme Court case, *Gagnon v. Scarpelli* (1973), which extended the rights afforded to parolees under *Morrissey* to offenders on probation as well. Basically, the *Morrissey* court ruled that parolees facing revocation must be given due process through a prompt informal inquiry before an impartial hearing officer. The Court required that this be through a two-step hearing process when revoking parole. The reason for this two-step process is to first screen for the reasonableness of holding the parolee since there is often a substantial delay between the point of arrest and the revocation hearing. This delay can be costly for both the justice system and the offender if it is based on circumstances that do not actually warrant full revocation. Specifically, the Court stated that some minimal

Video Link 6.4
Watch a video about the effectiveness of probation.

> inquiry should be conducted at or reasonably near the place of the alleged parole violation or arrest and as promptly as convenient after arrest while information is fresh and sources are available. . . . Such an inquiry should be seen as in the nature of a "preliminary hearing" to determine whether there is probable cause or reasonable ground to believe that the arrested parolee has committed acts that would constitute a violation of parole conditions. (p. 485)

The Court also noted that this would need to be conducted by a neutral and detached party (a hearing officer), though the hearing officer did not necessarily need to be affiliated with the judiciary, and this first step did not have to be formal in nature. The hearing officer is tasked with determining whether there is sufficient probable cause to justify the continued detention of the offender.

After the initial hearing is the revocation hearing. It is interesting to point out that the Court was quite specific on how the revocation hearings were to be conducted (Del Carmen et al., 2001). During this hearing, the parolee is entitled to the ability to contest charges and demonstrate that he or she did not, in fact, violate any of the conditions of his or her parole. If it should turn out that the parolee did, in fact, violate his or her parole requirements but that this violation was necessary due to mitigating circumstances, it may turn out that the violation does not warrant full revocation. The *Morrissey* Court specified additional procedures during the revocation process that include the following:

1. Written notice of the claimed violation of parole.

2. Disclosure to the parolee of evidence against him or her.

3. An opportunity to be heard in person and to present witnesses and documentary evidence.

4. The right to confront and cross-examine adverse witnesses.

5. A "neutral and detached" hearing body, such as a traditional parole board, members of which need not be judicial officers or lawyers.

6. A written statement by the fact finders as to the evidence relied on and reasons for revoking parole.

The *Morrissey* case is obviously an example of judicial activism (much like *Miranda v. Arizona* [1966]) that has greatly impacted the field of community corrections. The Court's clear and specific guidelines set forth in *Morrissey* have created specific standards and procedures that community supervision agencies must follow. Rather than ensuring that revocation proceedings include a just hearing and means of processing, the Court laid out several pointed requirements that continue to be relevant and binding to this day. The next pivotal case dealing with revocation proceedings and community supervision is *Gagnon v. Scarpelli* (1973). In the simplest of terms, the U.S. Supreme Court ruled that all of the requirements for parole revocation proceedings noted in *Morrissey* also applied to revocation proceedings dealing with probationers. However, this case is important because it also addressed one other key and critical issues regarding revocation proceedings. In *Gagnon v. Scarpelli*, the Court noted that offenders on community supervision do not have an absolute constitutional right to appointed counsel during revocation proceedings. Such proceedings are not considered to be true adversarial proceedings and therefore do not require official legal representation.

Common Reasons for Revocation

There are a number of reasons that offenders may have their probation revoked. Perhaps the most frequent reason that revocation hearings are initiated is due to a probationer's failure to maintain contact with his or her probation officer (Glaze & Bonczar, 2011). Of those probationers who experience a disciplinary hearing, the most frequent reason tends to be absconding or the previously mentioned failure to contact their probation officer (Glaze & Bonczar, 2011). Other reasons may include an arrest or conviction for a new offense, failure to pay fines/restitution, or failure to attend or complete an alcohol or drug treatment program (Glaze & Bonczar, 2011). Among probationers who have revocation hearings initiated against them, almost half may be permitted to continue their probation sentence. For those who are allowed to continue, they will almost always have additional conditions imposed against them, and their type of supervision will typically be more restrictive (Glaze & Bonczar, 2011).

Journal Article Link 6.3
Read about the problem of rising revocations.

Further complicating the picture is the fact that some conditions of probation result in what are often called technical violations. **Technical violations** are actions that do not comply with the conditions and requirements of a probationer's sentence, as articulated by the court that acted as the sentencing authority. Technical violations are not necessarily criminal, in and of themselves, and would likely be legal behaviors if the offender were not on probation. For instance, a condition of a drug offender's probation may be that he or she stay out of bars, nightclubs, and other places of business where the selling and consumption of alcohol is a primary attraction for customers frequenting the establishment. Another example might be if a sex offender is ordered to remain a certain distance from schools. For most citizens, going to nightclubs and/or setting foot on school grounds is not a violation of any sort, and neither of these acts is considered criminal. However, for the probationer, this can lead to the revocation of probation.

Any number of other behaviors can be technical violations. Additional examples might include the failure to attend mandated therapy, failure to report periods of unemployment, failing to complete scheduled amounts of community service, and failing to show up for routine appointments with the probation officer. Though it may be clear that these violations are substantially different from those that carry a new and separate criminal conviction, they still do carry the weight of a revocation (Hanser, 2009). These violations are obviously not as serious as true violations of criminal law, but they are important in demonstrating whether the offender is making genuine progress in the corrections process. Excessive technical violations would seem to indicate that reform is not a priority for the offender who continues to commit crimes.

APPLIED THEORY 6.1

Critical Criminology and Probation Supervision

The basic tenets of critical criminology are that inequality in power and material wealth help to create conditions that lead to crime. Critical criminologists contend that capitalism and the effects of the market economy are particularly prone to generating criminal behavior. This is largely due to the extreme inequality that impoverishes a large amount of the population. This also makes the less affluent groups open to exploitation and economic abuse at the hands of those who are more powerful. Thus, criminal behavior, according to conflict criminologists, has its etiology in the disparities between the rich and the poor, with the rich using their power and influence to dominate, subordinate, and exploit the poor.

Though it may not necessarily be the role of the community supervision officer to right the wrongs of society, it may be useful if such practitioners remain aware of the economic structures that impact society and may also impact how offenders see their plight. Most high-crime areas of the United States are also impoverished, consisting of populations that live in poverty and have great difficulty competing in the legitimate economy. Many of these high-crime regions, including those that offenders may return to once they are released on community supervision, may offer few legitimate employment opportunities. Due to the lack of monetary resources in the community, other social services and opportunities will be likewise limited. These areas also tend to consist of a population that may have had poorer access to education, medical care, and other services that impact the quality of life for community members.

In such communities, there may exist a culture of poverty, with little legitimate hope of breaking out of the economically debilitating circumstances. This culture is one that is far removed from that of middle-class America, though middle-class American youth may emulate the ghetto culture and/or sensationalized versions of such life that are portrayed by Hollywood and the media. This is unfortunate because it ensures that middle-class youth will not truly understand the pains of poverty, instead idealizing many of the negative criminogenic influences in such communities. Further, it labels, stereotypes, and reinforces the notion that poverty-ridden communities are criminogenic and even normalizes this so that youth in such communities accept it as their normal lot in life. Thus, the external portrayals exacerbate the problem. Incidentally, the portrayal of such underprivileged communities is done at the hands of rich and powerful media moguls, recording companies, and executive decision makers, all of whom fit within the upper-class and affluent society.

From these formulated expectations and due to the inequality of resources, the poor are again victimized as they are corralled into believing and accepting a fundamentally unfair system and they are, at least indirectly, told through media accounts that the life of crime is perhaps their most viable bet to achieving parity within a system of economic parity. It is with this in mind that police and other government agents are seen as being in league with "the man" who serves as a nefarious and obscure mastermind behind the lower class's woes. Such communities may also have family systems that teach children to fear and/or be disrespectful to police. Naturally, this extends to other government agents of the criminal justice system as well. With this in mind, the community in general and the offender in particular may actually hold the community supervision officer to be an agent to such inequalities.

This results in resentment that can build between the probationer and the community supervision officer, and this also can create a chasm between the community and the agency. This resentment may have little to do with the crime committed and the actual supervision provided by the officer, but it may instead be primarily due to years of under-class socialization that has conditioned the offender to see government agents as part of a system that deliberately and methodically seeks to exploit the poor and underprivileged. Thus an understanding of economic disadvantages, potential institutionalization, and/or marginalization to an inferior or subordinate role in society can aid community supervision officers to develop a rapport with the community and their clientele. An understanding of these factors that impact crime-prone and underserved communities can aid community supervision officers who find themselves engaged in correctional case management services for persons from such neighborhoods. This knowledge is also useful for correctional treatment specialists, who must understand the latent and manifest mistrust of treatment providers that is inherent in much of the underclass.

Community supervision officers and correctional treatment providers cannot single-handedly repair these communities. Further, these professionals cannot necessarily change the subculture of resentment and mistrust that may exist within some of these communities. But, they can encourage involvement in community development and stabilization projects, and they can be cognizant of the serious limits that face probationers and parolees who come from such communities. Agencies must work with persons in such communities who are receptive to forming multiagency partnerships, citizen volunteer groups, and the like. Above and beyond all else, such agencies and agency members must emphasize a sense of respect for the community in general since this sense of mutual respect is what has particularly been lacking among many such communities. An emphasis on community concern may help to take the sting out of the intergenerational resentment and distrust that may exist in such communities, allowing agency members to slowly change community attitudes and culture over the years that follow.

SOURCE: Cullen, F. T., & Agnew, R. (2006). *Criminological theory: Past to present* (3rd ed.). Los Angeles: Roxbury.

CONCLUSION

This chapter illustrates the importance of probation as a sanction within the correctional system. Whether one considers community- or institution-based corrections, the use of probation as a sanction impacts the overall correctional system quite significantly. This is especially true when one considers the impact that probation has on the jail facility. Without the use of probation, jail facilities would be even more overcrowded than they already tend to be. Thus, the use of probation as a means of controlling inmate flow into the jail is important.

Regardless of probation's use as a tool to mitigate offender flow into the jail system, probation's true purpose is to facilitate the reformation of offenders. This has been the case since its earliest inception when John Augustus first established this sanction in the United States. It is with this in mind that students should consider probation, a sanction that has reformative value. This means that the point and purpose of probation are consistent with this text's definition of corrections whereby the ultimate goal is to correct criminal tendencies among the offender population.

This chapter also highlights the importance of the presentence investigation (PSI), demonstrating that this report is important for judges who sentence offenders and it is also important during later points in the offender's sentence. Indeed, the PSI is even used in institutional settings when making early-release, treatment-planning, and custody-level decisions. Thus, the PSI is an important tool to the correctional system as a whole, and, consistent with this importance, probation officers tend to spend a significant amount of time constructing PSIs and/or referring to the information contained therein.

Probation officer qualifications and standards of training were also discussed. It is clear that the job of probation officer is not one that is easy. Indeed, this job requires a degree in most cases but pays little in comparison to other professions. Further, the work is stressful given the high caseloads that tend to exist for many probation officers. Qualifications and characteristics of probation officers demonstrate that this area of correctional employment may be quite different from institutional corrections and that this dimension of the correctional system has been underappreciated.

Lastly, revocation procedures were discussed in detail. Leading cases related to revocation for probation and the corresponding procedures for revocation were discussed. The stages of revocation and the processes used help to ensure that capriciousness does not occur when determining whether an offender should or should not remain on probationary status. The issue of technical violations, as opposed to those related to new criminal convictions, was also illustrated, showing that the types of infractions can vary considerably depending on the offender and the particular circumstances involved.

END-OF-CHAPTER DISCUSSION QUESTIONS

1. Who is the "father of probation," and how did he initially implement the practice of probation?

2. Discuss how probation impacts the jail and prison systems of a jurisdiction.

3. Discuss the means by which probation agencies might be organized.

4. Why is the presentence investigation report so important?

5. Identify and discuss the qualifications and characteristics of most probation officers.

6. Discuss the importance of *Morrissey v. Brewer* (1972) and *Gagnon v. Scarpelli* (1973).

7. How does critical criminology dovetail with probation supervision?

KEY TERMS

Global positioning system (GPS)

Hearing stage

John Augustus

Passive agent

Paternal officer

Preliminary hearing

Presentence investigation report

Probation

Punitive officer

Sentencing stage

Technical violations

Welfare worker

APPLIED EXERCISE 6.1

You are a senior probation officer in a midsize agency located in the suburbs of a metropolitan environment. You are troubled today by a dilemma that confronts you; you have two probationers who both have multiple technical violations, and you find it difficult to come to a determination for them that seems fair.

The first probationer, named Max, just failed his urinalysis and tested positive for alcohol, of all things. This is Max's third technical violation since he is supposed to refrain from consuming alcohol as one of the conditions of his probation. Max is on probation for assault. The assault was mutual—he got into an altercation with another man in a nightclub and put the man in the hospital. While Max had no previous violent record, he did have a documented problem with alcohol. Other than the fact that Max continues to drink occasionally and the fact that he has missed two prior appointments, Max fulfills the requirements of his probation. He pays all of his fees, goes to work on time, attends his Alcoholics Anonymous meetings, makes most appointments, and so forth. Max is always apologetic and respectful when he has a lapse in his conditions, and you believe that he is genuinely trying to improve.

The second probationer is Joe, who has failed to report for his appointment with you for the third time. Joe is routinely late to his appointments when he does make them, and he tends to have a surly attitude. Joe does not seem to care much when he is late, and he makes no overt attempt to try to assuage your concerns regarding his status on probation. Joe is on probation for writing a couple of hot checks, and he contends that, in most cases, full prosecution for his crime would not really occur, especially since the checks were small and written to the university that he attended. In reality, you know that Joe is correct in his appraisal of the situation. In fact, his case came through the courthouse at a time when the district attorney and judges had agreed to "crack down" on insufficient funds charges at the request of numerous businesses in the area. Thus, Joe was a victim of circumstances, in some respects. Further, Joe tells you that he thinks that it is irrelevant if he is all "nicey-nicey" at the probation office. After all, others have done far worse than him, and they get to stay on probation. As Joe puts it, "Hey, it ain't like I'm some gangsta or something—or one of those people who have some drug problem."

While here at the agency, you have recently had it brought to your attention that you probably exercise too much leniency on the job. Though your supervisor has outright given you official counseling on the issue, he contends that you need to be a bit firmer with your caseload. As it turns out, the jailhouse is a bit low this year; the county recently voted in favor of a referendum to build more space in the jail, and, with this in mind, your agency has been encouraged to utilize the space with those offenders who might benefit from a short stint in the jailhouse.

TO THE STUDENT: For this exercise, explain if you would put either of these offenders in jail for even a short period or if you would instead seek more restrictive conditions on their probation. If you place them in jail, explain how this might affect their employment and/or educational pursuits. Also, explain whether you believe that the offender's attitude should be relevant to your decision. Be sure to explain why you come to the conclusions that you do.

"WHAT WOULD YOU DO?"

You are a probation officer in a small rural agency. The chief probation officer explains to you that services have not been optimal and that many offenders are having difficulty finding employment. Further, many of them cannot travel the distances that are required to make many of their appointments. The local jail is full to capacity, and the state is not taking low-risk offenders. Your supervisor explains that this issue is not one of failure to meet the conditions of probation but is instead one where the offenders are unable to meet these conditions.

Your supervisor has established a steering committee made up of you, a member of the social services office, a person from city hall, a deputy from the sheriff's office, and another person from the regional hospital. She wants you to come up with some sort of action plan that will allow you to aid persons on community supervision in finding employment, making therapeutic and medical meetings, and meeting the conditions of their restitution requirements. She tells you that this is a very serious task, and she knows that it is a difficult task, particularly since your jurisdiction spans a large tri-county area with a total population of only 25,000 people. The local town of Maybury has a population of roughly 8,000 people. Though resources are scant, she encourages you to take this task seriously and notes that she will provide any support that is possible. In the meantime, she has lightened your caseload to make your new task more manageable.

What would you do?

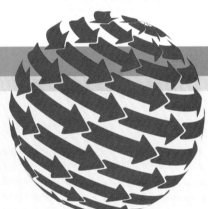

CROSS-NATIONAL PERSPECTIVE 6.1

The History of Probation in England

1876: Hertfordshire printer Frederic Rainer, a volunteer with the Church of England Temperance Society (CETS), writes to the society of his concern about the lack of help for those who come before the courts. He sends a donation of 5 shillings (25 pence) toward a fund for practical rescue work in the police courts. The CETS responds by appointing two "missionaries" to Southwark court with the initial aim of "reclaiming drunkards." This forms the basis of the London Police Court Mission (LPCM), whose missionaries worked with magistrates to develop a system of releasing offenders on the condition that they kept in touch with the missionary and accepted guidance.

1880: Eight full-time missionaries are in place, and the mission opens homes and shelters providing vocational training and develops residential work.

1886: The Probation of First Offenders Act allows for courts around the country to follow the London example of appointing missionaries, but very few do so.

1907: The Probation of Offenders Act gives LPCM missionaries official status as "officers of the court," later known as probation officers. The act allows courts to suspend punishment and discharge offenders if they entered into a recognizance of between one and three years, one condition of which was supervision by a person named in the "probation order."

1913: The first newsletter of the National Association of Probation Officers records the association's first annual meeting at Caxton Hall in London on December 11, 1912. The newsletter reports the address given to the Grand Jury of the London Sessions in September 1912 by Robert Wallace KC, who said that the calendar was one of the lightest in the history of the sessions. "Of 137 prisoners, 17 had been sent for sentence as 'incorrigible rogues' and 12 others were awaiting punishment. There were only nine women. There has been a steady diminution in the number of cases ever since the new method of dealing with offenders under the Probation of Offenders Act was adopted four years ago. Of those who had been dealt with in that way, very few had offended again."

1918: With juvenile crime increasing during and after the First World War, the Home Office concedes that probation should not be left to philanthropic or judicial bodies and that state direction is needed. The influential Molony Committee of 1927 stimulates debate about the respective roles of probation officers, local government, and philanthropic organizations. It encourages the informal involvement of probation officers in aftercare from both Borstal and reformatory schools.

1938: The Home Office assumes control of the probation service and introduces a wide range of modernizing reforms. The legal formula of "entering into a recognizance" is replaced by "consent to probation." Requirements for psychiatric treatment are also introduced, and it is made mandatory for female probationers to be supervised by women officers. LPCM concentrates on hostels for "probation trainees" and branches out into homes for children in "moral danger," sexually abused children, and young mothers.

1948: The Criminal Justice Act incorporates punitive measures such as attendance centers and detention centers, but the stated purpose of the probation order remains intact and is reaffirmed as "advise, assist, and befriend."

1970s and '80s: Partnerships with other agencies result in cautioning schemes, alternatives to custody, and crime reduction, while changes in sentencing result in day centers, special program conditions, the probation order as a sentence, and risk of custody and risk of reconviction assessment tools.

2000: The Criminal Justice and Court Services Act renames the probation service as the National Probation Service for England and Wales, replacing 54 probation committees with 42 local probation boards and establishing 100% Home Office funding for the probation service. It creates the post of director general of probation services within the Home Office and makes chief officers statutory officeholders and members of local probation boards.

2004: The government publishes *Reducing Crime, Changing Lives*, which proposes to improve the effectiveness of the criminal justice system and the correctional services in particular. The National Offender Management Service is established with the aim of reducing reoffending through more consistent and effective offender management. The government proposes to introduce commissioning and contestability into the provision of probation services, which it says will drive up standards further among existing providers and enable new providers to deliver services.

2007: The probation service in England and Wales is 100 years old.

Critical Thinking

Discuss the commonality of early religious involvement in corrections and explain how that affected correctional thought in both the United States and England. Next, after reading the chronological history of probation in England (see Cross-National Perspective 6.1), explain whether this religious emphasis continued or if it appears to have diminished over time. Is this the same as or different from developments in the United States? Explain your answer.

Adapted from: Probation Board Association of England and Wales. (2007). *Probation centenary, 1907–2007*. Retrieved February 2, 2011, from http://www.probationcentenary.org/contactus.htm.

For more information about probation in the United Kingdom, visit: http://www.probationcentenary.org/contactus.htm.

STUDENT STUDY SITE

Visit the Student Study Site at **www.sagepub.com/hanserintro** to access links to the videos, audio clips, SAGE journal articles, state rankings, and reference materials noted in this chapter, as well as additional study tools including eFlashcards, web quizzes, and more.

chapter 7

Intermediate Sanctions

LEARNING OBJECTIVES:

1. Know the definition and purpose of intermediate sanctions.

2. Identify the various types of intermediate sanctions and their placement within the continuum of sanctions.

3. Analyze the various means of ensuring compliance by substance abusers and sex offenders.

4. Compare the various ways intermediate sanctions are used in a variety of states around the nation.

5. Understand both the security and treatment functions associated with intermediate sanctions.

INTRODUCTION

Journal Article Link 7.1
Read about a proposal relating intermediate sanctions to social control.

Currently, there is no single definition of intermediate sanctions, nor is there any ironclad agreement about what ought to be included within such a definition. Some researchers contend that almost anything that falls between "regular" probation and a full prison term is an intermediate sanction; others deny inclusion in this category to any sanction that involves incarceration. However, the growing popularity of residential facilities like restitution centers (see Focus Topic 7.1), work release centers, and probation detention facilities, some with capacities in the hundreds, makes this distinction important (Guccione, 2002).

What intermediate sanctions do have in common is the presence of features designed to enhance the desired sanctioning purpose. Regardless of whether the intent is to achieve punishment, incapacitation, rehabilitation, or specific deterrence, intermediate sanctions provide more options than does simple probation. These sanctions also tend to vary in severity, leading to a continuum of sanctions that progress from the most restrictive (prison) to the least restrictive (suspended sentences, deferred adjudication, and so forth). This can lead to increased surveillance and tighter controls on movement, while enhancing the integration of more intense treatment to address a wider assortment of maladies or deficiencies. The use of intermediate sanctions can help to integrate supervision and treatment, offering options beyond what incarceration may usually offer. Indeed, intermediate sanctions should be perceived as a linking pin that integrates elements of the security and treatment spectrums, providing the glue between both orientations.

PHOTO 7.1

In many cases, the plea-bargain process allows for attorneys to discuss agreements on sanctions that will be given to an offender. This is a routine process in the courthouse.

One purpose in implementing effective and appropriate intermediate sanctions is to make available a continuum of sanctions scaled around one or more sanctioning goals. For example, the goal of incapacitation may be implemented through varying levels of surveillance or control of movement. Such a continuum permits the court or corrections authority to tailor sanctions that are meaningful with respect both to their purposes and to the kinds of offenders that come before them.

A current practice is to unload the complete list of sanctions on all offenders, setting up both offenders and the program for failure. A typical offender who is supporting two children, for example, is not likely to be able to pay restitution, perform extensive community service, and participate in frequent drug counseling. Targeting specific sanctions to specific offender profiles, on the other hand, increases the chances of success for both the program and the offender. This kind of policy-directed system can also be responsive to differing and changing behavior on the part of offenders.

Currently, as an alternative to the rising costs of incarceration, convicted offenders are being sentenced to community supervision with increasing frequency (Glaze & Palla, 2005). Despite supervising an overwhelming majority of offenders, community supervision (probation) departments have experienced budget cuts, which in turn have led to a reduction in staff and resources, regardless of the drastic increases in caseload sizes. Given the increased caseloads and the decrease in program funding, the need for alternative means of supervision and treatment is at a premium. To this end, intermediate sanctions have become the order of the day.

TYPES OF INTERMEDIATE SANCTIONS

When it comes to finding alternatives to punishment and rehabilitation for offenders, there is no shortage, particularly in terms of community-based rehabilitation. On a simplistic level, intermediate sanctions could be defined as alternatives to traditional incarceration that consist of sentencing options falling anywhere between a standard prison sentence and a standard probation sentence. Reflecting the versatile

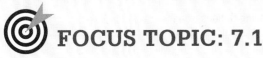

FOCUS TOPIC: 7.1

Doing Time in the Working World

Gina Faison takes the bus every morning to the downtown Los Angeles law office where she works.

She cannot leave the building for lunch with colleagues. She cannot stop at the mall after work. Nor can she go home to her husband and three young sons at night.

Faison, a paralegal and convicted thief, is serving an unusual three-year sentence at California's only restitution center for women.

"I don't know if I could have made it over the wall," said Faison, a 38-year-old first offender, referring to state prison.

She is one of 43 women now living at the minimum-security facility in Pico-Union, where inmates wear whatever they like, sleep two to six in a bedroom and sip their morning coffee outside under bright blue awnings.

The program is designed to move nonviolent inmates from prison into the work force to repay their victims, said Doris Mahlum, district administrator for the state Department of Corrections.

Participants have paid $250,000 in court-ordered restitution in the last two years, she said.

Despite increased prosecution of white-collar criminals and the popularity of alternative sentences for nonviolent offenders, the restitution center has operated in relative obscurity since 1971.

It serves inmates from throughout California, but rarely, if ever, have all its beds been occupied at once. Several are now empty.

To qualify, inmates must be nonviolent, must have been ordered to pay restitution and sentenced to three years or less. They are required to get a job and turn over two-thirds of their salary to their victims and the state to defray the costs of incarceration.

The women are housed in a beige one-story structure built in 1910 as the Chase Sanatorium in a residential area on West 18th Street near Union Avenue. A 50-bed men's center is in a renovated motel in an industrial section of South La Cienega Boulevard.

Unlike the general prison population, most of the inmates are educated and have marketable job skills, said Cheryl Atterbury-Brooks, the parole officer assigned to the women's center.

"We have doctors, lawyers, nurses," she said.

A few earn more than the staff that supervises them. Program manager Ernest Green recalled a geologist convicted of fraud who was paid $30 an hour.

SOURCE: "Doing their Time in the Working World. Restitution center is for women who stole, they pay their debts, avoid prison," by J. Guccione. *Los Angeles Times*, April 15, 2002. Copyright © 2002. Reprinted with permission.

nature of intermediate sanctions, the National Institute of Corrections (1993) has also defined intermediate sanctions as "a range of sanctioning options that permit the crafting of sentences to respond to the particular circumstances of the offender and the offense; and the outcomes desired in the case" (p. 18). For this text, the definition of these sanctions will consist of a blend of both definitions. Thus, **intermediate sanctions** are a range of sentencing options that fall between incarceration and probation, being designed to allow for the crafting of sentences that respond to the offender, the offense, or both, with the intended outcome of the case being a primary consideration. Tables 7.1 and 7.2 provide an examination of the various intermediate sanctions, their philosophical underpinnings, and their intended purposes.

The definition of intermediate sanctions, as just presented, provides a perspective that is highly consistent with the emphasis on reintegration found in this text. It is clear that these types of sanctions allow for a great deal of flexibility that can be adjusted to accommodate treatment and supervision considerations. These sanctions are guided by the intent of the sentencing body but allow for consideration of the various needs, challenges, and issues associated with the offender and the type of offending that he or she is prone to committing. This permits the calibration of sentences so that specific details are a better fit with the type of offense considered as well as the individual variables associated with the offender. Such flexibility is what provides the field of community corrections with its greatest source of leverage among the offender population, in terms of treatment and supervision.

This chapter will discuss the most commonly implemented and researched intermediate sanctions of intensive supervision, day reporting centers, day fines, home detention, electronic monitoring, shock incarceration, boot camps, community service, and various methods of compliance assurance. When considering the overcrowding problems in prison systems around the nation, it is clear that there is simply a pragmatic need for more space. As a result of the public's outcry for increased traditional sentencing of offenders, coupled with legislative action as a response to the public, the use of intermediate sanctions has grown. Recent reports indicate that many parolees and probationers are supervised under some form

Video Link 7.1
Watch a video about offenders in boot camps.

Warning Measures (Notice of consequences of subsequent wrongdoing)	Admonishment/cautioning (administrative; judicial)	
	Suspended execution or imposition of sentence	
Injunctive Measures (Banning legal conduct)	Travel (e.g., from jurisdiction; to specific criminogenic spots)	
	Association (e.g., with other offenders)	
	Driving	
	Possession of weapons	
	Use of alcohol	
	Professional activity (e.g., disbarment)	
	Restitution	
Economic Measures	Costs	
	Fees	
	Forfeitures	
	Support payments	
	Fines (standard; day fines)	
	Community service (individual placement; work crew)	
Work-Related Measures	Paid employment requirements	
	Academic (e.g., basic literacy, GED)	
Education-Related Measures	Vocational training	
	Life skills training	
	Psychological/psychiatric	
Physical and Mental Health	Chemical (e.g., methadone; psychoactive drugs)	
Treatment Measures	Surgical (e.g., acupuncture drug treatment)	
Physical Confinement Measures	*Partial or intermittent confinement*	Home curfew
		Day treatment center
		Halfway house
		Restitution center
		Weekend detention facility/jail
	Full/continuous confinement	Outpatient treatment facility (e.g., drug/mental health)
		Full home/house arrest
		Mental hospital
		Other residential treatment facility (e.g., drug/alcohol)

		Boot camp
		Detention facility
		Jail
		Prison
Monitoring/Compliance Measures (May be attached to all other sanctions)	*Required of the offender*	Electronic monitoring (telephone check-in; active electronic monitoring device)
		Mail reporting
		Face-to-face reporting
		Urine analysis (random; routine)
	Required of the monitoring agent	Sentence compliance checks (e.g., on payment of monetary sanctions; attendance/performance at treatment, work, or educational sites)
		Criminal records checks
		Third-party checks (family, employer, surety, service/treatment provider; via mail, telephone, in person)
		Direct surveillance/observation (random/routine visits and possibly search; at home, work, institution, or elsewhere)
		Electronic monitoring (regular phone checks and/or passive monitoring device—currently used with home curfew or house arrest, but could track movement more widely as technology develops)

SOURCE: National Institute of Corrections. (1993). *The intermediate sanctions handbook: Experiences and tools for policymakers.* Washington, DC: Author.

of intermediate sanctioning, and this trend is likely to increase in the future (Mitchell, 2011; Office of Program Policy Analysis and Governmental Accountability, 2010). While we must remember that the applicability of such programming is dependent upon the potential for harm in local communities and the ability of intermediate sanctions to reduce recidivism, there is little doubt that, in today's era of state-level budget cuts, many prison systems are using intermediate sanctions as alternatives to imprisonment (Mitchell, 2011). Students should refer to Figure 7.1 to see the cost difference between intermediate sanctions and prison.

Fines

Most offenders convicted of a criminal offense are assessed a fine as a punishment for committing the offense. A fine can be defined as a monetary penalty imposed by a judge or magistrate as a punishment for having committed an offense. In most cases, the fine is a certain dollar amount established either by the judge or according to a set schedule, depending upon the offense committed (see Chapter 3). The logic behind the fine is that it will deter the offender from committing another offense in the future for fear of being fined again. In most jurisdictions, the fines are assessed and paid in monthly installments to the receiving agency. In contemporary community supervision agencies, offenders are now able to pay their fines via credit or debit cards. The feelings are mixed regarding allowing an offender to pay in this manner. Officers sometimes feel that by delaying the effect of the monetary fine, it does not allow the offender to accept personal responsibility.

TABLE 7.2 Illustration of Scaling Possibilities for Criminal Sanctions: Type of Sanction, by Scaling Dimensions and Units of Measurement

Type of Sanction	Scaling Dimensions					
	Retributive Severity	Crime Reduction (A)	Recidivism Reduction (B)	Reparation	Economic Cost	Public Satisfaction
Sanction A Sanction B Sanction C Sanction D ...	Value in terms of pain and suffering (C)	Value in terms of impact on crime rate	Value in terms of impact on reoffense rate	Value in terms of compensating aggrieved parties (D)	Value in terms of cost efficiency	Value in terms of public approval ratings
Sanction Key:						
A = General deterrence effects						
B = Specific deterrence, incapacitation, rehabilitation effects						
C = Effects in terms of units of onerousness, intrusiveness, or deprivation of autonomy/ liberty						
D = Direct victims and possibly indirectly affected individuals, groups, or entities [e.g., family members, insurers, taxpayers, community, society]						

SOURCE: National Institute of Corrections. (1993). *The intermediate sanctions handbook: Experiences and tools for policymakers.* Washington, DC: Author.

As the offense seriousness increases from misdemeanor to felony, presumably the fines increase as well. This assessment of fines is totally dependent upon judicial discretion. Gordon and Glaser (1991) have demonstrated that most offenders are more likely to pay their fines in totality, and that the likelihood of recidivism for these offenders is significantly less than for those who are sentenced to traditional institutional incarceration after controlling for offender type and type of offense committed. At both the federal and state levels, fines are imposed. Traditionally, there was one set fine for certain offenses regardless of the financial standing of the offenders. As time has passed, many judiciaries have begun to understand that one set fine is more punishing to the offender who happens to earn the least amount of money and

FIGURE 7.1 Intermediate Sanctions Are Less Costly Than Incarceration

Intermediate Sanction	First Year Cost Per Offender 2008-09	Total First Year Cost For 100 Offenders[1]	Potential Savings Per 100 Offenders[2]
Prison	$20,272	$2,027,200	–
Supervision with GPS Monitoring	$5,121	$806,954	$1,220,246
Probation and Restitution Centers	$9,492	$1,639,211	$387,989
Day Reporting	$4,191	$917,823	$1,109,377
Residential Drug Treatment	$10,539	$1,419,529	$607,671

[1] The first year cost for 100 offenders is based on the actual program completion rates 2008-10. Offenders who do not complete the program are assumed to leave the program after 82 days and are sent to prison for the remaining 283 days of the year; the cost of prison for these offenders is included in the total first year cost estimate.

[2] The savings for 100 offenders represents the difference between the cost of prison for one year based on $55.54 per day and the total first year cost for intermediate sanctions.

SOURCE: Office of Program Policy Analysis and Governmental Accountability. (2010). *Intermediate sanctions for non-violent offenders could produce savings.* Tallahassee, FL: Author.

a "cakewalk" to those offenders who happen to be financially blessed. Given this, there has been a push for graduated fines that are dependent upon the income of the offender at time of sentencing. In this day of drastic budget cuts and pushes for alternatives to incarceration, fines are the order. They allow the offender an opportunity to pay for his or her treatment and punishment as opposed to the traditional method of placing the financial burden on the state.

Community Service

Perhaps the most widely known yet least likely to be used form of intermediate sanctioning is community service (see Chapter 5). Community service is the work that one is required to perform for repaying his or her debt to society after being found at fault for committing a criminal or deviant offense. In most cases, community service is ordered by the sentencing judge and supervised by the community supervision officer. Most judges prefer that offenders sentenced to complete community service do the work at a not-for-profit agency within their local jurisdiction. Types of community service range from trash pickups to caring for animals at an animal shelter or participating in menial labor jobs at the local public facilities.

Video Link 7.2
Watch a video about community service.

Community service is an alternative to paying fines for offenders who may not have the financial means to do so. The use of labor in lieu of money provides a means of holding offenders accountable, even if they do not have the ability to pay financial penalties. Due to the fact that many offenders are economically challenged, community service options began to spring up all around the country, particularly as an option for younger and less violent offenders. To date, community service is mostly used as an integral condition of probation or parole. In most cases, offenders are required to complete a set amount of community service hours a month.

Community service serves a dual purpose: to rehabilitate and punish offenders. In terms of rehabilitation, community service affords the offender time to participate in something constructive, all the while providing him or her with an opportunity to build "sweat equity" in something that is beneficial to the community. Community service is punitive, too, in that the offender is forced to give up his or her own time to work off a criminal debt without being paid.

Due to the low cost of overhead in funding community service programs, coupled with the added use of much-needed labor in communities, community service options will continue to be well utilized. One of the most pressing problems in evaluating community service is that such opportunities vary so widely, and often offenders participate in multiple community service sites and types throughout their time under supervision.

PHOTO 7.2

Some offenders must complete community service as part of their sentence. Offenders may be given community supervision or a split-sentences (includes both jail time and community supervision) which usually requires the completion of some type of labor, as seen here with this offender who prepares to do yard work.

In most cases, community service is completed anywhere the offender can get the hours. For example, an offender may begin community service at the local courthouse and complete his or her hours at the homeless mission. Despite the lack of research in this area, community service is clearly an integral part of intermediate sanctioning and provides a positive avenue through which offenders and the community can learn the rehabilitative and punitive ideals.

Intensive Supervision Probation

Perhaps the most commonly known form of intermediate sanction is **intensive supervision probation (ISP)**. ISP is the extensive supervision of offenders who are deemed the greatest risk to society or are in need of the greatest amount of governmental services (e.g., drug treatment). In most cases, ISP is the option afforded to individuals who would otherwise be incarcerated for felony offenses. The early forms of ISP operated under the conservative philosophy of increasing public safety via strict offender scrutiny. Today's ISP programs are focused on a host of components.

In the early days, ISP programs operated under the assumption that increasing an offender's contact with his or her supervising officer would increase public safety and simultaneously the offender's chances of rehabilitation. As an example, the California Special Intensive Parole Unit of the 1950s was created with an emphasis on increased supervision and a special interest in offender rehabilitation. A short time later, the field began to seek the optimal offender-officer ratio in terms of effectiveness. As a result of the inability to find that optimal ratio, intensive supervision suffered in credibility during the 1960s and 1970s.

When examining the various facets of modern-day intensive supervision, one finds that they are quite diverse. Some ISPs focus on specific offense and offender types (e.g., sex offending and younger offenders), while others vary in their level of supervision, which may range from 5 days per week to once every 2 weeks. The types of supervising officers vary from untrained community supervision officers to specialized officers who have been well trained in the supervision of at-risk offenders. In most cases, officers are afforded a lighter than normal caseload of approximately 10 to 20 offenders. Placement into intensive supervision is dependent upon the sentencing judge, the supervision officer, the parole board, or some combination of these. In today's agencies, the decision to place an offender on intensive supervision is made based on the level of assessed offender risk of rearrest.

Electronic Monitoring

Journal Article Link 7.2
Read about electrnoic monitoring used for sex offenders.

Perhaps the most widely used but least understood intermediate sanction is electronic monitoring. **Electronic monitoring** includes the use of any mechanism that is worn by the offender for the means of tracking his or her whereabouts through electronic detection. Electronic monitoring includes both active and passive monitoring systems. Active systems require that the offender answer or respond to a monitoring cue (such as a computer-generated telephone call), whereas passive forms of monitoring emit a continuous signal for tracking. With both types of electronic monitoring devices, offenders are required to wear an ankle bracelet with a tracking device. The active types are used in conjunction with the local telephone line. At random times throughout the day, the offender's home phone will ring, and the offender has a certain amount of time to answer. Once the offender answers the phone, a signal is transmitted via the tracking device, which validates that the offender is at home. With the passive type, the ankle bracelet transmits a continuous signal to a nearby transmitter, which transmits the signal to a monitoring computer. With each type, the supervising officer is sent a readout each morning of the offender's compliance.

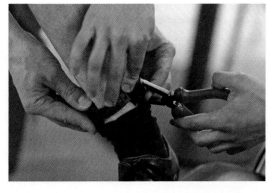

PHOTO 7.3

An offender on supervision is being fitted with an ankle bracelet that will be used for tracking purposes.

If an offender attempts to alter the connection, most devices have alarms that will sound and send an immediate message to the monitor. It is also not uncommon for an offender to be at home, not having tampered with the ankle bracelet, and yet it appears that he or she is noncompliant. Of the two electronic monitoring types, the active system has the lower rate of false alarms. Even though the passive system has the higher rate of false alarms, it is the fastest in determining noncompliance because it assesses the offender's whereabouts much faster.

Those in favor of electronic monitoring base their argument on the ability to increase public safety due to the knowledge of the whereabouts of each offender. Simply knowing they are being personally tracked may deter offenders from committing crime. Proponents also argue that electronic monitoring provides the least punitive alternative to incarceration, as it allows for offenders to be supervised in the community. Undoubtedly, electronic monitoring is a fiscally feasible intermediate sanction in terms of saving money while diverting offenders from incarceration (see Figure 7.2). However, questions remain as to the ability of electronic monitoring to assist offenders in the desistance from criminal behavior, whether supervision officer discretion helps or hurts the outcome, and the effects of community and family involvement on electronic monitoring.

Global Positioning Systems

In this new millennium, community supervision is beginning to utilize military capabilities to keep track of offenders. A global positioning system (GPS) receiver uses 24 military satellites to determine the exact location of a coordinate (see Chapter 6, Technology & Equipment 6.1). As we have seen earlier in Chapter 6, GPS tracking devices allow supervision officers to detect when an offender violates one of his

Video Link 7.3
Learn more about using GPS to track offenders.

FIGURE 7.2 Electronic Monitoring and Supervision Costs Much Less Than Prison

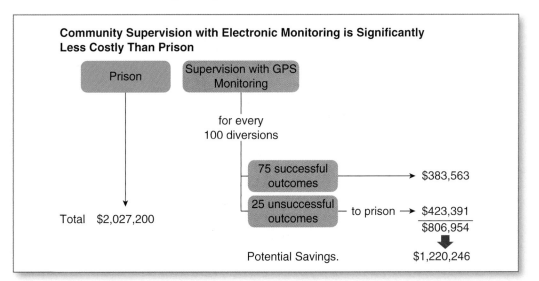

NOTE: Unsuccessful exits are program outcomes that denote non-compliance with program requirements and result in termination from the program. For purpose of estimating cost savings in this report, all offenders that unsuccessfully exit are assumed to be sent to prison.

SOURCE: Office of Program Policy Analysis and Governmental Accountability. (2010). *Intermediate sanctions for non-violent offenders could produce savings.* Tallahassee, FL: Author.

State Rankings Link 7.1
Percent of Adults on Parole Traced by Global Positioning Systems in 2009.

or her restrictions on movement due to a condition of his or her supervision.

Despite the advances that GPS technology has provided for community corrections, there are also some disadvantages. As noted in Chapter 6, GPS tracking devices often lose their signal during bad weather or in areas densely populated with trees. Further, this equipment is expensive and can be cost prohibitive for smaller, less affluent agencies. Because of this, only a small minority of offenders are tracked by GPS technology when compared with the entire offender population under community supervision. Nevertheless, when used in a strategic manner, this feature does provide an extra level of maintenance for those offenders where it is deemed appropriate. Table 7.3 provides a comparison of some advantages and disadvantages of GPS electronic monitoring.

TABLE 7.3   Advantages and Disadvantages of GPS Electronic Monitoring

	Advantages	*Disadvantages*
Active GPS Systems	• Seek to alleviate prison over-crowding • Immediate response capability • Date reporting in near-real time	• High daily cost • Reliance in wireless date service coverage • Labour intensive • Require immediate agency response • Greater agency liability • Tracing device size and weight
Passive GPS Systems	• Small, lightweight device • Can be independent of wireless date services • Lower daily cost • Less labor intensive	• "After-the-fact" tracking data • No immediate notification of zone violations

SOURCE: *Tracking sex offenders with modern technology: Implications and practical uses with law enforcement.* (2008). Alexandria, VA: International Association for Chiefs of Police.

Home Detention

Also known as house arrest, **home detention** is the mandated action that forces an offender to stay within the confines of his or her home or on the property until a time specified by the sentencing judge. It is the "father of modern science," Galileo, who provides the example of the first offender placed on home detention, after he proposed that the earth rotated around the sun. However, it wasn't until the late 20th century's "War on Drugs" that home detention gained notoriety. As a result of the massive numbers of drug offenders being sentenced to jail or prison, officials were seeking an alternative to supervision that would allow an offender to be supervised prior to trial or just before being placed into a residential treatment facility.

Many offenders sentenced to home confinement are required to complete community service and pay a host of fines, fees, and victim restitutions, while others are forced to wear electronic monitors or other detection devices to ensure that they are remaining in their residence during the specified time. In many cases, home detention is used for offenders during the pretrial phase or just prior to an offender

Prison Tour Video Link 7.1
Watch a discussion about electronic monitoring.

Audio Link 7.1
Hear an account of an offender who served home detention.

being let out of prison on a work or educational release program. If an offender leaves his or her residence without permission or against the policies set forth, the offender is seen as having technically violated the conditions of his or her supervision (Government Accounting Office, 1990).

Day Reporting Centers

Day reporting centers are treatment facilities to which offenders are required to report, usually on a daily basis. These facilities tend to offer a variety of services, including drug counseling, vocational assistance, life skills development, and so forth. The offenders who are likely to be required to report to day reporting centers may be one of two types: those placed on early release from a period of incarceration, or those on some form of heightened probation supervision. For those released early from a jail or prison term, the day reporting center represents a gradual transition into the community in which they are supervised throughout the process.

The advantage of day reporting centers is that they do not require the use of bed space and therefore save counties and states a substantial portion of the cost in maintaining offenders in their custody (see Figure 7.3). Focus Topic 7.2 provides a very good example of a day reporting center, this one operated by Hampden County, Massachusetts. This example demonstrates the various facets of day reporting centers and also dovetails well with future discussions in this text regarding police and community corrections partnerships for offender treatment. The Hampden County facility is operated by that county's sheriff's department and therefore provides a strong integration of law enforcement efforts and those of community supervision agencies.

Day reporting centers are similar to residential treatment facilities except that offenders are not required to stay overnight. In some jurisdictions, the regimen of the day reporting center is designed so that offenders attend 8- to 10-hour intervention and treatment classes. This is an important element of the day reporting center since it provides added human supervision. The implementation of creative and versatile forms of human supervision serves to optimize both treatment and security characteristics of offender supervision, and day reporting centers facilitate this concept. Indeed, one staff person conducting some form of instruction class (e.g., a life skills class, a psychoeducational class on effective communication, or perhaps a parenting class) can essentially watch over several offenders at the same time. Further, the offender's time is spent in prosocial activities with little opportunity to engage in any form of undetected criminal activity. Thus, day reporting centers enhance security processes while filling up the leisure times in an offender's day or evening with activities that are constructive and beneficial to the offender and to society; little time is left for distractions or unregulated activity.

Video Link 7.4
Watch a video about day reporting centers.

Prison Tour Video Link 7.2
Watch a discussion about day reporting centers and recidivism.

FIGURE 7.3   Day Reporting Centers Are Less Costly Than Prison

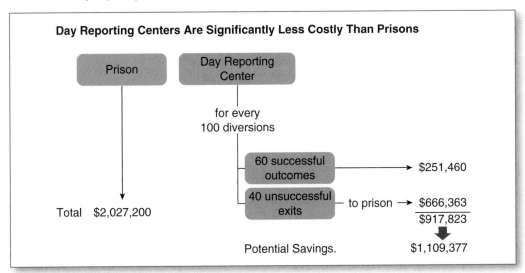

NOTE: Successful completions in substance abuse treatment programs are used as a proxy for successful completions in the day reporting program. Unsuccessful exits are program outcomes that denote non-compliance with program requirements and result in termination from the program. For purpose of estimating cost savings in this report, all offenders that unsuccessfully exit are assumed to be sent to prison.

SOURCE: Office of Program Policy Analysis and Governmental Accountability. (2010). *Intermediate sanctions for non-violent offenders could produce savings*. Tallahassee, FL: Author.

FOCUS TOPIC: 7.2

An Example of a Day Reporting Center

The Hampden County Day Reporting Center: Three Years' Success in Supervising Sentenced Individuals in the Community

In Massachusetts, the county correctional system incarcerates both those in pretrial detention and those sentenced to terms of 2.5 years or less for crimes such as breaking and entering, larceny, driving while intoxicated (DWI), and drug possession. Thus, each county facility is both a jail for pretrial detainees and a house of correction for sentenced individuals. The sheriff of each county, an elected official, is the administrator of the jail and house of correction.

Sheriff Michael J. Ashe Jr. has been in charge of the Hampden County Sheriff's Department and Correction Center in Springfield, Massachusetts, for more than 15 years. One of his early actions as sheriff was to choose not to live in the "Sheriff's House" that went with the job, but to turn it instead into a prerelease center. Inmates in residence at the center are within 6 months of release and are able to work and participate in community activities. These activities range from Alcoholics Anonymous and Narcotics Anonymous groups to individual counseling, religious services, workout regimens at the YMCA, and community restitution.

In October 1986, faced like many other correctional administrators with worsening overcrowding, Sheriff Ashe instituted what the Crime and Justice Institute refers to as the first day reporting center in the nation. The day reporting center was located in the country's prerelease center, so the new operation could draw on the prerelease center staff's experience in supervising offenders in the community. In addition, prerelease center staff member Kevin Warwick was selected to direct the day reporting center.

Program Description

The Hampden County day reporting center supervises inmates who are within 4 months of release and who live at home, work, and take part in positive activities in the community. Participants also are monitored randomly by "community officers." Under this system, each participant is contacted between 50 and 80 times per week.

Day reporting center participants meet with their counselors at the beginning of each week to chart out a schedule of work and attendance at positive community activities. They are responsible for following this schedule to the letter.

It is important to note that the Hampden County day reporting center is not a "house arrest" program; participants spend a good deal of time out of their homes, reentering the community. Day reporting is also not a diversion program. Sheriff Ashe was concerned that, if used as a diversion program, day reporting would just "widen the net" so that offenders who would not have otherwise gone to jail would be sentenced to day reporting.

Day reporting participants are still on sentence, in the custody of the sheriff, and have earned their way into the day reporting program by positive behavior and program participation. Some participants "graduate" from prerelease center in-house status to day reporting. Others, on shorter sentences, come right from the main institution to day reporting. All have been assessed for entrance into the program based on the likelihood of their being accountable for their behavior in the community.

Program Success

Nearly 500 individuals have participated in the day reporting center program to date, and, because of the program's close supervision, none has committed a violent crime in the community while in the program. Eighty percent of participants have successfully completed the program. Twenty percent have been returned to higher security, usually for lack of accountability (e.g., not following the required schedule) or a failed urinalysis test. Under the program, one "dirty" urine test (testing positive for either alcohol or drugs) results in a return to higher security. This strict policy was established because of the prerelease center's experience that alcohol or drug use was the primary reason that program participants caused problems in the community.

Pretrial Participants

During the past year, the day reporting program has expanded to provide some supervision of pretrial individuals who are released by the court on personal recognizance with the provision that they report daily to the day reporting center, even though they are not in the custody of the sheriff. These individuals do not receive the full services or supervision of day reporting, but their daily reporting is seen by the court as preferable to a release on personal recognizance with no stipulations for reporting at all.

Benefits

Advantages of the day reporting center to our department are numerous. Cell and bed spaces are saved for those who need them the most. Costs of supervising participants in the day reporting program are considerably less than costs for 24-hour lockup. Day reporting is also the ultimate "carrot" in our institutional incentive-based program participation philosophy; inmates who behave well in jail can serve the end of their sentences at home.

We have also found that individuals who earn the opportunity for home and community participation at the end of their sentences have an improved chance of successful community reentry. When sentences are a continuum of earned lesser sanctions, the final step to productive and positive community living is much easier than when inmates are released from a higher-security setting. Day reporting also benefits the community because participants work, pay taxes, and perform community service.

We in Hampden County would be happy to share information about our experience in implementing and operating the day reporting center with any interested jurisdictions. For more information, write to Richard McCarthy, Public Information Officer at the Hampden County Sheriffs Department, 79 York Street, Springfield, Massachusetts 01105, or call (413) 781-1560, ext. 213.

By Richard J. McCarthy, Public Information Officer, Hampden County, MA, Sheriff's Department.

SOURCE: National Institute of Corrections. (2006). *The Hampden County day reporting center: Three years' success in supervising sentenced individuals in the community.* Washington, DC: Author. Retrieved October 12, 2008, from http://www.nicic.org/pubs/1990/period74.pdf. Reprinted with permission.

Shock Incarceration/Split Sentencing

For certain offenders, the subjection to a loss of freedom is all that is needed to get their lives in order. As a result, the mechanism used for its stunning value is that of shock incarceration (see Chapter 5). Shock incarceration is a short term of incarceration followed by a specified term of community supervision in hopes of deterring the offender from recidivating. Because the brief stint of incarceration is meant to provide a sense of punitive reality to the offender, most shock incarceration programs are designed for juvenile offenders and those who have never been incarcerated before. Given the basic tenets of shock incarceration, it is mostly used in the form of mixed sentencing. In this case, offenders are given a short term of confinement and then placed on community supervision to complete their term of probation or parole. Under shock incarceration (sometimes called split sentencing), offenders are sentenced to a term of confinement only to be released after a set time and ordered to serve the remainder of their time on probation. The logic behind such action is that the offender will develop a natural dislike of incarceration and will seek to abstain from criminal behavior in hopes of avoiding such an unpleasant experience. Vito and Allen (1981) hold that shock incarceration should be viewed as a viable intermediate sanction because it (1) allows offenders the opportunity to realistically reintegrate into the community, (2) continues positive connections with existing family, (3) decreases the amount of time spent in prison, (4) decreases prison populations, and (5) decreases the amount of funding spent on prisons. Research has demonstrated that at least three quarters of all shock incarceration programs have shown some effectiveness.

Audio Link 7.2
Listen to a clip about juvenile reform.

Journal Article Link 7.3
Read about the impact of a Minnesota shock incarceration program.

METHODS OF ENSURING COMPLIANCE: DETECTING DRUG USE AMONG OFFENDERS

The detection of offender drug use is accomplished through a number of testing procedures that use a variety of body samples. The most common are obtained from the offender's urine, blood, hair, sweat, or saliva. According to Robinson and Jones (2000), urine testing is the most cost-effective, reliable, and widely used drug testing procedure. Nevertheless, it is important that staff understand the drug use demographics of their own region or jurisdiction so that they can determine the most appropriate drug testing strategy to employ. This will vary according to the type of drug use that is most common among drug abusers in the region as well as other considerations. In general, there are five sources from which samples are drawn for drug testing. The descriptions of these sources are taken from the U.S. government document written by Robinson and Jones and published by the Office of Justice Programs, and they are as follows:

1. **Urine Testing:** Due to price and accuracy of the testing process, urinalysis is considered the most suitable method for drug courts and most criminal justice agencies for detecting the presence of illegal substances. Generally, urine testing methods fall into two types: instrumental and noninstrumental (or "point-of-contact") testing (both defined further below). Both methods use some form of immunoassay technology to provide an initial determination of the presence of a drug (p. 3).

2. **Blood Testing:** Blood tests can provide discrete information regarding the degree of an individual's impairment, but the invasiveness of the procedure and the potential danger of infection make blood testing inappropriate for drug court programs (p. 3).

PHOTO 7.5

Drug testing equipment is routinely used by probation and parole officers as well as treatment specialists who work with drug courts and residential treatment programs.

TECHNOLOGY AND EQUIPMENT 7.1

Breathalyzers and Urine Tests

Breathalyzers, used with considerable frequency and at relatively minimal cost, can be particularly useful in detecting the presence and amount of alcohol that may not otherwise be detected through random urinalysis because of alcohol's relatively short life span in the human system. Breathalyzers can therefore be a very effective and relatively low-cost component of a drug court drug testing program, used in conjunction with urine testing for other substances. The breathalyzer must be calibrated according to certification standards established by the U.S. Departments of Transportation (DOT) and Health and Human Services (HHS) and/or the state toxicologist. The test must be administered by breath alcohol technicians who are trained in the use and interpretation of breath alcohol results. Local drug court officials may wish to contact their local law enforcement agencies regarding the use of breathalyzers in their local jurisdiction for requirements such as calibration settings, interpretation of test results, and the expertise available to administer and/or provide training on breathalyzer testing.

Urine testing, through both instrumental and noninstrumental devices, is also an accurate and reliable method for detecting the presence of alcohol if performed within the relatively short period following ingestion in which it can be detected. Because alcohol is more concentrated in urine than in blood, urine is the best specimen to use if one wants to determine if alcohol has been consumed. Generally, urine testing methods fall into two types: instrumental and noninstrumental. Both methods of analysis use some form of immunoassay technology to provide an initial determination of the presence of a drug and chromatography to confirm the presence and quantity of the drug. Regardless of the drug testing method used, the integrity of the collection, testing, and reporting process must be maintained to (a) ensure that the specimen is from the named defendant, (b) detect adulteration, and (c) ensure that no contaminants have been introduced that would affect the validity of the results.

Evidence of drug use may be present in the urine in the form of the parent drug and/or metabolites. Determination of the length of time that has elapsed between the time of ingestion and the time the test was conducted depends upon the rate at which the body metabolizes and eliminates the drug, physical characteristics of the individual's metabolism, and the sensitivity of the testing procedure. The time frame also can vary depending on the duration of abuse (e.g., long-term heavy doses or infrequent use), the amount of the daily dosage, and the route of administration (e.g., oral, injected, smoked, or inhaled).

SOURCE: Office of Justice Programs Drug Court Clearinghouse. (2003). *Drug testing in a drug court environment: Common issues to address.* Washington, DC: U.S. Department of Justice.

3. **Hair Testing:** The introduction of new, powerful instruments for hair analysis has increased interest in hair testing. Despite its increased popularity among agencies, caution should be used because hair analysis is subject to potential external contamination. Indeed, there are indications that hair analysis can produce tainted results, depending on the type of hair as well as the type of drug that is analyzed. For example, dark pigmented hair absorbs drugs more readily than blond or bleached hair. Male African American hair (black/brown) appears to absorb drugs more readily than hair of other groups, such as female African Americans (black/brown), male Caucasians (black/brown), and female Caucasians (black/brown and blond) (p. 3).

4. **Sweat Testing:** Sweat samples, which are obtained from patches that can be placed on a person for a number of days, have the advantages of a longer time frame for detection and the fact that they are difficult to adulterate. They do not, however, provide a correlation regarding the degree of impairment, and they are subject to individual differences in sweat production (p. 3).

5. **Saliva Testing:** Saliva samples permit a correlation with the degree of impairment and can be easily obtained. They are, however, subject to contamination from smoking or other substances (p. 3).

Audio Link 7.3
Listen to a clip about drug testing.

METHODS OF ENSURING COMPLIANCE: SEX OFFENDERS

Currently, every state has some type of notification process when sex offenders are released into the community. This is true whether the sex offender is on probation (having not been incarcerated) or has been released on parole (after serving a prison term). Commonly, these requirements fall under **Megan's laws**, which were passed as a result of the brutal rape and murder of a 7-year-old New Jersey girl named Megan Kanka. The victim's parents pushed for legislation in the state of New Jersey to mandate reporting of sex offenders who are released into the community, and in 1994, New Jersey was the first state to pass such legislation. The following year, the federal government passed similar legislative requirements. Since that time, other states have followed suit, with these laws often being informally referred to as Megan's laws out of respect for the crime victim who served as the catalyst for this reporting requirement.

PHOTO 7.6

Probation officers Holly Busby, right, and Bernie Sizer monitor about 50 people convicted of sex crimes. Here they visit with a recently released sex offender in his apartment.

The Center for Sex Offender Management (CSOM) is operated by the U.S. Department of Justice and is perhaps the leading national warehouse for training on sex offender-related issues and training. This organization is a federally operated program that provides a vast array of curricula, which are available to the general public and are ideal for community training. The CSOM (2008) notes that in addition to the typical notification programs that exist throughout the United States, there are many occasions where public agencies (such as police, prosecutors, and community supervision agencies) are required to provide specific information pertaining to individual sex offenders. This is conducted through a variety of means, including door-to-door citizen notification, public meetings, and the distribution of written and printed notices.

Audio Link 7.4
Listen to how the U.S. Supreme Court upheld Megan's law.

Further, the CSOM notes that as more comprehensive and collaborative approaches to the management of sex offenders emerge, community members, victims, the victim's family, the offender's family, and others are invited to become partners in the sex offender management process. It is against this backdrop that we emphasize CSOM's following point:

> As knowledge about the extensive occurrence of sexual assault becomes more widespread, the agencies responsible for sex offender management are beginning to recognize that community notification meetings and interactions with individual community members become opportunities to engage in sexual abuse prevention activities; to connect sexual assault victims with services; and, generally, to advance a community's ability to understand and protect itself from sexual abuse and its trauma. (p. 1)

Naturally, the ability of agencies to collaborate with community members will be specific to that region or location, as some areas are more amenable to such forms of notification and offender tracking than others. Such agency-community programs require that staff exercise sensitivity to the context and needs of individuals, families, and communities involved (CSOM, 2008). This process, while entailing a very important community education component, also requires a great deal of care since victim reactions can be quite varied.

Thus, this aspect of ensuring compliance consists of two parts. First is the notification process by which the community is made aware of the existence of a sex offender. Second is the community's involvement in ensuring that the offender is monitored by human observation, interaction, and general community awareness. This provides a strong preventative component for the offender and also ensures that other potential victims are vigilant regarding the possible threat that exists within their community. Nevertheless, these programs must also educate community members on the dynamics of sex offending and the likelihood of recidivism. For instance, in most cases, sex offenders do not recidivate; the majority of all sex offenses are actually not committed by an offender with a prior sex-offending history. This is important for community members to understand because it will increase the efficacy of reintegrative approaches while improving overall supervision of the offender.

CORRECTIONS AND THE LAW 7.1

Smith v. Doe *(2003) and the Constitutionality of Sex Offender Notification Laws*

The Supreme Court has given states the green light to continue posting the names and pictures of convicted sex offenders on the Internet. And justices have rejected attempts by sex offenders to prove they are no longer dangerous.

At issue is whether such laws amount to a second punishment for those already convicted for their crimes, and whether the laws violate an offender's due process rights. The Court has so far upheld the right of state legislatures to impose registries on sex offenders.

Every state has a so-called "Megan's law," named after Megan Kanka, a 7-year-old New Jersey girl kidnapped, raped, and murdered by a twice-convicted sex offender who lived across the street.

These laws require convicted sex offenders and certain other types of felons released from prison to register with local authorities. Such information is typically available to the public through print and Internet sources.

In this case (*Smith v. Doe,* 2003), the question was whether a state law violated the constitutional guarantee against punishment ex post facto, or after the fact.

One "John Doe" was convicted of abusing his young daughter, and the other man abused a 14-year-old girl. Both men were released in 1990, before the state passed its sex offender registration law. They argue they had served their sentences and wanted to put their crimes behind them.

The Court decided the state legislature intended the law to be regulatory, not punitive in nature.

Writing for a 6-3 majority, Justice Anthony Kennedy said: "Our system does not treat dissemination of truthful information in furtherance of legitimate governmental objection as punishment." And Kennedy noted, "The purpose and the principal effect of notification are to inform the public for its own safety, not to humiliate the offender."

But in her dissent, Justice Ruth Bader Ginsburg disagreed. "However plain it may be that a former sex offender currently poses no threat of recidivism, he will remain subject to long-term monitoring and inescapable humiliation," she said.

Supporters of these registration laws say citizens deserve to know if convicted sex offenders are living in their neighborhoods, and argue registration laws are not unfair, since their convictions are already a matter of public record.

Opponents of the law call it a "government-imposed stigma" preventing those who deserve to move on with their lives from doing so after serving their time. They say such laws represent an overly intrusive invasion of privacy, since other criminal records are not subject to such readily available public scrutiny.

SOURCE: Adapted from Mears, B. (2003). *Supreme Court upholds sex offender registration laws.* Retrieved from http://www.cnn.com/2003/LAW/03/05/scotus.sex.offenders/index.html.

INTERMEDIATE SANCTIONS IN DIFFERENT STATES

Reference Link 7.1
Read about a program used in Chicago.

This section will describe a series of programs offered in a variety of states around the nation. It is interesting to see that the use and application of intermediate sanctions can vary quite considerably by the type of offender being supervised, the type of program delivery, and the particular state that is examined. The key point in showcasing these various programs is to illustrate the utility of intermediate sanctions and the flexibility associated with their implementation. This is an important selling point for the increased use of intermediate sanctions, since it gives agencies a set of diverse responses that address a diverse array of challenges. We now turn our attention to a number of different programs from various states. The write-ups for these programs have been adapted from the public domain document titled *NIC Focus: Intermediate Sanctions,* a government publication released by the National Institute of Corrections (McGarry, 1990).

Kansas (Sedgwick County) Home Surveillance Program

The Sedgwick County Community Corrections Home Surveillance Program (HSP) provides an additional, restrictive level of intensive supervision in the community for identified high-risk offenders. This house-arrest program represents the most intensive supervision currently available short of placement

APPLIED THEORY 7.1

Routine Activity Theory as Applied to Community Supervision

For the most part, the tenets of routine activity theory, by Cohen and Felson (1979), reflect the general premise behind most intermediate sanctions. Cullen and Agnew (2006) provide a clear and effective synopsis of this theory in the following statement:

> Crime occurs when there is an intersection in time and space of a motivated offender, an attractive target, and a lack of capable guardianship. People's daily routine activities affect the likelihood they will be an attractive target and will encounter an offender in a situation where no effective guardianship is present. (p. 7)

Intermediate sanctions work to eliminate the likelihood that offenders will not have effective guardianship. In other words, an effective guardian will protect potential victims. This guardian is the use of surveillance devices and supervision programs utilized by community supervision agencies. Further, when agencies keep the community informed and when the community is encouraged to volunteer and partner with the agency, an additional layer of guardianship is added to the offender's supervision.

When the offender is released into the community, members of an informed and involved community are able to modify their routines to reduce the likelihood of victimization. Further, the offender is deterred from likely recidivism due to the understanding that he or she is being supervised by a number of different persons and through a variety of potential mechanisms. Thus, heightened community vigilance and increased controls placed on the offender work to augment one another, providing an ethereal prison, of a sort, when implemented correctly.

During this process, it is hoped that the offender learns to modify his or her own activities. While under supervision, many are restricted from certain areas of the community (an alcoholic may be restricted from bars and nightclubs, a sex offender may be restricted from approaching an elementary school, and so forth, as suggested in Chapter 6). Over time, graduated sanctions are lessened as the offender demonstrates that he or she is able to maintain his or her own behavior within the constraints of prosocial behavior. It is in this way that the reinforcement of routine activities theory leads to a form of internal social learning, being operantly reinforced upon the offender, whether the offender realizes it or not.

SOURCE: Cullen, F. T., & Agnew, R. (2006). *Criminological theory: Past to present (3rd ed.).* Los Angeles: Roxbury; Lilly, J. R., Cullen, F. T., & Ball, R. A. (2007). *Criminological theory: Context and consequences* (4th ed.). Thousand Oaks, CA: Sage.

---

in the residential programs. The county's residential center provides in-house, 24-hour supervision and could be compared to a work release facility. It offers residents self-help classes during their off-work hours. Because the residential center is usually full, the HSP becomes an even more important part of the agency's range of sanctions. Clients are sentenced to the HSP by the court, if recommended by community corrections evaluators, or are placed there after their graduation from the residential center or by other case managers who have experienced difficulty with them during intensive supervision.

The daily schedule at the HSP is explained to the offender prior to intake acceptance. All clients must agree to the HSP rules and regulations, which are explained in detail. Clients are required to keep a daily itinerary or agenda of their activities. They must sign out from their residence, stating where they are going and for what reason, and they must sign in upon their return. Each daily agenda is approved by the case manager. Offenders are also required to keep other records, such as Alcoholics Anonymous attendance forms and, in some cases, job search forms. Every client also must submit to a minimum of one urinalysis/drug screen or breath analysis per week.

Offender contacts are preferably made at the place of residence, place of employment, or other field sites. Staff conduct a minimum of four personal field contacts per week for each client, and daily contacts are attempted as time permits. Many contacts are made during the evening, usually after 10 p.m. because all clients have a 10 p.m. curfew. The HSP has two levels. Level I restricts clients to their homes with the exception of visits to their doctors or attorneys, which must be approved by the case manager. Clients who comply with Level I rules for 14 days progress to Level II, where they are allowed four 4-hour furloughs per week away from their residence, plus two 8-hour furloughs per week on their days off. All furloughs must be approved by the case manager. At the end of a 90-day period, staff review the case to decide whether the client will be placed on regular supervision. Clients not in full compliance or reasonably close to it will remain in the HSP.

Many offenders are placed in the program because they have failed to comply with the basic conditions of probation, such as reporting to their case manager and making regular payments on their court obligation. Frequent contacts in the HSP increase understanding of each client's needs and encourage clients to make their regular monthly payments. Because all HSP clients are considered high-risk to some degree, staff use a two-way portable radio assigned to the sheriff's channel. The radio provides a direct link to the dispatcher, who can summon any services that may be needed in the event of a field emergency or a threat to the staff. In addition, HSP clients use a voice 10-second pager to contact the staff when necessary. The pager has proved to be an invaluable means of communication, since staff are usually in a vehicle while on duty.

The HSP seems to be effective because staff get to know clients and their habits in a very short time. Frequent contacts help build rapport between clients and staff very quickly. In fact, clients have requested to stay in the program when it was time for their discharge. The cost of home surveillance obviously exceeds the cost of regular field services supervision. However, it is a more economical alternative than placement in a residential program or prison. In the future, the department may expand the HSP without increasing the number of staff, by adding electronic monitoring devices for higher-risk clients.

Missouri: A Control and Intervention Strategy for Technical Parole Violators

In an effort to effectively manage its offender population, the Missouri Department of Corrections has focused on a group that represents a significant number of prison commitments: technical parole violators. The department found that a large number of recommitments were offenders whose parole was revoked for technical violations rather than new convictions. Realizing that many of these violators were being returned to prison due to their inability to address alcohol and drug problems, the department, in concert with the Board of Probation and Parole, instituted a new concept in dealing with them.

The program's treatment center is designed for technical parole violators whose behavior has demonstrated their need for control and intervention. This facility offers more structure than other intermediate sanctions, such as intensive supervision, house arrest, or traditional halfway house placement, because offenders are confined to the facility with no passes during their 90-day stay. Offenders are screened by local field staff in conjunction with a coordinator from the facility to determine eligibility. Offenders must be technical violators who have not been charged with new law violations.

Further, it must be demonstrated that traditional strategies have been implemented and the offender has been unresponsive to them. Finally, the violation must be serious enough to warrant revocation and commitment to the Department of Corrections. This program facility is the final stop before recommitment to prison. Because the offenders in this program have been unable to remain on supervision within the community, they are placed on a vigorous treatment schedule. This program consists of three phases dedicated to building offender responsibility through a cognitive approach in a structured, didactic, interactional, and confrontational manner. The program follows a logical progression from problem awareness to skill building to relapse prevention and follow-up. The model relies on an Alcoholics Anonymous (AA) methodology, with study and work groups that enhance the daily education and therapy classes. Counseling groups help violators apply the class material to their own needs.

Phase I, which lasts 3 weeks, consists of intake, assessment, orientation, and intensive classes on the disease concept of chemical dependency. This work lays a foundation for violators to begin problem solving, using the tools furnished by AA and the 12-step recovery process. The skills violators learn through this general approach can be applied to their lives in the community, whether they have found chemicals to be a way of life or a component of an overall criminal lifestyle. Phase II makes up the next 6 weeks of the program. One topic is covered each week to bring about meaningful skill development. Topics include problem solving, understanding emotions, managing stress, assertiveness, relapse prevention, and the role of the family and others. The final 4 weeks, designated as Phase III, focus on vocational and job readiness, along with follow-up and placement planning sessions to provide the violator with a practical application of the techniques learned previously. All of these sessions are conducted by department staff, including psychologists, parole officers, and caseworkers. Custody personnel also receive training to help them adapt to the treatment approach as opposed to the traditional prison milieu.

Tennessee GPS Tracking of Sex Offenders

In 2007, the state of Tennessee published an evaluation of its experience utilizing GPS tracking of sex offenders. This detailed report provided a multifaceted examination that produced some fairly surprising results. Among the beneficial findings was that community supervision officers were better able to establish inclusion zones, or where the offender must be located during specified time periods, such as work or home during certain times of the day or evening. Further, GPS tracking aided in monitoring exclusion zones for places where the offender was not permitted to enter. Thus, the use of GPS tracking aided the overall supervision quality and monitoring of the offender. However, these same types of monitoring are able to be conducted using other methods. A key distinction with GPS tracking is the fact that it allows officers to see specific patterns of activity and then follow up on frequently visited locations. Because the supervision officer can track total movement of the offender, suspicious areas or those frequently visited by the offender can be more readily investigated. Further, it was held by most officers that GPS tracking seemed to deter sex offenders from engaging in other forms of deviant or criminal activity, simply due to the fact that these offenders were cognizant of the monitoring that they were under. In addition, when offenders did violate their community supervision requirements, officers were more likely to determine the specific violation that occurred. Thus, the overall supervision ability was enhanced, and the ability to pinpoint specific offense behavior improved the effectiveness of officers who sought to revoke or modify community supervision parameters.

Video Link 7.5
Watch how GPS is used to track sex offenders.

Moreover, GPS tracking helped to cultivate better partnerships between local law enforcement agencies, since this tool helped to more accurately confirm or eliminate allegations of potential criminal activity. This serves as an aid to both community supervision agencies and law enforcement agencies, as accuracy in detection allows for better placement of resources. Law enforcement officers are also provided an added benefit when attempting to resolve cases in their jurisdiction. Likewise, GPS data provide officers with information to investigate and verify citizen claims of inappropriate offender activity. This function would likely aid in further cementing partnerships between the agency and the wider community, a primary goal noted throughout this text.

However, it is also noted that GPS tracking has several limitations or challenges, both in implementation and in maintenance of the program. First, officers who have used this system point out that it is not necessarily the best approach for all sex offenders. This is consistent with prior research. In some cases, false positives may occur (remember Chapter 6), resulting in excessive forms of supervision that also create resentment among offenders who are making genuine efforts toward reform. In these cases, the offenders perceive the use of GPS as a punishment. It should be pointed out that research does indicate that lower-risk offenders who are supervised by strict levels of supervision recidivate more frequently and have overall higher recidivism rates than similar offenders supervised at less stringent levels (Champion, 2002; Tennessee Board of Probation and Parole, 2007). Much of this recidivism is thought to be due to the negative impact on offender motivation and the contrast between increased supervision and positive, reintegrative efforts (Hanser, 2007).

In addition, evaluative research by Middle Tennessee State University (MTSU, 2007) produced statistically significant descriptive and demographic results using subjects from both treatment and control groups. Briefly, the treatment group was administered GPS tracking while the control group was given some form of supervision that did not include GPS tracking. This allowed the evaluators to determine the impact of the GPS tracking itself, since other aspects of the supervision sentence were kept roughly equal or comparable between the groups. The evaluative research by MTSU found that offenders younger than 40 years old were more likely to commit new offenses (though not necessarily sex offenses) while under GPS supervision than were offenders over 40 years old. In addition, it was found that offenders in the 30- to 40-year-old age range were statistically more likely to gain new criminal charges than were offenders in any other 10-year age category investigated. Thus, it is clear that this group is perhaps most in need of enhanced supervision. Further, offenders who had less than a high school education were more likely to commit a new offense than were those who had a background that included high school or higher levels of educational attainment. Findings such as these are useful since they can be used to avoid false negatives to more accurately determine which offenders are most suitable for additional security through GPS tracking devices. This is particularly useful when only a finite number of tracking devices exist within an agency. From this discussion, it is clear that GPS tracking has many pros and cons. The detailed study conducted by MTSU, on behalf of the Tennessee Board of Probation and Parole, clearly provides a very detailed picture of the implementation of this intermediate sanction. This is important because GPS tracking is hailed as one of the most modern and sophisticated innovations. While it certainly has its place and while it does indeed provide a contribution to the range of supervision strategies, there are pitfalls that agencies must consider. Often, the balance between the pros and cons can be delicate when considering intermediate sanctions, and the use of GPS technology is no different.

CONCLUSION

This chapter has provided an overview of several types of intermediate sanctions that are used around the country. In addition, specific examples have been offered to demonstrate the variety of sanctions that exist and their flexibility in being utilized. The flexibility of intermediate sanctions gives community supervision agencies a range of potential responses to offender criminal behavior. This range falls along a continuum according to the amount of liberty that is denied the offender. These various penalties are interchangeable with one another and vary by level of punitiveness to allow community supervision agencies to calibrate the offender's punishment with the specific offense severity or tendency toward recidivism. In addition, intermediate sanctions help to connect the supervision process with the treatment process. Various intermediate sanctions, such as community service and the payment of fines, create a system of restoration, while the use of flexible supervision schemes such as electronic monitoring and GPS tracking allows the offender to engage in employment activities. Other programs, such as day reporting centers, ease the transition of offenders from incarceration to community membership and provide a series of constructive activities to ensure that the offender remains on task with respect to his or her reintegration process. Each of these sanctions can be used in conjunction with others to further augment the supervision process, all the while being less expensive and more productive than a prison term.

Reference Link 7.2
Read about community
service orders.

Finally, as has been noted consistently throughout this text, the use of community partnerships is again emphasized. In this case, the community partnerships come by way of citizens monitoring the offender who is tasked with completing various activities to fulfill his or her sentence. The use of human supervision is again shown to be important, and intermediate sanctions are well suited to citizen involvement when ensuring offender compliance. It is in this manner that intermediate sanctions are yet an additional tool that provides an external incentive for offenders to work their regimen within the community. These sanctions, when administered in a social vacuum, would not be expected to be effective. But when utilized against a backdrop of community involvement, agency collaboration, and solid case management processes, intermediate sanctions serve as interlocking supervision mechanisms that improve offender reintegration.

END-OF-CHAPTER DISCUSSION QUESTIONS

1. Provide the definition of intermediate sanctions and explain why they are important to corrections.

2. Identify and discuss the various types of intermediate sanctions and their placement within the continuum of sanctions.

3. Discuss the various means of ensuring compliance with substance abusers.

4. Discuss the various means of ensuring compliance with sex offenders.

5. Discuss the various means by which intermediate sanctions are used in various states.

6. Recall from earlier chapters the philosophical orientation for intermediate sanctions. Explain the underlying philosophy and model of correctional thought and, in light of readings so far, tell whether you believe these are good or bad options within the criminal justice system.

7. Provide a brief overview of the security functions related to intermediate sanctions and also provide a discussion of the treatment functions associated with intermediate sanctions.

8. Explain how routine activity theory applies to the use of intermediate sanctions. Explain the tenets of the theory and provide at least one specific example of how the use of intermediate sanctions dovetails with this theory.

KEY TERMS

Blood testing	Home detention	Saliva testing
Day reporting centers	Intensive supervision probation	Sweat testing
Electronic monitoring	Intermediate sanctions	Urine testing
Hair testing	Megan's Laws	

APPLIED EXERCISE 7.1

Read each of the case scenarios below and select the type of intermediate sanction that you think is best suited for each offender. The list of intermediate sanctions is presented after the scenario. Once you have made your selection, write a 50- to 150-word essay for each scenario that explains why you chose a particular intermediate sanction or combination of sanctions.

Students should remember that intermediate sanctions operate on a continuum, and students will need to avoid false positives when making their decisions. Total word count for this assignment is approximately 500 to 1,500 words.

Grading Rubric (This assignment is worth a maximum total of 100 points.)

1. Student provides a reasonable match between scenarios and intermediate sanction. (Each scenario is worth 3 points.)

2. Student provides adequate justification for each match between scenarios and intermediate sanction. (Each essay justification is worth 7 points.)

Applied Exercise Case Scenarios:

_____Scenario #1: A male juvenile who constantly sneaks out of the house despite his parents' attempts to prevent him. He leaves home at night to meet friends, use drugs, and commit acts of vandalism.

_____Scenario #2: A female offender who "keyed" the car of a neighbor who kept parking on the curb nearest to her own side of the street.

_____Scenario #3: A male delivery driver who is on community supervision for failing to appear in court for proceedings related to thefts in a neighborhood.

_____Scenario #4: A male gang offender who physically assaulted a man who smarted off to him.

_____Scenario #5: A female drug addict who has been busted for prostitution.

_____Scenario #6: A young male who has been committing petty acts of vandalism.

_____Scenario #7: A woman convicted of writing hot checks.

_____Scenario #8: A male teenager who made threatening prank calls to various people in the community.

_____Scenario #9: A middle-aged male who continues to drive while drunk. This is his second DWI offense. He has never been to prison.

_____Scenario #10: A bunch of youth who were playing pranks on elderly people in the community. They egged multiple homes and caused some light property damage to porch lights and other such components of victims' homes.

Applied Exercise Intermediate Sanction Choices:

A. Intensive supervised probation/parole

B. GPS tracking and probation

C. Standard probation and restitution

D. Home detention and electronic monitoring

E. Standard probation and community service

F. Shock incarceration, probation, and community service

G. Restitution

H. Community service

I. Day reporting center and the use of ISP

J. Standard probation

K. Home detention, electronic monitoring, and ISP

L. Drug court with ISP

NOTE: Students may use any of the above options more than once to apply to the scenarios provided. Likewise, there is no requirement that students use every one of the choices presented above.

"WHAT WOULD YOU DO?"

You are the executive director of a new day reporting center. You own this center and have invested a significant portion of your own time and money into this project. You have extensive experience as a case manager but have always dreamed of running your own place. The county-level jail and the state probation/parole department have agreed to send offenders to your center, and you have networked well to ensure that you are able to maintain a steady flow of clients. Further still, you recently completed a grant proposal for homeless drug abusers from the Substance Abuse and Mental Health Services Administration (SAMHSA). Thus, money seems to exist to ensure that you are able to maintain your facility.

However, the state department of probation/parole and the local jail facility want to know about the different types of services that you will provide to offenders who visit your facility during the day. You are asked to write a comprehensive outline of the different services that you plan to offer to clients.

In addition, SAMHSA informs you that it has a number of requirements for its grant recipients. SAMHSA is asking that you explain how you will demonstrate that your services are effective in the community. Though the organization does not require a statistical evaluation for this project at this time (not until after a year of funding), it does still want to know how you will ensure that your services are working.

What would you do?

CROSS-NATIONAL PERSPECTIVE 7.1

Electronic Monitoring in Sweden

In Sweden, approximately 13,000 people are under some type of noncustodial care, compared with only 5,000 sentenced to prison. Probation is the most common form of non-custodial care, but offenders may be sentenced to intensive supervision with electronic monitoring.

An offender may serve the sentence at home rather than in a correctional facility while under intensive supervision with electronic monitoring. In order to qualify, the offender must submit an application for electronic monitoring and have been sentenced to less than 2 months in prison. A local probation authority reviews the applications submitted and decides whether or not to recommend intensive supervision with electronic monitoring. Once approved, a transmitter is fastened around the offender's ankle, which sends signals to a receiver attached to the telephone line in the offender's home. A computer receives these signals and compares these signals with activities planned and registered by a probation officer. The probation officer prepares a timetable, which includes the exact time an offender may leave for work and return to his or her residence. Other activities may be allowed, such as community service programs or treatment programs, but must be preplanned as well. Should the offender fail to follow the timetable set by the probation officer, an alarm is triggered, and the offender may be subject to serve the remainder of the sentence in prison.

Offenders sentenced to intensive supervision with electronic monitoring must meet certain criteria, which include a residence equipped with electricity and phone line, being employed or a student, participating in rehabilitation programs, and remaining drug and alcohol free. If employed, a portion of the offender's income goes into a fund established for crime victims. Offenders are also subject to frequent residence checks and drug tests to ensure compliance with the conditions set by their probation officer.

SOURCE: Swedish Prison and Probation Service. (2008). *Kontakt*. Stockholm: Author.

Do you believe that a similar intensive supervision with electronic monitoring program would be effective in your area? Why or why not?

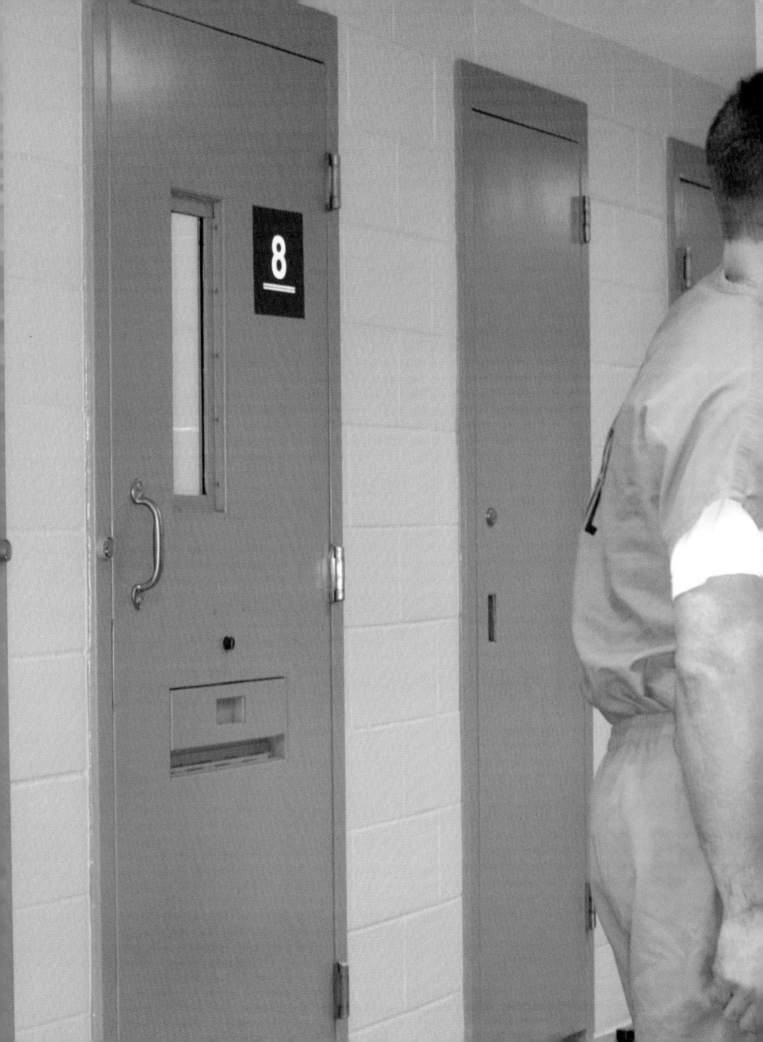

chapter 8

Correctional Facilities

LEARNING OBJECTIVES:

1. Identify the different types of prison facility designs.

2. Identify and discuss the different security levels inherent in prison facilities.

3. Discuss the various features that improve the perimeter security of an institution.

4. Identify and discuss the importance of auxiliary programs inside the prison.

5. Analyze technological developments in prison security.

INTRODUCTION

This chapter provides an overview of various physical facilities and their design. Students should understand that the physical design of a prison is very important to the facility's operation. Further, the physical features of the prison serve as its most prominent aspect. In addition, the general organizational climate, as well as the operations, of the prison is greatly impacted by the physical features of the facility. This chapter covers historical aspects of prison design. Even more important and also much more unique is the discussion on physical facilities related to prison services (kitchens, workshops, religious sections, recreational areas, etc.). This aspect of the physical facility can be very important in meeting programming and security requirements.

PRISON ARCHITECTURE THROUGHOUT HISTORY

Prison construction and development have evolved greatly in the United States. This evolution in the building of prison facilities has corresponded with the needs of correctional managers throughout the ages and the resources available for those who provided the construction. In other words, the needs of the persons operating a prison have typically determined how the prison was designed. It is clear from Chapters 1 and 2 that prisons can come in a variety of shapes and sizes—from abandoned quarries to old decommissioned ships all the way to huge monolithic structures, culminating in the high-tech designs of today's correctional environment. It is clear that prison construction has gone through phases that have met the need of social, penal, and managerial objectives, and the limits of what a jurisdiction is willing or able to finance.

Overall, there have been very few changes in the actual inmate housing unit; the basic human needs for a place to sleep, remove waste, and maintain daily hygiene management tend to remain the same. Jail cells, cell blocks, dormitory spaces, and other such arrangements tend to comprise the same basic facilities. Nevertheless, the form and appeal of these arrangements have changed in terms of cleanliness and/or type of material used. In this regard, innovations in both health and security issues have advanced the living standards for inmates in the United States.

Without question, the history of prison construction has been impacted by the use of certain well-known facilities. These facilities tend to influence construction in other areas of the world, depending on the correctional era and the corresponding needs of prison administrators. We begin our discussion of the different facilities and their construction by examining the French prison known as the Bastille. This prison was most famous for its eventual demise during the French Revolution in 1789. We provide a brief historical account of this facility (also discussed in Chapter 2) and its design.

The Bastille

The **Bastille** was a fortification built in the city of Paris and was a symbol of tyranny and injustice for both commoners and political prisoners in France. Citizens were held within its confines for an indefinite period without accusation or trial. During its early years, the Bastille was a prison for the upper class, consisting mostly of nobles who had been charged with treason. In addition, political and religious prisoners were held within its walls. By the late 1700s, however, this facility was used to house inmates of every class and profession. Ultimately, this facility was attacked and captured by a mob that revolted against the King of France, and the facility was eventually destroyed in 1789.

Video Link 8.1
Watch a video about the storming of the Bastille.

Originally called the Chastel Saint Antoine, the Bastille (French for "little bastion") was originally built as a fortress in the late 1300s but was later used as a prison. The Bastille was a four-story stone structure with eight closely spaced towers connected by a 15-foot-thick stone wall. The stone masonry of the fortress was contained within a thick, continuous wall that surrounded Paris. Amidst the towers, there were two enclosed courtyards. The walls themselves had several windows on each floor (George, 2008). This facility was, in many respects, a miniature castle within the workings of the walled fortifications of Paris. George (2008) notes that similar to "a medieval castle, it had a projected parapet (a series of stone shields running along the top of the wall) to protect defenders against arrows and other flying projectiles. Also like a castle, it was accessible only by drawbridge" (p. 338). Further, the entire fortification was surrounded by a moat that necessitated the draw-bridge and kept intruders at bay. The means by which the Bastille was designed makes it clear that its purpose was to contain people and to ensure that intruders were not able to aid in their release. This facility was secure, primitive, and gloomy and was the basis upon which the Second Western Penitentiary of Pennsylvania was built, near Pittsburgh, in the 1830s (George, 2008).

Pennsylvania Prisons

Though Eastern Penitentiary was discussed in detail in Chapter 2, this section will clarify the physical features of that facility, particularly since the Pennsylvania system was so instrumental to early American correctional development. Eastern Penitentiary featured cells that were arranged along the outer walls of a cell block. The cell blocks were all connected to a central rotunda, and each cell block jutted out in a radial fashion similar to spokes on a wheel. Thus, cells radiated from a central hub from which the open area of each cell block could be observed. The outer perimeter wall of the prison was rectangular; thus the prison was shaped as a rectangle with a round hub in the middle and eight "spokes" or cell blocks extending from the hub to the outer perimeter wall of the prison.

As noted in Chapter 2, this prison had many modern conveniences that did not exist in most prisons at the time. Advents such as modern plumbing systems and outside cell configurations with toilet and lavatory fixtures as well as showers were, until this time, unheard of within a prison environment. Thus, the design and physical features of Eastern Penitentiary were quite novel and progressive when compared to other institutions of the era.

PHOTO 8.1

The Bastille (French for "little bastion") was originally built as a fortress in the late 1300s but was later used as a prison. The Bastille was a four-story stone structure that had eight closely spaced towers connected by a 15-foot-thick stone wall.

PHOTO 8.2

The first sketch of Eastern Penitentiary is shown here. Eastern Penitentiary had many modern conveniences that did not exist in most prisons at the time.

Auburn/Sing Sing

The New York state system of prisons, opened at Auburn and Ossining, were based on a design quite different from the Pennsylvania system. In the original model, the Auburn/Sing Sing model utilized two back-to-back rows of multitiered cells arranged in a straight, linear plan. The typical cell might be around a total of 25 feet of space, measuring about 3.5 feet wide by 7 feet long. This is obviously a very small amount of room, especially considering that in today's prisons inmates are afforded 7 to 8 feet by 10 feet of space (approximately 80 square feet). These conditions were fairly cramped, and the design itself was unimaginative and inefficient. However, it was a simple design that was easy to construct and implement.

As time went on and as improvements in living standards brought in plumbing, electrical, and ventilation systems, the rows of cells were no longer joined in a back-to-back fashion, but instead, a small corridor was built between them.

Unlike cell blocks in the Pennsylvania model, those in the Auburn/Sing Sing model did not face one another. The distance that existed from the front of the cell to the outer building wall was usually from 7 to 10 feet, and this provided room for a long walkway along the front of the cells on the second tier and upward. In most all cases, the outer walls of the building had windows that allowed sunlight

PHOTO 8.3

This drawing shows the outside of a cell block at Sing Sing Prison. As seen here, the Auburn/Sing Sing model utilized two back-to-back rows of multitiered cells arranged in a straight, linear plan.

and air into the facility. Inmates could not reasonably reach these windows if locked in their cells since the distance was greater than their potential reach.

Correctional officers working the cell block would either walk the first floor or along the walkways in front of the cells of the upper floors. This type of design, sometimes described as a "telephone pole" design, made it necessary for officers to conduct their security checks by passing in front of each individual cell; otherwise, they could not view the inmate(s) inside. Despite the inefficiency of this type of supervision, the telephone pole design proliferated throughout the United States during the 1900s. In fact, these features are so common that when people envision correctional facilities, it is this design that comes to mind (George, 2008).

Panopticon

This prison model was created by Jeremy Bentham in 1785. Oddly enough, this design was never adopted in England, Bentham's home nation, but was used in the United States. A handful of facilities using this architectural design were built in Virginia, Pennsylvania, and Illinois (George, 2008). Even today, the panopticon at Stateville Correctional Center in Illinois is in operation. This facility consists of cells that face each other across a wide circular space with an enclosed observation post at the center of the structure. The individual cells are arranged on the thick masonry perimeter walls with narrow windows. The observation post consists of two stories and is accessible from the main floor. While movement on the ground level is easy enough, officers on the upper tiers must follow the curving, circumferential balcony for some distance to reach the stairs. If security staff must reach the observation post to an area near a cell block, the travel time can be quite significant.

PHOTO 8.4

The panopticon prison model was created by Jeremy Bentham in 1785. This design consists of cells that face each other across a wide circular space with an enclosed observation post at the center of the structure.

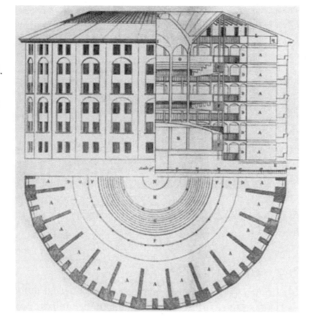

Reference Link 8.1
Read about the structural design of the original panopticon.

The **panopticon** was designed to allow security personnel to clearly observe all inmates without the inmates themselves being able to tell whether they were being watched. Indeed, the internal tower was constructed so that inmates could not tell if security personnel inside were watching them.

Direct Supervision

Audio Link 8.1
Listen to an account of the riot at New York's Attica Correctional Facility.

The direct supervision type of prison design was implemented by the Federal Bureau of Prisons (BOP) and was constructed due to the need to abate the conditions that contributed to a long deadly disturbance at New York's Attica Correctional Facility in 1971. This design greatly differed from prior models and, even today, features a large, open, central indoor recreational or day room space that can be effectively supervised by a single security person. Under the **direct supervision design**, cells are organized on the outside of the square space, with shower facilities and recreation cells interspersed among the typical inmate living quarters. These types of cell blocks may consist of multiple levels of cells. Security staff on each level can walk around that level of the unit and see through the interior space to nearly any other area of that space.

Journal Article Link 8.1
Read a review of the effectiveness of direct supervision.

Minimum-Security Facility Design (Modern)

Minimum-security prisons are, in many respects, not even prisons as envisioned by most of the public. On some occasions these are also referred to as open institutions due to the low-key security that is provided at these facilities. Minimum-security facilities and/or open institutions are typically designed to serve the needs of farming areas or public transportation works rather than being optimized for the offender's reform. Inmates may often work on community projects, such as roadside litter cleanup with the state department of transportation or wilderness conservation. Many minimum-security facilities are small camps located in or near military bases, larger prisons (outside the security perimeter), or other government institutions to provide a convenient supply of convict labor to the institution.

Minimum-security inmates live in less secure dormitories, which are regularly patrolled by correctional officers. These facilities typically have communal showers, toilets, and sinks. A minimum-security facility generally has a single fence that is watched, but not patrolled, by armed guards. At facilities in very remote and rural areas, there may be no fence at all. The level of staffing assigned to these facilities tends to be much lighter than at other facilities. The open nature of the facility is constructed and operated in such a manner that most inmates staying at such facilities can access showers, television, and other amenities on their own without oversight of security staff.

These facilities tend to consist of inmates who are not considered dangerous and are identified as somewhat industrious. In most cases, inmates are of "trustee" status, being offenders who have either committed minor crimes or served much of their sentence without institutional infractions. Many will have good prospects of being released into the community within a year or two. Freedoms afforded this group of inmates will be much greater than those for inmates of other custody levels. Many states even allow inmates in minimum-security facilities access to the Internet for personal reasons, job searches, and other purposes.

These types of facilities include plantation-style prison farms, as well as small forestry, forest fire–fighting, and road repair camps, depending on the type of labor that is needed.

Medium-Security Prison Design (Modern)

Medium-security facilities may consist of dormitories that have bunk beds with lockers for inmates to store their possessions. These facilities tend to have communal showers, toilets, and sinks. Dormitories are locked at night with one or more security officers holding watch and conducting routine patrols. Inside the dorm, supervision over the internal movements of inmates is minimal. The perimeter of these facilities, when not connected to another larger facility, is generally double fenced and regularly patrolled by armed security personnel.

Much of the newer prison construction during the past four to five decades has consisted of medium-security designs. Indeed, it is thought that close to one third of all state inmates are housed within medium-security facilities. These types of prisons tend to have tighter security than do minimum-security facilities, but they are not as restricted as are maximum-security facilities. Programs for inmates, opportunities for recreation, and the ability to move throughout the grounds are much better in these institutions than in maximum-security prisons.

In modern times, medium-security prisons may be designed along the lines of the community college campus, whereby residence areas are kept attractive and have single rooms rather than cells and open bunks as with dormitories (Allen, Simonsen, & Latessa, 2004). The use of external chain-link fences and other security features (e.g., cameras) may be the only clue that these grounds are, in fact, prisons for inmates. These types of facilities tend to implement more sophisticated technology than larger prisons and also tend to have less obtrusive security procedures when compared with maximum-security facilities.

Maximum-Security Prison Design (Modern)

Originally, when prisons were first designed, their primary and nearly only concern was security. Because of this, most all prisons were designed as maximum-security facilities. In most cases, they were surrounded by a high wall (up to 50 feet tall) that was usually made of brick-and-mortar material. Atop these stone walls could be found various forms of razor wire, and, at each corner and at different intervals along the walls, towers were built so that security personnel could look down upon inmates inside as well as outside of the facility. While in the towers, these armed guards were instrumental in preventing escapes and open-yard riots.

Nowadays, **maximum-security facilities** are not likely to have stone walls but will instead use corrugated chain-link fence. These fences will be lit by floodlights at night and may even have electric shock features for those who touch them. Chain-link fences, with razor wire atop them, tend to be just as effective at containing inmates as the stone walls but eliminate "blind spots" in security where inmates can hide. Rather, the open visibility makes it nearly impossible for inmates to approach the fence line without being detected. The perimeter is generally double fenced with chain-link and includes watchtowers that house armed security personnel. Add to this the use of cameras, sensors, and electric-deterrent fencing features, and the result is a fairly tightly maintained facility.

Pods

Most modern prisons are built with prefabricated sections, often referred to as **pods**. Within these pods, inmates will usually have individual cells with ding doors controlled from a secure remote control station. When out of their cells, prisoners remain in the cell block or an exterior cage. Movement out of the cell block or pod is tightly restricted, often requiring restraints as well as escorts by security staff. In maximum-security facilities, inmates may be housed in one- or two-person cells operated from a remote control station. Inside these facilities, inmates may be allowed to leave their cells to complete work assignments or correctional programs and otherwise may be allowed in a common area in the cell block or an exercise yard.

THE RISE OF THE SUPERMAX

During the 1990s, prison systems around the nation experienced problems with gang offenders and violent offenders who were serious threats to prison order. In fact, the late '90s saw the emergence of the term *security threat groups*, which referred to the various prison and street gangs that existed in and outside of prison. Other inmates, not necessarily linked with organized groups, proved a constant violent threat in many state systems, leading to a need for heightened security beyond maximum-security facilities.

Supermax facilities provide the highest level of prison security. These types of prisons hold the most dangerous of inmates, including inmates who have committed assaults, murders, or other serious violations in less secure facilities, and inmates known to be or accused of being prison gang members. Supermax facilities can either be freestanding, where the entire facility consists of this higher security level, or they can be a specified section of a larger facility with additional security features that make it a supermax facility. While most states have at least one such facility, the Federal BOP has several facilities located across the nation. The National Institute of Corrections provides a definition of supermax facilities that we will borrow for the use of this chapter and text. A **supermax facility** is a "highly restrictive, high custody housing unit within a secure facility, or an entire secure facility, that isolates inmates from the general population and from each other due to grievous crimes, repetitive assaultive or violent institutional behavior, the threat of escape, or actual escape from high custody facility(s), or inciting or threatening to incite disturbances in a correctional institution" (Riveland, 1999, p. 5).

USP Marion: The Protégé of Alcatraz

Though not technically labeled a "supermax" facility, the penitentiary on Alcatraz Island, California, should actually be given this title. **Alcatraz** was first opened in 1934 and held a number of notorious offenders such as Al Capone and other Mafia leaders. Though this facility was largely successful, public shift toward the medical model of correctional thought during the 1950s, along with a questionable escape, led to the ultimate closure of the facility in 1963. When Alcatraz closed, it was USP (United States Penitentiary) Marion, in rural southern Illinois, that was selected as the replacement facility to hold the challenging inmates who had called Alcatraz their home.

Ultimately at **USP Marion**, a special closed-custody unit was designed to house the BOP's worst inmates. While creating this addition, the BOP also created a new classification known as Level 6, which

Video Link 8.2
Watch a video about maximum security prisons.

Video Link 8.3
Take a look inside Alcatraz.

was over and above the other five security classifications that the federal government typically used to classify inmates. The entire prison was designated as the holding place for approximately 450 inmates who were drawn from the federal system and 36 other states—these offenders being among the most notorious around the nation. Despite the enhanced security features at Marion, in 1983, during two separate incidents, two officers were stabbed to death while four others were seriously injured (Ward, 1994). Four days later, another three officers were attacked, and an inmate was killed when neutralizing the incident. In reaction, a state of emergency was declared, and USP Marion was officially placed on lockdown status.

It is important to mention that USP Marion was eventually tested within the courts for the legality of its operations. A class action suit that included several inmate rights groups charged that Marion implemented controls that constituted cruel and unusual punishment. However, after several weeks of testimony, the federal district court in southern Illinois denounced these charges, and in *Bruscino v. Carlson* (1988), the Federal Circuit Court of Appeals upheld the district court's judgment (Ward, 1994). This meant that USP Marion had effectively passed the test of constitutionality. This was good news for Marion and also for many other states that had contemplated the use of a supermax security system but were hesitant due to concerns with the legality (Ward, 1994). Once it was determined the Marion was indeed constitutional, many states quickly set their sights on using similar facilities within their own prison systems.

States Utilize the Marion Model

Once word spread around the nation that the BOP had found a management strategy to control highly disruptive inmates, and once it was found that this strategy was constitutionally sound, correctional administrators from around the nation began to visit USP Marion to glean insights into its design and operation. This eventually became known as the "Marion Model" of prison design, at least informally. By the mid-1990s, at least 36 states had built some sort of supermax custody unit as an addition to already existing prisons or as a stand-alone facility. While the term *supermax* was commonplace, many states used different terms such as special housing units (SHUs) or extended confinement units (ECUs). As these units proliferated throughout the state systems, new constitutional challenges emerged that sometimes had results different from those associated with the rest of the Marion facility.

Indeed, other supermax facilities around the nation have had problems, in terms of both operations and legal criteria. Though problems have emerged, these facilities have operated effectively, for the most part. The resulting legal issues associated with this type of supervision demonstrate how progressive sanctions can invite progressive problems for a correctional system. The difficulty in containing disruptive inmates is compounded by the difficulty in appeasing civil rights requirements. The balance between these two concerns places administrators in a difficult position that is difficult to traverse.

USP Florence ADMAX: "The Alcatraz of the Rockies"

In 1994, the BOP opened its first true supermax facility at Florence, Colorado. Though Marion had a section that was a supermax security facility, it was not a stand-alone facility solely dedicated to supermax operations. The facility in Florence was designed for no other purpose than to operate as a supermax. This facility is officially referred to as the Administrative Maximum (ADX) facility, or ADX Florence. This prison housed over 400 inmates who were the worst of the worst in the BOP. These inmates were selected because they were either extremely violent, high escape risks, or identified gang leaders. Construction for this facility cost over $60 million, and each cell had a price tag of around $150,000, making this facility

one of the most (if not the most) expensive ever built and maintained. Annual maintenance for inmates is roughly $40,000 per year with the overall cost of prison maintenance being around $20 million a year.

USP Florence ADMAX is located on State Highway 67, 90 miles south of Denver, 45 miles south of Colorado Springs, and 40 miles west of Pueblo. The facility's design is nearly indestructible on the inside.

Video Link 8.4
Learn more about the inmate-staff violence at Marion.

Journal Article Link 8.2
Read about supermax prisons from a prisoner's point of view.

PHOTO 8.5

USP Florence ADMAX has cells that consist of a concrete bed, desk, stool, and bookcase, all constructed from reinforced concrete. This supermax prison was much more expensive to build than other prisons due to the enhanced security features of this facility.

The cell design consists of a concrete bed, desk, stool, and bookcase, all constructed from reinforced concrete and immovable. Each cells measures 7 by 12 feet, and each has a shower stall and reinforced plumbing within. Cell windows are designed so that all views of the outside are restricted, and inmates can only see the sky above them. In addition, cells are positioned in such a manner so that inmates cannot make eye contact with one another. Essentially, these offenders have no contact with humans. All food is given by tray through a door slot, and all visits are noncontact in nature. Further, recreation is for one hour a day and is alone. In many ways, it seems that, ironically, a Pennsylvania model of operation has been implemented, but, in this case, the intent is to simply incarcerate and hold the inmate in place; reform is no longer a priority with these hardened inmates who have a poor prognosis due to dangerous and repetitive behavior.

As one would guess, this supermax prison was much more expensive to build than other prisons due to the enhanced security features, higher-quality locks and doors, and outside-perimeter fencing designs. Advanced electronic systems, reinforced walls and ceilings, and other such security features add to the cost. Further, these facilities are expensive to maintain for two reasons. First, the advanced security features are costly to maintain, and the additional staff security adds an additional financial burden. Second, a large proportion of supermax inmates will never be released; their sentences are for very long terms, and this means that, over time, they will become more costly due to the need for geriatric medical care. Thus, the financial picture goes from bad to worse for these facilities.

CONSTITUTIONAL ISSUES WITH CONFINEMENT IN SUPERMAX CUSTODY

It has been found that, when kept in prolonged periods of confinement, inmates tend to exhibit mental health issues due to sensory deprivation, which include states of paranoia, irrational fears, resentment, inability to control anger, depression, heightened anxiety, and forms of full mental breakdown. Suicides tend to be higher among inmates who are confined for prolonged periods of time. Many of these issues, as students may recall from Chapter 2, are similar to those of inmates confined in solitude for prolonged periods in Eastern State Penitentiary under the Pennsylvania model of prison operation. This is an important observation because it demonstrates that history does, indeed, repeat itself, and it validates the fact that extreme isolation does cause human mental health problems. In modern correctional literature, the negative mental health effects of extended isolation may be referred to as **special housing unit syndrome**.

Supermax-specific case law to date is limited. The first case to capture national attention, *Madrid v. Gomez* (1995), was a wide-ranging attack on operations at the Pelican Bay SHU in California. This is a supermax-type control-unit facility where inmates identified as gang members; offenders with a history of violence, crime, or serious rule violations within prison; and other inmates considered major management threats are incarcerated. The Pelican Bay SHU was one of the first such facilities in modern American history explicitly planned and built as a state-level supermax facility.

LOCATION OF MANY PRISONS

Most early prisons tended to be located in remote areas of the state, away from metropolitan areas. This was especially true when prison farms and agricultural farm-lease agreements proliferated. Given the emphasis on agriculture, it was often necessary that such farms be in locations where there was plenty of ground space for the planting and harvesting of crops. Further, when prisons are located in remote areas of the nation, this adds a degree of security and a sense of public safety, at least in theory; the farther away offenders are from mainstream society, the less likely they can cause harm to additional victims. However, in reality this is not true since many inmates who concoct escape plans do not plan to escape on foot but instead often procure assistance from people outside of the prison walls. This is true with goods, transportation, and shelter once the escape has been effected. Thus, the location of a prison within a distant and rural area can help thwart unplanned escapes that take place on foot, but they are not foolproof against planned escapes.

Other prison facilities may be near metropolitan areas. There are many reasons for this, especially if the prison itself houses inmates with serious medical needs or other such specialized services. Placing

Video Link 8.5
View a video about well-known prisons in the U.S.

Audio Link 8.2
Listen to the controversy over solitary confinement.

Audio Link 8.3
Hear about life inside a supermax prison.

TECHNOLOGY AND EQUIPMENT 8.1

Dome Technology in Cell Block Design Versus Traditional Prison Construction

One innovative concept, not yet used by any correctional system in the United States, is dome construction in prison design. Dome structures are based on pod designs that are prefabricated, but it is the dome shape itself that holds substantial advantages for correctional agencies, in terms of both security and operational costs. The figure below, as part of this Technology & Equipment insert, provides a floor plan from Monolithic for a 1,200-bed-capacity prison that uses dome structures for cell block and dormitory living areas as well as other structures throughout the complex.

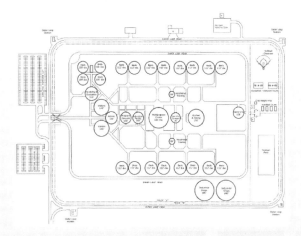

While in some ways the use of the dome configuration is reminiscent of Bentham's panopticon, the real advantage comes in the way of cost savings and additional security strength. With dome-shaped structures, the amount of heating and cooling is vastly reduced, and this has been found to be true with numerous residential and business facilities that have utilized this technology; prisons would be no different. Further, the speed of construction is increased, a benefit to any off-site construction as noted in other areas of this chapter. In addition, the use of sprayed concrete creates a much stronger structure than the use of traditional concrete; thus these facilities are more secure and more resistant to inclement weather. Likewise, the line of sight is maximized for security personnel, adding to the interior security of the structure. This means that this design is effective in eliminating the existence of blind spots in prison security

and observation—an issue that will be discussed later in this chapter. The elimination of such blind spots reduces the use of redundant and overlapping assignments of security personnel and eliminates the need for extensive technological surveillance equipment. On the other hand, if institutions do decide to use such equipment, the ability for it to detect institutional violations is enhanced by the open view provided by this construction design.

The diagram for this prison design features multiple two-story double-dome units that can house up to 120 inmates. This medium-security housing design has paired 112-foot-diameter, 37-foot-tall domes with 120 beds in single cells. Visitors enter between two 140-foot-diameter visitor's domes into the 108-foot-diameter administration and operations dome. Each visitor's dome has 11,484 square feet of open space. The Reception and Evaluation dome (110 x 37 feet) encompasses 9,500 square feet with all the modern facilities. Program Services, in a 100-foot dome, accommodates a pharmacy, an infirmary, a chaplain, a 2,500-square-foot multipurpose room, and offices. The educational facility, also in a 100-foot dome, comes complete with classrooms, library, and more. The centrally located kitchen in a 150-foot-diameter, 17,000-square-foot dome creates optimum work areas and easy access to the separate dining halls—two for inmates, one for staff—as well as private access to the storage/unloading area. Separate double gymnasiums are surrounded by locker rooms, exercise rooms, and offices in a 25,450-square-foot, 150-foot-diameter, multipurpose center. Located between the multipurpose center and dining hall a 90-foot-diameter dome houses the ample laundry and storage areas, commissary, canteen, and barber. A nondenominational chapel (60 x 25 feet) with rooms for ecclesiastical counseling provides an optional religious center.

As can be seen, this type of pod technology provides ample space and all the modern accoutrements that could be included in a state-of-the-art prison design. The fact of the matter is that these designs are, in reality, superior to traditional prison designs. They are structurally more tough than other designs, are less expensive to build and maintain, and save on the need for excessive security features since their design provides superior observation and security potential. All in all, this type of technology should be utilized by states that seek to improve their correctional system, making it both modern and cost-effective.

SOURCE: South, D. B. (2009). *The monolithic dome as a prison?* Italy, TX: Monolithic Domes. Reprinted by permission of Monolithic Constructors, Inc.

such facilities in and around areas where hospitals or other services are available may make practical sense. Also, some facilities (especially minimum-security facilities) may not have as many security concerns, especially with violent crime. In other cases, it may simply be that the facility is built on ground that is available to the agency. In fact, some communities may welcome the facility being located within their jurisdiction since it can mean additional jobs for the area. The reasons for a prison's particular location can be manifold, but in today's world of corrections, it is not always easy to determine the best location for a prison; the answer lies more with the point and purpose of the institution itself.

ACCOMMODATIONS FOR INMATES WITH DISABILITIES

The number of inmates with disabilities in prison facilities has continued to grow throughout correctional systems nationwide. Indeed, the aging inmate population, the effects of alcohol and drug abuse, and the injuries due to violence in facilities help to contribute to the disabilities and challenges that inmates possess (Appel, 1999). As inmate disabilities and different types of special needs are increasingly more important, the legal standards and requirements have also changed and become more rigorous.

Video Link 8.6
Watch a video about inmate rights.

Proof of this changing legal environment became most evident in 1990 when the **Americans with Disabilities Act (ADA)** was signed into action. This act became federal law, and it is important that correctional agencies ensure that staff are trained on the specific issues related to the ADA and inmates. This act created a whole set of legal obligations that, largely, did not exist for prison administrators. As such, when this act was first proposed, correctional administrators came together and produced over 7,000 pages of commentary and testimony regarding concerns and considerations with this act throughout the legislative process.

ADA Compliance

Prison Tour Video Link 8.1
Watch two wardens discuss ADA modifications.

According to the Civil Rights Division, Disability Rights Section, of the U.S. Department of Justice (2010), the ADA requires correctional agencies to make reasonable modifications in their policies, practices, and procedures that are necessary to ensure accessibility for individuals with disabilities, unless making such modifications would fundamentally alter the program or service involved. There are many ways in which an agency might need to modify its normal practices to accommodate a person with a disability. Some examples follow below:

> **Example 1:** An agency modifies a rule that inmates or detainees are not permitted to have food in their cells except at scheduled intervals, in order to accommodate an individual with diabetes who uses medication and needs access to carbohydrates or sugar to keep blood sugar at an appropriate level.

> **Example 2:** An agency modifies its regular practice of handcuffing inmates behind their backs, and instead handcuffs deaf individuals in front in order for them to sign or write notes.

> **Example 3:** An agency modifies its practice of confiscating medications for the period of confinement, in order to permit inmates who have disabilities that require self-medication, such as cardiac conditions or epilepsy, to self-administer medications that do not have abuse potential.

Lastly, state and local government entities should conduct a "self-evaluation" to review their current services, policies, and practices for compliance with the ADA. When such an evaluation finds that the agency has deficiencies, the agency should develop a "transition plan" identifying structural changes that needed to be made. As part of that process, the ADA has encouraged entities to involve individuals with disabilities from their local communities. Continuing this process will promote access solutions that are reasonable and effective.

PROTECTIVE CUSTODY SECTIONS

Protective custody is specialized, segregated housing that serves many purposes and is used in a number of circumstances. **Protective custody** is a security-level status, typically determined by the official classification process, that is given to inmates who are deemed to be at risk of serious violence that is predictable and likely to occur if they are not afforded protection. According to Angelone (1999), protection might be afforded to any of the following inmate types:

- Those afraid of sexual predators.
- Institutional informants.
- Those who are former law enforcement or corrections officers.
- Those who become government witnesses.
- Those whose lives now may be in danger from those they formerly preyed upon.
- Those who wish to exit membership from a prison gang.
- Those unable to pay off a gambling or other type of debt in prison.

Angelone (1999) notes that protective custody sections of state prisons are becoming more difficult to manage due to the variety of backgrounds and behavioral traits that exist among inmates afforded protection. In some of the larger institutions, it may arise that some form of separation within the protective custody section itself is necessary as a means of protecting protective custody inmates from one another; this is particularly true if one inmate has victimized the other prior to entering protective custody and is also true among rival gang members.

While in protective custody, inmates are entitled to almost all of the privileges and opportunities that they would have in the general population of a prison. Thus, modifications to educational programs, recreational activities, religious activities, legal resources, and so forth are all required. Naturally, this places an additional burden on administrators, in terms of both monetary resources and human resources. Thus, protective custody is a challenging aspect of prison operations that has become more frequently necessary as the prison population becomes more violent. This has been particularly true within the last three decades.

Audio Link 8.4
Hear about the efforts taken to prevent sexual violence.

Reference Link 8.2
Read a description of how and why prisoners are put into protective custody.

INNOVATIVE DESIGNS

Each correctional facility has its own challenges and needs that make it a bit different from other facilities in the respective correctional system. A variety of factors must be considered such as whether the site will be rural or urban, the security level needed, and operational concerns for security and programming—the security level of the institution, specific needs of inmates, the surrounding community support, the durability of materials needed, and so forth.

Prisons can vary widely in size, in terms of both inmate capacity and the physical area encompassed by the prison buildings. The *National Directory of Corrections Construction*, published by the National Institute of Justice, classifies prisons into the following general types:

1. Campus style: a number of individual buildings that are not connected.

2. Ladder, telephone pole: linear cell blocks arranged in parallel configuration off a central connecting corridor.

FIGURE 8.1   Various Prison Complex Designs

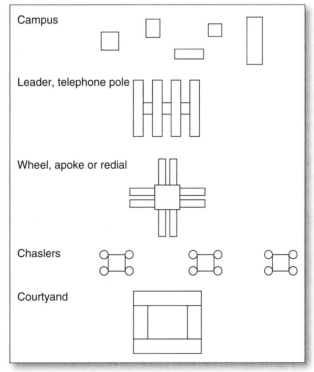

Source: General Accounting Office. (1991). *Prison costs: Opportunities exist to lower the cost of building federal prisons.* Washington, DC: GAO.

Although gang activity, drug culture, informers, rule relaxation, and the increasing rate of inmate damage suits (and the likelihood that prison officials may be held personally liable for inmates' injuries) have forced a trend toward protective custody (PC) units to safeguard certain inmates, the problems of overflow and unconstitutional restriction in these units have generated new litigation. Inmates assigned to these units are beginning to challenge the conditions of their confinement. For many inmates, the physical deprivation of PC is exacerbated by the sense that they are the objects of community contempt and by the fear of retaliation once they are released. Some prison psychiatric services personnel contend that depression, schizophrenia, and suicidal behavior may all be triggered by protective custody.

While a considerable amount of case law exists regarding both staff liability and inmate rights, very little case law exists that has dealt directly with protective custody. With respect to liability, the courts have determined that prison officials have a basic duty to take reasonable precautions to protect inmates under their care. However, in order to establish liability under the Eighth Amendment for a prison official's failure to protect an inmate, the inmate must demonstrate that the official was deliberately indifferent "to a substantial risk of serious harm" to the inmate (*Farmer v. Brennan*, 511 U.S. 825, 828 [1994]). To demonstrate deliberate indifference, an inmate must present evidence from which a trier of fact could conclude "that the official was subjectively aware of the risk" and "disregard[ed] that risk by failing to take reasonable measures to abate it" (829, 847). As noted above, the only issue before this court is whether the inmate introduces sufficient evidence to convince a trier of fact that the warden or other prison official was aware of a substantial risk of serious harm to the inmate. That awareness can be demonstrated through "inference from circumstantial evidence," and a prison official cannot "escape liability . . . by showing that, while he was aware of an obvious, substantial risk to inmate safety, he did not know that the complainant was especially likely to be assaulted by the specific prisoner who eventually committed the assault" (842–843).

Supreme Court cases following *Farmer* demonstrate that the converse is true as well: Where a specific individual poses a risk to a large class of inmates, that risk can also support a finding of liability even where the particular prisoner at risk is not known in advance. *See Curry v. Scott*, 249 F.3d 493, 507–508 (6th Cir. 2001) (where a particular prison guard had a history of racially motivated harassment of African American inmates, deliberate indifference could be demonstrated by factual record, without threat to a particular inmate).

Yet a 1979 Supreme Court decision upheld the idea that the courts should not interfere in matters of prison administration unless it can be shown that prison officials are making an "exaggerated response" to security problems. Legal observers believe that the decision will continue to limit the relief the courts grant to PC inmates in the future. This demonstrates that, overall, there is a lack of consensus among the courts regarding the rights of inmates to PC. The assignment of liability has become a fairly difficult task that is seldom able to be attached to the actions of prison staff.

This lack of consensus regarding the rights of inmates in PC coupled with the high standard for liability to attach, requiring proof of deliberate indifference, makes the process of obtaining protective custody status untenable. Further, Carlson and Garrett (2008) note that there is a bit of irony to the situation because while the Supreme Court has not addressed specific rights with inmates in protective custody, it has given extensive attention to inmates in administrative segregation. Administrative segregation is, in many cases, a status afforded to perpetrators of violence inside the prison. Thus, it appears that inmates in administrative segregation, some of whom are guilty of having victimized inmates in protective custody, have more due process rights that are defined than do the individuals being protected in protective custody.

Source: Anderson, D. C. (1980). *Price of safety—"I can't go back out there."* Washington, DC: U.S. Department of Justice. Retrieved from http://www.ncjrs.gov/App/abstractdb/AbstractDBDetails.aspx?id=69921.

Greene v. Boyles, 2004 FED App. 0078P (6th Cir. 2004).

3. Wheel, spoke, or radial: linear cell blocks that emanate from one central control area like spokes from the hub of a wheel.

4. Clusters: a number of individual buildings that are interconnected.

5. Courtyard: linear cell blocks interconnected around a central enclosed courtyard.

Figures 8.1 and 8.2 provide a basic illustration of each type of design and the manner in which it might be organized. There are numerous reasons that one design might be used rather than another, including the security level of the institution, the location of the prison, and/or the intended function of the facility.

FIGURE 8.2   Typical Cell Layout and Organization

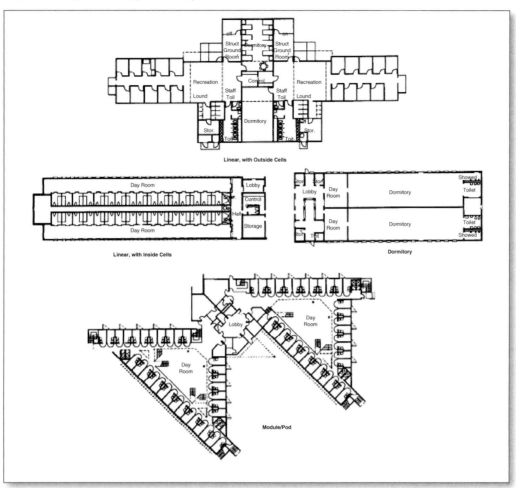

SOURCE: General Accounting Office. (1991). *Prison costs: Opportunities exist to lower the cost of building federal prisons.* Washington, DC: GAO.

Perimeter Security

A prison's **perimeter security system** is, ideally, a collection of components or elements that, when assembled in a carefully formulated plan, achieve the objective of confinement with a high degree of confidence. Keeping in mind that confinement is the ultimate objective, it is clear that anyone attempting to escape the institution by crossing the perimeter must be interdicted by responding officers before the perimeter is successfully penetrated. The perimeter system must ensure that this confrontation can occur. Figure 8.3 (not drawn to scale) shows a cross section cut through a basic two-fence security perimeter. It illustrates the components of a perimeter system and their relationship to each other. The perimeter itself is delineated by two chain-link fences with an isolation zone between them. All of the other components shown, including the camera towers and lighting, make up the security system applied to the perimeter, which must incorporate the sections of detection, assessment, and delay, all facilitating an armed response to the point at which an escape is being attempted.

Alarm Systems

When establishing alarm systems for perimeter security, camera video systems should be placed inside the inner fence and positioned to allow for viewing of the source object that triggers a given alarm. Positioning should ensure that the entire security zone is viewable rather than being narrow in scope and focus. Attention to lighting is important as well, since this will affect the effectiveness of camera systems at night. A primary issue when implementing a video surveillance system is being able to discriminate between person-sized alarm sources that could be escaping inmates and, conversely, small animals or other nuisance alarms (Crist & Spencer, 1991).

FIGURE 8.3   Fenced Perimeter of a Prison

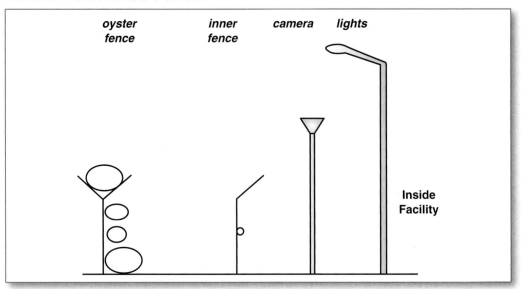

SOURCE: Crist, D., & Spencer, D. (1991). *Perimeter security for Minnesota correctional facilities*. St. Paul: Minnesota Department of Corrections.

Isolation Zone

The key idea with fencing is to provide enough of a delay so that security responding to the escape attempt will have time to intercept the escaping inmate before he or she can penetrate or clear the fence (Crist & Spencer, 1991). The area between the inner and outer fences is often referred to as the isolation zone. The **isolation zone** is designed to prevent undetected access to the outer fencing of the prison facility. This also forms an area of confinement where the inmate escapee is trapped once the alarm is triggered, which allows security staff time to respond and apprehend the inmate before the escape is successful.

The system shown in Figure 8.4 is based on a 20-foot-high wall with a thickness at the top of 16 to 24 inches. The construction is assumed to be solid stone masonry or reinforced concrete, which should discourage attempts to cut through the wall. Lighting features are also shown mounted on the top of the wall since this is typical of most stone-walled facilities. Sensor equipment is mounted on the wall and placed to detect an object or a person approaching the top of the wall or something leaning against or touching the wall. This same sensor equipment is also designed to detect persons who might scale the wall

FIGURE 8.4   Fenced Perimeter of a Prison With a Stone or Concrete Wall

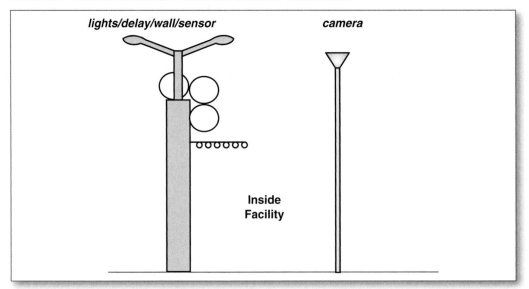

SOURCE: Crist, D., & Spencer, D. (1991). *Perimeter security for Minnesota correctional facilities*. St. Paul: Minnesota Department of Corrections.

from the outside since there would be no convenient way to get over the wall and inside the yard without encountering the sensor array. Thus, this security system also serves to thwart the attempt of outside accomplices.

Lighting

When providing lighting for these types of security designs, some problems are likely to be encountered. First, if the lighting is located atop the wall, the system will usually be about 15 feet from the sensor system and 5 or 6 feet inboard of the wall. This type of configuration produces hot spots in the lit areas that will exceed typical light-to-darkness ratios for optimal viewing. Because of this, some facilities may add light sources along the top of the wall while reducing their intensity. In addition, the lighting equipment may be directed away from the surface of the wall, just a bit, to reduce intensity and potential glare. However, the use of additional lighting fixtures is expensive, and this then adds further to the cost of the prison in terms of layout and maintenance.

Razor Wire

Three coils of razor wire create the barrier delay and are placed above the sensor, along the inner area of the wall, and along the top. Because determined inmates may be willing to concede detection with the thought that they can clear the wall prior to the response of security personnel, the razor wire is used to further prevent most inmates from taking the chance. To demonstrate how complicated security can be and how crafty some inmates may become out of desperation, consider that the lighting poles could be used to bypass this barrier. Thus, the poles should be made to give way and break if they are loaded with heavy resistance. When taken together, these collective features are customary to most basic perimeter security systems of older maximum- and medium-security-level facilities.

INTERNAL SECURITY

A number of features can be used within the facility to enhance internal custody and control of the inmate population. For instance, the use of touch screen surveillance systems in control rooms can provide centralized security staff with the ability to oversee security throughout various sections of the institution. Showcased in Figures 8.5–8.8, this type of equipment can provide a sense of organization to the overall security maintenance throughout the facility and help to organize the use of security staff resources, during times of both routine operation and crisis response.

However, Redding (2004) notes that although physical design and inmate classification may be key elements of the security process, it is the security staff who are integral to maintaining custody and control of the inmate population. Regardless of how well one builds a prison and of its attendant security features, the physical features of an institution's perimeter alone are useless without staff properly trained to be alert to their responsibilities while operating in their assigned capacities (American Correctional Association, 1998). Prison officials are responsible for the security measures that the physical design cannot control. Some duties include "access control, searching of prisoners and their belongings, and movement control both inside and outside prisons and during the transportation of prisoners" (Redding, 2004).

The only sure way of providing top-notch security is through education and training (Redding, 2004). The American Correctional Association (ACA) recommends that there be 120 hours of training after hire and another 80 hours before being placed on a shift. Some include inadequate training and education on the part of the officer. Also, some officers may be involved in scandals inside the prison. "All people—staff included—who move into and out of the institution must be considered possible avenues of contraband movement" (ACA, 1998). Thus, regardless of the types of technology that are developed and despite the physical barriers that may be built, there is almost always one unpredictable variable that exists within most security programs—human involvement. Successfully addressing this variable is perhaps the most important aspect of developing any true security process within an agency. Indeed, the use of other security tools will be minimized if not completely undermined if there is not appropriate human cooperation in the security process.

Given that the human element is so important to internal security, it is important that an appropriate form of organizational culture be developed within an agency that seeks to psychologically motivate

Journal Article Link 8.3
Read about threats to internal security.

FIGURE 8.5   Touch Screen Control Panel

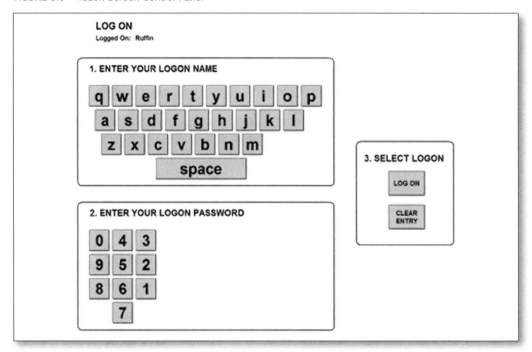

SOURCE: Reprinted by permission of Cornerstone Institutional Sales & Service, www.cisupply.com

FIGURE 8.6   Full View of Facility

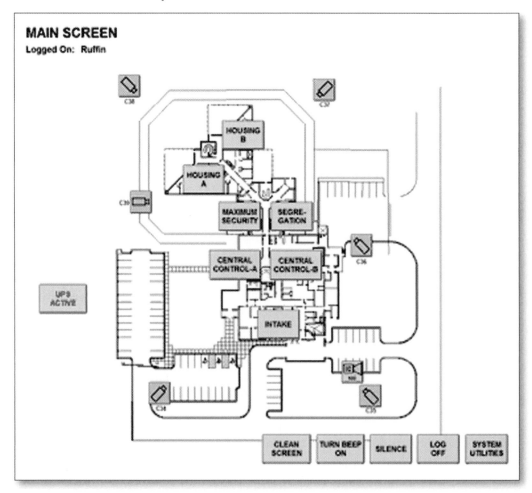

SOURCE: Reprinted by permission of Cornerstone Institutional Sales & Service, www.cisupply.com

FIGURE 8.7   Multilevel View of Pod

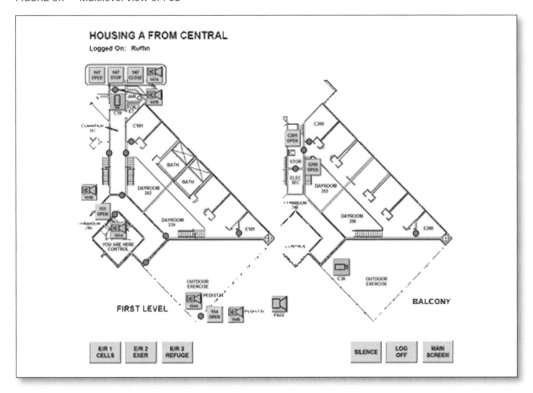

SOURCE: Reprinted by permission of Cornerstone Institutional Sales & Service, www.cisupply.com

FIGURE 8.8   View Segregation Pod

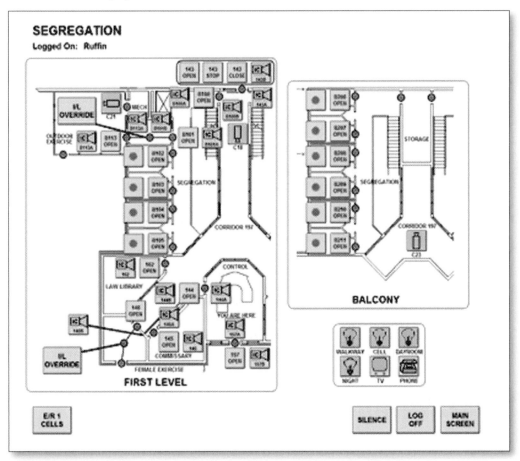

SOURCE: Reprinted by permission of Cornerstone Institutional Sales & Service, www.cisupply.com

employees toward security-minded objectives (Robbins, 2005). This sense of organizational culture refers to a system of shared meaning held by members of that organization. One shared meaning or belief is the need for security as well as the need for an attention to detail (Robbins, 2005). This attention to detail entails the degree to which employees are expected to exhibit precision, analysis, and attention to the specific routines that occur within the agency (Robbins, 2005). It is clear that such attentiveness would provide an environmental mind-set that is conducive to security-related issues. Without such a mind-set, truly disastrous results can occur.

Consider, for instance, that inmates in a San Antonio, Texas, prison managed to steal 14 revolvers, a 12-gauge shotgun, and a rifle before they drove away in a prison van without being checked. The key security breach had to do with personnel who did not follow agency policy and procedure related to security over the inmates. This escape led to a Christmas Eve robbery and the death of an Irving police officer (Associated Press, 2001). This example demonstrates that problems with security, particularly human compliance with security principles, can have a crucial and deadly impact on both the internal security of the prison facility and the outside community.

AVOIDING BLIND SPOTS IN CORRECTIONAL FACILITIES

Blind spots in correctional facilities can occur when the design has certain areas of the prison obscured from easy view of security staff and/or surveillance equipment. While the primary means of achieving internal security are the staff employed within, they cannot detect all things that occur. Surveillance equipment inside the facility is often used to add a security element to areas that are less patrolled and/or difficult for staff to observe in person. The use of closed-circuit television (CCTV) systems can provide good visual surveillance within a facility, but these types of systems can be costly. However, as noted in the previous subsection, this equipment is only as effective as the security personnel who use the equipment.

Thus, the best means of avoiding blind spots is to, at the design stage, leave as few areas out of restricted view as possible. In addition, staff should be aware, and provide more intensive physical monitoring, of these areas where obstructed view occurs. This prevents a number of problems that go beyond just escape. The blind spot areas of a prison leave a gap in security that can allow inmates to engage in inappropriate or illicit behaviors, such as trafficking and trading of contraband, inappropriate behavior within the institution, or assaultive actions against other inmates or staff. Thus, these areas are danger zones within the prison facility and should be given maximum attention by security personnel to offset the potential breach to internal or external security.

AUXILIARY SERVICES AND PHYSICAL SECURITY

The provision of auxiliary services is very important within the world of corrections. Though these services are auxiliary in nature, they are actually quite central to the survival of the inmate population. Indeed, the ability of an institution to feed its inmates, clothe them, provide for religious services and recreational services, and provide space where job skills can be practiced requires specialized facilities. This can also create additional security needs within the institution since staff must now do more than simply hold security; they must provide security with a population that is industrious and active. Keeping watch over inmates as they perform kitchen duties or other functions in the prison provides security staff with a whole new set of responsibilities and circumstances besides those encountered on the cell block or in the dormitory. It is with this in mind that we turn our attention to prison kitchens, their construction and design, and the need for secure kitchen facilities.

Kitchen Services and Facilities

The design and development of kitchen facilities in prison environments require that equipment be able to service hundreds or thousands of individuals on a daily basis yet, at the same time, facilitate security needs of the institution. This is a difficult balance in design since any mass feeding operation is, itself, a challenging process. When adding security issues to the kitchen operation process, the physical layout of the kitchen becomes very important.

Kitchens and related equipment tend to vary between facilities. For instance, older facilities tend to exist within the typical brick-and-mortar design with updated equipment placed therein as budgetary limits may allow. Newer facilities may have modern equipment that is energy efficient and likely to work much more rapidly and reliably than older equipment that may be found in older prisons.

In addition, the storage of cutlery equipment within the kitchen is critical. Strict monitoring of the use of culinary tools such as knives, forks, and meat saws is very important to institutional safety and security. Facilities must be designed so that the inventory of kitchen tools can be completed quickly and easily. This feature distinguishes a prison kitchen from most other types of commercial or mass feeding kitchens. The design of a kitchen is important when addressing the security issues that will confront kitchen security staff.

The most common method of serving food to inmates is through a cafeteria-style large open room. These rooms tend to have either long tables or a series of small tables with chairs that are secured to the ground. In such cases, inmates gather at the feeding line where the line may be open so that they can observe the persons who are serving their plates, but in other prisons a screen may extend down several feet from the ceiling so that inmates are not able to know who prepared their tray of food. This feature eliminates the possibility that inmates who do not like one another will have problems regarding the food that is served on the line.

Laundry Facilities

The need to continually clean clothes and bedding is also a routine issue in prison facilities. The facilities must have reliable washers and dryers and must have other services such as ironing equipment that is both heavy-duty and reliable. These facilities must be suitable for continual use and must also allow for adequate security over the inmate population. The constant wear-and-tear of equipment requires that all equipment be industrial in strength. Such equipment must be made to take abuse, as it is operated by inmates who, for the most part, have little incentive to adequately take care of it. Such equipment should be heavy-duty and oversized, and have commercially rated components.

As with kitchen facilities, laundry facilities should be designed so that security is able to be easily maintained. While in the facility, security staff should be able to maintain effective custody and control over inmates working in the facility. All products must be accounted for, including items such as irons and products like bleach and cleaning soap; such items hold value when traded throughout the inmate population. Laundry facilities must be designed to facilitate the need for inventory control of tools and equipment.

PHOTO 8.6

Prison kitchens and dining halls tend to be busy throughout the entire day and much of the evening. The continuous feeding process within the institution requires nearly round-the-clock work on the part of inmates and staff assigned to culinary duties. Pictured here is a jail facility kitchen (photo 8.6a) at Ouachita Correctional Center and a prison dining hall (photo 8.6b) at Richwood Correctional Facility.

PHOTO 8.7

Laundry work in a prison facility also requires all-day work among inmates and staff assigned to this service.

Recreational Facilities

Though the issue of inmate recreation may be controversial, it is inevitable that prison administrators will have to attend to this issue. Recreation for inmates comes in many shapes and forms, but, regardless of the type of recreation, the ability to offer such activities can be an effective behavior management tool inside the prison. The threat of exclusion from participation in recreation programs usually does gain compliance from most of the inmate population, and this alone demonstrates some operational value for such programs. When the leisure time of inmates is used in the construction of arts and crafts, the use of multipurpose activities, and participation in sports activities or physical exercise, they are less likely to be lured into other activities that are not prosocial. Institutional facilities for recreation might include any of the following:

- Intramural sports (e.g., basketball, handball, flag football, soccer).
- Games (cards, dominoes, bingo).
- Individual exercise (weight lifting and jogging).
- Arts and crafts (leather working, woodworking, painting).
- Clubs (Key Club, Jaycees, Toastmasters).

Each of the above activities will have different needs for facility space, some of which can even be provided outdoors. As with any additional prison service, the implementation of these programs also must be amenable to effective security maintenance. Naturally, some types of recreation include tools or instruments that can, if not kept under tight inventory, be trafficked among the inmate population. For instance, leather working tools, wood-cutting saws, and other types of instruments should be subjected to very close security scrutiny.

Religious Facilities

The impact of religion and faith-based programming in prison is undeniably important within the field of corrections. In some prisons, an actual religious gathering facility may exist whereas in other prisons a meeting room will be used with seats and speaking equipment provided. While the existence of full-fledged buildings devoted solely to religious services is rare in most prisons, the allocation of a gathering space that can be used for religious services is not rare. Given that different religious orientations may be found in prisons and that states do not wish to lay the ground for discrimination between different religions, it is probably prudent for administrators to simply provide space for religious services on an "as needed" basis.

Tool Shop Facilities

Tool shops tend to exist at many larger prisons where some type of industry is performed. Such facilities allow inmates to be productive while serving their sentence. Further, inmates can learn and perform repair work of appliances, lawn equipment, and even motor vehicles. Such shops produce tangible benefits for the prison and the inmate population. Nevertheless, security risks exist as such equipment can be used to make weapons and/or effect escape attempts. Thus, the design of tool shops must accommodate security concerns and allow for the easy inventory and control of equipment and tools.

TECHNOLOGY SYSTEMS IN PRISONS

The use of technology in prisons is becoming widespread and has impacted a number of operational aspects. While it is obvious that surveillance equipment such as alarms and cameras have had innovations, there are other developments that have been innovative and just as important. For instance, the physical security of the institution itself has been strengthened through improvements in building and fencing technology as well as technology related to ingress and egress from correctional institutions.

For example, prefinished concrete modules have become accepted in prison and jail design and construction. Examples from earlier parts of this chapter might include the design and building of the kitchen or of pod-like cell blocks. Precast concrete cells are thought to consist of a substantial percentage

APPLIED THEORY 8.1

Routine Activity Theory, Inmate Traffic Flow, and Institutional Infractions

According to routine activity theory (see Chapter 7), crime will occur at locations where a motivated offender, a suitable target, and a lack of capable guardians come together in confluence. Because, at least in theory, the entire prison consists of motivated offenders, there is a heightened likelihood that some form of criminal activity or victimization will occur. The presumption is that prison security—in terms of both personnel and security mechanisms—will be able to thwart the attempts of such offenders from committing crimes while in prison.

However, we know that trafficking and trading of contraband continue within the walls of the prison. Likewise, different forms of victimization also continue to occur within prisons. Lastly, illicit activities such as gambling also occur. Thus, it seems that there are indeed suitable targets (consisting of victims, or, when victimless crimes, activities), and, at least at times, the guardians of the prison (security staff) may not be capable of detecting and preventing this behavior.

The key to preventing institutional infractions and victimization within prisons consists of many prongs. First, security staff members' awareness of blind spots in prison will enhance their ability to detect and prevent institutional infractions. Second, the use of technology can be enhanced when it is placed within key areas that are vulnerable to inmate exploitation. Third, the design of the facility itself will naturally impact inmate traffic flow, creating areas where more contact between inmates will occur. Fourth, and lastly, the operational schedule of the institution will impact the ebb and flow of likely violations as inmates are moved from one function to another throughout the daily routine of prison operations.

An innovative design using pod-based dome technology has already been presented in this chapter as an ideal facility design to minimize security problems, both internal and perimeter based. Likewise, the use of CCTV has been touched upon briefly for its ability to detect crime. However, it is important to further showcase the use of CCTV, both with real cameras and with decoy cameras, since it enhances the deterrence, detection, and prevention of likely violations.

For the most part, many modern facilities already use camera surveillance to monitor and record inmate visitation rooms as a means of supervising visits and detecting the exchange of drugs or other contraband between inmates. Monitoring is conducted from remote areas of the prison, which means that inmates are not aware of whether they are being watched. In fact, institutions can even place decoy cameras (that are cheap to build but do not conduct surveillance) throughout some areas of the prison, and this alone can act as a deterrent for many inmates. This extends the deterrence value since inmates will not know which cameras work and which do not, while at the same time extending the budget of the institution that can afford a very finite number of cameras.

of all new inmate housing construction (Carlson & Garrett, 2008). Using traditional masonry construction typically would take longer because of the transportation of materials and weather delays. The use of modular building processes allows for good managerial control throughout the process and helps budgets to go further. These types of cells tend to have a longer period of low or no maintenance and are also less expensive to build. This is truly a win-win-win outcome between correctional facility operators, the community at large, and building contractors.

As another example, in California, Colorado, Missouri, and Alabama, innovations with lethal forms of electric fencing have been effective in deterring escape attempts (Carlson & Garrett, 2008). While these types of fences should not be seen as a full replacement of security staff, they do eliminate the need for so many staff to concentrate on perimeter security. Carlson and Garrett (2008) note that these developments

> truly do offer the opportunity to cut back on staffing in towers and external mobile patrols. California's Department of Corrections has found the installation of these fences has facilitated the deactivation of nearly all towers and has enabled administrators to redeploy staff to other important posts. (p. 417)

Thus, these types of innovations allow administrators to maximize the use of their employees by diverting them to areas of the prison that can benefit from more personalized and human-oriented job functions.

PRISONER IDENTIFICATION

In regard to inmate identification, new processes are being developed that greatly enhance institutional security and cost-effectiveness. For instance, mug shots are now taken with digital cameras and stored in computers; this allows for photographic images of inmates to be readily available for prison staff at a fraction of the cost that once was required and enhances inmate recognition by staff. Likewise, fingerprints are now maintained in online data systems while retina imaging and iris scanning equipment has seen innovations and improvements.

In addition, some facilities have begun to use wristbands with bar codes, and these tools are used to track inmates throughout the prison facility. In this way, through the use of touch-key control systems, prison staff can monitor the movement of individual inmates in real time. Similar tracking technology has been used in Los Angeles where the tracking of inmates in the nation's largest jail system is now conducted with radio-linked wristbands (Etter, 2005). These devices allow security staff to pinpoint inmates' location within a few feet. Los Angeles County has used these devices at Pitchess Detention Center in Castaic, about 40 miles northwest of downtown Los Angeles, with plans to expand the program to another 6,000 inmates at the county's central jail and then to other facilities (Etter, 2005).

Beyond tracking inmates around cell blocks, the technology has the potential to allow work-release crews to roam within an electronic fence that could be easily moved wherever it is needed (Etter, 2005). This is an important innovation because for prison farms, minimum-security facilities, and prison camps where inmates may provide work in wilderness and highway construction projects, the technology can make the process much more secure. Further still, with the use of surveillance systems inside the facility, the inmate can be tracked both centrally and by security in the vicinity of the inmate. Thus, officials are able to identify and hold security over specific inmates on an individual basis, from locations that are both near and far to the inmate's position inside or outside the prison facility.

Journal Article Link 8.4
Read about an innovative method of prisoner identification.

Prison Tour Video Link 8.1
Watch an assistant warden describe prisoner identification and tracking..

CONCLUSION

This chapter demonstrates that the physical features of a prison require forethought that occurs before the ground is even broken at the construction site. Issues related to the location of the prison facility, the types of custody levels and security, the function of the facility, and even logistical support for the facility are all important considerations. The design of the prison should be such that security is not compromised, but there is no true consensus on the best way to arrange a prison facility to address logistic issues while optimizing security features. In modern times, the use of large penitentiaries with gothic architecture has become antiquated. The formidability of modern security designs is obvious, particularly when one considers the introduction of the supermax facility to the realm of prison designs. Prison complexes have also emerged as a means of addressing the logistics of prison operational costs. Thus, both the design and the location of prison facilities can impact financial, operational, and security issues for correctional systems in the United States.

Further, the various services within a facility and the different functions of the prison are again emphasized. Attention to the design of kitchen and laundry spaces is important, both for security purposes and for institutional living standards. Other services, such as religious services, recreational services, and the use of tool shops for inmates to develop experience in specific trades, are also important as behavior management tools. These additional services eliminate idle inmate hands and minds and also give administrators some leverage in the control of inmate behavior; failure to comply with institutional rules can lead to restriction from these programs. Thus, the allocation of space and materials for these prison features can be important to future operational considerations. Though the cost to build such features can be high, the likely reductions in prison offenses and misbehavior may offset such financial concerns.

Lastly, technological developments in the field of corrections have led to numerous improvements in security. Improvements in cell block and electric fence construction have made facilities even more secure, in terms of both internal and perimeter security. Further, innovations in communication equipment and information sharing now allow prison facilities to be linked with outside agencies in a seamless fashion that aids in times of crisis and emergency. This data exchange can also aid law enforcement and community corrections personnel who deal with these offenders upon their release from the facility.

These advents in technology, along with those related to inmate identification and tracking, make the prison facility a part of a broader system that incorporates many other aspects of criminal justice and the outside community, enhancing security both inside and outside the prison itself.

END-OF-CHAPTER DISCUSSION QUESTIONS

1. Identify the panopticon and explain whether this design is used today.

2. Identify the various levels of security that classify prison facilities and/or cell blocks within facilities.

3. What is the supermax or Marion Model of prison facility construction? Discuss some of the constitutional issues that have emerged with this model of prison design.

4. Identify and discuss the primary components in perimeter security of a correctional facility.

5. Identify and discuss the primary components of internal security in a correctional facility.

6. Identify and discuss the integration of auxiliary programs inside a prison facility.

7. Explain how routine activity theory is related to inmate traffic flow and institutional infractions within a prison facility.

KEY TERMS

Alcatraz	Isolation zone	Pod
Americans with Disabilities Act (ADA)	*Madrid v. Gomez* (1995)	Protective custody
	Maximum-security facilities	Special housing unit syndrome
Bastille	Medium-security facilities	Supermax facility
Blind spots	Minimum-security facilities	USP Florence ADMAX
Bruscino v. Carlson (1988)	Panopticon	USP Marion
Direct supervision design	Perimeter security system	

APPLIED EXERCISE 8.1

You are the CEO of a large private prison company that is known for providing excellent correctional services. The time period is sometime between 2010 and 2014, and the current emphasis in the correctional industry is on offender reentry rather than incarceration. During the 1990s and early 2000s your correctional group experienced a boom in the inmate population and in the number of facilities needed. Because of this, you have a number of prisons within your state. However, the beds are emptying within your organization, and, since you are a private company, you know that you will need to do something within your organization to somehow modify your current organizational emphasis to dovetail with the current demands within the correctional industry.

At one of your board meetings, your chief of operations noted that there has been emphasis on prison industries, work release, and the need for offenders to have specified job skills in green technology and other forms of modern construction techniques. With that in mind, you, as CEO of the company, have decided to modify your prison facilities to create a variety of products and services that will appeal to various industries throughout the nation. Along the way, inmates participating in these programs will learn valuable job skills.

TO THE STUDENT: For this assignment, explain how you would design a prison facility so that it had both security features and auxiliary services that would, on the one hand, generate income for the prison organization and, on the other hand, provide job skill training for inmates scheduled to be released for reentry within a year.

In particular, you will need to address issues related custody levels of the inmates who would likely be utilized for these programs, security issues that would need to be considered with the inmate population, and the potential for financial success of industrial activities used in your design. Also, be sure to discuss any architectural considerations that may need to be considered when developing this program.

"WHAT WOULD YOU DO?"

You are the public relations officer for the state department of corrections. Recently, the state system has identified an area for a new prison site, but, once word of this decision was presented to the local community, a number of letters were sent to the governor's office expressing concern and resistance to this idea. You have been assigned the task of addressing these concerns and have been asked to mitigate public reactions to the idea of building a prison in the area. It is very clear that the state intends to build the facility but, at the same time, would like to resolve the public relations issue that has recently emerged.

The community is midsize, having a population of approximately 75,000 with some outlying towns also existing in the area. The nearest major metropolitan area is well over three hours' driving distance away. The community's economy is somewhat stable but lacks significant industrial development, being mostly agricultural in nature.

The prison is slated to be a minimum- to medium-security facility that will house 1,800 inmates. Many of these inmates will likely also be in various industrial and educational programs. There will be a need for security officers, educational specialists, and other employees within the prison. Further, this additional employment will draw persons from out of the area in some cases, which will increase the need for various goods and services (e.g., dry cleaning, groceries, restaurant services, home purchases) from business owners in the local area.

Your job is to showcase the positive impact that this facility can have on the community while also alleviating concerns about the potential pitfalls to having such a facility in the area. The governor's office has tasked you with this assignment.

What would you do?

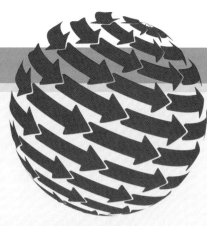

CROSS-NATIONAL PERSPECTIVE 8.1

Prison Programming and Design in India

As noted in this chapter, the design of a prison must accommodate numerous aspects of the facility's day-to-day operations. Among other things, facilities must be designed to accommodate a wide array of auxiliary services and/or industrial programs. The nation of India has 10 prisons, with Tihar being one of them. This prison has numerous industries that operate within its walls, some of which are included below:

Weaving: This section was initially established for manufacture of cloth for staff uniforms, convict uniforms, cotton durries, and so on. It has now started manufacturing terry cloth (white), woolen carpets, convict chador, woolen chador, fine chador, double-bed chador, dosuti cloth/cloth for cotton dresses, hand loom durries, and dusters. Introduction of up-to date technology with the installation of new power loom machines has not only augmented the production capacity of the section, but has also created a training ground for convicts working on these machines. Apart from meeting internal requirements of approximately 12,000 inmates, the prison has secured orders from various departments of the Government of National Capital Territory of Delhi and from the private sector. There are eight power looms and 52 hand looms in this section, and four additional power looms are being installed.

Carpentry: This is the largest section of the jail factory with a workforce of approximately 350 workers. During the last financial year more than 30,000 excellent-quality Meranti wood desks were supplied to various schools in Delhi. This section also trains convicts in the finer works of carving and carpentry, making furniture for sale to the general public. This is one flagship unit with the highest turnover. At present this unit is producing various types of office furniture, including office chairs and tables, visitor chairs, computer tables, center tables, sofa sets, and rocking chairs, for various private and government-run institutes. The furniture here is made from 100% teak wood.

Chemicals: Soap, phenyl manufacture, and oil expelling are the basic functions of this unit. Mustard oil of the finest quality is produced in the section. The unit was initially started for production of in-house consumption of these items, but at present the same is available for open sale to the public at much lower rates than on the market. By-products of oil from this unit, like oil cake, are also sold in the open market through open auction.

Paper: The only eco-friendly unit at the prison prides itself in the unique training section of Tihar where inmates are trained in the art of hand-made paper, from pulp to beautiful hand-made paper to various items like carry bags, fancy paper bags, file covers, file boards, envelopes, grass paper, tiger paper, leather paper, moon-rock paper, marble paper, tea paper, and cardboard paper, in addition to meeting internal stationary requirements of the jail administration. This unit supplies stationary items to various government departments, and old government files and paper from various departments are recycled in this unit.

SOURCE: Tihar Prison. (2009). New Delhi: India. Retrieved from http://www.delhi.gov.in/wps/wcm/connect/lib_centraljail/ Central+Jail/Home/Annual+Review+2009/Tihar+- +from+the+Eye+of+Media

chapter 9

Classification and Custody Levels

LEARNING OBJECTIVES:

1. Discuss the history and development of classification processes in corrections.

2. Identify the two primary functions of the classification process.

3. Identify different custody levels and the methods used for housing assignment.

4. Discuss legal precedent liability issues associated with classification.

5. Discuss how classification processes are central to prison service operations.

INTRODUCTION

> There are similar punishments and crimes called by the same name, but there are no two beings equal in regard to their morals; and every time that convicts are put together, there exists necessarily a fatal influence of some upon others, because, in the association of the wicked, it is not the less guilty who act upon the more criminal, but the more depraved who influence those who are less so.
>
> Gustave de Beaumont and Alexis de Tocqueville, 1833

The ability to predict future human behavior has, most often, been best accomplished through an examination of an individual's past behavior. When attempting to identify future criminal behavior, past behavior is perhaps the best basis that we have in forming our judgment. With this knowledge, prison systems attempt to separate those persons who have been identified as particularly ruthless from those whose criminality is much less severe. The desire to determine the severity of criminality between offenders is important so that those who are more severe will not negatively affect the reformation of those who are not. The desire to distinguish between offenders, based on the severity of the criminal tendencies, is reflected in the quote above by Beaumont and de Tocqueville in 1833. Nearly 180 years later, this quote seems to still be relevant to the field of corrections today.

HISTORY OF CLASSIFICATION

Students should recall from Chapters 1 and 2 that early periods of corrections focused more on punitive aspects than the actual correction of human behavior. Likewise, throughout the long history of punishment and corrections that existed prior to the early 1800s (which consists of the large majority of human history), the majority of all offenders were housed together. This was largely true whether the housing was in an actual penitentiary, aboard a ship used for confinement (a hulk), or in a gaol operated by a shire reeve. Over time, groups of offenders were separated into broad and ill-defined groups of offenders. For instance, juveniles, women, first-time offenders, and mere debtors were separated from hardened criminals. Even though this did begin to emerge, prisons were typically little more than human warehouses where behavior shaping was based purely on the administration of punishments.

Perhaps the first figure to have implemented an actual classification system was Alexander Maconochie, an officer in the British Royal Navy. Students may recall that Maconochie was mentioned briefly in Chapter 2 due to his influence on Zebulon Brockway's management of Elmira Reformatory. This should be a clue to students to understand that the contributions that Maconochie made to corrections have had far-reaching impact and results on the field. Maconochie was appointed over a convict farm on Norfolk Island, northeast of Australia. While serving as the commanding officer of this post, Maconochie implemented a system where the duration of an offender's sentence was determined by the inmate's behavior and willingness to work. Maconochie called this his **mark system** because "marks" were awarded to inmates for each day that they provided adequate work.

Under this plan, convicts were given marks and moved through phases of supervision until they finally earned full release. Because of this, Maconochie's system is considered indeterminate in nature, with convicts progressing through five specific phases of classification: (1) strict incarceration, (2) intense labor in forced work group or chain gang, (3) limited freedom within a prescribed area, (4) a ticket of leave, and (5) full freedom. Naturally, this classification system was designed to identify inmates who were good candidates for release. This was the primary means of motivation for good inmate behavior. Thus Maconochie provided a guide in predicting likelihood of success with convicts, making him well ahead of his time.

Reference Link 9.1
Read more about Alexander Maconochie.

PHOTO 9.1

Alexander Maconochie is quite well known for the development of his mark system on Norfolk Island. This is one of the earliest classification systems in correctional history.

Later, in the 1850s, a man by the name of Sir Walter Crofton was the director of the Irish penal system. When the **English Penal Servitude Act** of 1853 was passed during his term of office, he was naturally aware of the changes implemented in prison operations, and he was likewise aware of Maconochie's ideas, which he used to create a classification system that proved useful and workable within the Irish prison system. This classification system utilized three stages of treatment. The first stage placed the convict in segregated confinement with work and training provided to the offender. The second stage was a transition period whereby the convict was set to the task of completing public work projects while under minimal supervision. During the third stage, presuming that the offender proved reliable, he would then be released.

In implementing this classification system, inmates' classification level was specifically measured by the number of marks that they had earned for good conduct, work output, and educational achievement. This idea was, of course, borrowed from Maconochie's system on Norfolk Island. It is also important to point out that the Irish system developed by Sir Walter Crofton was also much more detailed, providing specific written instructions and guidelines that provided for close supervision and control of the offender (Cromwell, Carmen, & Alarid, 2002).

The next advent in classification then occurred in the United States when, in 1876, Elmira Reformatory opened. Elmira used a system of classification that had been produced due to Brockway's admiration of Maconochie's original ideas. Brockway was also aware of Crofton's adaptation of Maconochie's classification system and the refinements that had since been implemented within the Irish penal system. This was one of the earliest attempts at a true classification system in the United States, and it also appears that its origins were Irish in nature. Thus, correctional thought in Europe once again impacted and shaped the state of corrections in the United States. Likewise, this impact, largely due to Maconochie's insights, would continue all the way to current-day correctional thought and operation.

Thought regarding prison operations and the organization of inmate populations continued, and in 1920 the Wickersham Commission called for improved classification systems as a means of creating better treatment programs to reshape inmate behavior. At this time classification became part of the intent to provide individual treatment planning where clinical information, along with an offender's social and criminal history, was examined to improve offender rehabilitation outcomes. These advents were immediately followed by congressional acts in the 1930s that required classification of federal inmates. Carlson and Garrett (1999) note that these two periods culminated in another development during the 1960s where classification was used as the main process in balancing inmate protections against public safety concerns.

RATIONALE FOR CLASSIFICATION

In *Holt v. Sarver* (1969), the Supreme Court found that the totality of prison conditions should not become so deplorable as to violate constitutional expectations for inmates. Shortly after this, the first federal court ruling that a state must design and implement a classification system was *Morris v. Travisono* (1970). In this case, inmates of the Adult Correctional Institutions (ACI) system brought allegations against Rhode Island prison authorities in a class action lawsuit for alleged violations of the Eighth and Fourteenth Amendments of the Constitution. This case resulted in a detailed set of procedures for classifying prisoners that was overseen by the federal court system.

The Court approved and incorporated the procedures while continuing to enforce a consent decree where jurisdiction was maintained for 18 months while parties in litigation established the final legal scheme that would enforce compliance with these procedures. Later, in 1972, the district court entered a judgment as a final consent decree that established the Morris Rules as the minimal procedural safeguards to which inmates would be entitled. This federal case led to further precedent that would develop. The Morris Rules, amongst other things, established that classification is part and parcel to a well-run and orderly prison that contributes to treatment objectives as well as those related to custody, discipline, work assignments, and other facets of inmate existence within the prison walls. However, it is perhaps the case of *Palmigiano v. Garrahy* (1977) that best exemplifies the importance of classification processes to the operation of a prison system:

> Classification is essential to the operation of an orderly and safe prison. It is a prerequisite for rational allocation of whatever program opportunities exist within the institution. It enables the institution to gauge the proper custody level of an inmate, to identify the inmate's educational, vocational, and psychological needs, and to separate nonviolent inmates from the more predatory.... Classification is indispensable for any coherent future planning. (p. 22)

FIGURE 9.1 Overview of External and Internal Classification Systems

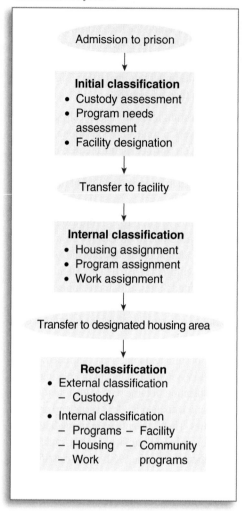

Admission to prison

↓

Initial classification
- Custody assessment
- Program needs assessment
- Facility designation

↓

Transfer to facility

↓

Internal classification
- Housing assignment
- Program assignment
- Work assignment

↓

Transfer to designated housing area

↓

Reclassification
- External classification
  - Custody
- Internal classification
  - Programs – Facility
  - Housing – Community
  - Work   programs

SOURCE: Hardyman, P. L., Austin, J., Alexander, J., Johnson, K. D., & Tulloch, O. C. (2002). *Internal prison classification systems: Case studies in their development and implementation.* Washington, DC: National Institute of Corrections.

It is clear that classification serves as the central organizing component when processing offenders within a correctional system. In order to avoid the potential for unconstitutional operations and avoid liability, states must have effective classification criteria.

The use of classification is imperative not just in prisons, but in jails as well. Indeed, the primary responsibility of the jail is to safely and securely detain all individuals remanded to its custody. Classification is an essential management tool for performing this function. Solomon and Baird (1982) note that

> corrections must recognize that classification is first and foremost a management tool. It should, in fact, be perceived as the veritable cornerstone of correctional administration. As a means of setting priorities, its purposes are to promote rational, consistent, and equitable methods of assessing the relative needs and risk of each individual and then to assign agency resources accordingly. (p. 98)

This has increasingly become a reality as the courts become increasingly involved in reviewing jail operations, just as they have done with prison system operations.

In addition to providing a consistent and documented rationale for assignment decisions, there are economic advantages of classifying inmates efficiently. Indeed, accurate classification allows for the redistribution of personnel according to the custody requirements of inmates and permits the facility to implement better crisis management response (see Figure 9.1). The reduction of false overpredictions (predictions of dangerousness that end up not being true) will save the facility money due to the fact inmates will not be inappropriately placed in costly, high-security housing but will instead be located within a less secure and less expensive environment—all without jeopardizing public safety.

MODERN CLASSIFICATION SYSTEMS

During the past decade, prisons have experienced increased pressure to improve their systems of classifying inmates according to custody, work, and programming needs. Fueled by litigation and overcrowding, classification systems are viewed as the principal management tool for allocating scarce prison resources efficiently and minimizing the potential for violence or escape. These systems are also expected to provide greater accountability and forecast future prison bed-space needs. In other words, a properly functioning classification system is seen as the "brain" of prison management, which governs many important decisions, including those that heavily influence such fiscal matters as staffing levels, bed space, and programming.

In times past, subjective forms of classification, based on the clinical opinions of professionals, were largely utilized. However, this has been eliminated in most modern systems of classification. Instead, objective forms of classification are used where decisions can be measurable and where the same criteria

Video Link 9.1
Watch an example of modern classification systems in action.

are used with all inmates in the same manner. The late 1990s in particular witnessed significant improvements in classification practices: The level of overclassification has been reduced, custody decisions are made more consistently, criteria for custody decisions have been validated, inmate program needs are assessed systematically, and institutional safety for both staff and inmates has been enhanced.

PHOTO 9.2

Modern-day classification centers in prisons serve as the hub for inmate housing and programming decisions.

Despite these improvements, additional issues remain unresolved within prison classification systems. In particular, decisions at the institutional or internal level that guide housing, program, and work assignments need to be as structured and organized as those made at the system or external level. As correctional facilities become more crowded, internal classification decisions play a more significant role. The widespread use of double celling in high-security units and the expanding use of dormitories for low- and medium-custody inmates have triggered the need for a systematic process for assigning inmates to beds or cells. As inmate populations continue to increase, decisions governing housing and programs, especially for inmates with extremely long sentences, will become increasingly difficult. The use of classification within a prison facility is often referred to as an internal classification system. An internal classification system is used to devise appropriate housing plans and program interventions within a particular facility for inmates who share a common custody level (minimum, medium, closed, or maximum). On the other hand, external classification processes have more to do with the placement of inmates at different facilities and/or on community supervision.

Prison Tour Video Link 9.1
Watch a work release director and an assistant warden describe classification systems.

THE GOALS OF CLASSIFICATION SYSTEMS

Essentially, there are four broad goals of classification. These four goals are fairly straightforward and commonsense but are nonetheless critical to effective prison management. Classification is intended to do the following:

1. Protect the public from future victimization by offenders who are already in the correctional system.

2. Protect inmates from one another by separating likely predators from less serious inmates.

3. Control inmates' behavior, which includes their ability to trade in contraband, engage in prison gang activities, or harm themselves (as with suicidal inmates).

4. Provide planning so that agencies can better allocate resources and determine programming accountability.

These four goals are what the day-to-day prison operations hinge upon. In one way or another, all of the operational aspects of the prison are designed to augment these four goals. Thus, classification sets the tone by which the institution operates through the matching of inmates with security and treatment services offered within the organization. We now turn our attention to each of the goals just noted.

Protect the Public

Public safety is an important element of corrections. In fact, it is the first and most paramount goal of the field of corrections. When we sentence offenders, we seek not only to hold them accountable for their injury to the public but also to protect the public from further injury. The key issue for classification is to determine how likely an offender is to cause further injury and to match that likelihood with a commensurate level of security that is not excessive but is sufficient to safeguard the public from further harm.

Protect Inmates

It is important to note that classification cannot and should not be expected to totally eliminate prison violence. As with protections for the public, the qualities of the risk prediction instrument, as a basis for classification, are important when protecting inmates from potential victimization. Effective instruments can identify and mitigate factors that can lead to prison violence, such as the separation of predatory inmates from likely victims, the placement of mentally disturbed inmates within the general population (where they are often victimized), or the need to separate rival gang members. Prisons that use effective screening and classification and base their security decisions on the outcomes of these processes will likely be effective in demonstrating good faith in providing reasonable protection of inmates in their custody.

Control Inmate Behavior

The control of inmate behavior often occurs through the ability to provide rewards or punishments for actions that are committed. Inmates who are repetitive rule violators can be reclassified to a level of custody that provides them with fewer privileges and prosocial activities. Inmates who maintain good behavior can be placed in less restrictive correctional facilities (e.g., minimum security) or may be given a special status, such as an inmate mentor on a given dorm or cell block, where they are looked to for their responsible nature and helpful assistance to other inmates as well as prison administrators. In addition, the screening for offenders who have special risks (e.g., suicidal inmates or those with medical or mental health conditions) can help to identify those inmates who will require special security or treatment assignments. Effective security and custody placement can reduce fear, violence, escapes, and potential litigation.

Provide Planning and Accountability

Classification systems allow correctional agencies to plan their resources by allocating them where they are most needed while not overspending on inmates who do not need as much supervision or intervention. Thus, these systems can save tax dollars and thereby provide the means for prisons to operate more efficiently. As mentioned before, the elimination of overclassification is very important when determining budgetary allocations. If inmates are repeatedly overclassified, they will be placed under restrictions that are more costly than is necessary, or they will be provided services that are not appropriate and thereby wasted.

Classification systems are extremely important for developing prison budgets, determining the types of units to build in the future, determining staffing levels, and providing services. Classification systems can also provide information on the characteristics of a system's prison population as a means of making security, custody, and staffing projections or even in determining if a new prison may need to be built within a system. These uses of classification systems can aid administrators so that they can avoid the error of overestimating the need for expensive maximum-security cells while underestimating the need for less expensive minimum-security beds. Thus, classification processes are critical to the management of any correctional system, whether it be a prison, a jail, or even community-based since the underlying goal of effective resource allocation applies to all spectrums of the correctional industry.

PHOTO 9.3

The use of automated classification systems is now standard practice in both prisons and community-based correctional agencies. These systems keep track of programming, sentence time served, and other important aspects of the offender who is serving time.

ELEMENTS OF ALL CLASSIFICATION SYSTEMS

Generally speaking, classification processes are divided into two phases, the initial classification phase and later points of reclassification. This means that classification is a continual process that follows inmates throughout their sentence. This is, in many respects, similar in concept to what Maconochie had

TECHNOLOGY AND EQUIPMENT 9.1

Automated Classification Systems

Information technology (IT) and computational developments have been found to enhance the productivity of prison classification systems in several jurisdictions. Because classification is data dependent, it requires high-quality data and sufficient computational capacity to make and evaluate classification decisions. With this in mind, classification productivity is categorized into two main components—efficiency and effectiveness—each with several subcomponents. Each element is important when considering how advances in IT and computer power may enhance productivity.

Brennan, Wells, and Alexander (2004) conducted case studies in seven prisons that had shown innovations in classification, management information systems, and IT. Several important findings emerged from their research. First, criminal justice databases are slowly becoming more integrated, and classification should gain profoundly from the speed, comprehensiveness, and integrity of the data. Second, prison classification is showing a trend toward more comprehensive systems, broader information, and multiple goals. This shift will increase the demands on IT for comprehensive data. Third, the management of change and innovation remains a challenge, but there have been many lessons learned regarding implementation and change management—especially with regard to IT and classification.

The state of Florida is one of the correctional systems that Brennan et al. (2004) examined. Florida's Department of Corrections has an excellent automated classification system known as CARS (the Custody Assessment and Reclassification System). Florida's classification and related inmate management applications are principally based on its mainframe-driven Offender Based Information System (OBIS), which is accessible by each facility. The two classification applications running under OBIS are CARS and the Risk and Needs System. OBIS is supplemented by minimainframe systems in each of the five reception and intake centers. The principal application is the Computer Assisted Reception Process (CARP). All three classification applications are integrated to facilitate data sharing and lookups and to minimize redundant data entry. Future plans call for additional local area network (LAN) and wide area network (WAN) personal computer (PC)-based applications such as drug testing, enhanced visitation tracking, implementing drug interdiction, and identifying gang activity to augment and integrate with the current systems. Plans also call for these PC-based applications to incorporate artificial intelligence engines to identify gang, drug, and contraband patterns throughout the entire prison system and overlay color-coded analysis on global positioning system (GPS) maps of the system.

With assistance from the Northeast Florida Center for Community Initiatives and the National Institute of Corrections, the Florida Department of Corrections Bureau of Classification and Central Records recently developed and implemented its new Risk and Needs System. This internal classification uses objective assessments (academic, vocational, and substance abuse, along with the inmate's risk factors) to determine internal placement decisions regarding housing and work assignments. Completing the Risk and Needs System requires the collection of information through a face-to-face interview with the inmate and through official data previously entered in OBIS. The information compiled and scored in the Risk and Needs System serves as the basis for the Inmate Management Plan.

Based on risk and needs assessment, the Inmate Management Plan is developed. This plan is the means by which classification decisions are made and documented and by which progress is tracked throughout incarceration. Management plans are reviewed at least every 12 months. The plan comprises primary work or program recommendations, housing recommendations, and goals and objectives to be achieved during incarceration.

While many state classification systems use automated programs (in fact, most all of them do), the state of Florida has one that is particularly well developed. The technology used in the Florida system allows classification to integrate a number of factors into the decision but with mathematical precision and much more quickly than could be done by a human being. This allows for more effective, more efficient, and more objective assessment as well as the development of logical and consistent Inmate Management Plans. While one of many state programs, Florida's has been found to be a good example of what correctional agencies might wish to implement in their own system.

SOURCE: Brennan, T., Wells, D., & Alexander, J. (2004). *Enhancing prison classification systems: The emerging role of management information systems*. Washington, DC: National Institute of Corrections.

implemented where commensurate good behavior would lead to a reclassification of their likelihood for release. The same is true today; as inmates exhibit behavior that is desired, their custody level and their overall time in prison can be greatly modified. Likewise, if inmates continue to exhibit antisocial behavior, their custody level can become more restrictive, and they will likely stay behind bars for the full duration of their sentence. If they should commit additional criminal acts when behind bars, they can be prosecuted and given additional time for these new crimes. In such cases, the classification process would again modify the inmate's overall standing within the system.

Security and Custody Issues

The **level of security** provided for particular inmates refers to the type of physical barriers utilized to prevent their escape and is related to public safety concerns. Indeed, as long as the inmates are kept within the prison grounds, it is less likely that they can harm persons in the community. On the other hand, the **custody level** is related to the degree of staff supervision needed for a given inmate. This is more related to safety and security within the prison facility itself, though this can also impact the likelihood that the inmate will be able to engage in activities that affect the public.

Initial Security Classification

The initial point of classification actually tends to occur well before the inmate arrives at the prison facility. Initial classification is usually conducted by community supervision staff prior to an offender's arrival to the prison, and this most often occurs right after the offender is sentenced. The federal system serves as a good example of how community supervision officers, often called pretrial services officers, provide the initial assessment that begins the later classification process in the federal prison system. This process entails the construction of a *presentence investigation (PSI) report*, as students may recall from earlier chapters, which is used to inform the judge of the circumstances associated with the offender prior to sentencing.

Because there are no specific standard forms of classification from state to state but all systems tend to have initial classification processes that are, by necessity, similar, a single system will be used as an example of how initial classification may be conducted. For purposes of this section, we will refer to the document titled *Program Statement: Bureau of Prisons Inmate Classification System* (2006) that serves as the basis of initial classification in the Federal Bureau of Prisons (BOP). Within the BOP, institutions are classified into one of five security levels—minimum, low, medium, high, and administrative—based on the level of security and staff supervision the institution is able to provide (see Figure 9.2). An institution's level of security and staff supervision is based on the following factors:

Audio Link 9.1
Listen to an explanation of presentence investigation reports.

- Mobile patrol.
- Internal security.
- Towers.
- Type of inmate housing.
- Perimeter barriers.
- Inmate-to-staff ratio.

FIGURE 9.2   Federal BOP Inmate Classification Scheme

Security level	Custody level	Male	Female
MINIMUM	COMMUNITY and OUT	0–11 points	0–15 points
LOW	OUT and IN	12–15 points	16–30 points
MEDIUM	OUT and IN	16–23 points	*
HIGH	IN and MAXIMUM	24+ points	31+ points
ADMINISTRATIVE	All custody level	All points totals	All points totals

SOURCE: Federal Bureau of Prisons. (2006). *Program statement: Bureau of Prisons inmate classification system.* Washington, DC: Author.

FIGURE 9.3 Inmate Load and Security Designation Form for the Federal Bureau of Prisons

INMATE LOAD AND SECURITY DESIGNATION FORM — FEDERAL BUREAU OF PRISONS

INMATE LOAD DATA

1. REGISTER NUMBER
2. LAST NAME 3. FIRST NAME 4. MIDDLE 5. SUFFIX
6. RACE 7. SEX 8. ETHNIC ORIGIN 9. DATE OF BIRTH
10. OFFENSE/SENTENCE
11. FBI NUMBER 12. SSN NUMBER
13. STATE OF BIRTH 14. OR COUNTRY OF BIRTH 15. CITIZENSHIP
16. ADDRESS–STREET
17. CITY 18. STATE 19. ZIP 20. OR FOREIGN COUNTRY
21. HEIGHT FT ___ IN ___ 22. WEIGHT ___ LBS 23. HAIR COLOR 24. EYE COLOR
25. ARS ASSIGNMENT

SECURITY DESIGNATION DATA

1. JUDGE 2. REC FACILITY 3. REC PROGRAM 4. USM OFFICE

5. VOLUNTARY SURRENDER STATUS   0 = NO   (-3) = YES
   IF YES, MUST INDICATE: 5a. VOLUNTARY SURRENDER DATE:
                          5b. VOLUNTARY SURRENDER LOCATION:

6. MONTHS TO RELEASE

7. SEVERITY OF CURRENT OFFENSE   0 = LOWEST   1 = LOW MODERATE   3 = MODERATE   5 = HIGH   7 = GREATEST

8. CRIMINAL HISTORY SCORE   0 = 0-1   2 = 2-3   4 = 4-6   6 = 7-9   8 = 10-12   10 = 13+

8a. SOURCE OF DOCUMENTED CRIMINAL HISTORY ___ = PRESENTENCE INVESTIGATION REPORT or ___ = NCIC III

9. HISTORY OF VIOLENCE   NONE   >15 YEARS   10-15 YEARS   5-10 YEARS   <5 YEARS
   MINOR   0   1   1   2   3
   SERIOUS 0   2   4   6   7

10. HISTORY OF ESCAPE OR ATTEMPTS   NONE   >15 YEARS   >10 YEARS   5-10 YEARS   <5 YEARS
    MINOR   0   1   1   2   3 (3)
    SERIOUS 0   3 (3)   3 (3)   3 (3)   3 (3)

11. TYPE OF DETAINER   0 = NONE   1 = LOWEST/LOW MODERATE   3 = MODERATE   5 = HIGH   7 = GREATEST

12. AGE   0 = 55 and over   2 = 36 through 54   4 = 25 through 35   8 = 24 or less

13. EDUCATION LEVEL   0 = Verified High School Degree or GED
    1 = Enrolled in and making satisfactory progress in GED Program
    2 = No verified High School Degree/GED and not participating in GED Program

13a. HIGHEST GRADE COMPLETED

14. DRUG/ALCOHOL ABUSE   0 = Never/>5 Years   1 = <5 Years

15. SECURITY POINT TOTAL

16. PUBLIC SAFETY FACTORS
    A-NONE
    B-DISRUPTIVE GROUP (males only)
    C-GREATEST SEVERITY OFFENSE (males only)
    F-SEX OFFENDER
    G-THREAT TO GOVERNMENT OFFICIALS
    H-DEPORTABLE ALIEN
    I-SENTENCE LENGTH (males only)
    K-VIOLENT BEHAVIOR (females only)
    L-SERIOUS ESCAPE
    N-PRISON DISTURBANCE
    N-JUVENILE VIOLENCE
    Q-SERIOUS TELEPHONE ABUSE

17. REMARKS

18. CMDT REFERRAL (YES/NO) ___

SOURCE: Federal Bureau of Prisons. (2006). *Program statement: Bureau of Prisons inmate classification system.* Washington, DC: Author.

- Detection devices.
- Any special institutional mission.

An inmate's security point score is not the only factor used in determining a commensurate security level. As one of the administrative processes, the SENTRY system cannot assign a security level unless prison employees complete an Inmate Load and Security Designation Form. This form serves as a basic data collection tool. BOP inmates are classified based on both security and treatment issues, as noted in earlier parts of this chapter. Specifically, the BOP considers the following factors:

- The level of security and supervision the inmate requires.
- The inmate's program needs (substance abuse treatment, educational/vocational training, individual counseling, group counseling, medical/mental health treatment, etc.).

In summary, just as with most other state correctional systems, the initial assignment (designation) of an inmate to a particular institution within the BOP is based primarily upon the following:

- The level of security and supervision the inmate requires.
- The level of security and staff supervision the institution is able to provide.
- The inmate's program needs.

Figure 9.3 provides students with a view of the Inmate Load and Security Designation Form, which helps to clearly demonstrate the information that is tracked when making initial classification decisions about the inmate. Figures 9.4 and 9.5 illustrate how the point system in the federal classification scheme also incorporates other factors related to public safety to determine the inmate's overall security point total; Figure 9.4 pertains to male inmates whereas Figure 9.5 pertains to female inmates.

FIGURE 9.4   Inmate Security Designation Based on Classification Score and Public Safety Factors—Male Inmates

SECURITY DESIGNATION TABLE (MALES)		
Inmate Security Level Assignments based on Classification Score and Public Safety Factors		
Security Point Total	*Public Safety Factors*	*Inmate Security Level*
0–11	**No Public Safety Factors**	**Minimum**
	Deportable Alien	Low
	Juvenile Violence	Low
	Greatest Severity Offense	Low
	Sex Offender	Low
	Serious Telephone Abuse	Low
	Threat to Government Officials	Low
	Sentence Length	
	Time remaining > 10 Yrs	Low
	Time remaining > 20 Yrs	Medium
	Time remaining > 30 Yrs (Includes non-parolable LIFE and Death penalty cases)	High
	Serious Escape	Medium
	Disruptive Group	High
	Prison Disturbance	High
12–15	**No Public Safety Factors**	**Low**
	Serious Escape	Medium
	Sentence Length	
	Time remaining > 20 Yrs	Medium
	Time remaining > 30 Yrs (Includes non-parolable LIFE and Death Penalty cases)	High
	Disruptive Group	High
	Prison Disturbance	High
16–23	**No Public Safety Factors**	**Medium**
	Disruptive Group	High
	Prison Disturbance	High
	Time remaining > 30 Yrs (Includes non-parolable LIFE and Death Penalty cases)	High
24+		**High**

SOURCE: Federal Bureau of Prisons. (2006). *Program statement: Bureau of Prisons inmate classification system.* Washington, DC: Author.

FIGURE 9.5   Inmate Security Designation Based on Classification Score and Public Safety Factors—Female Inmates

SECURITY DESIGNATION TABLE (FEMALES)		
Inmate Security Level Assignments based on Classification Score and Public Safety Factors		
Security Point Total	*Public Safety Factors*	*Inmate Security Level*
0–15	**No Public Safety Factors**	**Minimum**
	Deportable Alien	Low
	Juvenile Violence	Low
	Serious Telephone Abuse	Low
	Sex Offender	Low
	Threat to Government Officials	Low
	Violent Behavior	Low
	Prison Disturbance	High
	Serious Escape	High
16–30	**No Public Safety Factors**	**Low**
	Prison Disturbance	High
	Serious Escape	High
31+		**High**

SOURCE: Federal Bureau of Prisons. (2006). *Program statement: Bureau of Prisons inmate classification system.* Washington, DC: Author.

Other factors may be considered, depending on the circumstances. Factors that come into play when designating an inmate to a particular institution include, but are not limited to, the following:

- The inmate's release residence.
- The level of overcrowding at an institution.
- Any security, location, or program recommendation made by the sentencing court.

The **SENTRY system** is a comprehensive database used by the BOP to classify and track inmates within the system. Initial designations to BOP institutions are made in most cases by staff at the Designation and Sentence Computation Center (DSCC) in Grand Prairie, Texas, who assess and enter information from the sentencing court, U.S. Marshals Service, U.S. Attorneys Office or other prosecuting authority, and the U.S. Probation Office about the inmate into the computer database known as SENTRY. Once data are entered, SENTRY then calculates a point score for that inmate, which is then matched with a commensurate security-level institution (see Figure 9.2 for classification levels).

PHOTO 9.4

The first photo shows a jail control room with the lights on. This area serves as the security center for the facility. Correctional officers coordinate communications and surveillance from this room throughout numerous dormitories. Sgt. Amber Rawls and Warden Brown stand by and observe monitors and security screens. Note that the windows are one-way mirrors that turn opaque when the interior lights are on. The second photo shows a similar control when the lights are turned off. In this case, it is easy to see out into the dormitory and observe inmate movement therein.

Inmate Needs, Services, and Housing and the Classification Team

Determining an inmate's programming and housing needs requires that information be considered from a variety of sources. At intake, a medical screening of inmates is conducted within most correctional departments. This screening usually occurs within the first day of reception, and, if medical conditions warrant it, the inmate may be separated from the general population. If the inmate has only slight medical issues or issues that are able to be handled through routine visits in the prison infirmary, he or she will be housed as usual.

The initial screening for services also usually includes a review of the PSI report and, in the federal system, a scan of the information in the SENTRY system. Specifically, this screening is a search for a history of sexually aggressive behavior on the part of the inmate and/or to determine if the inmate has been the victim of such behavior. Other characteristics that the inmate may possess are considered to prevent victimization among other inmates. All of these procedures are conducted in the interest of the safety of the inmate and security of the institution.

Within the BOP, CFR Title 28, Part 524, Section 524.11(a) and (b) states,

(a) at a minimum, each classification (unit) team shall include the unit manager, a case manager, and a counselor. An education advisor and a psychology services representative are also ordinarily members of the team. Where the institution does not have unit management, the team shall include a case manager, counselor, and one other staff member.

(b) Each member of the classification team shall individually interview the newly arrived inmate within five working days of the inmate's assignment to that team.

The classification team is headed by a unit manager who supervises the other primary unit team members, who include case managers, correctional counselors, and staff representing education, psychology, and other disciplines contributing to an offender's law-abiding lifestyle. The **unit manager** directs the housing unit activities and is responsible for the unit's operation and quality control of all correspondence and programs. Figure 9.6 illustrates the authority level of the unit manager over the classification team and in relation to other management personnel within the prison facility.

The **case manager** is directly responsible to the unit manager and has major responsibility for case management matters within the unit. With other unit staff, the case manager will assist with unit inmates and participate in other unit operations as directed by the unit manager. The case manager's responsibilities include all the traditional duties required to move an individual through a correctional institution. They include awareness of policies, possessing the technical expertise to assess correctness of reports, knowledge about parole board procedures and the legalities involved, and so forth. In addition, since caseloads are small, the caseworker takes an active role in direct treatment intervention. That is, he or she will not only function as a full-fledged member of the unit team in all aspects of the programming process as it relates to residents on his caseload, but will also conduct counseling sessions or other treatment modalities that make up the unit's therapeutic approach.

The **correctional counselor** develops and implements programs within the unit to meet the individual needs of the inmates confined, including individual as well as group counseling. The correctional counselor may be assigned to either a general or a specialized unit, and is usually assigned, along with one case manager, a specific caseload. The correctional counselor plays a key role in maintaining and enhancing the security of the unit and institution by his or her extensive contacts with the inmates. The correctional counselor's role includes being a direct implementer of the agreed-upon treatment modalities, a fully functioning member of the classification team, a liaison between outside-the-unit activities (e.g., work assignment) and their implications for the classification process, an organizer and/or monitor of recreation and leisure-time activities, and so on. In general, the correctional counselor will have the most immediate, prolonged, and intensive relationship with many of the facility's inmates.

The **education adviser** is the unit team's consultant in all education matters, and this person normally will be a permanent member of the unit team. This person sees that all of the unit inmates are properly tested and informed of available education opportunities. The education adviser may also be responsible for monitoring and evaluating unit inmates in education programs, and will provide counseling in education matters as needed. Depending upon the specific needs of the prison population, it is the educator's responsibility to recommend training alternatives in order to help each individual reach goals mutually agreed upon in collaboration with the facility. He or she may also be required to develop special "classes" that provide inmates with information of relevance to the intent of the prison's program.

FIGURE 9.6   Administrative Lines of Authority for Classification Teams Among Prison Employees and Management

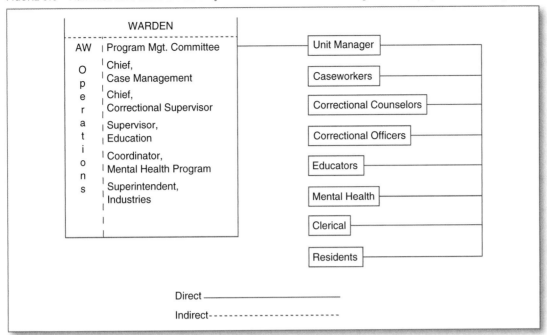

SOURCE: National Institute of Corrections. (1995). *Corrections information series: Unit management.* Washington, DC: Author. Retrieved from http://www.nicic.org/pubs/pre/000159.pdf.

The **psychology services representative** (psychiatrist, psychologist, psychiatric nurse) of the classification team has a multifaceted role. The psychology services representative is expected to be involved in the admission and information gathering process prior to classification; he or she is a member of the decision-making team. This professional is usually a psychologist and is generally responsible for the performance of diagnostic, therapeutic, research, educational, and evaluative functions relating to psychological services. This individual plans, organizes, participates in, and provides professional expertise for unit counseling programs. This function includes the assessment of inmate needs and the design of corresponding programs to meet those needs. This professional monitors, supervises, and/or conducts therapeutic sessions as needed within the facility.

PHOTO 9.5

Richwood Correctional Center has an extensive substance abuse treatment program. Pictured here are treatment team personnel, from left to right: Dr. Anissa Horne, Mr. Joe Key, Ms. Senalda, Mr. Fred Fulton, and Dr. Rob Hanser.

It is important to point out that the culture of the facility should be one that facilitates effective classification of inmates for both security and programming purposes (see Focus Topic 9.1). The use of classification teams with members from a variety of backgrounds can facilitate this. This means, however, that both treatment staff and security staff will need to find common ground in the day-to-day operations of the prison facility if classification processes are to have optimal outcomes.

Video Link 9.4
Watch a video about prison medical staff.

Reclassification Processes

At first, an inmate's custody is determined by the custody levels that exist within the facility that he or she is assigned to. The lowest level of custody, called community, is usually reserved for those inmates who meet the criteria for participation in community-based activities. Inmates within this custody level may be allowed to reside in the least secure housing, with some such facilities existing outside of the perimeter of the prison itself. These inmates may be allowed to work outside the prison with very little supervision, and they may participate in community-based programming activities on some occasions. The distinction between the status of offenders behind the walls and that of offenders on community supervision can become quite blurred, in some cases.

FOCUS TOPIC: 9.1

The Confluence of Assessment, Classification, and Staff Attitudes in Determining Program Effectiveness

In the state of West Virginia, an ingenious study took place in 2006 that examined the use of effective assessment and classification systems implementing the LSI-R (Level of Service Inventory–Revised). Because of the evaluation's rigor, this alone would have been sufficient for inclusion as a focus topic in this chapter. However, the researchers, Stephen M. Haas, Cynthia A. Hamilton, and Dena Hanley, also examined the effects of staff culture and attitudes toward reentry and rehabilitative orientations. Specifically, these authors examined West Virginia's implementation of the West Virginia Offender Reentry Initiative (WVORI). In doing so, these authors point out that research consistently shows that correctional staff can have a strong influence on the predicted success or failure of a program that is implemented by a correctional agency. This is an important aspect of the classification process that is rarely (if ever) considered a variable in most assessment and/or classification systems. It may well be that staff attitudes could explain some of the variance that exists between predicted offender outcomes and those that are different from what standardized instruments predict.

Thus, this research points to a underexplored area of assessment and treatment planning that may be applicable to any number of correctional programs. Some of the results that these researchers found are as follows:

1. Programs or interventions that depart substantially from the principles known to inform effective correctional programming are much less likely to observe reductions in recidivism.

2. Given that staff, such as case managers, counselors, and parole officers, interact with prisoners on a daily basis, they can determine the success or failure of any initiative undertaken by a correctional organization.

3. The identification of appropriate service and level of supervision after release should be contingent upon the accurate assessment of offender risk and needs.

4. Research has consistently shown that objective risk and needs assessments, based on statistical probabilities, more accurately predict the level of risk than personal or staff positions.

5. The success of a program can be significantly hampered by individual attitudes and personal opinions toward the new strategy, and the implementation of that strategy may be responsible for the success or failure of a new initiative.

6. Older organizations with well-embedded institutionalized organizational cultures and larger organizations with more layers of bureaucracy have more difficulty with communication and coordination.

7. Conflict between individual values of the staff and the values of the organization negatively impacts implementation strategies.

8. Detachment between staff attitudes and organizational values translates into role conflict. Role conflict produces stress and job dissatisfaction, contributing to a negative organizational culture.

9. Organizational culture drives staff behavior and knowledge of what is valued in the organization.

10. Staff tended to support the WVORI when they were supportive of rehabilitation, were more human service oriented, liked to work with others, liked their job, were empathetic toward inmates, and believed the department was committed to staff training and professional development.

11. A large majority of correctional staff were found to have a punitive orientation toward inmates, did not believe in the efficacy of rehabilitation, and were not oriented toward a human service career.

12. The initial report concluded that a substantial change in the human orientation of staff and greater support for rehabilitative efforts may be necessary for achieving greater support for reentry initiatives among correctional staff.

This study is important because it illustrates that the predictions of offender behavior can be mitigated and/or aggravated by the actions of supervision and treatment staff within an agency. This observation is not, in and of itself, particularly astute. However, the fact that this was specifically linked to the assessment and classification process makes this research innovative and very useful. Further, these factors are important both for the prognosis of individual offenders and when evaluating agency outcomes. These authors, through this research approach, have found a common linking pin between individual offender treatment planning and agency evaluation outcomes. Because of this, it is perhaps a good recommendation that future classification systems take into account data input regarding agency staff and organizational culture since these factors are seldom assessed and have direct bearing on the success or failure of offenders who are released to community supervision.

SOURCE: Haas, S. M., Hamilton, C. A., & Hanley, D. (2006, July). *Implementation of the West Virginia Offender Reentry Initiative: An examination of staff attitudes and the application of the LSI-R.* Charleston, WV: Mountain State Criminal Justice Research Services.

CORRECTIONS AND THE LAW 9.1

Court Cases and Legal Issues With Protective Custody

Throughout this chapter, we have explored a number of legal issues associated with both classification and the use of protective custody. The use of this security and housing assignment has been controversial in some cases. The article below, from the *New York Times*, demonstrates how, ironically, some of America's worst criminals end up getting enhanced protections, despite the crime(s) that they have committed. Students should ask if other alternatives were available to the Massachusetts Department of Correction and whether the state acted prudently. Such issues are what face federal courts when addressing the use of this and other restrictive assignments and when considering liability in regard to the protection of inmates in a system's custody.

BOSTON, August 28—John J. Geoghan, the defrocked pedophile priest strangled in prison by another inmate, was confined in the same protective custody unit as his attacker largely because the Massachusetts Department of Correction long shunned using protective housing for vulnerable inmates and has only two such units for its 9,500 prisoners, lawyers and experts familiar with the case say.

Mr. Geoghan, 68, who was convicted last year of groping a 10-year-old boy and was accused of molesting almost 150 boys, was killed on Saturday by Joseph L. Druce, the authorities say. Mr. Druce was sentenced to life without parole in 1989 for strangling a man he believed was gay.

Mr. Druce was constantly in trouble in prison, spending just three and a half years in the state's maximum security segregation unit at Walpole before being transferred to the protective custody unit at the Souza-Baranowski prison in Shirley where Mr. Geoghan had been sent after it opened four months ago, said Mr. Druce's lawyer, John LaChance.

In early August Mr. Druce was put in solitary confinement for several weeks at the Shirley prison for punching another inmate, prison officials said.

Leslie Walker, the executive director of Massachusetts Correctional Legal Services, which represented Mr. Geoghan in prison, said at a news conference today that putting the two men in the same protective custody unit was "a classification failure." The action showed that the Massachusetts prison system is broken, Ms. Walker said.

Jim Pingeon, the litigation director for the legal services agency, said, "The critical question that is really important here is the question of why Druce was in that unit with Geoghan to begin with."

Although it remains unclear why Mr. Druce was put in protective custody, given his predatory history, Mr. Pingeon said the trouble would never have happened if Massachusetts had an adequate number of protective custody cells and units in more prisons for endangered inmates. Prisoners in protective custody have been deemed in danger of attack from other inmates.

Mr. Pingeon traced the origin of the problem to a change in the 1980s, under Gov. Michael S. Dukakis, when the corrections commissioner at the time, Michael Fair, developed a strategy of putting all inmates in the general prison population, regardless of their vulnerability or dangerousness. Only a 30-cell protective custody unit was left, at the Massachusetts Correctional Institute at Concord.

This remained the strategy until the Department of Correction, recognizing the need to protect vulnerable prisoners better, opened the new unit at the Shirley prison four months ago, Mr. Pingeon said.

Mr. Geoghan had originally been in the protective custody unit at Concord, but after guards there urinated and defecated on his bed and encouraged other inmates "to kill him," Ms. Walker and Mr. Pingeon said, they asked that he be transferred to the new unit at Shirley.

It has a capacity of 64 inmates, though there are only 21 in it now, said Kelly Nantel, a spokeswoman for the correction agency.

Mr. Fair, who is now president of Security Response Technologies, a prison consulting company, did not return phone calls seeking comment. But even with the opening of the new protective custody unit, there were still not nearly enough cells for vulnerable inmates, Mr. Pingeon said. Even more troublesome, he said, there were not enough cells or units to separate violent inmates from those like Mr. Geoghan.

Peter Costanza, another lawyer with Massachusetts Correctional Legal Services, said the State Department of Correction frequently mixed several types of inmates in its few protective custody cells.

One group were sex offenders and people who were frail, like Mr. Geoghan, Mr. Costanza said. A second were mentally ill inmates, he said. A third were known informers. And a fourth were violent inmates who had developed bad relationships with more powerful gangs of prisoners and were therefore in danger of being attacked.

Mixing these vulnerable and predatory inmates together in protective custody is "crazy, a recipe for disaster," Mr. Costanza said.

Ms. Nantel, the spokeswoman for the Department of Correction, said she could not comment on why Mr. Druce had been placed in protective custody, given his background.

There was only one guard on duty for 22 inmates when Mr. Geoghan was killed, said John Conte, the Worcester County district attorney who is investigating the killing. Mr. Conte has said this appeared to be inadequate staffing.

Mr. Geoghan was buried today at Holy Hood Cemetery in Brookline, near the graves of his parents. His sister, Catherine, led the mourners, who included a few priests and nuns.

A funeral for Mr. Geoghan was held on Wednesday at Holy Name Parish in the West Roxbury section of Boston, the Rev. Christopher Coyne, a spokesman for the Boston Archdiocese, said.

A quirk in Massachusetts law will allow Mr. Geoghan's conviction to be vacated. Under the law, if an inmate dies in prison before his appeal is completed, his conviction is set aside.

Mr. Geoghan was convicted only once but was awaiting further criminal trials.

"It's a step back for me and for everyone who is involved," said Michael Linscott, who said he was molested by Mr. Geoghan at age 8. "He finally got what he deserved, and now I can't believe they're going to overturn it. It just makes a farce out of everything."

Jim Sacco, who said he was abused by Mr. Geoghan when he was 12, said: "Just because he's killed doesn't turn him into an innocent man. I don't know why they would even pursue that."

PHOTO 9.6

Individual housing units such as the ones pictured here consist of individual cells which are adjacent to a common dayroom, in a barred section of the jail facility.

Special housing assignments are provided for a number of reasons, but in this section we focus on those related to security. In earlier parts of this text, discussion was given for inmates in protective custody, particularly in Chapter 8 where the design of such facilities was considered. In this chapter, we look at the rationale and reasons for placing an inmate in special housing, which includes protective custody. The other primary form of special housing that is related to security considerations is administrative segregation. This type of special housing assignment is not punitive but is a housing designation intended to prevent potential disruption of institutional security, including the safety of staff and inmates who may be in danger if a given inmate is allowed to freely intermingle within the general population of the prison.

We begin with protective custody, followed with a discussion of administrative segregation. It is perhaps worth mentioning that the author of this text worked for several years in an administrative segregation department with violent and gang-related offenders, with occasional tours of duty in the protective custody section of the prison facility where he was employed. When appropriate, information regarding these types of special housing may be derived from professional experience derived from that employment within the Texas prison system.

Reference Link 9.2
Read about the first separate special housing unit for women prisoners.

PROTECTIVE CUSTODY

According to the National Institute of Corrections (1986), **protective custody** includes "special provisions to provide for the safety and well-being for inmates who, based on findings of fact, would be in danger in the general population" (p. 41). This general definition, provided by the premiere clearinghouse on correctional research, will serve as the definition of protective custody for this text. Regardless of definitional issues, the use of protective custody as an official classification did not officially emerge until the 1960s but grew in use during the mid-1980s, exceeding 25,000 inmates nationwide, but declined to around 7,500 inmates by 2001. Figure 9.7 provides an illustration of the trends in protective custody between 1980 and 2001. This trend is consistent with two other key occurrences within the field of corrections during these time periods. First, the 1980s saw a rise in the use of protective custody as a result of a number of federal court rulings and injunctions during the late 1970s and 1980s that required many prison systems to revamp their programs. Second, the populations in prison during the 1980s began to have more gang-related membership, followed with an influx of drug offenders in the 1990s, when another small increase (in 1990) was observed among those in protective custody. These trends impacted both protective custody and administrative segregation populations.

The reasons for being placed in protective custody can be many, but some are more common:

- Sexual harassment and/or pressure for sexual favors from other inmates.

- Providing information to correctional or law enforcement officials; being an informant.

- Being in debt to other inmates, usually through gambling of one sort or another.

- The type of crime that the offender committed prior to incarceration, such as with pedophiles.

- Having been previously employed in law enforcement or corrections.

FIGURE 9.7   Inmates in Protective Custody Nationwide

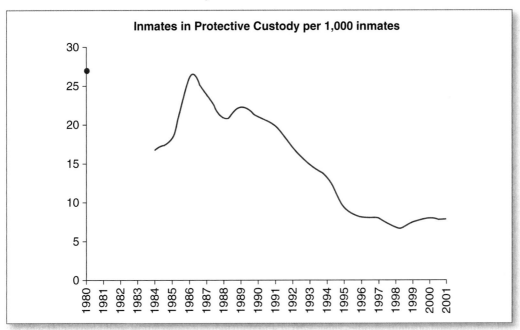

SOURCE: Association of State Correctional Administrators. (2004). *Fact sheet: Corrections safety: What the research says.* New York: Author.

Poore (1994) provides a very good overview of these reasons for assigning protective custody, and her work is presented here to highlight the complications behind those activities that may require use of this form of inmate classification and custody. According to Poore, each of the reasons below is usual for designation to protective custody along with the attendant concerns and considerations included:

Audio Link 9.2
Listen to a description of needs for protective custody.

- **Sexual Harassment.** Because most inmates know that sexual violation is considered inexcusable, there is a strong suspicion its frequent use as a reason for protective custody may be more for effect than for cause. Nevertheless, there are certainly cases when inmates have been seriously threatened and actually raped. This is a category frequently used by first offenders who fear such activity, even if they have not been subjected to it.

- **Assistance/Informants.** In the next category are those who may be paying for their assistance to law enforcement prior to coming to prison. Additionally, a large number of inmates have assisted the officials in prison with preventing escapes, curtailing drug traffic, or handling other illegal activity. These inmates often cannot live in the general prison population.

- **Debts.** Because of the availability of contraband in prison and the prevalence of gambling and other such activities, many inmates get into debt and are unable to pay. If there is no other arrangement to satisfy the debt, the lender is obligated to keep his other customers in line by handling those who will not pay. Many inmate arguments, fights, assaults, and even murders have been the end result of bad debts.

- **Type of Crime.** Contrary to the belief of many citizens, there are relatively few inmates who must seek protection as a result of an especially repugnant crime. Child molesters and rapists, who once faced great difficulties when living with other inmates, often are protected by rules of confidentiality and are aware that it would be in their best interests to lie about their crimes.

- **Former Law Enforcement.** Inmates who once worked in law enforcement may be at risk of harm due to the natural animosity that may exist between them and other offenders who are aware of their past line of work.

Aside from the reasons that protective custody may be initially granted, the classification process should continually reevaluate inmates in such custody, in regard to both their level of security and their participation in various types of programming. The courts have made it clear that inmates in both protective custody and administrative segregation should be afforded the same types of programming in any manner that is reasonable. With modification, these inmates have access to the same types of services and programs that are available to inmates in the general population. As security conditions for an inmate change over time in a prison, presuming that the inmate engaged in appropriate types of programming, it is feasible that he or she could be reclassified back to the general population, presuming the inmate's safety was no longer an issue.

ADMINISTRATIVE SEGREGATION

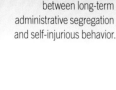

Journal Article Link 9.3
Read about the relationship between long-term administrative segregation and self-injurious behavior.

Administrative segregation is a type of classification that is nonpunitive in nature but requires the separation of inmates from the general population due to the threat that they may pose to themselves, staff, other inmates, or institutional order (see Figure 9.8 for rates of inmates placed in this custody level). Classification officials may use a number of reasons to impose this custody level upon an offender. One of the most common reasons for imposing administrative segregation is membership in a prison gang. Thus, many administrative segregation programs consist of a large number of gang members. Focus Topic 9.2 provides an interesting article on prison gang affiliation in Texas and the steps toward easing gang-related inmates from administrative segregation to the general population within Texas prisons.

Inmates in administrative segregation are usually housed in single cells where they receive the basic necessities and services, including food, clothing, showers, medical care, and even visitation privileges. Usually, these inmates are provided one hour of recreation time daily, on a confined recreation yard that has some type of fencing to prevent one inmate from having physical contact with another. Though they may be able to see one another through the fencing (such as with chain-link fencing), they are not allowed to engage in recreational activities in the same yard. Though many of the amenities available for general population inmates are provided to inmates in administrative segregation, some privileged activities and/or items may be restricted due to their gang status and the likelihood of dangerousness or because certain items may be used in the manufacture of homemade prison weapons. Indeed, the author of this text has a collection of prison weapons made by inmates while in administrative segregation; the types of deadly creations that can be made are limited only by one's imagination.

Lastly, as with inmates in protective custody, inmates in administrative segregation do receive routine reviews of their classification status. They may be eligible for reclassification, depending on the circumstances and whether they are gang-related. Typically, regardless of inmates' behavior, if they are known gang members, they will remain in administrative segregation due to their danger to the institution. Even in these cases, as

FIGURE 9.8   Inmates in Administrative Segregation Nationwide

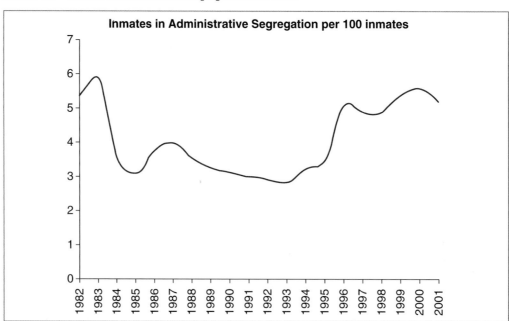

Source: Association of State Correctional Administrators. (2004). *Fact sheet: Corrections safety: What the research says.* New York: Author.

FOCUS TOPIC: 9.2

Leaving Gang Life and Administrative Segregation Behind in Texas

While gang life may have seemed like a good choice for some Texas offenders when they were on the outside, many inmate-gang members are starting to rethink that decision during their incarceration. With the Texas Department of Criminal Justice (TDCJ) sending all confirmed members of eight Texas gangs—ranging from the Mexican Mafia to the Aryan Circle—directly into administration segregation, those inmates have nearly 23 hours a day to sit alone in their cells and reevaluate their decision to belong to a gang.

To help inmates who want to break away from that way of life, TDCJ created the Gang Renouncement and Disassociation (GRAD) program to give them a way out.

"It gives the offenders an avenue to renounce their gang membership, to get out of the gang and to be able to go back to the general population," said *Kenneth W. Lee*, Program Administrator for TDCJ's STG Management Office. "Then, [they can] be released into the free world and thrive in society."

The GRAD program began four years ago at the Ramsey I Unit in Rosharon, Texas and targets offenders who belong to one of the eight security threat groups (STG) that TDCJ has identified for automatic placement into administrative segregation. All in all, about 6,000 inmates in the system belong to one of those gangs, which include the Aryan Brotherhood of Texas, Mexican Mafia, Barrio Azteca, Aryan Circle, Texas Mafia, Raza Unida, Texas Syndicate and Hermanos Pistoleros Latinos.

After conducting research on the best way to channel confirmed gang members out of administrative segregation and back into the general population, TDCJ came up with a nine-month program designed to transition former gang members back into the rest of the inmate population.

"The only way they can get out is to renounce their membership," Lee said. "If they meet all of the criteria for the program, they are put on a list."

Getting into GRAD

In order to be considered for the program, inmates must first submit a written statement to their STG officer stating their desire to renounce their membership to a particular gang. Afterwards, officers conduct a complete investigation of that inmate on their unit, to ensure that they truly intend to break their gang ties.

Beyond the written letter and the investigation, inmates must meet a variety of other requirements before they are accepted into the program:

- no offender assaults for a period of two years
- no staff assaults for a period of two years

- no major disciplinary cases for at least one year
- no extortion cases for a period of two years
- no weapons possession cases for a period of two years
- no sexual misconduct for a period of two years
- must be level one status for a minimum of one year
- must have renounced membership to a STG
- must not have been involved in any STG act for a minimum of two years
- can not have a security precaution designator of escape, staff assault or hostage situation

In addition, offenders have to fill out a form, which is reviewed by a committee on the unit level and then a regional coordinator, before it finds its way to Lee.

If an inmate is approved for the GRAD program, he is put on a waiting list, which now has 740 people on it, Lee said. And there are another 1,000 inmates who have submitted, in writing, their intent to renounce their gang memberships and are currently being monitored in their administrative segregation units.

"They're really wanting to get into the program," Lee said.

Every month, 16 new offenders are entered into the program and transferred to Ramsey I, where they live apart from the general population for the first two phases of the three-phase program.

Easing Back into the General Population

According to Lee, during phase one, the inmates live in single cells. He said it is an adjustment for a lot of the inmates to come out of administrative segregation—where they were handcuffed and shackled at all times when they were out of their cells—to an environment like Ramsey.

"There's a lot of rules they go by [at Ramsey], but it's completely different than administrative segregation," Lee said. "It takes a while [for the inmates] to adjust because some of the offenders have been in administrative segregation for as long as 18 years."

After the inmates become accustomed to living at Ramsey and spend two months in phase one, they enter phase two, during which inmates from different STGs live together in double cells for four months. According to Lee, the fact that former rival gang members are sharing a living space has never created any security issues.

"It has worked well," Lee said. "Of course we have had some disciplinary problems, but it has not been gang related—not at all."

Throughout phases one and two, the inmates attend four hours of educational programming each day, including anger management, cognitive intervention and substance abuse classes.

Once the inmates advance to phase three, they are mixed in with the other inmates at Ramsey, but still monitored by GRAD program officers. At this point, they take classes and work with the general population at the facility.

"They are separate from the rest of the general population while they are in phase one and phase two and, then, in phase three, they are put back into the rest of the general population [and] can continue [their] educational programming and [they are] given jobs to do to learn skills for when they do get out," Lee said.

After phase three, which lasts for three months, the inmates graduate from the GRAD program, their classifications are changed to reflect that they are now ex-gang members and they are transferred to other facilities, where they are integrated into the general population.

"There are a lot of different programs that are available to them once they have completed the GRAD process," Lee said. "Then they are treated like any other offender."

A Win-Win Situation

Although the STG officers in the units the offenders transition to are aware of their ex-gang member statuses and keep a closer eye on them in the general population, Lee said, so far, he has had no problems with offenders acting up or rejoining gangs after they have completed the GRAD program.

"Knock on wood, I've graduated 329 [offenders and] zero have gone back to a gang," Lee said.

Because of the program's success, Lee would like to see it expanded, a proposal that is currently being considered by officials at TDCJ.

"[We are] proposing to double it, so we'd be putting in 32 [offenders] a month and expanding [it] to 384 a year," Lee said.

It's a solid program, he added, because it benefits not only the offenders who are leaving gang life behind, but also the agency as a whole.

"It helps the security of the officers as far as lowering the number of confirmed gang members they have to watch," Lee said. "It's [also] cost-effective because it's freeing up administrative segregation cells and hopefully it will prevent these offenders from coming back into the system."

demonstrated in Focus Topic 9.2, programs may exist where inmates are able to eventually get out of administrative segregation, if they so desire. We will discuss gang offenders in jails and prisons extensively in Chapter 10 and will demonstrate how the emergence of gangs has impacted both prison operations and the general norms and culture of state prison systems around the nation.

SPECIALIZED OFFENDER CATEGORIES

Many inmates have a variety of characteristics, issues, or specialized needs that set them apart from the remaining prison population (Hanser, 2007). From a classification standpoint, the various needs that inmates may have can affect the decision to place them within a given facility, and, within that facility, these issues can affect individual housing decisions. However, it is important to note that each of these categories of the offender population creates the need for effective assessment and classification processes.

Further, one issue is very prevalent within the inmate population and directly relevant to the majority of the offender population: drug use. Because this issue is related to specific offender categories discussed later in this text and because this issue is a challenge for a large number of offenders in jail and prison, a section on drug use and the need for screening and classification has been included in this chapter. We now turn our attention to screening, assessment, and classification when faced with placement decisions for substance abuse treatment programs.

SUBSTANCE ABUSE ISSUES, ASSESSMENT, AND CLASSIFICATION

Many offenders in state and federal prisons are convicted of violating drug laws. In fact, 22.4% of all federal inmates and 32.6% of all state inmates reported being under the influence of drugs or alcohol at the very time that they committed the offense for which they were incarcerated (Bureau of Justice Statistics,

APPLIED THEORY 9.1

Differential Association, Minimizing Further Associations Through Effective Classification Processes

Differential association theory, according to Edwin Sutherland, is based on the premise that the excess of definitions favorable to crime, in excess of those definitions that are unfavorable to crime, will increase the likelihood for a person to commit criminal activity. Thus, the association that the person has with other criminals will increase his or her likelihood to engage in further criminal behavior.

Further, Sutherland asserts that criminal behavior is learnable and learned in interaction with other criminally minded persons. Through this association, the inmates learn not only techniques of certain crimes, but also specific rationale, motives, and so forth. This would then mean that inmates who interact with other inmates will likely increase their likelihood of further engaging in criminal behavior.

It is with this in mind that most classification programs will seek to separate low-risk inmates from high-risk inmates as much as is reasonably possible. Indeed, the separation of such inmate categories, as well as overall public safety, is the key reason for using classification systems. Thus, for the most part, it can be said that classification systems in the field of corrections are used for the same basic premises that differential association entails.

Such methods of separating the association of inmates with one another, or at least minimizing that association, are a perfect example of how theory and application meet one another within the real world of corrections. Given that prison has been found to have a criminalization effect where longer prison terms can lead to higher recidivism, it seems reasonable to presume that the less time an offender spends around criminal associations, the more likely he or she is to successfully reform. It is with that notion in mind that classification again becomes the important and central organizing aspect to the correctional processing of offenders.

SOURCE: Lilly, J. R., Cullen, F. T., & Ball, R. A. (2007). *Criminological theory: Context and consequences (4th ed.)*. Thousand Oaks, CA: Sage.

1998). In addition, more than 83% of all state inmates and more than 73% of all federal inmates reported past drug use, with most of that past drug use occurring during the year prior to their offense (Centers for Disease Control and Prevention, 2003). The problem is compounded by the fact that substance abuse is closely related to recidivism; inmates with prior convictions are significantly more likely than first-time offenders to be regular drug users.

Given the association between injection drug use and HIV/AIDS, detoxification also provides counseling to reduce AIDS-related risk behaviors (McNeece, Springer, & Arnold, 2002). Later, in Chapter 12, the student will see that drug abuse elevates the risk of contracting HIV/AIDS and other communicable diseases. This largely is associated with drug abusers who use intravenous drugs and those who engage in risky sex behaviors, particularly when prostitution and drug use are combined. In addition, students will learn in Chapter 12 that many cases of mental illness in jails and prisons co-occur with substance abuse disorders. We will expound on these interconnections in Chapter 12 but mention them here to demonstrate the importance of this issue and to, in addition, demonstrate the importance of having effective screening, assessment, and classification processes with the drug-abusing offender population.

Audio Link 9.3
Learn more about the prevention of AIDS in facilities.

Screening and Placement Criteria

Every form of treatment program involves some sort of screening. According to Myers and Salt (2000), screening serves two major purposes:

1. It attests to the presence of a condition that may go unrecognized if not detected.
2. It provides data to decide whether a client is appropriate for a specific treatment program or vice versa.

In the first use of screening, social, health, and criminal justice workers determine if there are sufficient grounds for referral of an inmate to a particular drug/alcohol treatment program. This screening is very important because the earlier the intervention takes place, the better the prognosis for the client. Obviously, the likelihood of reforming a drug experimenter (as described previously) is much better than

when treating a compulsive user. The second use of screening is to determine client appropriateness for a given treatment modality. It should be pointed out that the discretion in placement may not only consider the client's individual characteristics but also include the ability of a given agency to provide these services (e.g., fiscal constraints may be a factor despite the fact that the treatment program may be ideal for the client). In either case, it is this use of screening that provides the placement criteria for drug offenders in the criminal justice system.

Placement criteria are very important when processing drug offenders. The initial placement is important for both public safety and treatment-oriented concerns. When deciding upon placement criteria, a match must be made between the severity of the addiction and the level of care needed, ranging from medical inpatient care, to nonmedical inpatient care, to intensive outpatient care, to outpatient care (Hanson, Venturelli, & Fleckenstein, 2002). Further, matching the client's profile to a treatment modality is more likely to achieve lasting success translating to the enhanced evaluation of program effectiveness. For example, a client with attention deficit/hyperactivity disorder might be unsuited for the regimentation of a therapeutic community. Conversely, a person with low self-esteem, insecurities, and a fragile sense of self-worth would not be appropriate for a highly confrontational style of intervention.

Goldberg (2003) notes that several questions should be asked before placing clients in treatment. Further, agencies should also consider these issues before they begin to go into operation, or they should at least consider changing their program to address these questions. According to Goldberg (2003, p. 297), prior to matching clients to specific treatments, the following questions must be addressed:

1. Which treatment produces the best outcome for a specific group or person?

2. Do members of certain ethnic or socioeconomic groups respond similarly to certain types of treatment?

3. Is the effectiveness of a specific program linked to age of participants?

4. Do females and males differ in their response to treatment?

The matching of treatment to gender, culture, ethnicity, language, and even sexual orientation has been shown to improve the odds of achieving positive outcomes in a variety of treatment settings for a variety of treatment issues (Goldberg, 2003). In fact, the utilization of culturally competent programs for various racial/ethnic groups should be particularly addressed given the fact that minorities are highly prevalent within the correctional population. Goldberg (2003) also points out the importance of addressing issues relevant to female drug offenders, among these the need for prenatal care and treatment and the need for contact with their children. As will be seen in Chapter 11, a high proportion of female offenders on community supervision (72%) are the primary caretakers of children under 18 years of age (Bloom, Owen, & Covington, 2003). Thus, many female offenders may initially be motivated by the desire to reduce drug-related harm to their expected babies or to improve their relationship with and ability to attend to their children. This should not be overlooked, as this can be an effective source of motivation to encourage these offenders to complete their treatment, thereby improving their chances for long-term recovery.

Thus, the main point is that treatment programming must be effectively matched to the specific inmate. Certain groups of inmates may also have needs that are common to one another (e.g., as based on ethnicity, age, or gender), and they may have other more individualistic factors (divorce, abuse trauma, etc.) that may significantly affect their likelihood of success in treatment. In either event, treatment programs must rely on effective screening, assessment, and classification processes for inmate selection if they are expected to have successful outcomes. However, there is often a widespread tendency to simply place all inmates into drug treatment simply because the issues are so prevalent among the inmate population. As mentioned earlier, we will touch upon drug abuse issues with the inmate population in Chapter 11 and Chapter 12 where it will become clear that substance abuse is a primary co-occurring concern when working with female offenders, mentally ill offenders, and offenders who have HIV/AIDS or other communicable diseases.

CONCLUSION

The classification process is very important to institutional corrections. Indeed, it has been likened to the "brain" of the prison facility. For the most part, this is an appropriate description of the classification process and its importance to corrections. Effective classification is essential in determining both security needs and the specific needs of the inmate toward reformation. Without an adequate scheme for these types of decisions, corrections would likely be little more than guesswork. Thus, Maconochie changed the landscape of corrections with his mark system and, in the process, ushered in the future of corrections.

Given the scarcity of resources among most correctional agencies, it is important that they be able to predict how their funds can be most effectively allocated. Classification systems can help with this consideration. The elimination of overprediction of dangerousness is, in and of itself, one means by which classification keeps prison facilities from having even larger operational budgets. Couple this with the desire to keep the institution safe, and it becomes clear why classification processes are the cornerstone of any well-run facility.

Classification processes are important for both security and treatment purposes. From our readings, offender placement in various security levels within a prison can be important for the safety of staff, other inmates, and the offenders themselves. Thus, the welfare of everyone's safety hinges on the classification process. Likewise, appropriate classification is important regarding treatment approaches. The ability of classification and treatment staff to correctly place clients into the appropriate substance abuse intervention is critical to the program's success. As we move into future chapters regarding the prison culture and the processing of specialized offenders, it will become clear that effective assessment and classification a re critical to the correctional process. Without effective classification, we are likely wasting the tax dollars obtained from the public. Society counts on the field of corrections to ensure public safety and to maintain its security over offenders within its jurisdiction. This is an impossible mission without effective classification processes. Building a program on faulty assessment and classification processes is, arguably, a form of negligence to our obligation to protect society. Ultimately, public safety is *job one*, and it is, therefore, important that corrections fulfill its obligation to treat public safety with the due diligence that it deserves.

END-OF-CHAPTER DISCUSSION QUESTIONS

1. Provide a brief overview of the key historical figures in the development of modern-day classification systems.

2. Discuss the importance of the Supreme Court case of *Palmigiano v. Garrahy* (1977).

3. Identify and discuss the four broad goals of classification.

4. Identify the different custody levels and the methods used for housing assignments of inmates.

5. Identify the various members of a classification team (such as is used with the Bureau of Prisons) and explain the functions for each member.

6. Define the term *administrative segregation* and explain how it is usually used (and with what population it is usually used) within a prison.

7. Discuss four reasons for inmates being placed in protective custody in a prison facility.

8. Explain how the classification process and differential association operate along a similar set of premises.

KEY TERMS

Administrative segregation	Level of security	Protective custody
Case manager	Level of Supervision Inventory— Revised (LSI-R)	Psychology services representative
Correctional counselor		
Custody level	Mark system	SENTRY system
Educational adviser	*Morris v. Travisono* (1970)	Treatment
English Penal Servitude Act	*Palmigiano v. Garrahy* (1977)	Unit manager

APPLIED EXERCISE 9.1

Determine whether the following inmates should be given minimum-, medium-, or maximum-level security or if they should be given either administrative segregation or protective custody. Be sure to explain why you have answered as you have.

Inmate Al *is a member of a known street gang that is well represented in your own correctional system. He denies being a member of a gang but has been identified by law enforcement as a bona fide member when operating in the community.*

Inmate Nancy *is a female offender who has two kids and is incarcerated for check fraud. She has served the majority of her sentence and seems to be doing well in educational and vocational programs offered in the prison. She often reflects on getting out, getting a good job, and taking care of her children.*

Inmate Butch *is a known sexual predator who has sexually assaulted a number of inmates and even one female correctional officer throughout his life in prison. Butch is not liked by many inmates but is considered very masculine within the prison subculture. He seems to have no twinge of guilt or remorse for any of his acts.*

Inmate Tom *was a priest who was convicted of sexually abusing dozens of young boys within his church. He is slight of build and is a fairly docile appearing man. He just arrived at your facility a couple of days ago.*

Inmate Conway *minds his own business and does not talk much with prison staff. He keeps out of trouble, for the most part, but has an independent quality that keeps him a bit at odds with the programming aspects of prison. He has not been identified as dangerous (convicted of burglary), but he also does not seem to make great strides toward getting released early.*

For each of the above cases, determine their custody level from any of the following options:

> Minimum Security
>
> Medium Security
>
> Maximum Security
>
> Administrative Segregation
>
> Protective Custody

"WHAT WOULD YOU DO?"

You are a counselor in a substance abuse treatment program within a state prison facility. You run a group each morning from 8:30 to 10:00, Monday through Friday. The program is intensive, and the inmate participants are required to attend each and every session. As a reward for being selected as a participant and for successfully completing the program, inmates are given an extra 180 days of good time during the yearlong program. Further, these inmate participants are allowed to stay in a dorm specifically set aside for them.

While conducting group, you notice that one of your participants has not been attending group. When you inquire about this, you learn from the other inmate participants that this individual does not act as if he understands that he is supposed to go to group. Further, security staff have not been notified as to when he would need to attend group; thus security did not have any reason to require the inmate to leave the dorm.

The inmate participant has missed 8 days of group, and this is your first day to meet him. From your meeting, it is clear to you that this inmate has numerous challenges and that he really has a limited capacity to understand the requirements that he must adhere to. You are not sure what to do; on the one hand, you could remove him from group, and he will not gain good time and will likely be given disciplinary action within the prison due to his failure to attend. On the other hand, you could ignore this oversight and allow this inmate to continue through the program, knowing that he is likely to still have future mishaps as well. In addition, you are not sure what the other inmates will think, if you should deviate from the rules; they all know that this inmate was supposed to attend group.

You talk with your group about the situation and find that many of the group members are empathetic to his situation. Likewise, the clinical supervisor has indicated that he is understanding of the circumstances, but he is not sure how classification and/or the prison administration will process this situation.

You have some degree of discretion in resolving this situation and wish to be ethical and fair in your decision. Likewise, you want to ensure that you do not leave any loopholes for other offenders who might attempt to manipulate the program. Such inmates might find reasons to not attend therapy, using that time to attend to other self-identified priorities. Given the manipulative nature of the inmate population at this prison, this outcome is not an unthinkable concern.

How do you handle this situation, formally or informally? Who will you consult in resolving this? What do you tell the other members of the group? Do you ask classification about this situation, noting that this inmate may not have been placed into the correct treatment group?

In short, the question is . . .

What would you do?

CROSS-NATIONAL PERSPECTIVE 9.1

Electronic Monitoring of Housing, Classification, and Inmate Activity in Australia

As noted throughout this chapter, classification determines housing and programming issues within prison systems. Once inmates are assigned a custody level and programming regimen, they are subject to periodic review for reclassification. However, the means by which they are tracked throughout the completion of their sentence has also been an important issue, in terms of both public and/or prison safety and programming success. The nation of Australia has partnered technological advances with prison operations in a manner that enhances both prison security and programming options. We look at the following article as an example of how such advances can improve classification assignments and outcomes:

Two Australian companies, Alanco Technologies and NEC Australia, has begun the implementation and installation of a special Wi-Fi tracking system that is housed at the Alexander Maconochie Centre Prison, located in Canberra, Australia. These two companies have agreed to integrate their security system technologies as a means of offering state-of-the art, real-time tracking, to the more than 100 prison facilities that are located throughout Australia and New Zealand. Currently, the Maconochie Centre Prison is being used as the prototype implementation where multiple levels of prisoner classification is required for inmates in that facility. This facility includes young adults who are both male and female.

This security system will allow prison staff to monitor the physical location of inmates and will aid in controlling their movement between various segments of the population. This will also detect potential escape attempts and will therefore act as an enhanced security mechanism for public safety, not just institutional.

This system will also optimize staff efficiency and is expected to reduce long-term costs to the facility. The project is valued at over $1 million dollars but, due to the benefits in staff efficiency, the reduced likelihood of inmate infractions inside the institution, and the enhanced level of public safety, this cost is expected to result in a minimal investment. In short, the rewards will outweigh the costs of this program.

Naturally, because these private companies hope to sell this security product to as many buyers as are available, they have engaged in an intense marketing campaign. The use of this system at the Maconochie facility will allow for the public showcasing of this technology and the product that is available. While the market was originally intended for Australia and New Zealand, there is nothing to say that this same product could not and/or will not be available to other potential buyers in other nations around the world. This is especially true when one considers the state of globalization that impacts the criminal justice field in today's world, including the field of corrections, reaching even into prison facilities that are seemingly shut off from the rest of the world.

Question 1: From what you can tell, how progressive does the nation of Australia seem to be in relation to inmate security? Is this similar to or different from the state of correctional operations in the United States, in your opinion? Provide a brief explanation for your answer.

Question 2: Do you believe that such programs can enhance the outcomes and assignments derived from automated classification systems? Briefly explain why or why not.

SOURCE: GPS News. (2008). Alanco/TSI PRISM and NEC Australia partner for inmate tracking system. Scottsdale, AZ: Author. Retrieved from http://www.gpsdaily.com/reports/Alanco_TSI_PRISM_And_NEC_Australia_Partner_For_Inmate_Tracking_System_999.html.

STUDENT STUDY SITE

Visit the Student Study Site at **www.sagepub.com/hanserintro** to access links to the videos, audio clips, SAGE journal articles, state rankings, and reference materials noted in this chapter, as well as additional study tools including eFlashcards, web quizzes, and more.

chapter 10

Prison Subculture and Prison Gang Influence

LEARNING OBJECTIVES:

1. Discuss the prison subculture for inmates and correctional officers.

2. Compare importation theory with exportation theory.

3. Identify different aspects of prison culture that explain how offenders and officers view the world around them.

4. Discuss how professionalization and the diversification of correctional staff have impacted the prison subculture.

5. Discuss the impact that prison gangs have had on prisons, including the traditional prison subculture.

6. Identify the 13 gangs listed in this chapter as the primary prison gangs in the United States.

7. Explain what prison systems do to control gang problems that occur in their facilities.

I will stand by my brother

My brother will come before all others

My life is forfeit should I fail my brother

I will honor my brother in peace as in war

Aryan Brotherhood Oath

INTRODUCTION

This chapter provides students with a very unique aspect of the world of corrections. Students will learn that within the institutional environment, there is a commonality of experiences that arise between those who are involved; this is true for both inmates and staff. Indeed, many people may not be aware that, in fact, the mind and the world of the inmate often affect the mind-set of security personnel who work with the inmate. In essence, there is an exchange of beliefs and perspectives that often come together to produce a unique fusion between the two groups. This exchange of beliefs creates a unique subculture that is the product of both inmate norms being brought in from the outside and those taken from the prison to the outside community.

It is important for students to understand that prison staff are not immune to the effects of the profound social learning that occurs, and, over time, as they become more enmeshed in the prison social setting, they begin to internalize many of the beliefs and norms held by the prison subculture. While this may seem to be counterproductive and/or even backward from what one might wish within the prison environment, this is an inevitable process as prison staff find themselves interacting with the street mentality on a day-to-day basis. In actuality, this is a maturing of correctional workers as they begin to see a world that is not necessarily black and white but instead has many shades of gray. Issues become more complicated than being simple "good guy and bad guy" situations as correctional workers work with offenders on a personal level. The nuances and differences between different offenders tend to complicate what initially might seem like simple decisions.

Because correctional staff interact with these offenders on a daily basis, a sense of understanding develops both among correctional staff and between staff and the inmate population. Inmates come to expect certain reactions from correctional staff, and, just as certain, staff come to expect certain reactions from inmates. Amidst this are informal rules of conduct where loyalty to one's own group must be maintained, yet, at the same time, individual differences in personality among security staff and among inmates will affect the level of "respect" that an officer will get from the inmate population, and, for inmates, their conduct will also affect the amount of respect that they gain from others serving time. Likewise, correctional staff learn which inmates have influence, power, or control over others, and this may affect the dynamics of interaction. Further still, some inmates may simply wish to do their time whereas others produce constant problems; to expect security staff to maintain the same reaction to both types of inmates is unrealistic.

The dynamics involved in inmate-inmate, inmate-staff, and staff-staff interactions create circumstances that do not easily fall within the guidelines of prison regulations. Further, as a means of maintaining control of an inmate population that greatly outnumbers the correctional staff, many security officers will learn the personalities of inmates and will become familiar with the level of respect that they receive within the world of the convict. Likewise, and even more often, inmates watch and observe officers who work the cell block, the dormitory, or other areas where inmates congregate. They will develop impressions of the officer, and this will determine how inmates react to the officer. The officer is essentially labeled by the inmate population, over time, as one who deserves respect or one who deserves contempt. In some cases, officers may be identified as being too passive or "weak" in their ability to enforce the rules. In such cases, they are likely to be conned, duped, or exploited by streetwise convicts.

The various officer-inmate interactions impact the daily experiences of the individual officer and the inmate. Understanding how these various nuances impact these interactions is critical to understanding how and why prisons may operate as they do. In prisons that have little technology, few cameras, and shortages of staff, the gray areas that can emerge in the inmate-staff interactional process can lead to a number of ethical and legal conundrums. It is with this in mind that we now turn our attention to factors that create and complicate the social landscape of American prisons.

IMPORTATION THEORY

The key tenet of **importation theory** is that the subculture within prisons is brought in from outside the walls by offenders who have developed their beliefs and norms while on the streets. In other words, the prison subculture is reflective of the offender subculture on the streets. Thus, behaviors respected behind the walls of a prison are similar to behaviors respected among the criminal population outside of the prison. There is some research that does support this notion (Wright, 1994).

Regardless of what research may exist on this matter, most any correctional officer and most any inmate knows that the background of the offender (as well as the correctional officer) has a strong impact on how that person behaves, both inside and outside of a prison; this simply makes good intuitive sense. There are two key opposing points to consider regarding importation theory. First, the socialization process outside of prison has usually occurred for a much longer period of time for many offenders and is, therefore, likely to be a bit more entrenched. Second and conversely, the prison environment is intense and traumatic, being capable of leaving a very deep and lasting influence upon a person in a relatively short period of time. While this second point may be true, most offenders in prison facilities have led a lifestyle of offending and will tend to have numerous prior offenses. These offenses are only those for which they have been caught; there are still a wide range of criminal and noncriminal behaviors that may be unknown to the correctional system. This means that inmates will likely have led a lifestyle of dysfunction that is counter to what the broader culture may support. Thus, these individuals come to the prison with years of street life and bring their criminogenic view of the world to the prison.

It has been concluded by some (Bernard, McCleary, & Wright, 1999; Wright, 1994) that though correctional institutions may seem closed off from society, their boundaries are psychologically permeable. In other words, when someone is locked up, they still are able to receive cultural messages and influences from outside the walls of the prison. Television, radio, and mail all mitigate the immersion experience in prison. Visitation schedules, work opportunities outside of the prison, and other types of programming also mitigate the impact of the prison environment. Indeed, according to Bernard et al. (1999), "prison walls, fences, and towers still prevent the inside world from getting outside, [but] they can no longer prevent the outside world—with its diverse attractions, diversions, and problems—from getting inside" (p. 164). This statement serves as a layperson explanation of importation theory that is both accurate and practical.

INDIGENOUS PRISON CULTURE AND EXPORTATION THEORY

In contrast to the tenets of importation theory is the notion that prison subculture is largely the product of socialization that occurs inside prison. It was the work of Gresham Sykes (1958) that first introduced this notion in a clear and thorough manner. His theory has been referred to as either the deprivation theory of prisonization or the indigenous model of prison culture. Sykes (1958) referred to the pains of imprisonment as the rationale for why and how prison culture develops in the manner that it does. The **pains of imprisonment** is a term that refers to the various inconveniences and deprivations that occur as a result of incarceration. According to Sykes, the pains of imprisonment tended to gather around five general areas of deprivation, and it was due to these deprivations that the prison subculture developed, largely as a means of adapting to the circumstances within the prison. Sykes included the following five categories as being particularly challenging to men and women who do time:

1. The loss of liberty.
2. The loss of goods and services readily available in society.
3. The loss of heterosexual relationships, both sexual and nonsexual.
4. The loss of autonomy.
5. The loss of personal security.

Inmates within the prison environment essentially create value systems and engage in behaviors that are designed to ease the pains of deprivation associated with these five areas. Research has examined the effects of prison upon inmates who are forced to cope with the constrained prison existence.

PHOTO 10.1

These items are the "Prison Blues" line of clothing, manufactured by inmates in the correctional system of the state of Oregon. Their slogan is "Made on the inside, worn on the outside."

PHOTO 10.2

This inmate proudly displays his gang-affiliated tattoos.

For instance, Johnson and Dobrzanska (2005) studied inmates who were serving lengthy sentences. They found that, among those inmates who coped maturely to prison life, incarceration was a painful but constructive experience. This was particularly true for inmates who were serving life sentences (defined to include offenders serving prison terms of 25 years or more without the benefit of parole). As a general matter, lifers came to see prison as their home and made the most of the limited resources available in prison; they established daily routines that allowed them to find meaning and purpose in their prison lives, lives that might otherwise seem empty and pointless. The work of Johnson and Dobrzanska points toward the notion that, regardless of the environment, humans can be highly adaptable.

However, aside from the need to cope with prison life, there is also the idea that many of the mannerisms and behaviors observed among street offenders have their origins within the prison environment. Indeed, certain forms of rhyming, rap, tattoos, and dress have prison origins. For example, the practice known as "sagging" where adolescent boys allow their pants to sag—exposing their underwear—originates from jail and prison policies denying inmates the use of belts (because they could be used as a weapon or means to commit suicide). This practice is thought to have been exported to the streets during the 1990s as a statement of African American solidarity as well as a way to offend White society.

Other examples might be the notion of **"blood in—blood out,"** describing the idea that in order for inmates to be accepted within a prison gang, they must draw blood (usually through killing) in an altercation with an identified enemy of the gang. Once in the gang, they may only leave if they draw blood of the gang's enemy sufficient to meet the demands of the gang leadership or by forfeiting their own blood (their life). This same phrase is heard among street gangs, including juvenile street gangs, reflecting the fact that these offenders mimic the traditions of veteran offenders who have served time in prison. Consider also certain attire that has been popular, off and on, during the past decade, such as when Rhino boots became popular footwear, not due to their stylishness or functionality, but because they were standard issue for working inmates in many state prison systems.

THE INMATE SUBCULTURE OF MODERN TIMES

In all likelihood, the inmate subculture is a product of both importation and indigenous factors. Given the complicated facets of human behavior and the fact that inmates tend to cycle in and out of the prison system, this just seems logical. In fact, attempting to separate one from the other is more of an academic argument than a practical one. The work of Hochstellar and DeLisa (2005) represents an academic attempt to negotiate between these two arguments. These researchers used a sophisticated statistical technique known as structural equation modeling to analyze the effects of importation and indigenous deprivation theories. They found evidence supporting both perspectives but found that the key factor that determined which perspective was most accountable for inmates' adaptation to prison subculture was their level of participation in the inmate economy (Hochstellar & DeLisa, 2005).

Journal Article Link 10.1
Read about inmate adaptation to imprisonment.

This is an important finding because it corroborates practical elements just as much as it navigates between academic arguments regarding subculture development. The prison economy is one of the key measures of influence that an inmate (and perhaps even some officers) may have within the institution. An inmate who is active in the prison economy is one who is likely to have currency within the prison system. This currency can come in the form of actual money shifted in the inmate's commissary accounts, the possession and trafficking of cigarettes, ownership of desirable items, power over other inmates who can be prostituted for the pleasure of those willing to pay, or any number of other potentially valuable resources that can be brokered within the inmate economy.

Video Link 10.1
Watch a video about prison economy.

Regardless, the more resources an inmate has, the wealthier he or she will be in the eyes of the inmate population. Oftentimes, those inmates who are capable of obtaining such wealth are either stronger, more cunning, or simply smarter (usually through training and literacy, such as with jailhouse lawyers) than most other members of the inmate population. Thus, these inmates are likely to be more adept at negotiating the prison economy, and they are likely to have more influence within the prison subculture. They are also more likely to be successfully adapted to the prison culture (the influence of indigenous prison cultural factors) while being able to procure or solicit external resources (being a source of exportation outside the prison walls). In short, those who master the economy often have effective and/or powerful contacts both inside and outside of the prison. This is consistent with the findings of Hochstellar and DeLisa (2005).

THE CONVICT CODE AND SNITCHING

Going beyond the arguments related to this subculture's association with factors internal and external to the prison facility, the subculture itself has numerous characteristics that are often portrayed in film, in academic sources, and among practitioners (see Focus Topic 10.1). Chief among these characteristics is the somewhat fluid code of conduct among inmates. This is sometimes referred to as the **convict code**, which is a set of standards in behavior attributed to the true convict—the title of *convict* being one of respect given to inmates who have proven themselves worthy of that title. Among academic sources, this inmate code emphasizes oppositional values to conventional society in general and to prison authorities in particular. The most serious infraction against this code of conduct is for an inmate to cooperate with the officials as a snitch. A **snitch** is the label given to an inmate who reveals the activity of another inmate to authorities, usually in exchange for some type of benefit within the prison or legal system. For example, an inmate might be willing to tell prison officials about illicit drug smuggling being conducted by other inmates in the prison in exchange for more favorable parole conditions, transfer to a different prison, or some other type of benefit.

Video Link 10.2
Watch a video about snitching in prison.

Among all inmates, it is the snitch who is considered the lowest of the low. In traditional "old school" subcultures (i.e., those of the 1940s through the 1970s), snitches were rare and were afforded no respect. Their existence was precarious within the prison system, particularly because protection afforded to snitches was not optimal. During riot situations and other times where chaos might reign, there are recorded incidents where inmates have specifically targeted areas where snitches were housed and protected from the general population. In these cases, snitches were singled out and subjected to severely gruesome torture and were usually killed within the facility. Perhaps the most notorious of these incidents occurred at the New Mexico Penitentiary in Santa Fe. This prison riot occurred in 1980 and resulted in areas of the prison being controlled by inmates. These inmates eventually broke into "cell block 4," which housed known snitches in the prison. The details of how the snitch-informers were tortured and killed shocked the public conscience as news media provided reports.

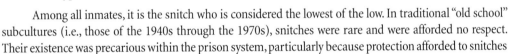

PHOTO 10.3

Jonathan W. Hilbun is an inmate at Richwood Correctional Center who is a dorm mentor in the Successful Treatment and Recovery (STAR) program. He stands here in front of a bookshelf that is part of the inmate library for the STAR program.

FOCUS TOPIC: 10.1

Focus From the Inside With Jonathan Hilbun, Inmate with Richwood Correctional Center.

The hyenas are the inmates who only prey on the weak inmates, and they will back off if the weaker inmate strikes back. But, if the weak one does not fend for himself, then the hyenas will devour him. A good description of a hyena attack is as follows:

> A new inmate arrives at a prison and is fresh on the dorm. There are all kinds of rules that go unspoken among the men in the dorm, and, in conjunction with the rules and regs of the prison, this is penitentiary law. The new inmate does not know the code, so he breaks a law and a "penitentiary G" checks him on it. If the new inmate does not fight the penitentiary G, then the hyenas will move in as well. Usually, the main hyena will move in first to take the bite, and, by this time, all have figured that the new inmate will not bite because they observed him get called out to fight and he did not. However, the main hyena will venture forth just in case the new inmate gives them a surprise.

The first form of engagement is based on the offer of false protection status. This is largely a psychological game where the hyenas try to instill fear into the new inmate, known as the "prey," and offer to assist him. A smart prey will turn the situation on the hyenas by fighting back against the leader. However, most new inmates are nervous and edgy, so if they are scared enough they will do anything the hyenas require. Sex, money, and whatever else the prey can offer are all on the table. But, if the prey fights the first hyena that approaches, then the penitentiary G who called him out at first will usually develop a little respect for the new inmate. This gives the new inmate some breathing space on the dorm, and his stay is then much easier. On the other hand, if the prey does not fight, then he is likely to go "under someone's wing," which can be good or bad, depending on who the protector is.

Another interesting point regarding inmate behavior, particularly hyena behavior, has to do with the inmates' interactions with security. In many cases, hyenas will have no respect for authority but, at the same time, be hesitant to directly challenge authority. Rather, they will tend to use subversive or indirect means of ridiculing the officer. For instance, when the "Freeman" (another term for a prison guard) comes on the dorm to count, an inmate may holler something across the dorm that is crude and crass. Comments may include "F—k that count," or "You don't even know how to count 'cause you flunked kindergarten," or "This dorm don't need no more police—go find a real crisis," or any other number of comments intended to disrespect the officer.

It is at this point that the officer must make a stand, and he really needs to do it quickly. If he or she does not, then the other hyenas will join along and will taunt and tease the officer to see how much they can get away with. This can actually get pretty bad as it may even set up an ongoing officer-inmate dynamic that can go on for the remainder of the officer's employment at the facility, if such misbehavior is left unchecked enough times.

In response, the officer will usually react by applying some type of punitive measures to inmates on the dorm. For instance, he will usually restrict the TV privileges and secure the phone lines as well, if the facility allows inmates to make phone calls. Likewise, he may decide to do a "special count" that requires all inmates to sit or lie in their own rack, prohibiting them from getting up and walking about the dorm. It can get pretty frustrating, over time, to sit in the bed for prolonged periods of time, and the officer knows this. It is doubly frustrating for those inmates who did not make the comment and who do not really respect the cowardly actions of the hyena.

During this time, the officer will usually leave the dorm and go back to the control room or observation post, leaving the dorm under observation until his return. Those who do not comply with the officer's order to stay on their rack will likely "catch a charge," meaning that they will get written up for disciplinary action. After a period of time, some inmates will begin to mumble and make statements like "Whoever said that coward sh__ better just take their charge," or "I gotta call my people, so you better just take your charge and get on with it," or "Whoever said that sh__ gots to get up outta here." This type of behavior can be the beginning of a long day or night, and it can even shape the meaning of life for this dorm and the officer(s) involved if it turns into a long-term problem.

Usually, one of the inmates will finally tell the officer the identity of the hyena who made the unruly comments, and, in many cases, this results in a type of understood bond of respect between the officer and the inmate. Though there is nothing necessarily spoken between the two, the officer knows that the inmate is going against the common wisdom of the prison subculture in doing this, and, at the same time, the inmate knows that the officer cannot get compliance until he or she breaks through the veneer of the hyenas who have openly and publicly challenged his or her authority and mocked the officer for all to see. It is a delicate interplay, in this middle-ground area, between officer and inmate, where both groups must learn to coexist with one another within a set of informal and formal parameters.

Naturally, it takes quite a bit of courage to tell on another inmate. Inmates usually will view the act of disclosing the identity of the person who commits an infraction as an act of snitching. Snitching, as we all know, is not respected in jail or prison and can be dangerous. This is usually not respected, but, in cases where a hyena has acted in a cowardly manner and where the rest of the dorm is made to pay for his action, respect is lost for the hyena, especially if he does not step forward and take his charge, so to speak. In addition, there is one other aspect that can make this approach actually respectable in the eyes of other inmates. This is when the informing inmate talks to the officer on behalf of the dorm and makes it clear that he cannot and will not take any incentives or benefits for the information. If he also makes it clear that he is not trying to get too cozy with the officer but, instead, is trying to simply live under the conditions of détente that exist within the prison subculture between inmates and officers, this will be considered acceptable. This is especially true if other inmates know, in advance, that this inmate will likely inform on behalf of the dorm.

At this point, the hyena is obviously crossed out among others on the dorm and is held in even lower regard by other inmates as a coward who sidesteps his charge and allows others to "pay his lick," so to speak. In some ways, this process of maintaining some semblance of decency and tangible respect for institutional authority is a means of redemption for the inmate and the dorm. In this regard, it is viewed that these men are capable of reform on at least a base level, contrasting with the typical saying that "there is no honor among thieves." In essence, even the inmate subculture has standards that the hyena has failed to maintain. Thus, the lack of respect goes to the hyena, and, so long as the officer conducts his job in a firm but fair manner, the officer is afforded his due respect.

It is worth mentioning that Mr. Hilbun has been incarcerated for 18 and a half years in a variety of institutions, including Angola and Richwood Correctional Center.

SOURCE: Jonathan Hilbun (personal interview, December 2, 2011). Used with permission.

However, one thing should be noted about snitches in the modern world of corrections; they are much more frequently encountered. Though there is a supposed code against snitching, the truth of the matter is that during the 1990s with the emergence of the War on Drugs, more and more inmates consented to being informants with law enforcement as a means of securing better sentencing deals. Further, the new breed of inmate that was observed during this time did not reflect behavior that was "honor bound" like the older inmates in prison. Though there continued to be verbal opposition to inmate snitching, wardens and other prison administrators noted the sharp increase in informants within their institutions during this time. It would appear that among modern-day inmates, the willingness to do one's time with honor is a lower priority. Many veteran prison officials and older inmates (particularly inmates who are serving life sentences) contend that this is reflective of modern society where people are not as accustomed to being inconvenienced—a fast-food and instant coffee generation.

Prison Tour Video Link 10.1
Watch an interview with two inmates.

SEX OFFENDERS AND PUNKS

Sex offenders, particularly child molesters, are also afforded no respect in prison. In the early to mid-1900s, child molesters typically had a high mortality rate and were often abused by other inmates. However, these types of offenses are becoming more prevalent and are more often detected by the justice system. Thus, there are higher proportions of these types of offenders in most prison systems. Further still, many prison systems have developed therapeutic programs that separate these offenders from the general population. Though this may be true nowadays, many are not placed in a separate treatment program and instead can be found within the general population of the prison.

For those inmates who are sex offenders, many are singled out by prison gangs to be "turned out." Turning out occurs when an inmate is forced to become a punk for the prison gang. The term **punk** is common prison vernacular for an inmate who engages in homosexual activity, but is a derogatory term that implies that the inmate is feminine, weak, and subservient to masculine inmates. In other words, the punk is considered a woman in prison and is often forced to engage in sexual acts for the pleasure of one or more inmates. Sex offenders in prison are disproportionately represented within this prison population and are considered to be at high risk for this type of victimization.

THE STOIC DEMEANOR AND THE USE OF SLANG

Other ideals within the prison subculture include the notion that inmates should maintain themselves as men who show no emotion, free from fear, depression, and anxiety. Basically, the "strong silent type" is the ideal. Today's young offenders may attempt to maintain this exterior image, but the effects of modern society (prevalence of mental health services, reliance on medications, and technological advances, as well as a fast-changing society) often preclude this stereotypical version of the convict from being reality for many inmates. Likewise, inmates are expected to refrain from arguments with other inmates. The general idea is that they must do their own time without becoming involved in the personal business of others. Getting involved in other people's business is equated to being a gossip, and this also is considered more of a feminine behavior. Thus, to be manly in prison, inmates must mind their own business.

Prison Tour Video Link 10.2
Watch two inmates discuss their relationships with other prisoners.

Inmates who stick to these two rules of behavior are generally seen as in control and not easily manipulated. Essentially, they are seen as psychologically strong of will and also fairly wise to the prison world. In some cases, these inmates may be referred to as a true convict rather than an inmate. In the modern prison culture, the title of **convict** refers to an inmate who is respected for being self-reliant and independent of other inmates or the system. Convicts are considered mature and strong, not weak and dependent on others for their survival. Convicts are considered superior to the typical inmate, and, while not necessarily leaders of other inmates (indeed, most do not care to lead others, but simply wish to do their own time), they are often respected by younger inmates who are themselves becoming acculturated into the prison environment.

APPLIED THEORY 10.1

Labeling Theory as a Paradigm for the Etiology of Prison Rape: Implications for Understanding and Intervention

According to labeling theory, group reactions are the key determinant to events later considered antisocial in nature. Labeling theory essentially asks why some acts are labeled deviant when others are not (Akers, 2000). This theory asserts that social group reactions serve to make certain behaviors deviant, regardless of the individual context in which they occur (Vold, Bernard, & Snipes, 1998). This begs the question as to who creates the label associated with deviant behavior. The answer to this inquiry lies with those who hold the power within a given social structure. Some sociologists have asserted that the more powerful members of society create the standard for labels applied to individuals who are less socially prominent (Schur, 1973). From this perspective, this manuscript will serve to demonstrate the labeling processes involved in homosexual rape within prisons.

In order to understand labeling theory, one must also understand the underlying power structures within a given social order where the labeling process occurs. This is crucial because the powerful members of a society impose labels upon those who are less powerful (Schur, 1973). The label is determined by the standards of the affluent and upwardly mobile, with those at the lower echelons being nearly, though not entirely, powerless to "throw off the yoke" of the labeling process (Becker, 1963).

For the upper and middle classes, power can effectively be expressed through economic, vocational, and academic avenues. For the lower classes, however, many of these routes to upward social mobility are denied, leaving only direct physical means for obtaining power or control (Miller, 1958). Correspondingly, a standard based on physical prowess and ability can develop (Messerschmidt, 1999). Many perform physically oriented jobs, and likewise find the physical realm of achievement to be their best hope in moving upward through the social order (Messerschmidt, 1999). Such an example might be the "ghetto kid" turned pro football or basketball star, or the rural small-town kid turned Marine Corps hometown hero. These images themselves are stereotypes that serve to maintain the power structure as well as the means of achievement.

With the prison population being drawn disproportionately from the less affluent members of society, it should come as no surprise that prison norms may, in various subtle ways, exemplify power status norms held by the lower classes (Miller, 1958; Tucker, 1981). The members of the "prison society" are even less socially powerful than their socioeconomic counterparts who are not incarcerated. For these members, physical prowess and coercion become the primary method of achieving power in the prison setting. Thus, aside from some rare exceptions, such as successful "writ writers" or inmates who have affluent family members, those who are physically powerful tend to also be the most socially powerful within the prison. Within the male inmate subculture, the expression of physical prowess as power

is frequently paired with roles of masculinity, which, in turn, reinforces the subculture of physical prowess within the prison setting (Messerschmidt, 1999).

The meaning of masculinity is different in prison than in mainstream society. In prison the meaning is reinforced as men in this location act to affirm their masculinity in the limited ways that are available (Messerschmidt, 1999). This results in a modified form of "hegemonic masculinity," which emphasizes negative attitudes toward authority, control over others, aggressiveness, and social reinforcement for violent acts (Messerschmidt, 1999). Previously learned sexual and social styles of masculinity, as exercised in the broader society, are adapted and altered within prison so that the male inmate does not lose his position of dominance and control. To fail to do so results in the male inmate accepting a subservient role, or as it is termed in the prison subculture, the role and label of a "woman" (Tucker, 1981). In essence, sexual violence among inmates is a statement of power, status, and control.

It is through both the means and the threat of violence that dominance and control are achieved, with the victim ultimately being given the label of "punk." This is true even in cases that prison officials may term "voluntary" or "consensual" sex. This connection between forced and voluntary homosexuality was illustrated in interviews conducted by Davis (1982), during which he found that "consensual" homosexuals tended to be subjugated heterosexuals who had been forced to engage in sex to avoid physical harm. This process, referred to as being "turned out" or "punked out," effectively redefines and labels the victim's role in prison as that of a punk, or subjugated homosexual (Tucker, 1981). Thus, the homosexual orientation and label placed upon the deviant is not one of self-choice or personal preference, but is forced upon him by more powerful members of the inmate subculture.

Labeling Theory as a Paradigm for Prison Rape Etiology

According to Lemert (1999), the deviant is a product of gradual, unconscious processes that are part of socialization, especially subcultural socialization. Lemert also asserted that the personality change that occurs from accepting and internalizing a deviant label is not always gradual but can be sudden. As Lemert (1999) states, "it must be taken into consideration that traumatic experiences often speed up changes in personality" (p. 386). This is especially true for inmates who are victims of prison gang rape in which multiple assailants attack and repeatedly rape an inmate-victim. For the victim of gang rape, entering into a sexual relationship with one man in return for protection can be an adaptive coping mechanism for survival within the prison subculture.

Lemert (1999) further states that "when a person begins to employ his deviant behavior or role . . . as a means of defense, attack, or adjustment to the overt and covert problems created by the consequent societal reaction to him, his deviance is secondary" (p. 388). In the previous example, the initial gang rape can be thought of as the source of primary deviance, whereas the deliberate decision to engage in "consensual" homosexuality with one partner essentially results in a more solidified self-identity. But this process creates a degree of cognitive dissonance within the individual, which, when resolved, tends to leave the victim more willing to engage in future homosexual conduct. Indeed, this dissonance is the crux of this adjustment process where the victim's original identity is juxtaposed against his or her newly ascribed identity, resulting in an eventual psychological metamorphosis from the point of primary deviance to that of secondary deviance through future acts of homosexuality (Festinger, 1958; Lemert, 1999). Throughout the process of coping with this dissonance, typical acute symptoms of this trauma, such as intrusive recollections and/or dreams about the assault, intense distress over stimuli that remind the victim of the assault, hypervigilance, difficulties sleeping and eating, and unexplained or exaggerated outbursts of anger, are likely to be experienced. Those who cannot successfully navigate this dissonance present with the previous symptoms on a chronic level, coupled with more serious and self-damaging psychological impairments associated with rape trauma (e.g., self-mutilation and suicide). The fact that these victims must repetitively subject themselves to subsequent victimization naturally exacerbates their likelihood for long-term psychological impairment and emotional injury.

But the victim of male prison rape will find it necessary to adjust to this new role since the sexual values of mainstream society are completely inverted within the prison subculture. The inmate perpetrator who willingly engages in predatory homosexual activity would typically be given the marginalized label of "homosexual" or "bisexual" in the broader society. Ironically, however, within the prison there is exactly the opposite effect with a corresponding increase in social status and "manhood" for the perpetrator of sexual assault. Within the prison subculture, rapists are considered masculine conquerors of effeminate punks (Weiss & Friar, 1974). The aggressor is not held as homosexual in orientation but is simply assuming a position of power within the subcultural norms of prison life. The victim of the prison sexual assault, however, suffers an injury greater than the sexual assault alone, as the victim's entire social position within the prison is effectively compromised and redefined.

Over time, many inmates who are forced into the subjugated role of punk learn that certain creature comforts can be obtained if they are willing to comply with sexual demands. Thus, many come to identify with and dress the part, to act the part, and even to rationalize their role. Indeed, this role can frequently go well beyond that of simple sexual services, extending to a relationship of complete and total servitude. Many will submit to cooking, cleaning, mending, and other activities typically held to be "feminine" by the prison subculture as well as mainstream society. Some inmates, upon acceptance of the punk label and resolution of the dissonance associated with secondary deviance, will even go so far as to involve themselves in competitive hypergamy, or the practice of achieving upward mobility through "marriage" within the prison subculture (Tucker, 1981).

While these inmates will frequently rationalize their activity as one of survival, their participation can lead them to a complete internalization of the role. With the label fully applied, many "homosexual" inmates will thus make the most of their remaining time in prison and will strive to obtain whatever securities their role can bring them. When the inmate begins to see himself as a punk and resolves his feelings of dissonance, the label becomes a source of self-identity. While the label of punk denotes lower status within the inmate pecking order, the punk learns to fulfill the role in a manner that allows a relatively trouble-free existence, so long as he continues to live the role. Thus, what was once a forced or coerced label effectively becomes a label with which the victimized inmate identifies and which he accepts as a definition of his self.

Structural Issues

Lemert (1999) maintains that role conceptions of the individual must be reinforced by the reactions of others. Many inmates have found that the institutional system simply does not care, lending tacit approval to sexual violence through a form of conscious disregard. According to Scacco (1975), "the shocking fact is that there is both overt and covert implication of officers in the attacks that take place in penal institutions" (p. 30). Likewise, Weiss and Friar (1974) assert that "prisoners are convinced that prison rape is an integral part of the prison punishment system," adding that inmates frequently contend that "prison rape is sanctioned by prison authorities. They view it as the ultimate method of control and punishment" (p. X). In this manner, members of the prison staff essentially serve to perpetuate and exacerbate the labeling process for "homosexuals" within the prison.

What is more, prison staff, both wittingly and unwittingly, serve to further marginalize the inmates labeled as punks when separating them from the general inmate population. These protective measures have a negative side effect since they can further reinforce the label punks are given. Likewise, the inmate punk is hesitant to go to prison authorities for assistance, due to further negative labels of being an informant or a snitch. Similarly, many inmates may be hesitant to discuss these issues with prison mental health staff for fear that such disclosures will be provided to authorities, ultimately making them a snitch for seeking psychological services for their difficulties. Such labels can have deadly results for the inmate. Thus, the inmate who seeks to avoid the labeling process finds himself with few avenues of escape or emotional assistance. The inmate either must fight off assaults or be cursed with one adverse label or another, if not both "punk" and "snitch." In either case, the prospects are frequently grim, with the most likely result being that the punk label is assumed by the inmate.

An inmate with the label of punk is cut off and isolated from participating in conventional activities that the dominant inmate enjoys. Once the status of punk is given, it is effectively ironclad, and the punk finds himself marginalized within the prison population, leading him to seek out others who share a similar set of circumstances (Tannenbaum, 1938). The role of punk is one that allows the "weaker" inmate within the prison power structure to exist, but through an exploitative (rather than consensual) relationship. The powerful residents within this inmate subculture have thus effectively labeled the punk, who "voluntarily" assumes the role. The superior masculine role, desired and maintained by the majority of inmates, has been denied the punk, who is now considered deviant by both inmate subculture and larger social norms.

SOURCE: Hanser, R. D. (2003). *Labeling theory as a paradigm for the etiology of prison rape: Implications for understanding and intervention.* Washington, DC: National Institute of Corrections. Retrieved from http://nicic.gov/Library/019245.

Within prison systems, there evolves a peculiar language of slang that often seems out of place in broader society. This slang has some consistency throughout the United States but does vary in specific terminology from state to state. The language often used by inmates, including slang, is also affected by their racial and gang lineage. For instance, members of the Crips or the Bloods will have certain terms that usually are only used by their groups, often as a means of identifying or denigrating the other group. Likewise, Latino gang members in the Mexican Mafia and/or the Texas Syndicate will also tend to have their own vernacular, with much of this being either Spanish phraseology or some type of unique slang. Terms like *punk* (an inmate turned out in prison), *shank* (a knife), *bug juice* (referring to psychotropic medications), and *green light* (referring to clearance to assault another inmate) are commonly known forms of slang found in most prison systems.

MAINTAINING RESPECT

In nearly every prison around the United States, one key fundamental issue is paramount among inmates: respect. This one word is perhaps the most important concept to understanding the inmate subculture. Inmate status revolves around the amount of respect given to an inmate and/or signs of disrespect exhibited toward an inmate. **Respect** is a term that represents an inmate's sense of masculine standing within the prison culture; if inmates are disrespected, they are honor-bound to avenge that disrespect or considered weak by other inmates. Any failure to preserve their sense of respect will lead to a question of the inmates' manhood and their ability to handle prison, and will lead others to think that they are perhaps weak. The fixation on respect (and fixation is an appropriate description in some prisons) is particularly pronounced among African American gang members in prison. This is also glorified in much of the contemporary gangsta music that emerged in the 1990s and continues today. This concept has become prevalent in the modern-day prison world. Because inmates have little else, their sense of self-respect and the respect that they are able to maintain from others is paramount to their own welfare and survival.

In addition, it is usually considered a sign of weakness to take help or assistance from another inmate, at least when one is new to the prison environment. Indeed, inmates will be tested when new to the prison world; they may be offered some type of item (e.g., coffee or cigarettes) or provided some type of service (getting access to the kitchen), but this is never for free or due to goodwill. Rather, inmate subculture dictates that a debt is thus owed by the *newbie* (a term for inmates who are new to a prison). New inmates may be required or coerced to do "favors" for the inmate who provided them with the good or service. For example, they might be asked to be a "mule" for the inmate or the inmate's gang. A **mule** is a person who smuggles drugs into prison for another inmate, often using his or her own body cavities to hide the drugs from prison authorities. In other cases, the inmate may be forced to become a punk for that inmate or for an entire prison gang.

THE CON AND THE NEVER-ENDING HUSTLE

Among inmates, there is the constant push and pull between the need to "con" others and, at the same time, the need to be streetwise enough to avoid being conned. Naturally, this constant and contradictory set of expectations completely impedes the ability for inmates to develop any sort of true trust; they must always remain vigilant for the potential "hustle" within the prison system. The term **hustle** refers to any action that is designed to deceive, manipulate, or take advantage of another person. Further, consider that the very term *convict* includes the word *con*, which implies that the individual cannot and should not be trusted. Thus, convicts are, stereotypically, always on the hustle, so to speak.

Inmates who are able to "get over" on others and or "skate" through work or other obligations in the prison system are considered particularly streetwise and savvy among their peers. In fact, some prison systems, such as the Texas prison system, have a term for this concept, known as "hogging." **Hogging** is a term that is used to imply that a person is using others for some type of gain or benefit, manipulating others into doing work, or fulfilling obligations on his or her behalf. When inmates are able to find some means to manipulate others into doing their dirty work, they are active in the art of the con. The process by which they encourage or manipulate a person to provide such a service is all part of the hustle.

A classic portrayal of this type of logic, though not a prison example, can be found in the story *The Adventures of Tom Sawyer* by Mark Twain. In this classic, Tom Sawyer, at one point, convinces other boys in the area that painting a fence (a chore that was assigned to young Tom) was a fun activity. So fun was it, according to Tom, that he would not allow anyone else to help him unless they paid him to do so. Ultimately, other boys paid Tom for the "opportunity" to paint the fence and join in the fun. Once several other boys had been solicited and had paid their fee for the privilege of painting this fence, Tom slipped off to spend the money that he had procured from those he had duped into doing his own assigned work. This example demonstrates all the fine points of the con, the hustle, and the act of hogging others.

THE IMPACT OF THE INMATE SUBCULTURE ON CUSTODIAL STAFF

Perhaps one of the most interesting dynamics within prison occurs between the inmates and the prison staff. This area of discussion is both complicated and paradoxical, in many respects. The paradox involved with this dynamic is that, while on the one hand, inmate subculture restricts inmates from "siding" with officers and officer culture restricts officers from befriending inmates, there is a natural give-and-take that emerges between both groups. In fact, a symbiotic relationship usually emerges between prison security staff and the inmate population. The **symbiotic prison relationship** exists between correctional staff and inmates as a means of developing mutually compliant and informal negotiations in behavior that is acceptable within the bounds of institutional security yet, at the same time, allows inmates to meet many of their basic human needs. This relationship is grounded in the reality of the day-to-day interactions that prison security staff have with inmates who live within the institution.

Because prison is a very intense environment that has a very strong psychological impact on both inmates and staff, it is only natural that this type of relationship often emerges. While the rules of the institution are often clearly written, these rules are often not pragmatic for the officers who must enforce them. For example, a rule to restrict inmates from having more than one blanket in their cell may, on the face of it, seem easy enough to enforce. However, consider the following scenarios when considering rule enforcement:

Scenario 1

A veteran officer with many years of experience may find that a given inmate, Inmate X who upholds the convict code and has respect within the institution, has the flu during the winter. The officer has access to additional blankets, and this is known among the inmates. Inmate X, in this case, tends to mind his own business and usually does as he is expected when the officer is on duty. The officer, in this case, may decide to offer Inmate X an additional blanket and would do so with no expectation that the inmate give something in return. Likewise, the inmate (as well as others watching) would know that the officer's kindness should not be taken for weakness, or no further empathy will be shown to convicts.

Scenario 2

This same veteran officer, having many years of experience, finds that Inmate Y who does not uphold the convict code and generally has average clout (at best) within the prison culture, has the flu during the winter. Inmate Y sometimes causes problems on the cell block for other officers and sometimes is sarcastic with officers. The veteran officer, in this case, would likely not give an additional blanket to Inmate Y, even if Inmate Y were to be courteous enough to ask for the additional blanket. In most cases, Inmate Y would know better than to ask, since he knows that he does not honor the convict code or work within the commonsense bounds of the symbiotic prison relationship. If he were to ask and especially if he were to push the issue, the veteran officer would inform him that "the rules are the rules" and would indicate that he needs to keep quiet and go to sick call when that option is available. Further discourse from Inmate Y would result in comments from the veteran officer that would imply that he is being a troublemaker and that he is not doing his time "like a man," leading to a loss of respect among others on the cell block. This would likely shame Inmate Y and cause him to lose status, yet, at the same time, the veteran officer would likely gain status among the inmates as being firm, streetwise, and cognizant of subcultural norms. Because he does not give in to Inmate Y, he would be perceived as strong and capable, not subject to manipulation and not an easy mark.

Journal Article Link 10.2
Read more about the impact of inmate subculture on custodial staff.

PHOTO 10.4

Sergeant Tatum talks with inmates regarding the organization of an upcoming function in a meeting hall of the prison. The means by which officers and inmates talk to each other sets the tone for respect or disrespect in the prison.

Obviously, Inmate X and Inmate Y are being given different standards of treatment. This is because implicit within the symbiotic prison relationship is the notion that "I will do my time and leave you to do your time," which is understood by veteran inmates and officers alike. Regardless of whether it is overtly stated or simply presumed, veteran officers will tend to leave convicts and/or trouble-free inmates unbothered and may, in some cases, even extend some degree of preferential treatment, within acceptable boundaries that allow them to maintain respect on the cell block. However, this does not mean that they will do so for all inmates, but they instead reserve the right to use discretion when divvying out the paltry resources available within the prison. In short, these veteran officers become effective resource and power brokers as a means of gaining compliance and creating an informal system of fairness that is understood informally among the inmates. Essentially, this type of veteran officer operates with this understanding:

I will let you do your time, but you will let me do my time—one shift at a time.

This concept is important because it creates a connection between both groups; they are both in a noxious environment, and both individuals have a role that they must uphold. Yet, at the same time, some degree of give-and-take is necessary to avoid extremes in rules that do not, ultimately, create just situations. So long as inmates allow the officer to generally do his time, one shift at a time, he will, in turn, leave them to serve their time without problems. On the other hand, if an inmate does not honor this type of understanding, he should expect no mercy or consideration from the prison security staff; the rules are the rules, and any sense of discretion will simply cease to be acted upon.

Officers who master these types of negotiations tend to gain respect from inmates and even from other officers. They may sometimes be referred to as "convict bosses" by inmates. The term **convict boss** or **convict officer** denotes an identity where the correctional officer has developed a keen understanding of convict logic and socialization and uses that knowledge to maximize control over his assigned post. This term is a form of respect that has been gained among inmates for that officer and generally comes with time, experience, sound judgment, and a cunning personality that is not easily deceived or manipulated. The officer is not perceived as weak but is instead thought to possess a good degree of common sense among inmates within the facility.

One important note should be added to this discussion. Students should keep in mind that the examples in the prior scenarios present a veteran officer with several years of experience. The use of this type of discretion by newer officers who do not have sufficient time and experience working with the inmate population will not have the same result. If a newer or younger officer attempted such discretion, he would likely be seen as a "sucker" and someone who could be easily marked for future exploitation. This person would not be perceived to understand the fine nuances in the gray areas of discretion within prison rules, norms, and mores. This person would also not likely be trusted among his peers who, generally, would expect him to stay "by the book" until he developed the level of expertise to make distinctions between blurred circumstances. This officer would likely be labeled "weak" among inmates and might even be considered an "inmate lover" by other officers. These labels should be avoided in hard-core institutions because once they are applied, it is very difficult (if not impossible) to be rid of them.

Lastly, the mannerisms that are displayed, both by inmates and officers, often reflect the type of upbringing that one has had and also tend to belie the value system from which that person operates. Within the prison, this is important because during an inmate or beginning officer's first few weeks of indoctrination to the prison experience, he or she is being "sized up" or appraised by others who observe them. Both the officers and the inmates begin to determine if the person is likely to be easily influenced and/or manipulated. This formative period whereby inmates and staff are socialized into the prison culture is important due to the influences of the prison subculture that include the inmate's subculture, the officer's subculture, and the need to master the symbiotic prison relationship between the two.

PRISONIZATION

Prisonization is the process of being socialized into the prison culture. This process occurs over time as the inmate or the correctional officer adapts to the informal rules of prison life. Unlike many other textbook authors, the author of this text thinks that it is important to emphasize that correctional officers also experience a form of prisonization that impacts their worldview and the manner in which they operate within the prison institution. Within his text on prisonization, Gillespie (2002) makes the following introductory statement:

> Prison is a context that exerts its influence upon the social relations of those who enter its domain. (p. 1)

The reason that this sentence is set off in such a conspicuous manner is because it has profound meaning and truly captures the essence of prisonization. However, for this chapter, students should understand that the influence of the prison environment extends to *all* persons who enter its domain, particularly if they do so over a prolonged period of time. Thus, prisonization impacts both inmates and staff within the facility. While the total experience will, of course, not be the same for staff as it is for inmates, it is silly to presume that staff routinely exposed to aberrant human behavior will not also be impacted by that behavior.

Prison Tour Video Link 10.3
Watch an interview with prisoners about prison culture and behavior.

Indeed, to some extent, prison is a traumatizing experience, even for those who work there. For security staff who must be involved in altercations (e.g., uses of force, the need to contain riots, observing and responding to inmate-on-inmate assaults), the impact of prisonization can be particularly traumatizing. The impact that prisonization has upon staff as well as inmates is an important consideration since it does, in part, dictate the contours of the guard subculture, which stands in competition with the inmate subculture. The prison experience can and often does impact relationships that guards have with persons who do not work in the prison setting, such as their spouses and/or children.

With respect to inmates, Gillespie (2002) found that both the individual characteristics of inmates and institutional qualities affect prisonization and misconduct. However, he found that individual-level antecedents explained prisonization better than did prison-level variables. This means that experiences of inmates prior to being imprisoned were central to determining how well inmates would adapt to the prison experience. For this text, this contention will also be extended to prison guards; their prior experiences and their individual personality development prior to employment within the prison will dictate how well they adapt to both the formal and informal exchanges that occur within.

THE GUARD SUBCULTURE

This area of discussion is both controversial and open to a great deal of debate. However, one reason for developing this text and providing a discussion on this particular topic is to provide students with a realistic and no-nonsense appraisal of the world of corrections, particularly as practiced in the prison environment. In providing a glimpse of the guard subculture (and this text does contend that a guard subculture exists), it is important to keep in mind that the specific characteristics of this subculture vary from prison system to prison system and even from prison to prison within the same state system. The reasons for this are manifold but are mostly due to the fact that, unlike inmates, guards are not forced to remain within the environment all day and night each day of the week. Rather, guards have the benefit of time away from the institution, and they can (and sometimes do) transfer from facility to facility, depending on their career formation.

Further, since guards are routinely exposed to external society (contact with family, friends, the general public, the media, etc.), they are able to mitigate many of the debilitating effects of the prison environment. Likewise, their integration into society mitigates the depth to which prison socialization will impact them personally and professionally. Thus, there is a greater degree of variability in the required adaptations of prison guards when compared to inmates. In addition, the type of institution that they find themselves working within can also impact this socialization. A guard who works at a maximum-security or violent institution will likely experience a different type of socialization than a guard assigned to a minimum-security dormitory. All of these factors can impact how the prison culture affects individual officers and the degree to which they become enmeshed into the guard subculture.

The discussion that follows is intended to address guard culture in maximum-security prisons or those institutions that have histories of violence among inmates. Larger facilities that have more challenging circumstances tend to breed the type of subculture that will be presented here. Though modern-day correctional agencies seek to circumvent and eliminate these subcultural dimensions, they nonetheless still exist in various correctional facilities.

The popular Hollywood image of prison guards is that they are brutal and uncaring and that their relationships with inmates are hostile, violent, and abusive. However, this is a very simplistic and inaccurate view of prison guards that simply makes good movies but does not reflect the reality behind why many people go to work at a prison. For many, it is a stable job available to persons in rural areas where few other jobs exist, producing a workable wage for the effort. For others, prison work may be a stepping-stone to further their career, particularly if they are interested in criminal justice employment. Indeed, the author of this text worked at Eastham Unit in Texas while attending school at a state university in the area, and this was a common practice among many students of criminal justice or criminology studies. This means that, at least in this context, many of the prison guards employed in the region actually possessed an above-average education, and they most likely possessed depth and purpose that exceeded the Hollywood stereotype.

The author of this text would like to acknowledge the work of Kelsey Kauffman (1988) in relaying the overall processes behind prison guard socialization and the development of prison guard subcultures. Like Kauffman, the author of this text encountered a similar transition experience where, over time, the aloof and distant feeling between himself and his fellow coworkers grew into a feeling of camaraderie and close connection in identity. To this day, this author considers himself, first and foremost, a prison guard at heart. However, it is Kauffman who so eloquently and correctly penned the formation and description of the guard subculture, and it is her work that will be used as the primary reference for this section.

According to Kauffman (1988), the guard subculture does not develop due to prisonization, indigenous factors, or importation of values. Rather, the culture is a product "of a complex interaction of importation, socialization, deportation, and cultural evolution" (Kauffman, 1988, p. 167). Kauffman notes that prison guards have a distinct and identifiable subculture that separates them from other professionals. The central norms of this subculture dictate how they proceed with the daily performance of their duties, such as with the example scenarios provided earlier when discussing the impact of the inmate subculture on custodial staff. In describing the prison guard subculture, Kauffman produced a basic structure that captures the main tenets behind this subculture. This same structure is presented in this text due to the author's own perception that Kauffman's description of prison guard subculture is reflective of most encountered throughout the United States. The following are the central tenets of the prison guard subculture's structure:

Audio Link 10.1
Hear more about prison guard subcultures.

1. **Always go to the aid of an officer in distress.** This is the foundation for cohesion among custodial staff. This tenet also can, in times of emergency, provide justification for violating norms within the bureaucratic system. This tenet applies to all guards, regardless of how well accepted the officer in distress may or may not be. This norm is key to officer safety and is fundamental. If an officer fails to uphold this norm, he or she will likely be ostracized from the group and will be treated as an outsider.

2. **Do not traffic drugs.** This is also considered fundamental because of the danger that it can create as inmates fight for power over the trade of these substances. In addition, the use of drugs is illegal and does not reflect well on officers who are supposed to keep such offenders behind bars. If an officer violates this tenet, it is considered justified within the subculture to inform authorities. While the guard subculture may allow members to inform authorities, most will not do so due to feelings of betrayal. However, it would not be uncommon for guards, amongst themselves, to put pressure on the officer who violates this norm through threats, intimidation, and coercion. In addition, officers will likely isolate the officer from interactions and will not invite him or her to functions outside of work. The officer will be treated as persona non grata.

3. **Do not be a snitch.** In many respects, this is a carryover from the inmate subculture. This comes in two forms of prohibition. First, officers should never tell information to inmates that they can use to get another officer in trouble. Generally speaking, officers are expected to not discuss other officers, their business, or their personal lives with inmates. The second prohibition applies to investigative authorities of the prison system. Officers are expected to stay silent and not divulge information that will "burn" another officer, particularly when the Internal Affairs Division (IAD) is investigating an incident. While it is expected that officers will not knowingly place their coworkers in legally compromising situations where they must lie for their coworkers (this would be considered abuse of the prohibition that places others in potential legal peril), it is still expected that coworkers not snitch on their fellow officer.

This tenet is perhaps one of the most difficult tenets because, in some cases, it puts officers in a position where they must lie to cover their coworkers, even when they were not directly involved. This can occur during investigations and even if officers are brought to court in a lawsuit. Officers who maintain their own behavior to comply with institutional rules still cannot be assured that they will be safe from liability because, in order to be trusted by their coworkers, they must be willing to "cover" for their fellow officer in circumstances where trouble might arise. This is regardless of whether the officer initiating the situation was or was not acting responsibly.

4. **Never disrespect another officer in front of inmates.** This tenet reflects the importance of respect and the need to maintain "face" within the prison culture. Officers who are ridiculed or made to look weak in front of inmates have their authority subject to question by inmates since inmates will talk, and the word will get around that the officer is not respected (and therefore not well supported) by his peers. This sets the officer up for potential manipulation in the future.

5. **Always support an officer who is in a dispute with another inmate.** This applies to all types of instances ranging from verbal arguments with inmates to actual physical altercations. Simply put, one's coworker is always right, and the inmate is always wrong. However, behind the scenes, officers may not get along and, in fact, may disagree on different issues related to the management of inmates. Indeed, one officer may conduct a write-up for disciplinary of an inmate while the other overtly objects when in the office out of earshot of the inmate population. The reasons for this may be many, but generally older more seasoned officers will be adept at informally addressing inmate infractions whereas junior officers will tend to rely on official processes. However, given the threat of employee discipline that exists within the system and given the need for control of the inmate population, most officers will ultimately maintain loyalty during the final stages where their official support is necessary.

6. **Do not be friends with an inmate.** This is another tenet that has complicated shades and distinctions. For veteran officers, this tenet is not much of a concern. They have already proven themselves to be reliable and/or are known to not be snitches. Further, most veteran officers are capable of enforcing the rules, regardless of their prior conversations with an inmate. However, it is not uncommon for veteran officers (and even supervisors) to have one or two inmates whom they talk with, at least on a topical level. Though they may not consider themselves friends with the inmate, they may allow that inmate some privileges and opportunities that others would not, simply because they have developed a symbiotic prison relationship with that inmate that has existed for a long period of time. In return, these inmates may do the officer small favors like reserving higher-quality food from the kitchen for that officer or even, in prisons where the subculture has truly created permeable boundaries, letting the officer know when supervisors or others are watching him or her while on duty. This allows the officer to operate his or her cell block in a more leisurely manner and, as such, the entire cell block benefits from the officer's laid-back approach.

7. **Maintain cohesion against all outside groups.** This tenet applies to members of the supervisory ranks, the outside public, the media, and even one's own family. This tenet is based on the belief that the general public does not understand the pressures placed upon officers and that the media tend to be sympathetic to the plight of the inmate, not the officer. Officers do not wish to implicate their family members and also do not want them to fear for their safety; thus details are seldom disclosed. Further, the administration is not seen as trustworthy but instead is seen as being politically driven. Administrators care only about their careers and moving up the corporate ladder and are too far removed from the rank-and-file to still understand the complexities of the officer's daily concerns. It is therefore better that officers not talk about what goes on in the institution to persons not within their ranks.

State Rankings Link 10.1
Correctional Officers and Jailers in 2009.

The above tenets, based on the work of Kauffman (1988), perhaps most clearly summarize the prison guard subculture. Again, this scheme may not be exactly as presented at all prisons, but in most larger and most older facilities, remnants of this thinking will have consensus among security staff.

As we have seen in prior chapters, numerous lawsuits emerged during the 1960s, 1970s, and 1980s, with their aftermath greatly impacting the field of corrections in the 1990s as well as the current millennium. Prison systems had to modify and adjust their operations to be considered constitutional, and this required that these systems incorporate strong incentives for organizational change among their prison staff. An emphasis on professionalism emerged throughout the nation, and, as the War on Drugs resulted in a swelling inmate population, so too swelled the number of prison guards who were hired within state prisons. Indeed, the elimination of building tender and trusty supervision schemes used in many southern states necessitated the recruiting and hiring of prison security staff. Likewise, during the 1990s, the term *prison guard* became outdated and was replaced with the official job classification of correctional officer in many state prison systems. The American Correctional Association advocated for the professionalization of correctional officers, and states began to adopt the standards set by that organization.

PROFESSIONALIZATION OF THE CORRECTIONAL OFFICER

Reference Link 10.1
Read about correctional officers' professionalization.

During the 1970s, amidst the increase in hiring that began to take place, concern arose regarding the training and competency of correctional officers. Indeed, in 1973 the National Advisory Commission on Criminal Justice Standards and Goals encouraged state legislators to take action to improve the education and training of correctional officers. Further, correctional administrators cited the need for security staff to study criminology and other disciplines that could aid in working with difficult populations. The National Advisory Commission on Criminal Justice Standards and Goals (1973) also indicated that "all new staff members should have at least 40 hours of orientation training during their first week on the job, and at least 60 hours additional training during their first year" (p. 494). This represents some of the first national-level attempts to mandate professional training and standards for correctional officers. Though these first steps were certainly headed in the correct direction, progress was slow. In 1978, it was determined that only half of all states were actually meeting the 40-hour entry-level training requirement, and even fewer were meeting the recommended 60 hours of training during the officer's first year.

The educational progress of correctional officers had not improved much during this time. Roughly 13% of the agencies did not even require a high school diploma, and the remaining 77% required only that—college was not even a remote consideration. Josi and Sechrest (1998), during a period when correctional officer standards were becoming a matter of priority, commented that "the job of correctional officer over the years has not been seen as requiring education at even the high school level, much less beyond" (p. 9). This comment was made in 1998, which was only about 14 years prior to the writing of the current text. Given the importance of this type of work, it is clear that more intensive training should be provided to correctional officers, and it is also clear that the acquisition of higher education should be encouraged.

The American Correctional Association has, throughout the past decade, generated a major push for professionalization of the field of corrections. This has resulted in a pattern of steadily increasing entry-level educational requirements consistent with a broader trend toward correctional officer professionalism. However, the term *professionalism* itself has been touted about by various correctional systems with much of an attempt to articulate

PHOTO 10.5

Brittany Naron is completing her bachelor's degree in criminal justice while employed as a correctional officer. She has also received POST-level training in corrections and completed internship experiences while working and attending college. Officer Naron was a student in one of the author's courses.

CORRECTIONS AND THE LAW 10.1

Nonlethal Force and Criminal and/or Civil Liability

Daniel Gordon and Eric Newsome, correctional officers at the Greenville Federal Correctional Institution, were indicted by a federal grand jury for violating the civil rights of an inmate and then lying to cover up the crime, Wan J. Kim, Assistant Attorney General for the Justice Department's Civil Rights Division and Acting United States Attorney Randy Massey, for the Southern District of Illinois announced today. The indictment alleges that the two defendants assaulted the inmate in his cell using fists and handcuffs to strike and injure the inmate. The grand jury charged both men with conspiracy to violate the inmate's civil rights and with filing false reports after the incident. Additionally, the grand jury charged Newsome with lying to a special agent of the United States Department of Justice's Office of the Inspector General. A trial date has been set for September 11, 2006.

Each defendant faces a maximum term of ten years in prison on each of the civil rights counts, ten years on the conspiracy count, and 20 years on each count of filing a false report. Newsome potentially faces an additional five years in prison for lying to the special agent of the Office of the Inspector General.

The indictment resulted from an investigation by Special Agent Kimberly Thomas from the Chicago Field Office of the Inspector General, Assistant U.S. Attorney Richard H. Lloyd from the United States Attorney's Office, and Trial Attorney Michael Khoury from the Civil Rights Division.

An indictment is an accusation and is not evidence of guilt. The defendants are presumed innocent and are entitled to a fair trial at which the United States has the burden of proving guilt beyond a reasonable doubt.

The Civil Rights Division is committed to the vigorous enforcement of every federal criminal civil rights statute, such as those laws that prohibit the willful use of excessive force or other acts of misconduct by law enforcement officials. The Division has compiled a significant record on criminal civil rights prosecutions in the last five years. Since FY 2001, the Division has increased the conviction rate of defendants by 30 percent.

SOURCE: U.S. Department of Justice. (2006). Two men indicted for violating the civil rights of an inmate at Greenville Federal Correctional Institution and lying to cover up the crime. Washington, DC: Author. Retrieved from http://www.justice.gov/opa/pr/2006/July/06_crt_462.html.

---

what this specifically means. While corrections is pointed in a progressive direction, there is definitely much more work to be done. Further, given the widespread budget cuts common in many states throughout the nation, money and resources for improved training and educational standards may be lacking. Yet, this is at a time when it is needed the most. How well prison systems fare in the future is yet to be seen, but one thing is clear: A failure to train and educate this workforce will only ensure that the potential corrective efforts of prison systems are minimized, and this then creates a potential risk to the public safety of society as a whole.

Audio Link 10.2
Hear about the affects of state budget cuts.

RACIAL AND CULTURAL DIVERSITY

Prior to the 1980s, prisons tended to be in rural areas and to hire staff from within the local area. The demographics of correctional staff in the United States have changed greatly from the late 1980s to the current time. This change toward a more multicultural setting is reflected in broader society and most all criminal justice agencies. This trend toward multiculturalism and diversity will only continue, both with the staff who are employed and with the inmates who are supervised.

The diversity that has developed in the correctional workforce has followed, in step, the move toward professionalization of the correctional profession. Indeed, prior to this shift, women and minorities were considered a threat to the cohesion of the correctional work group. During this time, women and minorities were often not treated fairly in the working environment, being subject to discrimination and harassment. Many African American and Latino American correctional staff reported bias in the workplace, and this was even more pronounced among women in corrections. However, the professionalization of corrections has opened the door for more fair and balanced work environments, and correctional staff have become more sensitized to different perspectives in the workplace.

Further, administrators of correctional facilities have made attempts to hire persons from diverse backgrounds since it has become increasingly clear that this is a benefit when contending with a diverse inmate population. This reflects the shift in prison operations where the primary purpose of prison is to simply respond to problematic behavior with force. Rather, the use of effective communication skills as a means of preventing problems and addressing issues in a more professional manner requires a sense of cultural competence among agencies and certainly among staff. One means of improving agency cultural competence is through the hiring of diverse workers who can relate to the inmate population's own diversity. Having officers of similar racial groups, with proficiency in various languages that are spoken in the facility, and from similar customs and beliefs enhances the ability of the agency to address problematic issues related to racial and/or cultural barriers. Thus, diverse work groups can mitigate many of the negative effects of the prison subculture as well as gangs that tend to be structured along racial lines.

FEMALE CORRECTIONAL OFFICERS

Prison Tour Video Link 10.4
Watch an interview with a female correctional officer.

The correctional field has traditionally been stereotyped as a male-dominated area of work. In later chapters, students will read more about women in the correctional field; an entire chapter is devoted to female offenders in correctional systems (Chapter 11). In fact, as with the current chapter, there is a general subculture that exists within women's prison facilities, and this subculture is separate and distinct from the male prison subculture. Likewise, the issues that confront women who work in corrections tend to be different as well. We will explore the various aspects related to both inmates and correctional workers who are female in the upcoming chapter.

Video Link 10.3
Learn more about the challenges faced by female correctional officers.

For now, it is simply important to note that women are increasingly becoming represented within the field of corrections. While women have had a long history of conducting prison work, they have typically been placed in clerical positions, teaching roles, support services, or the guarding of female offenders. They have not historically worked in direct supervision of male offenders. It was not until the late 1970s and/or early 1980s that women were routinely assigned to supervise male inmates (Pollock, 1986). The introduction of women into the security ranks has greatly impacted the organizational culture of many prison facilities and the subculture within them.

Women tend to not have the same aggressive social skills that men in prison tend to exhibit. Further, the prison environment tends to emphasize the desire to "be a man" and also denigrates the role of women as inferior. This means that women were not widely accepted among correctional officers and/or inmates. Since women have become integrated into the correctional industry, the male-oriented subculture has been weakened. The introduction of women into the security ranks, along with the inclusion of diverse minority groups, the professionalization of corrections, and the proliferation of prison gangs, has eroded the influence of the male-dominated and male-oriented convict code. While the convict code still exists and has its adherents, it is no longer considered a primary standard of behavior in many prison facilities but instead has become more of an ideal.

PROFESSIONALIZATION OF CORRECTIONAL OFFICERS AND THE CONVICT CODE

As indicated earlier in this chapter, the convict code, though still alive, is not universally found in all institutions, and newer generations of inmates do not seem to stay as loyal to the code as do prior generations. The professionalization of the corrections field has also limited the effectiveness of the convict code (Mobley, 2011). Authorities' unwillingness to allow inmates to enforce the convict code and to essentially police themselves (as with the building tender system discussed in prior chapters) has removed an important element of power from inmate groups (Mobley, 2011). The enforcement of rules through violence is no longer tacitly or implicitly permitted as it once was among prison guards (Mobley, 2011). Inmates who seek to enforce this code now get punished in some institutions and/or transferred as a means to disrupt their power.

Journal Article Link 10.3
Read about the legitimacy and authority of correctional officers.

The growing number of institutions in most state prison systems has enhanced the trend toward professionalization in corrections (Mobley, 2011). This has likewise resulted in more interest in this area of employment, particularly in 2009 and beyond where a depressed economy has made this area of employment more desirable for many of the working and middle class. Bureaucratic tendencies to centralize expanding prison systems and staff institutions with better-trained personnel stem largely from the same causes that have boosted incidences of snitching among the younger generation of inmates (Mobley, 2011). The criminalization of drug use during the 1990s and the prioritization of law enforcement resources against drugs—known as the War on Drugs—are the primary factors that have influenced prison systems to grow and professionalize, and have also aided in the slow but sure decline of the convict code within the inmate subculture (Mobley, 2011).

THE IMPACT OF GANGS UPON PRISON SUBCULTURE

Gang members are another group that tends to not adhere strictly to the tenets of the convict code (Mobley, 2011). This is particularly true among Latino and African American gangs. African American and Latino American gangs, which are the majority racial lineages represented among prison gangs, tend to view prison stints as just another part of the criminal lifestyle. As such, they have no true use for the convict code since it is their gang family who will protect them, not their reputation according to the convict code. Their alliances and their allegiance are uniformly tied to outside gangs that operate within prison walls (Mobley, 2011). So many young inner-city African American males and young Latino American males have been incarcerated that they are able to find some of their homeboys or hombres in nearly and correctional facility within their state. (Mobley, 2011) Thus, the young gang member does not, in actuality, need to trouble himself with adapting to the prison subculture (Mobley, 2011).

Video Link 10.4
Watch a video about prison gangs.

With their homeboys, gangsters comprise a distinct subculture whether on the street or in prison (Mobley, 2011). They "look out for" one another and protect each other, living in a nearly familial lifestyle. Few African American gang members speak to inmates outside of their gang "set," at least about anything of substance. Though most would claim that they do not snitch to "the man," and most would say that they just wish to do their own time, their true loyalty is to their gang family. Gang members "run with their road dogs" from "the hood" and meet up with each other in prison, forming bonds and making plans for when they reunite in their respective communities, the turf for their street gang activity (Mobley, 2011). This constant cycle, in and out of prison, creates a seamless form of support for many gang members.

THE IMPACT OF CROSS-POLLINATION: RECIPROCAL RELATIONSHIPS BETWEEN STREET GANGS AND PRISON GANGS

It is perhaps the emergence of gang life that has been the most significant development within prison subcultures throughout various state systems. In many texts on prisons and/or the world of corrections, there is a section on prison gangs. In most cases, these texts tend to present gang membership as isolated to the prison environment, with little emphasis on the notion that gang membership is permeable, found inside and outside the prison. Thus, while inmates may be gang members inside the prison, they do not simply discard membership once their sentence is served or when they are paroled out into society. Rather, their membership continues, and, in many cases, they will continue to answer to leadership who may still be locked up in prison. In other cases, they may be required to report to other leaders on the outside of the prison walls who will continue criminal work on behalf of the gang, plying their criminal trade on the streets and in broader society.

Conversely, many prison gang members were prior street gang members. Thus, an offender may engage in street gang criminal activity for a number of years, with short stints in jail being frequent. As noted earlier in this chapter, few inmates in state prison systems are locked up with long-term sentences for their first offense; rather they have typically committed several "priors" before that point, and some may have never even been detected by outside law enforcement. During their activity on the streets, these offenders will develop a reputation, particularly within their gang or their area of operation (if in an urban or a suburban setting) and will develop associations with other gang members. Once they finally do end up with a long-term sentence in a state facility, they have usually already embedded themselves within the gang structure on the outside that includes members who have been locked up inside the prison system.

In some cases, those doing state time may be the upper leadership of the street gang; these members will tend to direct prison gang activities internally while "calling the shots" for members on the outside. The term *shot caller* refers to these inmates and/or gang members who dictate what members will do within the gang hierarchy. The point to all of this is that a gang's membership does not begin or end with the prison walls. Rather, the prison walls are simply a feature that modern-day gangs must contend with—an obstacle that increases the overhead to conducting criminal enterprise.

Because gang membership is porous in nature, social researchers can only vaguely determine likely gang growth both inside the prison and outside the prison. In 1998, there were an estimated 780,000 gang members across the nation. A large proportion of these gang members also served time behind bars at one point or another throughout their criminal career. In fact, in some prison systems, such as the Texas prison system, gangs nearly controlled the prison system and even controlled many of the staff that worked within the system through various forms of friendships or occasional intimidation, all designed to manipulate staff within the organization.

Thus, prison gangs in some state systems were both persuasive and very powerful Potential recruits for existing prison gangs enter prison with natural feelings of anxiety and quickly learn the value of having some form of affiliation. Indeed, inmates without the protection of affiliation are likely to be the target of other inmates who are members of a gang. Likewise, this affiliation tends to be based along racial allegiances. In fact, most prison gang membership is strictly defined by the race of the member.

Traditional prison gangs include, but are not limited to, the Aryan Brotherhood, the Mexican Mafia, La Nuestra Familia, Black Guerilla Family, Texas Syndicate, and the Mexikanemi. Further, a confluence of street gangs has permeated several prison systems, particularly in California, Illinois, New York, Texas, and Florida. Common street gangs found in prisons are the Crips and the Bloods. In the Chicago area, most street gangs are aligned with either the Folk Nation or the People Nation. The Folks include notorious street gangs such as the Gangster Disciples and the Two Sixers (Fleisher & Rison, 1999). The People include groups such as the Latin Kings and the Vice Lords (Fleisher & Rison, 1999). Historically speaking, the main distinction between prison gangs and street gangs has been the internal structure and the leadership style of the gang (Fleisher & Rison, 1999). However, over time this distinction has become so blurred as to be meaningless in the offender world (Fleisher & Rison, 1999). In the correctional environment of today, the Gangster Disciples and Latin Kings, classic street gangs, are just as influential and powerful as are the Mexican Mafia and the Texas Syndicate (Fleisher & Rison, 1999). More telling is the fact that the Mexican Mafia, the Aryan Brotherhood, and even emerging local groups such as the Barrio Aztecas have become just as formidable in their own respective ethnic and/or culturally based neighborhoods or regions. Thus, both types of gangs have become "cross-pollinated" and are fully operational in both sectors of the criminal world. Indeed, it is sometimes common for leaders of the gang to be incarcerated, all the while giving orders for various actions to members who are still outside the prison operating within the community. For this text, this is effectively **gang cross-pollination**, when the gang has developed such power and influence as to be equally effective regardless of whether its leadership is inside or outside of the prison walls.

When discussing gangs that are cross-pollinated, the term **security threat group (STG)** will be used to describe a gang that possesses the following high-functioning group and organizational characteristics:

1. Prison and street affiliation is based on race, ethnicity, geography, ideology, or any combination of these or other similar factors (Fleisher, 2008, p. 356).

2. Members seek protection from other gang members inside and outside the prison, as well as insulation from law enforcement detection (use of safe houses when wanted).

Audio Link 10.3
Learn more about the prison violence committed by the Aryan Brotherhood.

3. Members will mutually take care of one another's family members, at least minimally, while the member is locked up since this is an expected overhead cost in the organization.

4. The group's mission integrates an economic objective, and uses some form of illicit industry such as drug trafficking to fulfill the economic necessities to carry forward other stated objectives (Fleisher, 2008). The use of violence or the threat of violence is a common tool in meeting these economic objectives.

Regardless of whether these groups are cross-pollinated to the point of being a disruptive offender group, other characteristics common to prison gangs go beyond racial lines of membership. These characteristics are common to most any gang within jail and/or prison, though not necessarily common to those based primarily on the street. First, prison gangs tend to have highly formal rules and a written constitution. The constitution and the rules are adhered to by all members who value their affiliation, and sanctions are taken against those who violate the rules. Second, prison gangs tend to be structured along a semimilitary organizational scheme. Thus, authority and responsibility are very clearly defined within these groups. Third, membership in a prison gang is usually for life. This has often been referred to, as noted above, as *blood in—blood out* among the popular subculture. This lifelong affiliation is also one of the root causes of parolees continuing their affiliation beyond the prison walls, and this lifelong membership is enforced against those who attempt to exit the prison gang. Thus, when gang members leave the prison environment, they are expected to perform various "favors" for the members who are still incarcerated. Lastly, as members circulate in and out of prison, they are involved in gang activities both inside and outside of the penal institution. Thus, the criminal enterprise continues to be an active business, and prison simply becomes part of the overhead involved in running that business.

Audio Link 10.4
Listen to a clip about prison gangs.

MAJOR PRISON GANGS IN THE UNITED STATES

During the 1950s and 1960s there was a substantial amount of racial and ethnic bias in prisons. This was true in most all state prison systems, but was particularly pronounced in the southern United States and in the state of California. During the late 1950s, a Chicano gang formed known as the Mexican Mafia (National Gang Intelligence Center, 2009). This gang was drawn from street gang members in various neighborhoods of Los Angeles and, while in San Quentin, began to exercise power over the gambling rackets within that prison. Other gangs soon began to form as a means of opposing the Mexican Mafia. Among the earliest to form were the Black Guerilla Family, the Aryan Brotherhood, La Nuestra Familia, and the Texas Syndicate.

This section provides a brief overview of some of the major prison gangs found throughout the nation. As accurately as possible, these gangs are presented in a manner that is historically correct, capturing the basic feeling of the time and context during their development (see Table 10.1). Because the federal government produces accurate resources and data on justice-related topics, information regarding most of these gangs has been obtained from the National Gang Intelligence Center, a think tank of the Department of Justice. Much of the information presented has been obtained from a recent document titled the *National Gang Threat Assessment 2009*. The following few pages provide an overview of 13 of the most prevalent prison gangs in the United States. Though not fully inclusive, this is a comprehensive listing of the major prison gangs that exist today. The history of each gang, criminal activity, and other relevant information is provided. The gangs are presented in the order in which they were formed, starting with the late 1950s and continuing through the early 1990s:

The **Mexican Mafia** prison gang, also known as La Eme (Spanish for the letter *M*), was formed in the late 1950s within the California Department of Corrections. It is loosely structured and has strict rules that must be followed by the 200 members. Most members are Mexican American males who previously belonged to a southern California street gang. The Mexican Mafia is primarily active in the southwestern and Pacific regions of the United States, but its power base is in California. The gang's main source of income is extorting drug distributors outside prison and distributing methamphetamine, cocaine, heroin, and marijuana within prison systems and on the streets. Some members have direct links to Mexican drug traffickers outside of the prison walls. The Mexican Mafia also is involved in other criminal activities, including controlling gambling and homosexual prostitution in prison.

Reference Link 10.2
Read about the proliferation of gangs in the U. S. and their impact on prisons.

TECHNOLOGY AND EQUIPMENT 10.1

Using Scanners to Detect Contraband Brought Into and Out of Prison Facilities

This was no ordinary telephone call. A Baltimore man allegedly used a cell phone to arrange a murder, offering to pay $2,500 for the crime, according to Maryland federal prosecutors. Moreover, the man should not have had a cell phone—he was in the Baltimore City Jail on the evening he allegedly placed the fateful call. Indeed, according to the federal indictment, he was being held on a murder charge and made the call to arrange the killing of a witness to the original murder. Cell phones and the electric chargers that power them are just the latest form of contraband that correctional institutions grapple with daily. Corrections officers also face attempts to smuggle drugs and weapons into the facilities, as well as inmates who fashion weapons out of ordinary materials. To help correctional managers detect contraband and run safer institutions, the National Institute of Justice (NIJ) is sponsoring several research projects and pilot programs, based on recommendations from expert practitioners, to test an array of technologies. Scanning and detection devices can help spot everything, from a cell phone to a knife.

Testing Airport Scanners in Prisons

One NIJ-sponsored pilot program that enjoyed success used a millimeter wave imaging system to scan visitors at the Graterford State Correctional Institution in Pennsylvania. The imaging system can look through clothing to detect weapons, cell phones, and nonmetallic objects. Currently used by the Transportation Security Administration (TSA) to scan passengers at an increasing number of airports, the system was tested and evaluated at Graterford, a maximum-security facility that houses about 3,100 inmates outside Philadelphia.

A person steps into a "portal," which looks like a booth. The system beams radio energy in the millimeter wave spectrum from antennas that rotate around the person. The energy is reflected, and scanners produce an image of the body and any objects hidden beneath the clothing. The system, called the SafeView, is manufactured by L-3 Communications. According to the manufacturer, the system produces less radiation than a cell phone transmission. Millimeter wave systems have been controversial because they present images of bodies so well—similar to nude photographs—that some people consider the systems intrusive. The TSA has taken various measures, such as immediately deleting the images, to win acceptance. This technology has much the same capabilities

PHOTO 10.6

This woman is being checked for contraband prior to entering a secure area of a prison institution.

and limitations as an alternative approach—backscatter X-ray systems—used for the same purpose.

The pilot project at Graterford involved scanning visitors. Thomas Dohman, Graterford's intelligence captain, said the system was used for more than a year, and officials believe it was successful. "It's very effective at discouraging smuggling," he said. To address privacy concerns, prison officials used a privacy screen that cut out the most explicit views but still allowed the system to signal if something was hidden beneath a person's clothing. Graterford officials also set up laptop computers when they introduced the system so visitors could see for themselves how the images looked. "The public accepted it," Dohman said.

The Graterford system completed between 400 and 600 scans in a typical week, and each scan was completed in seconds. "It really didn't slow down the [screening] process," Dohman said. The manufacturer made the system available for free during the testing period, and the NIJ coordinated the pilot project because it provided an opportunity to do an operational evaluation in a correctional environment that involved a commercially available system.

Overall, the millimeter wave system improved the contraband situation at Graterford, Dohman said. On several occasions, the system detected cell phones. Yet Dohman believes the system's greatest success is in its deterrent effect. According to Dohman, people who knew about the system did not even try to smuggle something through it. "It's infrequent that people had anything concealed," he said.

Although this technology detects contraband hidden under clothing, it does not detect contraband secreted in body cavities. To address this need, the NIJ is currently funding the development of a system that can identify contraband hidden in body cavities. The system, which is based on electric field tomography (EFT), is being developed by Quantum Magnetics Inc.

Portable Scanner Spots Improvised Prison Weapons Made by Inmates

Although millimeter wave portals can identify objects hidden under clothing, they are large, fixed, and relatively expensive. Corrections officials have told the NIJ that they would also like to be able to use inexpensive, handheld devices. These would give corrections officials more flexibility by allowing them to screen people at entrances and to perform spot checks anywhere. The NIJ is sponsoring the development of a handheld device that can detect everything from cell phones to Plexiglas. Many correctional institutions have reported that while their metal detection systems work well, the institutions face constant challenges in detecting nonmetallic objects, such as improvised weapons made of wood or hard plastics.

The NIJ awarded a grant to Luna Innovations Inc. to develop a new device that would spot contraband items regardless of what materials are used. The Weapons and Non-Permitted Devices Detector, or WANDD, is a handheld system similar to handheld metal detectors. The WANDD scans fully clothed people for contraband hidden under their clothing. Although designed specifically to spot nonmetallic contraband, it detects metal as well.

Unlike millimeter wave systems that use radio energy, the WANDD uses sound waves—akin to sonar—to detect objects. The WANDD includes an ultrasonic wave transmitter and an acoustic receiver. The device "listens" to the sound waves that bounce back to it, detecting hidden objects under clothing. Engineers at Luna tested the prototype at the Virginia Peninsula Regional Jail in Williamsburg. They found that the device works well with various clothing fabrics, including standard jumpsuits. The WANDD prototype successfully detected objects such as cell phones, plastic knives, guns, and credit cards.

SOURCE: Bulman, P. (2009). *Using technology to make prisons and jails safer*. Washington, DC: National Institute of Justice.

The **Black Guerrilla Family** (BGF), originally called Black Family or Black Vanguard, is a prison gang founded in San Quentin State Prison, California, in 1966. The gang is highly organized along paramilitary lines, with a supreme leader and central committee. The BGF has an established national charter, code of ethics, and oath of allegiance (see Figure 10.1). BGF members operate primarily in California and Maryland. The gang has 100 to 300 members, most of whom are African American males. A primary source of income for gang members is cocaine and marijuana distribution. Currently, BGF members obtain such drugs primarily from Nuestra Familia/Norteños members or from local Mexican traffickers. BGF members are involved in other criminal activities, including auto theft, burglary, drive-by shootings, and homicide.

The **Aryan Brotherhood** (AB; see Figure 10.2) was originally formed in San Quentin in 1967. The AB is highly structured with two factions— one in the California Department of Corrections and the other in the Federal Bureau of Prisons. Most members are Caucasian males, and the gang is active primarily in the southwestern and Pacific regions. Its main source of income is the distribution of cocaine, heroin, marijuana, and methamphetamine within prison systems and on the streets. Some AB members have business relationships with Mexican drug traffickers who smuggle illegal drugs into California for AB distribution. The AB is notoriously violent and is often involved in murder for hire. Although the gang has been historically linked to the California-based prison gang Mexican Mafia (La Eme), tension between AB and La Eme is increasingly evident, as seen in recent fights between Caucasians and Hispanics within CDC.

FIGURE 10.1   Sample Black Guerrilla Family (BGF) Code

BG Term	Meaning
Annette Brooks	Aryan Brotherhood
Bobby G. Foster	BGF
Central High	mainline
Compton	hole or segregation
D.C.	decision or deciding
Kiss	marked for death
Mary Mitchell	Mexican Mafia
Nelson Franklin	Nuestra Familia
Paula	police officer
Record shop	hospital
Salt	hacksaw
Sammy Davis, Jr.	bootlicking
Supermarket	killed or dead

FIGURE 10.2 Symbol of the Aryan Brotherhood

The **Crips** are a collection of structured and unstructured gangs that have adopted a common gang culture. The Crips emerged as a major gang presence during the early 1970s. Crips membership is estimated at 30,000 to 35,000; most members are African American males from the Los Angeles metropolitan area. Large, national-level Crips gangs include 107 Hoover Crips, Insane Gangster Crips, and Rolling 60s Crips. The Crips operate in 221 cities in 41 states and can be found in several state prison systems. The main source of income for the Crips is the street-level distribution of powder cocaine, crack cocaine, marijuana, and PCP. This gang is also involved in other criminal activity such as assault, auto theft, burglary, and homicide.

The **Bloods** are an association of structured and unstructured gangs that have adopted a single-gang culture. The original Bloods were formed in the early 1970s to provide protection from the Crips street gang in Los Angeles, California. Large, national-level Bloods gangs include Bounty Hunter Bloods and Crenshaw Mafia Gangsters. Bloods membership is estimated to be 7,000 to 30,000 nationwide; most members are African American males. Bloods gangs are active in 123 cities in 33 states, and they can be found in several state prison systems. The main source of income for Bloods gangs is street-level distribution of cocaine and marijuana. The gangs also are involved in other criminal activity including assault, auto theft, burglary, carjacking, drive-by shootings, extortion, homicide, identity fraud, and robbery.

Ñeta is a prison gang that was established in Puerto Rico in the early 1970s and spread to the United States. Ñeta is one of the largest and most violent prison gangs, with about 7,000 members in Puerto Rico and 5,000 in the United States. Ñeta chapters in Puerto Rico exist exclusively inside prisons; once members are released from prison, they are no longer considered part of the gang. In the United States, Ñeta chapters exist inside and outside prisons in 36 cities in nine states, primarily in the Northeast. The gang's main source of income is retail distribution of powder and crack cocaine, heroin, marijuana, and, to a lesser extent, LSD, MDMA, methamphetamine, and PCP. Ñeta members commit assault, auto theft, burglary, drive-by shootings, extortion, home invasion, money laundering, robbery, weapons and explosives trafficking, and witness intimidation.

The **Texas Syndicate** originated in Folsom Prison during the early 1970s. The Texas Syndicate was formed in response to other prison gangs in the California Department of Corrections, such as the Mexican Mafia and Aryan Brotherhood, which were attempting to prey on native Texas inmates. This gang is composed of predominantly Mexican American inmates in the Texas Department of Criminal Justice (TDCJ). Though this gang has a rule to only accept members who are Latino, it does accept Caucasians into its ranks. The Texas Syndicate has a formal organizational structure and a set of written rules for its members. Since the time of its formation—largely as a means of protection for Texas inmates in the California Department of Corrections—the Texas Syndicate has grown considerably, particularly in Texas.

FIGURE 10.3 Symbol of the Texas Syndicate

The **Mexikanemi** prison gang (also known as Texas Mexican Mafia or Emi) was formed in the early 1980s within the TDCJ. The gang is highly structured and is estimated to have 2,000 members, most of whom are Mexican nationals or Mexican American males living in Texas at the time of incarceration. Mexikanemi poses a significant drug trafficking threat to communities in the southwestern United States, particularly in Texas. Gang members reportedly traffic multikilogram quantities of powder cocaine, heroin, and methamphetamine; multiton quantities of marijuana; and thousand-tablet quantities of MDMA from Mexico into the United States for distribution inside and outside prison.

The **Nazi Low Riders (NLR)** evolved in the California Youth Authority, the state agency responsible for the incarceration and parole supervision of juvenile and young adult offenders, in the late 1970s or early 1980s as a gang for White inmates. As prison officials successfully suppressed Aryan Brotherhood activities, the Brotherhood appealed to young incarcerated skinheads, the NLR in particular, to act as middlemen for their criminal operations, allowing the Aryan Brotherhood to keep control of criminal undertakings while adult members were serving time in administrative segregation. Through their connections to the Aryan Brotherhood, the NLR was able to become the principal gang within the Youth Authority and eventually to move into penitentiaries throughout California and across the West Coast. The NLR maintains strong ties to the Aryan Brotherhood and, like the older gang, has become a source of violence and criminal activity in prison. The Aryan Brotherhood still maintains a strong presence in the nation's prison systems, albeit less active, while NLR has also become a major force, viewing itself as superior to all other White gangs and deferring only to the Aryan Brotherhood. Both gangs engage in drug trafficking, extortion, and attacks on inmates and corrections staff.

Barrio Azteca emerged in 1986 in the Coffield Unit of TDCJ by five street gang members from El Paso, Texas. This gang tends to recruit from prior street gang members and is most active in the southwestern region, primarily in correctional facilities in Texas and on the streets of southwestern Texas and southeastern New Mexico. The gang is highly structured and has an estimated membership of 2,000. Most members are Mexican national or Mexican American males. The gang's main source of income is smuggling heroin, powder cocaine, and marijuana from Mexico into the United States for distribution both inside and outside prisons. Barrio Azteca members also are involved in alien smuggling, arson, assault, auto theft, burglary, extortion, intimidation, kidnapping, robbery, and weapons violations.

Hermanos de Pistoleros Latinos (HPL) is a Hispanic prison gang formed in the TDCJ in the late 1980s. It operates in most prisons and on the streets in many communities in Texas, particularly Laredo. HPL is also active in several cities in Mexico, and its largest contingent in that country is in Nuevo Laredo. The gang is structured and is estimated to have 1,000 members. Members maintain close ties to several Mexican drug trafficking organizations and are involved in trafficking quantities of cocaine and marijuana from Mexico into the United States for distribution.

Tango Blast is one of largest prison/street criminal gangs operating in Texas. Tango Blast's criminal activities include drug trafficking, extortion, kidnapping, sexual assault, and murder. In the late 1990s, Hispanic men incarcerated in federal, state, and local prisons founded Tango Blast for personal protection against violence from traditional prison gangs such as the Aryan Brotherhood, Texas Syndicate, and Texas Mexican Mafia. Tango Blast originally had four city-based chapters in Houston, Austin, Dallas, and Fort Worth. These founding four chapters are collectively known as Puro Tango Blast or the Four Horsemen. From the original four chapters, former Texas inmates established new chapters in El Paso, San Antonio, Corpus Christi, and the Rio Grande Valley. In June 2008 the Houston Police Department estimated that more than 14,000 Tango Blast members were incarcerated in Texas. Tango Blast is difficult to monitor. The gang does not conform to either traditional prison/street gang hierarchical organization or gang rules. Tango Blast is laterally organized, and leaders are elected sporadically to represent the gang in prisons and to lead street gang cells. The significance of Tango Blast is exemplified by corrections officials reporting that rival traditional prison gangs are now forming alliances to defend themselves against Tango Blast's growing power.

United Blood Nation is a universal term that is used to identify both West Coast Bloods and United Blood Nation (UBN). The UBN started in 1993 in Rikers Island GMDC (George Mochen Detention Center) to form protection from the threat posed by Latin Kings and Ñetas, who dominated the prison. While these groups are traditionally distinct entities, both identify themselves by "Blood," often making it hard for law enforcement to distinguish between them. The UBN is a loose

FIGURE 10.4   Constitution of the Mexikanemi

1. Membership is for life ("blood in, blood out").

2. Every member must be prepared to sacrifice his life or take a life at any time.

3. To achieve discipline within the Mexikanemi brotherhood, every member shall strive to overcome his weakness.

4. Members must never let the Mexikanemi down.

5. The sponsoring member is totally responsible for the behavior of a new recruit. If the new recruit turns out to be a traitor, it is the sponsoring member's responsibility to eliminate the recruit.

6. When insulted by a stranger or group, all members of the Mexikanemi will unite to destroy the person or other group completely.

7. Members must always maintain a high level of integrity.

8. Members must never relate Mexikanemi business to others.

9. Every member has the right to express opinions, ideas, contradictions, and constructive criticism.

10. Every member has the right to organize, educate, arm, and defend the Mexikanemi.

11. Every member has the right to wear tattoo of the Mexikanemi symbol.

12. The Mexikanemi is a criminal organization and therefore will participate in all activities of criminal interest for monetary benefits.

SOURCE: Orlando-Morningstar, D. (1997). Prison gangs. Special Needs Offenders Bulletin. Washington, DC: Federal Judicial Center.

TABLE 10.1 Timeline History of Prison Gang Development in the United States

Year formed	Jurisdiction	Name of gang
1950	Washington	Gypsy Jokers
1957	California	Mexican Mafia
1958	California	Texas syndicate
1965	California	La Nuestra Familia
1966	California	Black Guerrilla Family
1967	California	Aryan Brotherhood
mid 1970s	Arizona	Arizona Aryan Brotherhood
1977	Arizona	Arizona Old Mexican Mafia
1980	New Mexico	New Mexico syndicate
early 1980s	Texas	Aryan Brotherhood of Taxes
early 1980s	Texas	Texas Mafia
mid 1980s	California	Bulldogs
1984	Arizona	Arizona's New Mexican Mafia
1984	Texas	Mexikanemi
1984	Texas	Mandingo Warriors
1985	Federal system	Dirty White Boys
1985	California	415's
1990	Connecticut	Los Solidos

SOURCE: Orlando-Morningstar, D. (1999). *Prison gangs*. Washington, DC: Federal Judicial Center.

confederation of street gangs, or sets, that once were predominantly African American. Membership is estimated to be between 7,000 and 15,000 along the U.S. eastern corridor. The UBN derives its income from street-level distribution of cocaine, heroin, and marijuana; robbery; auto theft; and smuggling drugs to prison inmates.

Gang Management in Corrections

Gang management requires a comprehensive policy that specifies legal precedents, procedures, and guidelines, including the verification of gang members. Over the years, most state systems have developed gang intelligence units and have trained correctional staff on gangs and gang activity. In modern times, state and federal corrections refer to gangs as security threat groups, or STGs, as noted above. Students may notice that, in the prior subsection, most of the 13 gangs listed have links to outside society and seek one another's protection while engaged in criminal activities that have an economic objective. This means that these gangs are all STGs because they operate inside and outside the prison and possess all the other characteristics discussed in previous subsections of this chapter.

When combating STGs in prison, the technical aspects, such as the paper classification and procedures needed to investigate gang members, are fairly straightforward. However, the human element is what makes the fight against STGs much more difficult. In correctional facilities that do not emphasize professionalism or encourage open communication among security staff, and do have a strong underlying prison subculture (both inmate and correctional officer), STGs are likely to proliferate. A lack of professionalism, stunted communication, and powerful subcultural norms that are counter to the prison administration serve as the breeding ground for gang development. Further, when selecting correctional staff to serve on gang task forces, the prison administrator must exercise care and remain vigilant. In some cases, an inmate's sibling, cousin, girlfriend, former wives, and companions may be employed within the facility. This is, of course, a common tactic used by gangs who seek to infiltrate the correctional system.

Gang Control, Management, and Administrative Segregation

In addition to the physical security of the facility, there are many psychological aspects of controlling gang activity. For instance, the immediate tendency of corrections officials may be to restrict privileges for gang-related inmates. But, as Fleisher (2008) notes, withdrawing incentives or placing these inmates in long-term states of restricted movement can have financial and social consequences for the prison facility. For instance, in Texas, many gang-related inmates are kept in administrative segregation. Administrative segregation is a security status that is intended to keep the assigned inmate from having contact with the general population. It is not punitive in nature, like solitary confinement. This custody status is intended to protect the general population from the inmate in segregation. However, this form of custody is very expensive.

Further, there is a tendency for prison systems that use administrative segregation to house inmates of the same gang in the same area. This prevents them from coming into contact with enemy gang members yet cuts costs that would ensue if they were kept on different cell blocks or dormitories. But doing this replicates the street gang culture as they are all together but with geographic isolation (i.e., one neighborhood, one gang) where there is one cell block and one gang. In other words, this can build solidarity for the group. This can also lead to problematic behaviors where inmates exercise power (through the gang rank structure) over a cell block or dormitory, encouraging security to work with those in power to maintain compliance over the other lower-ranking inmates of that gang. Naturally, this should be avoided because it validates the gang's power and undermines the security staff. Fleisher (2008) notes that other problematic behaviors can also emerge. For instance, gangs may attempt to run cell blocks, "sell" cells on the cell block, or "own" territory on the recreation yard. This simply reinforces their feeling that they have power over the institution. This should be avoided.

Gang Management Data

The modern prison facility has improved surveillance, layout, and intelligence-gathering strategies that have worked well to thwart the activities of gang members. One key aspect of a comprehensive gang intelligence program is the use of data that is continuously validated. Fleisher (2008) notes that prison administrators should do the following:

1. Develop strong nationwide ties to gang units in police departments.

2. Participate in national correctional conferences on gang intelligence.

3. Maintain good relations with fellow STG management persons in other agencies.

4. Establish strong contact with local police agencies and the state's attorney's office.

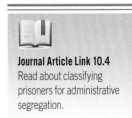

Journal Article Link 10.4
Read about classifying prisoners for administrative segregation.

It is important to point out that gang data are of no assistance if they are not well organized and carefully analyzed. The modern intelligence team should be well trained on databases and should have the ability to customize databases for various projects.

The first phase in developing an effective program is to initiate an effective intelligence and communications network that would accurately indicate how many inmates have gang affiliations, which gangs they are affiliated with, and their status within those gangs. The database should also provide information on which facilities gang members are in and their institutional classification. Further, all of this information can provide the department with data on the proliferation or concentration of any group, so that it can forecast where or when a buildup of a particular group could cause problems. Strategic transfers of inmates can assist the agency in controlling the establishment of gang power bases and can ensure that some individuals do not have undue influence over others.

In addition, good gang intelligence programs will have developed a digitized imaging program that offers numerous advantages for identifying gang members and their status, behavior, and control. The complete history and personal data of gang members can be recorded, and digitized images (front and side) can be taken. Digitized images should also be made of any tattoos, distinguishing marks, or scars. These images are usually clearer than those obtained by film, and this negates the need for taking additional photographs, or for film storage or development. The digitized images can also be entered into a computer and downloaded into the database. This type of process tends to take about two minutes per individual and can produce a permanent record that can be promptly updated as circumstances require.

Through this process, each facility is able to update records quickly. Changes are simultaneously downloaded to a central repository so the department has expedient, accurate information regarding new gang members or changes in the status of current members. An advantage of this system is that it is possible to conduct single and multiple searches on the basis of any data in the file. For instance, if one inmate gang member reports being attacked by another inmate but could not identify the inmate by name, a timely departmental search could be accomplished based on any information the victim could give. If the victim stated that the attacker was about 5 feet tall, with a moustache, and that he had a tattoo of a dragon on his right hand, a computerized departmental search could be expeditiously conducted. Every registered person in the entire gang network who fit that description would be displayed on the screen in a photo array—constituting a virtual "computerized lineup." These types of screens can also be altered to focus on points of interest, by enlarging images of areas in which there are scars, tattoos, or other distinguishing marks.

Lastly, prison staff should, of course, be appropriately trained on the use of these types of tools, and they should also be trained in gang recognition skills. This training also requires a good deal of ethics training since gang populations can be very manipulative. Ensuring that staff are well trained and confident will help the institution run well and will keep security at its peak. This will also curb gangs from growing and/or exerting undue pressure upon others. All in all, staff training will augment the policies and tools that agencies utilize. In fact, staff training will be the prime factor that determines whether policies and/or technical tools are utilized effectively.

CONCLUSION

This chapter has provided students with a glimpse of the "behind the scenes" aspects of the prison environment. The notion of a prison subculture, complete with norms and standards that are counter to those of the outside world, has been presented to give students an idea of the values and norms that impact the day-to-day operation of many prisons. There has been substantial debate as to whether this informal prison subculture is the product of adjustments and adaptations to prison life or if this subculture is more the product of norms brought in from the outside world—from the street life.

The informal subculture within prisons tends to be largely driven by inmates. The convict code has typically been presented as the "gold standard" of behavior among inmates. This code represents perceptions of eras that are now out of date and are not in sync with the modern era. The effects of professionalism within the correctional officer ranks, the diversity of correctional staff, and the difference in this generation of inmates all have led to the near demise of the honor-bound convict code. Within the informal subculture, it is clear that correctional staff also have some informal standards and expectations. The work of Kauffman (1988) has provided very good insight on the behavior of correctional staff who work in prisons.

The norms associated with both the subculture of prison staff and the convict code of inmates are in a state of flux and decline. The subculture among correctional staff has been impacted by the emphasis on professionalism and the diversification in staff recruiting. These two aspects related to employees in the system have, over time, changed the face of corrections and have also undermined the tenets of the prison subculture. What has resulted is a state of ambiguity where inmates often pay lip service to tenets of respectable behavior (according to prison logic) but often break the rules on this behavior when put under pressure. Simply put, there is truly no honor among thieves.

Gangs have emerged as a major force in state prison systems. The first recorded prison gangs began to emerge in the late 1950s and the early 1960s, primarily in the California prison system. Since that time, gangs have proliferated around the United States and have exerted substantial influence over the prison subculture and even dynamics in prison operations. In this chapter, we have covered 13 of the larger and more well-known prison gangs in the nation. From the coverage of these gangs, it is clear that they have networks that extend beyond the prison walls, and this, in turn, increases their power and influence within the prison walls. Indeed, when offenders in a street gang enter prison, they do not simply forfeit their membership in their gang. Likewise, when these inmates leave prison, they again do not simply leave their gang obligations behind. Rather, gangs have become porous groups that exist inside and outside the prison walls.

The methods used to control gang activity inside prisons have been discussed. Prison gang intelligence units must have effective means of investigating potential membership and collecting data on gang members. Utilizing electronic equipment for identification, storage, and retrieval is key to maintaining an effective antigang strategy. The ability to share data with other agencies enhances public safety within the region surrounding the prison and also improves security within. The truth of this issue is that, whether we like it or not, the prison has an impact on outside society, due to the manner in which the inmate population cycles into and out of prison. Thus, it is clear that prisons impact society, both in terms of keeping dangerous persons locked up and in terms of their learned behavior once they are released back into society.

END-OF-CHAPTER DISCUSSION QUESTIONS

1. How is the prison subculture for inmates and correctional officers often interrelated?

2. Compare importation theory with exportation theory and explain which one you believe is the stronger influence on prison subculture.

3. Explain some of the common outlooks and views of prison subculture. How does this contrast with the conventional logic of outside society?

4. How have professionalization and the diversification of correctional staff impacted the prison subculture?

5. Explain what is meant by "hyena logic" among inmates and provide some examples of how this impacts group behavior in some prison facilities.

6. Identify at least three prison gangs and explain how they have impacted corrections in their respective jurisdictions. Note their allies and adversaries in the prison and explain how this impacts prison operations.

7. Explain what prison systems can or should do to control gang problems that occur in their facilities.

8. Within the prison subculture, explain how labeling theory is related to prison rape.

KEY TERMS

Blood in—blood out	Importation theory	Respect
Convict boss/officer	Mule	Snitch
Convict code	Pains of imprisonment	Symbiotic prison relationship
Hogging	Prisonization	
Hustle	Punk	

APPLIED EXERCISE 10.1

You are the assistant warden of a large medium-security facility within a state prison system in the southeastern United States. Your facility has a disproportionate number of African American inmates (common in prison systems throughout the United States) and a disproportionate number of men, particularly Caucasian male officers.

In response to concerns from the Grievance Department regarding inmate allegations of racism from officers inside the facility, the warden has asked you to develop a comprehensive diversity training program for the security staff in your facility. Currently, your facility holds an annual one-day "refresher" course for staff. This course is actually only a four-hour block of instruction provided at the state training facility where employees around the state complete their annual in-service training to update their knowledge and skills. Everyone throughout the system knows that the four-hour block of instruction is not taken seriously and is simply offered as a means of documenting that the state has made the training available.

Your warden desires to change this within your facility for two reasons. First, it is just a good and ethical practice to take diversity seriously. Second, the dollars used from grievances and other allegations are getting costly enough to make diversity training a fiscally sound alternative to potential litigation.

With this in mind, you are given the following guiding information regarding the training program that you are to implement:

1. The program should be 1.5 days in length, given once annually.

2. The program should address numerous areas of concern, including race, gender, age, and religion.

Students should keep in mind that workplace diversity has two components: First it involves fair treatment and the removal of barriers, and second it addresses past imbalances through the implementation of special measures to accelerate the achievement of a representative workforce. Further, workplace diversity recognizes and utilizes the diversity available in the workplace and the community it serves.

Workplace diversity should be viewed as a means to attaining the organizational objectives of the correctional facility—not as an end in itself. The link between the agency objectives and the day-to-day processes that occur among staff in the facility is crucial to the success of workplace diversity initiatives.

For this assignment, outline the content that you would recommend for the 1.5-day training session and explain your rationale behind your recommendation. Also, explain how you will "sell" these ideas to prison staff to ensure that they take the training seriously. Lastly, explain how this training, if successful, can improve security and safety in the institution. Your submission should be between 500 and 1,000 words.

"WHAT WOULD YOU DO?"

You are a caseworker in a state facility and work closely with the institution's classification department on a routine basis. You have one inmate on your caseload, a pedophile named Jeff, who has presented with a number of challenges. Jeff is a 35-year-old male who is an inmate in your maximum-security facility. Jeff has recently been transferred to your facility from another facility, largely for protective reasons. Jeff has come to you because he is very, very worried. Jeff is a pedophile, and he has been in prison for nearly 8 years on a 15-year sentence. He is expected to gain an early release due to his excellent progress in prison and due to prison overcrowding problems and his own exemplary behavior. He has been in treatment, and, as you look through his case notes, you can tell that he has done very well.

But there were other inmates at his prior prison facility who did not want to see him get paroled. In fact, it is a powerful inmate gang, and Jeff had received "protection" from this gang in exchange for providing sexual favors to a select trio of inmate gang members. Jeff discloses that, while it was humiliating, he had to do this to survive in the prison subculture, particularly since he was a labeled pedophile. The gang knew this, of course, and used this as leverage to ensure that Jeff was compliant. In fact, the gang never even had to use any physical force whatsoever to gain Jeff's compliance. Jeff notes that this now bothers him, and he doubts his own sense of masculinity. Jeff also discloses that he has had suicidal ideations as a result of his experiences.

Jeff has performed well in treatment for sex offenders. But Jeff has also been adversely affected by noxious sexual experiences inside the prison. You are the first person that he has disclosed this to. As you listen to his plight, you begin to wonder if his issues with sexuality are actually now more unstable than they were before he entered prison. Though his treatment notes seem convincing, this is common among pedophiles. But not known to the other therapist was how Jeff had engaged in undesired sexual activity while incarcerated. This activity has created a huge rift in Jeff's masculine identity. Will this affect his likelihood for relapse on the outside? Does Jeff need to resolve his concerns with consensual versus forced homosexual activity? You begin to wonder.

Now, as you listen, you realize that if you make mention of this, then the classification system is not likely to release Jeff, and this condemns him to more of the same type of exploitation. The only real option that allows Jeff to be protected from such victimization is placing him in protective custody. However, Jeff adamantly refuses such a custody level due to fear that the gang will think that he is an informant who is giving evidence against them; they would essentially seek to kill him. If you do not mention any of this information and thereby allow someone to be released with a highly questionable prognosis, you run the risk of putting the public's safety at risk.

What would you do?

CROSS-NATIONAL PERSPECTIVE 10.1

Prison Gang Riots and Warfare in Guatemala and El Salvador

Gang members staged simultaneous riots in at least seven Guatemalan prisons on Monday (August 2005), attacking rivals with grenades, guns and knives in coordinated chaos that left 31 inmates dead, officials said.

The riots apparently began with attacks by members of the Mara Salvatrucha gang against rivals of the MS-18 gang, said Interior Minister Carlos Vielmann.

He said 31 inmates died before the riots were brought under control shortly after noon.

An Associated Press photographer saw 18 bodies, many riddled with bullet wounds, carried from El Hoyon prison,

which was specifically built to hold gang members in Escuintla, 30 miles south of the capital. A guard and 61 inmates were injured at El Hoyon, and tattooed gang members bleeding from knife wounds were carried from the prison on stretchers.

Escuintla Gov. Luis Munoz said the riot began with the explosion of two grenades.

As explosions echoed from inside the small, converted police barracks in downtown Escuintla on Monday morning, nearby storekeepers rattled metal shutters down over the shop windows and crowds of visitors pressed police for information.

The explosions stopped within an hour. Police first began removing the injured, then the dead.

Dozens of relatives, many of them the mothers of young gang members wept hysterically as stretchers were carried from the prison. The dead were taken to a morgue. So many were injured that they overflowed the capacity of the two local hospitals, forcing officials to take some elsewhere.

"Constant Communication"

Vielmann said visitors had brought guns into the prisons. "Until we have finished the high-security prisons (now under construction), that problem will persist," he said.

Speaking about the apparent coordination of the attacks, Vielmann said, "the gangs maintain constant communication. They have a Web page and not only synchronize in Guatemala, they synchronize with El Salvador, Honduras and with the United States."

He said they also use cellular phones and messages passed by prison visitors.

Human Rights Prosecutor Sergio Morales said there was evidence that police had helped gang members smuggle weapons into El Hoyon.

El Hoyon holds 400 alleged gang members. It was opened at an old police barracks after a December 2002 riot involving gang members at another prison in which 14 inmates died.

In the other riots Monday, three inmates died at the Canada Prison Farm 12 miles further south, and officials said eight died in rioting at Guatemala's top-security Pavon prison, about 15 miles east of the capital.

Two Stabbings

Two others were stabbed to death at a prison in Mazatenango, 85 miles southwest of the capital, according to officials.

Vielmann said smaller disturbances were quashed at three other prisons.

Law enforcement officials say the gangs emerged in Los Angeles and later spread to Central America when criminal migrants were deported back home.

Governments throughout Central America have been waging a campaign against the Mara Salvatrucha and related gangs, tightening laws and throwing thousands of the tattooed gang members into prisons, which have often seen clashes between feuding factions.

In May 2004, a fire swept through a prison in San Pedro Sula, Honduras, killing 107 inmates, most of them Mara Salvatrucha members.

That fire came 13 months after some suspected gang members were locked in their cells, doused with gasoline and set ablaze during a riot at the El Porvenir prison farm near the Honduran city of La Ceiba. Nearly 70 people, including prisoners, visitors, and guards, were killed.

In El Salvador, riots broke out in February when an alleged gang member was transferred to a top-security facility, and one inmate was killed. In September, 800 gang members rioted at two Salvadoran prisons.

Question 1: Discuss the reach of these gangs throughout their country of origin and even in other countries in the general region.

Question 2: In your opinion, what should these countries do to address the challenges associated with violent prison gangs in their correctional systems? Briefly explain your answer.

SOURCE: "At least 31 killed in Guatemala Prison Gang War." Associated Press, August 15, 2005. Used with permission.

STUDENT STUDY SITE

Visit the Student Study Site at **www.sagepub.com/hanserintro** to access links to the videos, audio clips, SAGE journal articles, state rankings, and reference materials noted in this chapter, as well as additional study tools including eFlashcards, web quizzes, and more.

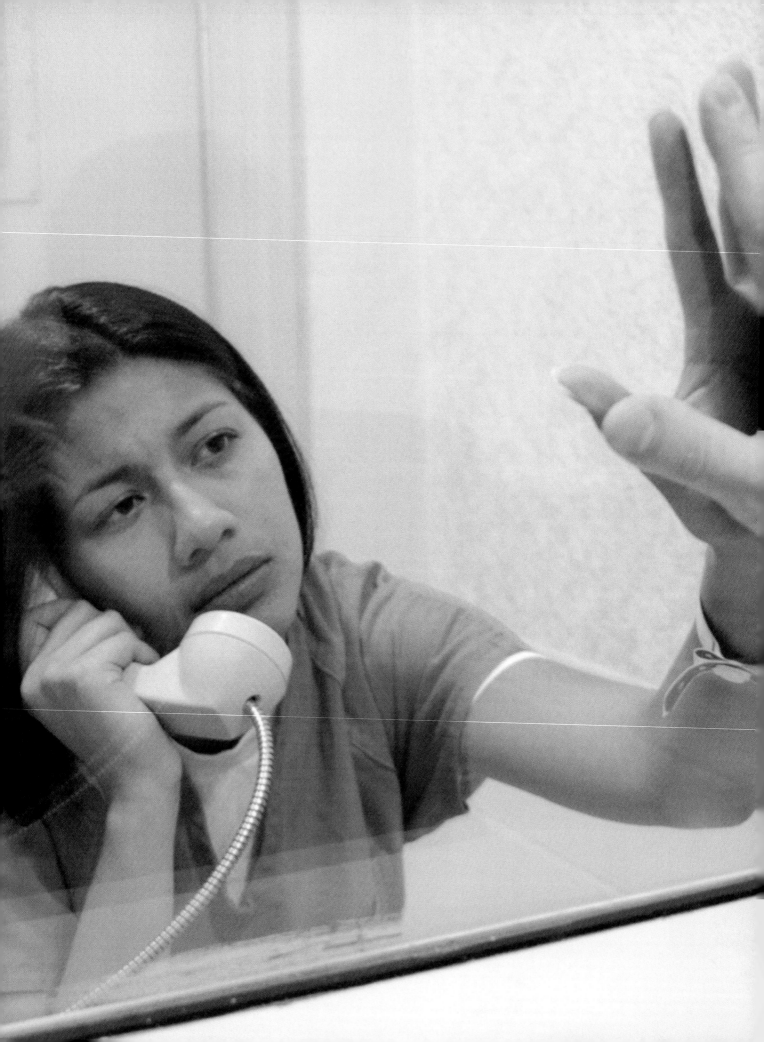

Female Offenders in Correctional Systems

LEARNING OBJECTIVES:

1. Discuss some of the characteristics of female offenders.

2. Compare rates of incarceration and terms of sentencing between male and female offenders.

3. Identify how patriarchy is thought to be a partial explanation for dynamics associated with women who are incarcerated.

4. Discuss the history of corrections related to female offenders.

5. Discuss the legal issues involved with female offenders in the correctional facility.

6. Identify some of the guiding principles associated with effective correctional operations when considering female offenders.

7. Identify various treatment implications related to female offenders.

This chapter will familiarize the student with the common problems associated with the female offending population. While the majority of this chapter will address issues regarding women in prison, some discussion regarding community-based orientations will also be found in this chapter. As will be seen in subsequent pages, women offenders have several physiological and psychological characteristics that set them apart from the male offending population. Some of these characteristics are quite often unique to the female population in broader society, whereas others are unique to females who find themselves involved in the criminal process. Of the offending population, no more than roughly 8% to 10% are women, depending on whether one is talking about jails, prisons, community supervision, or a combination of the three. On the other hand, the number of female offenders in the U.S. correctional system and the higher rate of growth of this offending population (as compared to male offenders) ensure that we cannot overlook this population. Indeed, considerations for the female offending population will become an increasingly important variable for the police, courts, and corrections, for some time to come.

State Rankings Link 11.1
Female Prisoners in State Correctional Institutions as a Percent of All State Prisoners in 2009.

FEMALE OFFENDERS BEHIND BARS: A DETAILED LOOK AT PERCENTAGES AND RATES

The number of women in state and federal prisons continues to grow at a rate faster than that for male inmates, with the incarceration rate for women increasing at nearly twice that for men (U.S. Department of Justice, 1994a). Further, a substantial portion of the female inmate population is held in three states. Data from 2005 show that these three states are (1) California, which held 21,601 women in prison and jail, (2) Texas, which held 21,344 female inmates in prison and jail, and (3) Florida, which had 14,094 women behind bars throughout the state (Hartney, 2007).

In 2009, there were over 106,000 women in prisons, substantially more than were locked up at the beginning of the millennium (see Table 11.1). While the total number of female offenders incarcerated has seen steady growth, recently there has been a slight downturn in this growth. The reasons for this are not clear, but may be due to a combination of factors related to more emphasis on reentry, treatment, and community-based sanctions.

Further, though the female population continues to grow in prison, women offenders are, in fact, a small proportion of the overall prison population, pushing perhaps 8% of the entire U.S. prison population (West, 2010). To ensure that the numbers are kept in perspective, consider that at the end of 2003, U.S. prisons held 1,368,866 men. This means that, in 2003, 1 in every 109 men was in prison. For women the figure was 1 in every 1,613.

Reference Link 11.1
Read how race, class and gender affect imprisonment rates.

Because of the War on Drugs, and because of the extended sentences associated with that era, many women were incarcerated for lengthier sentences, and this has helped fuel the growth in the female inmate population. Given the rates of drug use among female offenders, the growth in their numbers behind bars is not surprising. Currently, the United States incarcerates more women than any other country in the world. Students should see Focus Topic 11.1 for more information regarding the rate of incarceration for women in the United States.

According to numbers from the U.S. Department of Justice, the number of women in prison has grown by 48% since 1995, when the figure was 68,468. The male prison population has grown by 29% over that time, from 1,057,406. Over the years, the number of women incarcerated has grown by an average of 5%, compared with an average annual increase of 3.3% for men. Thus, the number of female inmates is rising in proportion to male inmates.

Audio Link 11.1
Learn more about the increase in the rate of incarcerated women.

Additional statistics reveal that the states with the greatest average annual increases in imprisoned women since 1995 were North Dakota (18.2%), Montana (14.1%), West Virginia (14.0%), Maine (13.6%), Utah (13.5%), and Vermont (13.2%). The only state with a decrease in that period was New York (−2.5%) (Harrison & Beck, 2006b).

However, prison statistics do not fully reflect the number of people behind bars. About 80,000 women were in local jails last year, along with more than 600,000 men. The federal prison system held a

TABLE 11.1 Number of Sentenced Female Inmates Under the Jurisdiction of State or Federal Correctional Authorities, 2000–2009

| Year | Number of sentenced female prisoners | | | Percent of all sentenced prisoners |
	Total	Federal	State	
2000	85,044	8,397	76,647	6.4%
2001	85,184	8,990	76,194	6.3
2002	89,066	9,308	79,758	6.5
2003	92,571	9,770	82,801	6.6
2004	95,998	10,207	85,791	6.7
2005	98,688	10,495	88,193	6.7
2006	103,343	11,116	92,227	6.9
2007	105,786	11,528	94,258	6.9
2008				
June 30	106,569	11,602	94,967	6.9%
December 31	106,411	11,578	94,833	6.9
2009				
June 30	106,362	11,898	94,464	6.9%
Annual change				
Average annual change, 12/31/2000–12/31/2008	2.8%	4.1%	2.7%	:
Percent change, 06/30/2008–06/302009	−0.2	2.6	−0.5	:

NOTE: Includes prisoners under the legal authority of state or federal correctional officials with sentences of more than I year, regardless of where they are held.

: Not calculated.

SOURCE: West, H. C. (2010). *Prison inmates at midyear 2009—Statistical tables.* Washington, DC: Bureau of Justice Statistics.

large share of female prisoners, with a population of 11,635 at the close of 2009. The state of Texas held even more female offenders, with numbers equaling 13,487 incarcerated females. California, which is the nation's largest prison system, held 10,656 women. Students should refer to Figure 11.1 for an illustration of state-to-state rates of incarceration for female offenders.

RATES OF WOMEN HELD IN STATE PRISONS, IN LOCAL JAILS, OR ON COMMUNITY SUPERVISION

Based on 2005 rates of incarceration in state prison or jail, the most punitive U.S. states for women were Oklahoma, Louisiana, Texas, Idaho, Georgia, and Wyoming (Hartney, 2007; see Figure 11.2 for details). Hartney uses the incarceration rates of different states as a measure of how punitive a state might be toward female offenders. While this may not be incorrect, it does ignore other measures, such as the death penalty, which would also demonstrate states' punitiveness toward female offenders.

FOCUS TOPIC: 11.1

Incarceration Rates of Women in the United States

The United States incarcerates the most women of any nation—183,400 in 2005. The rate of incarceration of women per 100,000 in the population is 123 (including federal prisons) in the United States compared to 88 in Thailand, 73 in Russia, 17 in England and Wales, and 3 in India. When one compares the number of incarcerated women in the nations of the world, Louisiana ranks 1st, Texas ranks 74th, and California ranks 7th.

SOURCE: Hartney, C. (2007). *The nation's most punitive states for women.* Oakland, CA: National Council on Crime and Delinquency.

FIGURE 11.1   Rates of Women Housed in State Prisons and Local Jails in 2005

SOURCE: Hartney, C. (2007). *The nation's most punitive states for women.* Oakland, CA: National Council on Crime and Delinquency.

In a different vein, those states with the lowest rates of incarceration were Rhode Island, Maine, Vermont, Massachusetts, Minnesota, and New Hampshire. It is perhaps interesting that these states are typically considered more progressive in different bodies of literature and that these states are also more prone to using treatment schemes, restorative justice approaches, and other innovations rather than prison. This is likely to at least partially explain why these states have such low incarceration rates. The opinion of this author is that these states tend to also be more affluent than those listed as having the highest incarceration rates. Affluent regions tend to have lower crime rates and, therefore, lower rates of imprisonment. In addition, the duration of these prison sentences tend to be less. The irony to this is that many states cannot afford to have increased expenditures for incarceration. Those who do have these higher incarceration rates tend not to be economically stable enough to afford it (Texas being the exception).

The states with the highest rates of women on probation in 2005 (see Figure 11.3 for details) were Montana (1,225), Minnesota (1,016), Texas (953), Delaware (917), and Georgia (857). Conversely, the states with the lowest rates of women on probation were New Hampshire (151), West Virginia (181), Nevada (191), Maine (198), Utah (220), and New York (222). Further, the states with the highest rates of

FIGURE 11.2   Rate of Women in Custody

FIGURE 11.3   Rate of Women on Probation

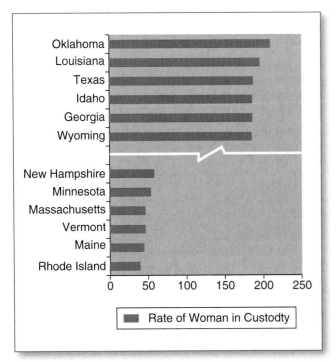

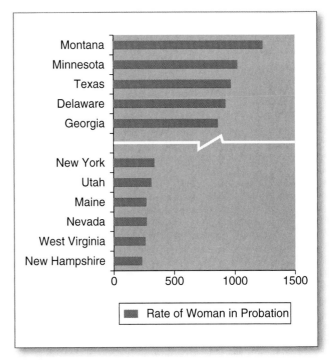

SOURCE: Hartney, C. (2007). *The nation's most punitive states for women*. Oakland, CA: National Council on Crime and Delinquency.

women on parole were Pennsylvania (219), Oregon (148), Arkansas (140), District of Columbia (131), and South Dakota (110). The states with the lowest rates of women on parole were Maine (0—Maine stopped using parole in 1975), Florida (3), North Carolina (4), Rhode Island (5), and several states with 10 (Glaze & Bonzcar, 2006).

Among women on community supervision (both probation and parole combined), about 6 in 10 tend to be Caucasian American, one quarter tend to be African American, and roughly 1 in 10 are Latino American (Bloom, Owen, & Covington, 2003). Of those women on community supervision, roughly 40% have no high school diploma or GED, 42% are single while under supervision, and 72% are the primary caretakers of children under 18 years of age (Bloom et al., 2003).

HISTORY OF WOMEN BEHIND BARS

Prior to the 1800s, women were generally imprisoned in the same facilities with men. As students may recall, this was true even back in England where women, children, and men were imprisoned together on floating gaols in the Thames. John Howard's work in the late 1770s helped to draw attention to the plight of women, and, with the developments in prisons in Pennsylvania, the issue of women inmates was squarely addressed. Though both men and women were separated during this time, the living conditions were equally unhealthy. Like the men, women suffered from filthy conditions, overcrowding, and harsh treatment.

In 1838 in the New York City Jail, for instance, there were 42 one-person cells for 70 women. In the 1920s at Auburn Prison in New York, there were no separate cells for the 25 or so women serving sentences up to 14 years. They were all lodged together in a one-room attic, the windows sealed to prevent communication with men (Rafter, 1985). Further, sexual abuse was reportedly a common occurrence at this time, with male staff raping women in prison. As an example, consider that in 1826, a female inmate named Rachel Welch became pregnant while placed in solitary confinement. Examples abound where women in prisons were routinely abused sexually, and, in the state of Indiana, there were accounts where prostitution of these women was widespread (Rafter, 1985).

Chapter 11: Female Offenders in Correctional Sy:

The Work of Elizabeth Fry

One activist who fought for women in prison during the early 1800s stands out. **Elizabeth Fry** (1780–1845) was a Quaker prison reform activist and an advocate for women who were incarcerated during these early years. Though most of Fry's work was done in England, she was perhaps the first person noted for spearheading the rights of women in prison, and her thoughts became known across continents. The work of Elizabeth Fry is noteworthy for several reasons. First, she was one of the first persons in the United States and Europe to truly highlight the plight of women in prison. Second, she was a Quaker, and, as we have seen in earlier chapters of this text, the Quakers were instrumental in effecting positive change in American prisons. Third, Elizabeth Fry was so influential as to be invited to share her thoughts across both the North American and European continents; seldom were women held in such high regard during this time.

In the early 1800s, Fry visited Old Newgate Prison in England. This prison was notorious for the squalid conditions that it provided for inmates. For female inmates, the circumstances were worse:

PHOTO 11.1

Elizabeth Fry reads to female inmates at Old Newgate Prison in 1823.

Approximately 300 women and children were collectively housed in two large cells. Cooking, the elimination of waste, sleeping, and all other activities were conducted in those cells. No fresh linens were provided, nor were nightclothes available. Fry would bring food, clothing, and straw bedding to those unfortunate enough to be at Newgate (Hatton, 2006).

Eventually, in 1817, Fry organized a group of women activists into the Association for the Improvement of the Female Prisoners in Newgate (Samuel, 2001). These women created a school curriculum for female inmates at Newgate, and provided materials so inmates could sew, knit, and make crafts that could be sold for income. Naturally, there was a religious orientation to these services, and the women at Newgate were given regular Bible studies to help them form a constructive and spiritually therapeutic outlook on their plight. Fry's concern for women in prison, and for the field of corrections in general, culminated in the completion of a book, *Observations on the Visiting, Superintendence, and Government of Female Prisoners* (Samuel, 2001), in which Fry discusses the need for prison reform extensively.

Prior to the 1800s and even during the early 1800s, judges in the United States were hesitant to sentence women for serious crimes unless they were habitual offenders (Feeley & Little, 1991). Indeed, it would appear that the chivalry hypothesis was the guiding notion behind viewing women and criminality. The **chivalry hypothesis** contends that there is a bias in the criminal justice system against giving women harsh punishments. This is true so long as the offenses that they commit are considered "gender appropriate," or consistent with the stereotyped role that women are expected to maintain.

This type of thinking is consistent with the **Victorian Era**, which viewed women from a lens of inflexible femininity through which women were to be considered pious and naïve of the evils of the world. Because this was the view toward women, the criminal courts were often hesitant to punish women whom norms had defined as pure, passive, childlike in their understanding, and primarily driven by emotion rather than reason. Further, Pollak (1950) has noted that during this era, men were expected to act in a fatherly and/or protective manner. Thus, the male-dominated criminal justice system (including police and judges) tended to downplay female crime, making it less likely to be detected, reported, prosecuted, and sentenced.

The stereotypes regarding appropriate conduct for women come from ideas about their "proper" place in society (Brennan & Vandenberg, 2009). Women who fell outside of these expectations were considered abnormal. Those who fell well outside of these expectations, such as female criminals who committed serious crimes, were considered evil or abhorrent. Thus, if women committed crimes that fell outside of what seemed understandable based on gendered stereotypes, their punishment was actually likely to be much harsher that what might be given to men. For instance, if women committed violent crimes such as murder or assault, they would tend to get a sentence that, in many cases, was more extreme than that given to male offenders. On the other hand, when women committed crimes more gender-based, such as prostitution, substance abuse, or theft, they were often given light sentences or simply avoided official action.

Female Criminality From 1850 Onward

Records of criminal convictions and imprisonment for women increased during and after the Civil War. In speculating why this was the case, it may be concluded that the absence of men (who were off to war), as well as the industrialization that occurred in the North, tended to impact views of women by creating circumstances where women were more visible within society (Kurshan, 1996). Further, an increase in crimes occurred throughout the nation among both men and women. This result meant that by midcentury there were enough women inmates to necessitate the emergence of separate women's quarters. The separation of women from men in prison facilities proved important to obtaining other changes in later years.

In 1869, Sarah Smith and Rhoda Coffin, two Quaker activists, were appointed to inspect correctional facilities, both in Indiana (the state in which they lived) and in other areas of the nation. They concluded that the state of morals and integrity among staff in female prisons was deplorable (Rafter, 1985). Further, these two activists spearheaded a social campaign against sexual abuse that they had discovered in Indiana prisons. Their work led to the first completely separate female prison, first opened in 1874. By 1940, 23 states had separate women's prisons (Kurshan, 1996).

The Evolution of Separate Custodial Prisons for Women and Further Evidence of the Chivalry Hypothesis

Eventually, as central penitentiaries were built or rebuilt, many women were shipped there from prison farms because they were considered "dead hands" as compared with the men. At first the most common form of custodial confinement was attachment to male prisons; eventually independent women's prisons evolved out of these male institutions. These separate women's prisons were established largely for administrative convenience, not reform. Female matrons worked there, but they took their orders from men.

Women in custodial prisons were frequently convicted of felony charges, most commonly for crimes against property, often petty theft. Only about a third of female felons were serving time for violent crimes. The rates for both property crimes and violent crimes were much higher than for the women at the reformatories. On the other hand, relatively fewer women were incarcerated for public order offenses (fornication, adultery, drunkenness, etc.), which were the most common in the reformatories. This was especially true in the South where these so-called morality offenses by Blacks were generally ignored, and where authorities were reluctant to imprison White women at all. Data from the Auburn, New York, prison on homicide between 1909 and 1933 reveal the special nature of the women's "violent" crime (Freedman, 1981, p. 12). Most of the victims of murder by women were adult men.

For many feminist researchers, this would not be surprising; the crime would be taken more seriously if it was against the male social order. Further, as we know from more current research today, most homicides committed by women tend to be domestic in nature. In many cases, issues related to long-term spouse abuse are at the heart of what ultimately turns out to be the victim-turned-perpetrator—the female partner killing her abuser in reaction to years of mistreatment. During the 1800s, issues related to spouse abuse were not identified as they are nowadays, and this means that, in most cases, concepts such as battered woman's syndrome—the term for when abused women show identifiable symptoms of trauma associated with domestic battering and psychological abuse—would have been alien in courthouses of that past era. Thus, the murders of men, particularly adult men, likely resulted from dynamics that were not acknowledged by courtrooms of that time. In fact, laws often gave husbands the right to use force in their household, including with their wives. Women, on the other hand, had no such right; they did not even have the right to vote at this time.

APPLIED THEORY 11.1

*Feminist Criminology and
the Female Offender*

Feminist criminology offers a variety of propositions regarding female criminality that are different from other theoretical perspectives. Among other points, feminist criminologists argue that traditional schools of criminology fail to account for the various issues that are specific to women, the female experience, and the causal factors associated with female criminality. If this is indeed true, then traditional criminological theory has failed to be gender competent, a derivative of cultural competence. This is an important point for both academics and practitioners alike; any failure to understand and appreciate the specific factors relevant to women means that causal factors tend to be misunderstood, and that supervision and treatment programs will be misdirected and ineffectual. Thus, it behooves practitioners to heed the call of feminist criminologists when designing and implementing their programs for female offenders. In summarizing feminist criminology, Cullen and Agnew (2006) state,

> Crime cannot be understood without considering gender, crime is shaped by the different social experiences of and power exercised by men and women. Patriarchy is a broad structure that shapes gender-related experiences and power. Men may use crime to exert control over women and to demonstrate their masculinity—that is, to show that they are "men" in a way that is consistent with societal ideas of masculinity. (p. 7)

From the reading thus far in this chapter and when considering the description of feminist criminology presented by Cullen and Agnew (2006), it should be clear to the student that there is a great deal of similarity between these two portrayals of female offending. From this chapter, it is evident that much of female crime is shaped by gender-related experiences and power. Activity in the sex industry, a prime area of involvement for female offenders, seems to indicate that much of the activity

related to female criminality is indeed rooted in gender-related experiences. Further, when one considers that the overwhelming majority of domestic violence victims are female and that female offenders experience higher rates of domestic violence perpetrated against them, this lends further credence to feminists who contend that men use crime to exert control over women and to demonstrate their power over them. Naturally, acts of sexual abuse directed at young girls also back up this theory, and, as this chapter demonstrates, female offenders generally have higher rates of prior childhood sexual abuse.

Finally, the effects of this abuse and the corresponding ravages associated with being raised in a criminogenic family environment tend to manifest themselves through various mental health symptoms and maladaptive coping mechanisms. It is perhaps for this reason, as well as other factors related to a poor sense of self-efficacy (common among many female offenders), that substance abuse may be so high among these offenders. The use of drugs, as well as comorbid problems with depression and anxiety, puts female offenders at further risk of having difficulties. Nevertheless, women to tend to be more verbally communicative than men, and this means that they also tend to do better in treatment regimens that utilize talk therapy. As a result, these offenders often have a better prognosis when in treatment than do their male counterparts. Perhaps, then, treatment programs for female offenders should continue to be intensified, with a continued focus on female-specific factors and theoretical frameworks that are consistent with feminist criminology. To fail to do so essentially puts the female offender, her children (as most female offenders have children), and the rest of society at risk for future criminality. In short, it simply makes good sense to integrate this theoretical perspective into the various supervision and treatment regimens designed for female offenders.

SOURCE: Cullen, F. T., & Agnew, R. (2006). *Criminological theory: Past to present* (3rd ed.). Los Angeles: Roxbury Publishing Company.

Other evidence exists that the chivalry hypothesis and/or stereotyped expectations of women may have been a partial explanation for female criminality. For instance, the Women's Prison Association of New York, which was active in the social purity movement, declared in 1906 that

> if promiscuous immigration is to continue, it devolves upon the enlightened, industrious, and moral citizens, from selfish as well as from philanthropic motives, to instruct the morally defective to conform to our ways and exact from them our own high standard of morality and legitimate industry.... Do you want immoral women to walk our streets, pollute society, endanger your households, menace the morals of your sons and daughters? Do you think the women here described fit to become mothers of American citizens? Shall foreign powers generate criminals and dump them on our shores? (Rafter, 1985, pp. 93–94)

The excerpt above demonstrates how, even in the 1900s, social views related to women and criminality were ties to moralistic outlooks regarding their sexuality and identity as mothers. Consider also that, during this time, performing an "illegal" abortion was classified as a violent crime that carried a sentence of imprisonment (Freedman, 1981, p. 12). Naturally, these abortions were illegal in every circumstance because there was no such thing as a "legal" abortion. Since abortion was considered murder, women who exercised autonomy over their own body and wished to avoid unwanted pregnancies had no choice but to commit the ultimate crime. This was regardless of the circumstances that led to their pregnancy. Because sexual abuse of young girls and women went largely unaddressed, many women (especially young girls) who were victims of rape and/or molestation were expected to endure this experience and to birth the offspring of their victimization. A failure to do so would be seen as contradictory to the nurturing and caring image that women were expected to maintain and would, therefore, be demonized by society and by the criminal justice system.

Minority Female Offenders Compared to Caucasian Female Offenders in American History

While discussion has been given regarding female offending and incarceration throughout past generations, one key point to understanding how women have been sentenced has been overlooked. This issue is the matter of racial disparities that have existed and continue to exist among the female population, particularly among those who are incarcerated. This is a very important point that deserves elaboration. It is also a point that is seldom discussed in many textbooks. Kurshan (1996) provides very good insight into this issue, and much of her work has been adapted in this chapter to elaborate on the inherent racism that existed in the justice system when processing female offenders.

Journal Article Link 11.1
Read about the historical role of race in imprisonment patterns of women in Maryland.

Consider that, in the South after 1870, prison camps emerged, and the overwhelming majority of women in these camps were African American; the few Caucasian women there had been imprisoned for much more serious offenses, yet experienced better conditions of confinement. For instance, at Bowden Farm in Texas, the majority of women were African American, were there for property offenses, and worked in the field (Freedman, 1981). The few Caucasian women there had been convicted of homicide and served as domestics. As the techniques of slavery were applied to the penal system, some states forced women to work on the state-owned penal plantations but also leased women to local farms, mines, and railroads.

An 1880 census indicated that in Alabama, Louisiana, Mississippi, North Carolina, Tennessee, and Texas, 37% of the 220 imprisoned Black women were leased out whereas only one of the 40 imprisoned White women was leased (Kurshan, 1991, p. 3). Testimony in an 1870 Georgia investigation revealed that, in one instance,

> there were no white women there. One started there, and I heard Mr. Alexander (the lessee) say he turned her loose. He was talking to the guard; I was working in the cut. He said his wife was a white woman, and he could not stand it to see a white woman worked in such places. (Freedman, 1981, p. 151)

Acknowledgment of the disparity between minority women and Caucasian women is important for two reasons. First, it is seldom addressed in most textbooks on corrections or correctional systems and practices. Second, we continue to see disparity between minority women and Caucasian women in today's society. Whereas, in generations past, much of the disparity was residue from the prior slave era, particularly in the South, the reasons for such disparity are perhaps no longer the same, yet they are real and still exist. It can be seen that, throughout history, women who commit crimes have been demonized, and, for those who were double minorities (particularly African American women), the treatment and type of prison experience received were significantly different. Indeed, female offenders were not (and still are not) all cast from one mold—they are diverse, and the experiences for minority women are even more noxious than they tend to be for Caucasian women. This is not to minimize the impact of incarceration upon Caucasian women but is meant to highlight even more the demographics and conditions of confinement for women throughout American correctional history. This provides a more historically correct view of how circumstances have evolved for women in the correctional system and also demonstrates that the disparity that we see today is simply an extension of past dynamics (see Focus Topic 11.2).

FOCUS TOPIC: 11.2

Disproportionate Sentencing and Incarceration of Minority Women

To further highlight the disparity between minority women and Caucasian women, consider that, in 2005, the national rate of women sentenced (per 100,000 in the general population) was 88 for Caucasian women, 144 for Latino women, and 347 for African American women. This means that the rate of sentencing for African American women was approximately 4 times higher than what was observed for Caucasian women.

In addition, 1 in every 300 Black females were incarcerated compared to 1 in every 1,099 Caucasian women and 1 in every 704 Latino women.

SOURCE: Harrison, P. M., & Beck, A. J. (2006, May). *Prison and jail inmates at midyear* 2005 (NCJ 213133). Washington, DC: U.S. Department of Justice, Office of Justice Programs, Bureau of Justice Statistics. Retrieved May 7, 2007, http://www.ojp.usdoj.gov/bjs/abstract/pjim05.htm.

PHOTO 11.2

A female inmate carries her property while being escorted to her cell.

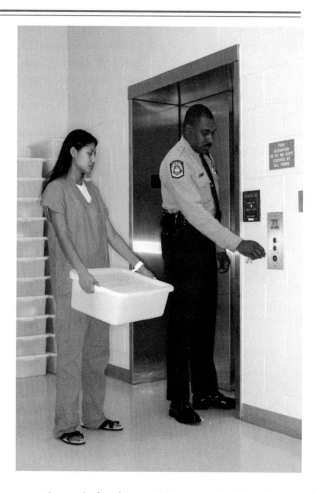

Early-20th-Century Women's Reformatories: A Feminist Perspective

Reformatories for women developed alongside custodial prisons. These were parallel, but distinct, developments. **Reformatories for women** developed due to the efforts of an early generation of women reformers who appeared between 1840 and 1900, but their use became more widespread as activists pressed for alternatives to the penitentiary's harsh conditions of enforced silence and hard labor (Kurshan, 1991; Rafter, 1985). The move to reformatories for women occurred at the same time that they were showcased for the male population; this was a time that many texts refer to as the reformatory era. The women who advocated reform for women behind bars were, in actuality, working in tandem with other prison reformers who have been discussed in earlier chapters of this text. Their work, though specialized to the plight of female offenders, was consistent with the times in which they lived.

In particular, these activists contended that the use of mixed prisons was problematic and provided female inmates with no privacy. This left them vulnerable to humiliation, physical abuse, and sexual abuse. But the reformatories, on the other hand, were more humane, and conditions were better than at the traditional female penitentiaries (Kurshan, 1991). The use of reformatories eliminated much of the risk of abuse at the hands of male inmates and even male prison staff. Reformatories also resulted in more freedom of movement and opened up a variety of opportunities for work that were often reserved for male inmates. Kurshan (1991) notes that

children of prisoners up to two years old could stay in most institutions. At least some of the reformatories were staffed and administered by women. They usually had cottages, flower gardens, and no fences. They offered discussions on the law, academics and training, and women were often paroled more readily than in custodial institutions. However, a closer look at who the women prisoners were, the nature of their offenses, and the program to which they were subjected reveals the seamier side of these ostensibly noble institutions. (p. 5)

As with most of the inmates in prisons throughout the nation, women in the reformatories were of the working class. Many of them worked outside the home. At New York State's Albion Correctional Facility, for instance, 80% had, in the past, worked for wages. Reformatories were also overwhelmingly institutions for White women. However, fewer minority women were placed in reformatories. This is not because they were sentenced less frequently but because African American, Native American, and Latino American women were more likely to be placed in a prison rather than a reformatory. Thus again, the racial discrimination seen among correctional systems of this era emerged in the operation of reformatories. Kurshan (1991), in discussing the racial discrimination among women processed in the criminal justice system, notes the following:

> Record keeping at the Albion Reformatory in New York demonstrates how unusual it was for black women to be incarcerated there. The registries left spaces for entries of a large number of variables, such as family history of insanity and epilepsy. Nowhere was there a space for recording race. When African Americans were admitted, the clerk penciled "colored" at the top of the page. African American women were much less likely to be arrested for such public order offenses. Rafter suggests that black women were not expected to act like "ladies" in the first place and therefore were reportedly not deemed worthy of such rehabilitation. (p. 5)

It is important to emphasize that reformatories existed for women only. No such parallel development took place within men's prisons. There were no institutions devoted to "correcting" men for moral offenses. In fact, such activities were not considered crimes when men engaged in them, and therefore men were not as a result imprisoned (Freedman, 1981; Rafter, 1985). A glance at these crimes for women shows the extent to which society was bent on repressing women's sexuality. More than half of women, however, were imprisoned because of "sexual misconduct" (Kurshan, 1991, p. 7). Women were incarcerated in reformatories primarily for various public order offenses or so-called moral offenses: lewd and lascivious carriage, stubbornness, idle and disorderly conduct, drunkenness, vagrancy, fornication, serial premarital pregnancies, keeping bad company, adultery, venereal disease, and vagrancy (Kurshan, 1991). In many cases, when young girls rebelled against abusive behavior (often sexual in nature), they were doubly victimized by the family and/or relatives who would have them sentenced and placed within a prison or reformatory (Kurshan, 1991). Naturally, these dysfunctional families would lie and concoct stories of inappropriate behavior, and, since belief systems were different and technology was primitive during these times, girls and young women had little ability to defend themselves from these false charges. Thus, this type of system is thought to have basically trapped girls and women in subjugation within a male-dominated society and a male-dominated criminal justice system.

Feminist criminologists have contended that reformatories were institutions of patriarchy and that, at their very inception, they were designed to reinforce stereotypes of women (Kurshan, 1991). **Patriarchy** is a term that describes any social system where fathers tend to be considered the head of the family and where men tend to hold economic, political, legal, and social power. At this time in history, it can hardly be argued that men hold the keys to power, whether this be economic, political, social, or legal power. This is easily just as true in penal operations. Thus, the arguments of feminist criminologists, combined with the types of offenses that were targeted for sentencing, plus the manner in which reformatories operated, create convincing accusations leveled at the purpose behind the use of these institutions. Though reformatories were not run in the same authoritarian style as in penitentiaries, they reinforced norms and expectations of the Victorian Era and stymied nonstereotypical behavior among women.

Further, the type of sentencing used was often open-ended or indeterminate. This meant that the length of time that a woman would have to serve under this type of system of socialization depended on her willingness to comply with institutional expectations. In other words, if she became more "lady-like," then she was more likely to be released. The length of time that she served had little to do with the actual offense and/or her likelihood of committing future crimes but had more to do with her meeting the expectations of a patriarchal system. However, this was disguised by a veneer of respectability with the official rationale for such undefined terms being the interests of the rehabilitative ideology. Thus, a woman's incarceration was not of fixed length, because the notion was that a woman would stay for as long

FIGURE 11.4 National Profile of Women Offenders

NATIONAL PROFILE OF WOMEN OFFENDERS

A profile based on national data for women offenders reveals the following characteristics:

- » Disproportionately women of color.
- » In their early to mid-30s.
- » Most likely to have been convicted of a drug-related offense.
- » From fragmented families that includes other family members who also have been involved with the criminal justice system.
- » Survivors of physical and/or sexual abuse as children and adults.
- » Individuals with significant substance abuse problems.
- » Unmarried mothers of minor children.
- » Individual with a high school or general equivalency diploma (GED) but limited vocational training and sporadic work histories.

as it took to accomplish the task of reforming her (Kurshan, 1991). Naturally though, her "reform" was determined on how well she obeyed and adhered to the patriarchal standards that had been established for her to follow.

ISSUES RELATED TO THE MODERN-DAY FEMALE OFFENDER POPULATION

When discussing female offenders, it becomes clear that the majority are minority members. Further, it likewise is the case that these women typically have few options and few economic resources. Thus, many of these offenders are marginalized in multiple ways from the access to success and stability commonly attributed to broader society. Of those women who are incarcerated, approximately 44% have no high school diploma or GED, and 61% were unemployed at the point of incarceration (Bloom et al., 2003). In addition, roughly 47% were single prior to incarceration while an approximate 65% to 70% were the primary caretakers of minor children at the point that they were incarcerated (Bloom et al., 2003). Lastly, over one third of those incarcerated can be found within the jurisdictions of the federal prison system, or the state prison systems of Texas and California (Harrison & Karberg, 2004).

Female offenders are disproportionately low-income women of color who are undereducated and unskilled, with sporadic employment histories. They are less likely than men to have committed violent offenses and more likely to have been convicted of crimes involving drugs or property. Often, their property offenses are economically driven, motivated by poverty and by the abuse of alcohol and other drugs. Women face life circumstances that tend to be specific to their gender, such as sexual abuse, sexual assault, domestic violence, and the responsibility of being the primary caregiver for dependent children. Approximately 1.3 million minor children have a mother who is under criminal justice supervision, and approximately 65% of women in state prisons and 59% of women in federal prisons have an average of two minor children.

Women involved in the criminal justice system thus represent a population marginalized by race, class, and gender. For example, African American women are overrepresented in correctional populations. While they constitute only 13% of women in the United States, nearly 50% of women in prison are African American. Black women are 8 times more likely than White women to be incarcerated. The characteristics of women under correctional supervision (community supervision, prison, or jail) are summarized in Table 11.2.

The Female Inmate Subculture and Coping in Prison

The conditioning of women in the United States regarding the traditional social role of motherhood and the forced separation from their family has a considerable effect on women in prison. A significant aspect of the female coping mechanism inside the prisons is their development of family-like environments with the other female prisoners. These fictional family atmospheres, or kinship structures, enable the women to

Video Link 11.1
Learn more about the lives of female inmates.

TABLE 11.2 Demographic Characteristics of Women Under Correctional Supervision

Characteristic	% Under Community Supervision	% in Jail	% in State Prison	% in Federal Prison
Race/ethnicity				
White	62	48	33	29
African American	27	44	48	35
Hispanic	10	15	15	32
Median age	32	31	33	36
High school diploma/GED	60	55	56	73
Single	42	48	47	34
Unemployed	Unknown	60	62	Unknown
Mother of minor children	72	70	65	59

SOURCE: Harrison, P. M., & Beck, A. J. (2006, May). *Prison and jail inmates at midyear 2005* (NCJ 213133). Washington, DC: U.S. Department of Justice, Office of Justice Programs, Bureau of Justice Statistics. Retrieved May 7, 2007, http://www.ojp.usdoj.gov/bjs/abstract/pjim05.htm.

create a type of caring, nurturing environment inside the prison (Brown, 2003; Engelbert, 2001). Associating with a prison family provides a woman with a feeling of belonging and social identity. Many of these relationships are formed based on friendships and develop into the companionship roles of "sister-to-sister" and "mother-to-daughter" bonds. These relationships can become intimate and include touching and hugging without having sexual overtones. However, sexual relationships in prison do exist and are not uncommon. In some instances a prison family will consist of "married" couples, with specific male and female roles. These relationships may only last while the women are incarcerated and do not necessarily signify homosexuality.

Some women who are in prison for an extended period of time may become involved with another female inmate in order to fill their needs for love and companionship. In many of these cases, one will act in a male role and take on male mannerisms. She may walk and talk like a man, cut or shave her hair, and attempt to dress in a manly fashion. On the other end, the other partner will typically behave in a traditional feminine manner. Some of these women become involved in these relationships only while in prison, and therefore do not consider themselves to be lesbian in the strictest sense of the word. Similar to male prison settings, sexuality inside the walls is considered separate from sexual identity outside of the walls.

For these women, involvement in a same-sex relationship is intended to simply fulfill their need to be "loved" and desired just as they would wish when outside the prison walls. There are additional advantages associated with belonging to a prison family structure. J. W. Brown, author of "The Female Inmate" (2003), explains: "In the female prison, 'family' members provide goods and services to those members of the family who demonstrate need. This 'kinship' network becomes the main conduit of illicit goods and services in the female prison." The meanings of the kinship relationships within the prison are many and varied. They provide support and protection, and they may be encouraged by the prison administration due to the social control aspect of keeping the female inmates out of trouble.

On the television series *Primetime Live*, Diane Sawyer spent a day and a night inside a women's prison as a mock inmate to witness firsthand the female inmate subculture. Like the male prison subculture, this culture is quite different from everyday society. The process of relationship development is one of the most uniquely affected components of the female prison experience. Kept apart from men for years at a stretch, the women of the Metro State Prison (the prison that Diane Sawyer visited) in Atlanta, Georgia, had developed a different approach to romance and family (ABC Primetime, 2004). From her newscast, it was clear that the hierarchy of desire in prison follows a guideline where the most desirable partners were inmates who are most masculine. These female offenders were referred to as "studs," while those who were submissive in a lesbian relationship were referred to as "femmes." Unlike in male prisons where sex is used as a tool of violence and intimidation, sex in the female inmate subculture tends to be more or

Journal Article Link 11.2
Read about the variety of types of relationships amont women in prison.

Video Link 11.2
Watch a video about prison families in female institutions.

Video Link 11.3
Learn more about the causes of violence in female institutions.

less genuinely consensual rather than coerced. In fact, most violence in women's prisons is often based on jealousy or possessiveness rather than violence.

Upon release, nearly all female inmates return to traditional heterosexual roles where they most often play a feminine role. Regardless of whether the kinship relationships are as defined as some believe, there is no doubt the studies have revealed interesting information pertaining to the female subculture within the prison system. Women, just like male inmates, are faced with surviving the term of their sentence inside the prison walls, and this requires that they create some type of acceptable social environment in which to cope with the situation.

A MYRIAD OF CONSIDERATIONS FOR FEMALE OFFENDERS

We now will turn our attention to several subcharacteristics that have been found to be commonalities among the female offending population. The remainder of this chapter will consider key issues associated with female offenders in an effort to demonstrate the multitude of difficult problems that confound effective intervention for many female offenders. The issues that affect most women who are processed in the justice system tend to be much different from those of men.

Domestic Violence

The research on the prevalence of **domestic violence** and its impact on women in the United States so abundant and obvious that it goes beyond the scope of this chapter to discuss. However, when limiting the discussion to female offenders and their experiences with domestic violence, it appears that they are at greater risk for physical abuse than those in the general population. According to the Women's Prison Association (2003), female offenders who are incarcerated are very likely to have histories of physical abuse; that is, 57% of adult women were victims of physical or sexual abuse. Furthermore, this study found that this violence is most likely to have been perpetrated by a boyfriend or husband.

Incarcerated women report being subjected to the most violence at ages 15 to 24 (Bloom et al., 2003). This means that this abuse tends to follow female offenders throughout their life span, indicating that these offenders return to a lifestyle that is self-damaging. Women on probation and parole are likely to be socially isolated from common social circles, and their peer network is likely to be limited (Bloom et al., 2003). At best it will include other women in a similar situation, or perhaps persons from employment (keep in mind the educational level, unemployment rate, and vocational skills of these women). More likely, these women will continue to associate within the subculture of origin, meaning that many of the friends and family that they return to are likely to be, or have been, criminal offenders themselves. This may be much more common since many women who offend often tend to do so as secondary accomplices with a male primary offender. Thus, these women are not likely to have many resources to rely on and may find themselves quite dependent on a man, including an abusive man.

Physical and Sexual Abuse

A study on the self-reported prior abuse conducted by Harlow in 1999 found that female offenders are abused more frequently than male offenders. State prison inmates reported both physical and sexual abuse experiences prior to being sentenced. The results found that 57.2% of females had experienced abusive treatment compared to 16.1% of males. Of this same group, 36.7% of the female offenders and 14.4% of the male offenders reported that the abuse occurred during their childhood or teenage years. Other findings from this study are as follows:

1. Males tend to be mistreated as children, but females are mistreated as both children and adults.

2. Both genders reported much more abuse if they had lived in a foster home or another structured institution.

3. Higher levels of abuse were reported among offenders who had an incarcerated family member.

4. Offenders reporting prior sexual abuse had higher levels of drug and alcohol abuse than those not reporting prior sexual abuse. Further, female offenders who were abused used drugs or alcohol more frequently than did male offenders.

Sex Industry Activity and Sexually Transmitted Diseases

A large body of research shows that female criminals often have some history of prostitution although the causal factor(s) and the order of causal factors are not very clear. A debate, indeed a schism, exists among researchers as to whether this is the case due to economic necessities or whether prior sexual victimization is at the root of this common form of female offense. Many researchers contend that prior victimization (especially sexual) is at the root, pointing toward the high rate of incidence of sexual abuse among female criminals and the high rate of female criminals' involvement in prostitution.

The rate of HIV/AIDS infection is higher for female offenders than for male offenders. According to the Women's Prison Association (2003), the percentage of women in state and federal prisons who are infected with HIV/AIDS is 3.6%, which is 12 times the national rate of infection. For men in prison, the percentage is 2.1%, which is a third lower than for women in prison (Women's Prison Association, 2003). In the general public, the rate for HIV/AIDS is twice as high for men as for women. Research indicates that female inmates tend to have higher rates of HIV due to involvement in risky sexual behavior. Interestingly, there is also a connection between this risky behavior and these women experiencing prior sexual abuse (Women's Prison Association, 2003).

Drugs

Drug use is a major contributor to female criminality. Female offenders use drugs more often than male offenders, though differences are not extreme and research focuses most on arrested and incarcerated subjects. Consider that, between 1985 and 1994, women's drug arrests increased by 100% whereas men's drug arrests increased only by about 50%. Regardless, the point is that when dealing with female offenders, addressing drug use is critical if you are to prevent recidivism. Further, female offenders engage in riskier drug habits than male offenders as they report higher levels of needle usage and needle sharing (Women's Prison Association, 2003). This social problem is further compounded because a high number of female offenders who are intravenous drug users likewise engage in prostitution and sex industry activity to support their habits.

Violent Crime

It is important to note that when it comes to violent crime, there is a huge disparity between male and female offenders. Simply put, female offenders do not commit violent crimes with great frequency. Most crimes revolve around larceny, theft, and fraud. Of those women who do commit homicides, the vast majority involve the killing of intimates usually in self-defense or in retaliatory response to long-term abusive relationships (Brown, 2003). Female chronic offenders are similar to male chronic offenders in that they are likely to be a minority group member, single, and a substance abuser, with a history of spouse abuse. But they differ in that they show differences in years of education (women typically have more), and female offenders tend to paradoxically score lower on IQ tests, are more likely to come from homes of divorce, and are more likely to come from criminogenic families. When both genders are compared, men are likely to be sentenced to prison for violent, property, and drug offenses while women are likely to be sentenced to prison for drug offenses and property crimes (Brown, 2003).

Given the high rates of abuse that the female offending population experiences (both in childhood and in adulthood), the female offender is commonly referred to as the victim-turned-offender. The prior victimization of female victims, particularly with domestic violence, is held as a primary causal factor in predicting female criminal behavior. This concept goes hand-in-hand with the tenets of the chivalry hypothesis and with feminist thought on criminality. While some may scoff at these types of concepts and explanations, it is hard to refute three key points. First, most crimes against women are from male perpetrators. Second, women tend to only attack men when they have been victimized. Third, women commit far fewer crimes that are about power and control.

Mental Health Issues

The experience of prison can exacerbate the prevalence and/or severity of mental illness. The experience of incarceration can deteriorate existing mental conditions, and it can lead to the breakdown in mental health among otherwise well-adjusted individuals. The mental health issues for female offenders are often tied to stages in their life cycle and development, such as with puberty, adolescence, and phases of reproductive development (Seiden, 1989). However, because a disturbing number of women are sexually and physically abused as girls and as adult women, attention has been focused on the anxiety, depression, and other psychological illnesses resulting from these events (Seiden, 1989). The trauma of early sexual and

TABLE 11.3 Female Inmates Presenting With Mental Health Problems in State Prisons and Local Jails

| Mental problem | Percent of inmates in— | | | |
| | Sate prison | | Local jail | |
	Male	Female	Male	Female
Recent history	22%	48%	18%	40%
Diagnosed	8	23	9	23
Overnight Stay	5	9	4	9
Medication	16	39	12	30
Therapy	14	32	9	23
Symptoms	48%	62%	59%	70%

SOURCE: James, D. J., & Glaze, L. E. (2006). *Mental health problems of prison and jail inmates.* Washington, DC: Bureau of Justice Statistics.

physical abuse may be manifested through a number of mental health symptoms and diagnoses as well as the more common post-traumatic stress disorders (PTSD) and alcoholism (Seiden, 1989). As with most forms of mental illness, these disorders develop largely in response to stressors that push an already over-taxed psyche. Indeed, because of their higher rates of abuse and victimization, coupled with their drug offending, female offenders may have numerous "predispositions" that make them prone to mental illness when the stressor of incarceration is presented as a life experience.

Depression is a very common mental illness among the incarcerated and is even more pronounced among the female offending population because this disorder tends to have higher prevalence rates among females in general society. Further, depression is a common symptom of dual diagnosis among drug abusers, so when the numerous problem variables are taken together, female offenders are very susceptible to bouts of depression and to the full array of mood disorders.

A recent study examined mental health issues among inmates in prisons and jails throughout the United States (James & Glaze, 2006). The study found that female inmates had much higher rates of mental health problems than male inmates (see Table 11.3). An estimated 73% of females in state prisons, compared to 55% of male inmates, had a mental health problem. In federal prisons, the rate was 61% of females compared to 44% of males; the rate in local jails was 75% of females compared to 63% of males.

Among female state prison inmates, 23% indicated that they had been diagnosed with some type of mental health disorder during the past 12 months (see Table 11.3). This same percentage was found for women in jail. This was almost 3 times the rate of male inmates (around 8%) who had been told they had a mental health problem. It seems that male offenders tend to mask their depression with anger and aggressive reactions that serve as defensive "fronts" or displays of force that mask their underlying depression. Much of this is due to socialization, but for women socialization tends to ensure that their symptoms of depression are recognized for what they are. Thus, men who are incarcerated may simply be diagnostically labeled as aggressive, and, when in a prison environment, this can go one step further into a classification of being assaultive. Though from the view of institutional security this is accurate, it nonetheless fails to detect the sense of depression that the male inmate may be experiencing.

On the other hand, for female inmates, socialization provides a ready tolerance for acts of depression and the expression of emotional sorrow, and thus prevalence rates among female and male inmates in prison may be compounded by social expectations and norms to which prison staff are accustomed. Further, as would be expected, prior abuse plays a role in addiction and depression, further cementing these two variables together as correlates among female offenders. Likewise, when it is considered that female victims of battering tend to present with depressive disorders and PTSD, and given the fact that domestic battering is targeted at female victims much more frequently than male victims, it is not surprising that this variable also aggravates rates of depression among the female offending population.

FEMALE OFFENDERS AS MOTHERS

In 1998, female offenders in the criminal justice system were mothers to approximately 1.3 million children. Many female offenders under criminal justice supervision face losing custody of their children. Some female offenders have relatives or friends who will care for their children while they are incarcerated, but many do not. For those who are able to arrange placement with relatives, the likelihood of permanent separation between mother and child is significantly reduced. It has been observed that maternal grandmothers most often care for the children of female prison inmates (Bloom, Brown, & Chesney-Lind, 1996). If a mother is unable to place her children with relatives or friends, the local child welfare agency will most likely place the child in foster care. When children of imprisoned mothers are placed in foster care, caseworkers are expected to make concerted efforts to sustain family ties and to encourage family reunification (Bloom et al., 1996). Most incarcerated mothers, particularly those who are mentally ill, do not have access to the resources they need to meet other reunification requirements imposed by the court, such as parent education, counseling, drug treatment, and job training. Upon release from custody to community corrections, mothers face numerous obstacles in reunifying with their children. They must navigate through a number of complex governmental and social service agencies in order to regain custody of their children. Although differences may exist across jurisdictions, in many cases, it is considered beyond the purview of probation and parole agencies to intervene in child custody cases.

When fathers are incarcerated, there is usually a mother left at home to care for the children. However, when mothers are incarcerated, there is not usually a father in the home. This situation is further exacerbated by the fact that there are fewer women's prisons, and because of the rarity of female prison units they tend to be great distances from one another and from the likely location where the female offender lived prior to incarceration. Because of this, there is a greater risk that female offenders will be incarcerated at a greater distance from their children than males (Bloom et al., 1996). Indeed, an average female inmate is more than 160 miles farther from her family than a male inmate, and at least half the children of imprisoned mothers have either not seen or not visited their mothers since they were incarcerated (Bloom et al., 1996). This low rate of contact between mother and child tends to weaken family bonds, which then causes psychological and emotional damage both to the child and to the incarcerated mother. Another negative effect on the female offenders caused by this low rate of contact is that recidivism rates tend to go up when inmate mothers have diminished contact with their children (Bloom et al., 1996).

Video Link 11.4
See how female inmates mother while incarcerated.

This separation between mother and child causes what has been called **collateral damage** to children and society by the current incarceration trends of female offenders who typically commit property and/or drug crimes (Crawford, 2003). Though female offenders separated from their children are at an increased risk of later recidivism, the damage done to the children is probably more serious than to the adult when a parent is incarcerated (Bloom et al., 1996; Crawford, 2003). A number of children display symptoms of PTSD, namely depression, feelings of anger and guilt, flashbacks about their mother's crimes or arrests, and the experience of hearing their mother's voice. Children of incarcerated mothers display other negative effects such as school-related difficulties, depression, low self-esteem, aggressive behavior, and general emotional dysfunction (Bloom et al., 1996).

CONDITIONS OF CARE FOR FEMALE OFFENDERS

It is considered a general fact that female prison institutions do not meet the inmate's needs as effectively as do male prisons. As a testament to the poor services that tend to be delivered to female inmates, consider the case of *Glover v. Johnson* (1988). This case involved the Michigan Department of Corrections and the issue of parity in service programming between female and male offenders. A class action lawsuit was filed on behalf of all female inmates in the state of Michigan, and this suit alleged that the constitutional rights of female inmates throughout the state had been violated because these inmates were being denied educational and vocational rehabilitation opportunities that were being provided to male inmates. Ultimately, the Michigan Department of Corrections was found liable, and a decree was issued for the Department of Corrections to provide the following to female inmates within its jurisdiction:

Audio Link 11.2
Listen to a clip about training programs in female prisons.

1. Two-year college programming.

2. Paralegal training and access to an attorney to remedy past inadequacies in law library facilities.

3. A revision of the wage policy for female inmates to ensure parity with male inmate wage compensation policies.

4. Access to programming that had previously only been provided to male inmates.

5. Prison industries that previously existed only at male facilities.

It appears that, despite such legal precedents, more recent practices have not improved substantially in other parts of the nation. Consider, for example, California, which has the largest state correctional system in the United States. An internal "watchdog" agency known as the **Little Hoover Commission** was tasked with providing recommendations to the state governor and legislature. This commission found that the correctional system was not doing well and that conditions were particularly bleak for female offenders (Vesely, 2004).

CORRECTIONS AND THE LAW 11.1

Legal Issues Regarding Female Offenders in Jail and Prison

When maintaining custody of female offenders, a number of legal issues arise that are unique to this population. This is particularly true in a male-dominated industry such as corrections. Agencies must be proactive in their policy approach, and they must ensure that their staff are knowledgeable on issues related to women in custody. Although lawsuits can be filed no matter how careful one may be, the evasion of liability, and even an end with a positive outcome, is more likely when the legal issues that arise have been anticipated and when one can articulate appropriate reasons for the policy, practice, or conduct in question. This legal insert will discuss many of the major areas in which gender has an impact.

Students should understand that, as with much of the content of this text, this legal insert is written from the perspective of the practitioner and/or the correctional administrator. As such, the tone and flavor of this insert are likely to be different from those of many introductory-level textbooks on corrections. This is because the author believes that you, as a potential practitioner in corrections, should be duly informed on the real-world issues and concerns within the field of corrections. A failure to expose students to these concerns is a failure to provide a usable and practical education for criminal justice practitioners.

Legal considerations in this section will refer to U.S. Supreme Court cases and/or federal cases as the basis for any stance taken. However, to the extent that a legal question has not been decided by the U.S. Supreme Court, any reference to specific cases should be viewed as persuasive but not necessarily predictive of how a different state or federal court will rule. This is because state and lower federal courts may have differences in their ruling, depending on the region and/or jurisdiction. This insert will address the following four legal issues concerning women offenders:

I.   Equal protection and access to facilities, programs, and services.

II. Staffing and supervision.

III. Sexual misconduct.

IV. Due process challenges.

These four themes or issues will serve as the overall thrust of discussion, and each area is, in and of itself, an important and somewhat broad point of concern. To the extent possible, these points of discussion will be distilled to specific points that students should keep in mind.

I. Equal Protection and Title IX: Equivalent Access to Programs and Services

Although the goal is to provide parity of treatment for all prisoners, regardless of gender, students should understand that administrators may not be required to provide the same level of facilities and services to men and women if they can justify the differences. For instance, there is no requirement that the same policies, facilities, programs, and services offered to male offenders be offered to female offenders. In many circumstances, differences will not run afoul of equal protection because male and female inmate populations are not deemed to be similarly situated. The modern trend treats gender as governed by *Turner v. Safley* (1987), unless the gender discrimination is purposeful (see Chapter 4 of this text regarding the standards set by *Turner v. Safley*), in which case regulations must satisfy protocols for exceptions (due to security or safety) that the Supreme Court has ruled on.

Regardless of whether the issue meets *Turner* guidelines or qualifies as an exception that has been given sufficient scrutiny, different policies, facilities, programs, and services can satisfy equal protection even if the populations are similarly situated, as long as a valid *penological justification* exists for the differences (again, see *Turner v. Safley* regarding valid penological justifications). Fairness and rehabilitative concerns dictate that parity should be the goal even when not constitutionally required.

II. Staffing and Litigation Issues

A number of lawsuits involving female offenders have been based on cross-gender supervision. Administrators must balance competing institutional claims with the privacy interests of women offenders. The law on cross-gender supervision and searches is very fact specific. However, challenges brought by female inmates appear to be treated more favorably than those brought by male inmates. Thus, women are more likely than men to be successful in suits that implicate privacy interests. This outcome stems from society's apparent view that women should be afforded more privacy than men. Also, because many female offenders have been victims of sexual and physical assault, cross-gender supervision can cause them additional trauma.

Cross-gender supervision also provides opportunities for sexual misconduct, which is one of the few areas in prison administration that is likely to generate high-profile litigation, and a substantial likelihood of liability being imposed. While inmates bring suits concerning cross-gender supervision, staff members or their unions sometimes challenge same-sex supervision policies. Generally, these issues require administrators to be proactive, to institute and enforce policies designed to limit the possibility of improper contact, and to be able to articulate reasonable explanations to justify staffing decisions.

When considering cross-gender strip searches and pat-downs, prison administrators should ensure that all strip searches are conducted between same-sex staff and inmates. In court, female inmates have tended to have more favorable outcomes than males when challenging either strip searches or pat-down searches. In some cases, general practices that allow opposite-gender searches may violate the Eighth Amendment rights of female inmates, such as with a female inmate who is known to suffer from trauma from sexual abuse.

However, as long as there are no egregious circumstances, opposite-gender searches of male inmates by females tend to be upheld, while cross-gender searches of females by male guards have a greater chance of being struck down. This is, to some extent, a double standard that relates to the differing expectations of privacy for each sex of inmate. In addition, this is grounded in the reality that most incidents of custodial sexual abuse occur among male officers and female inmates.

Another key area of consideration is the potential for lawsuits resulting from sexual harassment, sexual misconduct, or cross-gender supervision. The best means for agencies to defend against these lawsuits is to establish clear policies and procedures and ensure that employees follow them. This process should entail the following five actions:

1. Establish clear policies concerning inappropriate conduct.

2. Conduct training of staff concerning sexual misconduct and cross-gender supervision.

3. Establish multiple reporting mechanisms.

4. Establish protocols for investigating claims and insuring against retaliation.

5. Ensure that inmate complaints are investigated because they provide notice to the facility if the correctional staff member commits further misconduct.

Some administrators may wish to encourage same-sex supervision in their policies to lessen the likelihood of sexual misconduct claims arising from cross-gender supervision. While this will not protect them from all sexual misconduct claims (sometimes persons will commit these infractions against members of their own gender), this practice is likely to at least limit the number of claims that might emerge. In fact, it is very likely that these policies will prevent the majority of such claims since they are often based on cross-gender incidents; indeed, the most visible claims are those brought against males who are supervising female inmates.

III. Sexual Misconduct

It is important to understand that there are historical, cultural, and psychological reasons why women may feel more violated and/or intimidated by cross-gender supervision than men. Consider the problematic history that exists with custodial sexual misconduct in several female facilities throughout the nation. During the 1980s and '90s, roughly 23 correctional departments were involved in class action or individual lawsuits related to staff sexual misconduct with female inmates. One notorious case in particular occurred in Georgia and included staff throughout the entire institution and at all levels of supervision (*Cason v. Seckinger* [1984]). The U.S. Department of Justice filed civil lawsuits in two states (Arizona and Michigan) alleging systematic sexual misconduct by male correctional staff in women's prisons (Human Rights Watch, 1996).

Much of the **custodial sexual misconduct** included the use or threat of force targeted toward female offenders in multiple state correctional systems. Correctional staff also used their authority and ability to procure goods and services for the female inmates to encourage the inmates to engage in an exchange for sexual favors. Further, some of the misconduct was "consensual" between inmate and staff, but this is nonetheless abuse on the part of correctional staff. Many of the female offending population were themselves abused prior to incarceration, as children (in abusive families of origin) and/or as adults (as with domestic abusers or through involvement in the sex industry). Because of this, the dysfunctional exchange and confusion between sex and a mature emotionally intimate relationship is normalized for many of these women. In either event, it is the obligation of staff to ensure that appropriate boundaries are set and that these are not violated.

IV. Due Process Challenges

Typically, due process has not provided a useful tool for inmates to challenge their conditions of confinement. However, there is one area of concern related to female inmates that was mentioned earlier in this chapter: the mental health of women who are locked up. This can become a due process issue in cases where allegations of particularly brutal isolation and sensory deprivation is at issue, especially among female inmates who act out or attempt suicide in the general population. This may also raise Eighth Amendment and equal protection concerns. The higher percentage of mentally ill female inmates has been well documented.

In general, the interrelation of mental health care and security needs is a subject that calls for more attention with female offenders. Female inmates appear to be placed in solitary confinement for less problematic behavior than men, some of which is directed at themselves rather than others. Yet, their confinement appears to increase their violent behavior against themselves and may impose devastating psychological effects. Proactive administrators should consult with their mental health professionals to determine whether isolation is an appropriate response for the behavior in question.

Other due process issues sometimes arise around the issue of pregnancy and child-related questions. While inmate pregnancy is an issue usually dealt with in jails, it does also occur in prison settings. Most legal issues regarding the pregnancy itself tend to arise concerning access to nontherapeutic abortions and the conditions surrounding the birth of an inmate's child. Prison restrictions on the termination of pregnancies and on deliveries should be carefully monitored by administrators because they are likely to result in litigation.

Further, due process issues should be considered when addressing other child-related issues, such as termination of parental rights or placement of women in facilities close to their homes. As we have seen in earlier parts of this chapter, maintaining family relationships can be particularly important for female inmates. Understanding how such family-based legal issues impact female offenders is important in designing programs to ensure the best outcomes for these women and their children. Administrators must be sensitive to how family issues affect an incarcerated mother's programming in prison and her chances of rehabilitation when she returns to the community.

SOURCE: Bloom, B., Owen, B., & Covington, S. (2003). *Gender responsive strategies: Research, practice and guiding principles for women offenders.* Washington, DC: National Institute of Corrections. Retrieved from http://www.nicic.org/Library/018017.

Guiding Principles to Improve Services for Female Offenders

The foremost principle in responding appropriately to women is to acknowledge the implications of gender throughout the criminal justice system. The criminal justice field has been dominated by the rule of parity, with equal treatment to be provided to everyone. However, this does not necessarily mean that the exact same treatment is appropriate for both women and men. The data are very clear concerning the distinguishing aspects of female and male offenders. They come into the criminal justice system via different pathways; respond to supervision and custody differently; exhibit differences in terms of substance abuse, trauma, mental illness, parenting responsibilities, and employment histories; and represent different levels of risk within both the institution and the community. To successfully develop and deliver services, supervision, and treatment for women offenders, we must first acknowledge these gender differences (see Implementing Guiding Principle 1).

Research from a range of disciplines (e.g., health, mental health, and substance abuse) has shown that safety, respect, and dignity are fundamental to behavioral change. To improve behavioral outcomes for women, it is critical to provide a safe and supportive setting for supervision. A profile of women in most correctional facilities indicates that many have grown up in less than optimal family and community environments. In their interactions with women offenders, criminal justice professionals must be aware of the significant pattern of emotional, physical, and sexual abuse that many of these women have experienced. Every precaution must be taken to ensure that the criminal justice setting does not reenact female offenders' patterns of earlier life experiences. A safe, consistent, and supportive environment is the cornerstone of a corrective process.

Because of their lower levels of violent crime and their low risk to public safety, women offenders should, whenever possible, be supervised with the minimal restrictions required to meet public safety interests (see Implementing Guiding Principle 2). Understanding the role of relationships in women's lives is fundamental because the theme of connections and relationships threads throughout the lives of female offenders. When an understanding of the role of relationships is incorporated into policies, practices, and programs, the effectiveness of the system or agency is enhanced. This concept is critical when addressing the following:

1. Reasons why women commit crimes.

2. Impact of interpersonal violence on women's lives.

3. Importance of children in the lives of female offenders.

4. Relationships between women in an institutional setting.

5. Process of women's psychological growth and development.

6. Environmental context needed for programming.

7. Challenges involved in reentering the community.

Attention to the above issues is crucial to the promotion of successful outcomes for women in the criminal justice system (see Implementing Guiding Principle 3). Substance abuse, trauma, and mental health are three critical, interrelated issues in the lives of women offenders. These issues have a major impact on a woman's experience of community correctional supervision, incarceration, and transition to the community in terms of both programming needs and successful reentry. Although they are therapeutically linked, these issues historically have been treated separately. One of the most important developments in health care over the past several decades is the recognition that a substantial proportion of women have a history of serious traumatic experiences that play a vital and often unrecognized role in the evolution of their physical and mental health problems (see Implementing Guiding Principle 4).

Further, it should be obvious that programs will have to address both the social and material realities of female offenders, just as is true with the male inmate population. This is an important aspect of correctional intervention, particularly at the point of reentry. The female offender's life is shaped by her socioeconomic status, her experience with trauma and substance abuse, and her relationships with partners, children, and family. Most female offenders are disadvantaged economically and socially, and this reality is compounded by their trauma and substance abuse histories. Improving outcomes for these women requires preparing them through education and training so they can support themselves and their children (see Implementing Guiding Principle 5).

Video Link 11.5
Learn more about the reentry of incarcerated mothers.

TECHNOLOGY AND EQUIPMENT 11.1

Evaluating the Use of Radio Frequency Identification Device Technology to Prevent and Investigate Sexual Assaults in a Correctional Setting

In recent years, the problem of sexual violence in correctional facilities has gained national prominence, largely due to the passage of the Prison Rape Elimination Act (PREA) of 2003 (Public Law 108-79, now codified as 45 U.S.C. 15601 to 15609). As stated in the act, sexual violence may present serious problems in correctional facilities, affecting not just the victims of violence but the correctional population as a whole. In response to the increased attention on this issue, correctional administrators have sought ways in which to harness new training methods, management tools, and technologies.

The focus of this evaluation is to explore the use and effectiveness of one such measure: radio frequency identification device (RFID) technology, which enables correctional staff to track inmate locations in an effort to prevent prohibited acts, including sexual assault. The gravity of the consequences associated with custodial sexual abuse of females suggests that RFID technology designed to support prison management efforts to prevent sexual assaults, to effectively investigate them, and to increase inmates' perceptions of safety from sexual victimization would benefit the entire culture of a prison.

In correctional facilities, RFID transmitter chips can communicate the locations and movements of inmates within prison facilities to staff. The technology can be programmed to issue alerts when inmates are out of place, in prohibited locations, or in proximity to individuals with whom they have conflict. In addition, RFID historical records can be used to investigate allegations of inmate misconduct.

RFID technology enables users to authenticate, locate, and track objects or people tagged with a unique identifier (National Law Enforcement and Corrections Technology Center, 2005). In correctional settings, inmates can be fitted with RFID units on their ankles or wrists that enable correctional officers to track their locations and movements, potentially increasing the perceived risks of being detected when engaging in sexual assaults and other prohibited behaviors. RFID technology may deter inmates from committing prohibited acts by increasing their perceived risk of detection, especially when officers confirm inmates' perceptions by responding to RFID alerts and following through with disciplinary action. Similarly, it is feasible that RFID technology increases inmates' perceptions of safety from sexual assault based on the belief that perpetrators are more likely to be apprehended.

Because the system maintains historical data on inmates' locations, RFID technology may be a useful tool for investigating assaults, identifying which inmates were at the location where the assault took place, and aiding in the substantiation of allegations of sexual and other assaults. Thus, from a theoretical perspective, RFID technology should effectively increase an inmate's perceived risk of detection for both the perpetration of sexual assaults and the reporting of false allegations.

In 2006, the Urban Institute completed an assessment of RFID technology funded by the National Institute of Justice. The assessment investigated how RFID technology was being implemented in correctional settings across the country and found that 13 correctional facilities had implemented or were in the process of implementing RFID technology at that time. That study, however, simply identified likely evaluation sites, as evaluating the impact of RFID technology on prison management at these locations was beyond the scope of the contract. From a knowledge-building perspective, no published evaluations currently exist of RFID use as a correctional management tool, much less as a tool to prevent sexual and other violence. Correctional institutions across the country have expressed interest in obtaining RFID systems, but may be hesitant to expend scarce correctional resources in the absence of reliable evidence that the technology works.

SOURCE: La Vigne, N., Halberstadt, R., & Parthasarathy, B. (2009). *Evaluating the use of radio frequency identification device (RFID) technology to prevent and investigate sexual assaults in a correctional setting.* Washington, DC: Urban Institute. Reprinted by permission of the author, Nancy La Vigne.

FEMALE OFFENDERS AND TREATMENT IMPLICATIONS

In a study of 110 programs that deal with female offenders, it was found that programs conducive to treatment success of female offenders should use female role models and pay particular attention to

PHOTO 11.3

These female deputies work at the Louisiana Transitional Center for Women (LTCW) in Tallulah, Louisiana. LTCW is a reentry facility for female offenders who are leaving prison and will be returning to the community. These officers are shown here at North Delta Regional Training Academy while taking correctional officer training to meet certification standards set by the state.

gender-specific concerns not common to male offenders (Bloom et al., 2003). Treatment for female offenders requires a heightened need to respond to expression of emotions and the ability to communicate openly with offenders. Much of this has to do with socialization to be open and nurturing, emphasis on reciprocity, and so on.

Based on the research presented and the specific needs of female offenders, it becomes clear that treatment considerations for female offenders can be quite complicated. Indeed, it is plausible that a female offender could have the sundry challenges outlined in this chapter as well as numerous others included in various other chapters of this text. Thus, many female offenders can be viewed as "special needs plus" when considering the various issues that may be present. With this in mind, specific recommendations regarding treatment programs for female offenders are outlined as follows:

1. Treatment plans must be individualized in structure, including:
   a. Clear and measurable goals.
   b. Intensive programming with effective duration.
   c. Appropriate screening and assessment.

2. Female offenders must be able to acquire needed life skills:
   a. Parenting and life skills are taught—these are both *critical*.
   b. Anger management must be addressed.
   c. Marketable job skills are important because female offenders typically have few job skills and, unlike male offenders, have more difficulty obtaining jobs in the manual labor sectors that pay higher (construction, plant work, etc.).

3. Must address victimization issues:
   a. Programs should address self-esteem, which is typically tied into previous abuse issues, which in turn increase likelihood of substance abuse and prostitution, two main segments of female crime.
   b. Programs must address domestic violence issues. These are highly common among female offenders, both from family of origin and between previous boyfriends and/or spouses; often this is intergenerationally transmitted.

Audio Link 11.3
Learn more about the needs of incarcerated mothers.

Audio Link 11.4
Listen to a clip about aging female inmates.

Dolan, Kolthoff, Schreck, Smilanch, and Todd (2003) discuss the importance of having gender-specific treatment programs for correctional clients with co-occurring disorders. Their insights are important for a couple of key reasons that should be emphasized in this chapter. First, it is becoming increasingly clear within the treatment literature that therapists, caseworkers, and the curriculum that they use must be able to address diverse populations. Many law persons do not consider that women, the elderly, and the disabled are part of most diversity programs just as are ethnic and racial groups. This is important because it is also becoming clear that correctional programs must address these issues as well.

In Iowa, the First Judicial District Department of Correctional Services established a community-based treatment program in its correctional facility (incidentally, this also demonstrates how both correctional facilities and community supervision programs can successfully interface with one another). This program established a gender-specific female program to provide integration of treatment services designed to focus on dual diagnosis of female offenders. This is important since it is clear from the earlier introduction that female offenders may be at heightened risk of having dual diagnoses given their frequent prior abuse trauma, maternal concerns for their children, and the high rate of substance abuse.

The program addresses physical and sexual abuse issues, substance abuse, mental disorders, family-based counseling, and parenting issues. The program is founded on the notion that most of these clients have grown up in dysfunctional families, so it is difficult for these clients to even be able to conceive how a functional family actually operates on a routine basis. Further, this program specifically strives to include the children in the treatment process since it has been found that this increases likelihood of client program completion, and it helps the client's recovery from various other issues. Thus, treatment is optimized because the offender's role as a parent is used as a therapeutic tool to enhance the relevance of the treatment to the client.

Specific issues pertaining to physical health care, adult sexuality, preventative pregnancy education, education on sexually transmitted diseases, and grief/loss pertaining to their role as a parent are included within this program. A consortium of individuals and agencies are involved, including staff from the local Planned Parenthood, the local police force, community supervision, private therapists, and so forth. The topics covered by these individuals are also discussed in the group therapy sessions throughout the daily routine to reinforce the learning process. Specifically, Dolan et al. (2003) note that treatment for women with dual diagnoses and histories of violence is optimized when it does the following:

1. Focuses on a woman's strengths.

2. Acknowledges a woman's role as a parent.

3. Improves interactions between the parent and child.

4. Provides comprehensive, coordinated services for a mother and her children.

The program by Dolan et al. (2003) is an excellent example of how most programs for female offenders should be structured and should be considered a model program. The reasons for this are because it is comprehensive and demonstrates how the multitude of issues pertinent to female offenders can be addressed within a single facility while utilizing a wide array of services within the community. This program falls well within the theme of this text, demonstrating how community resources and public and private agencies can be combined to address complicated social ills with cost-effective methods. Because of this, it is suggested that other areas of the nation should look toward this program when designing treatments for their female offender population.

Journal Article Link 11.3
Read about how treatment programs for women must address multiple complicated goals.

CONCLUSION

While female offenders are a small proportion of the offending population, they are a rapidly growing group of offenders. It is becoming increasingly clear that services for female offenders are inadequate, within both institutional and community intervention programs. There is a need to address specific social ills that are fairly unique to female offenders since this population is likely to continue to grow in number. Among these social ills are domestic violence, sexual abuse, drug use, prostitution, sexually transmitted diseases, and child custody issues. Many of the problems associated with female offenders have hidden costs that affect the rest of society in a multifaceted manner. Any failure to improve services to this offending population will simply ensure that future generations likewise adopt criminogenic patterns of social coping. This is specifically the case given the "collateral damage" that emanates from the impairment of children whose mothers (and likely sole caretakers) are incarcerated. When thinking long-term, it becomes both socially and economically sound practice to work to improve services and ensure that accommodations are made for the special needs of the female offender.

Numerous legal considerations emerge with female inmates. These legal issues can range from the provision of services to pregnancy issues behind bars. The potential for staff misconduct is also a serious issue that resulted in a number of scandals during the 1990s. In addition, liability issues can emerge when employees conduct functions (such as strip searches and pat searches) where cross-gender interactions take place. Agency administrators must be sure to have clear and specific policies in place and that their staff are appropriately trained when supervising female inmates.

In order to prepare female inmates for reentry and to make their time in prison more constructive, agencies should follow several key guiding principles. First, agencies must recognize that gender does indeed matter, and agencies should provide an environment that fosters safety, respect, and dignity for women behind bars. Agencies should also develop policies and practices that are relational in nature and that promote good relationships with children, family, significant others, and the community. Agencies must address substance abuse, trauma, and mental health issues in a manner that is culturally competent. In addition, as with male inmates, agencies should provide female inmates with job and life skills that will allow them to change their socioeconomic circumstances. Lastly, effective and collaborative reentry processes must be utilized if agencies wish to realistically lower the likelihood of recidivism for female offenders.

END-OF-CHAPTER DISCUSSION QUESTIONS

1. What are some of the demographic and statistical characteristics of the female offender population?

2. Compare and contrast the rates of incarceration and the terms of sentencing for male and female offenders.

3. Who was Elizabeth Fry? Explain what she did to assist female offenders and why this was unique during her time in history.

4. Define patriarchy and then explain how this might be associated with the dynamics of women who are incarcerated.

5. Discuss how feminist criminology helps to explain criminal behavior among women.

6. Which states are the most punitive for female offenders? Speculate (based on your prior readings) as to why this may be the case for female offenders in those states.

7. What have been some common legal problems associated with female offenders in the correctional facility? What has been done in corrections to address these issues?

8. Identify and discuss at least three guiding principles associated with effective correctional operations when considering female offenders.

9. Discuss the various treatment considerations related to female offenders.

KEY TERMS

Chivalry hypothesis	Domestic violence	Patriarchy
Collateral damage	Elizabeth Fry	Reformatories for women
Custodial sexual misconduct	Little Hoover Commission	Victorian Era

APPLIED EXERCISE 11.1

For this exercise, students should consider how professionalism in correctional officer training has gained support during the past two decades of correctional history. This trend was discussed in the previous chapter (Chapter 10), and students were required to develop a training program on workforce diversity in Applied Exercise 10.1. While that training program was to be comprehensive, addressing multiple facets of diversity, such programs cannot go into the depth required when facilities are designed to meet the specific needs of a singly identified group, such as female offenders.

Consider your assignment in Applied Exercise 10.1. With that in mind, you are again asked to assume the role of the assistant warden who developed the diversity training program. As it turns out, you have done so, as your warden requested, and the program has been highly successful in reducing grievances based on racial differences. In fact, your warden made a point to praise your work, even letting the regional director know about your program and the positive impact that it has had on your facility. Further, the overall sense of professionalism possessed by officers in your facility has improved. Thus, your program has witnessed successes in numerous spheres of human resource operations.

It appears that you have done very well, indeed. The regional director ultimately created a region-wide position, the director of the new Office of Diversity and Specialized Needs. You were given this new job along with a pay raise. In short, you have been promoted. However, with every promotion comes added responsibility and duties. Your case is no different.

The regional director has asked that you go to the state's largest female prison, which is located in a remote area. He asks you to accomplish two tasks:

First, develop a training program for officers that is 1.5 days in length and that addresses *gender-specific* considerations in security, safety, and human services. You will need to develop an outline of the content as well as an explanation for that content. This training will be implemented within the facility during the next fiscal year, when budgeting allows for additional training.

Second, you are to write a brief memo that outlines the top five issues that you believe are important to meeting the special needs of female offenders in the facility. You must limit this memo to the top five issues that you think are a priority in delivering effective services to female offenders in your state. Among these, the remote location of the current facility, away from friends and family who can visit, might be one of the five potential recommendations.

For this assignment, students should create a brief outline of the 1.5-day training on gender-specific issues in security, safety, and human services. This aspect of the assignment will require anywhere from 250 to 750 words.

In addition, the brief memo, addressed to the regional director of state prison operations, should be approximately 500 to 750 words in length. A brief listing of the five recommendations and the reasons for those recommendations should be included.

WHAT WOULD YOU DO?

You are a correctional officer in a minimum-security facility that houses female inmates. While on your shift you are required to do a "shakedown" of the various inmates' living quarters throughout the day. In doing so, you happen to be in a dorm within the facility and are allocated a list of inmates whose property you are to search. Among these inmates is Lorianna Marisol Vasquez, her cubicle is ready to be searched, and she is standing close by in case you need to talk with her while conducting the search.

While searching her cubicle, you find a letter that she has written. It appears that the letter is written to one of the male guards at the facility who works the evening shift (you work the day shift). In the letter, it explains that Vasquez is in need of several hygiene products and also desires some cigarettes and sundry food products. Further, the letter seems to imply that Vasquez will make it well worth the officer's time to obtain these items.

However, the letter is written in a vague and comical manner, as if the entire idea were just a game or for sport, rather than being a serious-minded proposition. Likewise, from the letter, you cannot tell if this has been an ongoing arrangement or if this would be the initial proposition. You look, but find no letters from the officer to Vasquez.

But, you have heard rumors that this officer frequently talks with Vasquez for extended periods of time, and you have even detected a degree of jealousy among the other female inmates in the dorm. As it turns out, this officer is a good-looking fellow, and he is fond of being excessively polite to the women on the dorm. It makes you wonder if there is something more that may be occurring between inmate Vasquez and this officer.

What would you do?

CROSS-NATIONAL PERSPECTIVE 11.1

Free to Grow Up: Home for Female Inmates With Children in Europe

The province of Milan has recently opened a home for imprisoned women with children in the Lombardy capital in Viale Piceno, Italy. The home, opened as of a ministerial decree, was created in collaboration with the Milanese Penitentiary Administration and other area agencies that wish to end the intergenerational cycle of crime and criminal behavior. This program started life as a pilot institute based on a law passed in 2001, which focused on the issue that women with children under 3 years of age in exceptional cases should not be sentenced to stay in prison.

It is easy to comprehend the difficulties that small children in an institution can encounter in their psychic-physical development. Specifically, this program seeks to alleviate the trauma and sense of abandonment that youth tend to encounter when separated from their mothers. Conversely but just as useful is the fact that women in this program tend to fare better in their treatment programming and also tend to have better prognosis with various life-skills aspects in their day-to-day functioning. Thus, it is clear that children are, themselves, an important resource in the paths of change and growth of these sentenced women. It was this premise that moved the project experimented in Milan to the Institution of Attenuated Custody for Mothers (ICAM).

The project planning was set forth in the field of the consolidated collaboration with local territorial bodies with particular reference to the Milanese area and started with the sharing by all the bodies involved in pedagogic, juridical reflections, according to which the phenomenon, even if not having vast statistical dimensions, represents a particularly relevant aspect for all society due to the unexpected spin-offs on the infantile population of their stay in prison. Consequently society at large is involved in identifying solutions of mediation between the application of the mother's custody in prison and guaranteeing the child a serene infancy.

The child and the mother both require specific intervention. This program addresses the needs of both the child and the mother, simultaneously, and in a coordinated fashion that mitigates the affective impact on the child and optimizes the opportunities for the mother. In between, both maintain routine contact and are given therapeutic work that enhances the mother-child relationship, changing dysfunctional bonds to those that are likely much more healthy. For instance, issues of child parentification are addressed, and faulty parenting processes are redesigned through parent training and child education regarding the appropriate role of parent and child within the family system. Other dynamics are addressed as well, all with the intent to create a normalized family system that insulates both from the effects of unhealthy living.

This program is particularly suited for mothers who are addicted to drugs and alcohol. The Milan Prison has allocated a new housing building for the program, which is referred to as the attenuated custody institute for drug-addicted mothers. The ICAM is located in an urban area so that women can access all of the various services that are necessary. This is a superior location to a rural area where services would be hard to reach and where family and friends might have difficulty visiting. This location also enhances educational opportunities for the children.

The combination of effective programming and enhanced location has created an effective program that addresses the needs of parent and child. Overall, it would seem that the program is a success. The program has been designed to overcome many of the hurdles associated with female offender service delivery that occurs in most prison systems. It seems that these modifications and enhancements have worked well; current initial outcomes have proven to be positive. The Milan Prison's ICAM seems to hold promise as a showpiece that other programs around the world may desire to replicate. By all accounts, this might be an optimal approach in many countries that have noted the challenges for female offenders and their children.

Question 1: After reading this article, explain how this type of program addresses specific issues outlined in this chapter with female offenders. In other words, how are the issues between female offenders in this country similar to those in the United States?

Question 2: How does this type of program improve upon some of the deficiencies noted with many correctional facilities for female offenders?

SOURCE: European Programme for the Prevention of and Fight Against Crime. (2007). *Free to grow up: Home for female inmates with children.* Retrieved from http://praxis-psychosoziale-beratung .de/mcproject.htm

STUDENT STUDY SITE

Visit the Student Study Site at **www.sagepub.com/hanserintro** to access links to the videos, audio clips, SAGE journal articles, state rankings, and reference materials noted in this chapter, as well as additional study tools including eFlashcards, web quizzes, and more.

chapter 12

Specialized Inmate Populations

LEARNING OBJECTIVES:

1. Discuss some of the common issues facing prison systems when housing specialized inmate populations.

2. Discuss the prevalence of mental illness within state prison systems.

3. Identify various mental health diagnoses that might be found in prison settings.

4. Discuss the various challenges facing prison systems housing inmates who are HIV/AIDS positive.

5. Identify the various classifications of elderly inmates within an institution.

6. Discuss some of the challenges and issues that face correctional agencies when housing elderly offenders.

7. Discuss how the prison subculture impacts, interacts with, and reacts to inmates who are mentally ill, HIV/AIDS positive, and/or elderly.

INTRODUCTION

Prison Tour Video Link 12.1
Watch a clip about services provided for specialized populations.

As we have seen in Chapter 9, any modern correctional program relies on the notion that we must be able to reliably and validly classify and determine the needs of offenders. This ability to classify offenders ensures that we are able to match our responses in a manner that optimizes the outcome of our program. Further, from a legal and historical context, the concept of "needs" has been pivotal in designing responses to different types of offenders (juvenile offenders, mentally challenged offenders, etc.). However, when we use the term *need*, this implies that the issue involves something that is absolutely necessary, not something that is a mere desire or preference. Thus, if the individual does not have this need met, then he or she will experience some form of serious social, psychological, physical, or emotional impairment within his or her daily functioning. Because correctional institutions are liable for legally defensible standards of care for inmates in their custody, they must be prepared to address specialized needs that may emerge among their prison populations.

For purposes of this text, the term **offender with special needs** refers to specialized offenders who have some notable physical, mental, and/or emotional challenge. These challenges prevent either a subjective or an objective need from being fulfilled for that individual, the lack of this subjective or objective need impairs the individual's day-to-day ability to function within the confines of the criminal law.

CLASSIFICATION CONSIDERATIONS AND THE AMERICANS WITH DISABILITIES ACT

Reference Link 12.1
Read about issues concerning disabled prisoners.

During the first few hours of being received, an inmate should be given a medical screening or examination. While a full examination is the most effective approach, this may not always be practical. However, screenings can be easily conducted, even when large groups of inmates are being processed into the system simultaneously. The medical screening process is basically a preliminary triage to sort out serious issues from those that are likely to be more routine among other inmates on a cell block or within a dormitory. Likewise, this process can be used to identify medical issues that require immediate attention, thereby alerting staff to the need for a full examination and for additional medical service. During this process, mental health professionals should be available to assist inmates with issues that, while medical in nature, may impact an offender's state of mind.

Further, it should be a priority for prison systems to identify inmates who have disabilities. The Americans with Disabilities Act (ADA) defines a person with disabilities as one who has "a physical or mental impairment that substantially limits one or more major life activities, has a record of such impairment, or is regarded as having such an impairment" (p. 2). This definition is all-inclusive, meaning that it even applies to the inmate population, and the obligation to provide assistance extends to correctional agencies. Correctional administrators are compelled by law to comply with the provisions of the ADA. This act grants certain rights to citizens of the United States who are incarcerated.

MENTAL ILLNESS AND COGNITIVE DEFICITS AS SPECIAL NEEDS AND/OR DISABILITIES

Mentally ill inmates are those who have a diagnosable disorder that meets the specific and exact criteria of the **Diagnostic and Statistical Manual of Mental Disorders (DSM-IV-TR)**. This reference tome was formed by gatherings of psychiatrists and psychologists from around the world, and sets forth the specific guidelines in applying a specific diagnosis to a person presenting with a mental disorder. For the purposes of this chapter, **mental illness** will be defined as any diagnosed disorder contained within the DSM-IV-TR, as published by the American Psychiatric Association. Mental illness causes severe disturbances in thought, emotions, and ability to cope with the demands of daily life. Mental illness, like physiological forms of illness, can be acute, chronic, or under control and in remission.

The process of defining mental illness has been both controversial and subject to great scrutiny. Similarly, defining **mental retardation** has been a bit controversial as well. However, the definition provided by the American Association on Intellectual and Developmental Disabilities is the definition of

FOCUS TOPIC: 12.1

IQ Score Ranges for Mental Retardation (MR)

Severity	Percentage of MR Population	IQ
Mild	51–69	89.0
Moderate	36–50	6.0
Severe	21–35	3.5
Profound	Under 20	1.5

choice among the courts of America. According to this definition, "mental retardation refers to significantly sub-average general intellectual functioning existing concurrently with deficits in adaptive behavior and manifested during the developmental period."

Usually, to be considered mentally retarded, the individual must have an IQ of less than 70. Further, the person must demonstrate impairments in adaptive behavior. These impairments may come in many forms, such as slow overall emotional maturation, poor personal responsibility, or social skills below those normally expected of a person of similar age. Third, the individual must present with the disorder during the formative years, typically well before the age of 18.

According to the DSM-IV-TR (American Psychiatric Association, 2000), mental retardation is divided into four categories reflecting the severity of the retardation. The ranges of mental retardation, as noted by the American Psychiatric Association (2000), are listed in Focus Topic 12.1.

Generally speaking, it is estimated that mental retardation has a prevalence of 3% in society with roughly 89% having mild retardation. Similar percentages have been found to exist in the correctional population. Offenders with severe or profound retardation are often either unlikely to commit crime or diverted in the early stages of processing through the criminal justice system.

It is often difficult to identify mildly retarded offenders since their handicap is not especially pronounced so as to be easily identified. This is further compounded among the offender population when one considers that the offender population tends to have intellectual scores (IQ) that are slightly lower than the majority of the nonoffending population (much of this is due to lower socioeconomic status and lack of education among the majority of the lower-income offending population within the correctional system).

Moderately retarded offenders are more easily identifiable. Their deficits usually manifest in early childhood and involve some delayed muscular-motor development. These persons can usually learn to take care of themselves and do simple tasks. However, they often have difficulty with more complex tasks. They can usually progress to the third or fourth grades of academic ability. These offenders require fairly extensive training for community living and often need some form of structured employment setting.

Offenders with severe retardation often show marked delays in motor development early in life and are extremely hindered from functioning independently. These offenders need constant supervision to just function and communicate. These individuals often need constant nursing care and often have existing physical and/or mental impairments beyond their mental retardation. These individuals need extensive training for the simplest of basic skills. Because of this, they are seldom kept in the institutional or community correctional systems. Offenders with this level of impairment are extremely rare.

It is important to provide a clear distinction between mental retardation and mental illness. In technical terms, mental illness is a disease, whether temporary, periodic, or chronic. Mental retardation, on the other hand, is a developmental disability and therefore not considered a disease. A person suffering from mental illness may recover; however, the state of mental retardation is a permanent characteristic that will limit the individual's ability to learn indefinitely.

ACCESS TO PROGRAM ACTIVITIES AND AVAILABILITY

Access to specific programs, such as education, addiction treatment, and vocational training, can result in increased satisfaction and health while in the prison. Further, participation in these functions can increase the offender's likelihood of receiving early discharge through good-time accumulation, and this participation can improve the prognosis of the offender's later integration into the community. Because of these factors, implementing the ADA requirements may be prudent for correctional administrators to follow beyond the simple legal liabilities involved. Indeed, incorporation of these accommodations beyond the bare minimal requirements may also serve to ultimately improve the plight of corrections in the future if these problems are addressed in a proactive manner. As Appel (1999) notes, the ADA is the law, and, in much more than a monetary manner, compliance with the ADA is a classic case of "pay me now or pay me even more later." Thus, the long-term benefits for the wise correctional administrator will likely offset any of the short-term costs paid in the meantime.

SEPARATE CARE OR INCLUSION IN GENERAL POPULATION

Once the agency has identified special needs offenders, the next important step is to determine specifically how these offenders will be addressed. A primary question centers on whether these offenders should be kept in contact with the mainstream population of inmates or be segregated. This is an important issue because the welfare of the inmate is at stake, and, as we have seen in Chapter 4 and will see in Legal Insert 12.1, the agency can be held liable for a failure to protect inmates from assault or abuse, even when this is at the hands of another inmate. Other reasons often given for separating special needs inmates from the general population are as follows:

1. Cost Containment: It is generally more efficient and cost-effective if special needs offenders are kept in the same vicinity (both the same facility and the same housing area in that facility) where they can be treated as a group.

2. Managed Care: More effective care can be focused on a specialized unit where specifically trained staff can strategically target their skills to populations most in need.

3. Concentration of Resources: Relevant staff and resources can be more concentrated if special needs inmates are housed in one central location.

Mainstreaming, the integration of an inmate with a disability into the general prison population, is a general expectation of the ADA, and this is because it is expected that disabled inmates will be provided full and complete access to prison programs, activities, and services. However, the ADA does allow correctional administrators to remove an inmate from the general population if his or her health condition is a threat to other inmates, and they may also segregate inmates who are at risk of victimization from other inmates due to their impairment. What typically occurs is a mix of separate care and inclusion within prison facilities where some inmates are handled separately and apart from the main population while others remain in the general population, depending on the circumstances of a particular inmate.

SPECIAL FACILITIES AND HOUSING ACCOMMODATIONS

Prison Tour Video Link 12.2
Watch a correctional officer discuss housing for specialized populations.

Many special needs offenders need housing designed to accommodate their specific needs. Inmates who are mentally ill or who have cognitive deficits may need to be placed in specialized facilities. When considering facility and/or housing accommodations, both physical plant conditions and safety should be considered. It is often the physical plant issues that most concern correctional administrators because they have the potential for exceeding the capacity of already tight budgets. Although the overall spending for corrections has increased along with the increase in inmates throughout the nation, it has been found that even these larger budgets do not cover the specialized facilities and services required for facilities designed for the elderly and/or disabled. The main problems are with the cost to renovate already existing facilities since it is often the case that building a new facility with all of the features required by the ADA is cheaper than modifying older buildings. Equipment to accommodate this population and the physical modifications needed for existing facilities can result in tight operating budgets being stretched beyond their imaginable limits.

SPECIAL FACILITIES AND SUPPORT

When considering special facilities and physical plan support for special needs inmates, agencies should use a concept that Anderson (2008) refers to as universal design. **Universal design** refers to prison construction design that complies with ADA requirements and accommodates all inmate needs, in a universal fashion, regardless of how varied the needs may be from inmate to inmate. This type of design is ideal for agencies that wish to ensure that future construction efforts meet ADA and other standards of care.

This approach to prison facility construction and to implementing support services within future buildings will likely be the trend of the future throughout prison systems. Examples of universal design features might be wider doors, ramps rather than stairs, and heavier building materials that allow safety bars or railings to be added to the construction in later years, if needed (Anderson, 2008). The key issue is that this type of design planning allows for the accommodation of additional needs among the population housed. "While universal design is initially more expensive, it costs less over time as modifications are easier and not as expensive to implement" (Anderson, 2008, p. 364).

PRISON SUBCULTURE AND SPECIAL NEEDS OFFENDERS

In Chapter 10, extensive discussion was given to the prison subculture. This subculture idealizes certain standards of behavior, but, as noted in that chapter, these norms are in a state of flux due to the emergence of gang life inside and outside of the prison. The key issue related to the prison subculture and special needs offenders has two distinct points of concern. The first concern has to do with inmate reactions to the increasing representation of special needs inmates within prison facilities. Second, concerns regarding agency staff and their understanding of the issues associated with special needs offenders are important from the perspective of inmate welfare as well as agency liability.

With regard to the inmate population, serious concern should be given to special needs offenders because they are likely to be very vulnerable to exploitation among other inmates. This is true for elderly offenders who physically are weaker and may also not be as mentally adept as they were in younger years. This is also true for inmates with a variety of mental health conditions, such as anxiety-based disorders and affective disorders. These inmates are vulnerable to manipulation and are also likely to be victimized by predatory inmates due to their sense of fear (as with anxiety-related disorders) or their sense of self-neglect (as with affective disorders). Those with serious psychiatric disorders are likely to be taunted, ridiculed, and generally worked into heightened emotional states by other more stable inmates who may find their reactions amusing or entertaining. Inmates with cognitive impairments are likely to have their property stolen by other inmates, and they are likely to be duped by wiser cons who act as if they wish to befriend them. Sex offenders and inmates with alternative sex identities and/or preferences are likely to be sexually and physically victimized by other inmates.

As we have seen, respect within the prison subculture is very important. It should be clear to students that the previous examples consist of inmate groups who would command no respect within the prison environment. In fact, it is likely that inmates would be considered weak or soft if they were to associate too closely with these inmates, and with some (such as sex offenders or offenders with same-sex preferences) they would likely be ostracized from the main inmate power structure for respect. Even with the gang culture that has emerged as being a primary shaping mechanism for prison culture, these various types of offenders are not likely to gain respect, with one exception: the elderly inmate.

The elderly inmate who has lived by the convict code or is a veteran member of a gang is likely to have status among his peers. These inmates, for this text's purposes, will be referred to as greyhounds.

Video Link 12.1
Watch an account of
a long-term inmate.

Journal Article Link 12.1
Read about how officers
who supported punishment
had high levels of stress.

Greyhounds are older inmates who have acquired respect within the offender subculture due to their track record and criminal history, both inside and outside the prison; they are career criminals who have earned status through years of hard-won adherence to prison and criminogenic ideals. These inmates are hardly ever likely to be victims within the inmate subculture, and, in those cases where they may have been burned, they tend to have histories where they were able to "even the score" with those who committed a wrong against them. In short, greyhounds are not weak throughout their life of crime or while serving prison time.

Aside from inmate concerns, the training and understanding of correctional staff is also a key issue of concern with special needs inmates. Some staff may not understand mental illness and may be ill equipped to deal with inmates who present with odd or maladaptive behaviors. These inmates will have difficulty following institutional rules and may become a source of frustration for security staff. Thus, training is important for staff who will routinely deal with these types of inmates, and, within facilities designed for specialized inmates, security staff should be especially well trained in communication techniques, problem-solving approaches, the criteria for many mental health diagnoses, the means by which to address problematic or challenging inmate populations, sexual issues, communicable diseases, suicidal inmates, and so forth. As one can tell from this long list of criteria, the staff dealing with these populations should also be highly specialized.

Lastly, the officer subculture must definitely be professionalized among those who routinely work with various types of special needs inmates. In most cases, correctional officers see themselves as working in a helping capacity as much as a security capacity. This may be quite a stretch in job definition for many security staff, particularly those who see their role as more punitive in nature. These offenders are convicted felons, and not likely to elicit the sympathy of many correctional staff. This is particularly true for the sex-offending population. Training of correctional officers, along with organizational change, implemented by leadership within correctional agencies, is perhaps the best prescription for addressing staff obligations to these various groups of special needs offenders.

MENTALLY ILL OFFENDERS

In 2005, nearly 776,000 prison inmates were identified as possessing some type of mental health problem, according to James and Glaze (2006). This number included over 705,000 in state prison systems as well as another 70,000+ inmates in the Federal Bureau of Prisons. When added with another 479,900 inmates in local jails who were also found to have an identified mental health problem, the total count of incarcerated persons with a mental health issue in 2005 was over 1,255,000 offenders throughout the nation. The estimates mean that, during that year, approximately 56% of state inmates and 45% of federal inmates had some type of mental health issue, along with another 64% of all jail inmates (students should look to Table 12.1 for an illustration of these data). With the current trend toward increased sentence length, it is clear that this number will continue to rise. In fact, the proportion of inmates needing mental health assistance will most assuredly continue to rise from the current statistics as the correctional population continues to age behind bars.

The burden placed on institutional corrections is compounded by the significant number of inmates who have a dual diagnosis of both mental illness and substance abuse. Further still, numerous inmates have marginal levels of mental health problems but find these problems worsened by the conditions of incarceration, which causes them to deteriorate to a more severe state of mental illness. Because of this, it is absolutely mandatory that facilities screen for mental health problems at intake, and it is necessary to identify any inmate who may be at risk of suicide. Staff must not simply consider suicide data with respect to "profiles" of suicidal potentiality, but must ensure that they meet the legal objective criteria required (Hanser, 2002). This is important for the welfare of the offender but is also a necessity to evade liability, if nothing else.

Access to Care: The Four Standards of Mental Health Care

Correctional facility administrators are legally required to implement an adequate health care delivery system that can ensure inmate access to health care and health care providers (Johnson, 1999). This legal requirement for adequate health care also extends to mental health care (Hanser, 2002). An adequate care

TABLE 12.1   Recent Symptoms and History of Mental Health Problems Among Prison and Jail Inmates

Mental health problem	Percent of inmates in—		
	State prison	*Federal prison*	*Local jail*
Any mental health problem	56.2%	44.8%	64.2%
Recent history of mental health problem[a]	24.3%	13.8%	20.6%
Told had disorder by mental health professional	9.4	5.4	10.9
Had overnight hospital stay	5.4	2.1	4.9
Used prescribed medications	18.0	10.3	14.4
Had professional mental health therapy	15.1	8.3	10.3
Symptoms of mental health disorders[b]	49.2%	39.8%	60.5%
Major depressive disorder	23.5	16.0	29.7
Mania disorder	43.2	35.1	54.5
Psychotic disorder	15.4	10.2	23.9

NOTE: Includes inmates who reported an impairment due to a mental problem. Data are based on the Survey of Inmates in States and Federal Correctional Facilities, 2004, and the Survey of Inmates in Local Jails, 2002. See *Methodology* for details on survey sample. See References for sources on measuring symptoms of mental disorder based on a Structured Clinical Interview for the Diagnostic and Statistical Manual of Mental Disorders, fourth edition (DSM-IV).

[a]In year before arrest or since admission.

[b]In the 12 months prior to the interview.

SOURCE: James, D. J., & Glaze, L. E. (2006). *Mental health problems of prison and jail inmates.* Washington, DC: Bureau of Justice Statistics.

delivery system for mental health services in a correctional facility must address a range of specialized needs. In the Supreme Court case of *Ruiz v. Estelle* (1975), the Court focused on several issues required to meet minimally adequate standards for mental health care in a correctional environment. The following requirements articulated by the *Ruiz* Court are pertinent to this chapter:

PHOTO 12.1

Medications are routinely given to offenders who have mental health and cognitive impairments in prison. Sometimes, due to security issues for dangerous inmates, this is done through the cell bars, as pictured here.

1. Correctional administrators must provide an adequate system to ensure mental health screening for inmates.

2. Correctional facilities must provide access to mental health treatment while inmates are in segregation or special housing units.

3. Correctional facilities must adequately monitor the appropriate use of psychotropic medication.

4. A suicide prevention program must be implemented.

These **four standards of mental health care** are common to all jail and prison systems in the United States. The case of *Ruiz v. Estelle* was instrumental in laying much of the groundwork for correctional responsibilities to provide adequate mental health care. Other cases would soon follow that would clarify various fine points of law regarding liability issues, involuntary confinement, and so forth, but the four standards of mental health care for prison systems are generally considered to have evolved from the decisions in the case of *Ruiz v. Estelle*.

CORRECTIONS AND THE LAW 12.1

The Case of Ruiz v. Estelle and Mental Illness in Prison Environments

In 1972, David Ruiz sued the director of the Texas Department of Criminal Justice (William J. Estelle) over dangerous and inhumane working and living conditions. This was a long battled suit that ended in 1982 with a final consent decree that the Texas prison system was resolved to obey. In this class action suit, it was held that the Texas prison system constituted "cruel and unusual punishment," which is prohibited by the Eighth Amendment to the U.S. Constitution. Some of the specific problems noted from this case are as follows:

1. Overcrowding—the prison system had been placing two or three inmates within a single cell designed for only one inmate.

2. Inadequate security—the prison system utilized a system of security that incorporated selected inmates as guards. This practice led to numerous injustices and civil rights violations.

3. Inadequate health care—the prison system did not have an adequate number of medical personnel and also used the services of nonprofessional personnel (including inmate "surgeons" and orderlies) to deliver medical care. Likewise, the therapy for psychiatric patients was deficient.

4. Unsafe working conditions—unsafe conditions and procedures were the norm for inmate laborers.

Ultimately, all of these complaints were rectified within the Texas prison system. However, this case held even more stipulations that would affect the future of all mentally ill and mentally challenged inmates in Texas and throughout the entire nation. In this case, it was further ruled that it was cruel and unusual punishment to confine mentally ill inmates in solitary confinement. In response to this ruling, the prison administration in Texas developed the Administrative Segregation Maintenance Psychiatric Program to provide intensive counseling to inmates with serious mental illness in need of high-security housing as well as a program to transition these inmates back to the general prison population. Correction officials also increased mental health training for security staff and established oversight through regular on-site audits by various outside review bodies.

SOURCE: *Ruiz v. Estelle*, 503 F. Supp. 1265 (SD Tex. 1980), in Out of State Models.

Screening, Treatment, and Medication

Mental health care services begin at the point of screening. As discussed earlier in this chapter, this is a form of triage but is designed to sort out less serious mental health issues from those that require genuine psychiatric care. Given the volume of inmates entering the correctional environment and the fact that the presentation of these individuals is often unplanned, it is important to have a good initial mental health screening system in place. Inmates should be screened on a routine basis before they are placed on a cell block or dormitory. Such measures are good for the inmate's own mental health, but they are also good for the security and safety of institutional staff in the long term. Further, effective screening at the beginning is likely to prevent future problems and headaches for administrators. Thus, good screening practices will aid in the smooth running of the institution.

The primary goal of screening is to quickly identify emergency situations and inmates who might require more extensive intervention prior to placement in the prison population (Johnson, 1999). Further, proper mental health intake screening will determine the type and immediacy of mental health needs. The need for appropriate screening and identification of problem issues is important for both mental health and substance abuse issues. In fact, the two are very difficult to separate. When offenders abuse drugs, many of the drugs elicit symptoms of depression, mania, anxiety, and/or other characteristics that become full-blown diagnosable disorders. These mental disorders that occur in tandem with drug use are referred to as co-occurring disorders.

From the data provided in Table 12.2, it can be seen that a full 61% of prison inmates who had a current or past violent offense had some sort of mental health problem. In addition, 74% of these same inmates had some sort of substance dependence or abuse in their histories (see Table 12.3). The statistics among jail inmates are similar in that around three fourths of all jail inmates who have a mental health problem also have a substance abuse problem. The statistics are even more disturbing when one notes that

TABLE 12.2   Prevalence of Mental Health Issues Among Prison and Jail Inmates in the United States

High prevalence of mental health problems among prison and jail inmates				
	Percent of inmates in—			
	State prison		Local jail	
Selected characteristics	With mental problem	Without	With mental problem	Without
Criminal record				
Current or past violent offense	61%	56%	44%	36%
3 or more prior incarcerations	25	19	26	20
Substance dependence or abuse	74%	56%	76%	53%
Drug use in month before arrest	63%	49%	62%	42%
Family background				
Homelessness in year before arrest	13%	6%	17%	9%
Past physical or sexual abuse	27	10	24	8
Parents abused alcohol or drugs	39	25	37	19
Charged with violating facility rules*	58%	43%	19%	9%
Physical or verbal assault	24	14	8	2
Injured in a fight since admission	20%	10%	9%	3%

*Includes items not shown.

SOURCE: James, D. J. & Glaze, L. E. (2006). *Mental health problems of prison and jail inmates.* Washington, DC: Bureau of Justice Statistics.

even among prison inmates who do not have a mental health issue, half report drug use in the month right before arrest, and 42% of jail inmates without a mental disorder also report the use of substances during the month before arrest.

What these statistics mean is that the vast majority of inmates, whether in prison or in jail, are drug abusers. These statistics also demonstrate that these drug abusers are at an increased likelihood of having mental health problems while in prison. Thus, modern prison and jail systems should all have some sort of effective drug treatment component to mitigate the symptoms of inmates while they serve time behind bars. It behooves correctional agencies to provide these services to assist inmates serving time since this may lower the amount of institutional infractions among inmates.

PHOTO 12.2

Inmates participate in a group therapy session as part of a substance abuse program in the Iowa Correctional Institution for Women. Many correction institutions now offer programs to address substance abuse, mental health issues, and even family issues.

Beyond Screening: Mental Health Assessment

Inmates requiring further assessment should be housed in an area with staff availability and observation appropriate to their needs. The assessment should be assigned to a specific mental health staff member and consist of interviews, a review of prior records and clinical history, a physical examination, observation, and, when necessary, psychological testing. The types of mental health problems and services needed to address these problems are similar throughout each phase of the correctional system's process (e.g., jail detention, imprisonment,

TABLE 12.3   Substance Dependence or Abuse Among Prison and Jail Inmates, by Mental Health Status

Substance dependence or abuse	Percent of inmates in—					
	State prison		Federal prison		Local jail	
	With mental problem	Without	With mental problem	Without	With mental problem	Without
Any alcohol or drugs	74.1%	55.6%	63.6%	49.5%	76.4%	53.2%
Dependence	53.9	34.5	45.1	27.3	56.3	25.4
Abuse only	20.2	21.1	18.5	22.2	20.1	27.8
Alcohol	50.8%	36.0%	43.7%	30.3%	53.4%	34.6%
Dependence	30.4	17.9	25.1	12.7	29.0	11.8
Abuse only	20.4	18.0	18.6	17.7	24.4	22.8
Drugs	61.9%	42.6%	53.2%	39.2%	63.3%	36.0%
Dependence	43.8	26.1	37.1	22.0	46.0	17.6
Abuse only	18.0	16.5	16.1	17.2	17.3	18.4
No dependence or abuse	25.9%	44.4%	36.4%	50.5%	23.6%	46.8%

NOTE: Substance dependence or abuse was based on criteria specified in the Diagnostic and Statistical Manual of Mental Disorder, fourth edition (DSM-IV). For details, see *Substance Dependence, Abuse and Treatment of Jail Inmates, 2002,* <http://www.ojp.usdoj.gov/bjs/abstract/sdatji02.htm>.

SOURCE: James, D. J., & Glaze, L. E. (2006). *Mental health problems of prison and jail inmates.* Washington, DC: Bureau of Justice Statistics.

community supervision). As noted earlier, offenders may enter the system with a certain degree of mental illness that is further aggravated, or they may present new symptomology once incarcerated (Johnson, 1999).

The stress of being involved in the criminal justice process can itself serve as a causal factor for some mental illness. Stressors might include those induced by the legal system, separation from community and/or family support systems, and interactional problems with other offenders within the correctional facility. Indeed, if mental illness is already present, offenders are more subject to victimization from the remainder of the inmate population (Hanser & Moran, 2004). In fact, those who present with mental illness (particularly along the spectrum of mood disorders and/or anxiety disorders) are at an inflated risk of sexual assault within the prison environment (Hanser & Moran, 2004). Further, several documented cases link this victimization with later suicidal ideation and completion among the inmate population (Hanser, 2002).

Problems with sleeping and eating may be experienced as access to anxiety-reducing activities such as television, exercise, socialization, and smoking is much more limited (Johnson, 1999). All of this is compounded by a lack of control over one's environment and the diminished sense of autonomy that is experienced. Thus, inmates first appearing in the correctional facility must be closely watched and screened upon initial entry and during the first 90 to 180 days upon entry so that their integration into the institution can be appropriately monitored.

The correctional institution has an obligation to maintain security and control over the day-to-day routine for the welfare of staff and inmates involved. This means that inmates who present with psychological problems in coping must be kept in "check" so that they do not create a breach in institutional security. This is important and will likely be the primary (if not only) concern among security staff personnel. When disruptions do occur, it is common practice for security personnel to utilize methods of seclusion and/or restraint that are not necessarily consistent with clinical considerations. This can, to some extent, pit security staff against mental health staff on some occasions. However, these same mechanisms of control may be used as part of the treatment regimen when acutely disturbed psychiatric patients are involved (Johnson, 1999). A closely monitored review system must be implemented to ensure that these special security procedures are only used when necessary.

Limited reasons for the use of these special treatment procedures exist and are generally restricted to (1) the imminent risk of harm to self or others and (2) the imminent likelihood of serious damage to property. Inmates in seclusion require enhanced monitoring, which may mean continuous observation by line staff. This is especially true if self-injury is a potential risk. Inmates kept in restraints must be routinely assessed to ensure that they are not injured as a result of the restraining procedure and to ensure that they are able to maintain hygiene and nutritional requirements.

Malingering

Johnson (1999) notes that malingering may occur within institutions. Malingering occurs when inmates falsely claim and consciously fake symptoms of an illness. Inmates may malinger to avoid being responsible for their behavior because it may allow them to avoid certain consequences. Malingering may result in an inmate being referred for mental health evaluation or treatment. However, it is important that security staff do not attempt to discern between inmates who are malingering and those with a true mental illness. Security staff may be prone to do this when the inmate in question tends to be manipulative or if a security staff member has had previous disciplinary problems with the inmate. However, failure to assess correctly can simply compound the problems for the mentally ill offender, and this will ultimately lead to further problems for the institution as a whole, including security staff. Thus, this determination should only be made by qualified mental health professionals who have a detached and objective eye during the assessment period.

Legal Requirements, Transfers, and Involuntary Commitment for Psychiatric Treatment

Some offenders may exhibit behaviors that become progressively worse over their term of incarceration. Because of this, it is somewhat common that some of these offenders will be deemed more suitable for psychiatric hospitalization. Indeed, roughly 54% of all persons in secure mental hospitals were transferred from a prison system (Steadman, 1987). Though a substantial number of persons committed to psychiatric hospitals come from prisons, the reverse—that few prison inmates actually end up being committed to psychiatric facilities—is of course not true. This means that prisons then have become the essential "catch-all" or "dumping ground" for much of society's mentally ill. In 1980 the Supreme Court held in *Vitek v. Jones* that a transfer of any inmate to a mental health hospital required, at a minimum, an administrative hearing to determine the appropriateness of such confinement. While this is generally not a difficult process to comply with, the reality is that most hospitals are at maximum capacity just like prison systems. Thus, the option of mental hospitalization holds very limited utility for correctional administrators.

Broad Array of Pathology

Specific types of disorders have been found to be more problematic than others among the offending population. Among these are the mood, schizophrenic, and personality disorders. As we have seen in this section, a high proportion of offenders also have addiction or substance abuse disorders that are comorbid with the primary diagnosis (Sacks, Sacks, & Stommel, 2003). These are commonly referred to as co-occurring disorders within the treatment community, and this simply denotes the fact that the offender has two or more disorders. In most cases, when an offender is said to have a co-occurring disorder, the clinician is referring to a substance abuse-related disorder accompanied by some type of DSM-IV-TR-diagnosed mental health disorder.

Mood disorders include major depressive disorder, bipolar disorder, and dysthymic disorder. Major depressive disorder is characterized by one or more major depressive episodes (i.e., at least two weeks of depressed mood or loss of interest accompanied by at least four additional symptoms of depression). Major depressive disorder is the most common mood disorder associated with the offender population. Another type of depression, bipolar disorder, is characterized by one or more manic episodes usually accompanied by major depressive episodes. The individual afflicted with bipolar disorder will have mood swings that go back and forth between manic and depressive states. Dysthymic disorder is characterized by at least two years of depressed mood for more days than not, accompanied by additional depressive symptoms that do not meet the criteria for a major depressive disorder. There are multiple designations for depression within the DSM-IV-TR, and these various subcategories of diagnosis can be somewhat overly complicated for the layperson. To provide a complete overview of each of these types of depression would go well beyond the scope of this chapter, and, therefore, we will limit our discussion to the simple brief overview of depression that has been provided.

APPLIED THEORY 12.1

Individual Trait Criminological Theories and Criminal Activity

Cullen and Agnew (2006) note that research has suggested that genetic factors and biological harms of a nongenetic nature, such as head injuries, may increase the likelihood that individuals will develop traits that make them more prone to criminal activity. Among these are traits such as impulsivity or sensation seeking behaviors. David Rowe (2002) argues that physiological factors account for a substantial amount of criminal activity due to the effects of genetics or injury to various segments of the central nervous system.

In particular, Row has focused on the chemical messengers, called neurotransmitters, that exist within our nervous system and transmit electronic signals between the billions of neurons in our brain. The neurotransmitters are many, but serotonin and dopamine are particularly important because they affect our mood and emotional stability, and because even slight changes in the amount of each in our bloodstream can lead to different levels of emotional response or behavior. Further, Rowe (2002) and others have examined critical hormones such as testosterone that help to regulate various impulses such as sex drive and reaction to stressors.

This research is not just important from a mental health perspective, but it also ties in with many of the substance abuse issues that are corollary to inmates with mental disorders, to female offenders, to offenders with HIV/AIDS, and to elderly and juvenile offenders. Indeed, most illicit drugs impact our serotonin and dopamine levels of release. In fact, this release of neurotransmitters actually gives people their sense of "high" or release when using a substance. This provides direct reinforcement to the cerebral areas affected. Moreover, many drug users experience additional social reinforcers due to social contact with other drug users and acceptance within that crowd.

Though it may seem far-fetched, substantial research has demonstrated a connection between nervous system functioning and criminal activity (Hanser, 2010; Raine, 2004). This is true for both juvenile and adult offenders as well as for both nonviolent and violent offenders. Numerous cases exist where offenders were found to have various forms of imbalance in their neurochemistry. Andrea Yates, a female offender who drowned her own children during a serious bout of post-partum depression, is one classic example. Others abound throughout the literature, particularly in regard to the study of the classic psychopath whose central nervous system does not process anxiety-related impulses, making the person less able to acquire empathy for his or her victims. Indeed, brain imaging with MRIs and PET scans has pinpointed specific biological deficits involved in criminal dispositions among a variety of offender types; these deficits appear to be in the frontal cortex area of the brain, an area that regulates higher-order functioning.

Given the confluence of these physiological factors— mental illness, substance abuse, and criminal activity—the *individual trait theories* are important to consider. These theories are grounded in medical science and study specific physiological effects, producing results that are much more valid and reliable than the survey-based research attributed to most social-based theories. In effect, these theories seem to point toward inherent risk factors possessed by the person before any social learning takes place. Naturally, these theories hold serious implications for correctional agencies. Such theories seem to point to the utility of selective incapacitation strategies and to the notion that some offenders may simply not be able to change—at least without making modifications to their neurochemistry.

SOURCE: Cullen, F. T., & Agnew, R. (2006). *Criminological theory: Past to present* (3rd ed.). Los Angeles: Roxbury Publishing Company.

Generalized anxiety disorder is characterized by excessive anxiety and worry (apprehensive expectation), occurring more days than not for at least six months, about a number of events or activities. The individual also must report that it is difficult to control the worry to the point that it causes clinically significant distress or impairment in social, occupational, or other areas of functioning. A number of offenders may present with this disorder, though it may be difficult to determine because many of them will have objectively sound reasons for their anxiety. The hallmark of this disorder is when the individual worries when there is no specific reason for this worry. This is not necessarily a common disorder among offenders, but may be found among those who have particularly difficult backgrounds (e.g., abuse) or who had difficulty adjusting to their experiences within the criminal justice system. This disorder is most prevalent in female offenders because it is more prevalent among females in the general population.

Schizophrenic disorders, according to the DSM-IV-TR, have five characteristic symptoms, and at least two must be present before the diagnosis can be given to an individual. These symptoms are (1) delusions, (2) hallucinations, (3) disorganized speech, (4) grossly disorganized behavior, and (5) inappropriate affect. Further, the social, self-care, and/or occupational life of the individual must show signs of being well below the level achieved prior to the onset of the illness. Lastly, these symptoms must have existed for six months or longer.

Schizophrenic disorders are the second most frequent types of disorders. Only the cluster of personality disorders (discussed immediately hereafter) are found more frequently among the offending population. It should also be noted that schizophrenia is greatly compounded when offenders are locked in isolation for long periods of time. Offenders who are placed in administrative segregation, or those housed in so-called supermax facilities, either present with progressively worse cases of schizophrenia or may begin to develop schizophrenic "breaks" with reality. Thus, the occurrence of schizophrenia within the offending population is the result of the inherent disorder possessed prior to criminal involvement and also frequently a product of the offender's intensive contact with institutional seclusion from typical social stimuli and support.

Personality disorders are characterized by an enduring pattern of inner experience and behavior that deviates markedly from the expectations of the individual's culture, is pervasive and inflexible, has an onset in adolescence or early adulthood, is stable over time, and leads to distress or impairment. The focus of this section will be on antisocial personality disorder. Antisocial personality disorder is so problematic and encountered so frequently among the offender population that it warrants specific attention for students who wish to know about mental disorders within the institutional environment.

The offender with **antisocial personality disorder** is of most concern to the criminal justice system and to the public at large. This offender is likely to be violently dangerous and a true recidivist. It is this group of offenders that makes it hard to plead for mercy and leniency for other offenders presenting with other forms of mental disorder. The essential feature of antisocial personality disorder is a pervasive pattern of disregard for, and violation of, the rights of others that begins in childhood or early adolescence and continues into adulthood. Diagnosis with this disorder occurs if the individual presents with three (or more) of the following symptoms:

1. Failure to conform to social norms with respect to lawful behaviors as indicated by repeatedly performing acts that are grounds for arrest.

2. Deceitfulness, as indicated by repeated lying, use of aliases, or conning others for personal profit or pleasure.

3. Impulsivity or failure to plan ahead.

4. Irritability and aggressiveness, as indicated by repeated physical fights or assaults.

5. Reckless disregard for safety of self or others.

6. Consistent irresponsibility, as indicated by repeated failure to sustain consistent work behavior or honor financial obligations.

7. Lack of remorse, as indicated by being indifferent to or rationalizing having hurt, mistreated, or stolen from another.

For the most part, individuals with antisocial personality disorder rarely become independent and responsible adults. They spend much of their lives in one form of institutional setting or another (juvenile or adult correctional facilities, secure rehabilitation facilities, etc.), or they may remain dependent on family members. Further, it is estimated that up to 30% of all males in secure correctional facilities present with this disorder, with more inmates being progressively found to have antisocial personality as the level of institutional security increases (Gacono, Nieberding, Owen, Rubel, & Bodholdt, 2001).

Impact of Institutionalization on Mental Illness

Throughout this section, it has been pointed out that the effects of incarceration can aggravate mental health problems affecting inmates. Indeed, schizophrenia tends to be greatly magnified when inmates are placed in solitary confinement or segregation for prolonged periods of time. Other disorders, such as antisocial personality disorder, are particularly impacted by the inmate subculture, including the gang subculture. Because antisocial personality inmates are so criminogenic in orientation, the socialization from the inmate subculture simply entrenches them further into their disordered perceptions and beliefs. Likewise, inmates with this disorder provide an undue influence on the prison and, in the process, further exacerbate security problems within the prison and indoctrinate other inmates into the life of crime that the inmate subculture encourages.

Further, the prison experience is itself stressful and, as a result, will likely intensify reactions of inmates who are anxiety prone. In institutions where assaults frequently occur and where inmate safety is not a priority, this can be especially true. Rates of PTSD are high in prisons and particularly aggravated for those who are victimized within the prison environment. This is especially true for victims of prison rape and/or custodial sexual abuse. Lastly, rates of depression are often high among prison inmates due to the negative and restrictive environment (prisons are not cheery places, after all). Events that occur outside the prison (e.g., loss of a loved one, inability to assist family members, news of divorce) can also aggravate rates of depression and suicide.

SEX OFFENDERS

Sex offenders have been given quite a bit of media attention during the past two decades or so. Public fear of sex offenders, particularly child molesters, has generated strong emotional opposition to their being placed in the community. Though correctional systems cannot keep all sex offenders behind bars indefinitely, the general public consensus is that long-term incarceration is the best sentence for these offenders. Thus, many prison facilities are populated with a variety of sex offenders. Generally speaking, most sex offenders are housed within the general population of the correctional institution unless they are selected for some form of specialized program such as a residential therapeutic community.

Assessment and Classification

The assessment and classification of sex offenders is not always an easy process, even in prisons. Some of the reason for this is because official records are not always complete and/or may have missing information, especially if the case had extensive legal history, if the charge was plead down, or if offenders were charged for an offense other than the sex offense. Further, sex offenders are seldom forthcoming about their activity. Trained staff who have knowledge about typical sex offender profiles are ideal for the assessment and classification of sex offenders. These staff will usually be skilled at developing a rapport with these offenders while, at the same time, ensuring that they do not seem to condone their behavior. In addition, though the sex-offending behavior may be the primary issue of concern, persons conducting assessments should stay attentive regarding the other types of criminal activity that the offender may report. Often, these offenders are willing to discuss their other crimes as a form of psychological bargaining that evades their need to discuss their sex offending; the details of other crimes can be very helpful in properly classifying a sex offender.

Journal Article Link 12.2
Read about how sex offenders hide their crime from other prisoners.

Among sex offenders in prison systems, assessment processes will determine whether the offender is amenable to treatment. Most will be provided treatment if they are willing; however, those determined to be most motivated will likely be given a special form of incarceration through a therapeutic community. The **therapeutic community** environment provides necessary behavior modifiers in the form of sanctions and privileges that allow offenders immediate feedback about their behavior and treatment progress. This is important to note because these types of programs occur while offenders are theoretically "behind bars," yet eventually these types of treatments are utilized to reintegrate the offender into the community.

Basic Sex Offender Management

Institutions must focus on correctly identifying sex offenders as soon as possible after incarceration. For this to realistically occur, assessment and classification (just discussed) must take place. After the classification process, the offender should be separated from the general population of inmates, when possible. At a minimum, a separate area for sex offender treatment should exist, and, when possible, separate housing should be provided. Much of this has to do with the fact that these inmates are vulnerable to attack from other inmates since, as we have learned, these offenders are not respected within the inmate subculture and are specific targets within that subculture and among gangs active within a facility. While it is recommended that sex offenders be given separate housing, as was mentioned at the beginning of this chapter, this is not often the case. Most sex offenders are housed in the general population. This is because resources are scarce and because prison facilities are not required to separate all sex offenders from the population, so long as they are given reasonable protection.

Staff Issues With the Sex Offender Population in Prison

Ingram and Carlson (2008) perhaps says it best in noting that "the most essential step in developing and running a useful program for sex offenders is having trained staff who have the right attitude toward these inmates" (p. 377). Security staff should not view sex offenders as horrible persons who deserve the worst punishment possible. By the same token, these staff should not be sympathetic to sex offenders to the point that they entertain excuses for the criminal behavior, such as the unfairness of sex laws regarding consent, issues with a troubled home, and/or misunderstandings regarding appropriate sexual activity (Ingram & Carlson, 2008). Rather, security staff should be realistic and mature. They should view the behavior of the sex offender as inappropriate but should be willing to consider that these offenders can change.

The selection process for security staff who will work within sex offender treatment programs should set high criteria. Most staff who seek to work in this field will already have come to terms with the idea that treatment of sex offenders goes beyond punitive sanctions. However, the reasons that persons may seek these specialized assignments can be many, and some of them may not be healthy. Thus, careful screening and investigation of the person's background should be conducted.

Aside from security personnel, the treatment personnel involved with this type of program should be well qualified. Typically, a psychologist or psychiatrist is charged with supervising these types of programs. However, many treatment providers may be master's-level social workers and/or counselors. These individuals will often have specialized forms of education and/or training that is required as a means of being qualified to work with sex offenders. In fact, most states will have a registry or roster of mental health professionals who are given the legal authority to work with sex offenders. This demonstrates how important it is to ensure that those who work with this population are appropriately trained and credentialed.

Treatment of Sex Offenders

Sex offender programs today most often use a combination of cognitive-behavioral techniques and relapse prevention strategies (Ingram & Carlson, 2008). These programs usually include individual counseling sessions and group therapy sessions to break through offenders' denial of their activity and help them attempt to build empathy for victims of their crime (Hanser, 2010). When using group therapy, an effective technique to challenging denial is to invite offenders who are in an advanced treatment group to challenge offenders who are in denial in the less experienced group. The idea is that more experienced offenders in treatment will be more adept at challenging offenders in denial than others. In other circumstances, treatment staff may find it more effective to simply create a group of offenders who all exhibit levels of denial. This technique is called the "deniers group," consisting of sex offenders who are all in denial. Essentially, this is a "pre-group" that lasts from 12 to 16 weeks as a means of getting the offender in denial primed for the actual group therapy process. According to the Center for Sex Offender Management, treatment providers who employ this method report that the great majority of offenders are able to come out of their denial. This approach targets two major issues:

Video Link 12.2
Learn more about rehabilitative efforts for sex offenders.

- Eliminating cognitive distortions, which, left intact, allow offenders to continue denying or minimizing.

- Developing victimization awareness, which can allow offenders to understand the physical and psychological harm they inflict and, thus, render them more reluctant to commit future assaults.

One primary concern of group members is often related to confidentiality, particularly regarding information divulged by other group members. One way to address this concern is to ask the group participants to come to an agreement about their own confidentiality, and, in virtually every instance, the agreement they make among themselves is that what is discussed in group does not get discussed outside of group, as it pertains to anyone besides the person talking. Typically, it is best to have the group members come to this agreement among themselves rather than imposing such rules on them for three reasons. First, it is a simple way to begin their involvement in a discussion they are likely to understand and be interested in, without discussing any threatening content such as sex offending. This provides practice for what will be occurring in the group. Second, it requires that the group build cohesiveness and trust among its members, at least about this issue. Building trust among themselves can be a useful exercise because it leads to group members sensing that they can be helpful to each other.

Prison Subcultural Reactions and Treatment

In Chapter 10, extensive discussion was made regarding the prison subculture. Within this discussion, it was made clear that sex offenders tend to have no status behind bars, and, depending on the type of sex offender, they are likely to be victimized. This is particularly true for child molesters and other similar types of sex offenders. However, as with the outside community, social forces have changed some of the beliefs within the prison environment. Nowadays, it is not very uncommon for younger inmates to have some type of sex offense, but this is usually some type of rape of an adult female rather than the molestation of a child. While rape of women tended to also carry negative connotations within the older prison culture during the 1950s and before, the revulsion against this is not as great in today's modern prison environment.

There are many reasons for the shift in how the prison subculture responds to differing sex offenders. First, the gangsta movement during the 1990s consisted of rap music and attitudes that overtly denigrated women and referred to them through terms that implied they were to be exploited. This created an air of tolerance for female victimization among many younger offenders, particularly gang offenders. Second, youth now tend to be very sexually active, and boys are committing acts of violence more often than in past years; the shocking aspect of sex crimes has diminished. Thus, a culture has bred where women are considered lowly in status, and younger offenders no longer have incentives to be "gentlemen" but instead gain status points for "sexing" young girls and women into gang membership. Further, many gangs may engage in different types of rape as a preferred choice of criminal behaviors. These types of sex offenders will not be stigmatized in the prison culture but instead will be considered part of their gang family.

However, this is not the case for other sex offenders (again, particularly those who have molested children), inmates with sexual identity issues, or inmates who succumb to pressure for same-sex activity inside the prison. These individuals will be stigmatized and very likely sexually victimized in many of the older facilities and/or systems where the prison subculture predominates. In either event, these inmates will be afforded no respect by other inmates in the facility.

HIV/AIDS-RELATED OFFENDERS

In 2002, roughly 23,864 inmates in prisons and jails throughout the United States were HIV-positive, and 9,723 of these inmates had full-blown AIDS. This essentially means that, in 2002, about 2.0% of all state prison inmates, 1% of federal prison inmates, and 1.7% of all jail inmates were infected with HIV. In fact, this percentage continues to increase, with the federal prison system having 1.1% of its inmate population testing HIV positive during 2002 (see Table 12.6 for a detailed state-by-state count of **HIV/AIDS** cases in prison systems within the United States). This rate of infection is about 5 to 7 times that of the general population (Department of Health and Human Services, 2001).

It should be noted that roughly half of all the HIV-positive inmates are located within the state systems of Texas, New York, and Florida. This is not surprising since these three states and the state of California are the four largest and most prominent correctional systems in the United States, lending them the nickname of the "Big Four" among correctional system scholars (Clear, Cole, & Reisig, 2005; see also Chapter 2). During 1999, the state of New York had 7,000 infected inmates, Florida had 2,633, and Texas had 2,520. These numbers are fairly consistent with the relative prevalence of HIV/AIDS among injection drug users (commonly referred to as IDUs) in each of these states.

State Rankings Link 12.1
State Prisoners Known to Be Positive for HIV Infection/AIDS in 2008.

TABLE 12.6 Inmates in Custody of State or Federal Prison Authorities and Known to Be Positive for HIV, 2000–2002

Jurisdiction	Total Known to Be HIV Positive			HIV/AIDS Cases as a Percentage of Total Custody Population		
	2002	2001	2000	2002	2001	2000
U.S. Total Reported	23,864	24,147	25,333	1.9	1.9	2.0
Federal	1,547	1,520	1,302	1.1	1.2	1.0
State	22,317	22,627	24,031	2.0	2.0	2.2
Northeast	*7,620*	*8,136*	*8,721*	*4.6*	*4.9*	*5.2*
Connecticut	666	604	593	3.6	3.5	3.6
Delaware	128	143	127	1.9	2.1	1.9
Maine	—	15	11	—	0.9	0.7
Massachusetts	290	307	313	2.9	3.0	3.0
New Hampshire	16	17	23	0.6	0.7	1.0
New Jersey	756	804	771	3.2	3.4	3.2
New York	5,000	5,500	6,000	7.5	8.1	8.5
Pennsylvania	800	735	900	2.0	2.0	2.4
Rhode Island	86	148	90	2.5	4.4	2.6
Vermont	6	6	20	0.4	0.4	1.5
Midwest	*2,133*	*2,135*	*2,252*	*1.0*	*1.0*	*1.1*
Illinois	570	593	619	1.3	1.3	1.4
Indiana	—	—	—	—	—	—
Iowa	33	27	27	0.4	0.3	0.3
Kansas	48	41	49	0.5	0.5	0.6
Michigan	591	584	585	1.2	1.2	1.2
Minnesota	37	33	42	0.5	0.5	0.7
Missouri	262	262	267	0.9	0.9	1.0
Nebraska	24	24	18	0.6	0.6	0.5
North Dakota	4	4	2	0.4	0.4	0.2
Ohio	417	398	478	1.0	0.9	1.1
South Dakota	6	5	4	0.2	0.2	0.2
Wisconsin	141	164	161	0.8	0.9	1.0
South	*10,656*	*10,392*	*10,767*	*2.2*	*2.2*	*2.3*
Alabama	276	302	419	1.1	1.2	1.8
Arkansas	100	108	101	0.8	0.9	0.9
Florida	2,848	2,602	2,640	3.8	3.6	3.7

(Continued)

TABLE 12.6   (Continued)

Jurisdiction	Total Known to Be HIV Positive			HIV/AIDS Cases as a Percentage of Total Custody Population		
	2002	2001	2000	2002	2001	2000
Georgia	1,123	1,150	938	2.4	2.5	2.1
Kentucky	—	105	124	—	1.1	1.3
Louisiana	503	514	500	2.5	2.6	2.6
Maryland	967	830	998	4.0	3.5	4.3
Mississippi	224	234	230	1.9	2.0	2.1
North Carolina	602	573	588	1.8	1.8	1.9
Oklahoma	146	130	145	0.9	0.9	1.0
South Carolina	544	559	560	2.4	2.6	2.7
Tennessee	218	231	215	1.5	1.7	1.6
Texas	2,528	2,388	2,492	1.9	1.8	1.8
Virginia	425	507	550	1.4	1.7	1.9
West Virginia	24	16	14	0.7	0.5	0.5
West	*1,908*	*1,964*	*2,291*	*0.7*	*0.8*	*0.9*
Alaska	16	16	—	0.5	0.5	—
Arizona	130	122	110	0.4	0.4	0.4
California	1,181	1,305	1,638	0.7	0.8	1.0
Colorado	182	173	146	1.1	1.2	1.0
Hawaii	22	13	19	0.6	0.3	0.5
Idaho	18	14	14	0.4	0.4	0.3
Montana	8	11	11	0.4	0.6	0.7
Nevada	113	127	151	1.2	1.4	1.6
New Mexico	30	27	28	0.5	0.5	0.5
Oregon	42	30	41	0.4	0.3	0.4
Utah	58	34	37	1.4	0.8	0.9
Washington	101	88	90	0.6	0.6	0.6
Wyoming	7	4	6	0.6	0.4	0.5

SOURCE: Maruschak, L. M. (2004). HIV in prisons and jails, 2002. *Bureau of Justice Statistics Bulletin*. Washington, DC: U.S. Department of Justice, Office of Justice Programs.

While the concentration of HIV/AIDS in prisons poses a serious threat to inmates in general, research indicates that it poses an increasingly serious threat to female inmates specifically. Table 12.7 compares the rates of male and female inmates infected with HIV/AIDS over a 12-year period. The rate of infected women remains consistently higher than the rate of their male counterparts, with the most current data, 2002, indicating that women are infected at a rate that is approximately 50% higher than males.

TABLE 12.7   Number and Percentage of HIV/AIDS-Infected Prison Inmates, by Year and Sex

Year	Male /Female (Number)	Male/Female (Percentage)
1998	22,045/2,552	2.2/3.8
1999	22,175/2,402	2.2/3.5
2000	21,894/2472	2.1/3.4
2001	20,415/2,212	1.9/3.1
2002 (midyear)	20,273/2,164	1.9/2.9

SOURCE: From Franklin, C. A., Fearn, N. E., & Franklin, T.W. (2005). "HIV/AIDS Among Female Prison Inmates: A Public Health Concern," in *Californian Journal of Health Promotion, 3*(2), 99-112.

The ways in which women are exposed to HIV/AIDS reflect their lack of information and education related to infection as well as their propensity to engage in high-risk behavior. Women are infected through the use of intravenous drug needles and unprotected sex with infected partners. As we have seen in Chapter 11, more women than men suffer from drug addiction, and they tend to use drugs more frequently than men prior to incarceration. This has a direct effect on the likelihood that women will engage in high-risk drug-related behavior (e.g., intravenous drug use and needle sharing), thus increasing their chances of contracting HIV/AIDS. In addition, research has established the alarming rate at which women engage in prostitution in exchange for drugs or money to buy drugs.

The majority of female inmates enter prison already having contracted HIV/AIDS. There are, however, inmates (both male and female) who are infected while under correctional supervision. This occurs as a result of engaging in high-risk behaviors while incarcerated. Studies have indicated that inmates transmit HIV/AIDS through sexual activity where inmates participate in both consensual and coerced sex presenting the possibility of infection. In addition, inmates engage in illicit intravenous drug use, oftentimes sharing needles, further increasing their risk of HIV/AIDS transmission. Finally, inmates who receive tattoos while in prison increase the possibility of contracting communicable diseases, including HIV/AIDS, due to unsterile needles and inadequate protections against blood-borne transmission.

Inmate Medical Care and HIV/AIDS

For the most part, the quality and delivery of health and medical care in institutional corrections are poor. Inmates have reported extremely low satisfaction with regard to the accessibility and quality of medical service from general health concerns to specialized care. This is particularly the case for female inmates (Lindquist & Lindquist, 1999) as medical care offered in women's prisons has failed to provide constitutionally guaranteed standards of health care (see Anderson, 2003; Belknap, 2001; and Young & Reviere, 2001, for reviews). For example, specialized health care personnel such as gynecologists, obstetricians, and dietitians are often located off-site. This is specifically relevant where women in prison have a host of medical needs including gynecological concerns such as sexually transmitted diseases, reproductive-related health problems, and high-risk pregnancies and may need access to on-site medical treatment and counseling.

When medical specialists are not available on-site, inmates must be transported to receive medical care. This often results in transportation and scheduling conflicts (Belknap, 2001) as well as additional expenses and potential safety concerns where the outcome is less immediate health service. In order to increase access to medical specialists, many prisons have experimented with telemedicine where specialists provide consultation to prisoners via videoconferencing (students should see Technology Insert 12.1 for more on the use of telemedicine).

Research has indicated that roughly 25% of institutions do not screen or test for HIV/AIDS. This can be seen in Table 12.8, which shows the various screening and testing procedures employed by U.S. correctional facilities. Moreover, most institutions have screening methods that rely on inmate requests for HIV/AIDS testing. While some facilities screen inmates based on specific clinical indications, others rely on blind or unlinked studies where blood is tested but there is no identifying information that links the inmate to the results of the test. This form of testing provides aggregate numbers of infected inmates but does not allow for any type of medical treatment or educational follow-up. Lack of screening has problematic consequences when a host of women with the disease or infection are unaware of their HIV-positive status.

Reference Link 12.2
Read about HIV/AIDS issues in prisons.

TECHNOLOGY AND EQUIPMENT 12.1

Telemedicine Can Cut Medical Costs for Inmate Populations

The use of telemedicine has been hailed as a technological tool that can save correctional agencies substantial financial resources. Telemedicine is a process whereby physicians at a prison conduct different procedures and/or services with the consultation and guidance of more senior and specialized medical staff who are contacted by either phone, Internet, or both. In the late 1990s, a leased telemedicine network was installed to serve four federal prisons. The purpose of this demonstration was to test the feasibility of remote telemedical consultations in prisons and to estimate the financial impacts of implementing telemedicine in other prison systems. Abt Associates Inc. was contracted to evaluate the demonstration and estimate the costs and savings associated with the use of telemedicine in these selected prisons. As in most federal prisons, medical care was traditionally delivered through a combination of four types of providers:

- Routine primary care was largely the responsibility of prison employees. Telemedicine was not intended to substitute for any of these encounters.

- Specialty care was provided in regularly scheduled, in-person clinics for which the prisons entered into annual contracts with local specialists.

- Inmates requiring other less common specialties or hospital care were transported outside the prison to nearby health care facilities (usually hospitals).

During the demonstration period, a fifth mode of care—remote encounters with specialists via telemedicine—was added to determine whether the prisons could use telemedicine to overcome local problems in accessing needed specialists and improve security by averting travel outside the prison walls. The demonstration was also designed to supply data on costs and utilization to support a decision about whether and where to implement telemedicine in other prisons. During the period in which telemedicine processes were evaluated by the Bureau of Prisons (BOP), the following seven observations were noted:

1. Telemedicine was adopted quickly and used frequently in several medical specialty areas. By the end of the demonstration, 1,321 teleconsultations had been conducted.

2. Physicians reported that telemedical consultations were effective substitutes for direct, in-person consultations in some specialties (e.g., psychiatry and dermatology), but less than adequate in others (e.g., cardiology and orthopedics). Consequently, a nearly complete substitution of telemedicine for in-person psychiatric care took place quickly. Telemedical consultations were also used routinely for dermatology and orthopedics, although conventional consultations in these specialties continued. Telemedical consultations were used with several other types of specialties, but relatively infrequently.

3. The use of telemedicine averted 13–14 transfers by air charter to a federal medical center (FMC). Nearly all of these transfers would have been for psychiatric reasons. The availability and skill levels of prison psychiatrists at FMC Lexington (Kentucky) contributed to better management of psychiatric patients at the demonstration prisons. These prisoners would have been transferred to the psychiatric wards at MCFP (Medical Center for Federal Prisoners) Springfield (Missouri) had telemedical services not been available.

4. In an operational telemedicine system with optimal design, the savings generated by approximately 1,544 encounters would equal the purchase cost of the telemedicine equipment. The demonstration produced about 100 encounters per month; therefore, the initial cost of equipment would be recovered in approximately 15 months, with monthly savings of about $14,200 thereafter. If all capital costs are included, the time to recover the costs is still less than 2 years.

5. Telemedicine also improved some indicators of the quality of care available to prisoners. The

time between a prisoner's referral to a specialist and an actual consultation with the specialist declined in the demonstration prisons; probably specialists were more frequently available by telemedicine. The enhanced communications system also enabled the Pennsylvania prisons to obtain services in at least one specialty not available locally: infectious disease expertise for the care of HIV-positive prisoners. Even in fields in which specialists were locally available, telemedicine provided access to doctors with more experience in the treatment of prisoners.

6. Prison administrators in the project hypothesized that the prisons were calmer, with fewer incidents of violence because of the improved psychiatric care available through telemedicine. There were fewer assaults at FCI (Federal Correctional Institution) Allenwood and USP (United States Penitentiary) Allenwood after the demonstration began than in the previous year. However, we are unable to draw any consistent conclusions about the value of telemedicine in improving the social climate of the demonstration prisons.

7. The evaluation demonstrates convincingly that, after telemedicine was established within the prisons, it was widely embraced by officials and prisoners. Further, the evaluation establishes that a correctional agency such as the BOP can add telemedicine to its medical program with the expectation that taxpayer dollars will not be wasted, and, if anything, substantial savings associated with the new technology may be realized.

It should be clear that telemedicine can have some advantages for prisons, particularly for prison facilities designed to house specialized offender populations. For elderly offenders, offenders with HIV/AIDS, and mentally ill inmates, this type of service delivery may be more effective, create fewer security risks, and be less expensive than traditional methods of providing medical services. Thus, the use of telemedicine procedures can and should be seriously considered as a means of offsetting some of the costs associated with the expense of housing a special needs population.

SOURCE: Nacci, P. (2000). *Telemedicine can reduce correctional healthcare costs: An evaluation of a prison telemedicine network.* Washington, DC: National Institute of Justice.

TABLE 12.8   Screening and Testing Policies for the Identification of Female Inmates With the HIV/AIDS Virus, as Reported by Correctional Officials

Population Screened	1990	2002
All inmates/residents (at some time)	18.5%	7.6%
High-risk inmates	11.2	14.2
Inmate request	48.5	51.2
Clinical indication	48.9	39.4
Court order	21.0	26.2
At admission	23.6	13.6
At release	7.7	3.1
Random sample	6.0	.8
Other criteria	4.3	10.0
Inmates not tested	14.2	24.7

SOURCE: Franklin, C. A., Fearn, N. E., & Franklin, T. W. (2005). *Californian Journal of Health Promotion, 3*(2), 99–112.

Rights to Privacy and Inmate Subcultural Views

In addition, correctional staff must understand that inmates may have difficulty trusting that staff will keep their health and security as a concern. But for treatment programs to be successful (and this is the only way to improve long-term safety for both inmates and staff from the virus), a solid relationship must exist between the inmate client and medical staff or clinicians. Facilities and clinicians must:

- Deal with the inmate's mistrust of authority and unfamiliarity with health care providers and services.

- Be clear and open about the limits to, and likely success of, various interventions.

HIV/AIDS counseling and testing includes HIV antibody testing and individual, client-centered risk reduction counseling. These types of programs are designed to assist individuals in deciding if they will get further help. These programs may take place in different forms (e.g., during and following the initial intake medical screening, during or following education and prevention sessions). The counseling and psychoeducational programs should also be available to noninfected inmates.

By counseling noninfected inmates on how to avoid infection, these programs can reduce further infection and can save both correctional agencies and society an enormous amount of money and future grief and misery. It should be noted that the estimated lifetime treatment cost for an inmate with HIV/AIDS varies from $165,000 to $267,000 for correctional agencies that must foot the bill. Thus, HIV/AIDS prevention and psychoeducational interventions can save a great deal of money, even if just a handful of cases are prevented.

Just as with the broader population outside of the prison environment, the confidentiality of HIV/AIDS test results is a crucial concern when providing effective services. This is due to the fear of disclosure that may cause a person to avoid or refuse testing. Confidentiality in the correctional setting can be difficult because privacy is harder to maintain. This is particularly true when one considers that everyone within the prison may know when and where appointments for HIV-positive inmates occur. Information may leak fast through inmate orderlies, and inmates visiting prison infirmaries during the allocated time and/or place may quickly be identified by other inmates and/or staff as being positive for HIV/AIDS.

This can have serious and damaging consequences for individuals who seek medical services for their infection, and these potential consequences can prevent other inmates from seeking testing. This then simply aggravates the problem with HIV/AIDS in the prison setting since the virus is then left unchecked due to social concerns. It should be noted that this simply places both inmates and staff in potential jeopardy and at risk of being infected in the future.

The point regarding prison staff and inmate informal identification of other inmates suspected of having HIV/AIDS is very important when one considers the effects of the informal subculture within many state prison systems. Hanser and Moran (2004) discuss at length the effects of the prison subculture on sex and sexuality identification within the prison setting. Inmates who are at risk or identified as such may be targeted by inmate perpetrators who are sexually assaultive (and are also HIV positive) since the newly diagnosed inmate is considered to be already infected. This places the inmate as "fair game" among HIV-positive sexually assaultive inmates and among the inmate subculture that is not HIV positive. Inmates who are not HIV positive are likely to condone this victimization since this prevents spreading of the infection to other inmates who are not HIV positive and since the subculture will see the inmate as a punk and therefore deserving of further victimization. Thus, whether the inmate is or is not positive becomes a moot point as he becomes singled out among the already HIV-positive perpetrators as a likely target.

Video Link 12.3
Watch a video about HIV-positive inmates.

Likewise, the inmate suspected of potentially being HIV positive will likely be shunned by many other inmates who desire to avoid infection. This inmate will find his or her standard of living and social inclusion to be very limited. Opportunities to recreate and engage in other activities may be substantially impaired due to social pressure from other inmates who seek to eliminate HIV-positive inmates from mutually participating in group functions. In fact, in some prison systems, HIV-positive inmates may be segregated from the remainder of the prison population.

The segregation of HIV-positive inmates has drawn substantial debate in recent years. The state of Alabama is regarded as one of the toughest correctional systems in the nation on HIV-positive inmates. Alabama's prison populations are tested upon entry into the Department of Corrections, and HIV-positive inmates are segregated and placed in separate dormitories. Some correctional experts consider this to be a more practical and effective manner of delivering services to the HIV-positive prison population. This argument for segregation may be very sound regardless of the social penalty that inmates may perceive with this type of intervention.

Indeed, it is thought that the use of segregation can allow agencies to extend their resources by identifying gaps in services and filling those gaps during incarceration all the way through reentry into society.

The Alabama Department of Corrections does address prevention and in-house care that continues with effective aftercare while on community release. The program's aftercare is titled "Be Free Stay Free—Life Enrichment Modules Program" and has leveraged the assistance of community-based organizations to provide primary and secondary education about HIV/AIDS and the treatment of the virus. These programs include numerous classes and services, both inside the prison and during aftercare with classes on addiction, tuberculosis, vocations, and the method of obtaining and using medications when on community supervision. The intent is to empower these offenders to take responsibility for themselves upon release, being less of a burden and/or health risk to society.

HIV/AIDS and Custodial Staff Safety

From the discussion in the previous section, it should be clear that custodial staff are likely to be concerned about their own personal safety when dealing with inmates who have HIV/AIDS; this is completely understandable. However, it should also be clear that the prison subculture perpetuates fear and builds upon that fear to the point that those offenders who are even suspected of having HIV/AIDS are subject to direct and indirect victimization; this should be avoided.

As we have seen earlier in Chapter 10, there is a move toward increased professionalization among correctional personnel. This trend toward a professional workforce has helped to mitigate many of the negative effects of the prison subculture as well as the gang influences within prison facilities. In keeping with this trend, it is suggested that agencies provide ongoing training to their employees regarding the nature of HIV/AIDS as well as safety precautions that will aid staff to avoid being infected with a communicable disease. Employees should be trained to use universal precautions, which refers to a method of infection control in which all human blood and other potentially infectious materials are treated as if known to be infected with HIV/AIDS (Norman, 1991).

Journal Article Link 12.3
Read about how officers' knowledge of HIV relates to their perception of risk.

Legal Liabilities for Staff

As with any issue of safety and security that must be afforded to inmates, there is the potential for those inmates to file suit if the conditions of care are perceived to be substandard. In most respects, jail or prison staff must only make reasonable efforts to ensure that appropriate medical care is provided to HIV/AIDS-positive inmates. In most cases, if suit is filed by an inmate, it will be under Section 1983 of Title 42 U.S. Code, commonly referred to as a Section 1983 suit. These types of lawsuits were discussed in Chapter 4 of this text. As students may recall, these suits allege that jail or prison staff, while acting under color of law, have violated an inmate's constitutional rights. This is the most common avenue from which inmates will file suit, alleging that their Eighth Amendment rights against cruel and unusual punishments have been violated due to the use of some type of restriction or regulation that has, allegedly, impeded their ability to obtain adequate medical services.

However, as we have seen earlier in Chapter 4, the Supreme Court has provided good guidance to aid decision makers tasked with crafting policies and procedures related to the health and welfare of staff and inmates within their institution. In *Turner v. Safley* (1987), the Court noted that a regulation or procedure was valid if it could be shown to be "reasonably related to legitimate penological interests" (p. 89). This test continues to be the primary basis in determining the constitutionality of a facility's restrictions.

Despite the fact that such regulations must be minimally restrictive, the real world of prisons requires that some pains of imprisonment may be unavoidable regardless of how practitioners implement protective policies. For instance, as we have seen, an inmate who is suspected of being HIV positive will likely be shunned by many other inmates who desire to avoid infection. This inmate will find his standard of living and social inclusion very limited. However, these concerns, though substantive, are likely to be secondary if the welfare of the institution is optimized.

ELDERLY OFFENDERS

The graying of America is a phenomenon that is now fairly common knowledge among most persons in the public, particularly among those who keep up with recent news and events. While this is widely understood, there remains a consequence to the aging phenomenon that stays largely out of view of the public eye. This consequence is that of an elderly inmate population that is burgeoning within state prison

PHOTO 12.5

Elderly offenders and offenders with disabilities are very costly to correctional facilities.

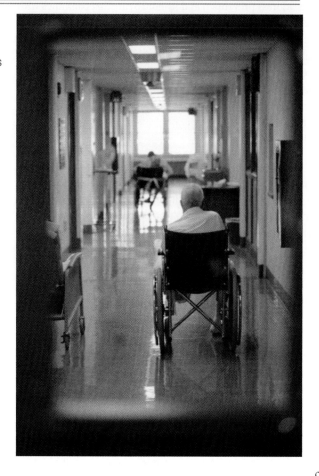

systems. This ever-growing and ever-aging population tends to also have a multiplicity of problems. Indeed, elderly inmates tend to have physiological symptoms that mimic health conditions that are roughly 10 years in advance of these inmates' actual chronological age. Thus, a 50-year-old inmate will, on the average, actually tend to have the physiological health of a 60-year-old in outside society (Fabelo, 1999).

Further, it is a simple legal fact, indeed a constitutional fact, that prison systems are responsible for the safety and security of the inmates in their charge. Administrators simply cannot run from this responsibility; standards of decency and human treatment require that appropriate medical attention be provided to inmates within their stead. The Eighth Amendment itself ensures that inmates are free from cruel and unusual punishment. Thus, prison administrators cannot inflict harmful conditions upon inmates if these could be considered cruel, malicious, or unusual. In addition, the Supreme Court has ruled cases like *Estelle v. Gamble* (1976) and *Wilson v. Seiter* (1991) that administrators cannot remain deliberately indifferent to the safety and/or security needs of inmates in their custody. Thus, turning a blind eye to the needs of elderly inmates is not, and will not be, an option for correctional practitioners.

Classification of Elderly Offenders

Perhaps the first step in ensuring that any offender's needs are appropriately met is the process of assessment. This assessment then must classify the elderly offender into categories that will ensure that the right standard of care is given. This accomplishes three goals: The process (1) ensures that the inmate received adequate care, (2) ensures that precious resources are not wasted on inmates not needing more intensive care, and (3) provides a guide when deciding housing and security levels for offenders to protect them and others from possible harm.

It is also important to note that any classification system for elderly inmates should include a protocol that distinguishes between inmates who entered the prison system before age 50 and those who reached that age while in prison. In essence, the data should clearly and prominently note if the offender falls within the category of an **elderly first-time offender**, a **habitual elderly offender**, or an **offender-turned-elderly-in-prison**. This is an important security consideration that most correctional administrators will find useful when running their institution. Once the elderly offender has been appropriately classified and once any necessary security precautions are resolved, prison staff will then be able to adequately ensure that the needs of these offenders are met.

The rise in numbers of habitual elderly offenders and offenders-turned-elderly-in prison has to do largely with the advent of "three strikes" felony sentencing in many states (Anno, Graham, Lawrence, & Shansky, 2004). These sentences require that third-time felony offenders serve mandatory sentences of 25 years to life. It should be noted that the felony does not necessarily mean that the offender is violent in nature. Also adding to these statistics are the punitive sentencing measures associated with the War on Drugs of the 1980s and 1990s where drug-using offenders were locked up at an all-time high, regardless of whether the crime involved violence or any form of drug trafficking (Anno et al., 2004).

Thus, habitual elderly offenders and offenders-turned-elderly-in-prison are the result of a confluence of social factors and criminal justice polices. These offenders, for various reasons, have been given enhanced penalties that preclude their release in the community. This greatly distinguishes them from the elderly-first-time-offender who does not share a similar criminogenic background. Though they may look the same while in inmate clothes in the prison facility, they are usually quite different from one another, and the public would be well served to keep this squarely in mind. States that have abolished parole and other community outlets may be well served to establish specialized court interventions for this type of offender. It is at this point that we turn our attention to the three typologies of elderly offenders, with each being briefly discussed in the paragraphs that follow.

Audio Link 12.3
Learn more about programs developed for aging inmates.

Elderly First-Time Offenders

It is estimated that approximately 50% of elderly inmates are first-time offenders, incarcerated when they were 60 or older. New elderly offenders frequently commit crimes of passion. Conflicts in primary relationships appear to increase as social interactions diminish with age. Older first-time offenders often commit their offenses in a spontaneous manner that shows little planning but is instead an emotional reaction to perceived slights or disloyalties. These offenders do not typically view themselves as criminal, per se, but instead see their situation as unique and isolated from their primary identity. Elderly first-time offenders are those who commit their offense later in life. For those who commit violent crimes, these are usually crimes of passion rather than premeditated crimes.

First-time offenders are more likely to be sentenced for violent offenses. These offenses will usually be directed at a family member due to proximity, if nothing else. Some experience crises of one sort or another due to disparity regarding the aging process, and this is also thought to instill a sense of abandon and resentfulness that may lead to aberrant forms of coping. Also, sexual offenses involving children are common among the first-time offending elderly. For persons over the age of 65, aggravated assault is the violent offense most often committed, followed by murder (Aday, 1994).

These offenders are also the most likely to be victimized in prison as their irascible behavior and demeanor are likely to draw the attention of younger inmates rather than providing any form of deterrence from victimization within the institutional setting (Aday, 1994). These offenders are the most likely to have strong community ties and are therefore usually the most amenable for community supervision because of this.

Habitual Elderly Offenders

Habitual elderly offenders have a long history of crime and also have a prior record of imprisonment throughout their lifetime. These offenders are usually able to adjust well to prison life because they have been in and out of the environment throughout a substantial part of their life. Thus, they are well suited and adjusted to prison life. They are also a good source of support for first-time offenders and, if administrators are wise enough to implement this, are able to act as mentors for these first-time offenders. These offenders quite often fit the mold of greyhounds within the prison facility and will often command a degree of respect within the prison subculture. While they may cope well with prison life, these offenders typically have substance abuse problems and other chronic problems that make coping with life on the outside difficult. Some of these inmates are not considered violent, but instead serve several shorter sentences for lesser types of property crimes. This is the group most likely to end up as geriatric inmates who die in prison.

Offenders-Turned-Elderly-in-Prison

Offenders-turned-elderly-in-prison who have grown old while incarcerated have long histories in the system and are the least likely to be discipline problems. Long-term offenders are very difficult to place upon release because they have few ties in the community and limited vocational background from which to earn a living. These offenders are often afraid to leave the prison and go back to the outside world because they have become so institutionalized within the predictable schedule of the prison. This also means that suicide may be considered among these individuals particularly prior to release, or even within a short time after release. This phenomenon is no different from that noted in the classic movie *The Shawshank Redemption* that portrays a released inmate who cannot cope with life on the outside, choosing instead to end his life prematurely by a self-hanging suicide.

Video Link 12.4
Watch a video about an offender-turned-elderly-in-prison.

Health Care Services and Costs

It should be clear to students that elderly offenders require substantial medical attention. The provision of this medical attention is very expensive and, in actuality, impairs many state prison systems around the nation. Because of the health care expenses, the cost of incarcerating an inmate who is 60 years of age or older is around $70,000 a year—roughly 3 times the cost for the average inmate. These inmates require specialized housing facilities, special programming, and even hospice and/or palliative care. Further, prison agencies must remain compliant with standards set by the ADA, which was discussed in the beginning section of this chapter. All of the various requirements just noted create a serious price tag for prisons, and, since the population continues to age, it is only likely that these expenses will continue to climb. How states and the federal government will afford these costs is a question often on the mind of many prison wardens and correctional administrators, particularly during times of economic challenge. The answer has yet to emerge, and this represents yet another challenge facing correctional agencies of the modern era.

CONCLUSION

This chapter has provided the student with an overview of specialized offenders, sometimes referred to as special needs offenders. These offenders tend to have special physical or mental needs that require extra concern and/or consideration from correctional agencies. These offenders also tend to entail considerable costs for agencies and present challenges to the institution's ability to ensure their safety and/or security. However, correctional agencies are obligated to provide sufficient resources and services for these offenders; this has been established by prior rulings made by the Supreme Court.

Among the various types of specialized offenders, those who have mental disorders have emerged as particularly problematic. These offenders tend to have high rates of institutional infractions, and they also tend to present with more problematic behaviors than do other inmates. Safety of these inmates is a bit more difficult to manage, and security is compromised from various details such as the administration of medications to their supervision in the population—a population that may victimize or dupe these offenders when the opportunity presents. Further still, these inmates tend to have substance abuse problems that are comorbid with their mental illness. In many cases, the substance abuse may be their primary disorder, and the presenting mental illness may be co-occurring.

Inmates with HIV/AIDS have also become an issue in corrections. HIV/AIDS is more prevalent among the offender population due to the offenders' risky lifestyles. Further, this disease is transmitted between inmates due to unhealthy sexual practices, intravenous drug use, and/or tattooing that occurs in prison. The sharing of needles between drug users when outside of the prison, unsafe sex practices, and the use of unsanitary needles in prisons for tattooing all compound the likelihood for inmates to contract HIV/AIDS. Further, female inmates have been identified as particularly susceptible to this disease, and it has been shown that they have higher rates of infection than do male inmates. This presents an additional area of concern when providing adequate care for the female population.

Lastly, elderly offenders were presented in this chapter as having distinct groupings or classifications, determined by their prison history. Inmates' particular history, whether they have engaged in a life of crime or committed a single crime resulting in a long-term sentence, and whether they were a late-life offender all affect the dynamics of their experience and the manner by which they are perceived within the prison subculture. Elderly inmates are a costly group to house, and, as we have seen, this cost is only going to continue to rise as we see a continued graying of the prison population.

END-OF-CHAPTER DISCUSSION QUESTIONS

1. Identify some of the common problems encountered with specialized inmate populations in prison.

2. What is the definition of mental illness? How prevalent is it within state prison systems?

3. Provide a discussion of two different personality disorders and explain how they may be problematic in managing the offender, whether in prison or on community supervision.

4. What is antisocial personality disorder, and why is it such a common disorder within the correctional population?

5. What are some safety and security concerns associated with the housing of inmates who are HIV/AIDS positive? Do these inmates have special legal protections that should be considered? If so, what are these rights or protections?

6. Identify and define the various classifications of elderly inmates within an institution.

7. What are some of the specialized requirements/considerations for prisons when housing elderly offenders?

8. Discuss how the prison subculture impacts, interacts with, and reacts to inmates who are mentally ill, HIV/AIDS positive, and/or elderly.

9. How do individual trait criminological theories explain criminal activity among some specialized criminal populations?

KEY TERMS

Antisocial personality disorder

Bipolar disorder

Co-occurring disorders

Diagnostic and Statistical Manual of Mental Disorders (DSM-IV-TR)

Dysthymic disorder

Elderly first-time offenders

Four standards of mental health care

Generalized anxiety disorder

Greyhounds

Habitual elderly offenders

HIV/AIDS

Malingering

Mental illness

Mental retardation

Mood disorders

Offender-turned-elderly-in-prison

Offender with special needs

Schizophrenic disorders

Therapeutic community

Universal design

APPLIED EXERCISE 12.1

In the case of *Farmer v. Brennan*, 511 U.S. 825 (1994), the Supreme Court of the United States ruled that a prison official's "deliberate indifference" to a substantial risk of serious harm to an inmate violates the cruel and unusual punishment clause of the Eighth Amendment. The case concerned Dee Farmer, a pre-op male-to-female transsexual, who had been incarcerated with the general male population after being transferred to USP Terre Haute in Indiana. Farmer was repeatedly raped and beaten by the other inmates and acquired HIV/AIDS as a result. Farmer claimed that the prison administration should have known that she was particularly vulnerable to sexual violence.

Consider this Supreme Court case and what you have learned in prior chapters regarding your legal liability as a prison staff member.

Answer the following questions in a 500- to 1,000-word essay:

1. Do prison personnel have a legal responsibility to safeguard effeminate inmates who have same-sex preferences? Why or why not? Be sure to explain your answer.

2. What measures should be taken to safeguard offenders with alternative sex identities and/or characteristics? How is this relevant to the reduction of HIV/AIDS in a prison facility?

3. What complications and challenges might occur for prison staff who safeguard inmates who engage in behaviors that are counter to the tenets of the prison subculture, discussed in Chapter 10 of this text?

4. Are prison staff required to protect inmates from potential exposure to HIV/AIDS?

"WHAT WOULD YOU DO?"

You work within the administrative segregation unit of a maximum-security prison as a sergeant. You supervise approximately 25 officers on your shift, each of whom works in a different position throughout the five cell blocks that you supervise. One day, while doing your rounds and signing paperwork maintained by your officers, you notice that a pair of officers are on the second level of the cell block standing in front of a cell. You listen closely, and you can hear them; they are laughing at, mocking, and ridiculing an inmate in the cell who is known to take a variety of medications due to symptoms of schizophrenia. Their joking is not violent, but it is demeaning, and it is clear that this is only likely to further aggravate the inmate's future mental condition.

The officers do not know that you have overheard them. In addition, this particular inmate attempted to stab an officer two months ago with a homemade blade. Thus, this inmate is not liked by many of the other officers. However, you wonder (based on information from other inmates) whether the officer who was nearly stabbed had been taunting this inmate and humiliating him for weeks. As their sergeant, you are expected to identify with the other officers and to not befriend inmates, nor should you, according to the tenets of correctional officer subculture, take the word of inmates over that of other officers.

You can see that this situation has created a bit of a dilemma, but, if left unresolved, it can escalate to another potential stabbing incident in your department. You consider the options that you may have, and, meanwhile, you can hear the laughter from the officers and from other inmates listening in the cells next door.

What would you do?

CROSS-NATIONAL PERSPECTIVE 12.1

Japan to Upgrade Care of Elderly Inmates

The swelling number of elderly inmates in Japan's prisons has prompted the government to begin a major revamp of its jails to provide elevators, handrails and wheelchair ramps for incarcerated seniors.

Renovation plans are set to begin by the end of March [2007] in three of the country's 75 prisons to accommodate seniors who require assistance, the Justice Ministry said this week.

The government will spend $76 million to create senior-friendly facilities for about 1,000 inmates, the first step in a program likely to be expanded in the future, ministry officials said.

The number of inmates 60 or older was 8,700 at the end of 2006, close to a threefold increase from a decade earlier. Older inmates make up about 12 percent of all inmates in Japan, according to the Justice Ministry.

Most elderly convicts are repeat offenders and have been convicted of theft or fraud, according to the National Police Agency. Less than 1 percent committed violent crimes such as murder, the agency said.

Experts believe some elderly inmates deliberately get themselves jailed because they see few options in the outside world.

"The number of elderly repeat offenders is on the rise because it is extremely difficult for them to start their life over again after release," said Maiko Tagusari, a lawyer specializing in prison conditions.

"Some of them even intentionally repeat petty crimes in an attempt to return to prison," she said.

In 2006, the total number of arrests across all age groups fell by 2.3 percent from a year earlier, but the number of arrested senior citizens rose by more than 10 percent, according to the National Police Agency.

About 900 elderly prisoners have trouble walking, feeding themselves or fulfilling prison duties, according to the ministry. A larger number have significant health problems but are able to take care of themselves well enough to live in prison without substantial assistance, the ministry said.

While those with dementia or serious health problems are kept at prison hospitals, most elderly inmates are in ordinary prisons and are required to provide compulsory labor.

The new prison facilities will be equipped with elevators, ramps and handrails in hallways and bathrooms, as well as medical staff trained for nursing care. Many prisons do not have full-time doctors.

Hisato Honda, a ministry official in charge of corrections, said the changes will improve living conditions for the inmates and make taking care of them easier for guards and prison officials.

"The idea is to relieve prison officials' burden of attending to the senior inmates," Honda said. "When they're in good health, senior inmates are fine. But once they get weaker, they're a big burden for everyone."

The graying of the prison population reflects a shift in Japan's overall demographics.

People over 60 account for about 27 percent of Japan's population, and that percentage is rising. The aging trend has caused concerns about Japan's fiscal future, as well as the welfare and living conditions of the elderly— including those in prison.

Question 1: After reading this article, how similar do circumstances in Japan regarding elderly offenders seem to be when compared to those in the United States? Provide a brief explanation for your answer.

Question 2: In your opinion, what should prison systems do to address the challenges associated with housing elderly inmates? Briefly explain your answer.

SOURCE: "Japan to Upgrade Care of Elderly Inmates" by M. Yamaguchi. Associated Press, January 9, 2007. Used with permission.

STUDENT STUDY SITE

Juvenile Correctional Systems

LEARNING OBJECTIVES:

1. Discuss the unique aspects of juvenile corrections when compared to adult corrections.

2. Discuss the history and development of juvenile corrections.

3. Identify how abuse and mental health issues aggravate a juvenile's ability to reform.

4. Identify racial disparities that exist for youth who are placed in confinement.

5. Discuss the various types of facilities and institutions used to house juvenile offenders.

INTRODUCTION

This chapter is unique from all of the other chapters in this text because it addresses an area of corrections that, in most respects, is separate and distinct from the other segments of the criminal justice system, including the correctional system. The juvenile system has a different orientation, emphasis, and set of terms and concepts that make it unique from adult corrections. For instance, the use of secure facilities is avoided if at all possible. The vast majority of youth who are processed through the juvenile justice system are placed on some form of community supervision. While this is also true in the adult system, this trend is even more pronounced within the juvenile system. Likewise, youth are not considered to be as culpable as adult offenders, and it is presumed that they are more impressionable than adults. Thus, the use of restrictive environments can have negative and counterproductive outcomes. Again, this is true with adult offenders as well, but it is not as pronounced as with juveniles.

Further, the means by which we process juvenile offenders is grounded in historical occurrences and legal precedents that have led to many unique considerations for youth. It is important that students understand this history so that the philosophical underpinnings to our current juvenile correctional system will be better understood. Because of this, we will first focus on the history of juvenile justice, punishment, and corrections, followed with a discussion of the legal precedents that have shaped our modern-day understanding of juvenile justice. In doing so, much of this discussion has been adapted from *Juvenile Justice* by Cox, Allen, Hanser, and Conrad (2011). This is because the author of this text has contributed to this historical account of the juvenile system and is therefore familiar with this content. Further, this account of juvenile correctional history is well written and succinct when one considers the scope and breadth of history and developments that have occurred within the field of juvenile justice. We now turn our attention to the historical precursors to the field of juvenile corrections.

HISTORY OF JUVENILE CORRECTIONS

The distinction between youthful and adult offenders coincides with the beginning of recorded history. Some 4,000 years ago, the Code of Hammurabi (2270 B.C.) discussed runaways, children who disowned their parents, and sons who cursed their fathers (see Chapter 1). Approximately 2,000 years ago, Roman civil law made distinctions between juveniles and adults based on the notion of **age of responsibility**. In ancient Jewish law, the Talmud specified conditions under which immaturity was to be considered in imposing punishment. There was no corporal punishment prior to puberty, which was considered to be the age of 12 years for females and 13 years for males. No capital punishment was to be imposed for those under 20 years of age. Similar leniency was found among Muslims, where children under the age of 17 years were typically exempt from the death penalty (Bernard, 1992).

By the 5th century B.C., codification of Roman law resulted in the Twelve Tables, which made it clear that children were criminally responsible for violations of law and were to be dealt with by the criminal justice system (Nyquist, 1960). Punishment for some offenses, however, was less severe for children than for adults. For example, theft of crops by night was a capital offense for adults, but offenders under the age of puberty were only to be flogged. Adults caught in the act of theft were subject to flogging and enslavement to the victims, but children received only corporal punishment at the discretion of a magistrate and were required to make restitution (Ludwig, 1955). Originally, only children who were incapable of speech were spared under Roman law, but eventually immunity was afforded to all children under the age of 7 years as the law came to reflect an increasing recognition of the stages of life. In general, only children who approached puberty were considered to know the difference between right and wrong and were held accountable.

English Origins

Roman and canon law undoubtedly influenced early Anglo-Saxon **common law** (law based on custom or use), which emerged in England during the 11th and 12th centuries. For our purposes, the distinctions made between adult and juvenile offenders in England at this time are most significant. Under common law, children under the age of 7 years were presumed to be incapable of forming criminal intent and, therefore, were not subject to criminal sanctions. Children between the ages of 7 and 14 years were not subject to criminal sanctions unless it could be demonstrated that they had formed criminal intent, understood the consequences of their actions, and could distinguish right from wrong (Blackstone, 1803, pp. 22–24). Children over the age of 14 years were treated much the same as adults.

Another important step in the history of juvenile corrections occurred during the 15th century when chancery or equity courts were created by the King of England. Chancery courts, under the guidance of the king's chancellor, were created to consider petitions of those who were in need of special aid or intervention, such as women and children left in need of protection and aid by reason of divorce, death of a spouse, or abandonment, and to grant relief to such persons. Through the chancery courts, the king exercised the right of *parens patriae* ("parent of the country") by enabling these courts to act *in loco parentis* ("in the place of parents") to provide necessary services for the benefit of women and children (Bynam & Thompson, 1992). In other words, the king, as ruler of his country, was to assume responsibility for all of those under his rule, to provide parental care for children who had no parents, and to assist women who required aid for any of the reasons just mentioned. Although chancery courts did not normally deal with youthful offenders, they did deal with dependent or neglected children, as do juvenile courts in the United States today.

Throughout the 1600s and most of the 1700s, juvenile offenders in England were sent to adult prisons, although they were at times kept separate from adult offenders. The Hospital of St. Michael, the first institution for the treatment of juvenile offenders, was established in Rome in 1704 by Pope Clement XI. The stated purpose of the hospital was to correct and instruct unruly juveniles so that they might become useful citizens (Griffin & Griffin, 1978, p. 7). The first private separate institution for youthful offenders in England was established by Robert Young in 1788. The goal of this institution was "to educate and instruct in some useful trade or occupation the children of convicts or such other infant poor as [were] engaged in a vagrant and criminal course of life" (Sanders, 1974, p. 48).

Evolution of Juvenile Corrections in the United States

Meanwhile in the United States, dissatisfaction with the way young offenders were being handled was increasing. As early as 1825, the Society for the Prevention of Juvenile Delinquency advocated separating juvenile and adult offenders (Snyder & Sickmund, 1999). Up to this point in time, youthful offenders had been generally subjected to the same penalties as adults, and little or no attempt was made to separate juveniles from adults in jails or prisons. This caused a good deal of concern among reformers who feared that criminal attitudes and knowledge would be passed from the adults to the juveniles. Another concern centered on the possibility of brutality directed by the adults toward juveniles. Although many juveniles were being imprisoned, few appeared to benefit from the experience (Dorne & Gewerth, 1998, p. 4).

In 1818, a New York City committee on pauperism gave the term *juvenile delinquency* its first public recognition by referring to it as a major cause of pauperism (Drowns & Hess, 1990, p. 9). As a result of this increasing recognition of the problem of delinquency, several institutions for juveniles were established between 1824 and 1828. These institutions were oriented toward education and treatment rather than punishment, although whippings, long periods of silence, and loss of rewards were used to punish the uncooperative. In addition, strict regimentation and a strong work ethic were common.

Under the concept of *in loco parentis,* institutional custodians acted as parental substitutes with far-reaching powers over their charges. For example, the staff members of the New York House of Refuge, established in 1825, were able to bind out wards as apprentices, although the consent of the child involved was required. Whether or not such consent was voluntary is questionable given that the alternatives were likely unpleasant. The New York House of Refuge was soon followed by other such institutions in Boston and Philadelphia (Abadinsky & Winfree, 1992).

"By the mid-1800s, houses of refuge were enthusiastically declared a great success. Managers even advertised their houses in magazines for youth. Managers took great pride in seemingly turning total misfits into productive, hard-working members of society" (Simonsen & Gordon, 1982, p. 23, boldface added). However, these claims of success were not undisputed, and by 1850 it was widely recognized that houses of refuge were largely failures when it came to rehabilitating delinquents and had become much like prisons. As Simonsen and Gordon (1982) stated, "In 1849 the New York City police chief publicly warned that the numbers of vicious and vagrant youth were increasing and that something must be done. And done it was. America moved from a time of houses of refuge into a time of preventive agencies and reform schools" (p. 23).

PHOTO 13.1

This picture of a reform school demonstrates the sterile and formal nature of these types of programs for troubled youth.

Reference Link 13.1
Read about juvenile reformatories.

In Illinois, the Chicago Reform School Act was passed in 1855, followed in 1879 by the establishment of industrial schools for dependent children. These schools were not unanimously approved, as indicated by the fact that in 1870 the Illinois Supreme Court declared unconstitutional the commitment of a child to the Chicago Reform School as a restraint on liberty without proof of crime and without conviction for an offense (*People ex rel. O'Connell v. Turner,* 1870). In 1888, the provisions of the Illinois Industrial Schools Act were also held to be unconstitutional, although the courts had ruled previously (1882) that the state had the right, under *parens patriae,* to "divest a child of liberty" by sending him or her to an industrial school if no other "lawful protector" could be found (*Petition of Ferrier,* 1882). In spite of good intentions, the new **reform schools,** existing in both England and the United States by the 1850s, were not effective in reducing the incidence of delinquency. Despite early enthusiasm among reformers, there was little evidence that rehabilitation was being accomplished.

The failures of reform schools increased interest in the legality of the proceedings that allowed juveniles to be placed in such institutions. During the last half of the 19th century, there were a number of court challenges concerning the legality of failure to provide due process for youthful offenders. Some indicated that due process was required before incarceration (imprisonment) could occur, and others argued that due process was unnecessary because the intent of the proceedings was not punishment but rather treatment. In other words, juveniles were presumably being processed by the courts in their own "best interests."

During the post–Civil War period, an era of humanitarian concern emerged, focusing on children laboring in sweatshops, coal mines, and factories. These children, and others who were abandoned, orphaned, or viewed as criminally responsible, were a cause of alarm to reformist "child savers." The child savers movement included philanthropists, middle-class reformers, and professionals who exhibited a genuine concern for the welfare of children. As a result, the 1870s saw several states (Massachusetts in 1874 and New York in 1892) pass laws providing for separate trials for juveniles, but the first juvenile or family court did not appear until 1899 in Cook County, Illinois. "The delinquent child had ceased to be a criminal and had the status of a child in need of care, protection, and discipline directed toward rehabilitation" (Cavan, 1969, p. 362).

LEGAL PRECEPTS AND ORIENTATION OF THE JUVENILE JUSTICE SYSTEM

By incorporating the doctrine of *parens patriae,* the juvenile court was to act in the best interests of children through the use of noncriminal proceedings. The basic philosophy contained in the first juvenile court act reinforced the right of the state to act *in loco parentis* in cases involving children who had violated the law or were neglected, dependent, or otherwise in need of intervention or supervision. This philosophy changed the nature of the relationship between juveniles and the state by recognizing that juveniles were not simply miniature adults but rather children who could perhaps be served best through education and treatment. By 1917, juvenile court legislation had been passed in all but three states, and by 1932 there were more than 600 independent juvenile courts in the United States. By 1945, all states had passed legislation creating separate juvenile courts.

The period between 1899 and 1967 has been referred to as the era of socialized juvenile justice in the United States (Faust & Brantingham, 1974). During this era, children were considered not as miniature adults but rather as persons with less than fully developed morality and cognition (Snyder

& Sickmund, 1999). Emphasis on the legal rights of the juvenile declined, and emphasis on determining how and why the juvenile came to the attention of the authorities and how best to treat and rehabilitate the juvenile became primary. The focus was clearly on offenders rather than the offenses they committed. Prevention and removal of the juvenile from undesirable social situations were the major concerns of the court.

It seems likely that the developers of the juvenile justice network in the United States intended legal intervention to be provided under the rules of civil law rather than criminal law. Clearly, they intended legal proceedings to be as informal as possible given that only through suspending the prohibition against hearsay and relying on the preponderance of evidence could the "total picture" of the juvenile be developed. The juvenile court exercised considerable discretion in dealing with the problems of youth and moved further and further from the ideas of legality, corrections, and punishment toward the ideas of prevention, treatment, and rehabilitation. In 1955, the U.S. Supreme Court reaffirmed the desirability of the informal procedures employed in juvenile courts. In deciding not to hear the *Holmes* case, the Court stated that because juvenile courts are not criminal courts, the constitutional rights guaranteed to accused adults do not apply to juveniles (*in re Holmes*, 1955).

Then, in the 1966 case of *Kent v. United States*, 16-year-old Morris Kent Jr. was charged with rape and robbery. Kent confessed, and the judge waived his case to criminal court based on what he verbally described as a "full investigation." Kent was found guilty and sentenced to 30 to 90 years in prison. His lawyer argued that the waiver was invalid, but appellate courts rejected the argument. He then appealed to the U.S. Supreme Court, arguing that the judge had not made a complete investigation and that Kent was denied his constitutional rights because he was a juvenile. The Court ruled that the waiver was invalid and that Kent was entitled to a hearing that included the essentials of due process or fair treatment required by the Fourteenth Amendment. In other words, Kent or his counsel should have had access to all records involved in making the decision to waive the case, and the judge should have provided written reasons for the waiver. Although the decision involved only District of Columbia courts, its implications were far-reaching by referring to the fact that juveniles might be receiving the worst of both worlds—less legal protection than adults and less treatment and rehabilitation than promised by the juvenile courts (*Kent v. United States*, 1966).

In 1967, forces opposing the extreme informality of the juvenile court won a major victory when the U.S. Supreme Court handed down a decision in the case of Gerald Gault, a juvenile from Arizona. The extreme license taken by members of the juvenile justice network became abundantly clear in the *Gault* case. Gault, while a 15-year-old in 1964, was accused of making an obscene phone call to a neighbor who identified him. The neighbor did not appear at the adjudicatory hearing, and it was never demonstrated that Gault had, in fact, made the obscene comments. Still, Gault was sentenced to spend the remainder of his minority in a training school. Neither Gault nor his parents were notified properly of the charges against the juvenile. They were not made aware of their right to counsel, their right to confront and cross-examine witnesses, their right to remain silent, their right to a transcript of the proceedings, or their right to appeal. The Court ruled that, in hearings that may result in institutional commitment, juveniles have all of these rights (*in re Gault*, 1967). The Supreme Court's decision in this case left little doubt that juvenile offenders are as entitled to the protection of constitutional guarantees as their adult counterparts, with the exception of participation in a public jury trial.

JUVENILE RIGHTS

During the years that followed, the U.S. Supreme Court continued the trend toward requiring due process rights for juveniles. In 1970, in the *Winship* case, the Court decided that in juvenile court proceedings involving delinquency, the standard of proof for conviction should be the same as that for adults in criminal court—proof beyond a reasonable doubt (*in re Winship*, 1970). In the case of *Breed v. Jones*

Audio Link 13.1
Listen to the *McKeiver v. Pennsylvania* oral arguments.

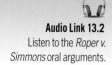

Audio Link 13.2
Listen to the *Roper v. Simmons* oral arguments.

(1975), the Court decided that trying a juvenile who had previously been adjudicated delinquent in juvenile court for the same crime as an adult in criminal court violates the double jeopardy clause of the Fifth Amendment when the adjudication involves violation of a criminal statute. The Court did not, however, go so far as to guarantee juveniles all of the same rights as adults. In the case of *McKeiver v. Pennsylvania* (1971), the Court held that the due process clause of the Fourteenth Amendment did not require jury trials in juvenile court. Nonetheless, some states have extended this right to juveniles through state law.

In the case of *Roper v. Simmons* (2005), the U.S. Supreme Court reversed a 1989 precedent and struck down the death penalty for crimes committed by people under the age of 18 years. The Court held that "evolving standards of decency" govern the prohibition of cruel and unusual punishment and noted that there is a scientific consensus that teenagers have "an underdeveloped sense of responsibility" and that, therefore, it is unreasonable to classify them among the most culpable offenders (Bradley, 2006). This was despite the fact that the crime involved in this case was heinous and barbaric in nature.

Process Involved With Juveniles in Custody

Initially, youth enter the juvenile justice system through some sort of contact with law enforcement. A juvenile can be taken into custody under the laws of arrest or by law enforcement if there are reasonable grounds to believe that the child is in immediate danger from his or her environment or if the youth has run away from home. In addition, court orders may be executed that require that youth to be taken into custody. The Uniform Juvenile Court Act (UJCA) is a document that provides guidance on how courts should process juveniles. Section 16 of the UJCA states that delinquent youth can be kept in a jail or another type of adult facility when other options are not available. In such a case, the detention space must be a room separate from adults, and the youth can be kept in detention only if it seems warranted as a means to ensure public safety. The UJCA further adds that delinquent youth "shall not be detained in a jail or other facility intended or used for the detention of adults charged with criminal offenses or of children alleged to be delinquent." The purpose of this section is to protect youth from exposure to criminals and the negative effects that jails and other secure adult environments may have upon the youth.

SCREENING AND CLASSIFICATION OF JUVENILE OFFENDERS

The need to classify juvenile offenders is important once it has been determined that they will be charged. Students may recall that assessment and classification issues were discussed in depth in Chapter 9. Further, students may also recall specific mention of an instrument used in corrections for supervision and treatment decisions when classifying inmates, the Level of Service Inventory–Revised (LSI-R). This instrument is widely recognized in the field of corrections and comports well with many of the treatment programs for adults and juveniles that are grounded in cognitive-behavioral types of interventions. One instrument that has emerged as particularly useful with juvenile offenders is the Youth Level of Service/Case Management Inventory (YLS/CMI), which was developed and adapted from the Level of Service Inventory (LSI) and is consistent with the theory and structure of the LSI-R (Flores, Travis, & Latessa, 2003).

This instrument is currently used in a variety of juvenile correctional settings in a number of jurisdictions. This same instrument has been employed to classify youth for judicial disposition decisions, placement into community programs, institutional assignments, and release from institutional custody. Proponents of the Y-LSI claim that the instrument is a valid risk prediction tool for youth, as well as a valid needs assessment tool that provides information relevant to intervention decision making. In many states, juvenile courts, probation offices, and residential programs have adopted the Y-LSI for case classification. This is true for a very substantial number of juvenile correctional systems throughout the nation.

One specific area of importance in screening and assessment is related to substance abuse for juvenile offenders. As noted in Chapter 9, substance abuse issues are tied to the criminality of many adult offenders in both the state and federal correctional systems. Substance abuse is likewise a very important aspect of juvenile treatment because many young offenders experiment with drugs and alcohol. Further, persons who are under the influence of drugs or alcohol or who have a tendency to use drugs and alcohol tend to have a higher rate of suicide when in jails or prisons. Lastly, suicide rates tend to be higher than average among teens. Thus, juvenile offenders are at particular risk for substance abuse–related suicide and/or additional mental health problems (e.g., depression and anxiety) when they are detained and/or placed in a secure environment.

The use of screening tools has become commonplace in many juvenile facilities; however, only 50% of youth in custody are in places that use standardized assessment tools to identify youth with substance use problems (Sedlak & McPherson, 2010). Despite the high rate of substance-related problems, nearly one fifth (19%) of youth in custody are in facilities that do not screen any youth for substance use problems, and more than one third (36%) are in facilities that screen some, but not all, youth. Table 13.1 provides additional data regarding the substance abuse screening practices used for youth admitted into detention or residential facilities.

Regardless of the specific instrument used, the decisions regarding juvenile justice treatment for thousands of youth in all types of correctional settings are based on some type of screening, assessment, or classification process. While Chapter 9 discusses the importance of assessment with various offenders, this is even more important with juvenile offenders because of temporal considerations in the youth's development. Indeed, at this point the criminal justice system makes its first determination of a juvenile offender, and this determination is likely to have a very long-range outcome. All types of treatment and intervention given to these offenders will be based entirely upon the results of the assessment(s) given. Thus, at this point the trajectory for future offending or future reformation is initialized. It is at this point that juveniles can be found to be limited to their detected involvement of delinquency or that they can be inappropriately treated, increasing the likelihood of their becoming an adult criminal.

EMPHASIS ON TREATMENT

As we have seen, the primary purpose within the juvenile justice system is to treat and reform youth rather than to punish them. The system has been specifically designed with the mind-set that youth should be spared the stigma of a conviction and the trauma of full incarceration, when practical. The juvenile

TABLE 13.1   Youth in Custody by Their Facility's Practices for Screening Youth to Identify Substance Abuse Problems

Facility Screening Practice	*Percent*
Who does the facility screen? When?	
All youth, definitely within 24 hours	27
All youth, at least some in 24 hours	13
All youth, none in 24 hours	24
Some youth, some in 24 hours	7
Some youth, none in 24 hours	10
No youth	19
What screening methods are used? (*all that apply*)	
Staff-administered question/interview	63
Standardized self-report instruments	50
Visual observation, medical exam, drug tests	47
Self-report checklist inventory	41
Records of previous tests, treatments	5

SOURCE: Sedlak, A. J., & McPherson, K. S. (2010). *Youth's needs and services: Findings from the survey of youth in residential placement.* Washingtone, DC: Office of Juvenile Justice and Delinquency Prevention.

FOCUS TOPIC: 13.1

Adolescents With Mental Health Needs

In an effort to improve services to this specialized population, the Texas Juvenile Probation Commission (TJPC) was tasked with creating a mental health screening instrument to be used by all departments. The TJPC has developed a comprehensive array of mental health services to this population. The project was named the *Special Needs Diversionary Program* and consists of juveniles with mental health issues that are supervised by juvenile probation officers who, in turn, work closely with mental health practitioners (eliminating the "organizational cracks" in the intervention process that are discussed in this chapter), guaranteeing the delivery of the necessary mental health services. The goals of the project are to keep the offenders at home within the community, reduce recidivism of those in the project, and have juvenile probation officers work closely with local mental health providers to ensure both proper assessment and interventions for juvenile probationers in the program. Some of the elements contained in this project's package of interventions are listed as follows:

1. Coordinated service delivery and planning between probation and mental health staff.

2. Provision and monitoring of medication.

3. Individual and/or group therapy.

4. Skills training.

5. In-home services such as multisystemic or functional family services.

6. Family focus support services.

7. Co-location of supervision and treatment services.

Youth participation is determined by indicators on the mental health screening instrument and the availability of a caretaker/guardian willing to work with the mental health and probation departments. At this point, an additional clinical assessment is made to determine the child's ability to function in society. Just as a side note, it was found that 22% of all of these youth suffered from depression, 19% qualified for the diagnosis of oppositional defiant disorder, 18% had the diagnosis of conduct disorder (a precursor to antisocial personality disorder), and 9% percent had attention deficit/hyperactivity disorder.

The Special Needs Diversionary Program illustrates how important assessment can be to both community supervision and mental health services. This program also demonstrates how public safety and offender needs can be better served when disparate community agencies create partnerships in providing service to special needs populations. Such partnerships, when coupled with accurate assessment instruments and procedures, can provide better interventions that are tailored for the offender. Interventions then will be more likely to have a better "goodness of fit" with the needs of the juvenile offender and will be better able to target those most at risk of recidivating when released on community supervision.

SOURCE: All material for this special insert was adapted from Spriggs, V. (2003). Identifying and providing services to Texas: Juvenile offenders with mental health needs. *Corrections Today, 65*(1), 64–66.

Video Link 13.1
Learn more about the treatment needs of juveniles.

Audio Link 13.3
Learn more about treatment of juveniles with mental health issues.

justice and mental health fields have increasingly recognized the scope of the mental health needs of youth involved in the juvenile justice system and the inadequacy of services to meet these needs (see Focus Topic 13.1 for more details). As we discussed in the prior subsection, standardized screening instruments have gained more acceptance within most treatment programs. Further, more service providers have turned toward evidence-based treatment approaches, and more juvenile justice and mental health agencies have collaborated to devise solutions (Cox, Allen, Hanser, & Conrad, 2011).

Youth in juvenile facilities tend to present with affective disorders, adjustment difficulties, and issues related to trauma and stress. For instance, symptoms of depression and anxiety were found to be very common among nationally surveyed youth in treatment facilities, with 51% of the custody population reporting that nervous or worried feelings have kept them from doing what they want to do over the past few months, and 52% indicating that they feel lonely for significant periods of time (Sedlak & McPherson, 2010).

Mental health services in the form of evaluation, ongoing therapy, or counseling are nearly universally available in the facilities, with 97% of youth living in places that provide one or more of these services either inside or outside the facility. However, despite the relatively high suicide risk in the placement population, individual screening for suicide risk is not common. More than one fourth (26%) of youth are in facilities that do not screen all youth for suicide risk. Despite the importance of early identification, 45% of youth are in facilities that fail to screen all youth within 24 hours, and 26% are in facilities that do not screen any youth at intake or during the first 24 hours (Sedlak & McPherson, 2010).

Further, suicide is the third leading cause of death among adolescents, and a prior suicide attempt is the single most important risk factor for death by suicide (Wintersteen, Diamond, & Fein, 2007). One fifth of youth in placement admit having two or more recent suicidal feelings. The prevalence of past suicide attempts (22%) is more than twice the highest rate for their peers in local surveys of the general youth population and nearly quadruple the rate in national samples.

COMMONALITY OF JUVENILE AS VICTIM OF PRIOR ABUSE

When delinquent behavior occurs, it may bring about further abuse, resulting in a vicious cycle that generates behavior that continues to get worse and worse. Children and adolescents who exhibit patterns of delinquency that emanate from the home often imitate the behaviors of parents or other family members. In some extremely dysfunctional homes, children may even be instructed on how to commit crimes. Though this may sound unusual, it is not unheard of, and there have been court cases where such occurrences have specifically been noted. Consider also that the crime of **contributing to the delinquency of a minor** is a form of neglect where an adult specifically facilitates the ability of youth to commit delinquent or criminal acts and encourages these youth to engage in such acts.

Journal Article Link 13.1
Read about the history of abuse differences in male and female delinquents.

Aside from circumstances where adults deliberately teach youth to commit crimes, it seems that abuse and neglect also foster delinquency in children due to the abuse and trauma produced from such experiences. For instance, Ireland, Smith, and Thornberry (2002) examined official records and utilized longitudinal survey data and found a strong relationship between maltreatment and delinquent behaviors. The research by Ireland et al. (2004) is important because it aids in demonstrating where much of the more serious offending among youth and young adults may come from. Though this does not explain all juvenile misbehavior, it does tend to be consistent in explaining etiology within a substantial portion of the more serious youthful offending as well as later adult offending.

Consider also the research by English, Widom, Spatz, and Brandford (2002) who note that there is strong support for a relationship between child abuse, neglect, delinquency, adult criminality, and future violent criminal behavior. The research by English et al. clearly underscores our contention that, for the majority of hard-core youthful offenders, the prior home life circumstances are interlaced with the youth's offending behavior. English et al. further note that abused and neglected children were 4.8 times more likely to be arrested as juveniles, 2 times more likely to be arrested as adults, and 3.1 times more likely to be arrested for a violent crime than were subjects who were members of a matched control group.

From the research just presented, it should be clear that youth who come from abusive homes indeed have an increased likelihood of engaging in serious delinquency, drug abuse, and later adult criminality. While a large number of youth engage in minor forms of delinquency, most forms of minor delinquency (e.g., teenage sex, use of alcohol at an occasional outing, speeding and minor traffic violations, violating minor ordinances) are actually part and parcel to the development of many teens. Indeed, these activities are often simply considered the process by which youth experience their newly budding sense of adolescent autonomy. However, when delinquency goes beyond the minor types of activity, such as with full-fledged burglaries (as opposed to petty shoplifting), drug use that goes beyond alcohol and marijuana, assaultive behavior, and other actions such as teen rape, we contend that in many cases prior childhood socialization and exposure to noxious family and peer influences are a common thread in etiology.

Other researchers share similar views on minor delinquent behavior among adolescents, going so far as to say that it is statistically normal among young boys growing up in the United States (Moffitt, 1993). According to Terrie Moffitt (1993), youthful antisocial and risk-prone acts are personal statements of independence. For example, these youth may engage in underage drinking or cigarette smoking, particularly with their peers, as a means of displaying adultlike behaviors. Another common form of delinquency for this group might be minor vandalism that is often perceived more as a "gag" than as an act of victimization (actions such as the defacing of road signs, the destruction of residential mailboxes, and other petty forms of destruction). Shoplifting in various stores may also be encouraged among some members of this group for the occasional "five-finger discount" in chosen music and/or clothing stores that are frequented by the adolescent peer group—displaying bravado among one's peers and, incidentally, obtaining an item that is valued by the individual and the peer group in the process. Lastly, some of these individuals may engage in occasional truancy from school, particularly if they are able to hide their absence. These adolescents typically commit acts of defiance or nonconformity simply as a means of expressing their developing sense of autonomy. However, these adolescents are not likely to continue their activities into late adulthood. Moffitt (1993) refers to these youth as **adolescent-only offenders**.

Chapter 13: Juvenile Correctional Systems   **335**

APPLIED THEORY 13.1

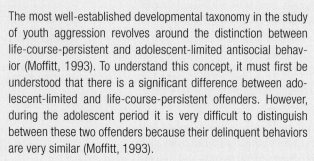

Adolescent-Limited Versus Life-Course-Persistent Juvenile Offenders: The Theoretical Work of Terrie Moffitt

The most well-established developmental taxonomy in the study of youth aggression revolves around the distinction between life-course-persistent and adolescent-limited antisocial behavior (Moffitt, 1993). To understand this concept, it must first be understood that there is a significant difference between adolescent-limited and life-course-persistent offenders. However, during the adolescent period it is very difficult to distinguish between these two offenders because their delinquent behaviors are very similar (Moffitt, 1993).

The majority of individuals who are delinquents during childhood and adolescence stop offending before they reach adulthood. According to Moffitt (1993), those adolescents who desist from delinquency are referred to as adolescent-limited juvenile delinquents. Many adolescents may be inclined to mimic their antisocial peers, who appear to have attained adult status in many ways. Through antisocial conduct, adolescents reject the ties of childhood and demonstrate that they can act independently. Under Moffitt's theory, youthful antisocial and risk-prone acts are personal statements of independence. It should be noted that self-report studies indicate that most teenage males engage in some criminal conduct, leading criminologists to conclude that participation in delinquency is a normal part of teen life (Scott & Grisso, 1997). Thus, adolescent-limited delinquents are likely to engage in crimes that are profitable or rewarding, but they also have the ability to abandon these actions when prosocial styles become more rewarding (Bartol & Bartol, 2010). The adolescent-limited youths are relatively free from personality disorders or poor decision making based on life skills deficiencies. Because of this, this group usually has adequate social skills to both compete and cooperate within the strictures of day-to-day society.

Some adolescents, however, continue their delinquent behavior into and throughout adulthood, and these are the life-course-persistent juvenile delinquents. Unlike the adolescent-limited delinquent, these adolescents lack many of the necessary social skills and opportunities possessed by the adolescent-limited delinquent. The reason for this difference in development is quite startling but nonetheless a common phenomenon to this group. For these offenders, the clue to their difference in conformative ability lies less in their adolescent years than in their early childhood development.

Indeed, it has been found that many life-course-persistent delinquents are children with inherited or acquired physiological deficiencies that develop either prenatally or in early childhood. To compound this problem, many of these same children often come from high-risk social environments as well, reflecting the parental deficiencies thought to be genetically transmitted intergenerationally from parent to child (Moffitt, 1993). This combination of the difficult child and an adverse child-rearing context serves to place the child at risk for future delinquent behavior, setting the initial groundwork for a life-course-persistent pattern of antisocial behavior during years when the child is usually most impressionable (Moffitt, 1993). Moffit also found that early aggressive behavior is an important predictor of later delinquency and could possibly be a marker for the life-course-persistent offender. This means that most violent youths begin their violent behavior during adolescence. However, of those youth who commit the most serious violent acts and who continue their violent behavior beyond adolescence, their violent natures can frequently be traced back to early childhood (Moffitt, 1993).

The greater prevalence of late-onset youth violence refutes the myth that all serious violent offenders can be identified in early childhood. In fact, the majority of young people who become violent show little or no evidence of childhood behavioral disorders, high levels of aggression, or problem behaviors—all predictors of later violence. Despite the fact that early predictors may not accurately assess the most *numerous* violent offenders, this process *is* more likely to correctly identify the most *dangerous* juvenile offenders (Surgeon General Executive Summary, 2002). It is for this reason alone that appropriate assessment is so critical; it may not necessarily lower overall delinquency rates significantly (a phenomenon considered "normal" among American adolescents), but it *is* likely to reduce violent crimes against members of society. Certainly, this is the category of crime that concerns the public most.

This distinction is important from an assessment point of view. Knowledge of these early indicators can allow the appropriate specialists an advantage in identifying children most at risk for delinquency. This knowledge then translates to an enhanced ability to provide effective interventions during an age when the child is likely to be more receptive. During early childhood, negative behaviors such as aggression have not been as clearly reinforced as they are by the time the child reaches adolescence. Thus, the earlier the intervention, the better the chance of saving the potential life-course-persistent offender from a life of misery and trouble.

SOURCE: Based on Moffitt, T. E. (1993). Adolescence-limited and life-course persistent antisocial behavior: A developmental taxonomy. *Psychological Review, 100,* 674–701.

While youth who might be classified as adolescent-only offenders may occasionally be in need of some sort of counseling for any number of life-course issues, they seldom will need to see a treatment provider who specializes in the offender population. In more instances than not, these youth will age out of their behavior and will have no need for a correctional counselor. Rather, general counseling that addresses teen development, social pressure, peer groups, and other common aspects of development are likely to be more effective for this group. On the other hand, some adolescents continue their delinquent behavior into and throughout adulthood, and these are what Moffitt (1993) referred to as the **life-course-persistent juvenile** delinquents (see Applied Theory 13.1 for more information on Moffitt's work).

TYPES OF CHILD ABUSE AND DETECTION OF ABUSE

In many cases, juvenile youth are victims of various forms of neglect or abuse. This is a very important aspect of juvenile offending, particularly when trying to provide treatment services for juvenile offenders. In many cases, community supervision officers will find themselves networking with child protection agencies, and they will likewise tend to have offenders on their caseloads who are in need of parent-

ing assistance, whether the offender realizes it or not. Further, one must consider that over 70% of female offenders on community supervision are also the primary caretakers of their children. This is an important observation, especially when one considers that the number of female offenders on community supervision is much higher than the number of those incarcerated. This means that community supervision officers are likely to come across issues related to the welfare of children on a fairly frequent basis. Further still, among a high number of delinquent youth, disproportionate rates of abuse and neglect occur.

In discussing these issues, we first turn our focus to child neglect since such maltreatment is often a precursor to later forms of abuse and since neglect also often occurs in conjunction with abusive treatment. **Child neglect** occurs when a parent or caretaker of the child does not provide the proper or necessary support, education, medical, or other remedial care required by a given state's law, including food, shelter, and clothing. Child neglect also occurs when adult caretakers abandon a child that they are legally obligated to support (Cox et al., 2011). Neglect is typically divided into three types: physical, emotional, and educational (Cox et al., 2011). **Physical neglect** includes abandonment, the expulsion of the child from the home (being kicked out of the house), a failure to seek or excessive delay in seeking medical care for the child, inadequate supervision, and inadequate food, clothing, and shelter (Cox et al., 2011). **Emotional neglect** includes inadequate nurturing or affection, allowing the child to engage in inappropriate or illegal behavior such as drug or alcohol use, and ignoring a child's basic emotional needs (Cox et al., 2011). Lastly, educational neglect occurs when a parent or even a teacher permits chronic truancy or simply ignores the educational and/or special needs of a child (Cox et al., 2011).

Beyond child neglect, acts of abuse are even more serious forms of maltreatment and include both physical and psychological forms of harm. **Child abuse** occurs when a child (youth under the age of 18 in most states) is maltreated by a parent, an immediate family member, or any person

PHOTO 13.3

Yolanda Love, a Child Protective Services specialist, poses with a doll used to mimic the size, weight, and movements of a real child to educate about the dangers of Shaken Baby Syndrome. Community supervision officers often find themselves networking with child protection agencies, and frequently have offenders on their caseloads who are in need of parenting assistance.

responsible for the child's welfare (Cox et al., 2011). According to Cox et al. (2011), **physical abuse** "can be defined as any physical acts that cause or can cause physical injury to a child" (p. 266). It is not uncommon for such parents to have been abused as children, resulting in an intergenerational transmission of violence through their abusive behavior. Psychological abuse is another frequently reported form of child abuse. **Psychological abuse** is also sometimes referred to as emotional abuse and includes actions or the omission of actions by parents and other caregivers that could cause the child to have serious behavioral, emotional, or mental impairments. Often, there is no clear or evident behavior of the adult caregiver that provides indication of psychological abuse. Rather, the child displays behavior that is impaired and/or has emotional disturbances that result from profound forms of emotional abuse, trauma, distance, or neglect with no direct evidence of the abuse usually existing.

Sexual Abuse

Sexual abuse of youth consists of any sexual contact or attempted sexual contact that occurs between an adult or designated caretaker and a child. It should be noted that it is rare that physical indicators of sexual abuse are found. This means that most sexual abuse is detected due to behavioral indicators and/or when the youth discloses such acts. Possible behavioral indicators include observations such as an unwillingness to change clothes or to participate in physical education classes; withdrawal, fantasy, or infantile behavior not typical of a teen; bizarre sexual behavior; sexual sophistication that is beyond the child's age (a bit hard to gauge with teens); delinquent runaway behavior; and reports of being sexually assaulted.

The behavior of parents also may provide indicators of sexual abuse. Such behaviors may include jealousy and being overprotective of a child. A parent may hesitate to report a spouse who is sexually abusing his or her child for fear of destroying the marriage or for fear of retaliation. In some cases, intrafamilial sex may be considered a better option than extramarital sex. Lastly, sexual abuse of children can have numerous side effects, including guilt, shame, anxiety, fear, depression, anger, low self-esteem, concerns about secrecy, feelings of helplessness, and a strong need for others. In addition, victims of sexual abuse have higher levels of school absenteeism, less participation in extracurricular activities, and lower grades.

FEMALE JUVENILES IN CUSTODY

As with adult female offenders, the needs of female juvenile offenders differ from those of males, as do the services they receive. Female juvenile offenders in placement have more mental health and substance use problems and worse abuse histories (Sedlak & McPherson, 2010). Higher percentages of females report an above-average number of mental or emotional problems and traumatic experiences, compared to male juveniles. The work of Sedlak and McPherson (2010) has been integrated into this section to illustrate some of the differences between male and female juveniles. According to their research, females reveal nearly twice the rate of past physical abuse (42% vs. 22%), more than twice the rate of past suicide attempts (44% vs. 19%), and more than 4 times the rate of prior sex abuse (35% vs. 8%) as males. As we have seen in earlier sections of this chapter and as we saw in Chapter 11, prior childhood abuse (particularly sexual abuse) produces long-term damage to female offenders; often this translates into long-term criminality for the most severely troubled girls and women who are victimized.

Female juvenile offenders are more commonly placed in residential treatment programs (compared to other types of programs), and nearly all youth in residential treatment programs are in facilities that provide onsite mental health services. Among these female youth, more receive individual counseling (85% vs. 67%), and fewer receive group counseling. Females also give their counseling less positive ratings (Sedlak & McPherson, 2010). This last point is a bit troubling and points toward the need for correctional programs to improve services for young female offenders, just as is needed for adult female offenders (see Figure 13.1).

Lastly, female juvenile offenders report significantly more drug experience than males, with 91% saying they had used at least one of the drugs listed (including marijuana, cocaine/crack, ecstasy, meth, heroin, inhalants, and an "other illegal drug" category) compared to 87% of males. More females than males report using nearly every substance listed, and 47% (compared to 33% of males) report having ever used four or more of the listed substances.

Audio Link 13.4
Listen to a clip about the special treatment needs of female juvenile offenders.

FIGURE 13.1   Percentage of Males and Females With Above-Average Numbers of "Yes" Responses to Mental and Emotional Survey Questions

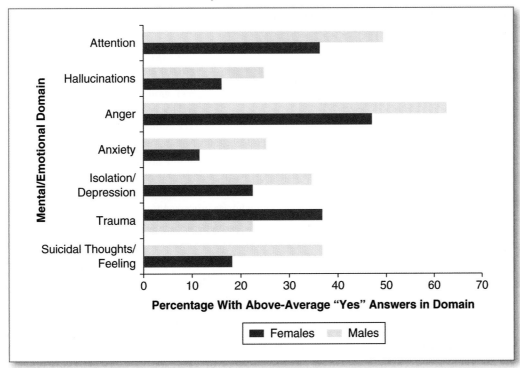

SOURCE: Sedlak, A. J., & McPherson, K. S. (2010). *Youth's needs and services: Findings from the survey of youth in residential placement.* Washington, DC: Office of Juvenile Justice and Delinquency Prevention.

Although males and females use drugs and/or alcohol at the same frequency just before entering custody, more females report recent substance-related problems (71% vs. 67%). Despite females' greater substance abuse problems, they are often housed in facilities that provide less access to substance abuse treatment. In comparison to males, fewer females are housed in facilities that offer substance abuse education (Sedlak & McPherson, 2010).

JUVENILE GANG MEMBERS

When working with juveniles in the correctional setting, gang membership will be encountered on a fairly frequent basis. This is particularly true if the community supervision agency referring the youth is in a large or midsize metropolitan area or if the correctional counselor works with youth in a state-operated facility. For correctional staff who work with juveniles, it is advisable that they develop a working knowledge of the different gang groups in their area and among their juvenile population. An understanding of the tenets of a particular gang, how leadership structures operate, and gang alliances can be important in rapport building and can also provide staff with an understanding of the youth's world, which will, undoubtedly, be influenced by the activities of his or her gang. This basic knowledge—and correctional staff should strive to learn more basic information—will provide staff with the bare basics to competently provide services to these youth.

Lifestyle, Peer Groups, and Youth Subculture

Peer groups are important for youth, and the peer group will likely be the primary source of socialization aside from the youth's family. Indeed, if the family was seriously dysfunctional, it is likely that the youth only identifies with his or her peer group. Among youth who are processed in the juvenile and/or criminal justice system, there exist a number of subcultural groupings that will be important reference points for youth seen by the counselor. In particular, it should be noted that the "gangsta" movement has had a particularly strong impact on youth culture, particularly among delinquent youth. The "thug" look and/or genre of music is fairly common among youth who are processed throughout the juvenile system. While other subcultural groups exist (Goths, alternative, etc.), they are not as well represented among the hard-core juvenile offender population. This is not to say that knowledge of such groups is not relevant to correctional counseling, but it is to say that these groups will not be as prevalent, largely due to the fact that they are simply not as widespread in popularity among today's youth and the public media.

Further, a disproportionate amount of minority youth are processed through the justice system. Thus, in many juvenile systems, youth will tend to congregate along racial lines just as they might along subcultural lines. African American and Latino American youth are particularly represented, and these youth will likely affiliate with their own racial categories. In many cases, the youth from these minority groups will also come from families who are not affluent, with economic challenges common to their background. These factors will tend to impact the socialization process that has been experienced by these youth, and this is likely to be quite different from the backgrounds of many counselors. Because of this, correctional workers must also understand the cultural backgrounds common to youth in their intervention programs.

Reasons for Joining

There has been considerable debate as to why youth join gangs. It is our contention that many youth join gangs for a number of reasons, but, among all others, the primary reason is to have some sort of need met. Considerable research has demonstrated that gangs provide many youth with basic human needs related to belonging. Some of these needs include security, acceptance, friendship, food, shelter, discipline, belonging, status, respect, power, and money (Valdez, 2009). Thus, gangs and gang membership likely result from any variety of personal, social, or economic factors.

Video Link 13.2
Watch an interview with a juvenile gang member.

In some cases, youth may be pressured into gangs. This is particularly true where rivalries are rampant and the need to recruit members exists. Peer pressure and intimidation may be the causal factor for some youth. Likewise, protection from victimization at the hands of other gang groups in the community might be another motivator. In addition, there may be expectations from older siblings and/or family members who have also joined a given gang. This is an important consideration because gangs in some areas of Chicago, Los Angeles, and New York have family memberships that span three or more generations. Indeed, some neighborhoods in these metropolitan areas have members throughout who are current members or who, now well into adulthood, were once members before settling down. In such cases, it is not uncommon for that neighborhood to sympathize with the gang and to provide it with support.

Amidst these neighborhood social conditions, the internal influences of the gang membership also work on the youth's development. The youngster may grow up knowing older gang members prior to himself becoming a member. He may learn to admire these members. Over time, an informal familiarization with the gang may develop. Eventually, the gang psyche is taught via the gang formal indoctrination process. This transformation of a youth into a gang member involves a slow process of assimilation. Once these young people reach an age at which they are able to prove their worth to the gang leadership, they are required to engage in some sort of ritual. In most cases this may consist of getting "jumped in," which is when the gang members beat the youth and the youth is expected to fight until he cannot continue to do so, or it may consist of getting "sexed in," in which some females may be required to have sex with male members to obtain affiliate status.

Consider further that many hard-core juvenile offenders come from abusive and/or neglectful homes. This is one key motivator for youth from these homes to join gangs. This motivation holds true for both male and female juvenile gang members. The family of origin is the primary source for developing the youth's sense of belonging and self-worth. If these youth do not get this support at home, they are likely to seek this support from some other source; gangs provide that source.

DETENTION VERSUS INCARCERATION

Detention facilities are secure residential facilities for youth and are separate from adult prisons. Though separate, they still resemble adult prisons in appearance and have locked doors and barred windows. These facilities are, in theory, supposed to be reserved for the most serious juvenile offenders—those who are violent and require secure confinement as a means of protecting society. Nevertheless, it is not uncommon for other youth such as runaways, homeless youth, and those who are abandoned to end up in these types of facilities.

Reference Link 13.2
Read more about juvenile detention centers.

Further, these facilities may hold youth who are scheduled for trial but have not been sentenced, or who may be waiting for the imposition of their sentence. This means that youth of differing custody levels may be kept within these facilities. Other youth may be in violation of their probation and being held for revocation or modification proceedings. In recent years, the juvenile justice system has made efforts to remove status offenders and neglected or abused children from these detention facilities, when and where appropriate. Despite the ongoing effort to limit the use of detention, juveniles are still detained in about 20% of all delinquency cases.

The overarching goal of juvenile corrections is to provide treatment services for youth and to avoid traumatizing or stigmatizing such youth in the belief that such restrictive measures will orient these youth toward further criminality. The use of juvenile waiver for serious offenders who are sentenced to periods of incarceration is presented in the following section. But for now, this sentencing option is presented to distinguish it from the use of detention. When youth are sent to prison, they are incarcerated with adult offenders. These youth are usually charged for adult offenses, and their sentencing terms are for several years. The types of incarceration that youth may face, whether in a juvenile detention facility or in prison itself, are discussed in the next few sections.

JUVENILE WAIVER FOR SERIOUS JUVENILE OFFENDERS

Video Link 13.3
Watch a clip about a juvenile incarcerated in an adult prison.

For those child and adolescent offenders who are incarcerated for violent crimes, a special form of incarceration may be employed. This occurs when the juvenile case is transferred to adult court and results in what is commonly known as juvenile waiver. Waiver to adult court can theoretically be utilized for any offense, but this process is usually reserved for serious, violent felonies or for property crimes with which juveniles are repeat offenders. Juveniles who are tried in adult criminal court are most often kept in a juvenile facility or separate wing until they are of sufficient age to be transferred to the adult population. Those who are placed in an adult prison are usually separated from the adult population.

The disposition of a juvenile who has been tried and sentenced in an adult court varies from state to state. The usual procedure is that younger offenders who are found guilty are sent to a juvenile detention facility until they are at least 16 to 18 years of age. Their treatment there is basically the same as that of juveniles who were tried under the juvenile justice system. Nevertheless, some youth who are charged as adults may be sent to an adult facility if the crime and circumstances warrant this. The disadvantage to this process is that it sends a message of hopelessness to the youth and society regarding the likelihood of reformation. Further, there is the possibility that this approach will only increase the criminality of juveniles as they are exposed to the adult criminal population. The adult prison system's mission is primarily the punishment of offenders, and this naturally includes those juveniles included within its confines as well. Perhaps these offenders are best considered to be targeted by a form of legal "selective incapacitation" where the most severe offenders are removed from society for no other reason than to protect society from any further harm from that offender. However, this automatically translates to an admission from the justice system in its ability to reform the youth—something that can be disturbing when one considers the sheer number of years left to transpire for a young offender of, say, 14 or 15 years of age.

TABLE 13.2   Offense Profile of Cases Waived to Criminal Court

	Number of Waived cases		*Percent of Waived cases*	
Most serious offense	*1985*	*2005*	*1985*	*2005*
Total delinquency	7,200	6,900	100%	100%
Person	2,400	3,500	33	51
Property	3,800	1,900	53	27
Drugs	400	800	5	12
Public order	600	700	9	10

SOURCE: Sickmund, M. (2009). *Delinquency cases in juvenile court, 2005.* Washington, DC: Office of Juvenile Justice and Delinquency Prevention.

In 2005, juvenile court judges waived jurisdiction over an estimated 6,900 delinquency cases, sending them to criminal court. This represents less than 0.5% of all delinquency cases handled. The number of cases waived was relatively flat from 1985 to 1988, rose sharply from 1988 to 1994 (93%), and then fell back to the levels of the mid-1980s and remained there through 2005. For many years, property offense cases accounted for the largest proportion of waived cases. However, since the mid-1990s, person offenses have outnumbered property offenses among waived cases. In 2005, half of waived cases involved person offenses. Table 13.2 provides specific details regarding the number and percent of cases waived

FIGURE 13.2 The Use of Juvenile Waiver Has Declined Since the 1990s

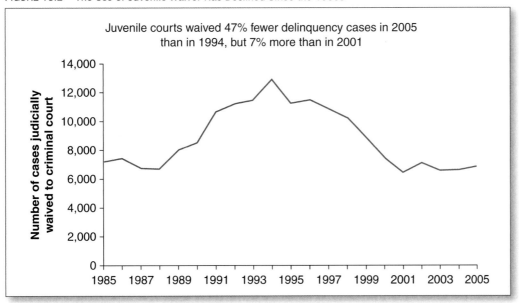

Juvenile courts waived 47% fewer delinquency cases in 2005 than in 1994, but 7% more than in 2001

SOURCE: Sickmund, M. (2009). *Delinquency cases in juvenile court, 2005*. Washington, DC: Office of Juvenile Justice and Delinquency Prevention.

from juvenile court to adult court. As can be seen, the numbers of youth waived to adult court are quite small, and even fewer of these are actually sent to an adult prison by the time that the process is over. Further, it is clear that the use of waiver processes has declined since the 1990s. Though a slight increase occurred from 2001 to 2005, the overall impact since the 1990s has been a reduction of 47% in the use of juvenile waivers (see Figure 13.2).

INCARCERATION OF JUVENILES

The most severe dispositional alternative available to the juvenile court judge considering a case of delinquency is commitment to a correctional facility. There are clearly some juveniles whose actions cannot be tolerated by the community. Those who commit predatory offenses or whose illegal behavior becomes progressively more serious might need to be institutionalized for the good of society. For these delinquent juveniles, alternative options may have already been exhausted, and the only remedy available to ensure protection of society may be incarceration. Because juvenile institutions are often very similar to adult prison institutions, incarceration is a serious business with a number of negative consequences for both juveniles and society that must be considered prior to placement.

Although incarcerating juveniles for the protection of society is clearly necessary in some cases, correctional institutions frequently serve as a gateway to careers in crime and delinquency. The notion that sending juveniles to correctional facilities will result in rehabilitation has proved to be inaccurate in most cases. Not only do "graduates" from correctional institutions

PHOTO 13.7

Juvenile court judges must make important decisions regarding both the welfare of the youth who are processed in their court and the interests of public safety.

CORRECTIONS AND THE LAW 13.1

Graham v. Florida: Justices Limit Life Sentences for Juveniles

The Supreme Court ruled that juveniles who commit crimes in which no one is killed may not be sentenced to life in prison without the possibility of parole.

Five justices, in an opinion by Justice Anthony M. Kennedy, agreed that the Eighth Amendment's ban on cruel and unusual punishment forbids such sentences as a categorical matter.

"A state need not guarantee the offender eventual release," Justice Kennedy wrote, "but if it imposes the sentence of life, it must provide him or her with some realistic opportunity to obtain release before the end of that term."

The ruling marked the first time that the court excluded an entire class of offenders from a given form of punishment outside the context of the death penalty. "'Death is different' no longer," Justice Clarence Thomas wrote in dissent.

The overall vote was 6-to-3, though that is a little misleading. Chief Justice John G. Roberts Jr. voted with the majority in saying that the inmate who brought the appeal had received a sentence so harsh that it violated the Constitution. But the chief justice endorsed only a case-by-case approach, saying that an offender's age could be considered in deciding whether a life sentence was so disproportionate to the crime as to violate the Eighth Amendment.

The case involved Terrance Graham, who in 2003, at age 16, helped rob a Jacksonville restaurant, during which an accomplice beat the manager with a steel bar. Mr. Graham was sentenced to a year in jail and three years' probation for that crime.

The next year, at 17, Mr. Graham and two 20-year-old accomplices committed a home invasion robbery. In 2005, a judge sentenced Mr. Graham to life for violating his probation.

The Supreme Court has carved out categories of offenders and crimes that are not subject to the death penalty, including juvenile offenders and those who do not take a life. Monday's decision [*Graham v. Florida*] applied those two decisions to life-without-parole sentences.

Justice Kennedy, who was joined by Justices John Paul Stevens, Ruth Bader Ginsburg, Stephen G. Breyer and Sonia Sotomayor, said both national and international practices supported the court's ruling.

Justice Thomas said the majority was wrong about the facts in the United States and abroad and wrong as a matter of principle to take account of international opinion. Justice Antonin Scalia joined all of Justice Thomas's dissent and Justice Samuel A. Alito Jr. most of it.

Thirty-seven states, the District of Columbia and the federal government have laws allowing life-without-parole sentences for juveniles convicted of non-homicide offenses. That represents, Justice Thomas said, a super-majority of states in favor of the punishment.

Justice Kennedy responded that a study relied on by Mr. Graham and supplemented by the court's own research had located only 129 juvenile offenders convicted under such laws. Seventy-seven were in Florida, the rest in 10 other states. Those numbers, Justice Kennedy said, make the sentence "exceedingly rare" and demonstrate that "a national consensus has developed against it."

Justice Thomas drew a different conclusion from the same numbers. "That a punishment is rarely imposed demonstrates nothing more than a general consensus that it should be just that—rarely imposed," he wrote. "It is not proof that the punishment is one the nation abhors."

Justice Kennedy added that the sentences at issue had been "rejected the world over." Indeed, only the United States and perhaps Israel, he said, impose the punishment even for homicides committed by juveniles.

"The judgment of the world's nations that a particular sentencing practice is inconsistent with basic principles of decency," Justice Kennedy wrote, "demonstrates that the court's rationale has respected reasoning to support it."

Justice Thomas disputed Justice Kennedy's math, saying 11 nations seem to allow the punishment in theory. More important, he said, "foreign laws and sentencing practices" are "irrelevant to the meaning of our Constitution."

He added that most democracies around the world remain free to adopt the punishment should they wish to. "Starting today," Justice Thomas wrote, "ours can count itself among the few in which judicial decree prevents voters from making that choice."

Although the majority limited its decision to non-homicide offenses, advocates may try to apply its logic more broadly to the some 2,000 inmates serving life-without-parole sentences in the United States for participating in killings at 17 or younger.

Justice Thomas questioned the distinction drawn by the majority between killings and other sorts of violent crimes. "The court is quite willing to accept that a 17-year-old who pulls the trigger on a firearm can demonstrate sufficient depravity and irredeemability to be denied re-entry into society," he wrote, "but insists that a 17-year-old who rapes an 8-year-old and leaves her for dead does not."

Justice Alito, in a separate dissent that seemed directed to sentencing judges, said the majority's opinion did nothing to affect even quite long fixed sentences.

Justice Thomas predicted that Monday's ruling would give rise to years of litigation about just what sort of parole or other processes states must provide to provide the required "meaningful opportunity to obtain release."

As usual in cases involving the Eighth Amendment, the justices debated whether the Constitution should consider, in a one common formulation, "the evolving standards of decency that mark the progress of a maturing society."

Justice Thomas said the court should look to the practices at the time the Bill of Rights was adopted. Given that capital punishment could be imposed on people as young as 7 in the 18th century, he said, Mr. Graham's punishment would almost certainly have been deemed acceptable back then.

SOURCE: "Justices Limit Life Sentences for Juveniles," A. Liptak in *The New York Times*, May 17, 2010.

reappear, but also their experiences while incarcerated often seem to solidify delinquent or criminal attitudes and behavior. Most studies of recidivism among institutionalized delinquents lead to the conclusion that although some programs may work for some offenders some of the time, most institutional programs produce no better results than does the simple passage of time.

There are a number of alternative forms of incarceration available. For juveniles whose period of incarceration is to be relatively brief, there are many public and private detention facilities available.

Public detention facilities frequently are located near large urban centers and often house large numbers of delinquents in a cottage- or dormitory-type setting. As a rule, these institutions are used only when all other alternatives have been exhausted or when the offenses involved are quite serious. As a result, most of the more serious delinquents are sent to these facilities. In these institutions, concern with custody frequently outweighs concern with rehabilitation. A number of changes have occurred in juvenile correctional facilities during the past half-century. Cottage-type facilities have been replaced by institutional-type settings, and the number of juveniles incarcerated has increased, as has the severity of their offenses (Gluck, 1997). Typically, we see fences, razor wire, and guards at these facilities more often than we see treatment providers.

Journal Article Link 13.3
Read about balancing treatment and custody in a juvenile maximum security facility.

SECURE CORRECTIONAL FACILITIES AND YOUTH

Youth may be kept in prisons if they are transferred to adult court. While this can happen, we will separate this aspect of juvenile processing from our discussion because, at the point of waiver, the juvenile is not longer treated as a juvenile; he or she is treated as an adult. However, one interesting point regarding youth and incarceration should be brought out. Youth who are sentenced to prison for anything but murder cannot be sentenced to life without the possibility of parole, so long as they were a juvenile when the offense was committed. This became true when the U.S. Supreme Court issued its historic ruling in *Graham v. Florida* (2010) that held sentences of life without parole for juveniles convicted of nonhomicide offenses to be unconstitutional. Those who do commit acts of murder can be, and sometimes are, given sentences to serve their time as adults. In such cases, either they will be kept in a secure lockdown detention facility until they are 18, at which time they will be transferred to the state's adult prison system, or, if they are sent immediately to adult prison (a rare likelihood), they are kept separated from the adult population.

As one might guess, secure correctional facilities are not the best places to mold juvenile delinquents into useful law-abiding citizens. Sending a delinquent to a correctional facility to learn responsible, law-abiding behavior is like sending a person to the desert to learn how to swim. If our specific intent is to demand revenge of youthful offenders through physical and emotional punishment and isolation, current correctional facilities will suffice. If we would rather have those incarcerated juveniles return to society rehabilitated, a number of changes must be made.

It is important to consider the effects of peer group pressure in juvenile correctional facilities. There is little doubt that behavior modification will occur, but it will not necessarily result in the creation of a law-abiding citizen. The learning of delinquent behavior may be enhanced if the amount of contact

PHOTO 13.8

Students line up near their bunks in a dormitory at the West Texas State School. This is one example of a juvenile correctional facility.

with those holding favorable attitudes toward law violation is increased. Juvenile correctional facilities are typically characterized by the existence of a delinquent subculture that enhances the opportunity for dominance of the strong over the weak and gives impetus to the exploitation of the unsophisticated by the more knowledgeable.

We should not then be surprised when juveniles leave these institutions with more problems than they had prior to incarceration.

TECHNOLOGY AND EQUIPMENT 13.1

Using COMPSTAT in Juvenile Corrections

As Chad returns from lunch, Jimmy grabs his shirt, spins him around and hits him repeatedly in the face and chest. Chad is a 16-year-old chronic juvenile offender and gang member who recently arrived in secure care. Jimmy is a 17-year-old chronic juvenile offender from a rival gang. A few juveniles circle around the combatants and yell encouragement to one or the other, but most drop to their knees as they are supposed to during any fight or facility disruption. Staff immediately stop line movement and separate the juveniles, while praising those who refused to participate in the melee. Both Chad and Jimmy are taken to separation where Chad is assessed and treated by a nurse for his broken nose, and Jimmy is interviewed by treatment and security staff to find out why he initiated the assault. Jimmy and Chad are later interviewed by the department's gang specialist.

Many juvenile correctional agencies across the nation struggle with the challenge of institutional violence. Indeed, "if a male will ever be involved in violence, adolescence is when it will happen." A typical week within the Arizona Department of Juvenile Corrections (ADJC), which houses an average population of 611 males and females in one of four secure care facilities, includes 11 juvenile-on-juvenile assaults and seven juvenile assaults on staff.

Assaults and fights frequently result in injuries to juveniles or staff, and can involve costly medical expenses. Fights disrupt the smooth functioning of a correctional facility and upset the treatment milieu. Unless assaults are handled properly, they can increase juvenile and staff fear, damage the institutional culture, and increase staff turnover. Director Michael D. Branham convenes a biweekly Central Office COMPSTAT review of assaults and other safe environment incidents, which include any crime or behavior that would endanger others. Branham ensures that advice is provided by staff from all of the key ADJC areas including top, mid-level and line facility managers, and representatives from the Education, Clinical, Legal, Inspections and Investigations, and Research and Development departments. During the Central Office COMPSTAT meeting, each facility superintendent presents his or her top problem areas, as well as top successes. A common topic in COMPSTAT meetings is classroom safety. Applause and congratulations are regularly given to unit staff who have reduced violence in the classroom or anywhere else within their respective facilities. Current and proposed intervention strategies to reduce assaults are discussed and input is provided by all disciplines. Time-bound action plans are presented to address the violence, and they commonly include Individual Behavior Plans for assaultive juveniles, and various management initiatives to promote safe environments.

The ADJC COMPSTAT program was initiated in June 2007 and a comparison of assault rates before and after COMPSTAT was implemented indicates a reduction in violence has occurred. Given all of the other juvenile and institutional factors that affect violence it is impossible to attribute the decline solely to COMPSTAT, but there is a strong feeling among ADJC staff that COMPSTAT is making a difference. If the heart of the ADJC COMPSTAT program is the proactive and cross-disciplinary approach toward the management of violence, the soul of the program is real-time data. Facility crime maps that identify hot spots of assault activity by location and time are located on the agency intranet and all employees have access to them. Incident reports are entered into an automated records system, which all employees also have access to. Icons that represent the number of incident reports by location (called crime data points) are placed on each facility map by the computer. Employees can select from more than 20 incident types, and by pressing a button, the computer will reconfigure the facility map to show where those incidents occurred. Employees can then see the actual incident reports by selecting the location that interests them. Facility maps automatically display the crimes occurring during the last 14 days; however, employees can select the time frame and incident type that interests them. Through the intranet, employees also have access to daily incident summaries, as well as real-time data on such things as type of incident, day of week and time of day. The maps permit local facility and Central Office analysts to understand which juveniles are involved as suspects and/or victims. They are linked to demographic and delinquency histories of the respective juveniles, allowing for the development of relevant intervention strategies to prevent further violence. The maps, along with the associated links, were created by the tireless efforts of ADJC's Management Information Systems staff.

ADJC has taken the COMPSTAT technique and applied it to juvenile corrections. The resulting violence reduction strategies are using real-time data and cross-disciplinary teams to develop plans that promote institutional safety. A safe correctional environment will allow Deputy Director Kellie Warren and her treatment teams to implement evidence-based programs to address the criminogenic needs of the juvenile offenders committed to the department's care and custody.

SOURCE: Dempsey, J. & Vivian, J. "COMPSTAT for juvenile corrections," in *Corrections Today*, February 1, 2009. Reprinted with permission of the American Correctional Association, Alexandria, VA.

DISPARITY IN JUVENILE DETENTION
AND INCARCERATION

During the late 1980s and early 1990s, the disparate minority representation in juvenile lockdowns became a topic of controversy. Most of the data available on this issue emerged during the late 1990s and during the early parts of the new millennium. As a means of demonstrating how disparate the juvenile system was, in terms of detention and incarceration, consider that, in 1997, minority youth constituted 34% percent of the juvenile population nationwide but represented 62% of the juveniles detained and 67% of those committed to secure juvenile correctional facilities (Snyder & Sickmund, 1999). In 1997, there were 7,400 new admissions of youth younger than 18 years old to adult prisons, and three out of four of these youth were members of a minority group (Poe-Yamagata & Jones, 2000). Table 13.3 shows that the overrepresentation of minority youth in secure juvenile detention and correctional facilities increased between 1983 and 1997, although it decreased slightly between 1995 and 1997.

TABLE 13.3   Percent of Minority Youth in Secure Detention and Correctional Facilities in the United States
for Selected Years From 1983 to 1997

	Total Youth Population (%)	Minorities (%)	
		Secure Detention	Secure Correction
Year			
1983	32	53	56
1991	32	65	69
1995	32	68	68
1997	34	62	67

SOURCES: Sickmund, Snyder, and Poe-Yamagata, 1997, and Synder and Sickmund, 1999.

Hsia, H. M. (2004). *Disproportionate minority confinement 2002 update.* Washington, DC: Office of Juvenile Justice and Delinquency Prevention.

Overrepresentation of African American youth occurs at all stages of the juvenile justice system, and African American youth are overrepresented more than any other minority group. In 1996–1997, African American youth constituted about 15% of the nationwide juvenile population but represented 26% of all juveniles arrested, 45% of those who were detained, and 40% of those in residential placement. However, for all stages of juvenile justice processing, except arrest and delinquency cases involving detention, the African American proportion of the national totals was smaller in 1996–1997 than in 1990–1991 (Hsia, 2004).

The number of Hispanic youth in the United States has increased faster than the number of youth of any other racial or ethnic group, growing from 9% of the juvenile population in 1980 to 16% in 2000 (Hsia, 2004). State studies show overrepresentation of Hispanic youth at arrest and other decision points in some states (DeJong & Jackson, 1998). Colorado is one example. Although Colorado does not have arrest data for Hispanics because they are included as White, the state's data for July 1998 to June 1999 show that Hispanics were overrepresented at all later decision points in the juvenile justice system (Hsia, 2004).

The Census of Juveniles in Residential Placement showed that Native American youth ages 10–17 constituted 2% of youth in secure correctional facilities nationwide but were only 1% of the national youth population (Snyder & Sickmund, 1999). Although national data suggest that Native American youth are placed in correctional facilities at twice the expected rate, state data give evidence of an even greater overrepresentation. For example, North Dakota's 1998 data indicate that Native American youth made up 8% of the state's total juvenile population but accounted for 13% of arrests, 21% of the secure detention population, and 33% of secure correctional placements (Hsia, 2004).

Asians and Pacific Islanders are the least studied racial groups. Research from the Census of Juveniles in Residential Placement revealed that Asian youth constituted 4% of the national juvenile population but represented only 2% of youth in secure correction. The available state data for Asians alone or Asians and Pacific Islanders combined also show, for the most part, that these youth are underrepresented in the population of confined juveniles at the state and even at the county levels. In cities with high concentrations of Asian youth, however, indications of overrepresentation exist. For example, a study of juvenile transfers to adult court in California showed that, in 1996, the composition of Los Angeles County's juvenile population ages 10–17 was 25% White, 51% Hispanic, 13% African American, and 11% Asian and other races (Hsia, 2004).

From the above information, it is clear that minority youth are disproportionately represented, regardless of the group examined. Even more telling is the fact that, in those states where a given minority group might tend to be more commonly represented, the proportional difference in the rate of confinement is increased. This basically implies that, in jurisdictions that find it necessary to work with minority groups, the disproportionate use of confinement is exacerbated—particularly when this is compared with jurisdictions that have marginal representation of a given group of minority youth.

FACTORS THAT CONTRIBUTE TO DISPARATE MINORITY CONFINEMENT

PHOTO 13.9

It is clear from statistics in juvenile research that African American youth are represented in the juvenile justice system at a proportion that greatly exceeds that of the broader U.S. population. This photo illustrates a situation where all the youth entering a facility are African American.

The reasons for the disparity in juvenile confinement are many. Most published literature on this issue notes that these statistics are not likely to be due to a racist system. While we cannot possibly answer this question within the scope of one discussion within one section of a single textbook, it should have become clear to students that, throughout the history of corrections in the United States, African American men and women have been disproportionately incarcerated. Given the various historical precedents associated with the civil rights era and other indicators that our society held minorities in a weakened position, and given the common knowledge regarding the existence of institutional racism that officially existed until the 1960s, it is not unreasonable to presume that, in some cases, racism may be part of the explanation.

Recent research by Huizinga, Thornberry, Knight, and Lovegrove (2007) investigated the often-stated reason for disparate minority confinement—that it simply reflects the difference in offending rates among different racial/ethnic groups—and they found no support in their rigorous study examining disparate minority contact with the justice system. Huizinga et al. (2007) note that "although self-reported offending is a significant predictor of which individuals are contacted/referred, levels of delinquent offending have only marginal effects on the level of DMC" (p. i). They found these results in terms of both total offending and more focused data that examined violent offenses and property offenses separately. Thus, it would appear that minority youth are no more delinquent than Caucasian youth.

The work of Hsia (2004) is a compilation of surveys and official investigation into the juvenile correctional systems of all 50 states. Hsia notes the following reasons for why such disparities existed in many state systems:

1. **Racial stereotyping and cultural insensitivity:** Eighteen states identified racial stereotyping and cultural insensitivity—both intentional and unintentional—on the part of the police and others in the juvenile justice system (e.g., juvenile court workers and judges) as important factors contributing to higher arrest rates, higher charging rates, and higher rates of detention and confinement of minority youth. The demeanor and attitude of minority youth can contribute to negative treatment and more severe disposition relative to their offenses. The belief that minority youth cannot benefit from treatment programs also leads to less frequent use of such options.

2. **Lack of alternatives to detention and incarceration:** Eight states identified the lack of alternatives to detention and incarceration as a cause of the frequent use of confinement. In some

Video Link 13.4
Learn more about disproportionate minority confinement and contact.

states, detention centers are located in the state's largest cities, where most minority populations reside. With a lack of alternatives to detention, nearby detention centers become "convenient" placements for urban minority youth.

3. **Misuse of discretionary authority in implementing laws and policies:** Five states observed that laws and policies that increase juvenile justice professionals' discretionary authority over youth contribute to harsher treatment of minority youth. One state notes that "bootstrapping" (the practice of stacking offenses on a single incident) is often practiced by police, probation officers, and school system personnel.

4. **Lack of culturally and linguistically appropriate services:** Five states identified the lack of bicultural and bilingual staff and the use of English-only informational materials for the non-English-speaking population as contributing to minorities' misunderstanding of services and court processes and their inability to navigate the system successfully.

Based on the research by Hsia (2004), it is the general contention of this author that much of the reason the disproportionate confinement exists among minority youth has to do with a confluence of issues that plague members of society who have suffered from historical trauma and, generation after generation, have had restricted access to material, educational, and social resources. Indeed, issues such as poverty, substance abuse, few job opportunities, and high crime rates in predominantly minority neighborhoods are placing minority youth at higher risk for delinquent behaviors. Moreover, concerted law enforcement targeting of high-crime areas yields higher numbers of arrests and formal processing of minority youth. At the same time, these communities have fewer positive role models and fewer service programs that function as alternatives to confinement and/or support positive youth development.

Further, it has been found that a disproportionate number of youth in confinement came from low-income, single-parent households (female-headed households, in particular) and households headed by adults with multiple low-paying jobs or unsteady employment. Family disintegration, diminished traditional family values, parental substance abuse, and insufficient supervision contribute to delinquency development. Poverty reduces minority youths' ability to access existing alternatives to detention and incarceration as well as competent legal counsel. Thus, all of these factors, associated with historical deprivations over time, have contributed and culminated in the state of affairs that we now witness among minority juveniles in the United States.

Journal Article Link 13.4
Read about approaches for reducing disproportionate minority confinement (DMC).

CONCLUSION

This chapter has introduced the student to some of the differences between juvenile corrections and adult corrections. From early history, the means by which juveniles are processed has been a bit of a debate with the notion of intent and culpability being a key area of concern. While juveniles may have, at one time, been housed with adult offenders, it became clear over time that a separate system of detention and confinement would be necessary.

We place our emphasis on juveniles who are kept in secure environments and/or incarcerated throughout this chapter. This is because, for the most part, this text is oriented toward the institutional aspects of corrections. Though most youth do get sentences of probation, a demonstration of the issues in detention centers and similar facilities warrants specific and separate consideration. It is clear that numerous issues confront juvenile correctional systems, including disparity issues and the need to attend to specific needs of offender groups, such as female juvenile offenders.

Lastly, we have discussed the use of waiver to transfer youth to adult court. This is often reserved for the most serious juvenile offenders and is an option that has decreased in popularity in many states. It is clear that the primary objective in processing youth is to reform them and, if possible, refrain from stigmatizing them. This is key and fundamental to juvenile corrections. The vast majority of youth are treated as if they are salvageable, and, in fact, the entire juvenile system is based on the notion that youth should be given intervention-based programming as opposed to punitive-based reactions.

Further, many youth have been victims of crime and abuse in their own right. In fact, problems with child abuse and neglect tend to correlate with increased levels of delinquency. Further, these youth report high levels of trauma, substance abuse, and mental illness. This is especially true with female juvenile offenders. Thus, juveniles demonstrate a need for mental health interventions. Current juvenile corrections systems attempt to address these issues to minimize the likelihood that these youth will become further entrenched in crime. As we have seen, some youth engage in delinquency that is specific to their adolescent years whereas others tend to progress well into their adulthood. It is the hope of modern juvenile correctional systems to avoid this later outcome by providing interventions that can change their trajectory toward a life of difficulty.

END-OF-CHAPTER DISCUSSION QUESTIONS

1. What is the primary intent in juvenile corrections when processing youthful offenders?

2. Identify, define, and discuss the different categories of abuse and neglect.

3. How does child abuse and neglect connect to delinquency among some youth?

4. How does the juvenile system contrast with the adult system? Does this also include differences specifically related to the means by which correctional practices are implemented? Explain your answer.

5. Identify and discuss at least two key Supreme Court cases that have impacted the field of juvenile corrections. Explain why you selected these two cases.

6. Identify how abuse and mental health issues aggravate a juvenile's ability to reform.

7. Identify and discuss how racial disparities exist among youth who are placed in confinement. Why do you think that these disparities exist?

8. Identify and discuss the types of facilities that are used to house juvenile offenders.

9. Discuss the theoretical work of Terrie Moffitt and explain whether you believe her theory does or does not do well in explaining juvenile delinquency.

KEY TERMS

Adolescent-only offenders

Age of Responsibility

Breed v. Jones (1975)

Child neglect

Educational neglect

Emotional neglect

Graham v. Florida (2010)

Houses of refuge

In loco parentis

In re Gault (1967)

In re Holmes (1955)

Life-course-persistent juvenile

McKeiver v. Pennsylvania (1971)

Parens patriae

Physical abuse

Physical neglect

Psychological abuse

Reform schools

Roper v. Simmons (2005)

APPLIED EXERCISE 13.1

Create an antigang program at a juvenile facility and in coordination with the state juvenile justice system.

For this exercise, students will need to read *Report No. 08-56* by the Florida Office of Program Policy Analysis & Government Accountability titled "DJJ Should Use Evidence-Based Practices to Address Juvenile Gang Involvement," available on the student study site or found independently at http://www.oppaga.state. fl.us/MonitorDocs/Reports/pdf/0856rpt.pdf. This document outlines the rise in juvenile gang members that has been found throughout the juvenile justice system of Florida.

Students should read this document and then explain how they would implement an antigang program within a detention facility in Florida. For this assignment, presume that there are currently gang members within the facility and that you are the head administrator for the facility. What means of prevention would you use to keep the gang membership from spreading? Would there be constitutional issues to consider? How would you follow up to demonstrate that the program worked?

Also, keep in mind that, as we have learned, gangs tend to cycle in and out of the custodial environment. This is also true with juvenile gangs. Thus, you should explain how you would coordinate with juvenile probation and outside community leaders as a means of identifying new gang members who enter your facility and as a means of providing interventions.

Your Applied Exercise should be from 500 to 1,000 words in length and should provide a well-organized plan of approach that incorporates both community and facility resources.

"WHAT WOULD YOU DO?"

You are a juvenile caseworker, and you have been working with Tanya, a 15-year-old at your detention facility. You have worked with Tanya for over a year and have noted that she has made considerable progress in treatment and the other aspects of programming. In fact, Tanya is scheduled to be released to aftercare in the near future. During a session, just two weeks prior to her release, Tanya discloses to you that her stepfather (who still lives at the domicile) molested her several times when she was young. Neither Tanya nor her mother ever reported this. As Tanya nears release, you do not know how to handle this situation.

What would you do?

CROSS-NATIONAL PERSPECTIVE 13.1

Overview of Family Court Jurisdiction in Juvenile Cases in Japan

The family court handles cases involving delinquent juveniles under 20 years of age. "Delinquent juveniles" include not only juveniles who have committed criminal crimes under the penal acts but juveniles whose tendencies indicate that they might commit crimes in the future as well. The family court has primary jurisdiction in regard to all delinquent juveniles, whether the crimes are felonies such as homicides or arsons, or misdemeanors such as traffic offenses. Thus, all criminal cases concerning juveniles must primarily be sent to the family court as juvenile delinquency cases for investigation and hearing.

The present Juvenile Act provides that the family court has jurisdiction over juveniles who (a) habitually disobey the proper control of their custodian, (b) repeatedly desert their home without proper reason, (c) associate with persons who have a criminal tendency or are of immoral character, or immoral persons, or frequent places of dubious reputation, and (d) habitually act so as to injure or endanger their own

morals or those of others, provided that from their character or environment there is a strong likelihood that the juveniles involved will become offenders.

Children under 14 years of age are primarily handled by the child guidance center, as provided by the Child Welfare Act, when they have committed acts that, if committed by a person aged 14 or over, would constitute a crime under the penal acts. These children come under the jurisdiction of the family court only when the prefectural governor or the chief of the child guidance center refers them to the family court. The family court ordinarily has jurisdiction over any juvenile under 20 years of age.

Proceedings for Juvenile Delinquency Cases

Family court proceedings involving juveniles are generally commenced in the following cases:

1. A judicial police officer or public prosecutor sends a juvenile case to the court.

2. A prefectural governor or chief of the child guidance center refers a juvenile case to the court.

3. A family court probation officer who has found a delinquent juvenile reports the case to the court.

4. Someone who is in charge of the protection of a juvenile, a schoolteacher, or any other person informs the court of the case.

When a case is filed in the family court, the judge assigns the case to a family court probation officer and gives directions for the investigation. The officer then undertakes a thorough and precise social inquiry into the personality, personal history, family background, and environment of the juvenile. When the juvenile needs to be taken into protective custody, the judge may detain the juvenile in a juvenile classification home (*Shonen-kanbetsu-sho*). The maximum detention period is 4 weeks in general. However, the detention period may be extended up to 8 weeks only when the examination of evidence is necessary because the juvenile denies the facts constituting the alleged delinquency.

Upon completion of social inquiry by the family court probation officer, the officer sets down the juvenile's social record and his or her opinion as to the case together with the recommendations about its disposition, and submits this as a report to the judge. Taking this report into consideration, the judge sets a time and place for a hearing. The hearing is nonpublic, and no person other than the judge, the court clerk, the juvenile, the persons in charge of the protection of the juvenile (parents or guardians), the family court probation officer, the attendant, and persons specially permitted by the judge may be present. The family court may permit the public prosecutor to be involved in the proceedings on the condition that it is necessary to prove the fact constituting the alleged delinquency, only when a juvenile over 14 years old has committed crimes resulting in death by acts done with criminal intent (e.g., homicides, injuries resulting in death) or crimes whose statutory penalties are capital punishment or imprisonment with or without work for life or not less than 2 years (e.g., robbery, rape).

The Family Court Judge Renders a Decision

The determination of the judge may take one of several forms. It is made on the basis of the family court probation officer's report, the judge's own research and inquiry, and the results of the hearing. The possible forms are as follows:

1. A decision to refer the case to a child guidance center. This action is taken when it is deemed that the juvenile should be dealt with under the Child Welfare Act rather than be placed under protective measures.

2. A decision to dismiss the case. Such a decision is reached when the court finds it unnecessary to make any particular disposition of the juvenile.

3. A decision to refer the case to the public prosecutor. The basis of this decision is the view that the juvenile should be subjected to normal criminal court proceedings due to the serious nature of the crime or the circumstances of the case, on condition that a juvenile was 14 years old or over when he or she committed the crime.

4. A decision to place the juvenile under protective measures. There are three kinds of protective measures.

   a. *The juvenile is placed under the probation of the probation office*. This is an organ of the Ministry of Justice with one office located in the district of each family court. The actual supervision over juveniles is undertaken by the probation officers of the district offices, and they are aided in their work by volunteers from among the public called volunteer probation officers.

   b. *The juvenile is placed in a support facility for development of self-sustaining capacity* (Jidojiritsushien-shisetsu) *or a home for dependent children* (Jido-yogo-shisetsu). Both of these institutions are provided for under the Child Welfare Act. The support facilities for development of self-sustaining capacity are established by the national or prefectural governments, or private persons to take care of children who are delinquents or are likely to become delinquents, while the homes for dependent children are private or prefectural institutions designed to care for dependent, abused, or neglected children.

   c. *The juvenile is placed in a juvenile training school* (Shonen-in). *This is an institution of the Ministry of Justice to provide corrective education to juveniles committed to it by the family courts*. The juvenile training schools are divided into four groups: (1) primary, caring for juveniles 14 to 15 years old without necessity of medical care; (2) middle, caring for juveniles aged 16 or over without aggravated criminal tendencies; (3) advanced, caring for juveniles 16 to 22 with aggravated criminal tendencies; and (4) medical, caring for all juveniles 14 to 25 who need medical treatment. Two types of programs are given in juvenile training schools: the long-term program and the short-term program. The latter is divided into the general short-term program and the special short-term program. The special short-term program offers extensive educational programs outside the juvenile training school.

Question 1: From what you can tell, how is the juvenile justice process in Japan similar to that in the United States? Provide a brief explanation for your answer.

Question 2: What are the similarities and differences in the use of juvenile confinement in Japan and the United States?

SOURCE: *Supreme Court of Japan: Juvenile Delinquency Cases.* Retrieved January 8, 2011, from http://www.courts.go.jp/english/proceedings/juvenile.html

STUDENT STUDY SITE

Visit the Student Study Site at **www.sagepub.com/hanserintro** to access links to the videos, audio clips, SAGE journal articles, state rankings, and reference materials noted in this chapter, as well as additional study tools including eFlashcards, web quizzes, and more.

chapter 14

Correctional Administration

LEARNING OBJECTIVES:

1. Discuss the history and organization of the Federal Bureau of Prisons.

2. Discuss common organizational features of state prison systems.

3. Identify key differences and similarities between managers and leaders.

4. Identify the characteristics of an effective correctional leader.

5. Discuss women in supervision.

6. Discuss correctional management and private prison systems.

7. Identify specific issues involved with emergency management.

INTRODUCTION

This chapter introduces the student to some basic issues involved with correctional management, supervision, and leadership. Before providing students with information regarding supervision processes in corrections, we begin with a discussion of the federal and state correctional systems to provide an understanding of their organization and the means by which oversight in operations is maintained. The administrative features of correctional systems are important because this puts a general template to the means by which policies and administrative regulations are promulgated down to individual prisons. Further, students will examine specific traits associated with management and leadership, as well as the differences between these terms. Specialized topics within this chapter include the experiences of women in correctional work who are promoted to supervisory positions as well as management schemes within private prison systems. Lastly, students will gain some insight on issues related to emergency management including the means of response, managerial considerations, and the need to work with agencies external to the prison facility itself.

FEDERAL BUREAU OF PRISONS ADMINISTRATION—CENTRAL OFFICE

Reference Link 14.1
Read more about the
Federal Bureau
of Prisons .

The head office of the Federal Bureau of Prisons (BOP) is known as the Central Office. The Central Office serves as the BOP headquarters, which is overseen and managed by the director of the BOP. This office includes eight divisions that provide oversight of major BOP program areas and operations, as well as the National Institute of Corrections. The Central Office is located in Washington, DC, providing ready access to the U.S. Capitol, federal courts, and the Department of Justice's headquarters building. Each division that is administered from the Central Office oversees its respective functions throughout all six regions of the BOP (see Figure 14.1 for an illustration of each region). From the Central Office, regional offices oversee these same functions that are carried out in prison facilities located in their jurisdiction. The eight service divisions are as follows:

1. The Administration Division is responsible for the BOP's financial and facility management. This division is responsible for budget development and execution, finance, procurement and property, and the inmate trust fund program.

2. The Correctional Programs Division ensures that national policies and procedures are in place that provide a safe, secure institutional environment for inmates and staff and encourage inmate activities and programs designed to eliminate idleness and instill a positive work ethic.

3. The Health Services Division is responsible for medical, dental, and mental health (psychiatric) services provided to federal inmates in BOP facilities, including health care delivery, infectious disease management, and medical designations.

4. The Human Resource Management Division coordinates the BOP's personnel matters, including pay and leave administration, incentive awards, retirement, work-life programs, background investigations, adverse and disciplinary actions, and performance evaluations.

5. The Industries, Education, and Vocational Training (IE&VT) Division is responsible for education and vocational training programs within the BOP. Each federal prison has its own education department that provides educational activities to federal inmates. This division manages literacy and occupational training programs, parenting programs, and adult continuing education activities, which are formal instructional classes designed to increase inmates' general knowledge in a wide variety of subjects, such as writing and math. Lastly, this division also oversees Federal Prison Industries (FPI), one of the most important correctional programs operated by the BOP. Created by federal statute in 1934, it operates as a wholly owned, self-sustaining government corporation under the trade name UNICOR. FPI employs and provides skills training to federal inmates at its diverse factory settings and contributes to the safety and security of BOP facilities by keeping inmates constructively occupied.

6. The Information, Policy, and Public Affairs (IPPA) Division collects, develops, and shares useful, accurate, and timely information to BOP staff, the Department of Justice, Congress, other government agencies, and the public.

7. The Office of General Counsel represents the BOP on a broad range of legal, policy, and management issues. This division includes seven Central Office branches, six regional legal offices, and 24 consolidated legal centers in the field. The primary responsibility of the regional legal offices is to provide litigation support for inmate litigation arising out of the prisons located within the region, and to provide legal advice to regional office and prison administrators.

8. The Program Review Division (PRD) was created in 1988 to establish a self-monitoring system that provides oversight of BOP program performance and compliance. Oversight involves monitoring specific program areas, conducting risk assessments for the purpose of creating review guidelines, and analyzing program performance trends and other data to achieve continuous program improvement. This division conducts reviews of all BOP programs.

Lastly, the **National Institute of Corrections (NIC)** is an agency within the BOP that is headed by a director appointed by the U.S. Attorney General. A 16-member advisory board, also appointed by the Attorney General, provides policy direction to the institute. The NIC provides training, technical assistance, information services, and policy/program development assistance to federal, state, and local corrections agencies. Through cooperative agreements, the NIC awards funds to support its program initiatives. The NIC also provides guidance with respect to correctional policies, practices, and operations nationwide in areas of emerging interest and concern to correctional executives and practitioners, as well as to the makers of public policy.

FEDERAL BUREAU OF PRISONS ADMINISTRATION—REGIONAL OFFICES AND JURISDICTIONS

Aside from the Central Office in Washington, DC, the BOP has six regional offices that directly oversee the operations of prison facilities within their respective regions of the country. These six regional offices include the Mid-Atlantic Region (MXR), North Central Region (NCR), Northeast Region (NER), South Central Region (SCR), Southeast Region (SER), and Western Region (WXR). Students should see Figure 14.1 for a mapped illustration of these regional jurisdictions.

Regional office staff maintain close contact with staff who work in various prisons and correctional facilities in their jurisdiction. For example, they provide management and technical assistance to facility and community corrections personnel. They also conduct workshops, conferences, and specialized

FIGURE 14.1   The Regional Jurisdictions of the Federal Bureau of Prisons

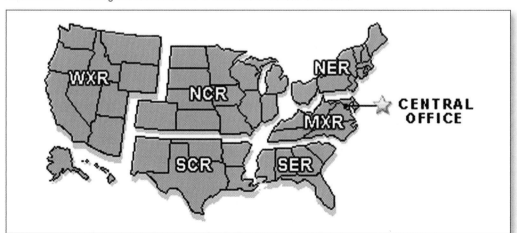

SOURCE: Federal Bureau of Prisons. (2010). *About regional offices.* Washington, DC: Department of Justice. Retrieved from http://www.bop.gov/about/ro/index.jsp.

training programs; give technical assistance to state and local criminal justice agencies; and contract to provide offender placement in residential reentry centers.

The Central Office and the Regional Offices serve as the primary administrative components that coordinate safety and security of inmates as well as human resources and training for staff within the BOP. At a more local level, each individual prison facility will also have its own human resources office as well as various offices that address specific functions of prison operation, such as security, education, recreation, medical services, and psychological services. These offices each answer to the warden(s) of their facility at the local level as well as the next highest office within the regional chain of command. Then, all reports and records are sent from the regional offices to the Central Office, as deemed appropriate.

STATE CORRECTIONAL SYSTEM ADMINISTRATION

Every state is tasked with responsibility for the incarceration, rehabilitation, and street supervision of offenders within its borders. However, states differ by several important aspects, including whether the incarceration, probation, and parole functions are combined into a single agency or placed within separate agencies. In addition, some states merge the probation and parole functions into a single function. Likewise, there is some variation as to whether probation and parole are state or local functions. Because we have covered several state systems throughout this text in prior chapters and because the degree of variability is so great among different state systems, only a simple and broad overview will be included here regarding the administration of state prison systems.

As we have seen in earlier chapters (particularly Chapters 1–4), each type of state correctional system has developed due to historical and legal occurrences that were more a matter of happenstance than intentional planning. The initial administrative bodies that coordinated and oversaw the operations of these systems often developed in a haphazard manner as well and often were the product of a politicized process where position appointments were grounded in patronage and nepotism. This early history of state correctional administration caused many problems with efficiency and the ability to create an objective and open form of administrative control. However, this was often offset by the paramilitary structure of most prison facilities and the fact that inmate labor served as a source of revenue for many states, particularly in the southern United States.

In today's world of corrections, state agencies are usually organized into a separate department of corrections, and these organizations will usually have a director who is appointed by the governor, or the prison system may be a division within a larger state department. For example, in Texas, the Texas Department of Criminal Justice—Institutional Division (TDCJ-ID) oversees the prison facilities of the broader TDCJ. Students should examine Figure 14.2 for a schematic on the organizational structure of the Correctional Institutions Division of the TDCJ.

Though this is a common type of organizational arrangement, many correctional administrators consider the separate department to be a more effective means of managing prison systems. One of the key reasons for this is that a separate department is able to control its own use of financial and personnel resources, and it does not have to compete internally with other divisions for its funding base. In addition, executive directors of departments have more flexibility when establishing policies and procedures.

LOCAL CORRECTIONAL SYSTEM ADMINISTRATION

Local correctional systems come in the way of county or city jurisdictions, as well as private institutions. The most common type of local correctional system is the county-based system, which is, most often, run by the sheriff's agency of that county. Most county-level jails house inmates for one year or less and are operated by jailers within the sheriff's department. This is common throughout the nation, and it is not uncommon for jail systems in major metropolitan areas to have populations that parallel some state organizations.

FIGURE 14.2 Organizational Structure of Correctional Institutions in the Texas Department of Criminal Justice

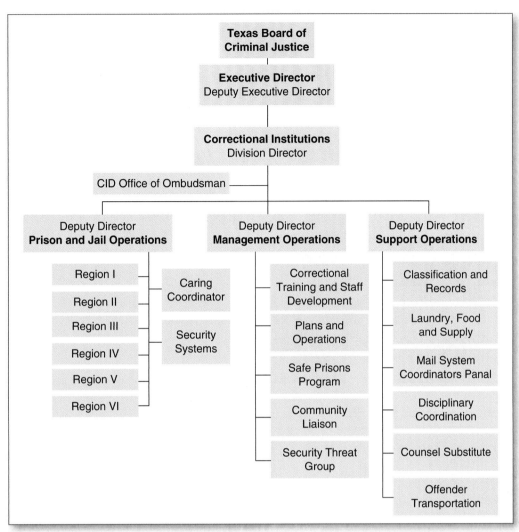

SOURCE: Texas Department of Criminal Justice. (2010). *Organizational charts: Correctional Institutions Division*. Retrieved October 11, 2011, from http://www.tdcj.state.tx.us/orgchart/orgchrt-cid.htm.

While these types of systems may actually consist of misdemeanant inmates, this is not always the case. For instance, in the state of Louisiana, it is common for many parish-level (in Louisiana, the term *parish* is used to denote a county, a product of its unique French cultural heritage) jails, operated by local sheriffs, to house inmates from the state department of corrections. These inmates will have committed felony crimes and have multiple-year sentences. The state-level correctional system contracts out the obligation for security and safety for these inmates, and, for a fee, these jail systems house the inmates. This process is conducted throughout the state because it is less expensive than building newer prisons and because this optimizes jail space throughout the state. Further, this system provides more flexibility in housing inmates in various areas of the state that are near to the inmate's family and/or reentry objectives. The author of this text is the administrator of a regional correctional training academy, North Delta Regional Training Academy, that is tasked with training parish-level jailers to ensure that they meet state-level standards of care.

In addition, private prisons can be considered more local in their orientation, though they are, in fact, a unique model of correctional system, unto themselves. Private prison systems also contract out with the state prison system to aid in housing the inmate population. These private facilities may also house inmates from within the local area, depending on the circumstances and the agreements

Journal Article Link 14.1
Read about new generation jails.

PHOTO 14.1

Warden Brian Newcomer of Ouachita Correctional Center is pictured here with fellow staff.

PHOTO 14.2

Sgt. Amber Rawls of Morehouse Parish is pictured at North Delta Regional Training Academy with local and regional correctional officers who must have this training to be qualified to work with inmates in state custody who are kept in their jail facilities.

Audio Link 14.1

Listen to a clip about private prisons.

made between the company owning the prison and the outlying cities and counties of the region. While private prisons are usually owned by private companies that operate several prison facilities, they are included here because the individual facilities operate under more flexible terms that tend to allow them to be of assistance to local law enforcement and municipal planners in a much more fluid manner than most state facilities.

For example, as mentioned a few moments ago, the author of this text administers a training academy that provides jailer training to parish-level correctional officers. This same academy has provided similar training to private correctional officers for **LaSalle Corrections**, a private company that owns and operates prisons in Louisiana and Texas. Even more to the point, this company has a prison facility, Richwood Correctional Center, which houses both state-level inmates and city-level inmates for the city of Monroe. This private facility has been active in the local region in housing city-, parish-, and state-level inmates, as the need may arise. In addition, this private prison has an administrative structure that is similar to Louisiana's state system but is flexible in its ability to make rapid decisions due to the private nature of ownership; there are fewer obstacles that interfere with the decision-making process for the owners of the company, unlike state-run programs. Further, this private facility provides all the same treatment and programming services of its state, county, and city counterparts. In fact, the author of this text is a therapist for a substance abuse treatment program in that same facility.

Aside from county-level correctional systems and private prison systems, the existence of city-level prison systems should not be overlooked. While these are not the most common types of prison systems (indeed, we usually refer to them as jail systems rather than prison systems), there are some exceptions. Some cities and their outlying suburbs are so large that they require their own adult prison institutions, complete with the requisite programming that one would expect in a prison system. For example, consider the **Philadelphia Prison System (PPS)**, which of course has its roots in the initial Quaker movements when the Walnut Street Jail was established. Today, the PPS offers a full range of services to offenders in its care. This system formally developed as a city-run prison system during the 1930s, during the same era when the federal BOP was established. With the start of educational programs for adults in the 1930s, the introduction of professional social workers, and the expansion of recreational programs in the 1950s, as well as the development of new vocational training and work-release programs in the 1960s, it is now true that this city-run collection of facilities is a formal prison system.

Within most state correctional systems, there exist three general levels of management. The first level consists of **system-wide administrators**, or managers who are at the executive level and direct the entire system throughout the state. These administrators conduct the broad planning of the agency that often includes a strategic planning process (see Focus Topic 14.1). The second level of administration includes **regional-level administrators**, or managers who oversee a specific region of a state. Usually, these regions will consist of a northern, southern, eastern, and western region that may be given a name or number for identification. The third level of administration in state agencies comprises the **unit-level administrators**, or personnel who manage the individual prison facility. In most cases, there will be a handful of regions within a state that have a number of prisons within the region's borders. We proceed with a more detailed discussion of the various level administrators in state prison systems.

System-wide Administrators

Within a department of corrections, there is usually a chief executive officer along with a set of deputies who implement various policies as determined by agency needs and by state-level politics that impact the agency. This level of administration is also usually responsible for obtaining funds and resources from state budget lines so that the agency can operate effectively, and these administrators will also be responsible for creating strategic plans that guide the spending of allocated money. **Strategic plans** are broad managerial documents that include goals and objectives of the agency, and they state the general direction in which an agency intends to operate. An example of a strategic plan from the state of Texas is included in Focus Topic 14.1, which also includes the mission and philosophy of the agency.

This level of management will also coordinate with other state agencies to ensure that services are integrated within the overall state system. For instance, it may be necessary for the department of corrections to work closely with the state police, local and state-level court systems, emergency response agencies, and so forth. This is especially true when major disasters impact a state or when there is an inmate escape. For instance, in the state of California, inmates may be used to help fight forest fires that wrack that state's ecosystem; this tends to require planning and coordination between many agencies. Lastly, in cases where inmates escape, public safety initiatives may require that prison staff work along highways, bus stops, airports, train stations, and so forth, in search of escaped inmates. These personnel will naturally work in tandem with law enforcement personnel in the area and throughout the state until the inmates are found or the search is disbanded.

Regional Administrators

If a state correctional system is large enough (in terms of both number of inmates and geographical area), there may be the need to divide the system into regions. This is usually found among systems that have numerous facilities. Regional administrators will address a number of issues related to resource planning among the various prisons within their jurisdiction (see Figure 14.3). This often includes inmate transfers within the region and outside of the region, the sharing of supplies and resources between prison facilities, and the screening of legal issues that often emerge from within individual prison facilities. Often, when an inmate grievance reaches the regional level of review, various regional administrators will screen and review the issue in a manner of best determining the most prudent response in resolving problems.

Institutional-Level Administrators

The head administrator of a prison is the warden. Below the warden is usually the assistant warden, followed by security ranks that include majors, captains, lieutenants, and sergeants. The position of warden is prestigious and often is one based on appointment by the executive director of a prison system. Thus, appointments are usually made at the state level, not the regional level. The political nature of this job should not be underestimated. Both internal demands from the prison system itself and external demands from the surrounding community, families of inmates, and the state political system cause this job to be very stressful. As Stephan Kaftan (2007), an expert on correctional administration, has noted, "wardens and superintendents operate in highly political and complex environments" (p. 2). This situation is made even more complex with when one considers issues related to media coverage, inmate litigation, and correctional officer unions that affect employee supervision.

Video Link 14.1
Watch a video about prison wardens.

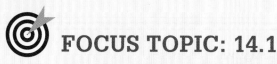

FOCUS TOPIC: 14.1

Strategic Plan for the Texas Department of Criminal Justice—Institutional Division

Texas Department of Criminal Justice
FY2011–2015 Agency Strategic Plan

Relevant Statewide Goals and Benchmarks
Public Safety and Criminal Justice

Priority Goal: To protect Texans by preventing and reducing terrorism and crime; securing the Texas/Mexico border from all threats; achieving at optimum level of statewide preparedness capable of responding and recovering from all hazards; and confining, supervising, and rehabilitating offenders.

The statewide benchmarks directly applicable to the Texas Department of Criminal Justice are:

> ➤ Average rate of adult re-incarceration within three years of initial release
>
> ➤ Number of correctional officer and correctional staff vacancies
>
> ➤ Average annual incarceration cost per offender
>
> ➤ Percent increase in the number of faith-based prison beds
>
> ➤ Percent reduction in felony probation revocations
>
> ➤ Percent reduction in felony probation technical revocations
>
> ➤ Total number of cameras in state correctional facilities
>
> ➤ Number of contraband items seized through the use of correctional security equipment

Texas Department of Criminal Justice Mission

The mission of the Texas Department of Criminal Justice is to provide public safety, promote positive change in offender behavior, reintegrate offenders into society, and assist victims of crime.

Texas Department of Criminal Justice Philosophy

The Texas Department of Criminal Justice will be open, ethical and accountable to our fellow citizens and work cooperatively with other public and private entries. We will foster a quality working environment free of bias and respectful of each individual. Our programs will provide a continuum of services consistent with contemporary standards to confine, supervise and treat criminal offenders in an innovative, cost effective and efficient manner.

SOURCE: Agency Strategic Plan for the Fiscal Years 2011–2015. Huntsville: Texas Department of Criminal Justice.

FIGURE 14.3   Regional Administrative Offices in the State of Texas

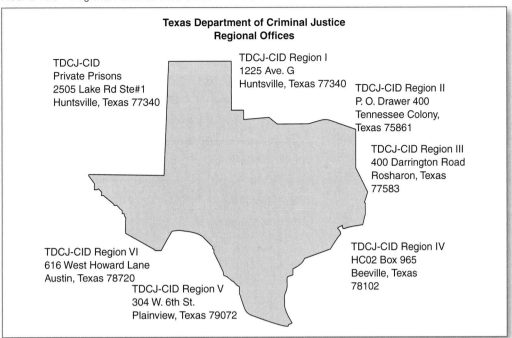

Texas Department of Criminal Justice
Regional Offices

TDCJ-CID
Private Prisons
2505 Lake Rd Ste#1
Huntsville, Texas 77340

TDCJ-CID Region I
1225 Ave. G
Huntsville, Texas 77340

TDCJ-CID Region II
P. O. Drawer 400
Tennessee Colony,
Texas 75861

TDCJ-CID Region III
400 Darrington Road
Rosharon, Texas
77583

TDCJ-CID Region VI
616 West Howard Lane
Austin, Texas 78720

TDCJ-CID Region V
304 W. 6th St.
Plainview, Texas 79072

TDCJ-CID Region IV
HC02 Box 965
Beeville, Texas
78102

SOURCE: Texas Department of Criminal Justice–Institutional Division. (2007). *Offender orientation manual.* Huntsville: Author.

Wardens of prison facilities are also required to learn quite a bit of information related to any variety of diverse issues. For instance, the author of this text worked at the Eastham Unit, in the Texas prison system, which is a sprawling farm that sits on 12,789 acres of territory. This facility and its attendant farming fields, barns, and support buildings produce agricultural products that include the following:

1. Cow/calf and heifer development operations.
2. Egg-laying operations.
3. Farm shop.
4. Feed mill and grain storage.
5. Edible and field crops.
6. Security horses/dogs.
7. Swine farrowing/nursery.
8. Wood finishing operations.

PHOTO 14.3

A Texas Department of Corrections "field boss" watches over inmates going to work in the fields outside the prison in Huntsville.

Obviously, these diverse agricultural and production operations require complicated oversight on the day-to-day management of the work itself, and this does not even consider the various issues related to security that must be considered, or medical issues that may be involved for different inmates. Even more, this also does not consider the employee issues that will come into play; not all correctional officers will have sufficient knowledge of agricultural work to be effective at supervising inmates who work in these types of operations.

The job of the prison warden is even more demanding when one considers that modern corrections now has expectations that inmates will be rehabilitated and that programs will be offered toward that purpose. The following types of programs (among others) might be included within the walls of a prison: substance abuse treatment, adult education programs, life decisions programs, financial planning, and religious services. The warden will be responsible for overseeing all of these types of programs. Students should see Focus Topic 14.2 for a list of the various responsibilities that a warden will have in fulfilling his or her job function.

Journal Article Link 14.2
Read about holding wardens responsible for recidivism rates.

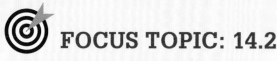

FOCUS TOPIC: 14.2

Job Duties of a Warden

Coordinates activities by scheduling work assignments, setting priorities, and directing the work of subordinate employees.

Evaluates and verifies employee performance through the review of completed work assignments and work techniques. Assigns, coordinates, and outlines the work methods of subordinate employees.

Identifies staff development and training needs and ensures that training is obtained.

Ensures proper labor relations and conditions of employment are maintained.

Maintains records, prepares reports, and composes correspondence relative to the work.

Establishes and maintains custody, security, and control measures at a state correctional facility.

Supervises and controls the inside movement of prisoners, including initial assignment to prison units and transfers within the institution.

Implements policies and develops procedures in area of responsibility (housing, treatment, custody, or security).

Supervises the classification and orientation of new prisoners.

Reviews written communications from prisoners and interviews them regarding special or personal problems.

Develops and implements procedures for educational and treatment programs based on department policies.

Represents the facility to the Department of Corrections' central office, other state departments, local agencies, and the public.

Reviews job résumés of candidates, prepares and conducts hiring interviews, and selects the most qualified candidate.

Plans, coordinates, and supervises leisure time activities of prisoners such as intramural and varsity sports, music, and library services.

SOURCE: Job specification. Michigan Civil Service Commission.

James Meko (2010) provides a very good overview of the typical work schedule of a warden who oversees a correctional facility. Meko points toward the need for wardens to be cognizant of developments outside of the prison and indicates that, on a routine day, wardens often review the local newspaper as well as television and radio broadcasts to determine if there are local developments that may impact their institutions. Examples might include a death in the community, a high-profile court case from within the community, adverse weather that may be expected, community perceptions regarding the prison or employees of the prison, the closure or opening of a local business, or statements from local political figures that might be relevant to inmates or employees in their prison. This alone demonstrates how wardens must consider the world that surrounds their prison facility as they manage the world within.

Typically, wardens will review shift logs of the shift commander or major, as these logs will tend to summarize important incidents or developments that have occurred the day or week before. Beyond this, wardens will usually begin their day with a meeting that includes their assistant or deputy wardens, the chief of security operations, and other high-ranking staff within the institution. This meeting, according to Meko (2010), is important for two key reasons:

> First, it keeps vital lines of communication open. Honest feedback, in both directions, ensures high-quality institutional operations. Such feedback also ensures that key players understand what is important to the warden and the agency, and empowers them to act accordingly. Second, this meeting enables the warden to give direction to one or all members of the group with the benefit that all hear the direction and are able to ask questions. This promotes mutual respect, shared values, and camaraderie. (p. 236)

Lastly, counterbalanced against the concerns for staff, the warden must be in touch with the inmate population. According to Meko (2010), a proactive warden will require assistant wardens and other high-ranking staff to attend at least one meal a day with and/or around inmates in the facility. This provides these high ranking staff with the opportunity to interact with the inmate population and provides a clear message that these staff are making an active effort to understand the world of the inmate. This is also an opportunity to assess the atmosphere of the correctional facility and random concerns that may be expressed. These staff will further encourage a sense of transparency within the facility since it opens the door to direct communication with the inmate population.

PROACTIVE CORRECTIONAL MANAGEMENT

Managers can respond to organizational problems by two different means, either reactively or proactively. A **reactive style of management** is used when a supervisor waits until a problem develops and then, after it has emerged, responds to remedy the situation. **Proactive styles of management** seek to anticipate and correct problems before they develop. In the previous subsection that discussed techniques that wardens can employ to enhance communication and awareness for inmates and staff, the intent is to provide the opportunity for senior administrators (the warden and assistant wardens) to act proactively to potential problems that may surface in the future. Essentially, proactive management has a preventative basis that eliminates or reduces factors that may escalate into a more serious circumstance.

The key feature of proactive management is ensuring adequate access to information. In most typical prison settings, managing staff react to problems after they have occurred. When this is the case, problem inmates provide the spark that sets off a chain of pretrained reactions. In many cases, these types of reactive responses are fashioned in a cookie-cutter style that has been repetitively rehearsed. Naturally, this creates an artificial style of response that is not always suited to the conditions that may exist.

In addition, consider that most reactive organizations do not have an open flow of communication. Rather, the communication is often from the top down to the bottom. This stymies the ability of conduct planning to adjust with changes in a situation. In essence, decision making is less nimble when the flow of communication does not go back and forth. Wardens and other senior staff must be visible and accessible to other security and support staff in the prison. Procedures and forums must be in place to ensure that communication is timely, intelligence is accurate, and critical information reaches the management team to ensure that decisions reflect the best information available.

AUTHORITARIAN FORMS OF MANAGEMENT

In authoritarian institutions, all major decisions are made by one person or a very small group of persons. The authoritarian system of management prevailed from the very beginning of prison management in the United States to about the mid-1950s. This was often linked to a system that emphasized punishment and consequences. Specifically, it is thought that this system of management in prisons was engineered by Elam Lynds, who is considered the innovator behind the Auburn system of prison management (see Focus Topic 14.3).

The key defining feature of the **authoritarian model** of prison management is strict control over staff and inmates with communication that flows from a top-to-bottom process. In addition, this model does not consider input from those outside of the system or facility. Thus, this tends to be a closed system of management that does not grow or improve through the processing of additional information from the environment. In fact, it is usually the case that authoritarian agencies and authoritarian managers tend to deal with new problems using the same types of responses that they have with older and previously encountered problems. Obviously, this is not very adaptive and leads to a failure of management to react appropriately to challenges that emerge. Instead, these types of managers tend to change, modify, or contort the issue into one that is consistent with their current repertoire of responses, all of which tend to be punitive in nature. Thus, this type of management stymies all sense of creative problem solving and also kills the human spirit.

BUREAUCRATIC FORMS OF MANAGEMENT

Bureaucratic methods of running agencies have some advantages over the authoritarian model, but, for the most part, this type of system is not truly superior to the previously discussed system. The **bureaucratic model** of prison management creates a formal organizational system that operates in a system that is not dependent upon the specific personnel or personalities assigned within it. So long as each person performs his or her basic job functions, this type of system will continue to operate, though not necessarily

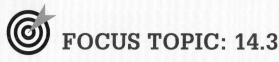

FOCUS TOPIC: 14.3

Back to the Future in Prison Management

Though authoritarian forms of prison management are not the primary model used in corrections today, this type of management has had a long and influential history. One primary figure who was instrumental in refining this type of approach was Elam Lynds, who was a think tank behind the Auburn or congregate system of prison management (students may recall that we discussed this type of prison system, developed in New York, in earlier chapters of this text).

As a captain in the Auburn system, Elam Lynds led the development of this system through the use of strict punishment-oriented management. He believed that all inmates should be treated equally and used a highly regimented schedule of activities that included the use of the lockstep marching model of movement. The key was to create uniform and machine-like behavior from inmates. Inmates were all dressed identically in black-and-white striped uniforms and engaged in a regimented routine of work and prayer. Advocates of this type of prison management believed that it had the best chance of reforming inmates into productive citizens. This type of system also ensured that the prison would be at least marginally profitable and did well in maintaining order.

This oppressive type of managerial system was based on an extreme military model that impacted the guards of the facility almost as much as the inmates. Infractions among employees were treated in a punitive manner, and there were few rewards or positive incentives for guards working in the facility. Naturally, since their job entailed the constant enforcement of severe forms of control, the personalities of officers and the climate of the institution were tense, stiff, and uncomfortable. This type of oppressive management (both of inmates and of the staff in employ) built an abusive and calloused culture within the institution. Strict adherence to orders, with no feedback loop to question the orders given, intensified the fear that was the primary source of motivation throughout the institution. Thus, fear was the tool of management in this authoritarian model, and it was used on both inmates and prison staff in the institution.

SOURCE: Excerpted from Carlson, P.M. & Dilulio, J. J. (2008). "Organizational management," in Carlson, P. M. & Garrett, J.S. (Eds.). *Prison and jail administration: Practice and theory.* Boston, MA: Jones and Bartlett.

---

in the most efficient manner. These types of systems tend to have a hierarchical structure with a formal and defined chain of command. Authority within this system is established along vertical communication patterns that flow from the top of the hierarchy to the bottom with strict channels of communication. Naturally, this type of communication is not the most adaptive because it does not allow for direct feedback from lower-level staff, but it is superior to the authoritarian model because this communication system is not dependent on one sole source of guidance and/information, making it capable of continued operation, even when the highest-ranking administrator is absent.

However, this type of a situation tends to produce what we will refer to as "holding pattern management" within the institution. **Holding pattern management** is where the system continues to operate but in a pattern of stasis where there is no true growth, nor is there a blockage in the systemic flow. Rather, information and operational procedures continue to show activity and movement, but, over time, no truly appreciable progress toward achieving goals or objectives is realized. Rather, the system continues to simply maintain the status quo throughout the period of operation. This type of system operates on standard operating procedures that follow extensive policies that complicate the process of operation and become the means to the end, in their own right. In other words, staff will tend to focus on doing tasks exactly as prescribed, regardless of whether the process actually works well to achieve the stated objective.

THE PARTICIPATIVE METHOD OF MANAGEMENT

This model of management requires that administrators elicit the input and ideas from persons being governed. Thus, **participative methods** of management include opinions and feedback offered from both inmates and staff when making decisions regarding the operations and governance of the prison facility. This type of management is actually a bit pragmatic in today's world of corrections because most prison facilities are operated with an inmate-to-staff ratio that is quite high. In other words, there are many more inmates than staff, and, even though staff have the upper hand in the long term when inmates become unruly, it is easy for inmates to gain a short-term advantage on a cell block or dormitory due to their sheer numbers compared to prison staff charged with watching them. Thus, in many cases, prison staff will use aspects of the prison subculture to gain leverage and maintain control over inmates as a means of maintaining compliance.

Administrators run into a paradox where too much control and discipline results in a system that is oppressive and plagued with problems from the effort to maintain a strong grip over the population while too little control can result in a security risk. Participative methods allow for a third means of management that attempts to balance these extremes. Indeed, in our earlier discussion regarding proactive correctional management, several examples were given where the warden or other top administrators in the facility might solicit input from inmates during mealtime or other points in the day. Likewise, this same form of management advocated for these administrators visiting with prison staff to solicit input from those staff.

Thus, the proactive approach to correctional management works hand-in-hand with the participative method of management because both seek the input of prison staff when identifying problems and formulating decisions. However, the participative method of management emphasizes one additional key feature; it also seeks the input of the inmate population, through both formal and informal venues. Thus, inmates as well as staff are treated as a formal component of the organization and therefore have at least some input on the day-to-day processes that occur within the facility (Silverman, 2001).

In addition, consider that—through informal networks—many administrators as well as general prison staff tend to be kept abreast of the happenings within a prison. This is sometimes called the prison grapevine and yields a considerable amount of information. The **prison grapevine** is grounded in the informal organization of the prison subculture and is an informal network that consists of information passed through the personal communications of employees to employees, inmates to inmates, employees to inmates, and inmates to employees. When examining the power of the prison grapevine, consider the fact that informal bargaining goes on between inmates and prison staff and that this shows some basis for cooperation among both populations; this then demonstrates that even though both populations are pitted against one another in the prison environment, they can and do work in mutually participative relationships. These relationships tend to be mutually exploitative in many respects but, nevertheless, result in informal deals and negotiation whereby participative approaches emerge. The wise administrator will, at least to some degree, embrace this natural symbiotic relationship between those who govern and those who are governed to create an atmosphere where mediation of the governance process is encouraged.

CENTRALIZED VERSUS DECENTRALIZED MANAGEMENT

Centralized management consists of tight forms of control in the communication process that ensure that decision-making power is reserved to only a small group of people. This type of managerial style tends to be reflective of bureaucratic models of prison management. The advantage of this type of management system is that decisions tend to be consistent and also reflect the need to operate the facility in a safe and secure manner. On the other hand, disadvantages emerge when mid-level and low-level supervisors do not feel empowered, and, lacking a sense of ownership, they may have little incentive (and authorization) to address issues that emerge but are unnoticed by higher-level management.

Decentralized management occurs when the authority and responsibility of management personnel are divided and distributed amongst various levels of the supervisory chain so that each level of supervision may make decisions that correspond to the problems that confront it at its particular level of management. This approach tends to speed up the decision-making process and allow for the integration of detailed information specific to a particular problem that must be addressed. However, there is less consistency from supervisor to supervisor in how problems are solved, and, without clear policies and guidelines, the entire facility can develop into several subunits that have inconsistent and even confusing forms of operation (Carlson & DiIulio, 2008).

When determining the best form of management between centralized and decentralized approaches, this author's answer is that both are equally useful but depend on the context. In situations of serious emergency when institutional safety and security are under grave threat or danger, the best approach is one that is centralized but directly involves the decision makers in the immediate response that is necessary. In these cases, it is important that the most experienced personnel are vested with concentrated decision-making powers so as to be able to react quickly to the threat while minimizing confusion amidst the ranks; this approach ensures clarity of operations. The use of centralized decision making is also more appropriate to strategic planning than to tactical planning. **Strategic planning** consists of the determination of long-term goals and objectives for an agency, usually spanning a period of one or more years in scope. On the other hand, **tactical planning** consists of ground-level planning that is narrow in focus, usually structured around the resolution of a particular issue or something that confronts the agency on a short-term basis. Higher-level administrators usually set the overall mission of the agency and are therefore best suited to make long-term strategic decisions for the agency. It is appropriate that such decision making is centralized to the upper administration because it is these administrators who are most informed of the macro-level issues that confront the agency as a whole.

Decentralized management is best utilized in situations where routine decision-making takes place and where there is more direct interaction between a particular level of management and the frontline staff who do the work of the agency. While these issues may be routine in nature, it is important to not underestimate the stress involved for employees and inmates who must continually, day in and day out, deal with some seemingly petty nuisance that builds up a continued sense of frustration. These issues can lead to explosive circumstances if not dealt with and thus allowed to remain a continued problem. Empowering staff so that they can address these types of routine problems can eliminate much of the job stress that they might experience, and also provides them with a sense of control (or at least influence) over their environment. The decentralized approach is also the best approach when attempting to maximize input from informal groups as well as the prison subculture (in regard to both inmate and staff subculture). Where centralized forms of management will ensure that decision makers are far and away from these types of communication networks, decentralized management structures will typically be adept at integrating information that is disseminated through the organizational grapevine.

MANAGEMENT VERSUS LEADERSHIP

In many respects, management differs markedly from leadership. Yet, in many other respects, these two characteristics of supervision may exist within the same individual. Regardless, the term **management** refers to persons who have been vested with an official title by the agency and who tend to be focused on the process of completing functions of operation within the prison facility. These personnel oversee the details of job assignments given to correctional officers and ensure that employees are maintaining behavior that is consistent with the stated policy and procedure of the agency. **Leadership**, on the other hand, entails skills and talents that motivate and influence persons toward a common goal or idea. Persons with leadership talent are often able to elicit commitment from employees that goes beyond mere compliance to the rules and regulations; they are adept at getting people to be inherently committed to a cause, goal, or objective of the agency.

Journal Article Link 14.3
Read about an experiment in the dynamics of leadership.

In reality, it may not be easy to separate management from leadership without creating an artificial distinction or category. This artificial distinction is not usually reflective of the "real world" of prison operations but is more a means of distinguishing between the multifaceted roles of various supervisory staff. The key point in discussing these two concepts is to demonstrate that the supervisor's job is hands-on in nature (Carlson & DiIulio, 2008). This means that supervisors should be visible and available to their employees; this is especially true with the upper management of the prison facility. As mentioned earlier in this chapter, wardens should "make their rounds" throughout the facility and solicit input from employees and inmates to get an informal sense of how the prison is running and to identify concerns of employees and inmates in their facility. In practice, this is done routinely among prison wardens throughout the United States.

Experience, Intelligence, and Emotional Intelligence in Leadership

There has been some degree of debate as to whether experience is more valuable than intelligence in leadership (Robbins, 2005). While it is certain that leaders should have the requisite intelligence to do their job correctly, it is debatable as to whether someone with a genius-level intellect would make a great leader. Indeed, such persons may find it quite difficult to interact with people who are not similarly brilliant, and, when considering the behavior of inmates within the facility, they may do a very poor job in working with the correctional population. By the same token, leaders with a great deal of experience may be very familiar with their job, but that does not necessarily mean that they have done that job in the most effective manner possible. In fact, some people may do a job for years and consistently achieve mediocre results; this should not be considered success. Even worse is the case where someone may have done a job for years and done it incorrectly; this is a disastrous outcome.

Within the field of corrections, there are circumstances where one trait is perhaps more important than the other. Naturally, the ideal situation is to have a leader who is both intelligent and experienced, and in most cases leaders will indeed have at least some degree of respectable intellectual ability as well as some degree of experience since many correctional supervisors tend to be promoted from the lower ranks. However, the likelihood of having a perfect balance between both intelligence and experience is very seldom achieved; thus, it is of importance to know how to assign leaders, depending on their own particular strengths along the intelligence and experience continuum.

In most cases where long-term planning is concerned, leaders who have high levels of intelligence tend to produce superior results. This is particularly true with long-term problem solving and/or strategic planning. The reason for this is that these types of decisions allow for thoughtful and reflective analysis, and, since the various contingencies of these decisions are far-reaching, the level of detailed outcome analysis requires a more thorough examination of the issues decided upon. Persons with high intellects tend to be good at these types of analyses, or they at least tend to be better than persons who are not as intellectually gifted.

On the other hand, in situations where quick, tactical-level decisions must be made, experience tends to be the better arbiter in determining who will lead most effectively. This is especially true in crisis situations where there is less reliance on textbook-like processes and more need for a well-practiced approach. Leaders with years of experience are more likely to have traversed other crises and/or demanding situations and will therefore have more previous and incident-related knowledge to draw from. While they may not necessarily have a high intellect, their prior exposure to similar incidents in their past can give them an edge in how they approach a situation and what they do in response. Obviously, those leaders who are experienced and who also have a high degree of intellect will be the best types of responders and reflect the optimal type of correctional supervisor.

Aside from the debate between intelligence and experience, another factor to effective leadership is very important to consider: emotional intelligence. **Emotional intelligence** describes how adept a person is at noticing and responding to the emotional cues and information exhibited by others with whom they interact. Emotional intelligence is a factor found to be especially useful in jobs that require a high degree of social interaction. Naturally, the field of corrections entails constant interaction between inmates and staff, staff and staff, and staff and the public. Indeed, human interaction lies at the heart of the correctional field of work, and this, therefore, means that emotional intelligence is even more important.

Leadership and the Custodial Staff (What Gets Respect)

Wardens and senior administrators must establish a vision of a successful correctional operation. In developing this vision, administrators must be able to sell their goals to those within the organization so that all persons provide earnest commitment. The best way to do this is through an understanding of the organizational culture that exists within an agency. Supervisory staff play a critical role in shaping and forming organizational culture, and it is through the emphasis on the mid-level and lower-level supervisory staff that upper administrators can best disseminate their vision plan for the future.

It is important that supervisors develop an image of involvement with the rank-and-file staff and that they communicate to all levels of staff the goals of the organization and why they are important. This type of management is based on the idea that the effectiveness of the organization depends on the example that the leaders set for other employees. There is a direct correlation between the expectations of leadership within the facility and the resulting behavior that is observed. When leaders or managers (keep in mind that they can be distinct from one another and in other cases one and the same) tolerate mediocrity, the result will be mediocre at best. On the other hand, when professionalism and excellence are expected, the momentum of the organization increases, and employees perceive the ways they may serve as helpful contributors.

Wright (2008) makes the point that the field of corrections is a "people business" where human relations skills are critical. The staff of any correctional agency tends to be made up of common people. In other words, most of the rank-and-file staff will be your average citizen; this is not a bad thing. Rather, leaders within correctional agencies should consider that it is important to understand the perspective from which most of their employees view the world, their job, and their role within the agency. An understanding of the day-to-day concerns of most of their staff will allow leaders to more easily develop a rapport with employees and more effectively motivate them toward agency goals. In addition, agency goals should be set with the agency staff in mind. Administrators must ask themselves, are my goals compatible with my employee population's ability and interest? If the answer to this question is no, then these administrators must consider training staff to make them capable of pursuing the identified goals, or they must consider revising the goals that they have set. A failure to choose at least one of these options will lead to bigger organizational problems in the future.

Supervisors must ensure that staff understand that they must follow agency guidelines and be consistent in performing their duties and enforcing rules (Wright, 2008). While this may seem like an obvious point, incidents where employees claim to not be aware of existing guidelines abound as do circumstances that consist of inconsistent rule enforcement. It is important that supervisors make active efforts to prevent the emergence of "rogues and mavericks" within the facility. **Rogues and mavericks** are employees who tend to act as if they are independent of the broader institution. In such cases, these employees act as if they are the law rather than persons charged with enforcing the laws of the institution. These employees are dangerous to the institution, and they undermine the authority of supervisors and administrators by exacting undue influence through the informal prison subculture. Further, other employees will watch to see if these independent-minded individuals are allowed to run free, and, if it seems to be true, they will tend to either emulate these behaviors or resent the fact that these employees get away with their behavior; neither outcome is favorable to the institution. Thus, these employees must be dealt with, and, if they refuse to modify their behavior, they must be eliminated from the ranks of the prison staff.

Span of Control and/or Influence

Span of control refers to the number of persons that an administrator supervises. This can vary greatly from as low as one person to several hundred or even thousands of people. In theory, the more people that the supervisor has responsibility for, the wider his or her span of control. However, for this text's purposes, we will modify this traditional understanding of a supervisor's span of control because even though, on an organizational chart, the regional administrator may have authority over persons in several prison facilities in his or her region, it is very unlikely that the regional administrator does, in fact, exert any true control over persons who are at the lowest ranks of the agency. Rather it is more likely that the regional administrator exerts influence over those agency employees through the acts and deeds of lower-ranking supervisors, the effects of organizational culture and tradition, and the willingness of the employees to tacitly submit to the authority of someone whom they may have never met (few entry-level correctional officers ever have any true face time with the regional director of their prison system).

Thus, the **span of control** in correctional institutions refers to the sphere of control that supervisors have over employees that they encounter and interact with on a routine basis and whom they are able to consult with to gain observable compliance with their requests, recommendations, and directives. On the other hand, the **span of influence** refers to the extended impact that a supervisor has upon employee behavior that may occur beyond his or her own actual observation but, through the effects of other organizational members, is carried forth as the desired means of operation. This has more to do with the effects of other members of the chain of command who repeat and enforce directives promulgated by the higher-level supervisor and less to do with the upper-level supervisor's own actual ability to exert control over individual employee behavior.

TECHNOLOGY AND EQUIPMENT 14.1

Strategic Planning Process in Determining the Acquisition of Technology and Equipment for Facility Security Purposes

The flow chart below has been provided to demonstrate to students the various concerns that administrators may have to consider when deciding upon security-related technology. This is particularly true with technology involved in the use of force against inmates or technology that will be used in response to prison disturbances, riots, or escapes.

Strategic Planning Framework

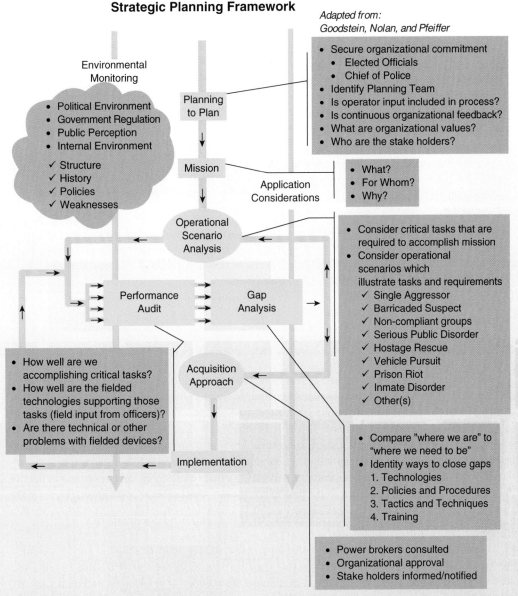

Adapted from: Goodstein, Nolan, and Pfeiffer

Environmental Monitoring

- Political Environment
- Government Regulation
- Public Perception
- Internal Environment
  - ✓ Structure
  - ✓ History
  - ✓ Policies
  - ✓ Weaknesses

Planning to Plan

Mission

Application Considerations

Operational Scenario Analysis

Performance Audit

Gap Analysis

Acquisition Approach

Implementation

- How well are we accomplishing critical tasks?
- How well are the fielded technologies supporting those tasks (field input from officers)?
- Are there technical or other problems with fielded devices?

- Secure organizational commitment
  - Elected Officials
  - Chief of Police
- Identify Planning Team
- Is operator input included in process?
- Is continuous organizational feedback?
- What are organizational values?
- Who are the stake holders?

- What?
- For Whom?
- Why?

- Consider critical tasks that are required to accomplish mission
- Consider operational scenarios which illustrate tasks and requirements
  - ✓ Single Aggressor
  - ✓ Barricaded Suspect
  - ✓ Non-compliant groups
  - ✓ Serious Public Disorder
  - ✓ Hostage Rescue
  - ✓ Vehicle Pursuit
  - ✓ Prison Riot
  - ✓ Inmate Disorder
  - ✓ Other(s)

- Compare "where we are" to "where we need to be"
- Identity ways to close gaps
  1. Technologies
  2. Policies and Procedures
  3. Tactics and Techniques
  4. Training

- Power brokers consulted
- Organizational approval
- Stake holders informed/notified

Administrators at the executive level (i.e., regional directors and above) and even at the facility level (i.e., prison wardens) must consider how well the equipment or technology will meet agency needs, the expense involved, potential legal issues that can emerge, the reliability of the equipment, and training of staff who will use the equipment, as well as likely perceptions generated by the media if the equipment is used in an incident. All of these issues can be very important concerns to administrators. In developing their decisions, executive administrators often develop strategic plans specifically related to the integration of technology, particularly when considering lethal and/or less lethal devices. Such a plan not only provides the general guidance necessary but establishes priorities, allocates resources, and assigns responsibilities. This is of particular importance with regard to less lethal devices because there are no universally accepted standards, no commonly accepted taxonomy, no standardized training requirements, and no reliable methods for comparison. Consequently, each agency is left to develop its own protocols and policies. It seems prudent, then, to establish some criteria for devices that promise to fulfill the particular requirements for a given agency and to avoid those that seem promising but are expensive, awkward, publicly unacceptable, or otherwise inappropriate.

A strategic plan is not a static document—it is a dynamic process that anticipates requirements and provides a means by which those requirements might be addressed. It is essential that this process be integrated into the overall strategic planning process for the entire agency. While there are numerous frameworks available, most have common features. Most simply, strategic planning is a thought process that includes three major considerations: *the ends* (the agency goals that support the mission), *the ways* (the methods that the organization uses to achieve those ends), and *the means* (the resources used to accomplish the ways). There are a number of strategic planning frameworks that can be integrated into the correctional agency's processes as a means to "think through" the ends, ways, and means in a more rigorous fashion.

Strategic planning for technological devices, particularly those involved with the use of force, should determine equipment necessary to accomplish tasks that support the agency mission. This part of planning provides the necessary focus and ensures that the efforts of all involved are complementary, not competing or counterproductive. Considering different operational scenarios that illustrate and support required tasks and their relative frequency is one method of identifying potential technology requirements. Most strategic planning involves a review process and feedback loops. Situations change, and assumptions often prove invalid. A review process ensures that the plan is continually "tuned" to adapt to changes in the environment and overcome obstacles. A dynamic strategic planning process enables the exploitation of opportunities and avoids or mitigates emerging threats. Such planning often proves an advantage when opportunities for acquiring new technologies and/or obtaining funding unexpectedly present themselves. The process also ensures both proper consideration of "stakeholder" input (e.g., from the officers in the field and the community) and necessary support of "powerbrokers" (e.g., the governor, the superintendent of corrections, elected officials, the community).

SOURCES: Goodstein, L. D., Nolan, T. M., & Pfeiffer, J. W. (1993). *Applied strategic planning: How to develop a plan that really works*. McGraw-Hill.

Weapons and Protective Systems Technologies Center. (2010). *A guidebook for less-lethal devices: Planning for, selecting, and implementing technology solutions*. Philadelphia: Pennsylvania State University.

WOMEN IN CORRECTIONAL MANAGEMENT

Journal Article Link 14.4
Read about female wardens' roles as reformers in corrections.

With the professionalization of corrections has come the understanding that diversity in the workforce necessitates transparency and ethical behavior behind the walls. In other words, when correctional staff consist of various persons from various groups and backgrounds, there is less likelihood that biases in operations can continue undetected. This is particularly true in cases where the prison subculture, steeped in a staunch male-oriented view, is concerned. The inmate subculture tends to be quite sexist in orientation with feminine characteristics being considered weak and inferior. Having women in the workforce can counter these biases among inmates, and having female supervisors can be even more effective in developing acceptance of women in the field of corrections. The key issue is whether agencies make a point to facilitate the careers of female security staff; it is very important that they do so in order that subcultural influences can be countered.

Carlson and Garrett (1999) has noted that many women tend to adopt a service-oriented approach that is less confrontational than that used by their male counterparts. This is actually a very valuable asset to agencies because it minimizes the number of grievances, potential lawsuits, personal injury claims, and other legal pitfalls associated with conflicts in prison. Likewise, the overall climate on cell blocks and in dorms that are handled in a less aggressive manner tends to be calmer; this can add to institutional safety. Though this approach has its benefits, there have been mixed results. In jail settings, research has found that women officers are perceived by male officers to be less effective in breaking up fighting inmates or controlling large and/or aggressive inmates.

On the other hand, male officers tend to view women as skilled at calming inmates and working with those who are mentally or emotionally disturbed (Carlson, 1999). Female supervisors tend to have these same skills and abilities, and, even in cases where male inmates are aggressive, women who hold rank seem to be just as adept as men at maintaining control of the cell block or dormitory.

It is advisable that correctional agencies continue to recruit and promote more female representation within the management circles. As we have seen, the role of the supervisor requires effective communication skills and the ability to share the agency's mission and values. If the agency is truly sincere about professionalism, ethical behavior, and a desire to develop a safe institution, then having optimal female representation can add to all of these objectives. This is especially true since the inclusion of women with supervisory power will tend to counter the negative aspects of the prison subculture, which will create an organizational culture that does not promote the sexist views that male inmates tend to hold within the institution.

Challenges to Upward Mobility

There is some debate as to whether the glass ceiling still exists within corrections. The **glass ceiling** is a term for official or unofficial barriers to promotion that exist for women within the workforce. For all practical purposes, it should be considered that some sort of barrier does indeed exist because, if for no other reason, there are substantially fewer female supervisors than male supervisors within correctional facilities. Further, throughout history, women who worked in corrections tended to do so in facilities for women, and, since the female offender population was proportionally smaller than the male offender population, the need for women to work in corrections was much less than that for men.

In addition, there are social constraints in society that tend to frown upon women working within the prison environment. Historically, this type of employment was not considered ladylike and therefore instilled a social aversion toward this type of employment. Coupled with the intensely masculine nature of the prison subculture, the hard-nosed population of male guards who already worked in prisons, and the dangerousness of the job, it is not surprising that during the past 100 years women were not commonly employed in this field. However, the modern era of corrections is seeing a change, and women are more commonly seen within this area of employment.

People placed in situations in which they are powerless and have limited promotional potential tend to lower their goals and develop approaches to work that are defensive and not postured for upward mobility. In many cases, women may not utilize the same set of aggressive social skills that their male counterparts employ and may therefore be at a socialized disadvantage. These skills may need to be learned on the job, and, for women in particular, there may be a need to learn about the prison environment's social cues. This means that women may have to adjust their body language and facial expressions to assert an authoritative image rather than one that is pleasant. In all cases, the stereotyped subservient image of women must be avoided. Likewise, attempts to make themselves attractive are also problematic within a prison setting. This means that the prison environment is often counterintuitive to the socialization that many women may receive.

However, many women in corrections report that, even when they have the skills and desire to work in corrections, they are often still at a disadvantage. This is due to the effects of the glass ceiling, which prevents them from being included in informal social circles, gaining appropriate mentoring and on-the-job training from their senior male counterparts, or having access to positions that are more dangerous but more prestigious within the informal guard subculture. Indeed, paternalistic desires to protect female officers may prevent them from working some job assignments, and this places female officers at a disadvantage in terms of training and experience, resulting in impaired promotional ability.

Prison System Culture

Further still, the problem of sexual harassment affects the prison work site, just as is the case in outside society. However, it is much more pronounced and pervasive in prisons. Harassment can include behaviors such as cussing, intimidation, or inappropriate humor. In the prison or jail setting, male staff as well as inmates may present challenges to women through an atmosphere that is demeaning to women. For instance, a male staff member may say to a group of male inmates working in the field, "OK, c'mon ladies, let's get back to work," which implies that women are less accepted and respected than are men. The fact that the guard is referring to the male inmates as "ladies" is meant to be demeaning and reinforces the notion that women have lesser stature within the prison. In cases where inmates "punk one another out" or say "you just got punked out" the implication is that the person holds a sexual role that is passive or subservient; this is typically equated to female behavior and/or a nonaggressive (and therefore weak) person. All of these biases toward women and anything that is effeminate exist in many prison environments and are juxtaposed against an environment of hypermasculinity.

In order that women can be integrated more fully into the world of prison operations, it is necessary that sexist opinions, beliefs, and informal exchanges be minimized by administrators. However, higher-level supervisors must do more than craft a policy and act punitively to enforce the policy; this will likely breed resistance to the idea. Rather, upper administrators should ensure that positive accomplishments of female staff and supervisors are showcased and rewarded within the agency. At the same time, administrators should ensure that these rewards are balanced with those given to male employees. The key is to change the image of the agency by demonstrating support for female officers and supervisors while doing so within the framework of acknowledging, showcasing, and rewarding *all* officers within the agency. This will be particularly effective if women who perform difficult duties in close contact with inmates are specifically noted within the agency.

Further, it is important that female supervisors be present and represented in male facilities, not just female facilities. While this can lead to some complications in certain situations, agencies must be committed to working around and through legal issues related to cross-gender searches, privacy issues for male inmates in shower areas and/or locations where strip searches may occur, and so forth. Ultimately, this acknowledgment of women in corrections is healthy for the sexist subculture that tends to exist among inmates and some correctional officers. Providing training on sexual equality, sexual harassment, and other similar topics is also important and should not be made optional but should be mandatory.

Video Link 14.2
Watch female correctional officers as they work in a prison.

EMERGENCY MANAGEMENT

The subsection on emergency management issues is not meant to be comprehensive or all-encompassing but is intended to simply address the fact that administration, management, and leadership must focus on the likelihood that the unexpected can and does occur within prison environments. It is good practice to ensure that, prior to the actual emergency event, administrators have put into place appropriate forms of reaction. Further, it should be pointed out that there is a difference between emergency preparedness and emergency response. **Emergency preparedness** consists of the planning, training, and budgeting process that is involved prior to the occurrence of an emergency. **Emergency response** consists of the actual intervention that is used, the management of that intervention, containment of the emergency, and the successful resolution of the emergency event. In planning these two stages, correctional administrators should be informed of their facility's general inmate and staff cultural climate since this will typically provide some advanced notice of developments that can become problematic. Thus, we now turn our attention to the need to gauge the climate within the prison facility, all in the interest of alleviating problems before an emergency state of affairs develops.

Video Link 14.3
Learn more about prison evacuations during an emergency.

Gauging the Climate

In prior chapters, we have examined the impact of the prison subculture on prison operations, and we have determined that a significant underground economy exists within the prison. Further, we have also noted that it is important that administrators "walk the rounds" throughout their facility to be seen both by inmates and by officers. With this in mind, administrators should conduct routine tours of the facility. Further, correctional supervisors should engage inmates and staff regarding rumor control, which requires that leaders identify rumors that occur (Armstrong, 2008). **Rumor control** is the active process of administrators to

Prison Tour Video Link 14.1
View a clip about preparing for emergencies.

APPLIED THEORY 14.1

Conflict Theory and Prison Management

Conflict theory contends that individuals and groups within society will have disparate amounts of resources, both monetary and property-based, and that groups with more power will use that power to exploit persons and groups who have less power. Conflict criminology extends the basic tenets of social conflict theory by noting that groups who are exploited will tend to use crime as a means of gaining material wealth, revenge, or a sense of control over their lives, all in reaction to the stress of their unequal plight. It is important to note that not all criminals will engage in criminality with the conscious intent of equalizing their circumstances, but, rather, the stresses of being without make criminal behaviors more likely among the underclass and lower socioeconomic classes. These classes are continually given short shrift among other members of society, and this creates an increased likelihood of crime commission.

Further, underprivileged neighborhoods tend to have less social and political clout and are therefore subject to poorer representation in society. This also occurs in the legal system where those without money are more likely to be prosecuted and much more likely to receive prison sentences. This means that much of the inmate population will be drawn from backgrounds of poverty and/or lower-income backgrounds. The means by which this can impact prison operations are many, but beyond anything else, this is likely to lead to challenges in communication between prison staff and inmates as well as an understanding among inmates of many of the social ideals that espouse the "work hard to get ahead" ethic that is common in society. For many inmates from this background, their hardworking families have remained poor. The payoff is therefore hard to see.

Further, many prison administrators understand that the job of correctional officer is not very prestigious. In fact, many of the personnel who work corrections may come from economic conditions that are not too different from those of the inmates that they supervise. This may also impair the overall ability of prison managers to empower prison staff to achieve levels of performance that go beyond minimal expectations. Further still, since exploitation will have been a fact of life for these individuals, they may see their role as exploitative by nature and intent. Regardless of whether conflict theory adequately explains criminality, it is certain that those who have fewer material resources are more often represented in prisons than are those groups who have substantial monetary resources. It is important for prison administrators to keep this in mind when addressing the inmate population as well as when working with the inmate subculture. Just as importantly, administrators must consider how this can and does impact correctional staff who may also view the world as one where the rich subjugate the poor.

The question is, then, whether prisons, as institutions, are simply mechanisms designed to keep poor people—who act out against the stresses of their poverty—contained and separated from persons who have economic power. If so, does this mean that persons who work in corrections are simply slaves to the system who unwittingly contribute to the exploitation by enforcing the will of those who are rich and therefore powerful? Naturally, these questions can only be answered on the basis of opinion. But, it is important that students consider these possibilities. These thoughts and questions likewise open the door for prison leaders to demonstrate to staff that they are able to impact something much broader than their own individual plight. With motivation and vision, the effective correctional leader can empower prison staff to understand that, for every inmate who does reform and for every officer who is not harmed by crime, the ability to break out of an exploitative economic system is increased. An understanding of the social dynamics that have, perhaps, brought inmates, officers, and administrators together in the prison environment can thus serve as the catalyst for a positive purpose behind the mission of the prison—that purpose being to eliminate further exploitation of persons without money through the creation of nonviolent environments and the reduction of criminal tendencies.

circumvent faulty information that is disseminated among staff or inmates and has the potential to cause unrest or disharmony throughout the facility. To be informed of rumors, a rapport with inmates and officers is necessary. Once a rumor is identified, the administrator should bring it up to inmates or staff in a non-confrontational manner and either confirm or deny the rumor, depending upon whether it is true or false. This will take away the power of the rumor and those who generate the rumor, and it will also eliminate the perception of defensiveness among the upper administration. A willingness to engage in rumor control will prevent and/or reduce many problems that might emerge within a facility (Armstrong, 2008).

Different levels of response are required, depending upon the type of emergency or crisis that occurs within the facility. For each type of response, different teams with incident-specific training should be used (Stepp, 2008). Regardless of the type of incident training, certain characteristics should exist

PHOTO 14.5

This team is suited in special protective equipment that allows the officers to safely engage inmates who are violent and dangerous. These types of response teams are critical to institutional security during emergency operations.

among all response team members. All teams should be composed of volunteers, and they should receive specialized training and skills that ensure that they are experts on their specific area of response. Further, they should be knowledgeable on policy and law regarding their type of response. Further still, these personnel should be required to pass rigorous physical, academic, and psychological screening.

When using teams for emergency management, the most common and the least lethal type of team is the disturbance control team. **Disturbance control teams** are specialized teams trained to respond to, contain, and neutralize inmate disturbances in prisons. These teams are trained in riot control formation and the use of defensive equipment such as batons, stun guns, and chemical weapons. Disturbance control teams are trained to contain both large and small disruptive groups. These response teams use less lethal technology for circumstances where life-and-death issues are not at stake. It is strongly recommended that some type of certification process be included that requires knowledge of agency policy and emergency plans as well as proficiency in the use of related equipment.

The next level of response includes armed disturbance control teams. **Armed disturbance control teams** deal with disturbances that have escalated to matters with life-and-death outcomes. Training and certification for these teams must be even more intense than for teams armed with nonlethal weaponry. Further, there may be more potential for liability with this type of team. When using armed teams, it is important to not use weapons unless administrators are sure that they can be protected and there is no danger of them being seized by inmates. Further, administrators should not establish policies where staff may be expected to shoot to disable an offender. It is unlikely these officers will have the continual training necessary to maintain the needed skill level. Further, if they shoot to disable and kill the offender, liability issues may ensue as well.

Lastly, tactical response teams are the most highly trained and skilled emergency response security staff. These teams are often referred to as **Special Operations Response Teams (SORT)**, which are teams designed to respond to crises within a prison facility where the security of the institution is seriously at risk, posing a threat to public safety. They are similar to the typical special weapons and tactics teams found in many police departments. Within the Federal Bureau of Prisons, a typical SORT has 15 members, including an emergency medical treatment specialist, a firearms instructor, a rappel master, a security/locking systems expert, a blueprint expert, and several firearms and tactical planning/procedures experts. All members must be proficient with weapons used in emergency response situations and, within 90 days of becoming a team member, must become proficient in tactical responses, riot control techniques, and rappelling. Each candidate also undergoes a panel interview with an associate warden, captain, team leader, and staff psychologist before being placed on the team. Lastly, SORT team members receive collateral specialty training that reinforces the special skills of individual team members. For example, each team has at least one medical specialist, blueprint specialist, chemical agent specialist, and sniper. To meet both the rigorous mandatory training requirements and the collateral specialty training, most team members participate in a substantial amount of training on their personal time.

Video Link 14.4
Watch a clip about special operations training.

ADMINISTRATIVE COOPERATION WITH OUTSIDE AGENCIES

During times of emergency, administrators must be sure that emergency response plans include mutually agreed-upon cooperative plans with outside agencies, particularly the local law enforcement agencies. The cooperative plans should be signed by the outside agency administrator and the unit warden. This also means that preexisting memoranda of understanding that establish the terms and conditions for

CORRECTIONS AND THE LAW 14.1

Conditions of Confinement and Case Law—Implications from Wilson v. Seiter

The following brief article is adapted from the article cited below this insert and is an earlier publication from the National Institute of Corrections. This article, in a very succinct manner, examines the primary case law from the U.S. Supreme Court and determines that, while some administrators may believe that they are largely insulated from concern over conditions of confinement, they are actually mistaken. Because most liability cases are settled out of court, administrators may find that their facility can be the source of extreme financial loss due to conditions of their facility and the need of the agency to settle out of court to avoid even larger losses. Naturally, this does not bode well for the career of a prison warden or another administrator who is responsible for the conditions of his or her facility.

The author of this article encourages administrators to not become complacent but to instead maintain safe facilities, humane conditions of incarceration, appropriate standards of medical and mental health care, protection of inmates from abuse, and appropriate staff conduct. Those who do will ultimately be administrators who are likely to be promoted, and those who do not may miss promotion or, worse yet, may find themselves liable in a legal suit. We now turn our attention to the ruling from *Wilson v. Seiter* (1991), the primary case addressing conditions of confinement, and the article (Wallenstein, 2008) that explains the modern-day importance of this ruling made in 1991 that is still legal and binding today.

> A prisoner alleging that the conditions of his confinement violate the Eighth Amendment's prohibition of cruel and unusual punishment must show deliberate indifference on the part of the responsible prison officials. (*Wilson v. Seiter*, 501 U.S. 294 [1991])

Justice Antonin Scalia, writing for the majority in remanding an appeals court decision regarding conditions of confinement, noted that the state of mind of these involved in the specific conditions was an appropriate area of inquiry. He suggested that the conditions themselves might not rise to an Eighth Amendment violation unless a standard of "deliberate indifference" or wantonness could be shown. The most unusual thought process in the majority opinion may suggest that a broad range of prison and jail conditions might be sustained, even if wholly deficient, in the absence of malicious intent by the administrator or the system.

Some have even suggested that future constitutional challenges to prison and jail conditions may be defended by reference to insufficient funding by state or local government.

I do not concur with this interpretation, nor do I believe that *Wilson v. Seiter* retreats significantly from twenty years of court-developed doctrine of appropriate jail and prison conditions and administrative responsibility for same. Twenty years of federal court examination of jail and prison conditions, policies, behaviors, and treatment issues have not been swept away.

Let us assume that some major conditions of confinement cases may be made somewhat more difficult to prove under the "deliberate indifference" doctrine. However, this is not likely to inhibit successful challenges to hundreds of jail and prison policies and procedures that are well established in case law and practice as well as in the standards of the field and profession. It is well to remember that the vast majority of federal cases are settled out of court and are not the subject of formal opinions. They are settled out of court because government units recognize that a court will not sustain unconstitutional practices. The hundreds of cases that address injuries to inmates through assaults, self-inflicted injuries or suicide, institutional failure to meet prevailing standards of health care practice, and the like will continue to fall within the area of substandard practice.

Prevailing professional standards accepted throughout our profession require safe facilities, humane conditions of incarceration, appropriate standards of medical and mental health care, protection of inmates from abuse, and appropriate staff conduct. Any administrator who believes that *Wilson v. Seiter* diminishes the constitutional responsibilities inherent in administration will find little protection in the "deliberate indifference" standard offered by the Court. A thoughtful and conservative jurist, Justice Byron White, reminded all administrators several years ago in *Wolff v. McDonnell* 418 U.S. 359 (1974) that "There is no iron curtain drawn between the Constitution and the prisons of this country." Case law extended these doctrines to jails, and conscientious improvements in jail practices and the responsibility of administrators for same have not been undone. Quality correctional practices will continue to reduce the likelihood of lawsuits.

SOURCE: Wallenstein, A. (2008). A wholly false sense of security: *Wilson v. Seiter* and jail litigation. Washington, DC: National Institute of Corrections. Retrieved April 18, 2010, from http://nicic.gov/Library/period94.

assistance should be on file. These prewritten documents help to reduce confusion during hectic times of response. Administrators must be able to implement plans and take actions to resolve the situation and not debate on the issues involved. As noted earlier in this chapter, leaders operating in this type of situational response will need more centralized management, and this is where experienced leaders will tend to fare better than their more junior counterparts. It is during these times that many of the managerial orientations used in their typical day-to-day schedule will likely be reversed, with less open communication and more directive decision making that is similar to the responsibilities of a field commander rather than a person-oriented manager. Understanding these differences in demands can be the difference between institutional security and pure chaos within the facility.

CONCLUSION

This chapter has provided an overview of the organizational structure of both the federal and state prison systems in the United States. Organization by levels of management and organization of services provided throughout the agency are both addressed, and it becomes clear that prison agencies are responsible for a disparate array of services and facilities. In addition, students must understand how these systems are organized and how rules and regulations from a central office are carried out within the prison facility. From this point, it is also important to understand how the lead manager of a facility, the prison warden, must then take these rules and regulations and implement them within his or her own facility. In the process, wardens must emphasize an active form of management whereby they are seen throughout the prison facility and where they communicate routinely with staff and inmates. This informal aspect of prison management is important in dealing with the prison subculture, addressing rumors, and getting a general feel for the climate of the institution.

This chapter makes it clear that the use of participatory styles of management as well as the delegation of responsibility and authority (when appropriate) can empower staff and allow the institution to better adapt to needs throughout the facility. The importance of effective training and employee development is critical to the overall welfare of the facility and also to developing effective supervisors in the future. The distinction between managers and leaders is also discussed in this chapter, and students will recall that some supervisors may be both good managers and good leaders, but, usually, supervisors tend to gravitate more in one direction or the other, seldom achieving mastery of both functions.

Issues related to women in corrections have also been discussed, and it has been noted that women often were restricted to work within specific areas of corrections, such as in facilities that held female inmates. Further, there has been a tendency to not allow women access to specialized areas of correctional work unless it is clerical or office-related. However, this is changing within the field of corrections, slowly but surely. Women now work within the security ranks and are promoted as supervisors, including wardens and executive-level administrators. Despite this, women are still the minority in these areas of work, and some wonder if the glass ceiling is still holding many women back from attaining career ascension. Perhaps the best means for ensuring that this is not the case is to work to change the culture within prison systems, among both staff and inmates.

Topics related to private prison management were also included, and it was seen that such organizations also operate programs of excellence. Through the use of its unit management system, this organization has provided very clear and very effective means of governing its employees while, at the same time, including their input in addressing day-to-day challenges within the organization. From the Focus Topics provided, it is clear that this organization places an emphasis on gender equality, diversity amongst employees, and the effective training of employees. As with the Federal Bureau of Prisons, many private prisons have prison facilities in numerous states throughout the nation.

Lastly, the reality is that prisons are dangerous institutions, and, as a result, the unexpected can occur where the security and safety of the institution and of the public itself are jeopardized. Administrators must be ready to deal with these possibilities, and they must be informed of the protocols and guidelines that are in place in the event of an emergency or a disturbance. The use of emergency response teams is necessary during these times of disruption. There are a variety of response teams that exist; all should be rigorously tested, and the selection of members should be restricted to the most qualified personnel. The means by which these teams are managed, including decisions for operational control and partnering with outside agencies to ensure public safety, are all concerns of the correctional administrator.

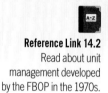

Reference Link 14.2
Read about unit management developed by the FBOP in the 1970s.

Audio Link 14.3
Hear more about efforts to improve workplace safety for correctional officers.

END-OF-CHAPTER DISCUSSION QUESTIONS

1. What are some key features of the organizational structure of the Federal Bureau of Prisons?

2. Identify and discuss the different levels of management in state prison systems.

3. Explain the difference between centralized and decentralized forms of management.

4. Identify and discuss the various models of managerial motivation and supervision.

5. What is the difference between a manager and a leader?

6. How well are women represented in today's world of corrections? What are some of the challenges that have faced women working in the correctional field?

7. What are some of the key advantages associated with private prisons? Are there any potential problems that may exist for these types of prisons? Explain your answer.

8. What are some key issues to note when considering emergency management procedures in a prison facility?

9. Refer to Applied Theory 14.1. Explain how conflict theory might be related to dynamics among the prison population and/or the prison subculture.

KEY TERMS

Authoritarian model	Leadership	Span of control
Bureaucratic model	Management	Span of influence
Centralized management	National Institute of Corrections	Special Operations Response Teams (SORT)
Decentralized management	Participative methods	Strategic plan
Disturbance control teams	Philadelphia Prison System (PPS)	Strategic planning
Emergency preparedness	Prison grapevine	System-wide administrators
Emergency response	Proactive styles of management	
Emotional intelligence	Reactive styles of management	Tactical planning
Glass ceiling	Regional-level administrators	Unit-level administrators
Holding pattern management	Rogues and mavericks	Unit plan
LaSalle Corrections	Rumor control	

APPLIED EXERCISE 14.1

Students must conduct either a face-to-face or a phone interview with a correctional supervisor who currently works in a prison facility in their state. The student must set up a day and time with that practitioner and interview him or her to gain the supervisor's insight and perspective on several key questions related to work in the field of institutional corrections. Students must write the practitioner's responses as well as their own analysis of those responses, and submit their write-up by the deadline set by their instructor. The submission should be written in the form of a minipaper that addresses each point below. The total word count should be 1,200 to 2,000 words.

When completing the interview, students should ask the following questions:

1. What are the most rewarding aspects of your job as a supervisor of other prison staff?
2. What are the most stressful aspects of your job?
3. What are some challenges you find in working with the inmate population?
4. Why did you choose to work in this field?
5. What type of training did you receive for this line of work?
6. What are your future plans for your career in institutional corrections?
7. What would you recommend to someone who was interested in pursuing a similar career?

In addition, students should ensure that their submission has appropriate spelling and grammar throughout.

Last, students are required to provide contact information for the person interviewed. Please have students obtain the following information from the correctional supervisor they interview. While you will probably not need to contact that person, it may become necessary in order to validate the actual completion of the interview.

Name and title of correctional supervisor: _____

Correctional agency: _____

Practitioner's phone number: _____

Practitioner's e-mail address: _____

Name of student: _____

"WHAT WOULD YOU DO?"

You are a warden of a medium-security facility. Lately, as you have made your rounds throughout the prison, you have noticed that there seems to be more tension between African American and Caucasian American inmates. One aspect of concern is the fact that your Internal Affairs Division and your Grievance Office has reported an all-time low in the number of complaints against officers or other inmates during the past two months.

While you would like to think that your prison facility is operating more smoothly and that this is the reason for the low complaints, you are skeptical. Rates of violence between inmates (some of this gang-related) and justified use-of-force incidents among staff are the same or a bit higher than usual, yet complaints are lower. Generally, when more incidents occur, you have more complaints. It seems as if something is amiss, and you recall in some training that you had at a conference for wardens that prior to major disturbances there tends to be a lull in communication with the inmate population.

You think to yourself, that trainer had said that "when it comes to prison riots, just remember that it is usually very quiet just before the storm."

Could this be occurring now? you wonder to yourself. You ponder over this as you make your way to the visitation area of the prison unit and, upon arrival, notice that one of the key leaders of the Aryan Circle is in a visitation chair, and sitting across from him is another important leader from that gang who has been watched by police street gang units. This other leader has always managed to evade arrest but is thought to be active in several incidents of gang-related violence and is also suspected in the burning of an African American church located in the area. There is no law or regulation that prevents him from visiting inmates in the prison since he has no official record and since he has been cleared by the prison agency. However, you know that, in order for him to make the visit himself (rather than sending some other member), something important is likely to occur.

Lastly, as you leave visitation and go through the prison, you notice that many of your officers do not interact with one another. Indeed, it seems that the Caucasian officers stand with one another most of the time while the African American officers do so with one another; there is little dialogue between officers of different racial groups.

You begin to wonder if racially driven differences among inmates and staff may be leading toward serious problems for the institution. As you are wondering this, you continue your rounds throughout the prison and look inside a dayroom where several inmates are watching the TV, and then it becomes clear that something is amiss, both inside and outside of the prison. On the TV you see a local news reporter who explains that an influential African American reverend of a local church has been murdered in his own home. Swastikas were spray-painted within the home, and it is clear that the murder was based on racial hatred.

You are not sure where to begin but realize that these issues in the community are very likely to impact the behavior among inmates within your institution. You fear that you may have a race-related disturbance and wonder how well your officers are addressing these issues. In fact, you are now concerned about how well your officers will support one another, given that there seems to be distance (and perhaps tension) between those of differing racial orientations. You decide something proactive must be done.

What would you do?

Write an essay response of at least 1,200 words that addresses, at a minimum, the following:

1. How you would address the racial friction within the inmate population.

2. How you would address staff cohesion and navigate potential employee problems.

3. How you would address the effects of the community and the outside media.

You can be creative in your responses but should refer to this chapter and prior chapters in addressing this issue.

STUDENT STUDY SITE

Visit the Student Study Site at **www.sagepub.com/hanserintro** to access links to the videos, audio clips, SAGE journal articles, state rankings, and reference materials noted in this chapter, as well as additional study tools including eFlashcards, web quizzes, and more.

chapter 15

Prison Education, Work, and Basic Services Programming

LEARNING OBJECTIVES:

1. Identify the primary forms of prison programs and services that are provided to inmates.

2. Discuss how educational and vocational programs are connected in their effects on recidivism.

3. Explain the medical and food service requirements in prison and how they are typically addressed.

4. Identify various legal issues associated with inmate prison programming.

5. Explain how inmate programming is important to facility operations and to preventing future recidivism.

INTRODUCTION

This chapter will focus on the various prison programs and services that are typical to any facility. It is important to understand that there are two competing views regarding prison programs for inmates; they tend to be polar opposites. The first view is the **work/education reform view**, which is thought to save society untold millions due to the lack of recidivism that has been shown to follow for inmates who have obtained employment and/or education. The second view is the **minimal services view**, which contends that inmates are entitled to no more than the bare minimum that is required by law. While this second view is certainly true, it is unrealistic and, in all honesty, simply ensures that recidivism will be a continual problem in the United States.

One famous and historical supporter of prison services and prison industries was **Chief Justice Warren Burger**. While Warren Burger believed in swift, certain punishment, he also believed in giving offenders an opportunity to reform themselves. "When society places a person behind walls and bars, it has an obligation—a moral obligation—to do whatever can reasonably be done to change that person before he or she goes back into the stream of society" (Burger, 1983, p. 4). Further, in his famous Prisons Without Fences address, he extolled on the need to provide such services to impact recidivism by stating:

> It is predictable that a person confined in a penal institution for two, five, or ten years, and then released, yet still unable to read, write, spell or do simple arithmetic and not trained in any marketable vocational skill, will be vulnerable to returning to a life of crime. And very often the return to crime begins within weeks after release. What job opportunities are there for an unskilled, functionally illiterate [person] who has a criminal record? (Burger, 1983, p. 5)

The quote from Warren Burger captures the essence of this chapter and its intent to demonstrate to students that while grown men are locked up behind bars, it is not prudent to have them passing the time in an idle manner. Instead, the productive use of that time benefits both the inmate and society, both economically and in terms of future crime rates. This chapter will provide an overview of these various services and will demonstrate that these services are necessary for three key reasons: (1) They provide options for inmates who do not wish to return to a life of crime, (2) the Supreme Court has mandated that most of these services be provided, and (3) offering these services gives administrators leverage over inmates to maintain compliance with institutional rules. Thus, these programs serve a function that is important both inside and outside the prison setting.

EDUCATIONAL PROGRAMS

Of all the prison programs available for inmates, education is perhaps the most important (see Focus Topic 15.1). The reasons that this is true are twofold. First, basic academics are fundamental to functioning in the day-to-day world of work. Without the ability to read, write, and do simple arithmetic, offenders will find it difficult to maintain gainful employment. Second, the majority of the inmate population has challenges with literacy and/or basic mathematics. In this section, we will examine some of the basic history behind correctional education and illustrate how this has been an integral component of corrections throughout history.

Reference Link 15.1
Read about education programs in prison.

Educational Programs Throughout History

The use of education in the institutional setting can, as it turns out, be traced all the way back to America's first penitentiary, the Walnut Street Jail. At this time, education and religious instruction tended to be combined. The Quakers were largely behind the use of education behind bars, and they were even the first to encourage secular education. However, there was a general fear that criminals would become even more crafty if they were educated, and this, therefore, resulted in minimal education being provided to those who were locked up.

After the Civil War, there was a search for methods to reform offenders; educational programs were identified as a preferred option. Further, education was at the heart of the reformatory model that prevailed during this time. The origins of this system were largely rooted with the efforts of Zebulon Brockway at the Elmira Reformatory (see Chapter 2). However, some researchers such as Schlossman and Spillane (1995) have contended that the credit given to Brockway is perhaps a bit excessive. They note that his programs were largely just replications of programs for adults that had been made available to juvenile offenders.

Work at Elmira was centered on a contract-driven, factory-based production of goods for the private sector. There tended to prevail a fundamental faith among prison administrators of the late 1800s that hard work was the touchstone of discipline and rehabilitation, regardless of the type of work that it might be. As Brockway had commented in 1888, "there is not any proper education and test of character that does not include training in industry" (Brockway, 1912, p. 268). Largely speaking, most of Brockway's efforts were centered on vocational education, which was designed to prepare inmates for the world of work. This did not include much emphasis on what we would today consider basic primary or secondary education. In most cases, this program was driven by the economic climate outside of the prison system where labor for certain specific skills was needed.

Schlossman and Spillane (1995) conducted an extensive review of the policies and practices of correctional systems in New York, Ohio, Texas, and Virginia during the 1920s and 1930s, and they found that, while some advancements had been made, they lagged well behind the innovations provided by Brockway. There was, however, one exceptional emergence during the 1930s that is noteworthy. This is the work of **Austin MacCormick** titled *The Education of Adult Prisoners*.

MacCormick was a professor at Bowdoin College when his well-known work was completed. Prior to this, he was an administrator at a U.S. Navy prison in Portsmouth, New Hampshire. Even before that, as a means to gain a firsthand understanding of the life of an inmate, he had anonymously had authorities in New York commit him to a prison; only a handful of administrators in the prison knew that he was not actually a convicted inmate. Even before this, MacCormick had written his own thesis on penological principles. *The Education of Adult Prisoners* was the result of efforts within the New York prison system to improve educational efforts. New York, in tandem with the Carnegie Corporation, hired MacCormick as a consultant to conduct the most comprehensive survey ever undertaken of educational programs for adults in prison in the United States.

During the 1960s and 1970s correctional education began to emerge as a priority within many state systems. This was true with both academic and vocational programming (Simms, Farley, & Littlefield, 1987). This was especially true due to the passage of the Adult Education Act of 1964, which provided funding for programs that serviced adults who had deficiencies in communication, basic math skills, or social skills that impaired their ability to gain or retain employment. During the 1970s this act was widely attributed with providing the funding needed for the recruitment of professional educators in prison systems around the nation.

The 1980s is perhaps the period in the history where the most fervor and public attention were given to prison-based education. There were several reasons for this, but one key factor was that the prison population had grown considerably during this time. This was exacerbated by another factor: A number of rulings from the Supreme Court during the 1960s and 1970s that addressed prison conditions and inmate rights tended to cite the need for better educational programs. In addition, the climate during

FOCUS TOPIC: 15.1

Correctional Education—Because It Works

Fox Lake inmate Antonio P. remembers first visiting Fox Lake Correctional Institution as a child. He had come to visit his father. The irony of this isn't lost on him and he wonders about his children's fate, with good cause. Generational incarcerations are closer to the norm than an aberration. Some families pass on the shackles of incarceration like heirlooms. Can we, as a society, break this cycle? Can we stop this revolving door before it creates a permanent underclass? Research tells us the answer is yes. Correctional education is the key to unlocking the shackles of intergenerational incarceration. In fact research shows that correctional education protects the public's safety, in the long run, better than any other type of correctional program.

If the public's safety is our main mission, doesn't it stand to reason that the best way to ensure public safety post-release, is by keeping recidivism numbers as low as possible? In the face of fiscal restraints it is imperative to understand the positive impact correctional education has in successful reentry programs. Many studies underline the false economy of curtailing correctional education in times of government belt-tightening.

The Cost-Effectiveness of Correctional Education

In the face of the correctional budgetary crisis, cost-effective programming must be found. The term "cost effective" is a mantle that rests well on correctional education, especially when one considers the results Audrey Bazos and Jessica Hausman found in their 2004 study, Correctional Education as a Crime Control Program. They reported that $1 million spent on correctional education prevents 600 new crimes, while that same money invested in incarceration prevents 350 crimes. In this era when cost-effectiveness has become a premier consideration, an expansion of educational opportunities may be corrections' most viable alternative. Reducing recidivism is the cost-effective approach.

Bazos and Hausman's study states that Wisconsin, specifically, found a 20 percent reduction in recidivism in offenders that completed an educational program. This reduction occurs after taking into account, and controlling, factors that are known to predict recidivism, such as age, race and length of sentence.

Bazos and Hausman's work speaks directly to corrections' need to be cost-effective. They found that the cost of correctional education would break even with a 6 percent reduction in recidivism. The collected field research shows that the true effect of correctional education on reductions in recidivism falls somewhere between 10 percent and 20 percent. Bazos and Hausman's study indicates that every $1 million spent on correctional education yields a savings of $1.6 million in a state's re-incarceration costs (due to the reduction in recidivism/reincarceration). In other words, correctional education rises above the break-even point by $600,000 for every $1 million spent.

Education Is the Eraser on Society's Pencil

Victims of crime disproportionately reside in diverse communities in major urban areas. Not coincidently the largest segment of our offenders comes from these same areas. Traditionally these areas have school systems with high dropout rates. Approximately 50 percent of all high school dropouts will be incarcerated at one point in their lives. The link between a lack of education, crime and incarceration is a strong one. If corrections is to meet its goals of "being responsive and sensitive to victims, victims' families and a diverse community" and ". . . the development of constructive offender skills . . ." the importance of access to correctional educational opportunities is self-evident.

Increasing Offenders' Employability

The 2001 Three State Recidivism Study by Stephen J. Steurer, Linda Smith and Alice Tracy is one of the more comprehensive examples of field work employing the scientific method to establish the connection between correctional education and lower recidivism rates. This in-depth study also includes data about the importance of correctional education on the earning power of offenders upon their return to society. This study found that offenders who had participated in correctional education while incarcerated earned roughly 23 percent more than a control group of nonparticipants in their first year after release.

It is imperative to note, particularly when politicians overseeing corrections suggest that performance measurement is crucial to the business plan and all department actions, that the higher earnings achieved by offenders were not a product of a specific educational or vocational diploma program but rather the product of participation in correctional education in general. This is a fact that must be considered when attempting to evaluate [program] effectiveness. As the next study examined establishes, recidivism rates go down as time spent in correctional classrooms goes up. A meaningful measure of program effectiveness might well be the offenders' self-report of post-program satisfaction.

Correctional Education's Impact on Offenders

The 1995 study, Prison Education Program Participation and Recidivism: A Test of the Normalization Hypothesis, by Miles D. Harer explores the theory that correctional education programs have a "normalizing" effect on offenders, that increases prison safety, reduces recidivism, nurtures pro-social norms, and negates the effects of "prisonization (criminogenic norms that facilitate the growth inmate subcultures that favor criminal behaviors post-release)."

Harer's study finds that there is approximately a 15 percent greater rate of recidivism among offenders with no educational participation than offenders who participated in [merely] .5 courses during each six-month period of their incarceration. The study further finds that the greater the rate of participation the lower recidivism rates drop. "The greatest decline in recidivism, with educational program participation, is among those who come to prison with a high school degree."

Conclusion

The research that has been done indicates that correctional education is the most effective approach to fulfilling the mission of corrections. Correctional education reduces recidivism rates. It goes beyond being cost-effective by producing a measurable savings for every dollar invested. Correctional education has a direct impact on the quality of life in our country and most particularly in ethnically diverse urban areas. Correctional education may be the bulwark that prevents the currently undereducated from becoming a permanent underclass. Correctional education promotes a successful reentry to society by improving the potential wages for the returning offender. While we can measure and prove that correctional education is the most cost-effective way to produce the most significant reductions in recidivism rates, proving or measuring why is a more complex proposition.

SOURCE: From Kaiser, J. "Correctional education: Because it works," in *Corrections Today*, August 1, 2010. Reprinted with permission of the American Correctional Association, Alexandria, VA.

this time was more punitive, and less emphasis was placed on correctional treatment programming; education, however, was an exception since it was not steeped in mental health jargon but was more clearly understood by the general public.

The 1990s saw an intense interest in prison education programs. Indeed these types of programs proliferated throughout the United States. Programs such as the Windham School District in the state of Texas became a major segment of prison operations in Texas, which, as students should know by now, is one of the major prison systems in the United States. In addition to the growth of these programs, there emerged an abundance of research on inmate education systems. Numerous state and federal studies were published during the mid- and late 1990s that have demonstrated that educational programs can and do lower recidivism.

Likewise, the birth of a new office in the Department of Education occurred in 1991, the **Office of Correctional Education (OCE)**. The OCE was created to provide national leadership on issues related to correctional education. To this day, the OCE provides technical assistance to states, local schools, and correctional institutions and shares information on correctional education. The office was authorized by the Carl D. Perkins Vocational and Applied Technology Education Act Amendments of 1990 (Public Law 101-392).

In addition to the functions just enumerated, the OCE provides extensive grant funding to various correctional education programs around the nation. This type of funding includes the **Life Skills for State and Local Prisoners Program**, which provides financial assistance for establishing and operating programs designed to reduce recidivism through the development and improvement of life skills necessary for reintegration of adult prisoners into society. "Life skills" include self-development, communication skills, job and financial skills development, education, interpersonal and family relationship development, and stress and anger management.

Video Link 15.1
Learn more about how prison education programs lower recidivism.

PHOTO 15.2

Inmates work on computer literacy skills in a correctional facility.

Despite this seeming victory for educational programming, the 1990s are known for one key policy change that has negatively impacted the ability of inmates to obtain a higher education while in prison: the elimination of the federal Pell Grant for inmates seeking college education. Up through the mid-1990s, the federal government had allocated a very small fraction of Pell Grant dollars to those who were incarcerated. **Pell Grants** are need-based federal monies set aside for persons who pursue a college education. The use of the Pell Grant in prisons was the result of legislation in 1965, where Congress passed **Title IV of the Higher Education Act**, which permitted inmates to apply for financial aid in the form of Pell Grants to attend college. Despite abundant research from the Federal Bureau of Prisons (BOP) and in states such as Alabama, Illinois, Ohio, New York, Texas, and Wisconsin that showed that college-level education caused a clear and consistent reduction in recidivism rates, this program was ultimately discontinued (Karpowitz & Kenner, 2001).

During the 1990s, the effects of the War on Drugs were being felt, and there was a mass prison building boom throughout the nation. Politicians heralded "tough on crime" platforms including "three strikes" initiatives, the elimination of parole, and enhanced penalties against drug offenders. During this time, politicians introduced legislation that prohibited tuition assistance to inmates. The U.S. Department of Education resisted this change of policy, and continued to support the use of Pell Grants in prisons. As part of this effort, the OCE issued facts and commentary in a 1995 report titled *Pell Grants for Prisoners*, in which it stated that "Pell grants help inmates obtain the skills and education needed to acquire and keep a

Reference Link 15.2
Read about the loss of Pell Grants for prison college courses.

Prison Tour Video Link 15.1
Watch a clip about educational funding.

job following their eventual release" (Department of Education, 1995, p. 1). Furthermore, the Department of Education (1995) published the following facts in support of Pell Grant eligibility for inmates:

1. Of the $5.3 billion awarded in Pell grants during that time, only $34 million were awarded to inmates. This is less than 1/10 of a percent of the overall money available.

2. The annual amount of award given per inmate was less than $1,300.00.

3. The money is given to the education providers and not to the inmates; this ensures that the money goes only to educational costs.

4. Death row inmates and those serving life sentences without parole were not eligible for this funding.

Thus, it is clear that this funding was marginal, at best, and it is clear that the money did not line the pockets of inmates in prison. Rather, the funding was well accounted for and went to assist inmates who had a reasonable chance for reentry—increasing their odds for successful reintegration. Despite this, the passage of the Violent Crime Control and Law Enforcement Act eliminated the use of the Pell Grant and, in the process, all but completely killed the offering of higher education in American corrections.

Though the Pell Grant has been eliminated from prison funding opportunities, the attention to college-level education for inmates is still a serious concern among scholars and practitioners of correctional education programming. This is so true that the bill, known as H.R. 4137, the Higher Education Opportunity Act, was passed by the House of Representatives on February 7, 2008. This bill includes provisions that would make all age groups eligible for the Incarcerated Youth Offender grant and will expand the spending cap from $1,800 per year to $3,300 for each offender (Contardo & Tolbert, 2010). Since 2008, the act has been in force, but many state systems are new to the particulars of the act. Regardless, this movement within Congress demonstrates that even politicians are beginning to clearly see the connection between education and the reduction of future crime rates. This provides a sense of optimism for many correctional educators and prison administrators.

Types of Education Programs in Corrections

The federal system tends to be the premier correctional system and also tends to include a wide range of services that are common to most other states. Because many states essentially follow the standards of the federal system, it is perhaps easier to showcase the federal system and/or a handful of examples from one state or another. The Federal BOP has long recognized the importance of education both as an opportunity for inmates to improve their knowledge and skills and as a correctional management tool that encourages inmates to use their time in a constructive manner.

Each federal prison has its own education department that provides education and recreational activities to federal inmates. While BOP inmates have access to a variety of educational programs, literacy education receives the highest priority. With few exceptions, an inmate who does not have a General Educational Development (GED) diploma must participate in a literacy program for a minimum of 240 instructional hours or until he or she earns a GED credential. The English as a Second Language (ESL) program enables inmates with limited English proficiency to improve their English language skills. Due to legislation passed in 1990, non-English-proficient inmates must participate in an ESL program until they pass competency skills tests at the eighth-grade level.

Distance Learning and Inmates

Though this approach to inmate education may seem strange at first, online education has reached the prison world and is now a routine part of inmate programs for higher education. However, this method of delivery has proven to be cost-effective and workable within the prison environment. Admittedly, there are security concerns with the availability of e-mail, and Internet access may provide obstacles to the implementation of distance learning. New surveillance technology, however, helps reduce security problems. Equally interesting is that some institutions have integrated a method of facility management that has established a good-behavior system in which inmates in prison can earn their computer privileges.

Programs such as the one in the Arizona Department of Juvenile Corrections (ADJC) have forged partnerships with outlying community colleges and other institutions to provide inmates with online postsecondary education. In this case, the use of technology and the Internet has provided the correctional agency with the means to offer higher education to juvenile inmates throughout the state while, at the same time, minimizing the costs associated with onsite classes and full-time instructors (Nink, Olding, Jorgenson, & Gilbert, 2009).

In response to concerns regarding security, information technology experts have developed firewalls to limit students' access to the college's online learning system and library services (Nink et al., 2009). This alone ensures that inmates are not able to use the computer system for anything other than what it is intended for. Further, partner colleges provide the necessary websites for student access to materials hosted outside of the college's network. In addition, partner colleges have utilized restricted e-mail access so that inmates can only receive e-mail from their instructors. The e-mail system is also set up to enable the continual audit of student e-mail communications. Lastly, computer labs are available to inmates during specific times of the day for online class activity. During the use of computer equipment, educational staff monitor the classrooms and online activity of inmates.

Programs such as the one from the ADJC demonstrate that sufficient security features can be implemented to make online education safe as a venue for achievement among inmates. When protections are in place, this can be a very feasible means of increasing opportunities for inmates and, in the process, reducing recidivism among those who return to the community. The use of this type of technology is a fairly recent advent for inmate correctional education but has even extended into the world of work for inmates serving time. In some instances, inmates are not only taking courses online, but they also may work by phone and online in various customer service facets. Thus, both education and work can be performed at a distance by inmates who are cleared for such activity and when sufficient security precautions are in place.

Celebrating Achievements

One of the most rewarding aspects of educational programs is the sense of empowerment and achievement that is obtained. Inmates who are recognized for their efforts, whether educational, vocational, or treatment oriented, gain positive esteem and tend to be more motivated as they approach their eventual release into society. For some inmates, this may be one of the few times that they have actually been recognized for their accomplishment. This alone can provide the offender with a new sense of self. We will also discuss the offering of life skills education and programming as a means of furthering offenders' sense of esteem and ability to effectively cope with stressors that may make them prone to further recidivism. However, for now, students should consider that, for many offenders, life has not been one in which they have received much positive attention, if any at all. Showcasing their positive outcomes is likely to reinforce that behavior and will serve to instill prosocial norms within their psyche.

PRISON WORK PROGRAMS

Prison work for inmates tends to consist of two types. The first type includes those jobs that maintain the functioning of the prison itself. These types of jobs might include the preparation of meals, working in the laundry, and cleaning of various prison areas and do not usually provide inmates with a trade or a skill by which they can earn a living in the outside community. The second type of work is industrial or vocational in orientation. These jobs include production, agriculture, craftsmanship, carpentry, construction, and even clerical positions in prison offices where genuine professional skills might be learned.

Audio Link 15.1
Hear about the various work programs in prisons.

Inmate Labor Throughout History

The origin of labor in prisons can be traced back to English jails of the 11th and 13th centuries when inmate labor paid for the costs of imprisonment as well as the salaries of the jailers and the sheriff. During the 1300s, hard labor was considered part of one's payment for keep and was the mainstay activity in workhouses of that time. The emphasis on work continued throughout history, but the types of work selected usually did not compete with free labor outside of the prison walls. During the mid- to late 1700s, prison reformers such as John Howard and Cesare Beccaria considered inmate labor a key factor in the reformation of offenders.

TECHNOLOGY AND EQUIPMENT 15.1

The Use of Computers and Online Technology in Inmate Education

To demonstrate that distance learning opportunities can and do work, a couple of examples are provided in this special insert. These brief excerpts demonstrate that distance education can occur through various media and formats. While there are understandable security concerns, many state systems have found the means to minimize the grounds for such concerns.

Computer Use For/By Inmates

In a survey that examined computer use among inmates in Canada and the United States, researchers found that inmates have personal computers available to them in nine state correctional systems. Access is restricted to word processing in Kansas and to legal purposes for federal detainees in Maryland, and is restricted for all inmates in Manitoba and Newfoundland in Canada. While sending or receiving e-mails is not permitted in the Canadian correctional systems, this is allowed in six state correctional systems in the United States, with some restrictions. Time limits are generally applied to inmates' use of computers, primarily being restricted to class periods. Inmate computer use is allowed during recreation in Maine, and 5 hours of use for legal purposes is allowed for federal detainees in Maryland. Access to the Internet is denied in all but four jurisdictions. The four jurisdictions that allow inmate Internet use allow this for legal and job-search purposes. In all cases, computer use is monitored closely by security and educational staff.

Distance Learning, Iowa Department of Corrections

Since the mid-1990s, the Iowa Department of Corrections, through the Iowa Communications Network (ICN), has provided individuals who are incarcerated the opportunity to take "courses online at their personal expense." Some 15 to 20 students per semester take 10 to 15 courses at community and private colleges and universities over the ICN, earning college degrees and certificates.

Educational Videoconferencing, Ohio Department of Rehabilitation and Correction

Using videoconferencing technology, the Ohio Department of Rehabilitation and Correction has implemented an education network that allows prisoners to participate in distance education programs, leveraging the effectiveness of teachers. In addition, some staff education/training programs are now provided via the video network, allowing instructors to deliver quality information without traveling to multiple locations or requiring staff to drive to a central location.

SOURCES: Hill, C. (2009). Survey summary: Computer use for/by inmates. *Corrections Compendium, 34*(2), 24–31.

Reentry Police Council. (2009). *Policy statement 15: Education and vocation training.* New York: Council of State Governments.

Much of the information regarding workhouses, prison industry, prison farming, and key figures who advocate for reform in these systems can be found in Chapters 1 and 2 of this text. From indentured servitude to workhouses and houses of correction, including the lease system and chain gangs, to the development of the prison farm, all the way through the Industrial Era to prison farming systems from 1900 and after World War II, significant discussion has already been allocated to inmate labor and working conditions throughout early history in the first two chapters of this text, so we will not repeat this discussion here.

Rather, we will follow with a more modern history of inmate labor, and we will focus our discussion on the federal system of inmate labor. The primary reason for this is that it has a defined history that is far-reaching and, at the base of it, contains all the elements of historical development that are common to most of the state systems. However, the federal system is not given to peculiarities of history and geography that are common to other state prison systems, such as those in the southern United States that relied largely on agricultural operations. It is with this in mind that we turn our attention to the federal system of inmate labor.

The History of Inmate Labor in a Model Program: UNICOR

In June 1934, President Franklin D. Roosevelt signed a law that established an organization for federal prison labor, named the **Federal Prison Industries Inc. (FPI)**. From this action emerged a full-fledged corporation owned by the U.S. government. This corporation was designed to operate various factories and to ensure that inmates were gainfully employed, when and where appropriate, during the course of their sentence. During the next few years, the number of inmates who were employed increased, and, in 1940, roughly 18% of the entire federal inmate population was employed through FPI. From this point onward, FPI grew into a major corporation, with a growing inmate workforce that was skilled in numerous trades and also produced a variety of goods and services. By the end of World War II, FPI was a producer of more than 70 categories of products at 25 separate shops and factories.

During the World War II era, FPI was a major contributor to the war effort. During this time, inmates worked double and even triple shifts throughout the day and night, with 95% of all products being sold to the military. Among these products were items such as bomb fins and bomb casings, TNT cases, parachutes, welded products, aircraft sheet metal work, shipbuilding crafts, auto/aviation mechanics, and drafting and electrical products. Many people are not aware that the inmate population, at least at the federal level, has been such a strong contributor to our national defense. During the tough times of World War II, federal inmates working for FPI were a primary source of labor. The impact that these inmates had upon America's war effort continued even after they served their time because many were able to move into defense-industry jobs upon release from prison. The federal government created job placement centers at several institutions, and this helped hundreds of inmates each year find employment.

During the Korean War of the 1950s, federal inmates again contributed to America's war effort. Indeed, sales by FPI exceeded $29 million, and over 3,800 inmates were employed by this corporation. Following the Korean War, FPI retooled factories and renovated outdated equipment to produce new products in response to changing markets. FPI opened shops that specialized in the refurbishment of furniture, office equipment, tires, and other government property. In addition, FPI introduced new vocational training programs that provided medical benefits for consumers by manufacturing artificial limbs and dentures, and providing inmate labor for hospital attendant work.

During the Vietnam War, there was another growth in production levels, but this was a short-term occurrence as FPI sought to ease its inmate population out of wartime production and into more mainstream forms of industry. By the late 1960s, military sales had declined significantly and nearly all but ceased at the close of the Vietnam War. With the close of the Vietnam War and the desire to transition to a more civilian-oriented sector, FPI was reorganized to have seven separate divisions, each responsible for a specified type of product. These districts provided goods and services in the following areas: (1) automated data processing, (2) electronics, (3) graphics, (4) metals, (5) shoe and brush, (6) textiles, and (7) woods and plastics. In addition, a program for the marketing of products as well as the quality assurance of those products was formally set in place.

During the late 1970s, FPI changed its name to **UNICOR Inc.** as a means of creating a new civilian and corporate-based identity. As this new identity formed, UNICOR introduced new lines in stainless steel products, thermoplastics, printed circuits, modular furniture, ergonomic chairs, Kevlar-reinforced items (such as military helmets), and optics, in an effort to increase its competitive position. State-of-the-art production techniques were embraced, including modern printing equipment. Such efforts led to improved product offerings, which, in turn, created new inmate work opportunities to better prepare inmates for post-release employment.

Also important was a seven-year study in the 1990s, the **Post-Release Employment Project (PREP)**, conducted by the BOP's Office of Research and Evaluation, that validated, conclusively, that UNICOR successfully achieved its mission of preparing inmates for release and therefore provided long-term benefits to society. Further, the PREP study showed that the inmates who participated in UNICOR's industrial or educational programs were less likely to incur misconduct reprimands while incarcerated, less likely to commit crimes following release, and less likely to return to prison than inmates who did not take advantage of such programs.

During the new millennium, UNICOR embarked on a corporate-wide campaign to become a leader in eco-sensitive practices, and to set the standard for government. This eco-sensitive industry, commonly known as green technology, became a primary area of industrial growth for UNICOR. To ensure that it fulfilled its commitment to green technology, a senior-level task force was formed to develop a five-year environmental plan, complete with measurable, corporate-wide objectives. This demonstrates how UNICOR has operated as a forward-thinking operation, providing products and services that are useful to society and that also reform offenders who are subject to release in the community.

Other Prison Work Programs

In many states and especially among three of the largest state correctional systems, Texas, California, and Florida, the employment of inmates in agricultural, forestry, and roadwork services has been a traditional focus of inmate labor (again, students should refer back to Chapters 1 and 2 of this text). These were especially popular forms of labor in the southern prison systems of the United States. Typically, this work included cotton picking, cutting lumber, harvesting crops, road construction, fire fighting, and the maintenance of state grounds and property. While this type of work offsets costs of prison system budgets, it does not prepare offenders for work on the outside and therefore does little to decrease recidivism, particularly when compared with skilled labor experience that allows offenders to support themselves once they are released.

Conversely, there are examples of state prison systems that operate both agricultural programs and industrial programs that reduce the costs of prison operations and also prepare inmates for work on the outside. We will examine both the Texas and California industrial systems as a means of exploring this point. However, some comments regarding the benefits of agricultural production should be provided.

In Texas, the prison system continues to operate under a directive to be as self-sufficient as fiscally possible while meeting all constitutional requirements. As a result, this prison system's agricultural division grows most of the food consumed by the staff and inmates. The Texas prison agricultural system includes farms that produce millions of pounds of fresh cannery vegetables, substantial dairy products, and poultry products, as well as eggs. These operations are so successful that they produced surpluses during the 1990s and the early 2000s and kept food costs down to approximately $2 per inmate per day (Benestante, 1996). These benefits are obviously beneficial to the state prison budget but also to Texas taxpayers who are free of the additional fiscal burdens that would be placed upon them if these programs did not exist. However, as noted earlier, they do not tend to prepare inmates for work that will provide them opportunities on the outside. Thus, the answer is to allow inmates who are nearing release to train in other job sectors. This is done in both Texas and Florida. As a result, we will briefly showcase both programs in the subsections that follow.

PHOTO 15.3

This inmate sews a laundry bag in a garment factory.

The Texas Prison Industry—Texas Correctional Industries

Texas Correctional Industries (TCI) was established in 1963, with the passage of Senate Bill 338, the Prison Made Goods Act of Texas (see Figure 15.1 for organization of prison manufacturing and logistics in Texas). The specific charge of TCI is to provide offenders with marketable job skills to help reduce recidivism through a coordinated program of the following:

1. Job skills training.

2. Documentation of work history.

3. Access to resources provided by various employment services upon release.

In addition, as noted in earlier parts of this chapter, TCI helps to reduce prison system costs by providing products and services on a for-profit basis to the Texas Department of Criminal Justice (TDCJ) and other eligible entities and to agencies or political subdivisions of the state.

TCI manufactures goods and provides services to state and local government agencies, public educational systems, public hospitals, and political subdivisions. TCI comprises six divisions: Garment, Graphics, Furniture, Metal, Marketing and Distribution, and Offender Work and Training Programs. TCI

FIGURE 15.1 Organizational Structure of Manufacturing and Logistics Division of Texas Prison System

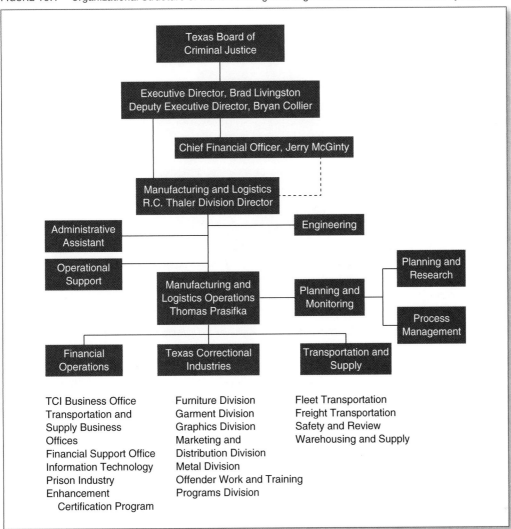

SOURCE: From Texas Department of Criminal Justice (2010). *Manufacturing and Logistics Annual Report Fiscal Years 2008 & 2009.*

has 37 facilities that manufacture items such as shirts, pants, coats, shoes, sheets, pillows, mattresses, signs, stickers, printed materials, janitorial supplies, soaps, detergents, license plates, stainless steel goods, park equipment, dump beds, a variety of office and institutional furniture, and modular office systems. All total, sales generated from these activities exceed $95 million annually. The work and training programs offered to offenders help reduce idleness and provide opportunities for offenders to learn marketable job skills and work ethics. On-the-job training and accredited certification programs, along with the Work Against Recidivism (WAR) Program (described in more detail in the following pages), are specifically targeted to successfully reintegrate offenders into society.

The division collaborates with the **Windham School District** (a secondary education program in Texas prisons) and other entities to establish work and training programs directed toward the effective rehabilitation of offenders, promoting a seamless integration of training opportunities, such as apprenticeship programs, diversified career preparation programs, short-course programs, on-the-job programs, and college vocational courses. These programs provide offenders with opportunities to acquire workplace knowledge and skills and help offenders develop a work ethic. The division is composed of Engineering, Operational Support, Financial Operations, Planning and Monitoring, Transportation and Supply, and TCI.

In Texas, the **Prison Industry Enhancement (PIE) Certification Program** is a partnership between the TDCJ and a private company, which allows the company to employ offenders who have volunteered to be a part of the program. The offenders are paid by the private company, and deductions are taken from their

FIGURE 15.2   Texas Prison Industry Enhancement Offender Contributions, 1993–2009

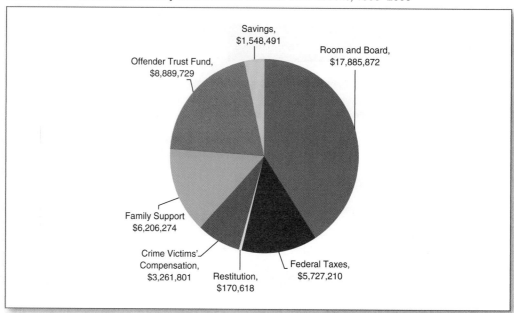

SOURCE: Texas Department of Criminal Justice. (2010). *Manufacturing and logistics annual report fiscal years 2008 and 2009.*

wages for their taxes, room and board, dependent support, and restitution, and a contribution is made to a crime victims' fund. This program has successfully offset correctional expenses for inmates who participate. Indeed, more than $17 million of offender earnings (room and board deductions) have been deposited in the state's General Revenue Fund since the program's inception. On average, for each offender employed, $5,071 is deducted for room and board, $1,431 is deducted for family support, $508 is deducted for the state's crime victims' compensation fund, and another $42 is deducted for restitution to victims (see Figure 15.2 for details).

PHOTO 15.4

These inmates are working on a computerized education employment program, which allows inmates to work at their own pace; teaches job, employment, and academic skills; and can assist the inmates upon their release.

The PIE Certification Program demonstrates how prison work programs can save taxpayers substantial amounts of money, but, at the same time, these programs are also able to give back to victims of crime. Thus, in addition to aiding in recidivism reduction for offenders who have useful job skills on release, their participation while incarcerated derives benefits for the prison system, society, and victims in a direct manner that can be measured. This means that these programs are invaluable within the field of corrections as they provide tangible benefits almost immediately after implementation.

Lastly, the **Work Against Recidivism (WAR) Program**, includes a joint effort between the Manufacturing and Logistics Division, the Texas Parole Division, the Texas Workforce Commission, and private sector enterprises, with a goal to facilitate the successful reentry of offenders upon release from the TDCJ. The WAR Program tracks offenders who are provided job skills while assigned to Manufacturing and Logistics facilities. WAR is administered by the Offender Work and Training Programs Division of TCI. TCI-designated training facilities continue to provide employable skills to offenders, while providing services that directly benefit customers and, less directly, benefit society as a whole.

For instance, since 2009, a program designed for computer recovery has existed within two prison facilities in Texas. This program provides inmates with experience in working on computers that have malfunctioned and provides them the ability to troubleshoot and repair these computers. In addition to giving inmates hands-on training, this program provided Texas public schools with a total of 6,366 refurbished computers in 2009 alone. This example demonstrates that inmates in Texas are not only being given job skills, but, in some cases, they are being taught highly technical skills that are hard to find in broader society. This also harkens back to Technology & Equipment 15.1, which demonstrates how computers and online technology have impacted inmate education and inmate vocational training throughout the nation.

Further, it is noteworthy to demonstrate how some of these inmate work programs provide altruistic benefits for society and can, in some instances, ease the difficulties for persons who are less fortunate in society. One specific example is the Braille facility in Texas, where inmates produced thousands of pages of transcribed Braille and tactile graphics for students who are visually disabled. This outcome illustrates how inmates can provide a worthwhile benefit to society while learning valuable skills and, in the process, can make the world a better place for those in need.

Journal Article Link 15.2
Read about a prison pet program.

The Florida Prison Industry—Prison Rehabilitative Industries and Diversified Enterprises

In the state of Florida, prison industries are frequently linked with inmate reentry initiatives to ensure that returning offenders are productive in the community. **Prison Rehabilitative Industries and Diversified Enterprises Inc. (PRIDE)** is an independent company that aligns its job training initiatives to the needs of the correctional system in the state of Florida. PRIDE Enterprises is recognized throughout the nation as a premier company that operates general manufacturing and services facilities throughout Florida. The vision of PRIDE is "to be the best company in the world at transitioning inmates to successful citizens" (PRIDE,

PHOTO 15.5

This inmate works on a manual transmission on Wednesday, February 24, 2010, at a prison auto mechanics class.

2008, p. 3). This is a very lofty vision, but it belies a genuine commitment to returning offenders to the community as productive citizens. Because this is the primary goal of corrections and because PRIDE is so well recognized and respected, it will be given a full subsection in this text. All information regarding this program has been adapted from PRIDE's 2008 annual report titled *PRIDE in Our Mission*.

Within PRIDE Enterprises, there exists a company initiative known as the **PRIDE Re-Entry and Transition Program**. This program directly supports the primary statutory mission in Florida, which is "to provide a joint effort between the department, the correctional work programs, and other vocational education, training and post-release job placement and help reduce recommitment." From this mission statement, it can be seen that vocational programs in Florida are directly tied to an offender's likely outcome once released; this comports with other research that has been showcased throughout this chapter and demonstrates that the state of Florida is following a model that is consistent with sound research and practice.

The reentry program prepares inmates for eventual release into the community by providing vocational training opportunities in correctional industry settings that function in a manner similar to independent profit-making enterprises. One key feature of the reentry program is an extensive on-the-job training (OJT) program that occurs in PRIDE's manufacturing facilities. A total of 41 different types of operation provide training to inmates in 29 prison facilities throughout the state. Inmate workers receive instruction in occupations ranging from field worker to dental lab technician. All training conforms to Florida Department of Education Curriculum Framework standards and is made available to the inmate worker through OJT, instruction, demonstration, and practical work experience. This instruction is provided to the inmate worker by industry supervisors who are considered "masters of their trades" (PRIDE, 2008, p. 6).

Upon successful completion of the curriculum, the inmate is awarded a certificate of achievement from the Florida Department of Education or another certifying authority attesting to mastered skills. But PRIDE not only focuses on the mastery of skills. This company also desires to ensure that inmates are indeed employed upon leaving prison. Skills that are not used cannot be translated into a beneficial outcome for the offender or for society. As a means of optimizing outcomes, the Florida Department of Education designated PRIDE as an assessment center for its **Ready to Work Program**. Ready to Work,

PHOTO 15.6

This inmate replaces spools of cotton while working in a garment shop.

sponsored by the Florida Legislature, was developed to ensure that Florida's workforce possesses the competencies necessary to succeed in the competitive marketplace. Its focus is to match employee skill levels to specific job requirements. Program participants are initially assessed in four areas: reading for information, locating information, applied mathematics, and workplace readiness. This program has been integrated within the inmate job training process to ensure that levels of functioning for inmates are on par with the remaining workforce in Florida.

The Ready to Work Program provides offenders with targeted instruction and course work to enable them to improve any deficiencies. When a participant achieves the required scores, a Florida Ready to Work certificate is awarded, which recognizes the specific skill levels attained. Job candidates may present this credential to employers as documentation that they have achieved mastery of the four key skills. The preparatory Ready to Work courseware is provided to the inmate workers as e-learning, hosted on the inmate local area network server. This is yet another example of how technology, computers, and electronic learning has permeated the inmate job training arena within correctional systems.

In determining participants of this program, the initial criteria require that inmates be within two years of release from incarceration to participate in Ready to Work. Use of the Ready to Work courseware reinforces computer skills, and the program content prepares workers for the GED examination and the **Test of Adult Basic Education (TABE)**. The TABE is one of the most comprehensive and reliable assessment products in the education industry, providing a solid foundation for effectively assessing the skills and knowledge of adult learners (McGraw-Hill, 2010). The TABE provides a system of diagnostic assessments and instructional materials that test and assess adults on their educational achievement and functioning in reading, math, language, language mechanics, vocabulary, and spelling (McGraw-Hill, 2010). Inmate participation in the OJT program requires the achievement of minimum TABE score levels in math, language, and reading.

In order to assist inmate workers in the achievement of their OJT certification, selected staff members receive TABE administration training and are certified as TABE administrators. The TABE testing process helps to ensure that eligible inmates will receive their certificates of achievement prior to their release from institutional custody. This then optimizes the time spent training these offenders because PRIDE and the Florida correctional system can be assured that their investment in the training process will translate to more frequent program completion and, incidentally, more effective offender reintegration in the community.

It is important to expound on this point because the various benefits of this process may not be directly clear to students of corrections. First, the fact that the state of Florida has these types of basic academic requirements for its workforce helps to improve and bolster the overall functioning of the entire state's population. Further, the benefits of being literate go beyond the ability to simply keep a job. They allow offenders to further their education and also empower offenders toward upward mobility, in terms of both education *and* vocation. This has a two-ply effect on their likely success in reentry, and this, therefore, helps to reduce the likelihood of recidivism even further among released offenders. Thus, the state of Florida has much to gain from this program that, in all likelihood, saves untold millions of dollars from reduced future crime. Further, Figure 15.3 demonstrates that, similar to inmate work programs in Texas, PRIDE also provides direct benefits to victims of crime.

When considering reentry initiatives in Florida, the PRIDE Transition Program is the community piece of a comprehensive system. This structure provides a seamless transition from the initial assignment of an inmate worker to a PRIDE correctional industry work program to the culminating employment of the offender in a local community business upon release. Transition specialists assist former PRIDE workers who have been released from incarceration in locating employment in the state of Florida. Any inmate assigned to PRIDE during his incarceration is eligible to apply for entry into the Transition

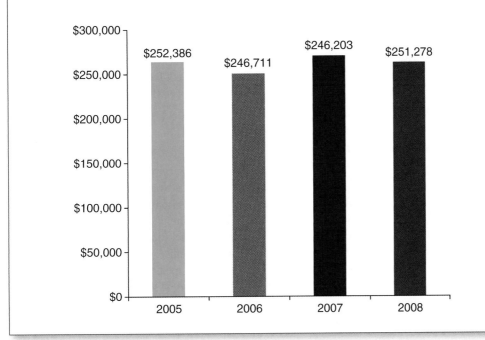

VICTIM RESTITUTION CONTRIBUTIONS

Under its Victim Restitution Policy, PRIDE accrued $251,278 in 2008. This amount represents 15% of traditional inmate compensation earned in 2008 and is paid into a State of Florida fund, which pays court-ordered victim restitution on behalf on PRIDE workers. Victim restitution funds are paid from PRIDE's net income and are a voluntary contribution on the part of PRIDE; a deduction for victim restitution is not taken from the traditional wage of inmate workers.

Program. Preference is given to offenders who left the PRIDE industry in good standing, were assigned to PRIDE at the time of their release, worked for PRIDE for at least six months, and earned a certificate of achievement.

The focus of the Transition Program is sustainable employment, which means a full-time job with benefits and the potential for advancement. Program participants are assessed to determine their needs and given intensive case management that assists them in managing barriers to successful community integration. This type of assistance often utilizes community service providers with whom PRIDE has established reciprocal relationships. This demonstrates how effective partnerships among agencies and private companies can augment correctional outcomes. Once offenders are released, they are provided case management for one year to assist them in job retention and to serve as a buffer against potential recidivism.

The Future of Prison Work

It is likely that prison work programs will continue to increase in use among prison systems around the nation. In fact, the current economic circumstances all but ensure that these programs will be popular in a variety of state systems as well as the BOP. The costs offset by inmate labor are too beneficial for correctional systems to operate otherwise, and, given that state budgets around the nation are so strapped, it would be foolhardy to think that these programs will not continue in the future.

Further still, the more contemporary emphasis on reentry in the field of corrections also dovetails with institutional programs geared toward work-related development among offenders. Without employable skills, offenders will have little success in the community. Thus, inmates will need to be trained, and they will need to be given experience so that they can competently use that training when outside of the prison environment. Prison work programs provide both the training and experience necessary and, when coupled with educational programming, provide offenders with the tools necessary to support themselves in the community. It is these two types of programming—educational and vocational—that are most

Prison Tour Video Link 15.2
Watch a clip about work programs for prisoners.

concretely related to an offender's ability to reintegrate into society. When taken together with substance abuse interventions (because a large majority of offenders have problems with substance abuse), the largest share of challenges for most inmates are addressed, and, when collectively implemented, these types of programming reduce recidivism considerably. It is with this in mind that we now turn our attention to substance abuse programming within the institutional environment.

PRISON HEALTH SERVICES

Reference Link 15.3
Read about prison health care.

Outside of prison, citizens must find a way to afford their own health care, and, in the absence of being able to do so, they will usually have to gain minimal health care from public government service. Regardless, free-world persons have at least some minimal say over the types of services that they will receive, and, if they desire, they can seek alternatives that may be available in society. For inmates, this is not the case, and, because prison health care is not always satisfactory, this has been the basis of many legal actions taken against prison systems.

History of Prison Health Care

During early jail and prison history, the public generally did not perceive inmates as having rights to health care. Indeed, the general consensus was that the lack of health care was perhaps deserved as a result of being sent to prison. The state of affairs with medical services in prisons stayed this way for hundreds of years. However, in the United States, attitudes toward medical care of inmates changed in observation of a prison riot that took place in 1971 at the Attica Correctional Facility in the state of New York. The Attica riot has been noted as a critical point in the reform of medical services in prisons due to the fact that, among inmate grievances, complaints against insufficient medical services were pronounced. Investigations followed this riot and found that unsanitary conditions existed and that correctional staff actively prevented inmates from obtaining medical services. In many cases, personnel working in the medical sector were unqualified and could not legally practice medicine in outside society.

Deliberate Indifference Revisited

Audio Link 15.2
Listen to the *Estelle v. Gamble* oral arguments.

During the 1970s, following the Attica Prison Riot, medical care drew more attention among correctional officials and the public. However, the Supreme Court decisions in a series of cases surrounding prison conditions hastened attention to medical care. In particular, the case of *Estelle v. Gamble* (1976) ushered in an era where medical services for inmates were normalized and required better than marginal care for inmates. In *Estelle v. Gamble*, the Supreme Court articulated the obligation of the state to provide inmates with adequate medical care.

The decision by the Court established a test to determine whether treatment given by prison officials was so insufficient as to constitute cruel and unusual punishment, in violation of the Eighth Amendment. The implication is that, in such cases, prison officials know that an inmate is in need of medical services, but, almost as an extension of their punishment, they are denied such services. In this case, the idea is that officials were being deliberately indifferent to the serious medical needs of inmates. In other words, they were ignoring the inmates' needs while being quite deliberately aware that the needs existed and were serious, not minor in nature. Some examples of deliberate indifference include denial or delay in providing treatment, providing inadequate treatment, or a failure to have qualified medical staff. Incidentally, prison systems will not evade liability if they cite inadequate funding as a reason for failing to provide medical services.

The Vagaries of Prison Life

While most inmates are young (crime tends to be a young man's game), they tend to have comparatively more medical issues than do other persons their age in mainstream society. There are several reasons that this is true. First, many offenders live unhealthy lifestyles prior to coming to prison such as the use of tobacco, drug and alcohol use, subsistence on a poor diet, risky sexual behaviors, and so forth. This lifestyle alone tends to put them at risk for illness, fatigue, infection, and diminished immune system functioning. Further, many have sexually transmitted diseases, tuberculosis, and other infectious diseases (Hanser, 2007).

FOCUS TOPIC: 15.2

Prison Medical Services Provide Assistance for Communicable Diseases Among Inmates in Baton Rouge

Prison Medical Services, the newest division under East Baton Rouge Emergency Medical Services, assumed operations of the medical services provided to all inmates incarcerated at the East Baton Rouge Parish Prison in Louisiana. Prison Medical Services is a unique system in that it provides 24-hour clinical care in addition to 24-hour advanced life support coverage. Prison Medical Services attends to the needs of approximately 1,500 inmates daily using a team of medics and nurses. The inmates have access to seeing one of two licensed physicians five days a week, a psychiatrist twice a week, and a dentist, social worker, and X-ray technician once a week.

Just months after its inception, Prison Medical Services implemented the Blood-borne Pathogens Program, which provides education and safety for all employees. Included in this program is the three-shot series of the Hepatitis B vaccine, the tuberculosis Tine skin test, and continuing education. In-services educates employees on the signs and symptoms of tuberculosis as well as prevention of this disease. Together with the Department of Public Health, Prison Medical Services has initiated the Sexually Transmitted Disease (STD) Program at the prison in which every inmate booked is tested within 24 hours of booking and treated, if necessary, within 48 hours. This program also educates every inmate on the dangers as well as the signs and symptoms of STDs.

Prison Medical Services' STD Program has proven so successful that it has become the pilot program for other jails and prisons statewide.

SOURCE: Baton Rouge Government Website. (2010). *Prison Medical Services*. Retrieved from http://brgov.com/dept/ems/prison.htm.

Prison environments tend to be clean enough for safety standards and to provide enough food for basic subsistence, but this still tends to be a Spartan existence. Given that inmates, while in prison, are near to one another on a daily basis, and given that germs and illnesses pass quickly between them, prisons do not tend to be conducive to good health. Further, the psychological impact of prison life tends to affect the body's physiological functioning; the stressors of prison life can and do take their toll upon the inmate's immune system.

Lastly, the inmate population tends to cycle back and forth into and out of prison. This has been discussed in prior chapters but is again important in the current discussion. As inmates leave prison, go back to their unhealthy lifestyles, and then return to prison, they bring with them to the community their illnesses (see Focus Topic 15.2). Their use of drugs and their participation in risky life choices further deteriorate their bodies, and, as they return back to prison, any negative health effects from this lifestyle are exacerbated by the prison environment. Thus, all individuals (including both inmates and correctional staff) within the prison should be educated on communicable illnesses and take precautions to avoid contracting germ-based health problems.

Audio Link 15.3
Hear about prison efforts to reduce the transmission of disease.

Clinics, Sick Call, and Standards of Care

In many prison facilities, sick call often requires that inmates fill out a form to request a visit to the unit infirmary. Inmates should be appraised of the procedures used to obtain medical services since, unlike in the free world, they cannot simply decide to see a doctor whenever they wish. Perhaps the best time to ensure that inmates are informed of procedures in obtaining medical assistance is orientation, during which written materials are handed out to inmates and they are expected to ask questions.

In order to avoid the abuse of sick call and the likelihood of malingering (faking an illness), many prison facilities have instituted a modest inmate copay system. In essence, inmates must pay a small fee to see a medical professional, and this tends to discourage most inmates from taking trips to the prison infirmary unless the request is legitimate. Administrators must be careful so that these types of programs are not seen as punitive. If this were the case, and if this were able to be upheld in a court of law, a potential violation of Eighth Amendment rights against cruel and unusual punishments could be found against the facility. The key is for administrators to, in good faith, lend assistance to inmates who are truly ill while, at the same time, holding inmates partially accountable for medical services when the illness is not severe.

Video Link 15.3
Learn more about medical care within prisons.

In addition, some issues are unique within prisons regarding the standard of care to which inmates are afforded. First, there can sometimes be problems with confidentiality in prisons due to the close

FOCUS TOPIC: 15.3

National Commission on Correctional Health Care Sets the Tone for Standards of Care in Correctional Settings

The National Commission on Correctional Health Care is committed to improving the quality of health care in jails, prisons, and juvenile confinement facilities. The NCCHC's origins date to the early 1970s, when an American Medical Association study of jails found inadequate, disorganized health services and a lack of national standards. In collaboration with other organizations, the AMA established a program that in the early 1980s became the National Commission on Correctional Health Care, an independent, not-for-profit 501(c)(3) organization whose early mission was to evaluate and develop policy and programs for a field clearly in need of assistance.

Today, the NCCHC's leadership in setting standards for health services in correctional facilities is widely recognized. Established by the health, legal, and corrections professions, the NCCHC's standards are recommendations for the management of a correctional health services system. Written in separate volumes for prisons, jails, and juvenile confinement facilities—and now with a manual specifically for mental health services—the standards cover the areas of care and treatment, health records, administration, personnel, and medical-legal issues. These essential resources have helped correctional and detention facilities improve the health of their inmates and the communities to which they return, increase the efficiency of health services delivery, strengthen organizational effectiveness, and reduce the risk of adverse legal judgments.

SOURCE: Adapted from the National Commission on Correctional Health Care Home Page. Retrieved from http://www.ncchc.org/about/index.html.

quarters and constant traffic in and out of spaces, including prison infirmary spaces. It is important to remember that inmates have a right to medical privacy, which means that medical personnel may not share details about an inmate's health or medical status with other correctional staff. This is particularly true if these persons are not medical staff. This still does not prevent security staff and other personnel from gaining access to protected medical information in the process of completing work assignments or through conversations with inmates. However, there are several exceptions to privacy, which are delineated in the **Health Insurance Portability and Accountability Act (HIPAA)**. HIPAA guidelines are well known among medical personnel and mental health personnel, and, for the most part, this act guides professionals on matters regarding the confidentiality of medical information.

Lastly, modern standards of care are governed by the **National Commission on Correctional Health Care (NCCHC)**, which is now the body that sets standards in correctional health care and accredits correctional facilities (see Focus Topic 15.3). The NCCHC provides technical assistance, educational programs for correctional staff, and clinical guidelines for medical staff. The outcome of this governing body has been uniform and appropriate medical and dental services as well as mental health and drug treatment programming that is both adequate and timely in availability. These services are, for all practical purposes, commensurate with what would be provided to persons who are not incarcerated.

Medical Services for Female Inmates

Audio Link 15.4

Listen to a clip about medical services for female inmates.

Students may recall from their readings in Chapter 11 that the needs for female offenders tend to vary from those of male offenders. It would be remiss to discuss medical care of inmates without providing some commentary on the specialized medical issues common to the female inmate population. Ross and Lawrence (2002) note that, increasingly, female offenders as a group are immersed in the illicit drug culture as alcoholics, drug addicts, or intimate partners of alcoholics or drug addicts. They note that research on syphilis indicates that incidence follows that of cocaine use in such a manner as to suggest an increasing prevalence of a sex-for-drugs lifestyle. Ross and Lawrence further state that the medical problems of these inmates are associated with those lifestyles prior to arriving in prison.

Common medical problems include asthma, diabetes, HIV/AIDS, tuberculosis, hypertension, unintended pregnancy, a variety of sexually transmitted diseases, and other sundry medical problems. While some of these medical issues are also common to men, they are becoming more common to women. Nevertheless, issues related to pregnancy are, of course, unique to female inmates, and with this in mind we turn our attention to services for birth control and pregnancy. In doing so, information from the BOP is provided as an example of the services that can and should be offered to female inmates.

Birth Control and Pregnancy

Female inmates should have access to medical and social services related to pregnancy, birth control, child placement, and abortion. Inmates are medically screened for pregnancy upon admission and are instructed to inform medical staff as soon as they suspect they are pregnant. If necessary, the childbirth takes place at a hospital outside the institution, and arrangements are made with outside social service agencies to aid the inmate in finding an appropriate placement for the child. Newborn children are not permitted to return to the institution with their mothers. Children can visit their mother when under the supervision and care of an adult visitor.

In addition, the BOP provides a community residential program called **Mothers and Infants Nurturing Together (MINT)** for women who are pregnant at the time of commitment. The MINT program is a residential reentry center–based program that promotes bonding and parenting skills for low-risk female inmates who are pregnant. Women are eligible to enter the program if they are in their last three months of pregnancy, have less than five years remaining to serve on their sentence, and are eligible for furlough. The inmate or a guardian must assume financial responsibility for the child's medical care while residing at MINT. The mother has three months to bond with the newborn child before returning to an institution to complete her sentence. In select MINT programs, the inmate may stay for an additional period of bonding with the child. The decision to refer an inmate to the MINT program is at the discretion of the inmate's unit team.

Abortion

As per federal law, the BOP is not allowed to use government funds to facilitate the performance of an abortion. However, funds are used to pay for abortion services only when the life of the mother would be endangered if the fetus is carried to term or in cases of rape. In all other cases, non-BOP funds must be obtained to pay for an abortion. Inmates receive medical, religious, and social counseling regarding their decision to carry the pregnancy to term or to have an elective abortion. If an inmate decides to have an abortion, arrangements are made for these medical services to be provided in an appropriate clinic outside the institution.

Journal Article Link 15.3
Read about the impact of forced-separation on incarcerated postpartum mothers.

PRISON FOOD SERVICE

As noted in the first two chapters of this text, early correctional history in the United States did not routinely consist of the use of prisons. Rather, other types of punishment were used (e.g., whipping, execution, slavery, exile) that did not require that inmates be housed on a long-term basis. Even when prisons did come into vogue, in many instances, inmates had to pay for their own food or complete sufficient labor to earn their food. Porridge, bread and water, beans, stew, and bitter coffee were typical menus. This state of affairs continued, for the most part, until the early 1970s when the Attica Prison Riot occurred. During this time, the courts became more involved in determining prison operations, and the federal courts, in particular, were very directive. Nevertheless, there were no clear standards as this process unfolded.

The American Correctional Association (ACA) emerged as the primary body that administrators looked to for guidelines in operation. Started in 1977, this organization provided practitioners with assistance in resolving discrepancies in their prison operations from what courts were requiring that they do. Among the various issues addressed in prisons, food services were one key feature identified as needing improvement during this time. In today's world, the ACA provides prison administrators with guidance on how well-organized food service departments should operate.

Lastly, and even more specific to food service programming in the prison environment, another body known as the **American Correctional Food Service Association (ACFSA)** works to represent the correctional food service industry. This organization promotes professionalism and sets standards of performance within this specialized area of correctional operations. This organization also provides for national certification of professionals working in the food service industry in corrections. The ACFSA hosts conferences and provides training workshops for professionals in food services. This organization also conducts site visits and provides administrators with a background set of guidelines that they can use as guidance when governing correctional kitchen operations.

Prison Tour Video Link 15.3
Watch a discussion about prison food service.

CORRECTIONS AND THE LAW 15.1

The Use of Food Loaf Based on Prison Safety and Security

During the 1990s, substantial controversy was generated over the use of a particular type of food product in prisons: food loaf. The questions surrounding the use of this product eventually led to legal questions in the Section 1983 lawsuit of *LeMaire v. Maass* (1993). In this suit, the plaintiff, inmate LeMaire, considered the conditions of the Oregon prison (particularly the use of food loaf) to be unconstitutional. However, it is important to understand the circumstances surrounding this case because they help to provide context in the security conditions that existed. In the actual records of the court case, the federal district court had described the inmates at Oregon's Disciplinary Segregation Unit (DSU) as extremely dangerous, with staff working under "the constant threat of unpredictable assaults and bombardment with feces, urine, spit, food, and any available movable object" (*LeMaire v. Maass*, 1993, p. 1447). Inmate LeMaire's behavior was similar to that of other inmates in the DSU.

Inmate LeMaire constantly made threats to conduct further assaults, both while in and while out of lockup. Prior to being sentenced to prison, LeMaire had slit a man's throat and had assaulted correctional officers and inmates with sharpened poles, feces, and a homemade knife once inside. In a two-year period, he had accumulated over 25 serious disciplinary infractions. Further, while in lockup he was prone to assaulting staff by throwing urine and feces upon them and even tried to deliberately hit staff in the facial region with these noxious substances. Thus, he was dangerous, even while in the DSU. Among LeMaire's complaints in his lawsuit, it was the use of the Nutraloaf (prison food loaf) that proved to be interesting because the federal district court had agreed with LeMaire that the use of this food alternative was unconstitutional.

However, the 9th Circuit Court of Appeals disagreed with the lower court and overruled its decision. The 9th Circuit determined that the Eighth Amendment requires only that inmates be given food "that is adequate to maintain health; it need not be tasty or aesthetically pleasing" (p. 1456). The fact that the food occasionally contains foreign objects or sometimes is served cold, while unpleasant, does not amount to a constitutional deprivation (citing *Hutto v. Finney*, 1978). They further stated that "Nutraloaf provides an excess of nutritional requirements and LeMaire, unlike the *Hutto* inmates who lost weight, has actually gained some sixty pounds in confinement. LeMaire is not being starved. He is being fed, and he is being fed adequately" (p. 1456). The 9th Circuit concluded by using a familiar catchphrase in prison case law by indicating that the use of the prison food loaf was not "incompatible with 'the evolving standards of decency' that mark the progress of a maturing society" (citing *Estelle v. Gamble*, 1976).

In further clarifying its ruling, the 9th Circuit stated that in the *Hutto v. Finney* (1978) case, the Supreme Court observed that serving inmates a tasteless food concoction called grue, which provided approximately 1,000 calories a day, might be tolerable if just for a few days but could be unconstitutional if it were served over a period of weeks or months, the concern being starvation of inmates. However, the 9th Circuit determined that Nutraloaf and grue were not comparable because Nutraloaf was intentionally made to be nutritious and well balanced as a meal alternative. Thus, the fact that a food product is not tasty for inmates is irrelevant from a legalistic perspective. Simply put, prison administrators ultimately are only required to ensure that inmates are given a healthy diet that is nutritious, not one that is pleasant to the taste buds. It then appears that the use of food for purposes of social control is acceptable in the world of corrections, both as a reward for good behavior and as a consequence of bad behavior.

SOURCE: *LeMaire v. Maass*, 12 F. 3d 1444—9th Circuit (1993).

Planning the Menu

The menu planning process is usually done on a 28- to 30-day rotation cycle, and these plans are usually prepared by the overall supervisor of food services or the assigned dietitian. Menus are usually planned according to national standards set by the National Academy of Sciences. There tend to be a variety of factors to consider in food preparation. The state of Connecticut Department of Correction (2010), in its administrative directive (directive number 10.18) titled *Nutrition and Food Services*, denotes the planning criteria of the master menu as follows:

> Master Menu Planning Criteria. The Correctional Chief of Food Services shall prepare menus considering nutritional adequacy, inmate preferences, costs, physical layout, cost of equipment and staff complement, variety in method of preparation and frequency and other relevant factors to good dietary practice. Preparation shall consider food flavor, texture, temperature, appearance, and palatability. (p. 2)

Video Link 15.4

Watch a clip about the food menu in prisons.

According to the Connecticut prison system, **common fare** is a diet that meets all nutritional requirements and reasonably accommodates recognized religious dietary restrictions. This demonstrates that the planning of the menu can be somewhat complicated and that, at a minimum, general dietary health should be considered. Further, the inmate population can be quite diverse both ethnically and due to medical needs. Food service managers often take these issues into consideration as well when preparing their menu cycles.

Feeding and Security

Prison kitchens can be breeding grounds for contraband of all types within the prison. Naturally, contraband can include any sort of kitchen tool, such as knives and cutlery, poisonous substances, or food items that can be used to make homemade alcohol (e.g., fruits and yeast). When nonsecurity personnel are hired to work with inmates in food preparation, they should be trained in security techniques and practices. As a means of maintaining control over these items, an inventory is taken daily, and inmates are required to formally sign these tools out. Many kitchens use what is called a shadow board, which is usually a board with the silhouette of the item drawn on the board so that missing kitchen tools can be quickly identified.

The use of secure storage facilities for food products that can be used to manufacture alcohol is also required. Kitchen staff must be alert so that inmates are not able to sneak products out of the kitchen area. In addition to inspecting the inmates, they should ensure that these products have not been hidden in the kitchen, placed in the trash (so that the food product can be taken out of the kitchen area undetected), or hidden in items that go in and out of the dining facility. It is important to note that junior and/or inexperienced staff may not realize when certain foods can be problematic and therefore may not prevent much of the contraband that occurs from the kitchen. Because of this, they must be trained on food usage, both for meal preparation and as a means of contraband. This last comment brings us to our next section: the training requirements for prison kitchen staff.

Training Requirements

Training requirements for prison kitchen staff can vary, but the personnel must have documented understanding of the planning, preparation, and serving of nutritious meals using sanitary and safe conditions. These individuals usually must have knowledge of kitchen work such that they know how to direct and lead people who must work together in a coordinated fashion. In addition, it is important that the kitchen manager ensures that those working in the kitchen are ethical and that they are appropriate for the job. Because inmates can be unpredictable and spiteful of one another, the kitchen manager will need to ensure that none of the inmate workers (or staff, for that matter) acts in an inappropriate or unsanitary manner when serving other inmates. In addition, persons in the kitchen should not give "extra" food during meals to inmates who do not have an authorized basis for such allocations.

Food Service Facilities and Equipment

Food service facilities and equipment vary from one jail or prison to another (Johnson, 2008). Some facilities may have equipment that is not up-to-date and where kitchen workers must work with challenges inherent to the equipment itself. Most prison kitchen setups are in a cafeteria-style arrangement, and inmates are usually fed three meals a day. It is important to understand that the feeding times for inmates may not be during the hours that most people would expect. Indeed, there may be some pliability in the times that inmates are fed depending on programming requirements, work schedules, and other factors that may impact scheduling.

In addition, some areas of the prison may require that inmates be given a food tray within their cell. For instance, inmates in administrative segregation and/or solitary confinement will usually be given a plastic tray that is kept in a heated food cart or otherwise stored for portable delivery. In cases where lockdown facilities are being fed, officers in the department will usually provide the inmates with their food tray, utensils, and required liquid beverage.

Food Supplies and Storage

Johnson (2008) notes that food should be of the best quality possible within budgetary constraints. This is true for multiple reasons, but, among others, providing decent food minimizes the amount of inmate discontent that can exist within the facility. Having good quality nutritional food keeps inmates in good

Journal Article Link 15.4
Read about the implications of food allergies for correctional institutions.

Video Link 15.5
Learn more about security in prison kitchens.

health and therefore reduces the amount of illness and other health problems that might arise; this is important because lower medical costs translate to savings for prison administrators.

As to food service equipment within a prison kitchen, this is typically similar to what one would find in any large-scale cafeteria. However, the various kitchen products may have various security features not found in free-world kitchens. For instance, the company Jail Equipment World markets a maximum-security convection oven. The description of this product explains that this maximum-security version of the oven prevents "the tampering of control and product settings, protect[s] ovens and essential components from vandalism and abuse, eliminate[s] hiding places for contraband and prohibit[s] the removal of parts and components for weapon fabrication" (Jail Equipment World, 2010, p. 1). These ovens carry a price tag of $5,200 to $12,000 each (Jail Equipment World, 2010, p. 1). This example demonstrates that kitchen appliances must meet functional requirements as well as security requirements, and this type of equipment carries a hefty price tag in some cases.

The Quality of Food as Leverage for Social Control

While it is clear that prisons have a legal obligation to ensure that minimal standards for nutrition are met when feeding the inmate population, there is not any requirement that they go beyond this. However, there may be incentives for correctional administrators who budget additional funds within their menu list. For instance, during holidays, most prisons serve some type of meal that is consistent with the holiday that occurs. Wardens who are able to allocate additional funds for special meals and events will greatly improve morale among inmates.

This can also work for programming and therapeutic activities. For example, when inmates know that the prison will be serving cake at a particular social function, they look forward to what in prison is considered a delicacy, the fresh-made cake. This can work wonders in building motivation among inmates and in getting interest in other areas of programming that they might not necessarily find initially appealing. Further, when inmates know that upcoming special meals are likely to be served, they will tend to avoid disciplinary problems so as not to miss out on the opportunity. While this may only work for the short term, it does still provide some degree of leverage with much of the inmate population.

PHOTO 15.7

Prison food loaf, pictured here, is a concoction that mixes the ingredients of a given prison meal into one single baked loaf of food product.

Further still, the type of food that one is served in prison may be modified due to disciplinary reasons. While it is generally not considered good correctional practice to use food allocation for punishment, prison systems do alter the way it is served for inmates who have some type of special security status or disciplinary consideration. Focus Topic 15.4 provides insight on how "prison loaf" is used as a replacement meal for inmates in various disciplinary statuses. In particular, this type of meal alternative may be given to inmates who are hostile and in lockdown (i.e., solitary confinement for assaultive behavior). It is not uncommon for these inmates to throw their food or liquid beverages on correctional officers and/or to use their utensils as weapons. While this may not sound overly problematic, when hot coffee is thrown on an officer or when salt is thrown in the eyes of another officer or inmate, this can cause injury that lasts for days. The use of products such as the prison food loaf eliminates safety and security concerns when feeding inmates with this type of behavioral history.

APPLIED THEORY 15.1

General Strain Theory, Inmate Satisfaction, and Prison Control

General strain theory, developed by Robert Agnew (1992), is based on the premise that persons experience strain when they are not able to obtain goals that they desire. These goals can entail money, status, and even self-efficacy. In some cases, persons may resort to criminal activities to alleviate this strain or to obtain their desired goal. However, strain is not caused only by the failure to achieve one's goals, often referred to as *goal blockage*; it can occur when some type of *undesired stimulus* presents itself or, just as important, when some *valued stimulus* is taken away from the offender.

This theory, though not very complicated, provides a good framework from which to understand the effectiveness of prison programming, life conditions in prison, and the maintenance of control over the inmate population. First, many inmates hope to get out of prison in a quick fashion and will often participate in programs to accumulate good time (early release) credit when completing those programs. Once they begin to put time and commitment into those programs and set their goal for completing a given program, the idea that they may be thwarted from obtaining their goal will tend to cause strain. The experience of strain is unpleasant, and most inmates will, generally speaking, seek to avoid this strain. Thus, prison administrators can and do place additional expectations upon inmates with the implication that, if they wish to complete a given program (and obtain the corresponding good time credits for early release), they must be willing to engage in certain prosocial activities and/or duties within the prison. This type of leverage over their behavior, when used in moderation (an excessive amount of strain for leverage can backfire), can achieve positive outcomes where inmates are guided—and essentially coerced—into positive behaviors. Thus, the desire to avoid goal blockage can be a motivator for inmates.

This type of strain-inducing technique can be used in prison-based drug treatment programs where inmates may be reluctant to commit to the program and/or complete activities within the program. As long as they wish to obtain the good time rewards, they must conduct themselves in a manner that ensures that treatment professionals observe positive behavior. While the inmates may be engaging in deception, they will tend to absorb some of the benefits from treatment, even if it is nearly accidental on their part.

Further, the use of undesired stimuli can be beneficial within prison programming for inmate services. Consider, for example, the use of prison food loaf (discussed in the food services section of this chapter). When inmates are under disciplinary provisions for assault and considered volatile toward staff, they may be given this food alternative rather than a typical meal. While the food loaf meets all nutritional requirements for an inmate's overall health, this food product has a taste described as bland, at best. Most inmates would agree that the experience of eating food loaf is an undesirable stimulus that, unless the circumstances made it necessary to eat such a product, they would rather avoid.

Lastly, strain can be experienced by taking some valued stimulus away from an inmate. This type of strain is not hard to imagine within the correctional setting. Indeed, one could say that the very act of imprisonment is the epitome of this type of strain because the most valued of stimuli—freedom—has been taken away from the inmate. It is expected that the strain from having their liberty (a valued stimulus) taken from them will deter many inmates from committing crimes in the future. Beyond this, any number of privileges can be restricted from inmates, such as the ability to engage in different forms of recreational activities. As we have seen in this chapter, recreational services can consist of a variety of artistic, active, or social endeavors that are often valued by inmates who seek to avoid boredom and idleness in prison. When these types of stimuli are restricted or removed, this will produce general strain for most inmates. In order to avoid this sense of strain, inmates are likely to comply with prison rules and regulations. This demonstrates how programming within prisons can be used to maintain prison control and also shows how prison officials can calibrate inmates' behavior based on their desire to avoid various aspects of general strain that can occur within the prison facility.

SOURCE: Lilly, J. R., Cullen, F. T., & Ball, R. A. (2007). *Criminological theory: Context and consequences* (4th ed.). Thousand Oaks, CA: Sage.

Prison food loaf is a food product that contains all the typical ingredients of a well-balanced meal that would be served to inmates who do not have disciplinary problems; these ingredients are mixed together and baked as a single loaf-like product that, while bland in flavor, is quite nutritious when considering vitamin, mineral, and caloric content. This type of food product is not used for punishment as much as it is intended to avoid the possibility of safety problems for inmates and staff. In other words, this type of food alternative is safer to serve to inmates who are dangerous and unpredictable. Legal issues related to this food product emerged during the 1990s with inmates contending that being fed prison food loaf was cruel and unusual punishment, in violation of their Eighth Amendment rights. One case, in particular, was *LeMaire v. Maass* (1993). Further information regarding this case is provided in Corrections and the Law 15.1.

CONCLUSION

This chapter has provided an extensive overview of many of the typical programs offered to inmates within the prison environment. The programs that have been discussed include educational, vocational, drug treatment, medical, recreational, food service, and religious programs. Though other types of programs are available to inmates, these types of programs tend to be universal in the means by which they are implemented, and they all tend to be used by nearly every inmate who serves time in the United States. This conclusion will not address each of these programs individually but will instead point toward one key theme that has been consistently mentioned throughout this chapter.

Throughout this chapter, students have learned that each of these programs works to improve inmate conditions within the prison and that, as a result, each program lowers observed infractions among inmates and also reduces the likelihood of lawsuits and/or prison riots. Further, most of these programs have legal requirements that make them at least marginally necessary within the prison environment. Regardless of whether each program is constitutionally required, it is clear that each provides benefits to both the inmates and the staff who work with them. This is an important observation because it can therefore be said that, in a roundabout manner, these programs reduce problems in prison facilities and, even more encouraging, they reduce recidivism when inmates are released into the community. Thus, prison programming is a smart investment that, in the longest of terms, saves taxpayers more money than it costs them and enhances public safety in future years when inmates are released from prison. To overlook the importance of prison programming is to be negligent in safeguarding our community's very safety.

END-OF-CHAPTER DISCUSSION QUESTIONS

1. What are some of the basic prison services offered to inmates in prison? How important are these services in maintaining institutional harmony in the prison?

2. Who is Austin MacCormick, and what is his significance to educational programming in corrections?

3. Refer to Focus Topic 15.1. Identify and discuss some of the key benefits to educational programming in corrections.

4. Provide an overview of one of the prison work programs presented in this chapter.

5. What are some distinct forms of programming that exist for female offenders?

6. Discuss some of the important legal issues associated with food services in corrections.

7. Explain how general strain theory provides a good framework from which to understand the effectiveness of prison programming and the maintenance of control over the inmate population.

8. Explain how general strain theory can be related to issues of prison control among inmates.

KEY TERMS

American Correctional Food Service Association (ACFSA)

Austin MacCormick

Chief Justice Warren Burger

Common fare

English as a Second Language (ESL)

Federal Prison Industries Inc. (FPI)

General educational development (GED)

Health Insurance Portability and Accountability Act (HIPAA)

Higher Education Opportunity Act

Hutto v. Finney (1978)

LeMaire v. Maass (1993)

Life Skills for State & Local Prisoners Program

Minimal services view

Mothers and Infants Nurturing Together (MINT)

National Commission on Correctional Health Care (NCCHC)

Office of Correctional Education (OCE)

Pell Grants

Post-Release Employment Project (PREP)

PRIDE Re-Entry and Transition Program

Prison food loaf

Prison Industry Enhancement (PIE) Certification Program

Prison Rehabilitative Industries and Diversified Enterprises, Inc. (PRIDE)

Ready to Work Program

Test of Basic Adult Education (TABE)

Texas Correctional Industries (TCI)

Title IV of the Higher Education Act

UNICOR Inc.

Windham School District

Work Against Recidivism (WAR) Program

Work/education reform view

APPLIED EXERCISE 15.1

Students must conduct either a face-to-face or a phone interview with a staff person in a prison facility who works in one of the following fields: (1) inmate education, (2) job training, (3) recreational supervision, (4) substance abuse treatment, or (5) religious programming. The student must set up a day and time with that practitioner and interview him or her to gain his or her insight and perspective on several key questions related to work in his or her field. Students must write the practitioner's responses, analyze those responses, and submit their draft by the deadline set by their instructor. Students should complete this application exercise as a minipaper that addresses each point below. The total word count should be 1,400 to 2,100 words.

When completing the interview, students should ask the following questions:

1. What are the most rewarding aspects of your job?

2. What are the most stressful aspects of your job?

3. How does your work help offenders to eventually reintegrate into society?

4. What are some challenges that you have in helping inmates?

5. Why did you choose to work in this field?

6. What type of training have you received for this line of work?

7. What would you recommend to someone who was interested in pursuing a similar career?

In addition, you should ensure that your submission has appropriate spelling and grammar throughout. Lastly, students are required to provide contact information for the auxiliary staff member. Please obtain the following information from the person that you interview. While instructors will probably not need to contact him or her, it may become necessary so that they can validate the actual completion of an interview.

Name and title of correctional supervisor: _____

Correctional agency: _____

Practitioner's phone number: _____

Practitioner's e-mail address: _____

Name of student: _____

"WHAT WOULD YOU DO?"

You are a correctional officer assigned to the agricultural section of a minimum-security facility. Your facility is large, with over 2,800 inmates who live on the property, most of them in dorm-like structures that have minimal security requirements. The classification of most of these inmates either is the level of "trustee" or is minimum security. None of them is known to have been violent.

You have recently been assigned to a field squad run by several "field bosses," as they are called, who are correctional officers with experience supervising inmates who work in agricultural settings. Each field boss has his or her own horse, field radio, revolver, and rifle to ensure that security is maintained during the day. The work is hot, and the inmates work very hard.

On your fourth day of work, you notice that the ranking officer, Sergeant Gunderson, allows two inmates, inmate Dooley and inmate Craft, to go off into a wooded section at the edge of the clearing. They emerge a little later and talk with the sergeant and then go back to work.

You watch this same routine continue during much of the month of July. You finally ask one of the other officers about what you notice, and he says to you, "You know, Mack, I just tend to watch over my assigned inmates and don't worry about too much else. So long as they ain't escaping and as long as the Sarge is happy, I just stay out of it. Maybe they gotta use the restroom or something . . . like, maybe they got bladder control problems or something." You ponder over it, and after two more days, you ask Sergeant Gunderson about what you observe.

Sergeant Gunderson says, "I would not be worried about them. They are old trustees who never hurt nobody and will likely be here forever. They kinda just wanna ride their time out, and I really do not see the need to rock the boat. Besides, you need to know that they have a long history with one of the assistant wardens here." He looks at you, pulling his straw-rimmed Stetson hat back a bit, and then says, "Believe it or not, those two like to work this detail, but, anytime that they want, they can pick another detail at the dorm or elsewhere, and they will get the job switch within 48 hours. They have their reasons, and I have mine, for why things work as they do. You understand?"

You shake your head up and down, say "Yeah, I get it," and leave the issue alone.

However, later that day, you happen to see, from a distance, the two inmates loading what appears to be a couple of watermelons into the back of a wagon that held work tools and sundry items. They also had several potatoes that were stacked on the wagon. They covered the produce with a tarp as you rode up and looked at you with a puzzled and worried look. You ask them what they are doing.

One of them, inmate Dooley, responds by saying, "We were just going to see if there were any additional work hoes available, but see that there aren't—why, what's wrong, Boss?"

You look at him and say, "Nuthin', just thought I would see what was going on—you guys get back to work." You watch them turn and go toward the main group.

The next day, you wait until Sergeant Gunderson is preoccupied with another officer and explaining the details of some work assignment. You quickly guide your horse to the edge of the woods where you have spotted inmates Dooley and Craft travel. You see a faint trail, and, when you careen your neck forward a bit and look, there is a small clearing where you view something that is unmistakable: a watermelon patch and, nearby, several potato plants.

Knowing what you know about inmates and the prison subculture, you recognize these two items as being prime ingredients for making homemade alcohol. In fact, you recall that some officers who work the dorms have noted that some inmates appear drunk on some occasions.

You come to your senses, look for Sergeant Gunderson, and also see that inmates Dooley and Craft have their backs to you, nearly 50 yards away. You quickly turn your gray gelding around, gently pulling the reins so as not to turn too quickly or too obviously. You ride slowly back to a location that provides a full field of vision over the inmates whom you are required to supervise. You count them and find that all are accounted for and think to yourself, "Those two inmates are growing products to make alcohol, and Gunderson knows all about it, but he is not doing anything about it." Then you wonder, "How long has this been going on, and who all knows about this?"

Lastly, you wonder to yourself, **"What should I do?"**

CROSS-NATIONAL PERSPECTIVE 15.1

Medical Services in Prison Systems in Other Countries

Before beginning this assignment, students should read the following excerpts related to United Nations and European Union standards on prison health care.

The International Covenant on Economic, Social and Cultural Rights

Article 12 recognizes

...the right of everyone to the enjoyment of the highest attainable standard of physical and mental health.

The UN Basic Principle for the Treatment of Prisoners

Principle 9 requires that:

Prisoners shall have access to the health care services available in the country without discrimination on the grounds of their legal situation.

The Standards Minimum Rules for the Treatment of Prisoners

Article 22 provides that:

...the medical services in prisons should be organized in Close relationship to the general health administration of the community or nation...

The United Nations Principles of Medical Ethics Relevant to the Roles of Health Personnel, Particularly Physicians, in the Protection of Prisoners and Detainees against Torture and Other Cruel, Inhuman or Degrading Treatment or Punishment

Principle I states that:

Health personnel, particularly physicians, charged with the medical care of prisoners and detainees have a duty to provide them with protection of their physical and mental health and treatment of disease of the same quality and standards as is afforded to those who are not imprisoned or detained.

Article 19:

Doctors who work in prisons should provide the individual inmate with the same standards of health care as are being delivered to patients in the community. The health needs of the inmate should always be the primary concern of the doctor.

Prisoners very often originate from the most vulnerable sectors of society – the poor, the mentally ill, those dependent on alcohol or drugs. These groups already have an increased risk of diseases such as TB. In prison, these problems are amplified by poor living conditions and overcrowding. A prison climate of violence and humiliation aggravates the situation, creating obstacles in accessing health care and promoting released back into society, bringing with them the illness and behaviours generated and worsened by their incarceration.

Question 1: How are the standards for prison medical care in other countries similar to those that we have discussed throughout this text?

Question 2: What can we learn when considering the medical challenges facing prison systems in other nations besides the United States?

Question 3: How are these challenges similar to those that prison systems face in the United States?

SOURCE: Prison Healthcare Project. (2004). *Improving prison healthcare in Eastern Europe and Central Asia.* London: International Centre for Prison Studies, Kings College, London.

chapter 16

Therapeutic, Recreational, and Religious Programming

LEARNING OBJECTIVES:

1. Identify components of substance abuse treatment in prison.

2. Discuss how substance abuse treatment programs affect potential recidivism.

3. Explain how recreation can affect inmate behavior in the prison.

4. Discuss some of the concerns for administrators with different types of recreational programming.

5. Identify some of the legal issues associated with religious programming in prisons.

INTRODUCTION

This chapter will focus on the various prison programs and services that are therapeutic, recreational, or religious in nature. These types of programming typically go beyond the basics of subsistence and housing offenders within a prison, but they tend to be very important in managing offenders' behavior and in aiding their outcomes once they are released from prison. In each type of programming, prison systems incur a cost of time and resources, and, for the most part, it is difficult for these facilities to realize a direct gain from their existence. However, the potential benefit to society outweighs the short-term institutional benefits. Further, these programs aid prison personnel in shaping inmate behavior behind the walls, giving them an additional tool for reward and restriction that can and does affect day-to-day inmate interactions amongst each other and with prison staff. It is for these reasons that these programs are offered.

DRUG TREATMENT PROGRAMS

"Studies have consistently shown that comprehensive drug treatment works. It not only reduces drug use but also curtails criminal behavior and recidivism. Moreover, for drug-abusing offenders, treatment facilitates successful reentry into the community."

Dr. Nora D. Volkow, director of the National
Institute on Drug Abuse (see Volkow, 2006)

Audio Link 16.1
Hear about how drug treatment programs can reduce recidivism.

The Bureau of Justice Statistics (BJS) and the National Center on Addiction and Substance Abuse (CASA) estimate that from 60% to 83% of inmates in the nation's correctional population have used drugs at some point in their lives; this is twice the estimated drug use of the total U.S. population (Office of National Drug Control Policy [ONDCP], 2001). Included in the 80% are inmates who used an illegal drug at least weekly for a period of at least one month, have been imprisoned for selling or possessing drugs, were under the influence of drugs or alcohol when they committed their crime, committed their offense to get money for drugs, or have a history of alcohol abuse. As stated before, drugs are commonly linked with crime, the issue being not if but how they are linked.

The primary modality implemented in most jails is simple chemical detoxification. Detoxification is designed for persons dependent on narcotic drugs (e.g., heroin, opium) and is typically found in inpatient settings with programs that last for 7 to 21 days. While many detoxification programs address only the addict's physical dependence, some provide individual or group counseling in an attempt to address the problems associated with drug abuse. Many detoxification programs use medical drugs to ease the process of overcoming the physical symptoms of dependence that make the detoxification process so painful for the addicted substance abuser. For drug offenders in jails in prisons, the mechanism of detoxification varies by the client's major drug of addiction. For opiate users, methadone or clonidine is preferred.

In all detoxification programs, inmate success depends upon following established protocols for drug administration and withdrawal. In a recent assessment of research literature on the effectiveness of detoxification, there appear to be promising rates of program completion (McNeece, Springer, & Arnold, 2002). Yet many clinicians note that mere detoxification from a substance is not drug abuse "treatment" and does not help people stay off drugs. This in no way ensures that relapse will not occur, and thus it is important for any program to have much more than a simple detoxification process. This should instead be viewed as nothing more than an initial step after the intake process of comprehensive treatment.

Peer Support Groups

Within many prison facilities, peer support programs are integral components of alcohol or drug intervention strategies. These programs are called "peer support" because, in many cases, the facilitators are also prior alcohol or drug abusers. In many prisons, peer support groups are facilitated by other inmates who have progressed to an advanced or senior level of involvement in the program. Perhaps the most widely known peer support group is the 12-step program, in which individuals meet regularly to stabilize and facilitate their recovery from substance abuse.

The best known is Alcoholics Anonymous (AA), in which sobriety is based on fellowship and adhering to the 12 steps of recovery (Hanson, Venturelli, & Fleckenstein, 2006; Myers & Salt, 2000). The 12 steps stress faith, confession of wrongdoing, and passivity in the hands of a "higher power," and move group members from a statement of powerlessness over drugs and alcohol to a resolution that they will carry the message of help to others and will practice the AA principles in all affairs. In addition to AA, other popular self-help 12-step groups are Narcotics Anonymous, Cocaine Anonymous, and Drugs Anonymous (Hanson et al., 2002; Inciardi, 1999; Myers & Salt, 2000). All of these organizations operate as stand-alone fellowship programs but are also used as adjuncts to other modalities. Although few evaluation studies of self-help groups have been carried out, the weight of clinical and observational data suggests that they are crucial to recovery. Research has failed to demonstrate that anonymous fellowship meetings by themselves are effective with heavy drug users.

The success of self-help programs in general, and AA in particular, may be explained by its comprehensive network, which supports abstinence and recovery; frequent attendance at AA meetings where role modeling, confession, sharing, and support take place; and participation in the member network between meetings, including obtaining and relying on a senior member or sponsor. Al-Anon, a fellowship for relatives and significant others of alcoholics, was founded in 1951, although it did not take off as a movement until the 1960s. Narcotics Anonymous, the third of the three major 12-step fellowships, was founded in 1953. It was relatively small throughout the 1950s and 1960s but obtained a great deal of popularity during the 1970s and 1980s (Myers & Salt, 2000).

Outpatient treatment is the most common form of treatment for substance-abusing offenders. This involves organized nonresidential treatment services that the client visits at least once a week for up to about 10 hours per week. Some of these programs are referred to as intensive outpatient (treatment) programs (IOPs) (McNeece et al., 2002), and provide fully structured treatment settings in which the client participates from 10 to 30 hours per week. The broad category of intensive outpatient treatment may include programs that term themselves day treatment or, in a medical setting, partial hospitalization. Clients in IOPs may remain living at home, in a therapeutic or long-term residence, or in apartment dwellings as part of a special program of comprehensive treatment (McNeese et al., 2002). All of the components of rehabilitative treatment should be provided including counseling (individual, group, and family), treatment planning, crisis management, medication management, client education, self-help education, and so forth.

The Therapeutic Community

Beyond the detoxification phase of "treatment," the residential therapeutic community is the next full-service form of treatment given to substance abusers in jails, prisons, or residential treatment centers. The therapeutic community is a total treatment environment in which the primary clinical staff are typically former substance abusers—"recovering addicts"—who themselves were rehabilitated in therapeutic communities (Inciardi, 1999; Myers & Salt, 2000). Recovery through this form of treatment depends on positive and negative pressures to change. This pressure is brought about through a self-help process in which relationships of mutual responsibility to every resident in the program are built. In addition to individual and group counseling, this process has a system of explicit rewards that reinforce the value of earned achievement. As such, privileges are earned. In addition, therapeutic communities have their own rules and regulations that guide the behavior of residents and the management of facilities. Their purposes are to maintain the safety and health of the community and to train and teach residents through the use of discipline. There are typically numerous rules and regulations within these facilities (Hanser & Mire, 2010).

Video Link 16.1
Learn more about substance abuse programs.

Journal Article Link 16.1
Read about the relationship between prison therapeutic communities and prison order.

THE BENEFITS OF SUBSTANCE ABUSE TREATMENT IN CORRECTIONS

Aside from education and employment, effective drug treatment is perhaps the most commonly needed form of inmate programming provided. Every state correctional system offers some variety of drug treatment programming, but it is the means by which these programs are offered that tend to determine their effectiveness. The best means of reducing recidivism among nonviolent drug offenders is through drug treatment admissions rather than imprisonment.

TECHNOLOGY AND EQUIPMENT 16.1

Computerized and Web-Enabled Addiction Severity Index

The Addiction Severity Index – Multimedia Version (ASI-MV®) interview is the client self-administered version of the widely used Addiction Severity Index (ASI). Inflexxion, with several grants from the National Institute on Drug Abuse (NIDA), developed and tested the ASI-MV and studies have shown it to have excellent reliability and validity. Since developing the ASI-MV in the early 1990s, Inflexxion also received NIDA grant support to research and develop the Spanish language ASI-MV and the Comprehensive Health Assessment for Teens (CHAT®).

Clients self-administer these interviews on a computer with audio and video using a mouse. Since these tools do not require staff time to ask the questions or collect data, they save agencies staff time and money, while increasing the consistency of data collection. It has been found that clients are able to easily use these programs, regardless of education level, reading ability, or prior computer experience.

In addition to clinical reports, which are immediately available for treatment planning and level of care placement, the system also includes the Analytics Data Center,

FIGURE 16.1   ASI-MV Graphic Profiles

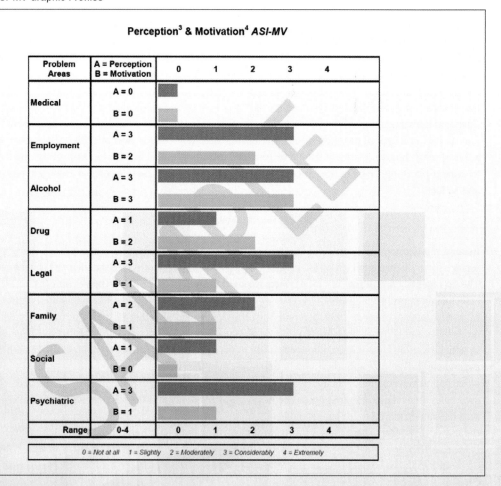

CLINICAL NOTE: Any Domain without a score (where there is an "X") is a result of the client not answering key questions in those areas. If this occurs, the clinician can go over the questions in that Domain with the client in a face-to-face meeting (Domain questions are provided in the "Question/Answer Report").

[3]Perception is a how troubled or bothered a client is by problems.

[4]Motivation is how important it is for the client to receive help for problems now.

SOURCE: ASI-MV (2012). Newton, MA: Inflexxion, Inc. Reprinted with permission from Inflexxion, Inc./ASI-MV. Retrieved from: https://www.asi-mvconnect.com.

which enables providers to anonymously track trends, characteristics and outcomes of their population.

The ASI-MV online system, which includes the ASI-MV and CHAT interviews and Analytics, are all part of the Behavioral Health Connect system of tools available only through Inflexxion (www.ASI-MVConnect.com).

ASI-MV Analytics is an online resource for substance abuse and mental health agencies, as well as treatment centers that provides easy access to de-identified, aggregate data uploaded from the ASI-MV system through a secure upload process. This enables organizations to easily view assessment, utilization, and outcome data associated with the ASI-MV interview.

The ASI-MV produces, on demand, numerous reports that can be used by treatment staff and administrators. Reports summarize client self-reported data from across all domains, and arrange the data in a useful manner to assist clinicians with treatment planning.

The summary includes problem lists and the following key clusters:

- Client's perception of problems
- Client's motivation to get help for problems
- Possible psychiatric risks
- Potential strengths/supports
- Recovery environment—assets and liabilities

These reports also contain an outcome comparison form, which a clinician can use to track progress; a blank treatment plan form or template; and a sheet listing available client handouts and worksheets. In the world of substance abuse treatment, the optimal integration of assessment and outcome data to maximize client programming makes for a well-designed and comprehensive means of treatment service delivery.

SOURCE: ASI-MV (2012). Newton, MA: Inflexxion, Inc. Reprinted with permission from Inflexxion, Inc./ASI-MV. Retrieved from: https://www.asi-mvconnect.com.

Indeed, increases in admissions to substance abuse treatment are associated with reductions in crime rates. According to the Justice Policy Institute (2008), admissions to drug treatment increased by 37.4%, and federal spending on drug treatment increased by 14.6% from 1995 to 2005. During the same period, violent crime fell by 31.5%. These figures are similar to other research in the field that consistently demonstrates that drug treatment programming reduces crime and recidivism.

Further, and even more specific to the point of this chapter, it has been shown that increased admissions to drug treatment are associated with reduced incarceration rates (see Figure 16.2). Indeed, of the 20 states that admit the most people to treatment per 100,000, 19 had incarceration rates below the national average. Of the 20 states that admitted the fewest people to treatment per 100,000, 8 had incarceration rates above the national average (Justice Policy Institute, 2008). For instance, California experienced decreases in incarceration rates when jurisdictions increased the number of people sent to drug treatment.

FIGURE 16.2   Relationship Between Increase in Drug Treatment Admissions and Federal Spending on Drug Treatment and Decrease in Violent Crime, 1995–2005

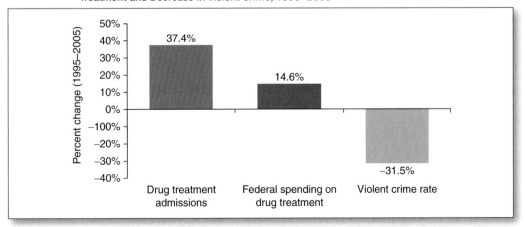

SOURCE: *Substance Abuse Treatment and Public Safety*. Washington, DC: Justice Policy Institute. Copyright © 2008 Justice Policy Institute. Reprinted with permission.

FOCUS TOPIC: 16.1

Drug Treatment Reduces Crime Rate and Incarceration Rate in the State of Maryland

Case Study: Drug Treatment, Imprisonment, and Public Safety in Maryland

"There's a long wait for the bed space in rehabilitation programs and if we can get people off drugs and get them clean and sober, they're not going to be committing any crimes and that's the ultimate goal." –Scott Rolle (R), Frederick Country state's attorney.[15]

In 2000, with growing support from the public, treatment providers, the community, and civil rights advocates, Maryland's focus from incarceration for drug offences to a more treatment-centered mind-set. This change in priorities saw criminal justice referrals for admission to drug treatment programs in Maryland rise by 28 percent from 2000 to 2004 and incarceration for drug offences fall 7 percent in the same period.[16] Six of seven areas in the state watched prison admission for drug offences decline over the four-year period.[17] Baltimore alone experienced a 10 percent drop in drug prisoner admissions while drug treatment admissions referred by the criminal justice system grew by 50 percent.

Reliance on drug treatment over incarceration varies greatly among Maryland countries. On average, Maryland jurisdictions admit 10 people to drug treatment programs for every one person serving a drug-based jail sentence. In Baltimore City, the ration was eight to one.[18] Most regions saw prison commitment for drug offences fall as criminal justice-referred drug treatment admissions increased between 2000 and 2005.

Eight of the 12 countries with above-average treatment-prisoner index scores saw their crime rate fall by at least 10 percent between 2000 and 2004.[19] Only two of the 12 countries with below average treatment-prisoner index scores saw their crime rate fall. Each of the five countries in Maryland that rely most heavily on treatment achieved a major crime-rate reduction compared to just two of the five countries that rely most heavily on drug imprisonment.

Although rising treatment admissions do not directly cause a drop in prison sentences, it is clear that a relationship between the two exists in most Maryland regions. In 2005, after reviewing sentencing patterns in the Baltimore City circuit court, the Campaign for Treatment, Not Incarceration discovered that sentencing practices shifted cases that resulted in 12 months or more of incarceration fell from 51 percent in 2000 to 44 percent in 2003.[20] At the same time, criminal justice drug treatment admission rose by a third. Evidently, the "treatment not incarceration" message has begun to take hold in Maryland.

SOURCE: Justice Policy Institute. (2008). *Substance abuse treatment and public safety.* Washington, DC: Author.

PHOTO 16.1

Ms. Gail Durban leads a psycho-educational class on gambling addiction with inmates at Richwood Correctional Center. Ms. Durban is a Certified Compulsive Gambling Counselor who works for the Office of Behavioral Health (OBH) in Louisiana.

Substance abuse treatment helps in the transition from the criminal justice system to the community. Community-based drug treatment programs have been shown to reduce the chance that a person will become involved in the criminal justice system after release from prison. This is important because it demonstrates that drug treatment can be an important alternative to prison and, at the same time, is an important aspect of offender reintegration after prison. Thus, regardless of the phase of the criminal justice system offenders find themselves in, drug treatment is likely to have positive benefits in terms of relapse and recidivism.

Many offenders with substance abuse problems are sentenced to intensive supervision probation (ISP) if they are not sent to prison. Others, when on parole, will tend to have similarly restrictive programming. In addition, drug offenders on probation or parole may be required to submit to drug screens to ensure compliance with treatment. Court and corrections officials will generally want to know if the offender is complying with treatment and remaining abstinent from drugs. In programs in which access to treatment is limited by available space or funding, those who do not comply may be discharged from treatment. Those who do not successfully complete treatment and continue to have positive drug screens

FOCUS TOPIC: 16.2

Drug Treatment Reduces Violent Crime and Incarceration in the State of California

Case Study: California—Proposition 36

The Substance Abuse and Crime Prevention Act of 2000 (SACPA), or Proposition 36, was put into effect in California in order to reduce the use if incarceration for nonviolent offenders, reduce drug-related crime and increase public health. It requires the use of drug treatment as an alternative to incarceration for nonviolent adult offenders convicted of drug possession for personal use.[22] From its passage in November 2000 to December 2005, the rate of people incarcerated for drug possession in California dropped 34.3 percent, from 59 to 58 people per 100,000.[23] Implementation of SACPA may not be the sole cause of this rapid decrease; there were, however, no other major public changes during this time.

According to the National Survey of Substance Abuse Treatment Services (NSSATS), this period saw a 25.9 percent increase in the number of drug treatment facilities in California, but a 2.83 percent decrease nationally when California is excluded.[24] Along with this increase in treatment facilities, the number of substance abuse clients in California increased 34.1 percent from 2000 to 2004. Excluding California, the nation as a whole only had a 4 percent increase in the number of treatment clients during the time.[25] As California violent rate decreased more rapidly than the nation's the number of California treatment facilities and clients increased.

Those opposing Proposition 36 feared that this decrease in incarceration would lead to an increase in violent crime. In fact, from 2000 to 2004 California's violent crime rate decreased 11.2 percent while at the same time the national average violent crime rate fell by 8.1 percent.[26]

Not only did California experience a decrease in violent crime, but the state also saved a substantial amount of money. Using the year 2000 as a baseline for drug possession prison, a Justice Policy Institute (JPI) report estimated that the state saved more than $350 million from 2000 to June 2006 (the end of the Initiative's funding) by using drug treatment as an alternative to prison.[27] (Researchers took the cost of the drug treatment programming into account in calculating savings.) Using a similar methodology, JPI found that California saved a total of $412 million on prison and jail operating costs alone over six and a half years.

The University of California's cost analysis of Proposition 36 also saw substantial cost savings. The study showed that California saved a minimum of $2.50 for every dollar spent on the treatment alternative, $4 per person who completed treatment, and a total of $173.3 million in savings to the California government in the first year alone.[29] The cost savings from Proposition 36 are available to be spent on more cost-effective public safety policies for Californians.

SOURCE: Justice Policy Institute. (2008). *Substance abuse and public safety*. Washington, DC: Author

---

may be sent back to court for further sentencing. While drug testing appears to serve a useful purpose in monitoring offenders with substance abuse problems, this testing alone is not sufficient to keep offenders from using drugs and reoffending. The best approach may be to combine random drug testing with forms of rehabilitative drug treatment to address the addiction and minimize the likelihood that the individual will engage in future criminal behavior.

Drug offenders on probation are usually placed in outpatient treatment programs, which usually include individual and group therapy, while some programs include family therapy and relapse prevention support. Outpatient drug treatment often includes a range of protocols, from highly professional psychotherapies to informal peer discussions (ONDCP, 2001). Counseling services vary considerably and include individual, group, or family counseling; peer group support; vocational therapy; and cognitive therapy. Aftercare, considered necessary to prevent relapse, typically consists of 12-step meetings, periodic group or individual counseling, recovery training or self-help and relapse-prevention strategies, and/or vocational counseling (ONDCP, 2001).

Prison Tour Video Link 16.1
Watch a clip about substance abuse counseling.

RECREATIONAL PROGRAMS

Recreational activities are an important aspect of prison management and operations. Well-designed recreational programs provide constructive options for inmates to spend idle time and, at the same time, can serve as incentives for good behavior. Though many people may balk at the notion that inmates are afforded recreational opportunities, it should be pointed out that access to such activities can (and does)

APPLIED THEORY 16.1

Social Learning and Behavior Management

Social learning theory is an integration of differential association and behavioral learning theories. In differential association theory, Edwin Sutherland posits that both criminal and law-abiding behaviors are learned in interaction with others. In American society, according to Sutherland, one is likely to associate, to varying degrees, with individuals who define law violations as favorable while also associating with individuals who define law violations as unfavorable. When exposure to people with behavioral patterns and attitudes favorable to crime exceeds exposure to people with behavioral patterns and attitudes unfavorable to crime, criminal behavior is likely to be learned. If the balance is struck in the opposite direction, law-abiding behavior is likely to be learned instead.

Unlike differential association, however, social learning theory also explains and specifies the learning mechanisms that lead to criminal behavior. According to social learning theory, the behavioral principles involved in the social learning of deviant behavior—and conforming behavior as well—include but are not limited to notions of operant conditioning, differential reinforcement, and discriminative stimuli. Concepts such as imitation of other social behaviors (if others have good outcomes from a behavior, we will tend to imitate that same behavior), self-reinforcement (where people do a behavior that they find self-fulfilling), the use of rewards for desired behavior (e.g., providing good time credit to inmates for completing a program), and punishment (being placed in solitary confinement for misbehavior in prison) are all components of this theory.

Further, the groups with which one associates can determine how different rewards and punishments are perceived. For instance, among gangs in prison, when one member is given solitary confinement for enforcing one of the gang's goals and when that member does his solitary confinement without letting prison administrators know details of the gang's activity, he might get respect from other members of the gang. In this case, the ironic outcome is that solitary confinement becomes a reinforcer of status among one's peers rather than a punisher for the undesired behavior. Thus, the learning processes can be complicated as they are affected by the existing prison subculture.

Because of this social learning component that can be both positive and negative, depending on the social circumstances, some treatment programs are separated from the main prison population. For example, the **Successful Treatment of Addiction and Recovery (STAR) program** at Richwood Correctional Center is a drug addiction program that consists of dorms that are separate from the housing units of the main compound. Inmates in this treatment program are kept separate from the general population because it is presumed that they will not be affected by negative associations with persons not in treatment. In addition, inmates in treatment together will likely be positive influences on one another and will, therefore, be likely to give messages and reinforcements conducive to treatment and recovery. Further, like many drug treatment programs, the STAR program emphasizes the people, places, and things that these inmates encounter that can affect likely relapse into drug use and recidivism into criminal activity. These messages demonstrate that associations with healthy people will aid in the offender's recovery from drugs and alcohol while associations with persons who lead unhealthy lifestyles will likely lead to associations that support drug and alcohol use. The same is true with the places in which offenders choose to spend their time as well as the things that they have in their environment. Thus, there is a reinforcing element (operant reinforcers) to this program and an element that also emphasizes the impact of the social setting.

In addition, Richwood Correctional Center places a strong emphasis on religious programming for both Muslim and Christian members. These groups tend to have teachings that are prosocial in orientation, from the perspective of both prison administration and crime prevention upon release into society. Religious programs provide structure and guidance with positive behaviors. The inmate's association with others who are like-minded to prosocial activities helps to socially reinforce the individual toward a healthy and positive lifestyle. Naturally, this reduces the procriminal and prodrug messages. Thus, religious programming serves as a very positive adjunct to treatment programming and behavior change among inmates.

Lastly, a social learning mechanism is involved with recreational programs. The use of physical recreation, particularly structured physical recreation, provides additional prosocial behaviors that are physiologically healthy, and this, in and of itself, translates to cognitive rewards: A healthy body leads to a healthy mind. Other recreational programs such as drawing and painting, music and singing programs, and so forth provide emotional benefits that are often self-rewarding for the inmate, thereby providing self-reinforcement. When individuals also receive recognition for these accomplishments, this adds an additional layer of reinforcement that can further support their continued activity in these healthy activities. Thus, recreational pursuits can have a therapeutic effect, and they also work hand-in-hand with the premises associated with social learning theory. In the end, any program that provides messages that are prosocial and, at the same time, minimizes those that are procriminal can be considered consistent with the tenets of social learning theory.

SOURCE: Sellers, C. S., & Winfree, L. T. (2010). *Akers, Ronald L.: Social learning theory*. In F. T. Cullen & P. Wilcox (Eds.), *Encyclopedia of criminological theory*. Thousand Oaks, CA: Sage.

keep the inmate population more manageable. Beyond this, many prison systems provide a set of additional rationales for their recreation programs. For example, the state of Washington Department of Corrections (2012) provides the following underlying purposes for providing prison recreational programming:

1. Contribute to a safe and secure environment and reduce idleness by allowing offenders an opportunity to participate in supervised and structured physical and prosocial activities.

2. Help offenders take responsibility for their health and wellness by adopting positive lifestyle habits.

3. Reduce the number of disciplinary problems, as well as injuries related to stress and strain.

4. Allow offenders to use recreation/wellness activities in conjunction with the offender release plan.

From the four purposes listed above, it can be seen that the state of Washington (like many other prison systems) views effective recreational activities as producing good outcomes for the offender and for the institution. For instance, the third purpose above denotes that disciplinary problems tend to be reduced when inmates engage in recreational programming, and there is also the implication that injuries or illness due to stress or strain may be reduced. Thus, we can conclude that, at a minimum, effective recreational programming saves the prison money in long-term medical costs and in terms of additional human resources for security staff who would otherwise need to contend with increased disciplinary incidents among inmates.

History

In America's early colonial jails as well as the Pennsylvania and Auburn system prisons, allocation for physical exercise was provided to inmates as part of the daily regimen. However, it was Elmira Reformatory, known for its progressive orientation toward inmate supervision and reform, that first offered a diverse array of programming options. At Elmira, inmates could participate in team sports, gymnasium activities, a variety of social clubs that would build esteem and social skills, as well as acting and artistic pursuits. In addition, inmates could opt to work for the inmate-run newspaper, titled *The Summary,* which first began in 1883. This paper was an eight-page weekly digest of world and local news. Importantly, **The Summary** was the first inmate-operated prison newspaper in the entire world (New York Correction History Society [NYCHS], 2008). In today's current prison environment, nearly every prison system (if not every major prison) has an inmate-run newspaper or newsletter.

During the late 1880s, the use of prison labor for profit was banned due to opposition from private corporations and businesses. This led Zebulon Brockway, the historical figure associated with the innovations at Elmira (see Chapter 2), to look for ways to keep the inmates busy with productive activities. As one of many programs, Brockway implemented a military program; when it was in full stride, the inmates were drilling five to eight hours a day. Inmates were organized into companies and regiments, with inmate officers and a brass band. Brockway also took this opportunity to shift the trade school program from evenings to days and to adapt the physical education program to the entire population. A gymnasium with marble floors, a swimming pool, and a drill hall, completed in 1890, allowed military and physical training in all weather (NYCHS, 2008).

Not until the 1960s would recreational options truly be considered a component of inmate treatment and reform. The **Attica Prison Riot**, mentioned in Chapter 15, drew attention to the need to provide inmates with a better standard of care, including recreational options that would be prosocial and healthy for inmates. This historical and also tragic event, along with various rulings from the Supreme Court and other lower courts, made it clear to prison systems around the nation that inmate programming would need to be improved. In 1966, the National Correctional Recreation Association (see Focus Topic 16.3) was established. The emergence of this association served as the formal acknowledgement of prison recreational services as a legitimate and central feature in prison operations and management.

During the 1990s, prison systems experienced enormous growth, and, at the same time, there was public fervor for the "get tough on crime" approach to incarceration. As a result, many states and even the Federal Bureau of Prisons (BOP) have limited the activity of prison recreation programs, including the use of television as well as weight lifting activities. In 1994, weight lifting in particular came into the spotlight

Video Link 16.2
Watch a clip about arts programs in prisons.

Reference Link 16.1
Read more about recreation programs.

FOCUS TOPIC: 16.3

The National Correctional Recreation Association

The National Correctional Recreation Association (NCRA) was founded in 1966 by a small group of correctional recreation leaders. These recreation leaders were largely custody officers who had displayed an interest in sports. Finding themselves assigned to the gym and yard areas, directing programs in weight lifting, baseball, and football, they banded together for mutual support and education.

Today, the NCRA is composed of practitioners at the federal, state, and local levels, including juvenile, medical, and community-based facilities. A growing emphasis on inmate health promotion and the professional preparation of future correctional recreation practitioners continues to expand the organization's scope.

NCRA Objectives

1. To create and maintain professional standards in the field of correctional recreation.

2. To create and foster interest in correctional recreation.

3. To inform professionals, inmates, and the public at large of the requirements and benefits of correctional recreation programs.

4. To encourage opportunities for constructive use of leisure time during incarceration and upon release.

5. To help reintegration of the inmate to society through recreational experiences.

6. To provide a means for communication among professionals interested in correctional recreation through formal and informal support mechanisms, an annual conference, a training institute, and publications.

SOURCE: National Correctional Recreation Association. (2010). *About the NCRA*. Retrieved from http://www.strengthtech.com/correct/ncra/ncra.htm#about.

PHOTO 16.2

These inmates are working out with recreational facilities designed for strength training. Though there are no weights shown, these types of exercises help inmates stay physically fit and increase their muscular strength as well as cardiovascular endurance.

of public scrutiny, and, between this time and 1997, several states banned or limited weight lifting in prisons.

One particular piece of legislation, passed by the U.S. Congress in 1996, is known as the **Zimmer Amendment**. This amendment restricted the purchase of several types of weight lifting equipment within the BOP. In recent years, the issue has moved to the back burner. Weight lifting remains banned or limited in approximately a dozen states. During the 1990s, weight lifting bans were part of a much larger "no frills" prison movement. In-cell television viewing, R-rated movies, pornographic materials, boxing, wrestling, judo, karate, electronic musical instruments, computers, and in-cell coffee pots and hot plates were among many items banned or limited.

From 2000 onward, a number of states have experienced budgetary problems, and this has severely impacted prison budgets. As a result, cuts in prison system spending have limited the types of recreation available. While recreational opportunities may exist in most prisons, they tend to be funded by the inmates themselves and are restricted to activities such as unstructured physical activity on a recreation yard, the ability to sing in prison choirs (especially for religious programming), watching films, and other no-cost programs that do not require anything more than marginal commitment on the part of prison systems.

Recreational Programming

Effective recreational programs require well-trained professionals, adequate equipment and supplies, and space for implementation. In addition, programs should include a variety of indoor and outdoor activities. As a means of example, we will refer to the Department of Corrections in the state of Montana and its policy document titled *Recreation Programs DOC 5.5.3*. This document lays out, in very clear terms, the expectations regarding personnel who supervise in recreational services as well as the structure of

FOCUS TOPIC: 16.4

The NCRA Position Statement on Weight Lifting Programs in Correctional Settings

It is the official position of the National Correctional Recreation Organization that weight lifting programs are an integral part of rehabilitation services within the spectrum of corrections.

Properly administered weight lifting programs are a vital tool in the daily management of a volatile environment as well as a potentially cost-effective measure. The benefits of these programs can be documented in several areas:

1. The vast majority of incarcerated criminals committed their offenses during leisure time. Programs such as weight lifting give offenders leisure skills to utilize during free time after parole or release.

2. In the commission of a crime, the major contributing factors are often the presence or use of intoxicants and/or firearms. Physical strength and size are insignificant in comparison.

3. Accreditation standards and some court decisions require that institutions offer a comprehensive recreation program with a variety of equipment and supplies. Such programs supply emotional, psychological, and physiological benefits. Weight lifting is a part of a comprehensive program.

4. Inmate idleness during incarceration has been cited as a cause of serious disturbances in institutions. Inmates who are involved in constructive physical activities such as weight lifting are less likely to become involved in disruptive behavior. Thus, weight lifting programs contribute to good institutional management by providing an outlet through which offenders can appropriately relieve stress and anxiety.

5. The positive self-esteem that comes from the self-discipline required to obtain improved physical condition is a vital part of the inmate's preparation for a successful return to society. This is especially true when combined with other programs such as education, vocational skills, and drug treatment.

6. Many correctional systems fund recreational equipment and programs out of monies generated by offenders (e.g., store funds, vending machines, and long-distance phone call fees). This reduces taxpayer costs in that government funds can be focused on educational, vocational, and security needs while inmates supply funding for their own leisure activities. This promotes a positive work ethic—linking vocational and recreation programs, enhancing the assimilation of societal norms within the institution, and increasing the likelihood that inmates will operate within these norms upon release.

The task of providing a safe environment of positive change is not an easy one, and our tools are few. The elimination of any of these tools would create a void that would be difficult and costly to fill. The reality is that nearly all inmates in our prisons will one day return to society. It is our responsibility to ensure that they have every opportunity to return as more productive citizens that when they came to us. Weight lifting is a vital part of correctional programming, and we strongly encourage its continued presence in America's prisons.

SOURCE: National Correctional Recreation Association. (2010). *About the NCRA.* Retrieved from http://www.strengthtech.com/correct/ncra/ncra .htm#about.

recreational programming. According to this document, each program will have a full-time recreation program administrator.

This **recreation program administrator** is often responsible for a number of duties, but, among them, this individual is expected to survey the recreational needs and interests of the offender population at least one time each year. This is important because it provides inmates with some voice in the matter and, as we have seen from prior history, detracts from the likelihood that inmates will be so disgruntled as to be unruly or, worse yet, resort to a riot. Throughout the year, the recreation program administrator will ensure that recreational facilities are maintained and in good condition. In addition, the equipment should be sufficient for the number of inmates in the facility.

The recreation program administrator will usually, carefully, select offenders to fill the role of program assistants. These inmates are chosen for their trustworthiness (within the limits that an inmate should reasonably be trusted), responsibility, and ability to work with groups. Lastly, the recreation program administrator will often provide for the integration of community members and local sports teams. When doing so, the recreation program administrator should complete a routine background check on all regular volunteers to verify their identity, occupation, and credentials for the type of activity involved.

Video Link 16.3
Learn more about programs designed for special needs offenders.

Prison Tour Video Link 16.2
Watch a clip about the importance of recreational programs.

Video Link 16.4
Watch a clip of the Louisiana State Prison rodeo.

Audio Link 16.2
Learn more about prison theater programs.

Lastly, recreation program administrators will oversee recreation programs in locked facilities and be adept at crafting programs for special needs offenders. This is an important aspect of the duties of the recreation program administrator. Programming for the elderly must be appropriate for this population, and this is increasingly becoming a requirement in many prison facilities. Often, such programs not only emphasize physical fitness, but they also integrate wellness programming into the overall service delivery. Lastly, programming for women and juveniles requires additional considerations. This can be true for a number of reasons ranging from the preferences of different groups to potential security or medical concerns.

The content of programs can be quite diverse. For instance, recreational activities can include softball, basketball, volleyball, table games, sporting competitions, holiday activities, hobby programs, and programs by outside groups. On the other hand, general population housing units with day rooms may provide activities such as dominoes, checkers, cards, and television. Recreational activities will be supervised and made available to each offender for at least one hour each day with the exception of segregation inmates. Further, inmates housed in locked units (i.e., administrative segregation or solitary confinement) will not exercise with general population offenders. These inmates are escorted to and from recreation, and should be searched prior to and after the recreation period and escorted by security personnel.

From this discussion, it should be clear that there are many recreation considerations, both in terms of programming and in terms of security. The recreation program administrator must be able to balance the lifestyle enhancement features of recreation against the security requirements of the institution. This can result in pushes and pulls between different components of the prison administration. Further still, we will see in a later subsection that, in some cases, recreation programs are used to augment or instill therapeutic benefits. In such cases, recreation-oriented staff may find that they work in tandem with treatment-oriented staff, which then creates a whole new set of considerations that go beyond merely ensuring that inmates are content with their leisure-time activities. In such cases, inmates are expected to derive mental health benefits from these activities as well.

Benefits for Inmates and Institutions

One of the key benefits of recreation is the tendency toward a reduction in violence and disciplinary problems. The fact that when inmates are provided constructive activities the institution will likely have fewer discipline problems is simply common sense; boredom can lead to chaos much more quickly than structured activity, particularly activity that is enjoyable. The leverage that prisons can maintain over inmates who desire such activities also helps to maintain a level of compliance that is otherwise difficult to obtain.

Another benefit related to recreational programs is that they can help to elevate the esteem of inmates serving time. Because most programs enable inmates to set their own standard for success, there is a high likelihood that they will be encouraged to participate, and this can add a sense of motivation. It is important that inmates feel motivated since this is a necessary experience if they are to participate in a positive manner in programs such as drug therapy, educational achievement, or job training. Sports such as jogging are intramural in nature and allow the inmates to compete with their own past performance and to gauge improvements in their own activity. Team sports allow inmates to practice group membership, anger control, and the ability to work with authority figures (team captains and such). Other endeavors such as theater acting and participation can teach delayed gratification and cooperation (Silverman, 2001).

Lastly, as most persons who have worked in prisons know, inmates can become quite skilled in producing crafts and hobbies that, while seemingly trivial to persons outside of the prison environment, can generate income for inmates. The crafts and products created tend to range from carvings to drawings to constructed items made from any number of materials that inmates can safely procure under institutional policy. These products tend to be unique from those found in retail settings, and persons who wish to order products usually can do so. The funds that inmates can generate from these activities are paltry, at best, in comparison to what they might command outside of the prison walls. But necessity often leads to desperation, and this translates to benefits for free-world persons seeking unique gifts or souvenirs. If nothing else, this gives prison administrators additional leverage over these inmates and saves prison dollars since inmates with their own income are likely to just purchase most of their necessities.

Recreational Programs as Tools for Rehabilitation

In many respects, recreational programs can be useful as tools for rehabilitation. One term used to describe rehabilitative recreational programs is therapeutic recreation. Therapeutic recreation is a type of recreational programming intended to augment treatment planning for clients so that they can obtain optimal physical and mental health. More specifically, **therapeutic recreation (TR)** programs are designed to meet the needs of individuals with a variety of disabilities, impairments, or illnesses by providing specific services such as recreational activities, leisure education, and skills training in the cognitive, physical, behavioral, social, and affective domains (Olson, 2004). The definition provided by Olson (2004) is connected to mental health orientations. It is this perspective that we will take for this subsection, and therefore the definition provided by Olson will be used.

For inmates who participate in therapeutic recreational activities, the most common types of special needs or disabilities include behavior disorders, substance and chemical abuse, chronic mental illness or personality disorders, and developmental disorders. TR specialists usually incorporate some type of initial assessment to address the functional and activity skill levels of their clients. Many of these specialists include individualized treatment goals from the completed assessments to guide them in planning the recreational program. Other specialists may provide treatment activities based on general needs, abilities, and interests.

Common activities used in TR programs are arts, crafts, board or card games, music, sports or physical fitness, gardening, and reading activities. Unique activities include relaxation therapy, experiential education, animal-assisted therapy, anger management, parenting groups, diet and wellness groups, martial arts, humor therapy, and current events. The more specialized programs are often conducted in a conjoint partnership with a mental health professional, such as a professional counselor, social worker, or psychologist. In these cases, there is often a fusion between the therapeutic group and some type of other recreational activity.

For instance, when considering anger management, stress management, and aggression control, inmates may be required to engage in physical activities with other inmates and, at the same time, cooperate with others in the group. Their ability to regulate their communications while also fully participating is intended to augment the sessions that they may have later in the evening related to anger management or emotional control. By using skills that they learn in the session when involved in physical recreation and, in turn, sharing their successes and failures at this application in their later group sessions, inmates engage in the classic talk therapy and have an opportunity to infuse these skills into their recreational experiences.

Another example comes from the research of Williams (2003) and Williams and Strean (2004), who found that physical strength training could have beneficial effects on substance abuse treatment programs. However, the connection between these two interventions was dependent on another variable: motivation of the inmate. Using an experimental design, Williams and Strean found that, for some offenders, strength training had positive treatment effects, but, for others who were not motivated to participate in the activity, it had negative effects since they may have perceived it to be coercive. Accordingly, they concluded that while the combination of recreation and therapy held promise, one has to be very careful in how recreation activities are utilized. Nevertheless, when effectively implemented, these activities can reduce crime and/or drug relapse.

Other research that shows how physical conditioning and recreation can improve treatment outcomes extends to juvenile offenders as well. Research by Williams, Strean, and Bengoechea (2002) demonstrates the potential benefits of sport, recreation, and leisure, and how they relate to rehabilitation of juveniles. This study found that the successes of the **Life Development Intervention**, a comprehensive approach to linking sport and recreation to counseling psychology that emphasizes continuous growth and positive change. This program demonstrates that, when clients are physically healthy, they have an enhanced ability to benefit from therapy. Williams et al. (2002) also note that many skills important to recreation and sport are life skills transferable to other endeavors.

Lastly, programs related to the use of gardening and therapeutic outcomes have been used in the past and are currently used today. Stemming from the early 1900s, a prison garden project was implemented by Warden Lewis Lawes of Sing Sing Prison in Ossining, New York. At that time, an influential inmate with ties to wealthy community members, inmate Charles Chapin, had successfully obtained support and materials to create a beautiful and well-maintained garden on prison grounds. This garden, attended by inmates (under the direction of inmate Chapin), grew to a major project and was purported to have resulted in numerous benefits for inmates. In demonstrating these benefits, consider the excerpt from Lindemuth (2007):

Reference Link 16.2
Read about prison music programs as therapy.

Audio Link 16.3
Listen to a clip about music programs.

In addition, several long-running prison garden programs have noted positive long-term outcomes for participating inmates. Rice (1993) investigated post-release outcomes for 48 participants in the San Francisco County Jail's horticulture therapy program, the Garden Project. His analysis showed that inmates benefited from involvement in the program both during incarceration and post-release. Participants reduced negative or self-destructive behaviors in several ways. These changes included reduction in illegal activities (from 66.7% to 25%), fewer friendships with criminal associates, limited reliance on damaging familial relationships, less drug use, and an increased desire for help. Psychological benefits included higher self-esteem and reduced anxiety, depression, and risk-taking behavior. (p. 89)

As demonstrated above, Lindemuth (2007) notes that naturalistic settings may offer benefits in terms of stress reduction and improved mental states. In several studies conducted within U.S. correctional facilities, access to views out and the quality of these views have been shown to have a measurable influence on the behavior and psychological outlook of inmates and staff. Lindemuth further showcases work by Moore (1981) that has shown that an inmate's view out from prison cells can have a significant impact on their physical well-being. More specifically, Moore found that the view out from a cell (exterior or interior), the cell's relative privacy, and the noise level within the cell are correlated with the number of sick calls to the infirmary.

Lindemuth (2007) shows how gardening recreation programs can have therapeutic effects for inmates. Indeed, one program is quite unique in the state of New York on the infamous Rikers Island. In 1997, the Horticultural Society of New York (HSNY) began GreenHouse, a program providing inmates at the Rikers Island jail complex horticulture training and work experience in the design, installation, and maintenance of gardens.

PHOTO 16.3

An inmate maintains the garden at the Rikers Island GreenHouse project. GreenHouse operates under the premise that jail can serve as a sustainable resource—one that generates benefits to constituents in jail as well as to entire communities across the city and region.

The garden at Rikers Island includes structures such as arbors, post and rail fences, birdhouses, a gazebo adjacent to a pond and a waterfall feature, a greenhouse, and a preexisting brick and cinder block building used as an office and a classroom. Walkways are constructed of gravel and brick. Several rabbits are kept near the office, and several guinea hens live near the garden (donated from a correctional officer's farm). The Rikers Island garden has a strong programming component. Horticulture classes are primarily taught in the winter months when conditions become inhospitable for garden activities. During this time, the greenhouse is transformed into a carpentry shop where inmates construct birdhouses, kestrel and bat boxes, planters, and other wood features for the Rikers garden and city-wide schools and parks.

PHOTO 16.4

The inmates at Rikers Island gardens build and maintain structures such as arbors, post and rail fences, birdhouses, as well as this gazebo adjacent to a pond with a waterfall feature.

As noted in earlier parts of this chapter, some of the work-related programs offered to inmates provide benefits to others in society, including youth and persons who have disabilities or financial challenges. For example, inmates involved in the GreenHouse program grow plants for schools and other public entities including libraries in low-income neighborhoods. Vegetables grown on Rikers are donated to cooking classes offered at the Rikers jails and also to area homeless shelters. This program offered at Rikers Island is a perfect example of how the volunteer work of inmates helps others in the community.

For the minimal time and effort necessary among prison staff, it seems that these types of programs offer huge incentives to everyone involved, and that they are able to improve the prognoses of inmates who also receive mental health services.

Before closing this subsection, one other program, also in New York, should be showcased because of its uniqueness and because it specifically relates to female offenders, making it a genuine rarity but one that, if replicated in other facilities, can generate enormous benefits. This program is located at Bedford Hills Correctional Facility (BHCF), a maximum-security facility for women. This program includes gardening but also grounds for mothers to see visiting children. Like the garden at Sing Sing, the contemporary Children's Center garden and playground at BHCF had strong support from individuals both within and outside the facility. The main goal of the Children's Center is to help women preserve and strengthen relationships with their children while incarcerated.

The gardens at BHCF are maintained by the women who serve time and are created to provide a pleasant area for child visitation. The entire program is quite extensive and includes a nursery, a parenting center, a day care center, a prenatal center, and a child advocacy office. It is important to emphasize that this type of programming affects not only the inmates, but their children as well. Thus, it has a direct impact upon persons in the community and, at the same time, helps to maintain the mental health of the female inmates serving time. In addition, this program demonstrates how two different types of programming (i.e., gardening and children's visitation programs) can have connections that improve the standards of confinement for inmates, reduce interpersonal problems within the institution, and reduce problems related to child maladjustment that can occur within the broader outside community. Thus, recreational programming can provide numerous benefits, including therapeutic benefits.

PHOTO 16.5a and 16.5 b

The Rikers Island gardens have walkways of gravel and brick with diverse floral plantings constructed and planted by the inmates. In the winter months the greenhouse is transformed into a carpentry shop where inmates construct a wide variety of wood features for their garden and citywide parks.

RELIGIOUS PROGRAMS

Religion has played a central role in American prisons since the days of the Walnut Street Jail and even before. Students may recall that the Quakers of Pennsylvania were instrumental in achieving jail and prison reform. Indeed, the term *penitentiary* is reflective of the word *penitence,* and the prison was initially meant to be a place where inmates could reflect on their wrongdoings, and where it was hoped that they would come to change their ways. The goal of religion in early corrections was to reform these offenders amidst the need to protect the community and amidst the community desires to see punishment of the offender. While religious programming today is a key aspect of prison facility operations, the role of hired

CORRECTIONS AND THE LAW 16.1

Legal Issues and Religious Practices

The First Amendment of the U.S. Constitution protects the freedom of religion as a fundamental right, and this extends to inmates. In essence, regardless of whether individuals are locked up, they still have a right to practice the tenets of their religious beliefs without obstruction. The right to religion in prison was not an issue identified as needing court intervention until the 1960s and 1970s. During this time a handful of cases emerged in federal courts that directly addressed religious practice within the prison setting. Most notable among these cases were *Fulwood v. Clemmer* (1962), *Cooper v. Pate* (1964), and *Cruz v. Beto* (1972). In the *Fulwood v. Clemmer* (1962) case, the U.S. District Court for the District of Columbia ruled that correctional officials must recognize the Muslim faith as a legitimate religion and not restrict those inmates who wish to hold services. While this is not a Supreme Court case, it was decided in the U.S. Capitol district (the District of Columbia) and is therefore considered a decision that is universally agreed upon throughout the nation. Two Supreme Court cases that addressed religion include *Cooper v. Pate* (1964), where the courts recognized that prison officials must make every effort to treat members of all religious groups equally, unless they can demonstrate reasonableness to do otherwise. In the case of *Cruz v. Beto* (1972), it was ruled discriminatory and a violation of the Constitution to deny a Buddhist prisoner his right to practice his faith in a comparable way to those who practice the major religious denominations.

These cases demonstrate support for the practice of religious observance from federal courts. However, the federal courts are receptive to the potential challenges that can emerge due to inmate manipulation of religious safeguards. Later, the Fifth Circuit Court of Appeals ruled in *Theriault v. Carlson* (1977) that the First Amendment does not protect so-called religions that are obvious shams, that tend to mock established institutions, and whose members lack religious sincerity. Though this was not a Supreme Court ruling, other legal precedents in state and federal courts indicate that, generally speaking, the judiciary does not expect prison officials to be foolish in their efforts to respect the religious rights of inmates; requests for religious consideration must be valid and sincere among inmates.

Further, though inmates have protected rights to exercise their faith, prison staff have the right to regulate religious practices within prisons to ensure that the safety and security of the institution are not compromised. As students may recall from their past chapter on legal issues in corrections (Chapter 4), *Turner v. Safley* (1987) established the ability of correctional officials to limit or curtail constitutional rights of inmates as long as there is a legitimate penological interest. However, another case emerged that further reinforced the ruling in *Turner* but was also specific to religious issues in prison. In the case of *O'Lone v. Estate of Shabazz* (1987), it was ruled that depriving an inmate of attending a religious service for "legitimate penological interests" was not a violation of an inmate's First Amendment rights. This fully affirms the fact that, ultimately, the safety and security of the institution is the paramount priority in prisons.

Thirteen years later, a significant piece of legislation emerged that has weathered the tests of litigation: the **Religious Land Use and Institutionalized Persons Act of 2000 (RLUIPA)**. The RLUIPA has helped to refine and clarify inmates' religious rights under the First Amendment. The primary intent of this law is to further safeguard (not restrict) the rights of inmates to practice their religious tenets in state and federal facilities. Specifically, this law prohibits the government from restricting inmates' opportunities to practice their religion unless there is a compelling government interest and only if the interference is the least restrictive means of securing that interest.

The Supreme Court issued a ruling in *Cutter v. Wilkinson* (2005) addressing the constitutionality of the RLUIPA and its application to nontraditional religions. In this case, the plaintiffs who filed were inmates of prison facilities in the state of Ohio's Department of Rehabilitation and Correction. These inmates asserted that they were adherents of "nonmainstream" religions, namely the Satanist (typically the Church of Satan, which opposes Christian churches), Wicca (nature worship that includes witchcraft), and Asatru (the name for a Nordic-based religion that reveres Odin) religions. In addition, some of the plaintiffs in this lawsuit included members of the Church of Jesus Christ Christian (CJCC), which has ties to an extremist group and criminal gang, the Aryan Nation. These inmates complained that Ohio prison officials, in violation of the RLUIPA, failed to accommodate their religious exercise in a variety of different ways, including retaliating and discriminating against them for exercising their nontraditional faiths, denying them access to religious literature, denying them the same opportunities for group worship that are granted to adherents of mainstream religions, forbidding them to adhere to the dress and appearance mandates of their religions, withholding religious ceremonial items that are substantially identical to those that the adherents of mainstream religions are permitted, and failing to provide a chaplain trained in their faith. (*Cutter v. Wilkinson,* 2005, p. 713)

The Court unanimously decided in favor of the inmates and found that the state of Ohio had violated the rights of the inmates and that Ohio's objections to several issues regarding the RLUIPA were mistaken. The state of Ohio had reasoned that, among other things, the RLUIPA (1) violated the Establishment Clause of the First Amendment, (2) gave religious inmates more rights and protections than nonreligious inmates, and (3) prevented prisons from enforcing appropriate security measures.

When addressing the Establishment Clause claim, the Court noted that the Religion Clauses of the First Amendment provide that "Congress shall make no law respecting an establishment of religion, or prohibiting the free exercise thereof" (*Cutter v. Wilkinson,* 2005, p. 719). The first of the two clauses are commonly called the **Establishment Clause**. The second, the **Free Exercise Clause**, requires government respect for, and noninterference with, the religious beliefs and practices of our nation's people. While the two clauses express complementary values, they often exert conflicting pressures. The Court has struggled to find a neutral course between the two Religion Clauses, both of which are cast in absolute terms, and either of which, if expanded to a logical extreme, would tend to clash with the other. In deciding the *Cutter* case, the Court noted that "our decisions recognize that 'there is room for play in the joints' between the Clauses" (*Cutter v. Wilkinson,* 2005, p. 719). With this in mind, the Court concluded that the RLUIPA neither established nor promoted any specific religion (indeed, the plaintiffs represented several separate religions, two of which—the Satanists and the CJCC—philosophically opposed one another) nor interfered with religious observance, including the right to *not* observe a religion or belief system. Thus, the Court reasoned, the RLUIPA did not violate the Establishment or Free Exercise Clause.

In addition, because inmates are free to choose their religion and because they are also free to choose no religion, the Court did not determine that religious inmates are afforded more rights than nonreligious inmates. Rather, if inmates wished to have a certain prescribed set of rights to activities that are part of a bona fide religion (not an obvious sham), then they had the unobstructed right to join that particular religion; the sincerity of their belief might be questionable, but was not the legal issue of argument and therefore was not addressed. Lastly, the Court rejected the notion that prisons could not provide sufficient security while respecting religious observances, again deferring to the prior ruling in *Turner v. Safley* whereby a balancing test should be utilized to ensure that neither the rights of inmates nor the security of the institution is compromised in an unreasonable fashion.

SOURCES: See References section for all court cases and referencing of the Religious Land Use and Institutionalized Persons Act of 2000 (RLUIPA).

staff and volunteers who provide religious services has become quite complex. In many cases, religious programming may be infused with treatment programming for addiction recovery, the development of life skills, and even the dietary requirements of various inmates.

History of Religion in Corrections

In earlier chapters, we have discussed the history of corrections and have noted the long and extensive role of religion throughout that history. The work of Dr. Harry Dammer, in the *Encyclopedia of Crime and Punishment* (Levinson, 2002), provides a very succinct and interesting historical overview of the role of religion in corrections. Because Dammer's work is so precisely congruent with the goals of several subsections in this chapter that address religion in corrections, it will be used extensively throughout this section. With this noted, we begin with a brief account of the history of religion in corrections, borrowing from the work of Dammer (2002).

Dammer (2002) notes that the influence and practice of religion in the correctional setting is as old as the history of prisons itself. Dammer speculates that the initial entry of religion into prison was probably carried out by religious men who themselves were imprisoned. The Bible stories of such prisoners include Joseph and Jeremiah in the Old Testament, and John the Baptist, Peter, John, and Paul in the New Testament. Beginning in the days of Constantine, the early Christian Church granted asylum to criminals who would otherwise have been mutilated or killed. Although this custom was restricted in most countries by the 15th century, releasing prisoners during Easter and requests by church authorities to pardon or reduce sentences for offenders were continued practices for centuries.

As noted in earlier chapters of this text, the early colonists continued the customs and common laws of England including the use of the pillory, the stocks, and the whipping post. During the 18th century isolating offenders from fellow prisoners became the accepted correctional practice. It was thought that long-term isolation, combined with in-depth discussions with clergy, would lead inmates to repent or become "penitent"—sorry for their sins. Thus the term *penitentiary* was derived. Pennsylvania Quakers were primarily responsible for many of the prison reforms. The prototype of this regime was the Walnut Street Jail in Philadelphia that in style reflected the Quakers' belief in man's ability to reform through reflection and remorse.

Even during the 19th century when daytime work was initiated by the Auburn system, solitary confinement at night was still the norm in correctional practice. The forced solitary confinement was thought to serve the same repenting purpose as the older penitentiary. Belief in education as a tool for reducing criminal activity also assisted in the growth of religion in prison. Because of the limited budgets of correctional institutions, chaplains were often called upon to be the sole educator in many American prisons.

Journal Article Link 16.2
Read about how prison religion took on new roles in the 19th century.

In the modern world of corrections, religion continues to play a very important part in prison operations. However, as we will see when discussing legal issues in correctional religion, the meaning of the term *religion* has broadened out a bit and now includes groups that, during the early colonial history of America, were not even in existence and also includes religions that were more prevalent in areas of the world outside of Europe. The religious pluralism in prisons means that inmates will (and often do) raise questions or requests that go beyond the expertise, training, or ecclesiastical endorsement of some experts (Van Baalen, 2008). In such cases, these inmates may have to defer to spiritual leaders in the community. In many cases, volunteers may fulfill that role, and, in other cases, facilities may hire contract chaplains or religious experts to address inmate issues if the need seems to warrant such an expenditure.

Religious Diets and Holy Days

Inmates of various religious groups will request specialized diets that are required for their particular faith. In most instances, prison staff can and do ask inmates to document that such a diet is a required part of their faith, in advance. Legitimate requests, based on recognized religious tenets must be accommodated (Van Baalen, 2008). Rulings related to the Religious Land Use and Institutionalized Persons Act of 2000 (RLUIPA) suggest that prison systems should refrain from requiring inmates to prove that their dietary regimens are part and parcel to their religious tenets, so long as the dietary requests are not so onerous as to require substantive budget challenges and/or provided that the safety and security of the institution are not compromised.

Audio Link 16.4
Listen to a clip about prison ministry.

Van Baalen (2008) notes that many religious observances for even traditional faiths may require the consumption of particular foods (e.g., Jewish Passover), and some religions may require that food

FOCUS TOPIC: 16.5

Focus From the Inside With Ronald "Raúl" Drummer; Criminal Charge: Aggravated Battery and Attempted Armed Robbery

My quest for self-identification started when I realized my own failure to make rational decisions. I was constantly driven by either my environment, emotions, or a desire rooted in unrealistic expectations. As the result of years of pondering and searching, I developed the Triangular Approach to Complete Liberation in Prison (TACLP). The basic tenet to this is that we function best when we have persistent stimulation in all three realms of existence, consisting of the spiritual, mental, and physical.

PHOTO 16.6

Ronald Drummer is an inmate at Richwood Correctional Center who is a dorm mentor in the Successful Treatment and Recovery (STAR) program. He stands here in front of a bookshelf that is part of the inmate library for the STAR program.

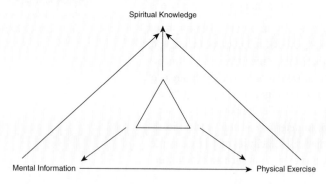

During this time, I had a choice to give credence to a higher power in accordance with Alcoholics Anonymous and the 12 steps. I also tried to rely on self-education and Islam, and I even studied under a cult leader named Dr. Malachiz York. I was introduced to Christianity with emphasis on the death, burial, and resurrection of Jesus the Christ. I noticed that this belief system challenged me more than anything else in my life, thus far. After being in the faith for about two years and practicing for over 11 years, I observed two types of Christians. One used the notion that faith is all that is needed of a person (thereby remaining on the surface level of their spiritual development), whereas the other consisted of those brave souls who plunged into their commitment to

the word with no reservations (there was no point of return). I wanted that sort of dedication, and it went so deep that it pierced my very heart.

However, I soon learned that the principles of the Bible would continually keep me at a crossroads. At every checkpoint I had to leave a piece of myself behind in order to advance to the next. This has made all the difference in my incarceration—total abandonment of my old way of thinking that would be inconsistent with what I now believed to be the truth. This process showed through my conduct in the prison. My disciplinary reports went down to none at all. I was once unapproachable—now people can hardly believe this is the same person they had known. In addition, prison officials liked to have me around and eventually trusted me with responsibilities. Most important of all, I had no "good time" incentives to influence my behavior based on early release. I simply was making these changes for my own good . . . and all the while I was serving "flat time" on my sentence.

With the spiritual aspect of development on the go, I eventually focused more on the mental aspects of functioning. With this, I focused on information dealing with addiction and drug rehabilitation. Although my faith was the rock, awareness of my addiction was the undergrowth. Taking classes in a therapeutic environment opened my mind to the threat of drug use to my body and mind. During this time, I delved into various philosophical readings and a series of thought-provoking tomes. Ultimately, my development of both spiritual and information-based areas gave me stability in mind and spirit, but I was still lacking in my physical development.

While my introduction to exercise was a much needed step in the right direction, I lacked motivation to maintain my regimen. I applied the same technique to physical fitness as I did to discovering God and comprehending available information about drug addiction. I started out jogging around the prison. I pushed myself until I went from 245 pounds to 178 pounds. Through access to the prison facilities, I took advantage of weight lifting. It turned out that I was well suited for this form of exercise, and, once results started coming, I felt a sense of motivation and gratification that was unparalleled in the physical world.

For the first time in my life I had found my point and purpose in the most unlikely of places. Now, I am completely liberated in every area of my life, which is the ultimate goal of the TACLP. If I did not have access to these resources, I would still be mentally, spiritually, and physically impaired and unfit. Now I am able to smile without effort, laugh and not hurt, and love without restraint. My life started when I was locked up. My family is my fellow prisoners and the staff. We give each other hope. I am connected openly with my prison brothers and discreetly with the staff. Coming to prison was the best thing that happened to me. I am only sorry that the incident that led to my incarceration hurt the victim of the crime. At this point in my life, I thank my mom, dad, and family for the support throughout the years. Most of all, I thank God for giving me a willingness to change.

As a side note, it is worth mentioning that Mr. Drummer has been incarcerated for 19 years.

SOURCE: Ronald Drummer (personal interview, December 1, 2011). Used with permission.

not be consumed at specific times during the day or night (e.g., Muslim Ramadan). Prisons around the United States routinely accommodate these dietary modifications based on religion. There are even some occasions where a religious group may require the setting of a group meal as part of a ceremony; such types of request should be accommodated so long as appropriate notice is given to prison administrators (Van Baalen, 2008). In these cases, the chaplain or another religious expert will aid security staff in providing the accommodations to ensure that misunderstandings are minimized.

PHOTO 16.7

Religious programming is an important element of the daily schedule in many correctional facilities.

Prison Tour Video Link 16.3
Watch a clip about religion in prisons.

Chaplain Functions and the ACCA

According to the American Correctional Chaplains Association, correctional chaplains are professionals who provide pastoral care to those who are imprisoned, as well as to correctional facility staff and their families when requested. In early U.S. prison history, chaplains held positions of relative importance, which is not surprising considering they were part of a system created by religious groups. They were responsible for visiting inmates and providing services and sermons, and also served as teachers, librarians, and record keepers. At times the chaplain would also act as an ombudsman for the inmates when issues of maltreatment would arise. During the 1800s and early 1900s, chaplains were often viewed as naïve and easily duped by inmates. Almost in response to this perception, the clinical pastoral education movement emerged during the 1920s and 1930s and promoted the serious study of chaplaincy. This field of study applied the principles, resources, and methods of organized religion to the correctional setting in a structured, disciplined, and professionalized manner. This resulted in the development of competent professional chaplains who were able to meld with the rehabilitation ideas that surfaced from the 1930s through the 1960s.

The chaplain of today is typically an educated and multiskilled individual who is generally accepted as helpful by those who live and work in correctional facilities. Chaplains serve a variety of functions. Their main purpose is to administer religious programs and provide pastoral care to inmates and institutional staff. In the past, this meant that the common duties were to provide religious services, counsel troubled inmates, and advise inmates of "bad news" from home or from correctional authorities. More recently, the role of chaplain has been expanded to include coordination of physical facilities, organizing volunteers, facilitating religious furlough visits, contracting for outside religious services, and training correctional administrators and staff about the basic tenets, rituals, and artifacts of nontraditional faith groups. In the case when an individual or a small group of inmates wishes to practice a religion not familiar to a current chaplain, a contract chaplain, an outside volunteer, or a spiritual adviser who specializes in that faith perspective may be brought into the institution to minister to inmates.

The specific types of religious groups vary from prison to prison and state to state. Nearly all state and federal correctional institutions provide support for at least some of the four traditional faith groups—Catholic, Protestant, Muslim, and Jewish. However, in recent years a number of nontraditional religious groups have been established in prison environments. These include, but are not limited to, Hinduism, Mormonism, Native American religions, Buddhism, Rastafarianism, Hispanic religions (Curanderism, Santeria, Espiritismo), Jehovah's Witnesses, Christian Scientists, and two of the newest faith groups to enter correctional facilities, Witchcraft and Satanism. The religious programs and practices conducted by the different faith groups differ according to the beliefs of the group, inmate interest, amount of time and space available in the prison, competence of the religious staff, and the support of the correctional authorities. It is not uncommon for a large prison to have numerous religious services on a daily basis. For example, a typical day could include a Bible study class, Catholic Mass, Islamic Ta'Leem, Jewish Faith Meeting, Spanish Gospel Group, and a Native American Sweat Lodge Ceremony. As one can see, the role of the chaplain in modern corrections can be quite complicated, and this is, in part, what has led to the various legal challenges noted in this chapter.

Lastly, correctional chaplains are now recognized as integral professionals in the field of corrections. The **American Correctional Chaplains Association (ACCA)** is a national organization that provides representation and networking opportunities for chaplains who work in various correctional environments. The organization also provides members with research on best practices in the field of correctional chaplaincy. This organization also provides training and certification for correctional chaplains as a means of furthering the standards of service that these professionals provide.

Religious Volunteers

Religious volunteers are a commonplace practice in most prison systems. The availability of volunteers to assist religious staff is a boon, but it does have its limits. Most volunteers are not necessarily trained with clinical skills to provide professional counseling, and they are usually oblivious to many of the security practices necessary to operate a prison. Indeed, many such volunteers tend to view security staff as stern on the inmate population, and, in return, many security personnel may view religious volunteers as misled in their perceptions of the inmates with whom they work. In most cases, faith-based volunteers will desire to minister to their own religious groups, and they are likely to be part of a larger church membership outside the prison within the community. This means that they will tend to have an agenda, of a sort, even though it may be spiritual in nature. Lastly, volunteers should be given very specific instructions regarding security at the very beginning of their involvement within a program. The volunteer, according to ACAA standards, should be provided some type of orientation, a tour of the prison, and materials that include a handbook and/or guidelines within the prison. The list of rules and regulations for inmates should also be provided to ensure that inmates cannot manipulate the volunteer into assisting them with something that is unauthorized.

PHOTO 16.8

Chaplain Sam Hubbard stands in his office at Richwood Correctional Center. "Chap," as he is commonly called by staff and inmates, coordinates religious programming at the facility. He is also active in inmate recreational competitions, as seen by the many trophies that he has helped inmate teams to obtain when competing with other prisons throughout the region.

Journal Article Link 16.3
Read about justifications to expand religious services in prisons.

Are Inmates Really Motivated by Religion?

There is perhaps a good deal of dissent among many practitioners in the field of corrections when answering this question. According to Dammer (2002), there is a belief among many who work in prison environments that inmates "find religion" for manipulative reasons (p. 1375). However, though this may sometimes occur, there is evidence that inmates have received positive benefits resulting from their incarceration and religious practice (Dammer, 2002). Research by Johnson, Larson, and Pitts (1997) found that participants in religious programming had significantly fewer infractions while in prison than did inmates who did not participate in such programs. Even more convincing of the positive effects of religious programming is the finding that inmates who participated frequently in religious programming services were less likely to be arrested when examined one year after their release. Thus, it would appear that prison religious programs have both short-term and long-term positive effects.

More recent research provides continued empirical evidence indicating that religious programming reduces crime and recidivism among adult offenders (Hercik, 2007). For instance, Johnson and Larson (2003) conducted a preliminary evaluation of the InnerChange Freedom Initiative, a faith-based prisoner reform program. Results show that program graduates were 50% less likely to be rearrested and 60% less likely to be reincarcerated during a two-year follow-up period.

It appears that numerous studies demonstrate the efficacy of faith-based programs, both within the prison facility itself and later when offenders are released into the community. Thus, it appears that most inmates really are motivated by religious programming. Contrary to dour views held by skeptics, these programs have been found to be effective by numerous researchers in the field of corrections. With empirical quantitative evidence of positive outcomes, it should be concluded that religious programs in corrections are just as important as other forms of programming.

CONCLUSION

This chapter has provided an extensive overview of many of the typical programs offered to inmates within the prison environment. The programs that have been discussed include drug treatment, recreational, and religious programs. Though other types of programs are available to inmates, these types of programs tend to be universal in the means by which they are implemented, and they all tend to be used by nearly every inmate who serves time in the United States. This conclusion will not address each of these programs individually but will instead point toward one key theme that has been consistently mentioned throughout Chapter 15 as well as this chapter.

Throughout this chapter, students have learned that these programs work to improve inmate conditions within the prison and that, as a result, each program lowers observed infractions among inmates and also reduces the likelihood of lawsuits and/or prison riots. Further, most of these programs have legal requirements that make them at least marginally necessary within the prison environment. Regardless of whether each program is constitutionally required, it is clear that each provides benefits to both the inmates and the staff who must work with them. This is an important observation because it can therefore be said that, in a roundabout manner, these programs reduce problems in prison facilities, and, even more encouraging, they reduce recidivism when inmates are released into the community. Thus, prison programming is a smart investment that, in the longest of terms, saves taxpayers more money than it costs them and enhances public safety in future years when inmates are released from prison. To overlook the importance of prison programming is to be negligent in safeguarding our community's very safety.

END-OF-CHAPTER DISCUSSION QUESTIONS

1. What are therapeutic communities? Explain how they are utilized in prison facilities.

2. Discuss how substance abuse treatment programs affect potential recidivism.

3. Explain how recreation can affect inmate behavior in the prison.

4. Discuss some of the concerns for administrators with different types of recreational programming (e.g., weight lifting).

5. Discuss at least two Supreme Court cases associated with religious programming in prisons. Be sure to explain why you selected those two cases for your discussion.

6. Explain how various physical conditions might affect the mental health of inmates in prison facilities.

7. What is the Triangular Approach to Complete Liberation in Prison (TACLP)? Explain how this concept ties in with the various types of programming in this chapter and an offender's likelihood of future recidivism.

8. Explain how social learning mechanisms can be both positive and negative within a prison environment. Provide an example of a treatment program that attempts to capitalize on the positive aspects and minimize the negative aspects.

KEY TERMS

Administrator

American Correctional Chaplains Association (ACCA)

Cutter v. Wilkinson (2005)

Cooper v. Pate (1964)

Cruz v. Beto (1972)

Establishment Clause

Free Exercise Clause

Fulwood v. Clemmer (1962)

Life Development Intervention

O'Lone v. Estate of Shabazz (1987)

Recreation program administrator

Successful Treatment of Addiction and Recovery (STAR) program

Theriault v. Carlson (1977)

Therapeutic recreation (TR)

The Summary

Zimmer Amendment

APPLIED EXERCISE 16.1

Students must conduct either a face-to-face or a phone interview with a staff person in a prison facility and who works in one of the following fields: (1) recreational supervision, (2) substance abuse treatment, or (3) religious programming. The student must set up a day and time with that practitioner and interview him or her to gain his or her insight and perspective on several key questions related to work in the field of the chosen practitioner. Students must write the practitioner's responses, conduct their own analysis of those responses, and submit their draft by the deadline set by their instructor. Students should complete this application exercise as a minipaper that addresses each point below. The total word count should be 1,400 to 2,100 words.

When completing the interview, students should ask the following questions:

1. What are the most rewarding aspects of your job?
2. What are the most stressful aspects of your job?
3. How does your work help offenders to eventually reintegrate into society?
4. What are some challenges that you have in helping inmates?
5. Why did you choose to work in this field?
6. What type of training have you received for this line of work?
7. What would you recommend to someone who was interested in pursuing a similar career?

In addition, you should ensure that your submission has appropriate spelling and grammar throughout.

Lastly, students are required to provide contact information for the auxiliary staff person. Please obtain the following information from the auxiliary practitioner that you interview. While the instructor will probably not need to contact this person, it may become necessary in order to validate the actual completion of an interview.

Name and title of correctional supervisor: _____

Correctional agency: _____

Practitioner's phone number: _____

Practitioner's e-mail address: _____

Name of student: _____

"WHAT WOULD YOU DO?"

You are a correctional officer assigned to a section of the prison dedicated to substance abuse treatment and reentry activities. As part of your day-to-day activities, you are required to have inmates in each of your assigned dorms go to "group" at different times of the day. This area of the prison consists of four dorms, and each dorm has four different groups of 10 to 12 men assigned to the group. One day, you are asked to let out the men on B Dorm who are in Group 6. As everyone in this program knows, the dorms are divided and classified as either A, B, C, or D, and there are four groups, identified by number, in each dorm. Groups 5 through 8 are on B Dorm, and, just before you unlock the heavy metal door to enter the dorm, you can hear the men who are already gathered waiting for your call—they are laughing. You listen for a few seconds and find out that they are laughing about their substance abuse counselor. You decide to hold off on opening the door and listen for just a bit, and you hear the following:

Inmate Joe: "Yeah, that guy has more problems than we do."

Inmate Frank: "No doubt about it . . . but what I think is funny is that whenever Jacob mentions something about his meth use, that counselor always has a story that is even bigger and better about his own recovery."

Inmate Jacob:	"Yep, that is why I just keep making up stories, just to see what he will come up with next."
Inmate Joe:	"Well, you know that he looks like he is high or something most of the time that we go to group . . . or like he was up all night drinking . . . I think he really is on the dope still."
Inmate Jacob:	"He can't be doing meth, we would know by now, you can't really hide that."
Inmate Frank:	"Naw, he ain't doin' meth, but I bet he has some kind of prescription pills, and I bet he is drinking all the time."
Inmate Jacob:	"As long as I am getting the good time for finishing the program, I do not care about everyone else's stuff, especially a counselor's problems."

Both inmates Joe and Frank shake their heads and indicate agreement with one another, saying "No doubt about that!"

You stick the key in the door, and, as usual, it makes a loud noise as you turn it in the lock. The large metal keys on your oversized key ring clang around as you open the door. Naturally, the men, waiting on the other side of the door, are quiet and do not continue talking about their counselor.

You call them out by announcing, "B Dorm, Group 6, time to go across the street!" which is a slang term for going across the hall to the group rooms where the addiction groups occur.

You walk with the men in the group to the room where they meet and see their counselor, Mr. Sam Friday, who by all appearances looks just fine. He smiles at you and thanks you for bringing them over. He starts up a little small talk as the men get situated into the room.

You leave and go back to your station in the hallway outside of the four dorms. Over the next several weeks, you continue to overhear comments from the inmates about this counselor and, from time-to-time, you notice that Sam Friday does seem a bit tired and/or aloof. Nothing is a major problem, but his appearance sometimes seems a little odd.

You know that if you mention this through your chain of command, the implications could be very serious, both for Mr. Friday and for yourself. If he does have some type of problem, then he would need to get help, and you would be commended for saying something. However, if he does not, your own supervisor would probably not like the fact that you have generated suspicion where, in fact, none needed to exist. This could also cause some problems for the programming within your area of the prison, regardless of the outcome.

You like working in this section of the prison. It is considered a better area to work that is much more relaxed and where you have more latitude throughout the day. The requirements are not as numerous as in other areas, and there tend to be fewer headaches.

The inmates all get 180 days of good time from finishing the program, and this makes them much more compliant. Essentially, most people would tell you that if it ain't broke, there is no need for you to fix it. As you think to yourself, you wonder . . .

"What should I do?"

CROSS-NATIONAL PERSPECTIVE 16.1

The Prison System of France and the Muslim Inmate Population

Home to Europe's biggest Muslim population and a robust counter-terrorism system, France has long kept a keen watch on Islamic radicalism. In recent years it has been spared big bombings of the kind seen in London and Madrid. But France is no stranger to attack by jihadists, and officials fear it is just a matter of time before they strike again.

The authorities are particularly worried about recruitment to militant Islam in France's overcrowded prisons. "French prisons are a preferred recruiting ground for radical Islamists," Michèle Alliot-Marie, the interior minister, told Le Figaro newspaper. She and her EU counterparts have been working on a joint handbook on how to counter the phenomenon, which touches many European countries, notably Britain. At the end of September, Ms. Alliot-Marie will host an EU seminar, in the heavily Muslim Paris *banlieue* of Saint-Denis, to discuss what to do.

Fiercely secular, France does not collect official statistics based on religion. But Farhad Khosrokhavar, a French specialist on the subject, estimates that Muslims make up well over half France's prison population—far higher than their 8% or so share of the total population. Among these there are currently some 1,100 people behind bars in France for terrorist-related activities, according to Alain Bauer, a criminologist. Ms. Alliot-Marie said that another 55 have been detained this year.

Proselytising among inmates is common. Security officials are worried that many radicals jailed around the time of the 1998 football World Cup, hosted by France, are starting to be released. "Radicalised Islamists become more influential in prison," says Mr Khosrokhavar. He reckons there are a few hundred Islamists actively recruiting behind bars in France.

It is hard to know how to counter this. Concentrating jihadists in one or two penitentiaries, as many countries do, may help them plot attacks from prison. Yet dispersing them, or regularly moving them between high-security prisons in order to disrupt networks, may spread radical ideology and increase recruitment.

Less crowded cells might help. France, whose jail population has grown by 30% since 2001, is building three new prisons to this end. Another idea is to provide more Muslim chaplains to offer a moderate spiritual outlet for Muslim inmates.

Azzedine Gaci, head of the Regional Council of the Muslim Faith in Lyon, makes such visits to the prison in Villefranche-sur-Saône, where he reckons 70% of its 700-odd inmates are Muslim. "They need a different interlocutor," he says. In the absence of competent chaplains, extremists fill the vacuum. France currently has 1,100 chaplains accredited to visit its 63,000 inmates across 195 prisons—yet only 117 of them are Muslim.

Question 1: How might it aid security within French jails and prisons to add more Muslim chaplains to their overall count?

Question 2: In your opinion, how appropriate is it for French administrators to have only 117 of their 1,100 accredited Chaplains be of Muslim orientation when approximately half of all its inmates are Muslims by faith?

SOURCE: "Jailhouse jihad: Fears that terrorism is breeding in French prisons" in *The Economist,* September 18, 2008. Copyright © *The Economist* Newspaper Limited, London 2008. Reprinted with permission.

STUDENT STUDY SITE

Visit the Student Study Site at **www.sagepub.com/hanserintro** to access links to the videos, audio clips, SAGE journal articles, state rankings, and reference materials noted in this chapter, as well as additional study tools including eFlashcards, web quizzes, and more.

chapter 17

Parole and Reintegration

LEARNING OBJECTIVES:

1. Know and understand the basics regarding state parole, its organization, and its administration.

2. Discuss the historical development of parole.

3. Be able to discuss the parole selection process, factors influencing parole decisions, and factors considered when granting and denying parole.

4. Be aware of the common conditions of parole and understand how parole effectiveness can be refined and adjusted to better meet supervision requirements that are based on the offender's behavior.

INTRODUCTION

PHOTO 17.1

Parole also means that offenders will have many more options than might be encountered in a dayroom such as the one shown in this photo.

This chapter addresses a type of offender outcome that represents a successful end to the offender's prison experience: the release from prison on parole. This response to offender behavior falls within the field of corrections but comes at the end of the institutional process. This early release from prison reflects the fact that the offender has been well behaved in prison and also represents a new beginning for that offender, basically, as a reward for his or her prosocial behavior in prison. It should be pointed out that, within the community-based correctional population, the parolee population tends to be quite small when compared with the probation population. Further, the parolee population exists within only a select number of states. This chapter is provided primarily to ensure that the text is complete in its presentation of the correctional system but should not be viewed as a fully comprehensive authority on the use of parole.

PAROLE AND PAROLEE CHARACTERISTICS

State Rankings Link 17.1
Adults on State Parole in 2009.

Parole is a mechanism that has been nearly as controversial as the death penalty (for more on this topic, students should refer to Chapter 18). Parole has had a tortured history in the federal system, resulting in a slow and ongoing effort to eliminate and/or restrict its use in the federal system, and it has also been eliminated in many states throughout the nation. Nevertheless, a substantial number of inmates are on parole throughout the nation, with some still serving sentences under the outdated federal system. **Parole** can be defined as the early release of an offender from a secure facility upon completion of a certain portion of their sentence. As of 2008, the nation's parole population grew to 828,169 offenders, with mandatory releases from prison due to good time provisions accounting for nearly 51% of those offenders who were released on parole (Glaze & Bonczar, 2009). This reflects the fact that the use of discretion in early release processes has declined. As Figure 17.1 demonstrates, it has been found that discretionary releases by parole boards have steadily declined from 55% in 1980 to 22% in 2004. Contrast this against the fact that mandatory parole releases have continued to increase since 1980, and it is clear that states are (by and large) relying more on legislative enactments than on the actual discretion of parole board members.

Among those on parole, roughly 1 out of 8 (or about 12%) are female offenders. During the past decade, the proportion of female parolees has increased from 10% to 12%, making this a 20% increase in the proportion of female offenders represented in the parolee population. In addition, the percentage of parolees who are African American tends to be around 40%. The proportion of Caucasian American offenders has increased during the past several years, coming to 41% of the overall parole population. Roughly 18% of all parolees nationwide are Latino American with another 2% being on other racial categories. Lastly, the largest percentage of parolees were convicted of drug offenses with 37% of the total parolee population having some drug-related conviction. A quarter of all parolees had violent offenses while another quarter had property offenses. Table 17.1 provides an examination of the U.S. parole population by offense.

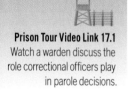

Prison Tour Video Link 17.1
Watch a warden discuss the role correctional officers play in parole decisions.

THE BEGINNING HISTORY OF PAROLE

Two primary figures are attributed to the development of parole: **Alexander Maconochie** and **Sir Walter Crofton**. Alexander Maconochie was in charge of the penal colony at Norfolk Island, and Sir Walter Crofton directed the prison system of Ireland. While Maconochie first developed a general scheme for parole, it was Sir Walter Crofton who later refined the idea and created what was referred to as the **ticket of leave**. The ticket

FIGURE 17.1   State Trends in Mandatory Versus Discretionary Parole

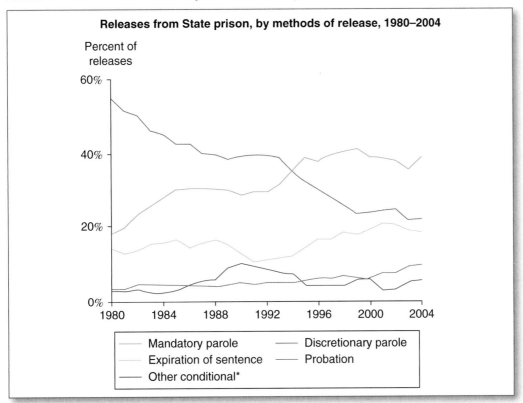

Releases from State prison, by methods of release, 1980–2004

NOTE: Data are from the National Prisoners Statistics (NPS-1) series.

*Other conditional releases include: provisional releases, supervised work furloughs, releases to home arrest or boot camp programs, conditional pardons, conditional medical releases, or unspecified releases.

SOURCE: Glaze, L. E., & Bonczar, T. P. (2006). *Probation and parole in the United States, 2005.* Washington, DC: U.S. Department of Justice.

of leave was basically a permit that was given to a convict in exchange for a certain period of good conduct. Through this process, the convict could instead earn his own wage through his own labor prior to the expiration of his actual sentence. In addition, other liberties were provided so long as the convict's behavior remained within the lawful limits set by the ticket-of-leave system. The ticket-of-leave system is therefore often considered the antecedent to the development of parole.

During the 1600s and 1700s, England implemented a form of punishment known as banishment on a widespread scale. During this time, criminals were sent to the American colonies under reprieve and through stays of execution. Thus, the convicts had their lives spared, but this form of mercy was generally only implemented to solve a labor shortage that existed within the American colonies. Essentially, the convicts were shipped to the Americas to work as indentured servants under hard labor. However, the war of independence within the colonies put an end to this practice, until 1788 when the first shipload of convicts was transported to Australia. Australia was the new dumping ground for convicts who were used as labor just as had been the case in the Americas. The labor was hard, and the living conditions were challenging. However, a ticket-of-leave system was developed on this continent in which different governors had the authority to release convicts who displayed good and stable conduct.

In 1837, Alexander Maconochie, a captain in the Royal Navy, was placed in command over the English penal colony in New South Wales at Norfolk Island, which was nearly 1,000 miles off the eastern coast of Australia. The convicts at Norfolk Island were the worst of the worst since they had already been shipped to Australia for criminal acts in England, only to be later shipped to Norfolk Island due to additional criminal acts or forms of misconduct that were committed while serving time in Australia. The conditions on Norfolk Island were deplorable—so much so that many convicts preferred to be given the death penalty rather than serve time upon the island (Latessa & Allen, 1999).

TABLE 17.1   Parolee Characteristics by Type of Offense

Types of offense	2002	2005
Violent	24%	25%
Property	26	25
Drug	40	37
Public order	…	6
Other*	10	7

NOTE: 2002 was the first year data for type of offences were collected

…Not available.

*In 2002 public order offenses were reported among other offenses.

SOURCE: Glaze, L. E., & Bonczar, T. P. (2006). *Probation and parole in the United States, 2005.* Washington, DC: U.S. Department of Justice.

APPLIED THEORY 17.1

Braithwaite's Crime, Shame, and Reintegration as Related to Parole

According to Cullen and Agnew (2006), John Braithwaite is different from most labeling theorists because he does not suggest noninterventionist approaches. Rather, Braithwaite holds that shaming is necessary for social control and the offender. However, the important issue is what follows shaming: reintegration or stigmatization. Reintegration is essential because shamed individuals are considered to be at a turning point in their lives. It is at this point where offenders can become reacquainted with society or find themselves further entrenched in the criminal subculture. It is when quality social relations exist that they provide the means through which offenders are given the forgiveness and support needed to become members of the community (Cullen & Agnew, 2006).

According to Cullen and Agnew (2006), "restorative justice programs most closely mirror Braithwaite's admonition to meld shaming with reintegration" (p. 277). Restorative justice programs seek to restore and heal the victim, repair the damage to the community, and reintegrate offenders after they have made their commitment to the victim. From this point, "repentant offenders potentially are granted a measure of forgiveness by victims and are reaccepted by their family and community" (p. 277). These attempts at shaming and further reintegration provide much more effective alternatives to stigmatizing sanctions used in the criminal justice system.

In this chapter, the mention of reintegration is particularly important since these offenders will be coming back into the community after serving years in prison. In addition, the "measure of forgiveness" that Cullen and Agnew (2006) refer to is important, since this will be a necessary ingredient if offenders are to have a chance at reintegrating into the community. Thus, Braithwaite's work specifically applies to the reintegration of paroled offenders and explains that, though reconnection with the community is the primary end goal, there is a shaming element that is both proper and necessary. In other words, there must be a genuine consequence to aberrant and/or illegal behavior if the learning mechanisms are to take place. However, once those consequences have been meted out and once the offender has experienced the full impact of those consequences, society has an ethical obligation to cease and desist from applying additional consequences to the offender; to do so is unethical, disproportional, and unproductive. In fact, excessive consequences that go beyond the norm are likely to produce more crime.

Given that there are serious labeling implications for ex-cons well after they have served their term in prison, it is clear that the consequences continue to follow them well after they have completed the duration of their sentence. This is true even after they finish their parole or early release obligations when coming out of prison. Further, these additional consequences affect the prior offender's ability to obtain jobs and necessary resources to function in society. Because of these additional consequences, the punishments are perhaps excessive, and high recidivism rates are therefore expected.

The primary point to Braithwaite's work is that a shaming process is indeed necessary, and this shaming process should be public and hold the offender accountable. However, once that process of accountability has been fulfilled, society must then assume the burden of reintegrating the offender back within the community. Otherwise, we should not be at all surprised when individuals turn back to criminal behavior. In fact, when we fail to offer the chance for reintegration, we essentially have contributed to the recidivism. As a society, it could be argued that if we continue to add consequences beyond the sentence, and if we do this with the knowledge that it is likely to increase recidivism, then we essentially make a knowing choice that encourages further criminality among those in need of our support and guidance.

SOURCE: Cullen, F. T., & Agnew, R. (2006). *Criminological theory: Past to present* (3rd ed.). Los Angeles: Roxbury Publishing Company.

Reference Link 17.1
Read about the idea that prisons are inherently shaming.

While serving in this command, Maconochie proposed a system where the duration of the sentence was determined by the inmate's work habits and righteous conduct. Though this was already used in a crude manner through the ticket-of-leave process in Australia, Maconochie created a **mark system** in which "marks" would be provided to the convict for each day of successful toil. His system was quite well organized and thought out, being based on five main tenets, as described by Barnes and Teeters (1959, p. 419):

1. Release should be based not on the completing of a sentence for a set period of time, but on completion of a determined and specified quantity of labor. In brief, time sentences should be abolished and task sentences substantiated.

2. The quantity of labor a prisoner must perform should be expressed in a number of "marks" which he must earn, by improvement of conduct, frugality of living, and habits of industry, before he can be released.

3. While in prison he should earn everything he receives. All sustenance and indulgences should be added to his debt of marks.

4. When qualified by discipline to do so, he should work in association with a small number of other prisoners, forming a group of six or seven, and the whole group should be answerable for the conduct of labor of each member.

5. In the final stage, a prisoner, while still obliged to earn his daily tally of marks, should be given a proprietary interest in his own labor and be subject to a less rigorous discipline, to prepare him for release into society.

Under this plan, as first described in Chapter 2, convicts were given marks and moved through phases of supervision until they finally earned full release. Because of this, Maconochie's system is considered indeterminate in nature, with convicts progressing through his five specific phases of classification: (1) strict incarceration, (2) intense labor in forced work group or chain gang, (3) limited freedom within a prescribed area, (4) a ticket of leave, and (5) full freedom. This system, as devised by Maconochie, was based on the premise that inmates should be gradually prepared for full release. It is apparent that Maconochie's system utilized versions of intermediate sanctions and indeterminate sentencing. *Indeterminate sentences* include a range of years that will be potentially served by the offender. The offender is released during some point in the range of years assigned by the sentencing judge. Both the minimum and maximum times can be modified by a number of factors such as offender behavior and offender work ethic. The indeterminate sentence stands in contrast to the use of *determinate sentences*, which consist of fixed periods of incarceration imposed on the offender with no later flexibility in the term that is served. This type of sentencing is grounded in notions of retribution, just desserts, and incapacitation. Due to the use of indeterminate sentencing and primitive versions of intermediate sanctioning, Maconochie's mark system is perhaps best thought of as a precursor to parole as well as the use of classification systems. In fact, the use of classification systems tended to be underdeveloped. Thus Maconochie provided a guide in predicting the likelihood of success with convicts, making him well ahead of his time.

However, Maconochie appears to have been too far ahead of his time; many government officials and influential persons in both Australia and England believed that Maconochie's approach was too soft on criminals. His methods of reform drew increasing negative publicity from Australian and English citizens who perceived the system as too lenient on convicts. Ironically, this is not much different from today where the common consensus among Americans is that prisons and punitive sanctions are preferred forms of punishment. Contrarily, Maconochie was fond of criticizing prison operations in England, his own belief being that confinement ought to be rehabilitative in nature rather then punitive (note that this is consistent with the insights of John Augustus and his views on the use of probation). Maconochie's ideas were not popular among government officials of the Crown or the general populace of England, and he ultimately was dismissed from his post on Norfolk Island as well as other commands for being too lenient with convicts. Nevertheless, Maconochie was persistent, and in 1853, he successfully lobbied the **English Penal Servitude Act**, which established several rehabilitation programs for convicts.

The English Penal Servitude Act of 1853 applied to prisons in both England and Ireland. Though Maconochie had spearheaded this act to solidify, legalize, and permanize the use of ticket-of-leave systems, the primary reason for this act's success had more to do with the fact that free Australians were becoming ever more resistant to the use of Australia as the location for banished English convicts. Though this act did not necessarily eliminate the use of banishment in England, it did provide incentive and suggestions for more extensive use of prisons. This law provided guidelines for the length of time that inmates should serve behind bars before being granted a ticket of leave and, according to Cromwell, Carmen, and Alarid (2002, p. 166), maintained the following:

1. The power of revoking or altering the license of a convict will most certainly be exercised in the case of misconduct.

2. If, therefore, he wishes to retain the privilege, which by his good behavior under penal discipline he has obtained, he must prove by his subsequent conduct that he is worthy of Her Majesty's Clemency.

3. To produce a forfeiture of the license, it is by no means necessary that the hold should be convicted of a new offense. If he associates with notoriously bad characters, leads an idle or dissolute life, or has no visible means of obtaining an honest livelihood, and so on, it will be assumed that he is about to relapse into crime, and he will at once be apprehended and recommitted to prison under his original release.

It should be clear that the above guidelines are the basis of a general form of parole. The conditions mentioned in the English Penal Servitude Act of 1853 are also common to today's use of parole in the United States, though, of course, there are now many more technical aspects to the use of parole in today's society. However, the guidelines mentioned (particularly the third item above) clearly demonstrate that the offender's early release is contingent on his or her continued good behavior and desistance from crime as well as criminogenic influences. Because of this and other significant improvements in penal policies in England, as well as Maconochie's contributions to early-release provisions in England, Maconochie has been dubbed the father of parole.

Reference Link 17.2
Read about the Irish (or Crofton) system.

During the 1850s, as first described in Chapter 9, Sir Walter Crofton was the director of the Irish penal system. Naturally, since the English Penal Servitude Act of 1853 was passed during his term of office, he was aware of the changes implemented in prison operations, and he was likewise aware of Maconochie's ideas, which he used to create a classification system that proved useful and workable within the Irish prison system. This classification system utilized three stages of treatment. The first stage placed the convict in segregated confinement with work and training provided to the offender. The second stage was a transition period whereby the convict was set to the task of completing public work projects while under minimal supervision. During the third stage, presuming that the offender proved reliable, he was eventually released on "license" (Dressler, 1962; Latessa & Allen, 1999).

In implementing this classification system, inmates' classification level was specifically measured by the number of marks that they had earned for good conduct, work output, and educational achievement. This idea was, quite naturally, borrowed from Maconochie's system on Norfolk Island. It is also important to point out that the Irish system developed by Sir Walter Crofton was also much more detailed, providing specific written instructions and guidelines that provided for close supervision and control of the offender, using police personnel to supervise released offenders in rural areas, as well as an inspector of released prisoners in the city of Dublin (Cromwell et al., 2002).

Release on license was contingent upon certain conditions, with violations of these conditions providing for the possibility of reimprisonment. "While on license, prisoners were required to submit to monthly reports and were warned against idleness and association with other criminals" (Latessa & Allen, 1999, p. 156). Thus, offenders released on license had to report to either a police officer or another designated person, had to meet specific requirements, had to curtail their social involvements, and could be again incarcerated if they did not maintain those requirements (Latessa & Allen, 1999). This obviously resembled several aspects of modern-day parole programs. In fact, it could be said that contemporary uses of parole in the United States mimic the conditions set forth by Sir Walter Crofton in Ireland.

Parole From 1960 Onward

During the period from 1930 through the 1950s, correctional thought reflected what was then referred to as the "medical model," which centered on the use of rehabilitation and treatment of offenders (see Chapter 2). In general, support for the medical model of corrections began to dissipate during the late 1960s and had all but disappeared by the 1970s. The medical model presumed that criminal behavior was caused by social, psychological, or biological deficiencies that were correctable through treatment interventions. The 1950s were particularly given to the ideology of the medical model, with influential states such as Illinois, New York, and California falling under the treatment banner.

Lasting until the late 1970s, the reintegration era advocated for very limited use of incarceration (only a small proportion of offenders being incarcerated with short periods of incarceration being most commonly recommended). Probation was the preferred sentence, particularly for nonviolent offenders. Indeterminate sentences were utilized, and deinstitutionalization was the theme for this period of corrections. However, this era in corrections was short-lived and received a great deal of criticism. Indeed, the prior medical model of corrections had hardly come to a full conclusion before the community model was also being seriously questioned by skeptics.

The mid- to late 1970s saw a slowly emerging shift take place due to high crime rates that were primarily perceived as the result of high recidivism rates among offenders. This skepticism of rehabilitation was brought to its pinnacle by practitioners who cited (often in an inaccurate manner) the work of Robert Martinson. As students may remember from Chapter 2, Martinson conducted a thorough analysis of research programs on behalf of the New York State Governor's Special Committee on Criminal Offenders. Martinson (1974) examined a number of various programs that included educational and vocational assistance, mental health treatment, medical treatment, early release, and so forth. In his report, often referred to as the **Martinson Report**, he noted that "with few and isolated exceptions, the rehabilitative efforts that have been reported so far have had no appreciable effect on recidivism" (Martinson, 1974, p. 22).

From this point forward, there was a clear shift from a community model of corrections to what has been referred to as a *crime control model of corrections* (see Chapter 2). During the late 1970s and throughout the 1980s crime was a hotly debated topic that often became intertwined with political agendas and legislative action. The sour view of rehabilitation led many states to abolish the use of parole. Indeed, from 1976 onward, more than 14 states and the federal government abolished the use of parole. The state of Maine abolished parole in 1976, followed by California's elimination of discretionary parole in 1978, and the full elimination of parole in Arizona, Delaware, Illinois, Indiana, Kansas, Minnesota, Mississippi, New Mexico, North Carolina, Ohio, Oregon, Virginia, and Washington (Sieh, 2006). In addition, the federal system of parole was also phased out over time. Under the Comprehensive Crime Control Act of 1984, the U.S. Parole Commission only retained jurisdiction over offenders who had committed their offense prior to November 1, 1987. At the same time, the act provided for the abolition of the Parole Commission over the years that followed, with this phasing-out period extended by the **Parole Commission Phaseout Act of 1996**. This act extended the life of the Parole Commission until November 1, 2002, but only in regard to supervising offenders who were still on parole from previous years. Thus, though the U.S. Parole Commission continued to exist, continued use of parole was eliminated, and federal parole offices across the nation were slowly shut down over time (see Figure 17.2 for further information on various developments in parole).

FIGURE 17.2 Historical Developments in Parole

1840	Maconochie creates his "mark system" in Australian penal colony.
1854	Sir Walter Crofton creates the ticket-of-leave system in Ireland.
1869	New York establishes indeterminate sentencing processes.
1870	American Prison Association publicly endorses parole.
1976	Maine abolishes parole.
1984	Federal government abolishes granting additional forms of parole leniency.
1996	State of Ohio becomes the 11th state to formally abolish parole.

SOURCE: Adapted from the *Parole Board Survey*, Association of Paroling Authorities International (2001).

PHOTO 17.2

Members of a Montana parole board listen to a victim's testimony at a parole hearing.

In addition to the eventual elimination of parole, many states implemented determinate sentencing laws, truth-in-sentencing laws, and other such innovations that were designed to keep offenders behind bars for longer periods of time. The obvious flavor of corrections in the 1980s was toward crime control through incarceration and risk containment (Clear & Cole, 2002). This same crime control orientation continued through the 1990s and even through the beginning of the new millennium, with an emphasis on drug offenders and habitual offenders during the 1990s. Also noted were developments in intensive supervision probation (ISP), more stringent bail requirements, and the use of three-strikes penalties. The period during the last half of the 1990s and beyond the year 2000 had a decidedly punitive approach. The costs (both economic and social) have received a great deal of scrutiny even though crime rates lowered during the new millennium. Though there was a dip in crime during this time, it was not necessarily made clear if this was, in actuality, due to the higher rate of imprisonment or due to other demographic factors that impacted the nation.

History of Federal Parole and Supervised Release

Parole of federal inmates began after enactment of legislation on June 25, 1910. At that time, there were three federal penitentiaries, and parole was granted by a parole board at each institution, with the membership of each parole board consisting of the warden of the institution, the physician of the institution, and the Superintendent of Prisons. By 1930, a single Board of Parole in Washington, DC, was established. This board consisted of three members, serving full time, who were appointed by the Attorney General. The Federal Bureau of Prisons performed the administrative functions of the board. In August 1945, the Attorney General ordered that the board report directly to him for administrative purposes. In August 1948, due to a postwar increase in prison population, the Attorney General appointed two additional members, increasing the Board of Parole to five members (Hoffman, 2003).

Legislation in 1950 saw the board increase to eight members with six-year terms. The board was placed in the Department of Justice for administrative purposes. Three of the eight members were designated by the Attorney General to serve as a Youth Corrections Division pursuant to the Youth Corrections Act. In October 1972, the Board of Parole began a pilot reorganization project that eventually included the establishment of five regions, creation of explicit guidelines for parole release decision making, provision of written reasons for parole decisions, and an administrative appeal process (Hoffman, 2003).

In May 1976, the **Parole Commission and Reorganization Act** took effect. This act retitled the Board of Parole as the U.S. Parole Commission and established it as an independent agency within the Department of Justice (Hoffman, 2003). The act provided for nine commissioners appointed by the President, with the advice and consent of the Senate, for six-year terms. These included a chairman, five regional commissioners, and a three-member National Appeals Board. In addition, the act incorporated the major features of the Board of Parole's pilot reorganization project: a requirement for explicit guidelines for parole decision making and written reasons for parole denial; a regional structure; and an administrative appeal process.

Eight years later, the **Comprehensive Crime Control Act of 1984** created a U.S. Sentencing Commission to establish sentencing guidelines for the federal courts and established a regimen of determinate sentences (Hoffman, 2003). The chairman of the Parole Commission is an ex-officio, nonvoting, member of the Sentencing Commission. The decision to establish sentencing guidelines was based in substantial part on the success of the U.S. Parole Commission in developing and implementing its parole guidelines. In 1987, the U.S. Sentencing Commission submitted to Congress its initial set of sentencing guidelines, which took effect that year. As set forth by this act, offenders whose acts were committed on or after November 1, 1987, serve determinate terms under the sentencing guidelines and are not eligible for parole consideration (Hoffman, 2003).

Thus, the Sentencing Commission promulgated a set of sentencing guidelines that were officially instituted within the federal system. During this legislation, parole for federal inmates was essentially abolished, but, unlike what many may realize, the use of supervised release from federal prisons was not, in actuality, entirely eliminated. While official parole and the use of parole boards no longer exist within the federal justice system, the modified version of early release is afforded some federal inmates based on requisites related to sentence completion. This postrelease supervision is termed **supervised release** and is provided as a separate part of the sentence under the jurisdiction of the court. This type of early release is administered by the sentencing court for a given inmate, similar to community supervision under probation. In the federal system, the court, not the parole board, has the authority to impose sanctions on released inmates if they violate the terms or conditions of their supervision.

At the same time, the act provided for the official abolition of the Parole Commission on November 1, 1992 (five years after the sentencing guidelines took effect). This phase-out provision did not adequately provide for persons sentenced under the law in effect prior to November 1, 1987, who had not yet completed their sentences. Elimination of, or reduction in, parole eligibility for such cases would raise a serious ex post facto issue. To address this problem, the **Judicial Improvements Act of 1990** extended the life of the Parole Commission until November 1, 1997 (Hoffman, 2003). However, this extension would still prove to not sufficiently address the complexities related to the residual paroled population, and this resulted in yet another act, the Parole Commission Phaseout Act of 1996, which again extended the life of the Parole Commission for the same reason. This act authorized the continuation of the Parole Commission until 2002. In addition, it required the Attorney General, beginning in 1998, to report to Congress annually on whether it was more cost-effective for the Parole Commission to continue as a separate agency or for its remaining functions to be transferred elsewhere. It is important to note the U.S. Attorney General has reported each year that it is more cost-effective for the Parole Commission to continue as a separate agency. Since then, another act, the 21st Century Department of Justice Appropriations Authorization Act of 2002, extended the life of the Parole Commission until November 1, 2005.

Currently, the U.S. Sentencing Commission oversees the supervision of offenders who leave federal confinement early due to credit for good behavior. According to the *2007 Federal Guidelines Manual*, the court

> is required to impose a term of supervised release to follow imprisonment if a sentence of imprisonment of more than one year is imposed or if a term of supervised release is required by a specific statute. The court may depart from this guideline and not impose a term of supervised release if it determines that supervised release is neither required by statute nor required for any of the following reasons: (1) to protect the public welfare; (2) to enforce a financial condition; (3) to provide drug or alcohol treatment or testing; (4) to assist the reintegration of the defendant into the community; or (5) to accomplish any other sentencing purpose authorized by statute.

Though the Sentencing Commission oversees the majority of federal offenders released from prison, there is apparent support for the continued use of the Parole Commission. On July 21, 2008, during the meeting of the 110th session of Congress, the **United States Parole Commission Extension Act of 2008** was passed to provide for the continued performance of the U.S. Parole Commission (U.S. Congress, 2008) and became Public Law No. 110-312. So strong was support for this act that the initial bill passed in the Senate by unanimous consent prior to going to Congress and, subsequently, being signed by then President George Bush (GovTrack.us, 2010). From this brief discussion of federal parole, it should be clear that this mechanism is a vestige from the past, but, at the same time, it continues to reemerge with new life as an operational organization. While it may be debated as to whether federal parole may, one day, return to its previous prominence, it is clear that the federal system, like state systems, will continue to have the need to supervise offenders released from prison, regardless of the agency mechanism that is ultimately used.

PAROLE AT THE STATE LEVEL

With respect to the administration and organization of parole boards, it is clear that there is a great deal of variation in their structure and implementation. Table 17.2 shows that many state parole board systems select members through a variety of means (most typically including selection by the state's governor). The term of service for parole board members, the number of persons serving on parole boards, and the use of either part-time or full-time members greatly varies from state to state. The types of activities that each board may perform and/or the sources of information that each board may use also vary greatly.

TABLE 17.2 State Parole Board Appointments, Structure, Terms, and Functions

	Governor Appoint	Leg. Confirm.	Term Years	Number on the Board	F (Full) or P (Part) Time	Use of Parole Analysis
Alabama	X		5	5	P	NO
Alaska	X	X	5	5	P	NO
Arizona	X	X	5	5	F	YES(6)(7)
Arkansas	X	X		5F, 2P	F	
California	X	X	7	6	F	YES
Colorado	X	X	6	7	F	NO
Connecticut	X	X	4	15P, 3F	F/P	YES(6)
Delaware	X	X	4	5P, 1F	F/P	NO
Florida	X	X	6	3	F	YES(6)(7)
Georgia	X	X	7	7	F	YES(6)
Hawaii	X	X	4	3P, 1F	F/P	NO

(Continued)

TABLE 17.2 (Continued)

	Governor Appoint	Leg. Confirm.	Term Years	Number on the Board	F (Full) or P (Part) Time	Use of Parole Analysis
Idaho	X	X	3	5	P	YES
Illinois	X	X	6	15	F	YES(7)
Indiana	X		4	5	F	NO
Iowa	X	X	4	5P, 2F	F/P	YES(8)
Kansas	X	X	4	4	F	NO
Kentucky	X	X	4	8	F	NO
Louisiana	X	X	11	7	F	NO
Maine						
Maryland	X	X	6	8	F	YES(9)
Mass.	X		5	7	F	YES(9)
Michigan	Dir. of Corr.		4	10	F	YES(7)
Minnesota	Dir. of Corr.					
Missouri	X	X	6	7	F	YES(6)(7)(9)
Montana	X	X	4	5	P	YES(6)
Nebraska	X	X	6	5	F	NO
Nevada	X		4	13P, 7F	F/P	YES(9)
New Hamp.	X		5	7	P	NO
New Jersey	X	X	6	15	F	YES(9)
New Mexico	X	X	6	9	P	NO
New York	X	X	6	19	F	
N. Carolina	X		4	3	F	YES(6)(7)
North Dak.	X	X		6	P	
Ohio	Dir. of Corr.		life	9	F	YES(7)(9)
Oklahoma	1		4	5	P	YES(6)
Oregon	X	X	4	3	F	YES(6)(7)
Penn.	X	X	6	9	F	YES
Rhode Is.	X	X	3(12)	7P, 1F	P	
S. Dakota	2	X	4	6	P	NO
Tennessee	X		6	7	F	YES(9)
Texas	X	X	6	18	F	YES(8)
Utah	X	X	5	5	F	YES(6)
Vermont	X	X	3	5	P	NO
Virginia	X	X	-11	3	F	YES(9)

	Governor Appoint	Leg. Confirm.	Term Years	Number on the Board	F (Full) or P (Part) Time	Use of Parole Analysis
Washington	X	X	5	3	F	YES(6)
West Virg.	X	X	6	5	F	
Wisconsin	X	X	2(10)	7	F	NO
Wyoming	X	X	6	7	P	
U.S. Par. Co.	President	X	6	5	F	YES(9)

(1) Appointed by the Governor, one by Supreme Court, one by Court of Appeals.

(2) Two by the Governor, two by the Attorney General, and two by Supreme Court.

(3) Three years for the Chair and two for the members.

(4) Eight years for the Chair and four to six for the members.

(5) Full-time five years and part-time three years.

(6) Case reports writing and interviews.

(7) Hold probable cause hearings.

(8) Hold revocation hearings.

(9) Hold parole consideration hearings.

(10) The Chair 2 years, others on merit.

(11) At the pleasure of the Governor.

(12) Chair is double appointment, three years as a member and two years as Chair.

SOURCE: Adapted from the Association of Paroling Authorities, International: Parole Board Survey (2001). Retrieved March, 11, 2009, from http://www.apaintl.org/Pub-ParoleBoardSurvey2001.html.

This demonstrates that there is a very great deal of disparity throughout the United States among the top organizationally ranked decision-making bodies that decide on issues related to parole.

When taken together, the variation in state implementation of the day-to-day supervision of parolees (e.g., as a separate function or when being combined with probation caseloads) and the variation that exists among parole boards themselves make it clear that the entire organizational structure can be quite complicated. While this may, on the face of it, appear to be the case, there is a great deal of similarity in the types of laws, forms of supervision, and regulations that are required throughout the nation. While each state naturally has the right and ability to administer community supervision functions in a manner that is most suitable for that state, it will become clear that there are as many similarities between probation and parole programs around the nation as there are differences. As you progress through the remaining chapters, common trends and tendencies will become more apparent.

The Granting of Parole in State Systems

In most states, offender cases are assigned to various individual parole board members who are tasked with reviewing the case so that they can formulate their initial recommendations. The recommendations that they provide are typically honored and accepted as written. Most states that follow this process hold a formal hearing where parole board members may share their views. When the parole hearing is conducted with the offender seeking parole, it may be that all members involved with the decision are present or just one member is present. It is not always the case that all parole board members meet with the inmate seeking parole, but the process may be modified considerably from what is typically presented on television. Lastly, when parole hearings are conducted, the board may convene at the facility where the inmate is located (requiring the board to travel), or the inmate may be brought to the board, wherever the board is located (in many cases, the state capitol).

The process and guidelines for parole selection tend to vary considerably from state to state. Some states have a minimum amount of time that must be served. Others have stipulations on the types of

crimes that were committed in the past. Naturally, some states have both of these criteria as well as others to regulate the parole process. However, the actual decision by any parole review decision-making body is often made by members who have a great deal of discretion. Indeed, it appears that parole boards are influenced by a wide variety of criteria, many of which are not necessarily noted by statute or official agency guidelines. Institutional infractions, the age of the offender, marital status, level of education, and other factors may all weigh into the parole board's decision making.

Naturally, one of the key concerns with granting parole is the probability of recidivism. To a large extent, the prediction process has been little better than guesswork. For decades, the development of prediction devices has continued with an attempt to standardize risk factors. Psychometric tools and statistical analyses have ultimately rested upon actuarial forms of risk prediction. In most cases, it is the objective use of statistical risk prediction that turns out to be more accurate than that which allows for individual subjectivity. There are, of course, some exceptions, since the context surrounding the statistical data may be important and may provide alternative explanations as to why a certain set of numbers and/or statistical outcomes may have been obtained. However, this often simply results in the overprediction of likely reoffending. Nevertheless, this is costly to prison systems, and, in some states, there may be a need to reduce prison system overcrowding. Indeed, parole mechanisms can serve as release valves for prison systems that become overstuffed with offenders. When this occurs, there may be a need for a certain amount of offender releases, and parole boards may have to make tough decisions that do not necessarily comport with the formal risk assessment that is based on a standardized instrument. This is where the difficulty tends to occur, and this demonstrates why, on the one hand, it is counterproductive for standardized risk assessment instruments to overpredict (as with the Wisconsin Risk Assessment scale), yet, on the other hand, subjective decision making is a necessary evil that is fraught with peril, resulting in mispredictions that ultimately lead to serious mistakes in determining an offender's likelihood to recidivate.

Other factors also affect the decision to grant parole. For instance, an inmate may (on a standardized instrument) have a high likelihood of reoffending. But, the type of reoffending may be of a petty nature. In such instances, parole boards may decide to grant parole despite the fact that the offender is not considered a good risk based on a pure analysis of whether he or she will, or will not, reoffend. Thus, it is clear that the specific type of reoffending is also an important consideration among parole board personnel. As just noted, this may be an especially important consideration when parole boards are aware that the state's prison system is overcrowded and that a certain number of releases will assist prison administrators in maintaining their prison population levels within required guidelines. Thus, it is better to release a person likely of relapsing on drugs and/or alcohol or who may commit some form of shoplifting than it is to release someone likely of committing some form of violent crime. It is with this next-best-solution approach that parole boards may be compelled (though not legally required) to make their releasing decisions.

It is important for students to appreciate the problems associated with prison overcrowding. As shown in past chapters, federal court rulings during the 1970s and 1980s penalized many state prison systems and essentially forced them to honor a variety of civil rights standards when incarcerating inmates. Thus, the issue of overcrowding cannot be taken lightly by prison administrators, and state systems resort to a number of alternatives to alleviate this overcrowding. Some states are better than others at finding innovative means of housing and/or supervising offenders. But, among those states that still use parole, it is a fact that this option is one of the means by which state prison systems resolve their overcrowding problems, meaning that these state correctional systems rely on their community correctional systems to augment and support their institutional correctional systems. Thus, parole boards may play a key role in bridging these two components in an effort to ameliorate challenges facing a state correctional system.

The fact that parole boards can play such a role should not be underestimated. They may, in fact, be under some pressure to assist the overall state system. Further, consider that these boards are often constructed by the governor of a given state. In some cases, state politics and state priorities may come into play, affecting the decision making of some parole board cases. This is particularly true when the parole board's administration is consolidated rather than independent in nature (as earlier discussed in this chapter). The point in this discussion is to demonstrate that parole boards do not operate in a complete vacuum. The influences of the surrounding contextual reality are inevitable, and these influences come from a number of directions. Indeed, prison wardens, state offices, victims, the parolee's family, and the public media may all have an impact upon the discretion employed by parole board members, individually and collectively.

Other points that may lead to premature release may be more relevant to the individual offender's circumstances. For instance, the offender may have been convicted when very young but may have committed a very serious crime (e.g., a multiple shooting) that carried a very lengthy sentence. It may be that the parole board simply considers the maturation of that offender and, as much of the criminological research demonstrates, considers that the offender is less likely to reoffend and more likely to remain crime free in the later years of his life. In addition, an occasional situation may develop where the offender considered for parole has extenuating circumstances in outside society such as an ill or dying family member who is close to the offender, or perhaps children of the offender who are in need of parental contact. In these cases as well, it may be that the parole board will grant priority in releasing that offender from incarceration while noting that appropriate levels of community supervision should be maintained. Lastly, there are various circumstances where offenders are given compassionate release. Hanser (2007) notes that this is one option given to numerous inmates who are terminally ill. Hospice programs and other forms of medically related release programs have been implemented in a number of states, even those that typically adopt a hardened stance on crime and offender processing (Hanser, 2007).

Journal Article Link 17.2
Read about attitudes regarding compassionate release of terminally ill offenders.

Video Link 17.2
Watch a clip about prison hospice.

PAROLE AS THE CORRECTIONAL RELEASE VALVE FOR PRISONS

The intent for using parole, at least initially, was to provide an incentive to inmates for prosocial behavior while also providing for a gradual process of reintegration into society. This process was intended to be based upon the behavior of the inmates and their progress in work assignments and programming while serving their sentence. The use of parole was not, however, intended to be a mechanism to assist prisons in maintaining population overflow within prisons. In fact, the soundest decisions for parole do not consider prison populations at all but, instead, are based entirely upon the factors relevant to the inmates and their behavior.

Nevertheless, states around the nation find themselves considering the increased use of parole or early release due to problems with prison overcrowding (see Figure 17.3). State correctional systems may find it difficult to house the influx of offenders when their budgets are not increased to accommodate this continual flow of new inmates. The state of Arkansas is a very good example of how prison overcrowding has become a basis for the increased use of parole options. In 2001, the Arkansas Board of Correction and Community Punishment implemented an accelerated parole scheme to release over 500 inmates, citing the need to free prison and jail space due to the state's record-breaking incarcerated population. The state's system was so backlogged that over 1,000 state inmates were being held in county jails due to a lack of prison space ("Arkansas Speeds Parole," 2001). This same problem has been noted in other areas of the nation.

The state of Arkansas, in dealing with the overcrowding issue, lowered the security level of many cell blocks and facilities from maximum to medium security and from medium to minimum security. Further, inmates who were classified as lower security levels were also eligible for parole at a much quicker rate and would therefore be released from confinement more quickly. Arkansas sought to lower security levels in prisons because this required fewer correctional officers to guard the inmates. In addition, the paroling of more inmates also reduced the number of inmates needing to be supervised. This addressed the shortage of correctional officers in Arkansas and was implemented by reducing the number of officers that would eventually be needed to maintain the prison population. It is clear that these policies—artificially lowering inmate security levels—were dangerous and based not on the security of the institution or society but on economic concerns.

Whenever correctional systems use parole with the intent to reduce correctional populations rather than facilitate reintegration of offenders, they are using parole as a **release valve mechanism** for their prison population. This is becoming increasingly more common in states, during recent economic challenges, that face state governments. In fact, many states are embracing the move toward reentry due, in part, to the fact that this trend reduces the number of inmates within their prison facilities. While reentry efforts can be useful in reforming offenders and thereby reducing their likelihood of

FIGURE 17.3   Parole Population Increases and Decreases by State (2002)

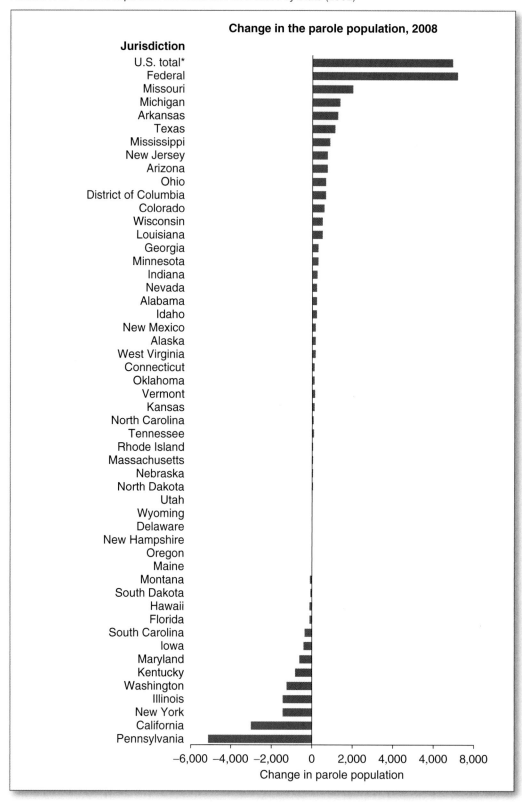

SOURCE: Glaze, L. E., & Bonczar, T. P. (2009). *Probation and parole in the United States, 2008*. Washington, DC: U.S. Department of Justice.

recidivism, such practices should operate regardless of prison population levels. If prison population levels determine the likelihood of release, then release decisions are made due to monetary, not public safety, considerations. This is a dangerous game to play in corrections, and puts the public at risk for future criminal victimization.

CORRECTIONS AND THE LAW 17.1

Liability of Parole Board Members for Violation of Substantive or Procedural Rights

For the most part, it is clear that parole boards are not typically liable for violations of substantive or procedural rights when determining initial parole decisions. This should not be confused with decisions during parole revocation hearings. In terms of revocation hearings, the Supreme Court case of *Morrissey v. Brewer* (1972) clearly established a number of rights related to due process through a prompt informal inquiry before some form of impartial hearing officer. However, initial decisions to grant parole are simply a privilege to which an inmate has not constitutionally secured the right. Though inmates do not have a right to parole, they do have a right not to be discriminated against on the bases of race, religion, sex, creed, and so forth, when such determinations are being made. One case, *United States v. Irving* (1982), was filed under Section 1983 of 42 U.S. Code in the Seventh Circuit. In this case, the offender alleged systematic racial discrimination against African American inmates with respect to parole board decisions for release. Interestingly, the circuit court did hold that the parole board members themselves had absolute immunity when faced with such suit. However, the Seventh Circuit noted that the offender could still sue for declaratory relief (essentially requesting an injunction that the parole board change its practices) due to the fact that the Seventh Circuit found evidence that tended to demonstrate discrimination on the part of the parole board.

Thus, it may be that individual parole board members are immune from liability when performing their functions. Yet, on the other hand, offenders still retain certain civil rights under the Fourteenth Amendment that must be honored by parole boards just as they must be honored by custodial corrections officials. This is a reasonable point since, after all, the desire to eliminate bias and discrimination among government officials was the actual reason that Section 1983 forms of redress were created.

Just as prison officials must provide constitutional treatment of prisoners, so should parole-granting bodies.

One additional point of interest regarding parole board liability revolves around the rights of offenders who are released on parole, only later to find out that such a release was a mistake on the part of the parole board itself. While such instances are not common, they have occurred frequently enough to be ruled on by more than one federal court. Indeed, two lower courts have held that the protections in *Morrissey* also confer some substantive protections for inmates who are mistakenly released. In both *Ellard v. Alabama Board of Pardons and Paroles* (1987) and *Kelch v. Director, Nevada Department of Prisons* (1993), it was determined that once a state confers a right to be released, the inmate's due process rights go beyond the contours set by *Morrissey*.

Indeed, it was determined that the grant of freedom places substantive limits on a state's power to reincarcerate an inmate who has been mistakenly released. In the *Ellard* case it was held that a mistakenly released inmate could not be reincarcerated unless the release violated some sort of state law and that this departure from state law substantially undermined a state's penological interests (see the 1987 U.S. Supreme Court case, *Turner v. Safley*, for a discussion on legitimate penological interests). A similar ruling was found in the *Kelch* case as well, demonstrating a consistency among circuit court rulings and thereby lending support for the point that parolees do not have a right to parole, prior to the parole-granting decision. However, this changes when they are actually released on parole, with *Morrissey* protections affecting revocation proceedings for those legitimately on parole and a subsequent expectation of parole surfacing when offenders are mistakenly and prematurely released from the prison environment by parole board officials.

SOURCE: Barton, B., & Hanser, R. D. (2011). *Community-based corrections: A text/reader.* Thousand Oaks, CA: Sage.

THE ROLE OF INSTITUTIONAL PAROLE OFFICERS

Institutional parole officers, often referred to as case managers, will work with the offender and a number of institutional personnel to aid the offender in making the transition from prison life to community supervision while on parole. These professionals are often referred to as caseworkers as well as institutional parole officers, denoting their reintegrative role in the parole process. Thus, this professional serves both a security function (assessing suitability for parole) and a reintegration function (providing casework services inside the prison and networks that extend beyond the prison). Much of the information presented in this section regarding prerelease planning and the role of the institutional parole officer follows information from the state of Oklahoma's Pre-Release Planning and Reentry Process guidelines (Jones, 2007).

Audio Link 17.1
Hear about the role that parole officers play in supervising offenders.

During prerelease planning, prison staff work together to provide a bridge of services that connect the offender to the outside world. A great deal of work can go into the planning and preparation process of an inmate's exit from prison. This section will shed some light on the other aspects of the institutional parole officer's job and function, since these professionals provide a linking-pin function between the prison world and the outside community.

Upon determining that an inmate is suitable for parole, the institutional parole officer will begin the prerelease planning process that attends to the offender's transition from prison to the community. This process typically begins about six months prior to release and involves a shift from institutional case planning to individual community preparedness. Prior to exiting the prison, the goal of a good reintegration program should be to ensure that the offender has the support, information, and contacts necessary to begin anew, without having to do self-exploration during the initial three- to six-month period of leaving the prison. Even small details must be attended to, such as providing offenders with essentials, such as proper clothing and shoes that are appropriate for the season and are not marked as being inmate clothing; proper identification; and appropriate referrals to community agencies that can assist with other services.

Throughout the process, agency administration will tend to track the offender's progress, keeping a careful eye on the six months prior to release. At this point, the offender may experience problems with anxiety due to nervousness over his or her newly expected freedom, the responsibilities of the outside world, and the effects of prisonization inside the facility. A good prerelease program will address these issues in advance, preparing the inmate psychologically for release. Aside from inmates' initial entry into prison, this period is often one of the most stressful points for offenders coping with prison life since so much of their future is unexpected and since they will be held to expectations that they have not had to meet in years.

Video Link 17.3
Watch a video about preparing for release.

Various forms and checklists will be completed during this time as interviews are completed as part of the review case plan that notes the offender's approach toward release. These interviews will seek to identify various needs that the offender might have upon release. Needs-based assessment instruments perform this function and are used to determine an offender's treatment needs. Identified needs can be many but often consist of some program that the offender did not complete while in prison, such as educational plans or substance abuse treatment programs. Other needs may be related to the payment of restitution, ensuring transportation, making provisions for child support, or other issues relevant to an offender. According to Jones (2007), of the Oklahoma Department of Corrections, the prerelease plan must, at a minimum, include the following:

1. The proposed residence of the offender or referral to temporary housing.

2. Information regarding the offender's financial obligations and identification of the proposed employment, a referral to assist the offender in locating employment, or the means in which the offender will lawfully support him- or herself.

3. Program referrals for any aftercare needed as a result of programs completed while incarcerated or for services to satisfy an identified need that was not addressed while the offender was incarcerated.

Video Link 17.4
Watch a video about employment after release.

Beyond this, staff should note any unique circumstances in the prerelease plan that might provide challenges to the successful reintegration of the offender. This will typically be included in the "Adjustment Review" and will also be included with what is often referred to as the Offender Accountability Plan. The **Offender Accountability Plan** addresses needs for restitution, the need to respect the rights and privacy of prior victims, and any particular arrangements that have been made with the victim, as well as provisions that might be included to ensure the offender's responsibility to the community at large.

The actual day of release is an important milestone for the offender and is actually critical to the offender's successful reintegration. This should be treated as more than a nostalgic moment, and the seriousness of the new challenge ahead should be kept in focus. Activities should focus on the last few tasks required for a seamless transition to the community. In addition, the offender should be provided a portfolio of the various services available, requirements of parole, and so forth, allowing the offender to keep the information and requirements organized. Organizational skills may be somewhat impaired given the newness of the release experience and the likely euphoria that will be experienced.

Lastly, Torres (2005) points out that although release from the prison facility can be a euphoric experience, it can also subsequently result in unexpected disappointment and frustration for the offender. Torres (2005) provides an insightful description of the psychological challenges associated with offenders' reintegration as they navigate between their life prior to incarceration and the life that they now face:

> The parolee's memories of family, friends, and loved ones represent snapshots frozen in time, but in reality, everyone has changed, moved away, taken a new job, grown up, or perhaps most disappointingly become almost strangers. The attempts to restore old relationships can be very threatening and eventually disappointing. In addition, the presence of almost complete freedom after years of living in a structured, confined prison setting can also add tremendous stress to adjusting to the open community where the offender must now assume major responsibilities of transportation, obtaining a driver's license, finding a job, reporting for drug testing, and so on. If married, with children, the spouse may unrealistically expect the offender to immediately begin providing financial relief to the family that perhaps has endured financial hardships while the breadwinner was away. Other barriers to success include civil disabilities that prohibit the felon from voting . . . and most importantly, from being employed in certain occupations. (p. 1125)

Institutional parole officers are cognizant of the situation that faces upcoming parolees. They must ensure that the offender has the full range of support necessary to face what can be actually traumatic as an adjustment demand. The offender will come to grips with issues that most people do not consider, making the experience of release sometimes a bit bittersweet. Offenders may (or may not) themselves realize the full range of emotional experiences that they will have upon release, and it is the job of the institutional parole officer to, among other duties and responsibilities associated with the offender's release, ensure that appropriate support for coping is provided to the offender who may be disappointed and/or overwhelmed by the experience.

COMMON CONDITIONS OF PAROLE

The terms and conditions for parolees, in most cases, are identical to many of those included for offenders on probation. For instance, the state of Oklahoma requires parole fees of $40 at a minimum and also clearly demarcates the potential outcomes if an offender violates the terms of his or her parole, providing a list of potential outcomes that include additional levels of supervision, reintegration training, addition of day reporting centers, weekend incarceration, nighttime incarceration, intensive parole, jail time, and incarceration. This is similar to probation when offenders violate the terms and conditions of their supervision. If possible, the offender will be kept on supervision (depending on the nature of the violation) but will experience a graduated set of increasingly restrictive sanctions and requirements that will become additional conditions to his or her parole requirements. Figure 17.4 provides an example of some of the terms and conditions of parole in the state of Connecticut. The terms and conditions, for the most part, tend to be very similar from state to state. In addition, conditions (such as noted in Number 14 of Figure 17.4) unique to the offender are not as frequently used aside from additional fines and/or community service, unless the offender happens to be in a specialized category of population typologies (such as with sex offenders), but even in these cases restrictions tend to be similar to most others required of other sex offenders.

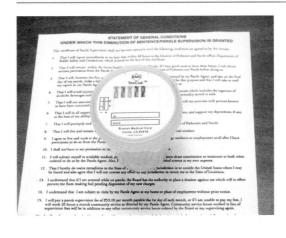

PHOTO 17.3

The sheet of paper underneath this urinalysis cup clearly identifies the conditions of an offender's parole. In this case, the parole officer is making it clear that the offender is expected to remain drug free by placing the urinalysis cup directly on top of the list of parole conditions.

Journal Article Link 17.3
Read about how retribution continues even after release.

TECHNOLOGY AND EQUIPMENT 17.1

New Dawn Technologies—Case Management Software as a Service, the JustWare System

For over 15 years, New Dawn Technologies has helped make communities safer by providing leading-edge case management, data integration, and public access solutions to government agencies, including courts, prosecutors, probation and parole agencies, pretrial services, and public defenders. One key service that this company provides to both probation and parole agencies is the use of an automated case management system hosted online. The hosted software as a service (SaaS) solution, named JustWare, provides complete case management functionality via a secure server site. New Dawn provides and maintains the servers, manages all backups, and conducts all hardware and server software updates. Of more critical concern to parole officers are the specific benefits that JustWare provides, as follows:

Increases Parole Officer Safety

JustWare enables agencies to set up notification features that will alert officers to any possible hazards associated with an offender (e.g., "vicious dog," "do not meet at offender's home"). This information can be entered into notes fields and/or put into an "attributes" field that will automatically pop up when the officer opens the offender's name record. As probation and parole officers are frequently on the road, they must be able to access the information about their clients when they are not at the office. JustWare is available from anywhere with a secure web connection, enabling officers to check an individual's record immediately before going to visit him or her and see if there is any safety information of which they should be aware.

Manage Client Personal, Case, and Condition Information

Each name screen can contain family details, physical identifiers, alerts, employment history, educational background, military record, medical and substance abuse history, and much more. Agencies can track unlimited amounts and types of contact information, family or other key relationships, identification numbers, unique attributes, events, notes, files, tasks, and more.

JustWare will also track case information and notes for any of the current and past cases in which clients have been involved. JustWare's case screens track all court conditions/sentencing (e.g., random drug/alcohol testing, electronic monitoring, community service), details about the crime and court case, intoxicants/drugs, treatments, referral to programs, service providers, contact with the client, locations, and much more. Officers can also link other closely related cases, even if none of the clients or other key people is the same within the cases. Because you define your case summary screens, they can display virtually anything for summary including treatment attendance, drug test results, financial obligations, offender photos, and much more. These summaries can be printed or exported to other programs. JustWare visually alerts agencies and parole officers of any important information regarding any personnel or cases. You can set up an unlimited number of attributes (e.g., "dangerous environment," "needs interpreter," "prior offenses," and more) and specify which of them should appear as a pop-up when officers or staff open a case. Lastly, JustWare's screens are set up to track the information frequently requested by other probation and parole agencies.

E-Mail Key Reports

Have key reports automatically e-mailed to a group or an individual interested party on demand or on a schedule. Agencies can subscribe to key, customized reports, such as caseload reports, monthly and quarterly reports, calendar reports, and more. Reports can be contained within the e-mail body or attached as a separate document (exportable to Adobe Acrobat, Microsoft Excel, Rich Text Format, XML, etc.). This is a great solution for elected officials, administrators, or even external stakeholders such as law enforcement or judicial staff who need regular key reports and updates at critical times.

SOURCE: New Dawn – JustWare Probation and Parole. Reprinted with permission from New Dawn Technologies. Retrieved from: http://newdawn.com/solutions/justice-solutions/probation/

REENTRY INITIATIVES

Before we can discuss offender reentry programs, we must understand what constitutes offender reentry. Some observers note that offender reentry is the natural byproduct of incarceration, because all prisoners who are not sentenced to life in prison and who do not die in prison will reenter the community at some

FOCUS TOPIC: 17.1

Freedmen, Inc. Halfway House for Offenders Released From Prison

Freedmen, Inc. is a faith-based organization that works with a variety of organizations in the community to provide offenders with housing, transportation, employment, job skills, spiritual guidance, mental health, and substance abuse assistance. This organization's board of directors includes numerous people who are active in reentry efforts in their community. The House of Healing, as it is called, is the primary home in which offenders are housed, but there are other homes as well.

It is important to understand that most of the efforts of this organization are funded through donations and church-based collaborations. Naturally, this means that there is a strong Biblical basis to much of the programming. While this may be problematic to some people, this program is designed for offenders who desire this type of reentry experience.

Though this program was originally designed for men, there is now a sister program that aids female offenders in reentry. This points toward the growing reentry needs of the community. These women engage in programming that is similar to the programs in which their male counterparts engage; however, they do not stay in the same facility as the male participants.

This organization is one example of how grassroots efforts in communities can provide services that aid persons trying to rebuild their life after incarceration while, at the same time, making the community safer by offering participants alternatives to crime.

SOURCE: Louisiana Department of Public Safety and Corrections (2010). Reentry in Louisiana. Baton Rouge, LA: LDOC.

---

point. According to this school of thought, reentry is not a program or some kind of legal status but rather a process that almost all offenders will undergo. A variant on this approach to reentry is the concept that **offender reentry**, simply defined, includes all activities and programming conducted to prepare ex-convicts to return safely to the community and to live as law-abiding citizens (Nunez-Neto, 2008).

Although this broad definition of reentry certainly encompasses all the activities that may impinge on or affect a prisoner's reentry into society, it may be a cumbersome one for the purposes of crafting and evaluating government policies. This has led many in the field to focus on a more narrow and thus more manageable definition of reentry. This more narrow definition is often stated in two parts: correctional programs that focus on the transition to the community (such as prerelease, work release, halfway houses, or other programs specifically aiming at reentry) and programs that have initiated some form of treatment (such as substance abuse, life skills, education, or mental health) in prison that is linked to community programs that will continue the treatment once the prisoner has been released (Nunez-Neto, 2008).

To demonstrate how the reentry effort has become a nationwide priority, consider that the Second Chance Act was signed into law on April 9, 2008, and was designed to improve outcomes for people returning to communities from prisons and jails. This first-of-its-kind legislation authorizes federal grants to government agencies and nonprofit organizations to provide employment assistance, substance abuse treatment, housing, family programming, mentoring, victim support, and other services that can help reduce recidivism.

PHOTO 17.4

Taffi Dupre and Amanda Peoples are parole officers who also work with the state of Louisiana's victim-offender dialogue program. These officers work their usual tasks as community supervision officers but also aid victims who wish to meet with offenders to gain understanding of the criminal incident that took place.

Audio Link 17.2
Listen to a clip about ex-offenders and medical care.

VIOLATIONS OF PAROLE, PAROLE WARRANTS, AND PAROLE REVOCATION PROCEEDINGS

No discussion pertaining to parole (and particularly an entire chapter on the subject) would be complete without at least noting some of the issues associated with the revocation of that sentencing option. The

FOCUS TOPIC: 17.2

Reentry in Louisiana

Approximately 15,000 state offenders are released each year from Louisiana prisons to Louisiana communities—usually the communities where they were living when they committed their crimes. Many offenders are released with only a bus ticket and $10. Once in the community, they are expected to get a job, earn a living, contribute to the well-being of a family, follow the law, and generally get along with their law-abiding neighbors. Within five years, half will be back in prison, either for violating conditions of their release or for committing new crimes. That translates into more dollars, more victims, more frustration, and diminished success when the offender is released the next time.

People are spending years, sometimes decades, cycling in and out of probation and parole offices and prisons, seemingly unable to disengage from the criminal justice system. In Louisiana, the recidivism (return-to-prison) rate is approximately 50% after five years. Reducing the return-to-prison rate by even 10% would result in significant dollar savings for the state and its citizens and, hopefully, an enhanced quality of life in communities across the state. The question of what happens to men and women when they leave prison has never been as urgent as it is today.

Louisiana's Response

In 2002, the Louisiana Department of Public Safety and Corrections organized and standardized programs and services to deal with these issues and to better prepare offenders for a successful reintegration into their communities. Offenders are provided the opportunity to participate in a variety of educational, vocational, faith-based, and therapeutic programs to aid their reentry efforts. Louisiana's response will improve public safety, reduce recidivism, decrease victimization, and reduce the financial burden of its correctional system.

Two unique forms of programming offered for offenders reentering the community include substance abuse and religious programming. While these types of interventions are common to most correctional systems, Louisiana has implemented two unique programs that merit specific mention and consideration.

Substance Abuse

Of the offenders in the state correctional system, 80% have substance abuse problems that contribute to their criminality. It is imperative that the department continue to provide substance abuse treatment and education for incarcerated offenders and subsequently link them with services in the community upon release. The department continues to develop and expand community partnerships with local government and community organizations through parish sheriffs, community volunteers, and private companies to improve substance abuse education and treatment to offenders.

Offenders are provided the opportunity to participate in a variety of substance abuse education programs including Alcoholics Anonymous, Narcotics Anonymous, and Dynamics of Addiction, Quitting Cocaine, and Relapse Prevention. Treatment facilities provided through the department include the Steve Hoyle Rehabilitation Center and Blue Walters Substance Abuse Treatment Program.

The Blue Walters Substance Abuse Treatment Program is a comprehensive program designed to rehabilitate eligible offenders nearing release with a history of alcohol and drug abuse. The program goal is to provide substance abuse treatment and prevention education, and to develop a collaborative relationship between outside treatment service providers and jail-based treatment programs, to assist offenders in developing a recovery base, as well as a safe and successful transition into society. The transition occurs through a combination of halfway house placement, aftercare, and/or work release. The author of this text is the program director of the Blue Walters Substance Abuse Treatment Program at Richwood Correctional Center in Louisiana.

Values Development

Most offenders have a values base that is inconsistent with what it takes to adjust in society. It is imperative that we continue to provide faith-based and character-based programs to offset these deficits. Faith-based programs can help an offender prepare for successful reentry into the community by establishing a spiritual foundation from which he can make sound, moral decisions. Developing partnerships with faith-based institutions that can help ex-offenders maintain their good intentions and positive efforts is crucial to the success of reentry.

Results of a three-year study by the department indicated that, when offenders are involved in an effective prison ministry, the percentage of those rearrested drops dramatically from 41% to 14%. According to an article in the *Justice Quarterly* (March 1997) titled "Religious Programs, Institutional Adjustment, and Recidivism Among Fellowship Programs," a study by the Academy of Criminal Justice Sciences found that those who attended 10 or more Bible studies during their incarceration were 67% less likely to return to prison than those who did not.

Chaplains working with hundreds of volunteers comprise the heart of religious programming, available daily to offenders in all institutions.

Additionally, faith- and character-based dormitory (FCBD) programs have been established at Dixon Correctional Institute, Louisiana Correctional Institute for Women, and Rayburn Correctional Center. The FCBD programs are aimed at maximizing the powers of personal faith or a positive belief system, positive peer pressure, and positive role modeling through mentoring.

Unique in the nation is the New Orleans Baptist Theological Seminary's "Angola Campus" at the Louisiana State Penitentiary. The seminary, established in 1995, offers two college-level degree programs for the offender population, a two-year associate degree in pastoral ministries, and a four-year bachelor's degree in theology. As many of Angola's offenders are serving life sentences, the department sees their role in the reentry process as mentors—helping other offenders' transition back into the community. Some offenders who have earned their bachelor's degree are being transferred to other institutions, where they work under the supervision of the chaplain to strengthen religious programming. Approximately 90 offenders are consistently enrolled in the seminary, which offers one of the most unique educational opportunities for state offenders and has proven to be a life-changing experience.

SOURCE: Louisiana Department of Public Safety and Corrections. (2010). *Reentry in Louisiana*. Baton Rouge, LA: LDOC.

revocation process is often a two-stage process that was initially set forth in the Supreme Court ruling of *Morrissey v. Brewer* (1972). The first hearing is held at the time of arrest or detention and is one where the parole board or other decision-making authority will determine if probable cause actually does, in fact, exist in relation to the allegations against the parolee that are made by the parole officer. The second hearing then is tasked with establishing the guilt or innocence of the parolee. During this hearing, the parolee possesses a modified version of due process, namely being provided with written notice of the alleged violations, having disclosure of evidence to be used against him or her (similar to discovery), the right to be present during the hearing and to provide his or her own evidence, the right to confront and cross-examine witnesses, the right to a neutral and detached decision-making body, and the right to a written explanation of the rationale for revocation.

PHOTO 17.5

Parole officer and supervisor Pearl Wise (middle) is pictured here with officer David Jackson (left) and Chris Miley (right) in tactical gear. As parole officers, they are required to complete in-service tactical training that includes non-lethal and lethal weapons proficiency. Though she works in a field that is law enforcement related and requires the use of authorized weapons, Ms. Wise is well known throughout her community as an active supporter of reentry efforts throughout the state of Louisiana.

One interesting development in response to revocation procedures is that of the parole revocations officer. In some states such as South Carolina, the **parole revocations officer** is primarily tasked with the routine holding of preliminary parole revocation hearings by reviewing allegations made by parole officers against parolees. These hearings are administrative and not nearly as formal as those held by a judge in a true court of law. Typically, these courts are routine in nature, but some situations may have rulings and findings of fact that vary. Though most hearings are not complicated, a degree of discretion is required on occasion when determining if the evidence has been presented well and/or to determine if the violation requires a true revocation of parole, as opposed to more restrictive sanctions. The position of parole revocations officer does not require formal legal training but instead simply requires that the hearing officer know the laws and regulations surrounding that state's parole system.

Cromwell et al. (2002) point out that that the process of revocation is actually a bit more in-depth and takes longer than many people may realize. In considering Burke's (1997) research, throughout the nation, it was found that the average time required to complete the revocation process, from the point of violation detection to the disposition by the parole revocation decision-making body, took anywhere from 44 to 64 days to complete. When taken in total with the safeguards afforded parolees during the revocation process, and the fact that many are returned to some more stringent form of parole (rather than prison), there is clearly an effort to work with offenders on parole.

Regardless of whether the decision-making body consists of the parole board itself or a parole revocations officer, there are some situations where the offender may be entitled to some form of legal counsel. In *Gagnon v. Scarpelli* (1971) it was held that parolees do have a limited right to counsel during revocation proceedings, as determined by the decision-making person or body over the proceedings and to be determined on a case-by-case basis. This is, quite naturally, relevant only to those circumstances where the parolee contests the allegations of the parole officer and at the parolee's own expense; there is no obligation on the part of the state to provide such representation.

Audio Link 17.3
Hear the *Morrissey v. Brewer* oral arguments.

Reference Link 17.3
Read about parole revocation proceedings.

CONCLUSION

This chapter has provided students with a view of correctional practices that occur at the end of the correctional process. Parole, as we can see, has had many critiques due to the concern for public safety when inmates are released. This concern is exacerbated when correctional systems use parole as a release-valve for large prison populations rather than an incentive for those offenders who truly exhibit reform while serving time.

The use of parole has been shown to be nearly as controversial as is the death penalty. Citizens around the nation read news reports of offenders who are released early from prison and commit heinous acts shortly after being released. This obviously makes it seem as if our justice system is being 'soft'

FIGURE 17.4   Example of Terms and Conditions of Parole in the State of Connecticut

State of Connecticut
Board of Pardons and Paroles

Statement of Understanding and Agreement

CONDITIONS OF PAROLE

NAME _____ CJIS NO. _____ RELEASE ON OR AFTER _____

1. **RELEASE, DIRECTION.** UPON RELEASE, YOU WILL REPORT TO YOUR ASSIGNED PAROLE OFFICER AS DIRECTED AND FOLLOW THE PAROLE OFFICER'S INSTRUCTIONS. YOU WILL REPORT TO YOUR PAROLE OFFICER IN PERSON, BY TELEPHONE AND IN WRITING WHENEVER AND WHEREVER THE PAROLE OFFICER DIRECTS.

2. **LEVELS OF SUPERVISION.** YOUR PAROLE OFFICER WILL ASSIGN YOU TO ONE OF SEVERAL LEVELS OF COMMUNITY SUPERVISION, DEPENDING UPON YOUR CIRCUMSTANCE. THESE LEVELS OF COMMUNITY SUPERVISION MAY INCREASE DEPENDING UPON CHANGES IN CIRCUMSTANCES, AT THE DISCRETION OF THE PAROLE OFFICER, AND MAY INCLUDE RESIDENTIAL PLACEMENT, ELECTRONIC MONITORING, CURFEW, AVOIDANCE OF SPECIFIC GEOGRAPHICAL AREAS AND AVOIDANCE OF SPECIFIC SOCIAL CIRCUMSTANCES OR INDIVIDUALS.

3. **RESIDENCE.** YOU WILL LIVE IN A RESIDENCE APPROVED BY YOUR PAROLE OFFICER AND YOU WILL COORDINATE ANY CHANGES IN YOUR PLACE OF RESIDENCE THROUGH YOUR PAROLE OFFICER BEFORE MOVING. YOUR PAROLE OFFICER HAS THE RIGHT TO VISIT YOUR RESIDENCE AT ANY REASONABLE TIME.

4. **EMPLOYMENT.** YOU WILL SEEK, OBTAIN AND MAINTAIN EMPLOYMENT THROUGHOUT YOUR PAROLE TERM, OR PERFORM COMMUNITY SERVICE AS DIRECTED BY YOUR PAROLE OFFICER. YOUR PAROLE OFFICER HAS THE RIGHT TO VISIT YOUR PLACE OF EMPLOYMENT OR COMMUNITY SERVICE AT ANY REASONABLE TIME.

5. **MARITAL/DOMESTIC STATUS.** YOU WILL KEEP YOUR PAROLE OFFICER INFORMED OF ANY CHANGES IN YOUR MARITAL OR DOMESTIC STATUS.

6. **FIREARMS PROHIBITED.** YOU WILL NOT USE, OR HAVE IN YOUR POSSESSION OR CONTROL, FIREARMS, AMMUNITION, OR ANY OTHER WEAPON OR OBJECT THAT CAN BE USED AS A WEAPON.

7. **SUBSTANCE ABUSE TREATMENT.** YOU WILL PARTICIPATE IN AN ADDICTION SERVICES EVALUATION AND TREATMENT AS DEEMED APPROPRIATE. YOU WILL FOLLOW THE INSTRUCTIONS OF THE PROGRAM STAFF AND YOUR PAROLE OFFICER AND WILL NOT MAKE ANY CHANGES WITHOUT THE EXPRESS PERMISSION OF THE PROGRAM STAFF AND YOUR PAROLE OFFICER. YOU WILL ALSO SUBMIT TO RANDOM URINALYSIS FOR THE BALANCE OF YOUR PAROLE TERM.

8. **MENTAL HEALTH TREATMENT.** YOU MAY BE REQUIRED TO PARTICIPATE IN A MENTAL HEALTH SERVICES EVALUATION AND TREATMENT AS DEEMED APPROPRIATE. YOU WILL FOLLOW THE INSTRUCTIONS OF THE PROGRAM STAFF AND YOUR PAROLE OFFICER AND WILL NOT MAKE ANY CHANGES WITHOUT THE EXPRESS PERMISSION OF THE PROGRAM STAFF AND YOUR PAROLE OFFICER.

9. **DRUGS PROHIBITED.** YOU WILL NOT USE, OR HAVE IN YOUR POSSESSION OR CONTROL, ANY ILLEGAL DRUG, NARCOTIC OR DRUG PARAPHERNALIA.

10. **TRAVEL.** YOU WILL NOT LEAVE THE STATE OF CONNECTICUT WITHOUT PRIOR PERMISSION OF YOUR PAROLE OFFICER.

11. **OBEY ALL LAWS, REPORT ANY ARREST.** YOU WILL OBEY ALL LAWS, AND TO THE BEST OF YOUR ABILITY, FULFILL ALL YOUR LEGAL OBLIGATIONS, INCLUDING PAYMENT OF ALL APPLICABLE CHILD SUPPORT AND ALIMONY ORDERS. YOU WILL NOTIFY YOUR PAROLE OFFICER WITHIN 48 HOURS OF YOUR ARREST FOR ANY OFFENSE.

12. **GANG AFFILIATION.** YOU WILL NOT ASSOCIATE OR AFFILIATE WITH ANY STREET GANG, CRIMINAL ORGANIZATION OR WITH ANY INDIVIDUAL MEMBERS THEREOF.

13. **STATUTORY RELEASE CRITERIA.** YOUR RELEASE ON PAROLE IS BASED UPON THE PREMISE THAT THERE IS A REASONABLE PROBABILITY THAT YOU WILL LIVE AND REMAIN AT LIBERTY WITHOUT VIOLATING THE LAW AND THAT YOUR RELEASE IS NOT INCOMPATIBLE WITH THE WELFARE OF SOCIETY. IN THE EVENT THAT YOU ENGAGE IN CONDUCT IN THE FUTURE WHICH RENDERS THIS PREMISE NO LONGER VALID, THEN YOUR PAROLE WILL BE REVOKED OR MODIFIED ACCORDINGLY.

14. **ADDITIONAL CONDITIONS.** YOU ALSO MUST ABIDE BY THE FOLLOWING INDIVIDUAL CONDITIONS:

FAILURE TO COMPLY WITH THESE CONDITIONS MAY RESULT IN THE REVOCATION OF PAROLE, AND, IF APPLICABLE, THE LOSS OF GOOD CONDUCT CREDITS EARNED WHILE IN PRISON.

I HAVE READ OR HAVE HAD READ TO ME, IN MY PRIMARY LANGUAGE, THE CONDITIONS OF PAROLE RELEASE. I FULLY UNDERSTAND MY OBLIGATIONS AND AGREE TO COMPLY WITH THESE CONDITIONS OF RELEASE ON PAROLE. IN ADDITION, I UNDERSTAND THAT THESE CONDITIONS SHALL APPLY TO ANY TERM OF SPECIAL PAROLE FOR WHICH I MAY HAVE BEEN SENTENCED TO SERVE.

_____ _____ _____ _____
Parolee   Date   Witness   Date

_____ _____ _____ _____
For the Board of Pardons and Paroles   Date   Hearing Location   Date

SOURCE: State of Connecticut Board of Pardons and Parole. Retrieved from http://www.ct.gov/doc/lib/doc/pdf/paroleconditions.pdf.

on criminals and makes it appear that prison authorities are indifferent to the safety of surrounding communities. However, prison authorities largely have their hands tied and must rely on the direction of their central state administration that generates parole decisions. Amidst the decisions that are made is the reality that prison overcrowding can and has led to legal complications; the overcrowding being a violation of Constitutional rights held by inmates in confinement. Thus, the only options are to build more prisons, house inmates in some other type of facility, or let them out on early release. Parole is one of the early-release mechanisms used by some prison systems and this has been likened to a release valve that opens when prisons are overstuffed with inmates. These types of "numbers game" release decisions are not safe for society and result in continued crime problems.

From this chapter, it should be clear to students that the correctional process is one fraught with public concern and controversy. It is almost as if the correctional system can never meet the competing demands placed upon it by society. On one extreme is the desire to punish, on the other is the desire to reform. Amidst this is the concern for the victim which has become increasingly more important to the

Prison Tour Video Link 17.2
Watch a clip about parole and re-entry programs.

field of corrections. Corrections, like all aspects of the criminal justice system, is a public concern that brings strong images to mind. Whatever may be in store for the correctional system and its practitioners is a matter of debate but, it is for certain, that the challenges associated with this system will never disappear.

END-OF-CHAPTER DISCUSSION QUESTIONS

1. Identify and discuss the contributions of Alexander Maconochie to the development of parole.

2. Identify and discuss the contributions of Sir Walter Crofton to the development of parole.

3. Discuss some basic concepts regarding state parole, its organization, and its administration.

4. Explain how the parole selection process works and the various factors that influence parole decisions.

5. What is meant by the "release valve" function of parole?

6. Explain how an effective reentry program is, in actuality, a component of any effective crime prevention model through the reduction of recidivism.

7. Discuss Braithwaite's theory on crime, shame, and reintegration and explain how it is related to the effectiveness of parole.

KEY TERMS

Alexander Maconochie

English Penal Servitude Act

Gagnon v. Scarpelli (1971)

Institutional parole officer

Judicial Improvements Act of 1990

Mark system

Martinson Report

Offender Accountability Plan

Parole

Parole Commission and Reorganization Act

Parole Commission Phaseout Act of 1996

Parole revocations officer

Release valve mechanism

Sir Walter Crofton

Supervised release

Ticket of leave

United States Parole Commission Extension Act of 2008

APPLIED EXERCISE 17.1

Students must conduct either a face-to-face or a phone interview with a parole officer or other parole specialist who currently works in a community corrections setting. The student must set up a day and time with that practitioner and interview him or her to gain insight and perspective on several key questions related to work in the field of parole supervision. Students must write the practitioner's responses, provide their own analysis of those responses, and submit their draft by the deadline set by their instructor. Students should complete this application exercise as a minipaper that addresses each point below. The total word count should be 1,400 to 2,100 words.

When completing the interview, students should ask the following questions:

1. What are the most rewarding aspects of your job in parole?

2. What are the most stressful aspects of your job in parole?

3. What is your view on treatment and/or reintegration efforts with offenders?

4. What are some challenges that you have in keeping track of your caseload?

5. Why did you choose to work in this field?

6. What type of training have you received for this line of work?

7. What would you recommend to someone who was interested in pursuing a similar career?

In addition, you should ensure that your submission has appropriate spelling and grammar throughout. Lastly, students are required to provide contact information for the parole practitioner. Please have students obtain the following information from the parole practitioner that they interview. While instructors will probably not need to contact this person, it may become necessary so that they can validate the actual completion of an interview.

Name and title of correctional supervisor: _____

Correctional agency: _____

Practitioner's phone number: _____

Practitioner's e-mail address: _____

Name of student: _____

"WHAT WOULD YOU DO?"

You are a state parole officer who has been active in various aspects of offender reentry. You currently work and live in a medium-sized community. On occasion, your supervisor asks you to serve on community committees and advisory boards as a means of increasing partnerships in your area and as a means of extending the sources and abilities of your own agency. Recently, you have been asked to serve with a group of agencies, some state-level, some county-level, and many of them private or nonprofit in nature. This group has been referred to as the Community Reentry Initiative (CRI) among persons in your area. They have had very good success in creating employment opportunities for parolees in the community, and this has been a great help in reducing recidivism. This group has also had some success in obtaining affordable housing for offenders who do not have a place to stay.

At this point, the CRI has decided to implement a restorative justice component to its efforts. This will require contact with prior victims and will require their consent in participating in the process. This is likely to provide a challenging aspect to the project. However, all victims must be allowed to provide their input in the process as offenders are paroled into the community and integrated into the restorative justice process.

While at the meeting, it became clear that many people looked to you as an expert on reentry issues. In fact, as time went on, several members suggested that a subcommittee be constructed to begin the development of the restorative justice program. At the close of the meeting, you were asked to lead this subcommittee.

However, there has been a recent backlash among community members who do not favor offender reentry initiatives in their own community. In fact, some citizens have gone to city hall to protest the implementation of these initiatives.

Naturally, you are a bit uneasy with this responsibility, but you know that your supervisor would be disappointed if you did not agree to help with this task. Your supervisor is very progressive and is fond of saying, "Change is good, so let's have more good by making more change!" So, with no real time to consider the implications, you hesitantly agreed to accept the position as head of the subcommittee.

Now, at this point, you want to help but do not know exactly what you should do. Your subcommittee consists of two local religious leaders, a police officer assigned to the neighborhood stabilization team, a victim's rights advocate from a local domestic violence facility, a low-ranking person from a local television station, a social services supervisor, a classification specialist who is employed by the prison that is in the region, and a counselor from a local substance abuse treatment facility. Your supervisor in your parole agency encourages you to help this group and even offers to give you a half-day off each week so that you can spend time in support of this initiative.

What would you do?

CROSS-NATIONAL PERSPECTIVE 17.1

Parole Officers in Canada

Driving up to the warehouse at 8 p.m. on a Thursday, the parole officer hopes his client will be hard at work inside. So far, every meeting with the client has gone well, as have the meetings with the parolee's employer. But this is an unscheduled meeting, and the probation officer knows a good start by someone on parole doesn't always mean the virtuous behavior will continue.

"I don't like it when the guys return to jail," explains Rob Christensen. "It can be a very (defeating) feeling. When you do see someone come out and succeed, it's very good." In his nine years on the job, the Calgary parole officer has seen his share of successes and failures. Regardless of what happens from case to case, though, his main goal remains to help offenders released from prison do well in the community while protecting the public at the same time.

It's a busy and demanding job. And, like other careers within law enforcement, it comes with its good and its bad, especially because parole officers must maintain constant contact with all aspects of the parolees' lives. "You see some really terrible stuff in the files, and you have to deal with these people professionally," Christensen says. "You're always looked at as the bad guy when all you're trying to do is help the guy. And it can be confrontational at times. But, for him, there are many pluses as well. I like the interaction with all the different characteristics of people. I like helping when I can and the law enforcement side of things."

Working for Correctional Service Canada as a parole officer in the community, Christensen's duties see him travel throughout the city meeting those on parole in their homes and at their jobs. Parole officers must also try and meet employers, family, friends, and others in regular contact with the parolee to ensure everything is on the straight and narrow, or to find a way to get more help to the parolee. This could include enrolling the parolee in a substance abuse program. As all these matters are legal issues, parole officers spend plenty of time taking notes and completing paperwork in the office as well.

The law always held an attraction for Christensen, who originally contemplated applying for the Royal Canadian Mounted Police while he was in college. "I was looking at law enforcement of some sort," he says. But the thought of moving all over the country held little appeal. In discussing his future with others, someone suggested applying at the Bowden penitentiary. He did, was accepted, and began work as a federal corrections officer in 1989 and worked his way up the ladder. (Provincial corrections officers deal with those who receive sentences of less than two years.) He spent six years as a parole officer in the institution before moving to Calgary.

He now puts in a regular workweek of 40 hours, but the days and times of his shifts may vary. Parole officers are paid on a sliding scale up to about $63,000 a year. Knowing the ins and outs of parole, however, is but a small part of what's required of a parole officer. Christensen says a parole officer needs solid communication skills, patience, and strong interpersonal skills. "You need to be able to interact on a professional level and a personal level. You have to be able to read people in a hurry."

Parole officers have been around for decades, and that's likely to continue, Christensen says. And he offers this advice to those considering this line of work: "Don't feel like you can change the world, and don't feel like you can change everybody. Take the satisfaction from the ones who do [change]."

1. In what ways do the functions of parole officers in Canada seem similar to those in the United States?

2. From the information in the article, does it appear that parole considerations in Canada follow a punitive model or a reintegrative model?

SOURCE: Sproxton, M. (2002). Parole officers constantly deal with the good and bad. Nextsteps.org. Retrieved February 7, 2010, from http://www.nextsteps.org/steps/dec02/mirror.htm.

STUDENT STUDY SITE

Visit the Student Study Site at **www.sagepub.com/hanserintro** to access links to the videos, audio clips, SAGE journal articles, state rankings, and reference materials noted in this chapter, as well as additional study tools including eFlashcards, web quizzes, and more.

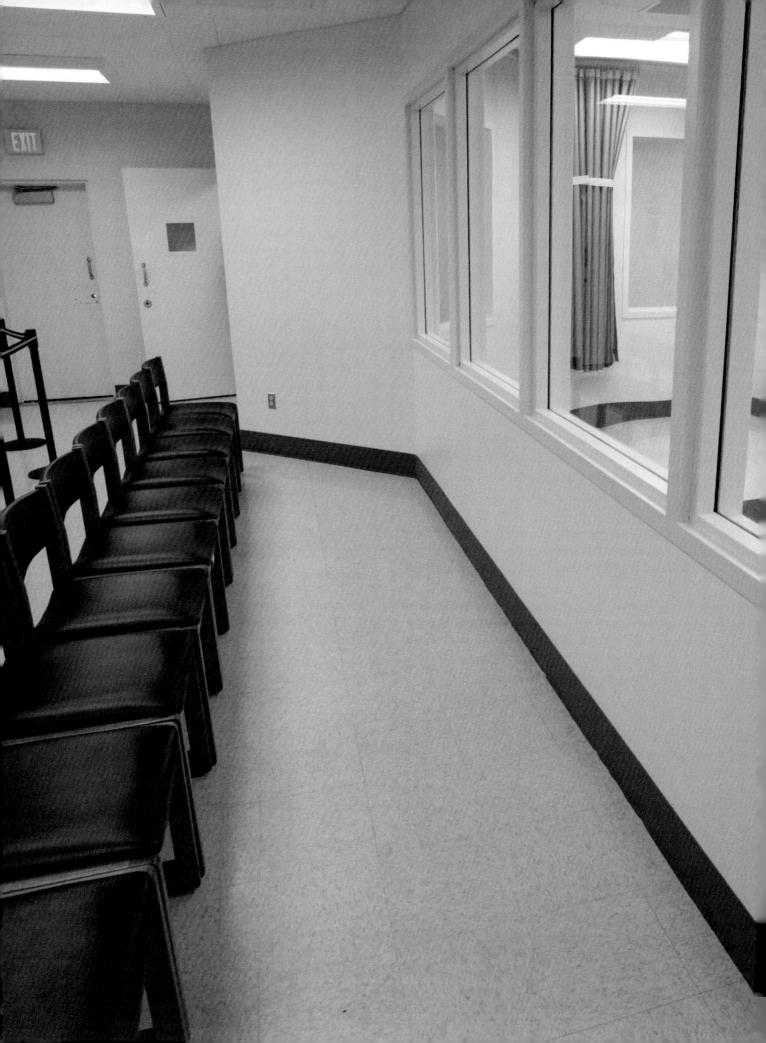

chapter **18**

The Death Penalty

LEARNING OBJECTIVES:

1. Analyze the various statistics associated with the death penalty and those who have received this sentence.

2. Discuss constitutional aspects and case law rulings on the death penalty.

3. Discuss the various controversial issues associated with the death penalty.

4. Identify the common philosophies related to the use of the death penalty.

INTRODUCTION

This chapter addresses the most extreme outcome when offenders are at the end of the correctional process: obtaining the death penalty. This response to offender behavior falls within the field of corrections but comes toward the end of the institutional process. Obviously, the death penalty results in the end of the offender's journey through the correctional process and entails no true rehabilitative orientation for the offender. Thus, this chapter covers the death penalty, but it should be noted that extensive focus is not given to the death penalty issue because it is, comparatively speaking, not a major area of focus in the day-to-day operation of correctional systems. However, this chapter is provided to ensure that the text is complete in its presentation of today's world of corrections.

CONSTITUTIONALITY OF THE DEATH PENALTY

The death penalty has always been the source of substantive debate in the United States. However, the key era in which this sanction was most often debated within the courts was during the civil rights movement of the 1960s. During the 1960s, numerous cases appeared that challenged the legality of the death penalty. Prior to this time, most proponents of the death penalty interpreted that sanction as conforming to the Fifth, Eighth, and Fourteenth Amendments of the Constitution. However, the notion that this penalty was perhaps a violation of the "cruel and unusual" punishment clause of the Eighth Amendment led some proponents to reconsider their stance.

In 1958, the Supreme Court made a ruling that was seemingly unrelated to concerns with the death penalty in the case *Trop v. Dulles.* In *Trop*, the Court developed a phrase that would be cited in future cases due to the meaning and essence of this catchphrase and because it fit so well with many compelling arguments in favor of reform within the correctional system. This phrase from the Court was that there existed "evolving standards of decency that marked the progress of a maturing society" (*Trop v. Dulles,* 1958, p. 86). The logic from this statement has been used by opponents of the death penalty to justify why the death penalty should be eliminated from the range of sentencing options.

Audio Link 18.1
Listen to the *Furman v. Georgia* oral arguments.

In 1968, the Supreme Court made an important decision regarding the jury selection process in cases where the death penalty might be given. The Court held that it was not sufficient to strike a potential juror from serving if he or she had doubts or reservations about the use of the death penalty (*Witherspoon v. Illinois,* 1968). Rather, it was determined that jurors could only be disqualified if it could be shown that they were incapable of being impartial in their decision making while on the jury.

Perhaps one of the most important cases, at least from a historical standpoint, was *Furman v. Georgia* (1972). In *Furman*, it was determined that the death penalty had been administered in an arbitrary and capricious manner. The Court, in ruling on Georgia's death penalty statute, noted the wide discretion given to juries who were largely unguided in the application of death penalty decisions. This was considered arbitrary in nature and a violation of the Eighth Amendment prohibition against cruel and unusual punishments. This decision resulted in the commutation of hundreds of death row sentences to life imprisonment.

In discussing the *Furman* decision, it is important to emphasize that the Supreme Court did not rule that the use of the death penalty, in and of itself, was unconstitutional. Rather, the Court simply ruled that the manner in which the death penalty was applied was

PHOTO 18.1

Correctional officers bring an inmate to his cell on death row at Ellis Unit in Huntsville, Texas.

unconstitutional. Thus, the process implemented, not the death penalty sanction, was the issue of concern. Once states were clear on this point, many quickly acted to revise their laws so that their own use of the death penalty would not be stricken down.

After this, states rewrote their death penalty statutes to avoid the problems noted in *Furman*. According to the Death Penalty Information Center (2004), Florida was the first state to rewrite its own death penalty statute, doing so just five months after the *Furman* ruling. Shortly after this, another 34 states proceeded to enact new death penalty statutes. Nevertheless, as we will see in the next subsection, the ability to apply the death penalty has been eroded over time within increasingly more challenging restrictions on its use being applied as the years progress. We now turn to several U.S. Supreme Court decisions that have shaped and tempered the use of the death penalty since the ruling in **Gregg v. Georgia (1976)** (see Chapter 4).

Constitutional Limits on the Death Penalty

Numerous Supreme Court decisions have followed the ruling in *Gregg v. Georgia* that have greatly limited the use of the death penalty. For instance, in 1977, just one year after the *Gregg* decision, the Supreme Court ruled in **Coker v. Georgia** that the death penalty was unconstitutional when used for the rape of an adult woman if she had not been killed during the offense. In other words, the commission of a rape—alone—was found to not be sufficient grounds for the death penalty. Later, in 1986, the Court further restricted the use of the death penalty for those who were insane in **Ford v. Wainwright.** Thus, defendants who could successfully use the insanity defense could avoid the death penalty. Much later still, in **Atkins v. Virginia**, the Court ruled in 2002 that the execution of the mentally retarded was also unconstitutional. This issue had been one of controversy throughout the past decade and beyond with earlier Court rulings allowing mental retardation to be used as a mitigating factor to reduce sentence severity of offenders eligible for the death penalty. With the rulings in *Ford v. Wainwright* and *Atkins v. Virginia*, it was clear that the death penalty was not likely to be considered legal if the offender suffered from some serious mental defect that impacted his or her knowing intent to commit the crime.

Later, the issue of juveniles and the death penalty was finally resolved after years of continued Supreme Court rulings that had slowly minimized the application of the death penalty to nonadult offenders. In **Roper v. Simmons** (2005; see Chapter 13), the Supreme Court ruled that the death penalty was unconstitutional when used with persons who were under 18 years of age at the time of their offense. This case once and for all settled the matter regarding the use of the death penalty with juveniles. The reasons for this were simply that juveniles were not considered culpable in the same manner that adults are and therefore could not have the intent necessary to qualify for a death penalty charge.

Prior to this, in **Thompson v. Oklahoma (1988)**, the Supreme Court found that the Eighth and Fourteenth Amendments prohibited the execution of a person who was under 16 years of age at the time of his or her offense, though only four of the justices fully concurred with this ruling. In *Stanford v. Kentucky* (1989) and in *Wilkins v. Missouri* (1989), the Supreme Court sanctioned the imposition of the death penalty on offenders who were at least 16 years of age at the time of the crime. The decision in *Roper* overturned these prior judgments.

Key U.S. Supreme Court Decisions

One area of concern with the death penalty has been the potential for racial disparity, both in how the case is treated and in the outcome of the case. Two key cases come to mind when considering racial factors and the death penalty. The first case is *Batson v. Kentucky* (1986), in which the Court addressed the manner by which juries are formed in death penalty cases. In *Batson*, the Court ruled that prosecutors had to provide nonracial reasons for their eliminating potential jurors from serving on the jury. Essentially, race is not allowed to be a factor in the jury selection process, and, when prosecutors remove a disproportionate number of citizens with the same racial identity of the defendant (the person facing the death penalty), they may be required to explain their actions.

Another key case regarding racial issues and the death penalty was *McClesky v. Kemp* (1987). In *McClesky*, the Court held that statistical data used to demonstrate disparities in the use of the death penalty were not sufficient evidence to invalidate its use. In other words, if it is shown that a higher-than-expected

Audio Link 18.2
Listen to the *Gregg v. Georgia* oral arguments.

Journal Article Link 18.1
Read about the Flynn correction when measuring IQ scores and its possible application to the death penalty.

Video Link 18.1
Learn more about the juvenile death penalty.

Audio Link 18.3
Listen to the *McClesky v. Kemp* oral arguments.

PHOTO 18.2

number of minority offenders are put to death when compared with Caucasians, this is not grounds against the use of the death penalty. In this case, *McClesky* contended that Georgia's application of the death penalty was discriminatory and used statistical analyses to show a pattern of racial disparities that were determined by the race of the victim. In this case, it was shown that, in particular, when the victim was Caucasian and the defendant was African American, the death penalty was much more likely to be given. However, the Court held that racial disparities would not be recognized as a constitutional violation of "equal protection of the law" unless deliberate racial discrimination against the defendant could be shown.

Aside from race, there have been other concerns with the use of the death penalty. Among these has been concern in allowing judges to determine if the death penalty will be given completely on their own. In *Ring v. Arizona* (2002), the Court held that juries, rather than judges, are to be the body that determines if the death penalty will be given to a convicted murderer. This ruling overturned the death penalty processes of several states that had, prior to this, allowed judges to make this determination on their own. Also important in the *Ring* decision is that any and all aggravating factors that would increase likelihood of getting the death penalty must be included in the initial indictment. This additional requirement made it to where the federal government itself had to revise some of its death penalty laws.

Two cases that address legal representation and/or procedural issues during death penalty proceedings are also mentionable. In *Strickland v. Washington* (1984), the Supreme Court ruled that defendants in capital cases have a right to representation that is objectively reasonable. To demonstrate that their representation was not sufficient, defendants must show that the ruling against them would be appreciably different if they had not used the specific legal counsel that had been afforded them; this is a very difficult standard to meet. In *Uttecht v. Brown* (2007), the Court made a ruling that seemed to have undermined its earlier ruling in *Witherspoon v. Illinois* (1968). In the *Uttecht* ruling, the Court held that it was, in fact, acceptable to remove potential jurors from service if they expressed mere doubts about the use of the death penalty. In this case, the trial court had removed a potential juror who had merely expressed doubts about, but not absolute opposition to, the death penalty.

Lastly, there is one case that is most unusual because it cited trends and legal rulings in other countries and also appealed to implications with other countries when the defendant—a citizen of another country—is put to death in the United States. In *Medellin v. Texas* (2008), a Mexican citizen who raped two young girls in Texas was given a death sentence. In this case, the nation of Mexico sued the United States because the Mexican national consulate had not been notified about Medellin's case, a requirement of the Vienna Convention on Consular Relations. The state of Texas rejected this notion and continued to pursue the death penalty for Medellin. What is most interesting about this case is that the Bush administration sought to influence the Supreme Court, entering the case on behalf of Medellin in an attempt to get the U.S. Supreme Court to overturn the Texas court's ruling.

The concern of the Bush administration was that the Texas ruling and the completion of the death sentence would place the United States in breach of its obligation to comply with the World Court and its oversight (Murphy, 2008). Despite the persistence of federal government officials, Texas maintained its stance on the death penalty and its own authority to implement judicial decisions within its jurisdiction. Ultimately, this led to an unexpected decision by the Bush administration where the U.S. government withdrew from the Vienna Convention's optional protocol that gave the International Court of Justice jurisdiction over disputes related to the treaty between the United States and Mexico. Even with this in mind, in July 2008 the International Court of Justice asked for a stay of execution for Medellin on the grounds of unfair trial practices. The state of Texas did not heed this request and executed Medellin in August 2008.

Audio Link 18.4
Listen to the *Uttecht v. Brown* oral arguments..

CORRECTIONS AND THE LAW 18.1

Racism and the Death Penalty: The Supreme Court Case of Miller-El v. Cockrell (2003)

In the 2003 Supreme Court case of *Miller-El v. Cockrell*, the Supreme Court ruled by a vote of 6-3 in favor of Miller-El that he should have the opportunity to prove that his death sentence was the result of discriminatory jury practices. Such practices included the so-called Texas shuffle to limit or eliminate African American jurors. Other practices included disparate questioning of potential jurors based on race, and a training memo instructing prosecutors on ways to skew juries based on race. In choosing a jury to try Miller-El, a Black defendant, prosecutors struck 10 of the 11 qualified Black panelists. The Supreme Court said the prosecutors' chosen race-neutral reasons for the strikes were suspicious and concluded that the selection process was replete with evidence that prosecutors were selecting and rejecting potential jurors because of race.

Justice Souter, writing for the majority, set out the evidence that race governed who was allowed on the jury, including disparate questioning of White and Black jurors, jury shuffling, a culture of bias within the prosecutor's office, and the fact that the prosecutor's race-neutral explanations for the strikes were so far at odds with the evidence that the explanations themselves indicate discriminatory intent.

Prior to this, in 2002, the Court had reversed a ruling from the lower federal court of appeals (the Fifth Circuit) that concluded that Miller-El had not provided sufficient evidence to obtain a habeas corpus appeal (habeas corpus, as students may recall, is an appeal that inmates can file after they are convicted and while in jail or prison). In this earlier ruling, the High Court voted 8-1 that the lower court had implemented a "dismissive and strained interpretation" of critical facts that ensured that claims of discrimination could not be sufficiently supported by Miller-El. In other words, the Supreme Court pointedly held that the Fifth Circuit Court of Appeals had been unrealistic and biased in its decision. Therefore, the Supreme Court reversed this ruling with the issue revolving around standards for obtaining a habeas corpus appeal under the **Antiterrorism and Effective Death Penalty Act of 1996**. According to the Fifth Circuit, this act required that the inmate provide clear and convincing evidence (about an 80% likelihood) of a constitutional violation before a certificate of appeal would be granted. However, the Supreme Court ruled that courts of appeal should limit their examination to a simple threshold inquiry (perhaps around a 25% likelihood), much less than the clear and convincing standard.

Consistent with prior rulings, the High Court noted that inmates must only demonstrate "a substantial showing of the denial of a constitutional right" in order to obtain an appeal. Providing a substantial showing only requires that the inmate demonstrate that jurists of reason could disagree with the lower court's decision regarding his constitutional claims. In considering the merit of Miller-El's claims of racial discrimination, the Supreme Court noted that Miller-El's criticism of the prosecution's use of jury shuffling had merit. This practice permitted parties to rearrange the order in which potential jurors were examined so as to increase the likelihood that visually preferable candidates would be selected. With no information about the prospective jurors other than their appearance, the party requesting the procedure literally shuffled the juror cards, and the members were then reseated in the new order. This shuffling process affected jury composition because any prospective jurors not questioned were dismissed, and a new panel of jurors appeared the following week. Thus, jurors who were shuffled to the back of the panel were less likely to be questioned and then less likely to serve on the jury.

On at least two occasions the prosecution requested shuffles when there was a predominant number of African Americans in the front of the panel. On yet another occasion the prosecutors complained about the purported inadequacy of the card shuffle by a defense lawyer but lodged a formal objection only after the postshuffle panel composition revealed that African American prospective jurors had been moved forward.

Further, the Court seemingly contradicted its own prior rulings in *McClesky v. Kemp* (1987) by pointing toward statistical data to support its concern with the practices of prosecutors in the Texas court system. The Court said that,

> in this case, the statistical evidence alone raises some debate as to whether the prosecution acted with a race-based reason when striking prospective jurors. The prosecutors used their peremptory strikes to exclude 91% of the eligible African-American venire members, and only one served on petitioner's jury. In total, 10 of the prosecutors' 14 peremptory strikes were used against African-Americans. Happenstance is unlikely to produce this disparity.

The Court stated that the Texas court's finding of no discrimination smacked of reality and was both unreasonable and erroneous. The facts and circumstances of the case determined that the Texas courts were, indeed, racially biased, resulting in a reversal of the lower court's rulings and granting Miller-El legal relief and a new trial.

SOURCE: *Miller-El v. Cockrell*.
(01-7662) 537 U.S. 322 (2003).
Cornell University Law School.

State Rankings Link 18.1
Prisoners Executed:
1977 to 2009.

Though the death penalty has carried a great deal of controversy, the statistics related to this sanction are somewhat controversial but also demonstrate that, when compared with the entire correctional population of the United States, offenders with death sentences are a small minority. The data in Figure 18.1 help to illustrate this point. From these data, it can be seen that the total number of death sentences throughout the nation in any given year does not typically exceed 300 offenders. While this is not to say that the death penalty should not be taken seriously, it does demonstrate that the number of sentences to death is actually quite low in relation to the overall population of offenders who are sentenced. Further still, in Figure 18.2, it can be seen that from 1976 to 2010, a grand total of 1,226 persons were put to death in the United States. Again, while this is not to minimize the severity or importance of examining this offense, it is clear that 1,226 offenders is a very small number, particularly when one considers that this is the total number of offenders executed over the span of 34 years. In fact, if one took this total number of executions and simply compared it to the entire prison population currently housed (there are over 1.2 million inmates in the United States), it is clear the combined executions over 34 years add up to no more than 1% of this year's current prison population. When one adds the offender population on community supervision, the portion of offenders who have been put to death is even lower. Indeed, the total number of offenders put to death in any given year (again, see Figure 18.2) is less than .05% of the prison population of that corresponding year. Simply put, the death penalty–eligible population is a very small population.

FIGURE 18.1   Number of Death Sentences per Year

Year	1993	1994	1995	1996	1997	1998	1999	2000	2001	2002	2003	2004	2005	2006	2007	2008	2009
Sentences	295	328	326	323	281	306	284	235	167	169	154	140	138	122	119	111	106*

SOURCE: Bureau of Justice Statistics: "Capital Punishment 2008." * Estimate based on DPIC'S research.

Death Penalty Information Center. (2010). *Facts about the death penalty.* Washington, DC: Author.

FIGURE 18.2   Number of Executions per Year

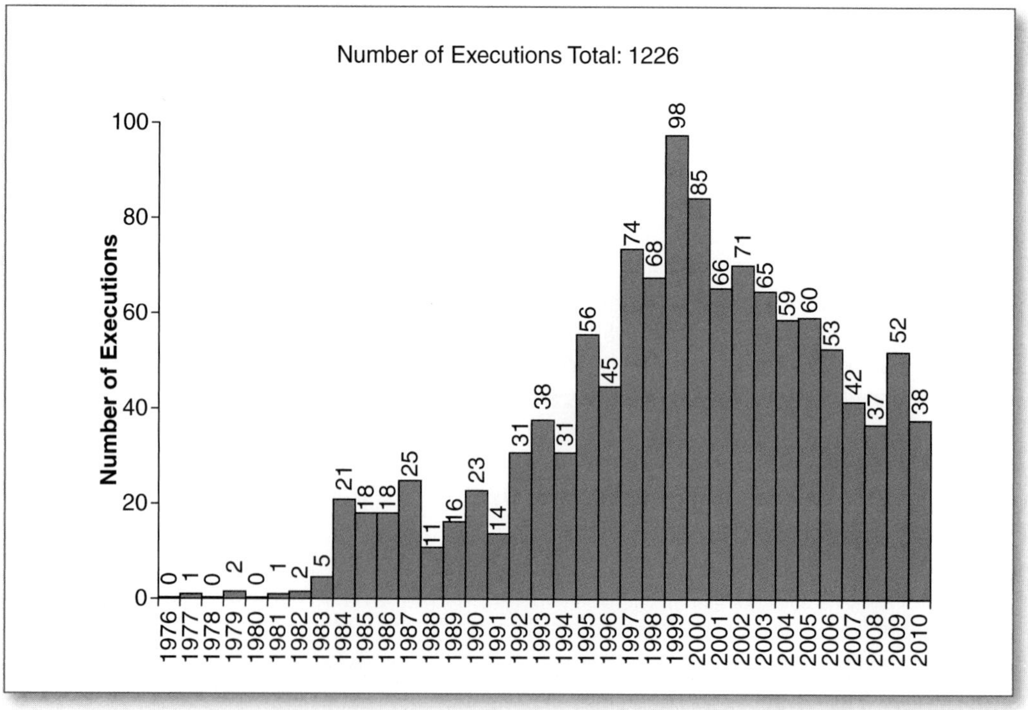

Number of Executions Total: 1226

All of the aforementioned is simply to point out that the controversy associated with this penalty perhaps outweighs the actual level of impact that it has on state correctional systems. Aside from the costs associated with the lengthy appeal process, this sanction has little impact on the criminal justice

FIGURE 18.3　Offenders on Death Row

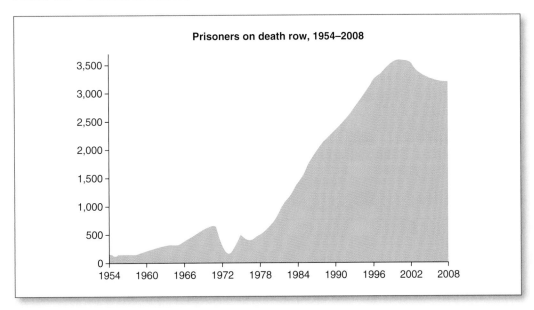

Prisoners on death row, 1954–2008

SOURCE: Bureau of Justice Statistics. (2008). *Capital punishment statistical tables*. Retrieved from http://bjs.ojp.usdoj .gov/index.cfm?ty=tp&tid=181.

FIGURE 18.4　Offenders Executed

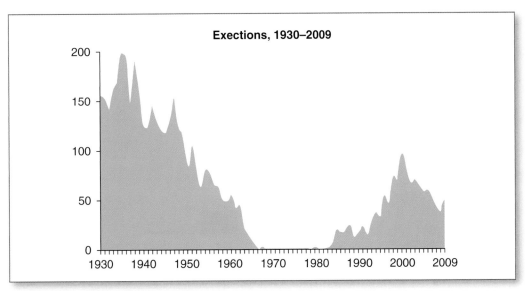

Exections, 1930–2009

SOURCE: Bureau of Justice Statistics. (2008). *Capital punishment statistical tables*. Retrieved from http://bjs.ojp.usdoj .gov/index.cfm?ty=tp&tid=181.

system. This is particularly true when one considers that the effectiveness of deterrence objectives is quite questionable. In essence, the death penalty is a minor aspect of the correctional process, especially at a systemic level, but, because of its unique permanence and severity, it receives a considerable amount of attention.

When taking a glimpse at Figures 18.3 and 18.4, students can see that the number of offenders on death row rose greatly from 1954 to about 2002, but there has been a slight downturn since that time. Indeed, the number of prisoners under sentence of death decreased for the eighth consecutive year in 2008, according to the BJS. On the other hand, the number of executions seemed to have increased with a sharp peak in 2000 that has also been followed by a decrease in executions until, in 2009, a total of 52 inmates were executed; this was 15 more than in 2008. These figures provide a visual depiction of the up-and-down nature of the death penalty as a sanction that is given during sentencing and actually used against offenders.

State Rankings Link 18.2
Prisoners under Sentence of Death as of January 1, 2010.

TABLE 18.1　Number Death Row Inmates by State

DEATH ROW INMATES BY STATE: January 1, 2010					
California	697	S. Carolina	63	Connecticut	10
Florida	398	Mississippi	61	Kansas	10
Texas	337	Missouri	61	Utah	10
Pennsylvania	222	*U.S. Gov's*	59	Washington	9
Alabama	201	Arkansas	42	*U.S. Military*	8
Ohio	168	Kentucky	35	Maryland	5
N. Carolina	167	Oregon	32	S. Dakota	3
Arizona	135	Delaware	19	Colorado	3
Georgia	106	Idaho	17	Montana	2
Tennessee	90	Indiana	15	New Mexico	2
Louisiana	85	Virginia	15	Wyoming	1
Oklahoma	84	Illinois	15	N. Hampshire	1
Nevada	77	Nebraska	11	**TOTAL**	3261

FIGURE 18.5　Executions by Region

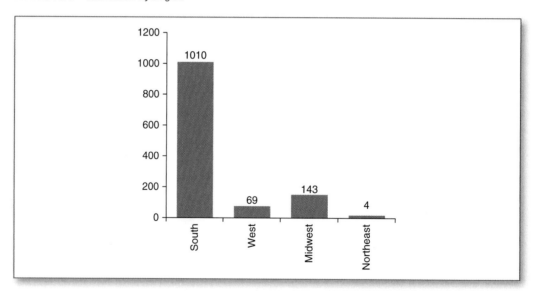

SOURCE: Death Penalty Information Center. (2010). *Facts about the death penalty.* Washington, DC: Author

　　Table 18.1 shows that, as of 2010, the three states with the largest death row populations were California, Florida, and Texas. This is an interesting point because we have, in earlier chapters, referred to these three states as being part of the "Big Four" in corrections due to the size of their correctional populations and the various characteristics of each state. Figure 18.5 examines these same data from a regional perspective, and, as we have noted in earlier chapters regarding prison operations, it appears that the southern region of the United States is particularly punitive in nature, having the highest number of executions when compared with other regions of the United States.

　　While the impact of the death penalty may be questionable in regard to the day-to-day operations of the criminal justice system, one thing is for certain—it is a very costly sanction to maintain. The costs associated with the death penalty tend to largely be due to the legal fees associated with the appeals process in death penalty cases as well as the cost for long-term and secure housing. The Death

Penalty Information Center (2010) has collected data on the costs associated with the death penalty and has reported the following information from a variety of sources:

Reference Link 18.1
Read more about death row.

1. The California death penalty system costs taxpayers $114 million per year beyond the costs of keeping convicts locked up for life.

2. Taxpayers have paid more than $250 million for each of the state's executions (*Los Angeles Times*, March 6, 2005).

3. The most comprehensive study in the country found that the death penalty costs North Carolina $2.16 million per execution *over* the costs of sentencing murderers to life imprisonment. The majority of those costs occur at the trial level (Duke University, May 1993).

4. Enforcing the death penalty costs Florida $51 million a year above what it would cost to punish all first-degree murderers with life in prison without parole. Based on the 44 executions Florida has carried out since 1976, that amounts to a cost of $24 million for each execution (*Palm Beach Post*, January 4, 2000).

5. In Texas, a death penalty case costs an average of $2.3 million, about 3 times the cost of imprisoning someone in a single cell at the highest security level for 40 years (*Dallas Morning News*, March 8, 1992).

It is clear that the death penalty is much more expensive than the use of a simple life sentence without parole. This truly calls to question the utility of the death penalty since it affects such a small group of offenders yet costs so much to implement. Since research on the deterrent effect of the death penalty is mixed, this makes it even more questionable as to whether the death penalty is truly a logical sentence to implement. Given that state budgets are strapped for income and that this penalty does not necessarily improve public safety, it may be that the use of life sentences is a superior means of punishment for heinous crimes.

An Analysis of Persons on Death Row

When we refer to persons on death row, it is perhaps important to explain what we mean by "death row" and that we also get a good idea of the characteristics of those who fall within this category. The term **death row** refers to persons who have been convicted and sentenced to be executed but are awaiting the time at which their execution will take place. As we can see in Table 18.2, during the year 2008, the federal government has record of just over 3,200 inmates who were on death row at the close of the year. Of these, the overwhelming majority of inmates were male offenders (98.2%), and this means that very few women are serving time on death row. It is also clear that most offenders on death row are either Caucasian (56.1%) or African American (41.7%) with only about 2% being of some other race. This means that there are very few Latino Americans or Asian Americans on death row.

Nearly half of all offenders on death row do not have a high school education. This is a common problem among the offender population and points toward the need for educational services for those inmates whose time has not run out and who are not on death row. Conversely, only about 9% of all offenders on death row have attained any type of college or university course work. Thus, it is most likely that offenders who end up on death row are in the lower socioeconomic categories of society, particularly when one considers that educational levels and income levels tend to correlate. Lastly, most offenders on death row were not married at the time of their offense. The information in Table 18.2 shows that over 50% were never married, indicating that these offenders report as not having spouses.

In regard to age, Table 18.3 shows that over 60% of all offenders on death row committed their offense prior to the age of 30 years old, meaning that crimes for which the death penalty is given tend to be committed in the mid-20s, being neither very young nor very old. According to the Bureau of Justice Statistics (2008), among those offenders for whom arrest information was available, the average time of arrest was 29 years old, with approximately 10% of the total death row population being age 19 or younger at the time of arrest.

In addition, only 58 women were on death row in 2008. The majority of these women came from two states: California and Texas. Students should consult Table 18.4 for a state-by-state breakdown of the number of women on death row. As can be seen, no state has more than 5 women on death row, aside from California and Texas. Naturally, this is a very small number of offenders on death row, particularly when

State Rankings Link 18.3
Female Prisoners under Sentence of Death in 2009.

State Rankings Link 18.4
Male Prisoners under
Sentence of Death
in 2009.

State Rankings Link 18.5
Percent of Prisoners
under Sentence of Death
Who are White: 2009.

State Rankings Link 18.6
Black Prisoners under
Sentence of Death
in 2009.

State Rankings Link 18.7
Hispanic Prisoners under
Sentence of Death
in 2009.

TABLE 18.2   Demographic Characteristics of Prisoners Under Sentence of Death, 2008

Characteristic	Prisoners under sentence of death, 2008		
	Yearend	Admissions	Removals
Total inmates	3,207	111	119
Gender			
Male	98.2%	97.3%	99.2%
Female	1.8	2.7	0.8
Race[a]			
White	56.1%	58.6%	61.3%
Black	41.7%	39.6	37.0
All other races[b]	2.2	1.8	1.7
Hispanic origin			
Hispanic	13.2%	19.8%	8.1%
Non-Hispanic	86.8	80.2	91.9
Number unknown	384	5	8
Education			
8th grade or less	13.5%	17.1%	19.2%
9th-11th grade	36.5	31.7	36.4
High school graduate/GED	40.8	41.5	35.4
Any college	9.2	9.8	9.1
Median	12th	12th	11th
Number unknown	528	29	20
Marital status			
Married	22.2%	18.3%	20.2%
Divorced/separated	20.1	19.5	27.9
Windowed	2.9	4.9	1.9
Never married	54.7	57.3	50.0
Number unknown	371	29	1.5

NOTE: Calculations are based on those cases for which date were reported. Detail may not add to total due to rounding.

[a]Includes persons of Hispanic/Latino origin.

[b]At yearend 2008, inmates in "all other races" consisted of 27 American Indians, 35 Asians, and 9 Self-identified Hispanics. During 2008, American Indian and 1 Asian were admitted; and 1 Asian and 1 self-identified Hispanic were removed.

SOURCE: Snell, T. L. (2010). *Capital punishment, 2008—Statistical tables.* Washington, DC: Bureau of Justice Statistics.

compared to the broader correctional population throughout the United States. In fact, only 11 women have actually been put to death since the moratorium on the death penalty was lifted in 1976. All of these women committed murders of one kind or another.

Among those women who have been put to death, Karla Faye Tucker stands out due to the violence and unique characteristics of her crime. With male accomplices available to help, Tucker, of her own volition,

TABLE 18.3 Age at Time of Arrest for Capital Offense and Age of Prisoners Under Sentence of Death at Year End 2008

Age	Prisoners under sentence of death			
	At time of arrest		On December 31, 2008	
	Number*	Percent	Number	Percent
Total number under sentence of death on 12/31/08	2,957	100%	3,207	100%
19 or Younger	311	10.5	0	
20–24	811	27.4	44	1.4
25–29	682	23.1	222	6.9
30–34	507	17.1	388	12.1
35–39	317	10.7	564	17.6
40–44	172	5.8	543	16.9
45–49	93	3.1	575	17.9
50–54	39	1.2	394	12.3
55–59	21	0.7	245	7.6
60–64	5	0.2	161	5.0
65 or older	2	0.1	71	2.2
Mean age	29 yrs.		43 yrs.	
Median age	27 yrs.		43 yrs	

NOTE: The youngest person under sentence of death was a black male in Texas, born in June 1988 and sentenced to death in June 2007. The oldest person under sentence of death was a white male in Arizona, born in September 1915 and sentenced of death in June 1983.

*Excludes 250 inmates for whom the date of arrest for capital offense was not available.

SOURCE: Snell, T. L. (2010). *Capital punishment, 2008—Statistical tables.* Washington, DC: Bureau of Justice Statistics.

killed a man and a woman in their domicile because they owed her money. What was most unique about this offender is that she murdered each person with a pickax, a bloody and savage means of killing individuals. Even more unusual for female offenders was the fact that she claimed to have experienced sexual gratification when committing both murders. These types of traits are usually only observed among male murderers, in terms of both the violence used and the sexual gratification associated with that violence. Tucker's execution drew national attention and included nightly reports from various major TV newscasters, as well as live nationwide coverage from the prison where she was executed. Tucker was the second woman to be executed in the United States since the death penalty was ruled allowable in 1976 by the U.S. Supreme Court.

Another well-known female who was executed was an infamous serial killer named Aileen Wuornos, who, while prostituting herself, lured multiple men to locations where she could kill them. During the 1989 and 1990 period, several male bodies were found along the highways of central Florida, all murders perpetrated by Wuornos. So rare is the female serial killer as a crime phenomenon that, within two weeks of her arrest, Wuornos had sold the movie rights to her story. This case ultimately resulted in several books and movies. Wuornos represents a classic case that feminist criminologists argue for when advocating for the victim-turned-offender hypothesis. Her father was a child molester who ultimately was killed in prison when Wuornos was 13. By age 14, Wuornos was pregnant, had dropped out of school, and eventually became a prostitute who hitchhiked along roadways and at truck stops. Wuornos was the 10th woman to be executed in the United States after the 1976 death penalty moratorium was lifted.

Students should see Focus Topic 18.1 for details on women who have been executed and the crimes that they committed. The types of murder committed have some degree of difference between these

Reference Link 18.2
Read more about Karla Faye Tucker.

TABLE 18.4   Women Under Sentence of Death, by Race and Jurisdiction, December 31, 2008

Jurisdiction	All races[a]	White[b]	Black[b]
Total	58	40	15
California	15	11	2
Texas	10	6	4
Pennsylvania	5	2	3
North Carolina	5	2	2
Alabama	4	2	2
Mississippi	3	3	0
Federal	2	2	0
Louisiana	2	1	1
Tennessee	2	2	0
Arizona	2	2	0
Ohio	1	1	0
Florida	1	1	0
Georgia	1	1	0
Kentucky	1	1	0
Oklahoma	1	1	0
Virginia	1	1	0
Idaho	1	1	0
Indiana	1	0	1

[a]Includes America Indians, Alaska Natives, Asians, Native Hawaiians, and other Pacific Islanders.

[b]Excludes persons of Hispanic/Latino origin.

SOURCE: Snell, T. L. (2010). *Capital punishment, 2008—Statistical tables.* Washington, DC: Bureau of Justice Statistics.

offenders but demonstrate how unusual these women are from most female offenders. It is arguable that these women were put to death due to the fact that they broke the social mold and expectations of our patriarchal society, as feminist scholars might contend (students should refer back to Chapter 11 for more on these points). One thing is certain: These offenders tended to, because of their rarity, generate substantial public attention.

Race of Offender and Victim in Death Penalty Cases

A primary source of controversy related to the death penalty relates to perceptions of racial bias in its application. Statistics such as those from Figure 18.6 show that approximately 56% of all persons who are executed are Caucasian and 35% are African American. While the argument can be made (particularly among those who are not familiar with demographics in the United States and/or are neophytes in research) that most persons executed are Caucasian, this still reveals disparity in the application of executions. When one considers that African Americans account for approximately 13% of the population, it seems that the percentage who are on death row and executed is disproportionately high. Conversely, when one considers that Caucasians account for around 70% to 75% of the population (depending on classifications of Hispanic Americans), it seems that the percentage of those given the death penalty and executed is disproportionately low (U.S. Census Bureau, 2000).

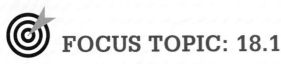

FOCUS TOPIC: 18.1

Women Who Have Been Executed Since Gregg v. Georgia *(1976)*

Velma Barfield	Executed in 1984 for poisoning multiple people with arsenic. Murders were committed to gain money for life insurance claims.
Karla Faye Tucker	Executed in 1998 for violently stabbing a man and a woman to death with a pickax.
Judy Buenoano	Executed in 1998 for poisoning a husband to death and also killed one of her children in a staged canoeing accident. Attempted to kill a boyfriend with a car bomb. Collected $240,000 in fraudulent life insurance benefits for the murders.
Betty Lou Beets	Executed in 2000. Had killed two husbands with a handgun and hid bodies for years before being caught.
Christina Riggs	Executed in 2000 for smothering to death her two young children with a pillow. She was a licensed nurse and used lethal drugs to attempt suicide and this failed. Suffered from depression and asked for no defense at her jury trial.
Wanda Jean Allen	Executed in 2001 for killing her same-sex partner outside of a police station. Her partner was in the process of filing a domestic complaint against Wanda Jean Allen, and Wanda Jean shot her before she could do so. They had met in prison as lovers when Wanda Jean was serving time for manslaughter of another prior intimate partner.
Marilyn Plantz	Executed in 2001. Hired two teenagers to kill her husband. She assisted them in disposing of husband's body.
Lois Smith	Executed in 2001 for stabbing and shooting her son's girlfriend. Lois Smith believed that the woman had conspired to kill her son and transported the woman to the crime scene, psychologically tortured her, and shot her 9 times.
Lynda Block	Executed in 2002 for fatally shooting a police officer. Shot the officer in partnership with her common-law husband in a Walmart parking lot.
Aileen Wuornos	Executed in 2002 for shooting seven men to death. In each case, Wuornos had hitchhiked and prostituted herself to lure the men to their death.
Frances Newton	Executed in 2005 for shooting her husband and her two children. Contended that the crime was committed by an unknown drug dealer who was collecting money from her husband.

Because of these and other observations, some contend that the death penalty is administered in a racially and class-biased manner. Although it was true that outright racism existed in the system during the early to mid-1900s, oversight by the Supreme Court helped to mitigate this a bit. Now, the issue of discriminatory application has shifted to the race of the victim who is killed. Students can see in Figure 18.6 that over 75% of murder victims in cases resulting in an execution of the offender were Caucasian. This is despite the fact that over 50% of the perpetrators of these crimes were Caucasian. Simply put, if you murder a Caucasian, you are more likely to be executed, but if you murder an African American, you have lower odds of being executed.

This is an important observation because it does perhaps underlie some bias in the justice system regarding the value of persons who are victimized. Where the race of the defendant may matter to some extent due to socioeconomics and the inability to obtain effective legal counsel, this should not matter in regard to victims. The prosecutor is the body responsible for seeking a death sentence, and, after this, it is the appeals process that generally determines how quickly the execution will follow. Because the resources available to district attorneys are often plentiful and because the same is true for the state (at least in comparison to the resources available to most offenders and their legal counsel), it would be expected that executions would not be influenced by the race of the defendant. All of this is mentioned because as an overall general economic demographic, Caucasians tend to have more affluence and property ownership in the United States than do most minority groups. The question is, then, what makes persons who kill Caucasians more likely to be executed than those who kill African Americans?

FIGURE 18.6   Race of Defendants and Race of Victims in Death Penalty Cases

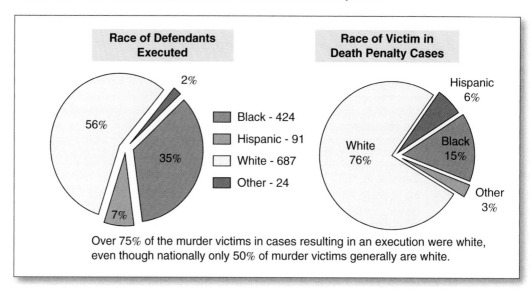

Race of Defendants Executed

56%
2%
35%
7%

Black - 424
Hispanic - 91
White - 687
Other - 24

Race of Victim in Death Penalty Cases

Hispanic 6%
White 76%
Black 15%
Other 3%

Over 75% of the murder victims in cases resulting in an execution were white, even though nationally only 50% of murder victims generally are white.

SOURCE: Death Penalty Information Center. (2010). *Facts about the death penalty.* Washington, DC: Author.

Before answering this question, let us further consider research that supports the notion that persons who kill Whites are more likely to get the death penalty than those who kill Blacks. Once study by the General Accounting Office (1990) of the federal government evaluated 28 other studies that covered homicide cases for different time periods throughout several states that had the death penalty. This meta-analysis of prior studies included different geographic regions of the United States. These studies found a pattern of evidence that indicated racial disparities in death penalty processing after the *Furman* decision.

In fact, in 82% of those studies, the race of the victim was found to influence the likelihood of being charged with capital murder or receiving the death penalty; that is, those who murdered Whites were found to be more likely to be sentenced to death than those who murdered Blacks. What was amazing is that these findings were remarkably consistent across data sets, states, data collection methods, and analytic techniques. The findings held for high-, medium-, and low-quality studies that the General Accounting Office analyzed (1990).

Thus, when we ask the question "What makes persons who kill Caucasians more likely to be executed than those who kill African Americans?" our answer has been provided, at least in part, by the research just presented. That answer has to do partly with prosecutorial discretion at earlier stages of the criminal justice process. But is this issue truly this simple, or is there perhaps some other factor at play? In this chapter, the contention will be that there is indeed another set of issues to explain this phenomenon. But before explaining, we will name this phenomenon the *Prosecutorial Death Discretion Outcome.* The **Prosecutorial Death Discretion Outcome** basically observes that prosecutors are overwhelmingly Caucasian and that, when determining whether to seek the death penalty, they tend to do so disproportionately more often when the victim is also Caucasian than when the victim is African American. The reasons for this, however, are not as likely to be due to racism as they are to be due to politics.

Most district attorneys (prosecutors) hold their positions by public election. This means that they are voted into office, and, as such, their communities must generally be happy with their performance. In many cases, it is the affluent within a community who tend to have more political power in that community, and they also tend to vote more. Prosecutors may be tempted to ensure that the affluent members of their community remain satisfied with decisions that are made, or, at the very least, they may try to ensure that they do not upset this socioeconomic strata of citizens too greatly. In addition, when members of this group are close to someone who is killed, their families tend to have more influence and likely will more effectively ensure that their case is prosecuted with more vigor, or to the maximum extent of the law. On the other hand, minority communities (particularly African American communities) tend to have fewer resources and less political clout. This does not mean that crimes of murder against members of this

Journal Article Link 18.2
Read about how minority death row inmates convicted of killing Whites face higher execution probabilities than other capital offenders.

TABLE 18.5   Method of Execution by State

Lethal Injection			Electrocution	Lethal gas
Alabama[a]	Kentucky[a,b]	Ohio	Alabama	Arizona[a,c]
Arizona[a,c]	Louisiana	Oklahoma[a]	Arkansas[a,d]	California[a]
Arkansas[a,d]	Maryland	Oregon	Florida[a]	Missouri[a]
California[a]	Mississippi	Pennsylvania	Kentucky[a,b]	Wyoming[a,e]
Colorado	Missouri[a]	South Carolina[a]	Nebraska	
Connecticut	Montana	South Dakota	Oklahoma[f]	
Delaware[a,g]	Nevada	Tennessee[a,h]	South Carolina[a]	
Florida[a]	New Hampshire[a]	Texas	Tennessee[a,h]	
Georgia	New Jersey	Utah[a]	Virginia[a]	
Idaho[a]	New Mexico	Virginia[a]		
Illinois	New York	Washington[a]		
Indiana	North Carolina	Wyoming[a]	Hanging	Firing Squad
Kansas			Delaware[a,g]	Idaho[a]
			New Hampshire[a,i]	Oklahoma[f]
			Washington[a]	Utah[j]

[a]Authorizes 2 methods of execution.

[b]Authorizes lethal injection for persons sentenced on or after 3/31/98; inmates sentenced before that data may select lethal injection or electrocution.

[c]Authorizes lethal injection for persons sentenced after 11/15/92; inmates sentenced before that data may select lethal injection or gas.

[d]Authorizes lethal injection for those whose offense occurred on or after 7/4/83; inmates whose offense occurred before that data may select lethal injection or electrocution.

[e]Authorizes lethal gas if lethal injection is held to be unconstitutional.

[f]Authorizes electrocution of lethal injection is held to be unconstitutional and firing squad if both lethal injection and electrocution are held to be unconstitutional.

[g]Authorizes lethal injection for those whose capital offense occurred on or after 6/13/86; those who committed the offense before that date may select electrocution by written waiver.

[i]Authorizes hanging only if lethal injection cannot be given.

[j]Authorizes firing squad if lethal injection is held unconstitutional. Inmates who selected execution by firing squad prior to May 3, 2004, may still be entitled to execution by that method.

SOURCE: Snell, T. L. (2006). *Capital punishment, 2005*. Washington, DC: Bureau of Justice Statistics.

community will not be prosecuted, but it does mean that there will be a stronger likelihood for plea bargains and life sentences without parole to be given. This is even truer when one considers that most crimes are intraracial, with Black offenders tending to kill Black victims. The general incentive to prosecute for death rather than to plea out of court is perhaps not as strong.

In addition, their voting potential tends to be less due to lower numbers in most jurisdictions and other factors. In inner-city jurisdictions that are largely African American, crime rates may be higher, and, stereotypically, violent crime tends to correlate. Given this observation, the fact that most crime is intraracial, and that drugs and gangs may be associated with these areas of the United States, the impetus behind a long and drawn-out legal prosecution may not be as strong, particularly if the crime involved offender-on-offender violence, such as with rival gang members or drug dealers.

All of these factors, more affluence (on the average) among families of Caucasian victims, the lack of socioeconomic power among much of the African American community, and crime dynamics in many African American urban communities tend to impact courthouse dynamics. Discretionary decisions made at the time of plea bargaining tend to favor those with more clout and not to be as favorable to those who do not have political clout. If the victim's family has substantive influence, then this too affects the overall total outcome of who is prosecuted to the fullest, up to and including the death penalty.

Federal Death Penalty and Death Row

In 1790, the first Congress established the death penalty for several offenses that today would not be considered constitutional. At that time, crimes of treason, forgery, piracy, counterfeiting, and crimes on the high seas were death penalty–eligible offenses. Today, only treason and crimes affiliated with some type of murder are eligible for the death penalty. Within the federal court system defendants who are found guilty have a second hearing to determine whether a sentence of death is justified (U.S. Department of Justice [USDOJ], 2001a).

The hearing to determine whether the death penalty will be given is held before a jury of 12 members (USDOJ, 2001a). At the hearing, the prosecutor presents evidence in support of the aggravating factors for which notice has previously been provided, and the defense is free to present evidence concerning any mitigating factors. The government must prove the existence of aggravating factors beyond a reasonable doubt, and the jury must unanimously agree that such a factor or factors have been established (USDOJ, 2001a). The defendant need only establish the existence of mitigating factors by a preponderance of the evidence, and each juror is free to conclude that such factors have been established, regardless of whether other members of the jury agree. To recommend a sentence of death, the jury must determine that the defendant had the requisite culpability with respect to the victim's death, and must unanimously agree that the aggravating factor or factors it has found sufficiently outweigh any mitigating factors to justify a capital sentence (USDOJ, 2001a).

Video Link 18.2
Watch a video about death row.

As of November 2009, there were a total of 48 inmates on death row in the federal correctional system. Of these, 21 were Caucasian, 26 were African American, and 1 was Latino. There were also 3 female inmates on death row in the federal system, and all three were Caucasian. Ages for inmates on death row ranged from 25 to 59 years old. As noted earlier, the overall population of death row inmates is quite small, and this is true in the Federal Bureau of Prisons as well. Regardless, this system, including its death penalty sentencing, has undergone extensive research and evaluation.

In 2001, an evaluation of the federal death penalty system was conducted. When released, the report prompted then Attorney General Janet Reno to note that the information in that report showed racial/ethnic disparities in the federal death penalty system, in comparison to the general population. Specifically, in the 682 cases submitted to the Department of Justice's death penalty review procedure between 1995 and July 2000, 20% involved White defendants, 48% involved Black defendants, and 29% involved Hispanic defendants (USDOJ, 2001a).

Despite this report, it is clear that up until 1995, federal executions were not a major concern to the U.S. justice system. Indeed, between 1963 and 1995, there were no executions conducted by the federal government. In 1995, the execution of David Ronald Chandler was set. Chandler had been convicted for his involvement in a 1990 drug-related murder of a police informant. Ultimately, the merits of his case ended with Chandler getting his death sentence commuted, and he now serves life in prison at Fort Leavenworth in Kansas. Nonetheless, others have been executed since then, including the infamous Timothy McVeigh who committed the Oklahoma City bombing of the Alfred P. Murrah building. Two others executed since this time are Juan Raul Garza (executed in 2001) and Louis Jones (executed in 2003). In comparison to state systems, the federal system does not execute offenders on a frequent basis.

When the ruling in *Furman v. Georgia* (1972) invalidated the death penalty in the United States, the federal branch of the justice system did not follow suit with the various state justice systems by revising its own statutes. Rather, the potential use of the death penalty lay dormant until 1988, when the President signed the **Anti-Drug Abuse Act of 1988.** A part of this law made the death penalty available as a possible punishment for certain drug-related offenses. The availability of **capital punishment** in federal criminal cases expanded signifi- cantly further on September 13, 1994, when the President signed into law the Violent Crime Control and Law Enforcement Act, which included the **Federal Death Penalty Act of 1994.** This act established constitutional procedures for imposition of the death penalty for 60 offenses under 13 existing and 28 newly created federal capital statutes, which fall into three broad categories: (1) homicide offenses, (2) espionage and treason, and (3) nonhomi- cidal narcotics offenses. Two years after the Federal Death Penalty Act was passed, the fed- eral government established the Antiterrorism and Effective Death Penalty Act of 1996, which added another four federal offenses to the list of capital crimes.

From this discussion, it is clear that the death penalty process has gone through substantial revi- sion in the federal justice system. As the laws related to the death penalty have changed, so too have the internal decision-making processes in federal death penalty cases (U.S. Department of Justice, 2001b). In 1995, the federal government adopted the policy—commonly known as the death penalty "pro- tocol"—under which U.S. Attorneys are required to submit for review all cases in which a defendant is charged with a capital-eligible offense, regardless of whether they actually desire to seek the death penalty in the defendant's case. The submissions are initially considered by a committee of senior fed- eral attorneys in Washington, DC, known as the **Attorney General's Review Committee on Capital Cases** (Review Committee), which makes an independent recommendation to the Attorney General. From January 27, 1995, to July 20, 2000—U.S. Attorneys submitted a total of 682 cases for review, and the Attorney General ultimately authorized seeking the death penalty for 159 of those defendants (USDOJ, 2001b). While a case progresses through the Department of Justice review process, it simultaneously continues in the U.S. Attorney's Office and in the court system. Some cases submitted for review are subsequently withdrawn due to events outside the review process (USDOJ, 2001b).

For example, the defendant and the U.S. Attorney may enter into a plea agreement that disposes of the case and results in the imposition of a prison term. In other cases, a judicial decision may result in the dismissal of either the entire case or the specific charges that are punishable by death. As a result, the total number of cases considered by the Review Committee is smaller than the total number submitted, and the total number of defendants considered by the Attorney General is smaller still. Furthermore, not all defendants who proceed to trial receive the death penalty (USDOJ, 2001b).

Due to this process of culling out offenders who will receive the death penalty, the federal govern- ment plays a relatively small role in administering the death penalty in this country. From 1930 to 1999, state governments executed over 4,400 defendants (USDOJ, 2001b). During the same time period, the federal government executed 33 defendants and has not carried out any executions since 1963 (USDOJ, 2001b). Furthermore, the Department of Justice's Bureau of Justice Statistics (BJS) reports that by the end of 1998 (the most recent year for which this statistic is available), there were 3,433 defendants with pending death sentences in the state system, compared to 19 defendants with currently pending death sentences in the federal system (USDOJ, 2001b). Thus, despite the expansion of the availability of the federal death penalty since 1988, federal defendants account for approximately one half of one percent of all the defendants on death row in the United States.

Lastly, and simply as a point of interest, the federal government has designated **United States Penitentiary (USP) Terre Haute** as the physical location for death row (see Focus Topic 18.2). At this facil- ity, the Special Confinement Unit was built and became the federal death row. During the years of 1995 and 1996, USP Terre Haute was modified to accommodate death row inmates and provide functions necessary for this population. On July 13, 1999, the Special Confinement Unit at USP Terre Haute opened, and the Bureau of Prisons transferred male federal death row inmates from other federal prisons and from state prisons to USP Terre Haute. The federal government chose Terre Haute as the location of the men's death row due to its central location within the United States.

Prison Tour Video Link 18.1
Watch a warden discuss death row housing.

FOCUS TOPIC: 18.2

Special Confinement Unit Opens at USP Terre Haute

On July 13 [1999], the United States Penitentiary (USP) Terre Haute, Indiana, opened a Special Confinement Unit to provide humane, safe, and secure confinement of male offenders who have been sentenced to death by the Federal courts. As a result of this action, this week, inmates with Federal death sentences have been transferred from other Federal and State correctional facilities to USP Terre Haute for placement in this Special Confinement Unit.

Based on the increasing number of Federal death penalty cases throughout the country, opening the Special Confinement Unit at USP Terre Haute has become necessary to implement Federal death sentences under applicable Federal statutes and regulations. This unit will be managed in a manner consistent with Bureau of Prisons' policies and procedures. The staff who work in this unit have received specialized training for managing this type of special offender.

The physical design of this two-story renovated housing unit includes 50 single-cells, upper tier and lower tier corridors, an industrial work shop, indoor and outdoor recreation areas, a property room, a food preparation area, attorney and family visiting rooms, and a video-teleconferencing area that is used to facilitate inmate access to the courts and their attorneys.

The Special Confinement Unit operations ensure inmates are afforded routine institution services and programs such as work programs, visitation, commissary privileges, telephone access, and law library services.

On July 19, 1993, USP Terre Haute was designated as the site by the Bureau of Prisons where implementation of the Federal death penalty would occur, including the establishment of a Special Confinement Unit for Federal death penalty cases. In 1995–96, the facility was modified to accommodate this responsibility. Prior to housing special confinement cases, this unit was used to house Cuban detainees.

USP Terre Haute was constructed in 1940. The grounds of USP Terre Haute cover 33 acres enclosed by a secure perimeter double fence. Today, USP Terre Haute is one of nine Federal high-security prisons which confine the Bureau's most dangerous offenders. Adjacent to the USP Terre Haute is a minimum-security camp for male offenders. USP Terre Haute's inmate population is currently 1,070; it has a rated capacity of 741. The minimum-security facility inmate population is 307; it has a rated capacity of 340.

SOURCE: Dunne, D. (1999). *Special Confinement Unit opens at USP Terre Haute*. Washington, DC: Office of Public Affairs Press Releases. Retrieved from http://www.bop.gov/news/press/press_releases/ipaspec.jsp.

METHODS OF EXECUTION

PHOTO 18.4

This picture shows a lethal injection table used in Texas.

In Table 18.5, students will see that there are generally three primary means of executing offenders on death row—lethal injection, electrocution, and lethal gas, which will be discussed briefly. While death by firing squad is used in three states—Idaho, Oklahoma, and Utah—the use of hanging is likewise very rare, and, again, only three states authorize the use of hanging; these are Delaware, New Hampshire, and Washington. Thus, this discussion will remain restricted to the more common forms of execution used in the United States.

Execution by Lethal Injection

The execution protocol for most jurisdictions authorizes the use of a combination of three drugs. The first, sodium thiopental or Sodium Pentothal, is a barbiturate that renders the prisoner unconscious. The second, pancuronium bromide, is a muscle relaxant that paralyzes the diaphragm and lungs. The third, potassium chloride, causes cardiac arrest. Each chemical is lethal in the amounts administered.

The inmate is escorted into the execution chamber and is strapped onto a gurney with ankle and wrist restraints. The inmate is connected to a cardiac monitor, which is connected to a printer outside the execution chamber. An IV is started in two usable veins, one in each arm, and a flow of normal saline solution is administered at a slow rate. At the warden's signal, the injection of intravenous chemicals occurs. The most common problem encountered is collapsing veins and the inability to properly insert the IV.

Currently, 20 states and the federal government authorize lethal injection as the sole method of execution (see Table 18.5). Other states provide for lethal injection as the primary method of execution, but provide alternative methods depending upon the choice of the inmate, the date of the execution or sentence, or the possibility of the method being held unconstitutional.

PHOTO 18.5

This is an older-model electric chair. Electric chairs are seldom used today as a means of execution.

Execution by Electrocution

The execution protocol for most jurisdictions authorizes the use of a wooden chair with restraints and connections to an electric current. The offender enters the execution chamber and is placed in the electric chair. The chair is constructed of oak and is set on a rubber matting and bolted to a concrete floor. Lap, chest, arm, and forearm straps are secured. A leg piece (anklet) is laced to the offender's right calf, and a sponge and electrode are attached. The headgear consists of a metal headpiece covered with a leather hood, which conceals the offender's face. The metal part of the headpiece consists of a copper wire mesh screen to which the electrode is brazened. A wet sponge is placed between the electrode and the offender's scalp. The safety switch is closed. The circuit breaker is engaged. The execution control panel is activated. The most common problems encountered include burning of varying degrees to parts of the body, and a failure of the procedures to cause death without repeated shocks. Witness accounts of many botched executions over the years have caused electrocution to be replaced with lethal injection as the most common method of execution.

Currently, only Nebraska currently uses electrocution as the sole method of execution. Nine other states provide for electrocution as an alternative method, depending upon the choice of the inmate, the date of the execution or sentence, or the possibility of the method being held unconstitutional. Interestingly, in 2008, the Nebraska Supreme Court ruled that the use of the electric chair as a method of execution violates the Nebraska Constitution. With no alternative methods of execution on the books, Nebraska is practically without a death penalty.

Execution by Lethal Gas

The execution protocol for most jurisdictions authorizes the use of a steel airtight execution chamber, equipped with a chair and attached restraints. The inmate is restrained at his chest, waist, arms, and ankles, and wears a mask during the execution. The chair is equipped with a metal container beneath the seat. Cyanide pellets are placed in this container. A metal canister is on the floor under the container filled with a sulfuric acid solution. There are three executioners, and each executioner turns one key. When the three keys are turned, an electric switch causes the bottom of the cyanide container to open allowing the cyanide to fall into the sulfuric acid solution, producing a lethal gas. Unconsciousness can occur within a few seconds if the inmate takes a deep breath. However, if the inmate holds his or her breath, death

Video Link 18.3
Watch a video about execution.

Journal Article Link 18.3
Read about methods of execution as fads.

can take much longer, and the inmate usually goes into wild convulsions. A heart monitor attached to the inmate is read in the control room, and after the warden pronounces the inmate dead, ammonia is pumped into the execution chamber to neutralize the gas. Exhaust fans then remove the inert fumes from the chamber into two scrubbers that contain water and serve as a neutralizing agent. Death is estimated to usually occur within 6 to 18 minutes of the lethal gas emissions.

The most common problems encountered are the obvious agony suffered by the inmate and the length of time to cause death. Currently, only four states—Arizona, California, Missouri, and Wyoming—currently authorize lethal gas as a method of execution, all as an alternative to lethal injection, depending upon the choice of the inmate, the date of the execution or sentence, or the possibility of lethal injection being held unconstitutional.

ARGUMENTS FOR AND AGAINST THE DEATH PENALTY

The debate over the death penalty has been active in the United States for generations. Generally, it is not difficult to find people who have strong views regarding this sanction, with some supporting and some opposing its use. Indeed, there is a multitude of arguments on both ends of the spectrum, and, because of this, these arguments will be presented along three key themes upon which many arguments depend. These three identifiable themes consist of deterrence, retribution, and arbitrariness, and each one will be discussed separately to allow for a more clear presentation of the arguments associated with them.

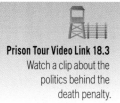
Deterrence

Students may recall that we discussed the notions of general and specific deterrence in Chapter 3 of this text. We again use these terms to explain the pros and cons used for the death penalty. When arguing over matters of deterrence, supporters of the death penalty contend that when murderers are sentenced to death and executed, other would-be murderers will reconsider their acts due to the fear of being executed. This is an argument of general deterrence and is based on the notion that, due to the observation of the death penalty being imposed, other criminals will equate this outcome to their own circumstances and will be deterred from committing crimes that can result in the death penalty. This naturally presupposes that offenders contemplate their actions to such an extent before committing those actions. Other supporters argue in favor of more specific deterrence rather than general deterrence. Specific deterrence is achieved in such cases because that specific offender who is put to death will not be able to commit another crime again because, simply put, he is dead. This is perhaps the most effective and most guaranteed means of preventing recidivism that is known.

Opponents of the death penalty who argue against the utility of deterrence as a rationale for using the death penalty note that while numerous statistical studies have been conducted, there is no conclusive evidence that the death penalty lowers crime. In fact, there may even be some indication that its use can increase crime (this will be discussed in more detail later in the brutalization hypothesis section of this chapter). Support for this can be seen when comparing states that do not employ the death penalty with those that do; generally crime rates and murder rates are lower in states that do not have the death penalty. Interestingly, the United States, an ardent proponent of the death penalty, has a higher murder rate than do countries in Europe as well as Canada, which do not have a death penalty.

Further still, most people who commit murders do not usually plan on being caught, and most commit their crimes due to moments of anger when in impaired states, such as with substance abuse. These types of

TECHNOLOGY AND EQUIPMENT 18.1

The Use of DNA Technology Frees Death Row Inmates, Brings Others to Justice

After five years on Louisiana's death row, Ryan Matthews received a second chance at life. He was exonerated last year with the help of DNA evidence.

"He was 17 years old at the time of his arrest and is borderline retarded," said Martha Kashickey, the public-education associate for the Innocence Project at Yeshiva University's law school in New York City.

"Post-conviction DNA testing on the mask the perpetrator left at the scene both exonerated Matthews and revealed the identity of the actual perpetrator," Kashickey said from New York City.

The Washington, D.C.-based Death Penalty Information Center (DPIC) reports that 13 other death-row inmates have also been exonerated with the help of DNA evidence.

"The assumption was that they were guilty [because] they were found guilty, unanimously, by a jury," said Richard Dieter, president of the DPIC. "But sometimes DNA kind of pierces through that and says that, despite what a witness says he saw, this person was not the one who left this evidence at the scene."

While many death-row inmates await only their execution, others hope for new tests that could spur their release.

"People are on death row sometimes as long as 15 or 20 years, so there are still quite a few people who were convicted at times when DNA testing wasn't prevalent [or as reliable as it is now]," Dieter said.

In 2004 the U.S. Congress passed legislation that encourages all states to enable post-trial DNA tests. The legislation also provides funding for such tests.

"Half of the [U.S.] states have processes to allow [DNA] testing" even after the appeals process is exhausted, Dieter explained.

Texas Department of Public Safety (DPS) spokesperson Tela Mange notes that her agency's crime lab has handled 49 such inmate requests (not all of them death-penalty cases) for DNA retesting. A significant percentage of the inmates have been exonerated.

"Eight tests were inconclusive, and there were nine individuals that were excluded as donors of the biological evidence left at the scene," Mange said from her Austin office.

Such post-trial exonerations are likely to become a thing of the past, because modern, accurate, affordable DNA testing has become a common pretrial practice.

"We have an increasing number of between 2,500 [and] 3,000 DNA cases each year," Mange said. "Juries are coming to expect it, especially because they are being trained by TV. But there is a disconnect between *CSI* and the things that we can do, and that's a concern. We can't get returns on DNA cases in an hour."

DNA evidence is also subject to human error. Confidence in many testing labs has been shaken by confirmed cases of botched, falsified, and otherwise erroneous procedures, most infamously at the Houston Police Department crime laboratory, where a 17-year-old boy was convicted for rape based on improperly processed DNA samples.

While exonerations of death-row inmates and violent criminals are usually subject to very stringent testing control, such has not always been the case with pre-trial DNA evidence.

"Just because you're doing DNA testing, people shouldn't always consider the results 100 percent reliable," Dieter explained. "Much depends on the quality of people collecting the evidence, doing the testing, doing the probability calculations—all of this is subject to human error."

Reform Needed?

Rob Warden, director of the Center on Wrongful Conviction at the Northwestern University School of Law in Chicago, said the United States' many labs and controlling agencies are in need of fundamental reform.

"The most fundamental reform would be to establish reliable scientific procedures in crime labs," he said. "They should be independent of law-enforcement agencies. Scientists should not know what the desired outcome of the test is. Instead, it sometimes happens [that officials say,] 'Here's a semen sample from the victim, and here's the suspect's sample—can you match them?' That shouldn't be the question."

Even when DNA evidence is accurately managed, using it to prove innocence or guilt is not always straightforward.

"People confuse the presence of biological material and DNA with its ultimate use," said John Bradley, the district attorney of Williamson County, Texas.

"DNA means that a biological material is present, but there is still a lot of work to be done to draw truthful inferences from it, from the prosecutors' or defendants' viewpoint. You can go into any room anywhere and likely find some DNA, but it doesn't resolve the question of what does that DNA mean?"

Bradley explained that not only are juries becoming more DNA savvy but defendants are as well.

"In a few interesting cases defendants have come close to manipulating DNA in ways that led the case away from themselves," he explained.

A Saskatchewan, Canada, doctor was accused of raping a sedated patient on 1992 but readily consented to DNA blood tests, which indicated that he was not the rapist. Only after the victim hired a private detective did the truth emerge.

The physician had twice implanted into his arm plastic tubes of another person's blood. He was eventually convicted in 1999 and served about four years in prison.

"It really opened my eyes," Bradley said. "As much as we can make mistakes as prosecutors, we have to be aware that defendants can also manipulate the system."

Bradley cites other complex examples of intentional DNA manipulation. For instance, a serial rapist paid prostitutes for semen-filled condoms and used the fluid to confound DNA testing. Also, several Texas prisoners switched identity armbands prior to blood sampling, fooling a nurse who did not know the inmates.

Despite the challenges, DNA is helping law enforcement to close the books on many cases that had been unresolved for years.

The United States' Combined DNA Index System (CODIS) compares DNA profiles of convicted sex offenders and other violent criminals with evidence from unsolved cases.

"We had a serial rapist who raped two little girls, and the detectives had decided that there was no way to solve the case," Mange, the Texas Department of Public Safety spokesperson, said. "But five years later we submitted the evidence [to CODIS], and we got a match. We never would have solved this case in a million years without CODIS, and these girls were living in fear, because they thought that this person was out there."

The booming use of DNA testing has led to enormous backlogs in many labs, and lack of public funding for the tests has frustrated prosecutors and defenders alike.

With DNA's importance likely to grow, both groups hope that increased funding will help the wheels of justice turn fairly and quickly.

SOURCE: "The Use of DNA Technology Frees Death-Row Inmates, Brings Others to Justice," Brian Handwerk in *National Geographic News*, April 8, 2005.

circumstances do not allow for the offenders to contemplate the outcome of their actions, and, depending on their emotional framework at the time of crime commission, it may be doubtful that the knowledge of this sanction would be a deterrent. When also considering that these factors are allowed to mitigate the punishment of offenders, it is clear that such circumstances may not truly justify the death penalty, at least not on a logical basis.

Lastly, life sentences, when given in total without parole, are just as effective as death sentences. Both can arguably deter crime in a general and specific manner. However, the life sentence allows for remediation in cases where it may later be found that an offender was, in fact, innocent. In addition, it is worth noting that most murderers on death row are very well mannered and do not represent an institutional hazard. When coupled with the fact that life sentences tend to be less expensive than death sentences, it seems clear that deterrence can be achieved for less cost and can include safeguards that allow for remediation of cases where mistakes in the guilt determination process have occurred.

Retribution

The second theme around which arguments for and against the death penalty tend to revolve is the desire for retribution. Students may recall that we discussed the concept of retribution in Chapter 3 of this text. The concept of retribution is sometimes given Biblical reference with the saying "an eye for an eye," which implies that offenders committing a crime should be punished in a manner that is commensurate with the severity of the crime that they have committed. This is also referred to as a "just desserts" model, which demands that punishments match the degree of harm that criminals have inflicted on their victims (Stohr, Walsh, & Hemmens, 2009).

Video Link 18.4
Watch a video about offenses and the death penalty.

While many people tend to confuse retribution with simple revenge, it is not the same thing. Rather, retribution is based on a logical premise that if a person commits an infraction the logical consequence is a penalty calibrated to the severity of that infraction, as much as is humanly possible, of course. It is recognized by most proponents of retribution that this approach cannot restore the victim and/or the victim's family members to their state of existence before a murder was committed, but it is thought that an execution of the offender will bring closure to the criminal activity and to the ordeal that faces the victim. This symbolic closure has a logical connotation and outcome.

While retribution has been couched as a logical approach, there is an emotional component that is also addressed; families of the victim can see that, if nothing else, there is some connection between the action and the consequences received. In addition, the death penalty can help to facilitate the grieving process as some families may desire reciprocation in the sense of loss that is incurred. To ask for a payment of anything less than a life would seem to indicate that the life of the victim was somehow less valuable. Thus, there may indeed be an emotional sense of justice that is fulfilled. While many critiques of retribution might not find this adequate as a rationale, supporters may contend that families of murder victims have a right to feel as they do and, correspondingly, are entitled to seek relief as they are allowed within the law.

Opponents of retribution may hold that, at the base of it, retribution is simply a form of revenge. The contention is that retribution simply provides a reason and rationale behind the pursuit of unbridled revenge. In fact, opponents of retribution tend to believe that the use of death itself contradicts the "evolving standards of decency" espoused by the Supreme Court. The mark of a civilization is the means by which it aids those who are troubled and not through the eradication of their existence. This is even more true when the offender has a diminished capacity and/or acted in an altered state of mind. Simply put, the use of the death penalty is considered barbaric, and justifications based on retribution do not make this penalty more civilized.

Arbitrariness

The last theme that many arguments involving the death penalty tend to entail is concerns over the arbitrary nature of the death penalty. Supporters of the death penalty argue that it is not arbitrarily applied and even note that, as a matter of fact, more Caucasian American offenders are executed than are minority offenders. On the other hand, the number of African Americans on death row tends to exceed their overall proportion within the broader population. Thus, the issue of racial disparity in the application can point to some degree of arbitrariness in the use of this sanction.

Consider also that one study found that nearly half of a total of 1,936 capital punishment cases ended with a plea bargain. This included cases where there were two or even three victims. From this, we can conclude that there is a degree of variability in determining exactly who is actually put to death. In fact, most plea bargains are made according to the evidence that exists in a case and/or the representation

APPLIED THEORY 18.1

Death Penalty and Rational Choice Theory

Rational choice theory is predicated on the idea that individuals consciously and deliberately choose criminal behavior of their own free will. The components of criminal behavior, under rational choice, are the immediate social situation, justification that the offender has for the action, and the likelihood of getting away with the criminal act. Thus, when we use the death penalty, we presume that offenders are able to rationally make a choice to commit a crime and therefore understand why they are given the death penalty when it is applied. It is for this reason that certain groups have been excluded from receiving the death penalty, such as with the mentally challenged and/or juvenile offenders.

According to Keel (2005), the concepts associated with rational choice theory are rooted in the analysis of human behavior developed by the early *classical theorists*, Cesare Beccaria and Jeremy Bentham. Keel (2005) notes the central points of this theory: (1) The human being is a rational actor; (2) rationality involves an end-means calculation; (3) people (freely) choose all behavior, both conforming and deviant, based on their rational calculations; (4) the central element of calculation involves a cost-benefit analysis: *pleasure* versus *pain*; (5) choice, with all other conditions equal, will be directed toward the maximization

of *individual* pleasure; (6) choice can be controlled through the perception and understanding of the potential pain or *punishment* that will follow an act judged to be in violation of the social good, the *social contract*; (7) the state is responsible for maintaining order and preserving the common good through a system of laws (this system is the embodiment of the social contract); and (8) the *swiftness, severity, and certainty* of punishment are the key elements in understanding a law's ability to control human behavior.

The key issue is that rational choice is a highly subjective concept. When determining whether offenders exercised rational choice, numerous conditions may have to be considered. Rather than consider these points, rational choice theory simply focuses on the act, itself, that was committed. Attention and focus are simply cast toward those variables that make the act less desirable in the future. However, it is clear from our readings that it is questionable if deterrence associated with the death penalty actually works at all. Given the tendency to ignore many of the mitigating factors that might be associated with an outcome, rational choice theory presumes that offenders were fully aware of their actions and the potential outcomes of their actions. This leaves substantial room for error.

that the offender is able to obtain. This means that determining whether the offender gets the death penalty has little to do with the ultimate outcome of justice but instead is reliant on other factors associated with the case. Obviously, this creates disparate and, arguably, arbitrary outcomes.

Regardless of whether racial disparities do indicate arbitrariness, there is general consensus that no matter how much we try, we can never perfectly calibrate a sanction to be exactly commensurate with the crime that is committed; this is impossible. Thus, to apply a permanent sanction that does not allow for later modification (such as with early releases) seems to be ludicrous when there is little guarantee that the punishment is not commensurate to mismatches in awarding capital punishment. The inability to ensure proportionality, therefore, undermines the argument for retribution and instead further illustrates how we, as a society, are at risk of enabling arbitrary practices.

BRUTALIZATION HYPOTHESIS

There is some evidence that the death penalty may not only be a failure at deterring crime, but may actually increase homicide levels in areas where executions occur. This observation is often based on the notion that violence begets violence and is referred to as the brutalization hypothesis. The **brutalization hypothesis,** first introduced in Chapter 1, contends that executions may cause an increase in murders because it reinforces the use of violence. Because of this, researchers such as Bowers and Pierce (1980) contend that "the lesson of the execution then, may be to devalue life by the example of human sacrifice" (p. 457).

Other researchers, such as Cochran, Chamlin, and Seth (1994), examined the reinstatement of the death penalty in Oklahoma. They found "no evidence that Oklahoma's reintroduction of the execution produced a significant decrease in the level of criminal homicides during the period under investigation" (Cochran et al., 1994, p. 129). Even further, they noted that the death penalty seemed to produce a brutalizing effect that further encouraged offenders to commit murders if they had feelings that their own life or circumstances were fundamentally unfair.

TABLE 18.6   Selected Studies of the Deterrent Effect of the Death Penalty

Study	Unit of Analysis	Period	Result
Sellin, 1959	Matched state comparison	1920–1962	No deterrent
Ehrlich, 1975b	US (aggregate)	1933–1969	7–8 fewer murders per execution (C.I. 0–24)
Bowers and Pierce, 1980	New York state	1907–1963	2 more homicides per month after an execution
Mocan and Gittings, 2003	State-level	1977–1997	5 fewer homicides per execution
Katz, Levitt, Shepherd, 2003	State-level	1950–1990	No systematic evidence of a deferent (+3.1 to −5.6)
Dezhb akhsh, Rubin, and Shepherd, 2003	Country-level	1977–1996	18 fewer homicides per execution
Shepherd, 2004	State-level	1977–1999	3 fewer murder per execution
Zimmerman, 2004	State-level	1978–1997	14 fewer murders per execution
Shepherd, 2005	Country-level	1977–1996	−21 states have brutalization effect −6 states have deterrent effect −23 states have no effect Overall, 4.5 fewer murders per execution
Donohue and Wolfers, 2005	Canada vs. US	1950–2003	No deterrent

SOURCE: Kohen, A., & Jolly, S. J. (2006). *Deterrence reconsidered: A theoretical and empirical case against the death penalty*. Paper presented at the annual meeting of the Midwest Political Science Association, Palmer House Hilton, Chicago. Retrieved from http://www.allacademic.com/meta/p140213_index.html

Regardless of the argument that one believes, it is very clear that the research is quite mixed on the utility of the death penalty. In short, no one can seem to prove whether "it works" at doing anything in a manner that is intended, and both advocates and opponents are able to generate evidence for their views. This makes the entire issue difficult to discern. Work by Kohen and Jolly (2006) demonstrates the mixed state of affairs in researching the efficacy of the death penalty. When looking at Table 18.6, it can be seen that there are numerous studies that have different results. Some studies find support for deterrence, and some do not; others occasionally find support for the brutalization effect. While Kohen and Jolly (2006) were making a case against the death penalty in their review of the research, it is our point now to simply understand that, despite years of debate, it seems that nobody has airtight proof of either side of the argument.

However, we will close our discussion of the death penalty with these final thoughts. While it may not be proven that the death penalty does not work, it is certainly not proven that it does work to deter crime. If we do not know, for a fact, that this sanction deters crime, then the most logical response is to not use this permanent sanction when other sanctions are available until the time that we do know, for a fact, that this sanction prevents crime. If we do otherwise, we must then admit that deterrence is not our rationale for using the death penalty. This then means that, simply put, the death penalty is a sanction that would be steeped in retribution, and, in this case, our government would be ethically obligated to uphold its social contract to take a life when one is taken. To fail to do so would mean that the government is fraudulently or negligently failing to uphold its end of the social contract. On the other hand, when the government does this to an innocent individual, it once again fails in meeting its social contract by infringing on the liberty of the innocent and subjecting a person to the terrifying experience of being on death row, knowing all the while that he or she was innocent, but that the world outside remained uncaring to his or her pleas. To further put this in perspective, let us close by noting that as long as humans

Journal Article Link 18.4
Read about citizens' attitudes towards wrongful convictions.

determine guilt or innocence, the use of the death penalty will always lead to an innocent person's death from time to time. This is the price of doing business in the justice system.

CONCLUSION

This chapter has provided students with a view of a correctional practice that occurs at the very end of the correctional process. In fact, the application of the death penalty is a confession that we cannot or do not wish to correct certain offenders. The death penalty is considered cruel and inhumane by a number of people in society and, as a result, has experienced scrutiny from persons who wish to see it abolished. When considering the types of crimes associated with the death penalty, it is clear that, for the most part, only offenders who have been convicted of murder will be found on death row. Further still, most of these offenders have committed prior offenses, with most also having served prior jail or prison sentences. This is important because it demonstrates that most have led a life of crime that goes beyond the single crime for which they are sentenced. Though their civil liberties must still be protected and though they are entitled to the full range of appeals guaranteed by law, this small group of offenders (remember, only a tiny minority of offenders are sentenced to death) does tend to have a long history of offending.

In addition, there is still a noticeably disproportionate difference in racial representation on death row, with African Americans being disproportionately represented. This is even more magnified if the victim was Caucasian. This disparity has been observed among various state systems and was even specifically noted within the federal system's use of the death penalty. While this may occur for any number of reasons, it is an interesting point that offenders are more likely to be given the death penalty if the victim is White. Different researchers emphasize this point for a variety of reasons. For our purposes, in this chapter, we conclude that much of this has to do with partisanship issues where the more affluent members of society tend to be Caucasian (on the average this is true throughout the nation), and these persons have a strong pull on outcomes within the justice system.

END-OF-CHAPTER DISCUSSION QUESTIONS

1. What are some arguments in favor of the death penalty?

2. What are some arguments against the death penalty?

3. Select two Supreme Court cases that you believe are important regarding the death penalty. Explain why you believe that they are important.

4. What is the victim-turned-offender hypothesis, and how does it comport with the tenets of feminist criminology introduced in Chapter 11?

5. Identify the different means of execution used in administering the death penalty.

6. How does racial disparity come into play regarding the death penalty?

7. In your own words, explain why you believe that deterrence theory is or is not a good justification for the use of the death penalty.

KEY TERMS

Anti-Drug Abuse Act of 1988	Death row	*Roper v. Simmons* (2005)
Atkins v. Virginia (2002)	Federal Death Penalty Act of 1994	*Thompson v. Oklahoma* (1988)
Antiterrorism and Effective Death Penalty Act of 1996	*Ford v. Wainwright* (1986)	*Trop v. Dulles* (1958)
Attorney General's Review Committee on Capital Cases	*Furman v. Georgia* (1972)	United States Penitentiary (USP) Terre Haute
Brutalization hypothesis	*Gregg v. Georgia* (1976)	
Coker v. Georgia (1977)	Prosecutorial Death Discretion Outcome	*Witherspoon v. Illinois* (1968)

APPLIED EXERCISE 18.1

Students must conduct either a face-to-face or a phone interview with either an inmate on death row or a correctional officer who has worked in a death row setting. The student must set up a day and time with that practitioner or inmate and interview him or her to gain insight and perspective on several key questions related to the death penalty. Students must write the responses of the inmate or practitioner, provide their own analysis of those responses, and submit their draft by the deadline set by their instructor. Students should complete this application exercise as a minipaper that addresses each point below. The total word count should be 800 to 1,100 words.

When completing the interview, students should ask the following questions:

1. What is the most unique aspect of death row from the typical prison facility?

2. What are some common things that you think about when on death row?

3. What do you think that the public needs to understand about death row?

In addition, you should ensure that your submission has appropriate spelling and grammar throughout. Lastly, students are required to provide contact information for the death row inmate or practitioner. Please have students obtain the following information from the person that they interview. While instructors will probably not need to contact this person, it may become necessary so that they can validate the actual completion of an interview.

Name and title of correctional supervisor: _____

Correctional agency: _____

Practitioner's phone number: _____

Practitioner's e-mail address: _____

Name of student: _____

"WHAT WOULD YOU DO?"

You are a religious services officer who works at Louisiana State Penitentiary Angola and you often work with the inmates on death row. One inmate in particular, nicknamed "Greyhound" because of his advanced years in age, is scheduled for execution within the next 48 hours. You are aware that he will not be given a "stay" on his execution and that he will, in fact, be put to death at that time. Over the years of working on death row, you have gotten to know many of the men who do their time until their execution date, and Greyhound is one of them.

You are also aware of one other detail that he recently divulged to you. He did not commit the crime for which he will soon die. The crime was one where the daughter of a small-town mayor was raped and killed back in 2004, and her body was found strangled and hidden in the woods near the town. Greyhound was seen near the area and ultimately confessed to the killing.

However, Greyhound has disclosed to you that it was, in actuality, his own son, James, who had committed the killing. Greyhound loved his son, who was expected to leave on a football scholarship to Notre Dame after the summer that the crime had been committed. According to James, the incident was accidental. You see, it appears that the two teens had a long history of experimentation with sexual activity. James had, in fact, had sex with the girl, Cheryl, and, while having sex, the two teens had experimented with different types of autoerotic asphyxiation. They had been seeing each other for over a year and had both learned of this type of sexual activity on the Internet. They experimented with this multiple times, and, on the last occasion, the situation went wrong.

James would usually hold Cheryl and, with some degree of force, would choke around her carotid arteries while penetrating her sexually. This particular evening, they had been drinking, and Cheryl was quite drunk. He thought that she had passed out while they had sex and, before completing his sex act, did not realize that he had, in fact, choked her. Between the tension on her neck and her drunken state, he had killed her, but by accident. The two were in the woods, late at night, on a blanket, near the shore of Lake Livingston. James, being scared, contacted his father rather than the police.

His father told him to not say a word, and they decided upon a plan. The plan that they came up with did not work. Cheryl's parents noticed her gone prematurely, and Cheryl's little brother, Timmy, knew of the location where Cheryl would meet James for their sexual trysts. Timmy told the parents who went to catch the teens in the act. James and his father were forced to leave the scene prematurely and Cheryl's body was found by her parents. The entire situation was heartbreaking and shocked the citizens of the town.

From there, Greyhound had told his son to keep quiet. He concocted a story and took the blame for the crime. James went on to Notre Dame, amidst his father's court involvement and ultimate sentencing to death. His son has often wanted to come forward, but given the cover-up of the murder and the circumstances, his father has been adamant that his son say nothing. Greyhound is telling you because he is, in actuality, a very religious man, and he wants to clean his soul. He does not want you to mention this, ever— he notes that you are required to keep this confidential and that he is expecting you to do so.

You know that, if you say nothing, the wrong person will be going to death for a crime that he did not do, all to protect the welfare of his son. On the other hand, if you do say something, it is likely that both Greyhound and his son will be in legal trouble, and this will also ruin James's life, who has graduated as an electrical engineer, is married, and has two kids. You struggle during your sleeping hours as you think about the dilemma in which you are caught.

What would you do?

STUDENT STUDY SITE

Visit the Student Study Site at **www.sagepub.com/hanserintro** to access links to the videos, audio clips, SAGE journal articles, state rankings, and reference materials noted in this chapter, as well as additional study tools including eFlashcards, web quizzes, and more.

chapter 19

Program Evaluation, Evidence-Based Practices, and Future Trends in Corrections

LEARNING OBJECTIVES:

1. Identify the process of evaluative research and distinguish between process and outcome measures.

2. Know and apply the assessment-evaluative cycle.

3. Be able to explain how evaluative research contributes to correctional agency effectiveness.

4. Identify and discuss the use of evidence-based practices in corrections.

5. Be aware of likely future trends in correctional agencies.

INTRODUCTION

Effective research and evaluation of correctional programs is critical if we are to begin to understand what is likely to produce lasting change in offenders. To not effectively research and evaluate such programs is, in essence, resigning our efforts to chance. Chance is not acceptable, however, when huge amounts of money and individuals' lives are at stake. Therefore, the question becomes "How do we effectively evaluate correctional programs, and how do we know that those programs are working?" In response to this question, we begin this chapter with an explanation of the specific function of evaluation research, which can be described as a form of explanatory research. We conclude the chapter with a discussion of trends likely to impact corrections in the future. This last aspect of the chapter is based on prior research as well as observations of policy and decision making that has been touted among numerous correctional agencies around the nation.

EVALUATION RESEARCH

In the past several years a massive effort on behalf of the U.S. Government has been aimed at enhancing evaluation practices and services. Various documents have been published and placed in the public domain to help community correction programs better understand the impact of various treatment services. Much of the following information is borrowed from the Center for Substance Abuse Treatment (2005), a government agency responsible for implementing and evaluating many treatment programs attempting to better serve offenders suffering from mental illness and co-occurring disorders.

Research and evaluation is a critical dimension of correctional programs. Evaluations are needed for program monitoring and for decision making by program staff, criminal justice administrators, and policy makers. Evaluations provide accountability, identify strengths and weaknesses, and provide a basis for program revision. In addition, evaluation reports are useful learning tools for others who are interested in developing effective programs. Many treatment programs in the criminal justice system have operated without evaluations for many years, only to find out later that key outcome data are needed to justify program continuation.

Conducting an adequate evaluation requires one to clearly formulate the treatment model and reasonable program goals and specific objectives related to client needs. General goals must be translated into measurable outcomes. The evaluator generally works closely with program administrators to translate the evaluation guidelines into operational components. For example, general goals of helping program participants to become drug and crime free can be operationalized into intermediate goals of changing behavior (e.g., reductions in rule infractions and fewer positive drug test results) while in a program. In essence, scientific principles for conducting research should be carefully adhered to in order to enhance the viability of findings.

There are three basic types of evaluation:

1. Implementation

2. Process

3. Outcome

An important note before we discuss the three main components of evaluation research is that, while implementation and process evaluations can begin when the program is initiated, outcome evaluation should not begin until the program has been fully implemented. Outcome evaluations are generally more costly than other types of evaluation and are warranted for programs of longer duration that are aimed at modifying lifestyles (such as therapeutic communities), rather than drug education interventions that are less intensive and less likely to produce long-term effects.

Implementation Evaluation

While programs often look promising in the proposal stage, many fail to materialize as planned in the security-oriented correctional environment. Other programs are rigidly implemented as planned and without adjustments for the realities of community corrections, often rendering them less effective. **Implementation evaluation** is aimed at identifying problems and accomplishments during the early phases of program development for feedback to clinical and administrative staff. Such evaluations involve informal and formal interviews with correctional administrators, staff, and offenders to ascertain their degree of satisfaction with the program and their perceptions of problems.

Process Evaluation

Traditionally, **process evaluation** refers to assessment of the effects of the program on clients while they are in the program, making it possible to assess the institution's intermediary goals. Process evaluation involves analyzing records related to the following:

- Type and amount of services provided.
- Attendance and participation in group meetings.
- Number of offenders who are screened, admitted, reviewed, and discharged.
- Percentage of offenders who favorably complete treatment each month.
- Percentage of offenders who have infractions or rule violations.
- Number of offenders who test positive for substances (this can be compared to urinalysis results for the general prison population).

Effective programs produce positive client changes. These changes initially occur during participation in the program and ideally continue upon release into the community. The areas of potential client change that should be assessed include the following:

- Cognitive understanding (e.g., mastery of program curriculum).
- Emotional functioning (e.g., anxiety and depression).
- Attitudes/values (e.g., honesty, responsibility, and concern for others).
- Education and vocational training progress (e.g., achievement tests).
- Behavior (e.g., rule infractions and urinalyses results).

Within institutional corrections, it is also important to evaluate program impact on the host prison facility itself. Well-run treatment programs often generate an array of positive developments affecting the morale and functioning of the entire inmate population. Areas to examine include the following:

- *Offender behavior.* Review the number of rule infractions, the cost of hearings, court litigation expenses, and inmate cooperation in general prison operations.
- *Staff functioning.* Assess stress levels, which may become manifest in the number of sick days taken and the rate of staff turnover. Generally, the better the program, the lower the stress, and the better the attendance, the involvement, and the commitment of staff.
- *Physical plant.* Examine the physical properties of the program. Assess general vandalism apparent in terms of damage to furniture or windows, as well as the presence of graffiti. Assess structural damage, for example, to walls and plumbing.

Outcome Evaluation

Outcome evaluations are more ambitious and expensive than implementation or process evaluations. **Outcome evaluation** involves quantitative research aimed at assessing the impact of the program on long-term treatment outcomes. Such evaluations are usually carefully designed studies that compare outcomes for a treatment group with outcomes for other less intensive treatments or a no-treatment control group (i.e., a sample of offenders who meet the program admission criteria but who do not receive treatment), complex statistical analyses, and sophisticated report preparation.

Journal Article Link 19.1
Read about outcome evalutaion of a drug abuse program for women.

FOCUS TOPIC: 19.1

Commonly Used Measures of Reentry Program Performance

Process Measures

  Substance Abuse Treatment Services Received

  Employment Services Received

  Housing Assistance Received

  Family Intervention and Parent Training Received

  Health and Mental Health Services Received

Outcome Measures

  Rearrest Rates

  Reincarceration Rates

Proportion Employed

Rates of Drug Relapse

Frequency and Severity of Offenses

Proportion Self-Sufficient

Participation in Self-Improvement Programs

SOURCE: Bureau of Justice Assistance, Center for Program Evaluation. (2007). *Reporting and using evaluation results*. Washington, DC: Author. Retrieved from http://www.ojp.usdoj.gov/BJA/evaluation/sitemap.htm.

PHOTO 19.1

Rob Hanser stands at the entrance to the Blue Walters and Successful Treatment for Addiction & Recovery (S.T.A.R.) section of Richwood Correctional Center. This is a section of the prison that consists of group treatment rooms, counselor offices, a programming meeting room, and two dormitories that house approximately 200 inmates.

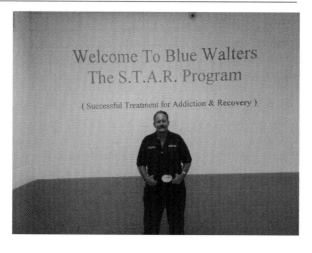

Follow-up data (e.g., drug relapse, recidivism, employment status) are the heart of outcome evaluation. Follow-up data can be collected from criminal justice records and face-to-face interviews with individuals who participated in certain programs. Studies that use agency records are less expensive than locating participants and conducting follow-up interviews. Outcome evaluations can include cost-effectiveness and cost-benefit information that is important to policy makers. Because outcome research usually involves a relatively large investment of time and money, as well as the cooperation of a variety of people and agencies, it must be carefully planned. A research design may be very simple and easy to implement, or it may be more complex. In the case of more complex studies, it is usually advisable to enlist the assistance of an experienced researcher.

Program Quality and Staffing Quality

Aside from outcome and process measures, there are a number of other areas that agencies may wish to evaluate. These other areas may or may not require the input of the offender, and they may or may not be dependent upon the offender population's outcome results. Some examples include when agencies wish to assess the quality of their program, their staff, or their curricula. Each of these three components is very important but may go well beyond simple outcome evaluation measures. In some cases, such as with program curricula, there may be a connection to the general process measures used to evaluate the program. However, it is important when agencies evaluate curricula that they keep this separate and distinct from the blurring effects of staff that may modify the general process with their own therapeutic slant and/or means of implementing aspects of a job requirement. In other words, the individual preferences of different persons employed in the agency are not what you hope to observe in a curricular assessment, but rather it is the uniform and written procedures that are of interest.

From the example with curricular assessment just noted, it is clear that evaluations can be quite complex and detailed, depending on the approach taken by the agency. The key to an effective and ethical

Prison Tour Video Link 19.1
Watch the author discuss outcome evaluation.

evaluation is evaluative transparency. **Evaluative transparency** is when an agency's evaluative process allows for an outside person (whether an auditor, an evaluator, or the public at large) to have full view of the agency's operations, budgeting, policies, procedures, and outcomes. In transparent agencies there are no secrets, and confidential information is only kept when ethical or legal requirements mandate that the information not be transparent, such as with a client's treatment files and/or a victim's personal identity. In such cases, the intent is a benevolent safeguarding of the client's welfare, not the agency's own welfare.

If one is to evaluate the quality of a program, it stands to reason that the program must be transparent to the evaluator who is tasked with observing that program. Agencies that seek to meet high ethical standards must be transparent. This is a core requisite to ensuring the quality of the program that is implemented. Further, programs of quality are accountable to the public, and this is, in part, an element of transparency. Public accountability is a matter of good ethical bearing, and this is consistent with the reason that ethical safeguards are put into place—to protect the public consumer. In the case of corrections agencies, the product that is "sold" to the public is community safety, and it is the obligation of the agency to be accountable and transparent to the public when providing services to its jurisdiction. Thus, the quality of the program should be appraised by its ability to deliver ethical, open, and honest services that hold community safety as paramount.

In regard to staffing quality, agencies should make a point to evaluate their standards as well as the support that they provide to their staff. Naturally, recruitment and hiring standards should be evaluated routinely, but it is also important that agencies examine their own support services for staff. Some examples might include the existence of an effective human resources division, sufficient budgeting for equipment to effectively do one's job, and the nature of the job design, particularly in regard to caseload. As one might guess, this is also related to the overall quality of the program.

Quite naturally, agencies should evaluate their hiring standards and should examine factors such as the number of complaints generated by the community regarding staff functioning. Grievances and/or complaints by offenders can also be examined if it should turn out that there is some legitimacy to such complaints. Likewise, employee standards of conduct are important as are incidents where employees do not meet standards that are expected by the agency. Further, staff should be consulted and evaluators should consider whether the line staff feel prepared and/or whether they consider their work environment to be on par with other agencies. All of this staff-related information provides a richer analysis of agency operations and also provides additional transparency to the day-to-day routines that occur.

Feedback Loops and Continual Improvement

In evaluating correctional agencies, it is important that the information obtained from the evaluation serve some useful purpose. The Bureau of Justice Assistance Center for Program Evaluation (2007) elaborates on the need for evaluations to be constructed in a manner that is useful to the stakeholders of the evaluation. **Stakeholders** in corrections evaluations include the agency personnel, the community in which the agency is located, and even the offender population that is being supervised. According to the Bureau of Justice Assistance (BJA), it is important for evaluators to be clear on what agency administrators wish to evaluate, and it is also important that evaluators ensure that administrators understand that evaluative efforts are to remain objective and unbiased in nature.

Beyond the initial understanding between administrators and evaluators, it is always important that evaluators provide recommendations for agencies, based on the outcome of the evaluation (BJA, 2007). It is through the use of these recommendations that agencies can improve their overall services and enhance goal-setting strategies in the future. Indeed, evaluation information can be a powerful tool for a variety of stakeholders (BJA, 2007, in Using Evaluation Result). Program managers can use the information to make changes in their programs that will enhance their effectiveness (BJA, 2007, in Using Evaluation Result). Decision makers can ensure that they are funding effective programs. Other authorities can ensure that programs are developed as intended and have sufficient resources to implement activities and meet their goals and objectives (BJA, 2007, in Using Evaluation Result).

Agencies that are adept at implementing evaluative information and recommendations are sometimes referred to as learning organizations. **Learning organizations** have the inherent ability to adapt and change, improving performance through continual revision of goals, objectives, policies, and procedures. Throughout this process, learning organizations respond to the various pushes and pulls that are placed upon them by utilizing a continual process of data-driven, cyclical, and responsive decision

What Are Policies, Activities, Goals, and Objectives?

Policy: A governing principle pertaining to goals, objectives, and/or activities. It is a decision on an issue not resolved on the basis of facts and logic only. For example, the policy of expediting drug cases in the courts might be adopted as a basis for reducing the average number of days from arraignment to disposition.

Activities: Services or functions carried out by a program (i.e., what the program does). For example, treatment programs may screen clients at intake, complete placement assessments, provide counseling to clients, and so on.

Goals: A desired state of affairs that outlines the ultimate purpose of a program. This is the end toward which program efforts are directed. For example, the goal of many criminal justice programs is a reduction in criminal activity.

Objectives: Specific results or effects of a program's activities that must be achieved in pursuing the program's ultimate goals. For example, a treatment program may expect to change offender attitudes (objective) in order to ultimately reduce recidivism (goal).

SOURCE: Bureau of Justice Assistance Center for Program Evaluation (2007). *Reporting and using evaluation results.* Washington, DC: Author. Retrieved from http://www.ojp.usdoj.gov/BJA/evaluation/sitemap.htm.

making that results in heightened adaptability of the organization. The ideal community corrections agency is a learning organization—one that can adjust to outside community needs and challenges as well as internal personnel and resource challenges. Lastly, in its ideal state, evaluation is an ongoing process that is embedded in the process of program planning, action setting, and later improvement. The BJA (2007) notes that evaluation findings can be used to revise policies, activities, goals, and objectives (see Focus Topic 19.2) so that community supervision agencies can provide the best possible services to the community to which they are accountable.

This is to demonstrate the importance of policy making as well as the setting of goals and objectives that guide a community supervision agency into the future. This cyclic pattern of going from assessment to implementation to evaluation demonstrates a continual circle of development that uses past data to better face future challenges. This is the most effective means of utilizing real-world research to tailor-fit programs to the challenges within a jurisdiction. With this in mind, we once again point toward the work of Van Keulen (1988) who roughly 20 years ago noted that

> goals and objectives also play a critical role in evaluation by providing a standard against which to measure the program's success. If the purpose of the program is to serve as an alternative to jail, the number of jail-bound offenders the program serves would be analyzed. If the program's focus is to provide labor to community agencies, the number of hours worked by offenders would be examined. Last, having a statement of goals and objectives will enhance your program's credibility by showing that careful thought has been given to what you are doing. (p. 1)

Van Keulen (1988) demonstrates the reasons why clarity in definition, point, and purpose behind a community corrections program is important. Thus, clearly articulated goals not only help to crystallize the agency's philosophical orientation on the supervision process, but they also provide for more measurable constructs that lend themselves to effective evaluation. Clarity in the goals and objectives allows the agency to perform evaluative research to determine if its efforts are actually successful or if they are in need of improvement. Such clarity then facilitates the ability of the agency to come "full circle" as the planning, implementation, evaluation, and refinement phases of agency operations unfold.

Community Harm With Ineffective Programs, Separating Politics From Science in the Evaluative Process

As we near the close of this text, it is important to reflect on the potential consequences that might be incurred if agencies are allowed to operate ineffectively. Public and institutional safety and security constitute the top priority for correctional agencies. However, one of the best long-term approaches to improving public safety is the use of effective reintegration efforts. Thus, programs that fail to adequately supervise offenders on community supervision run the risk of allowing the community to be harmed. Likewise, programs that fail to implement effective treatment approaches also put the community at risk.

Multiple means of maintaining supervision over offenders have been provided throughout this text. From the use of jails and prisons to the use of residential treatment facilities, to probation and then to the broad continuum of intermediate sanctions, all the way up to parole or, when we have run out of options, the use of the death penalty, these supervision interventions should be implemented in a manner that is a "best-fit" scenario for the offender and his or her likely level of risk. This comes back again to one of the most critical aspects of corrections, the assessment and classification process. As noted in Chapter 9, it is the assessment and classification process that sets the stage for determining how an offender is housed and supervised. It is also at this point where correctional resources can be optimized by ensuring the best fit between supervision resources and offender risk as well as treatment resources and offender needs.

The evaluation of correctional agencies is directly tied to the assessment component that occurs as the offender is first processed. Indeed, the assessment of the offender typically serves as the baseline measure when examining evaluation processes. Both process and outcome evaluations tend to examine data during the initial assessment against the data received when the offender exits a particular program or sentencing scheme. It is in this manner that the evaluation of correctional supervision programs serves to reinforce the initial assessment process. The initial assessment and classification process will be considered effective if, at the end of the offender's involvement in a given supervision program, the evaluation of the program demonstrates that the offender is indeed less likely to recidivate, particularly if this likelihood falls below that experienced at other agencies in the area and throughout the country. Thus, the evaluation process is a feedback loop into the initial assessment process, demonstrating to agencies that their programs are (or are not) working. If they are found to be in need of improvement, evaluators can then determine if this is due to the initial assessment or to some process issue further within the program's service delivery. Checking the initial assessment and ensuring that this process is adequate follows a "garbage in—garbage out" philosophy.

It can be seen that this process creates a systemic loop whereby the agency is constantly assessing and evaluating itself. This is known as the **assessment-evaluation cycle**, which is the process whereby assessment data and evaluation data are compared to determine the effectiveness of programs and to find areas where improvement of agency services is required. Agencies that successfully implement the assessment-evaluation cycle tend to use public resources more effectively and also are not prone to placing the community at risk of future criminal activity. In other words, agencies using the assessment-evaluation cycle will operate at an optimal level, avoiding harm to the community and the mismanagement of resources. On the other hand, agencies that do not successfully implement the assessment-evaluation cycle will be more likely to *both* waste agency resources and place the community at a level of risk that otherwise would be preventable.

Video Link 19.1
Learn more about a treatment program for offenders.

Audio Link 19.1
Hear how data is used to prevent recidivism.

EVIDENCE-BASED PRACTICES

Evidence-based practice is a significant trend throughout all human services that emphasize outcomes. Interventions within community corrections are considered effective when they reduce offender risk and subsequent recidivism and therefore make a positive long-term contribution to public safety. In this section of the chapter, students are presented with a model or framework based on a set of principles for effective offender interventions within state, local, or private correctional systems. Specifically, **evidence-based practice (EBP)** implies that (1) one outcome is desired over others; (2) it is measurable; and (3) it is defined according to practical realities (e.g., public safety) rather than immeasurable moral or value-oriented standards (Colorado Division of Criminal Justice, 2007). Thus, EBP is more appropriate for scientific exploration within any human service discipline, including the discipline of corrections. We now follow with the presentation of eight different EBP principles, taken from the Colorado Division of Criminal Justice (2007) and the National Institute of Justice (2005):

Prison Tour Video Link 19.2
Watch the author discuss how evidence-based practices are implemented.

EBP #1: Assess offender risk/need levels using actuarial instruments.

Risk factors are both static (never changing) and dynamic (changing over time, or having the potential to change). Focus is on criminogenic needs—that is, deficits that put an offender at risk for continued

Journal Article Link 19.2
Read about the relationship between gender and the predictive utility of the Level of Service Inventory.

criminal behavior. For example, many studies show that specific offender deficits are associated with criminal activity, such as lack of employment, lack of education, lack of housing stability, and substance abuse or addiction (Colorado Division of Criminal Justice, 2007). Actuarial instrument tools are available that can assist in the identification of these areas of service needs. One of the most common is the Level of Service Inventory (LSI). It is used in jurisdictions across the United States and Canada, and has been the subject of a considerable amount of research. Systematically identifying and intervening in the areas of criminogenic need are effective at reducing recidivism (Colorado Division of Criminal Justice, 2007).

EBP #2: Enhance offender motivation.

Humans respond better when motivated—rather than persuaded—to change their behavior. An essential principle of effective correctional intervention is the treatment team playing an important role in recognizing the need for motivation and using proven motivational techniques. Motivational interviewing, for example, is a specific approach to interacting with offenders in ways that tend to enhance and maintain interest in changing their behaviors (Colorado Division of Criminal Justice, 2007).

EBP #3: Target interventions.

This requires the application of what was learned in the assessment process described in #1 above. Research shows that targeting three or fewer criminogenic needs does *not* reduce recidivism. Targeting four to six needs (at a minimum) has been found to reduce recidivism by 31%. Correctional organizations have a long history of assessing inmates for institutional management purposes, if nothing else (Colorado Division of Criminal Justice, 2007). But when it comes to using this information in the systematic application of program services, most corrections agencies fall short. While inmate files may contain adequate information identifying offenders' deficits and needs, correctional staff are often distracted by population movement, lockdowns, and day-to-day prison operations. Staff training and professionalism become an essential component of developing a culture of personal change: Well-trained staff can—and must—role model and promote prosocial attitudes and behaviors even while maintaining a safe and secure environment (Colorado Division of Criminal Justice, 2007).

EBP #4: Provide skill training for staff and monitor their delivery of services.

Evidence-based programming emphasizes cognitive behavior strategies and is delivered by well-trained staff. Staff must coach offenders to learn new behavioral responses and thinking patterns. In addition, offenders must engage in role-playing, and staff must continually and consistently reinforce positive behavior change (Colorado Division of Criminal Justice, 2007).

EBP #5: Increase positive reinforcement.

Researchers have found that optimal behavior change results when the ratio of reinforcements is four positive to every negative reinforcement. While this principle should not interfere with the need for administrative responses to disciplinary violations, the principle is best applied with clear expectations and descriptions of behavior compliance. Furthermore, consequences for failing to meet expectations should be known to the offender as part of the programming activity. Clear rules and consistent consequences that allow offenders to make rewarding choices can be integrated into the overall treatment approach (Colorado Division of Criminal Justice, 2007).

EBP #6: Engage ongoing support in natural communities.

Research has confirmed the fact that placing offenders in poor environments and with antisocial peers increases recidivism. Prison-based drug and alcohol treatment communities show that the inmate code can be broken and replaced with a positive alternative and, in the process, teach offenders the skills they will need upon release. Likewise, parole supervision requires attending to the prosocial supports required by inmates to keep them both sober and crime free. Building communities in prison and outside of prison for offenders who struggle to maintain personal change is a key responsibility of correctional administrators today (Colorado Division of Criminal Justice, 2007).

EBP #7: Measure relevant processes/practices.

An accurate and detailed documentation of case information and staff performance, along with a formal and valid mechanism for measuring outcomes, is the foundation of evidence-based practice. Quality control and program fidelity play a central and ongoing role to maximize service delivery (Colorado Division of Criminal Justice, 2007).

EBP #8: Provide measurement feedback.

Providing feedback builds accountability and maintains integrity, ultimately improving outcomes. Offenders need feedback on their behavioral changes, and program staff need feedback on program integrity. It is important to reward positive behavior—of inmates succeeding in programs, and of staff delivering effective programming. Measurements that identify effective practices need then to be linked to resources, and resource decisions should be based on objective measurement (Colorado Division of Criminal Justice, 2007). Years of research have gone into the development of these evidence-based principles. When applied appropriately, these practices have the best potential to reduce recidivism (see Figure 19.1). These principles should guide criminal justice program development, implementation, and evaluation.

FIGURE 19.1   The Eight Evidence-Based Practices as Framework to Reduce Recidivism

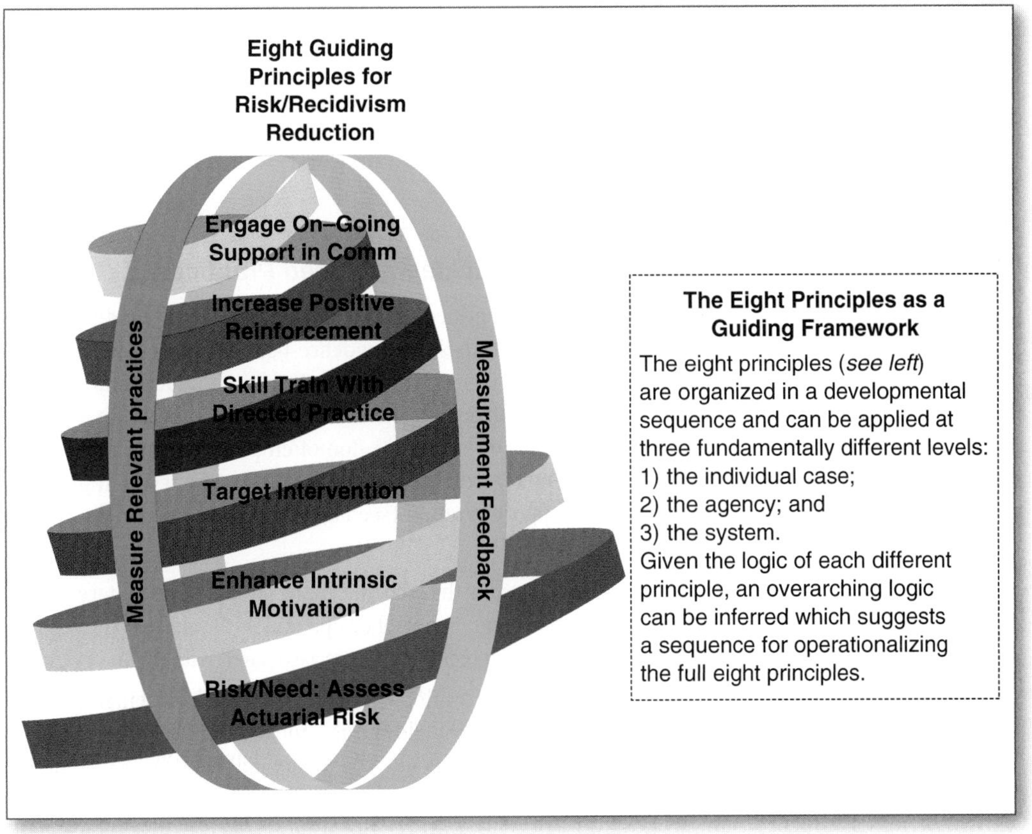

Eight Guiding Principles for Risk/Recidivism Reduction

Engage On–Going Support in Comm

Increase Positive Reinforcement

Skill Train With Directed Practice

Target Intervention

Enhance Intrinsic Motivation

Risk/Need: Assess Actuarial Risk

Measure Relevant practices

Measurement Feedback

The Eight Principles as a Guiding Framework

The eight principles (*see left*) are organized in a developmental sequence and can be applied at three fundamentally different levels:
1) the individual case;
2) the agency; and
3) the system.
Given the logic of each different principle, an overarching logic can be inferred which suggests a sequence for operationalizing the full eight principles.

SOURCE: National Institute of Justice. (2005). *Implementing evidence based practice in corrections.* Washington, DC: U.S. Department of Justice.

Individual Case-Level Implementation of Evidence-Based Practices

At this level of implementation, the logical implication is that one must assess (EBP #1) prior to triage or targeting intervention (EBP #3), and that it is beneficial to begin building offender motivation (EBP #2) prior to engaging these offenders in skill-building activities (#4). Similarly, positively reinforcing new skills (EBP #5) has more relevancy after the skills have been introduced and the offender has been trained (EBP #4) and at least partially in advance of the offender's realignment with prosocial groups and friends (EBP #6). The seventh (measure relevant practices) and eighth (provide feedback) principles need to follow the activities described throughout all the proceeding principles. Assessing an offender's readiness to change as well as ability to use newly acquired skills is possible anywhere along the case management continuum. These last two principles can and should be applicable after any of the earlier principles, but they also can be considered cumulative and provide feedback on the entire case management process.

Agency-Level Implementation of Evidence-Based Practices

The principles, when applied at the agency level, assist with more closely aligning staff behavior and agency operations with EBP. Initial assessment followed by motivational enhancement will help staff to prepare for the significant changes ahead. Agency priorities must be clarified and new protocols established and trained. Increasing positive rewards for staff who demonstrate new skills and proficiency is straightforward and an accepted standard in many organizations. The sixth principle regarding providing ongoing support in natural communities can be related to teamwork within the agency as well as with external agency stakeholders. The seventh and eighth principles are primarily about developing quality assurance systems, both to provide outcome data within the agency and to provide data to assist with marketing the agency to external stakeholders (National Institute of Justice, 2005).

System-Level Implementation of Evidence-Based Practices

The application of the framework principles at the system level is not much different than at the agency level in terms of sequence and recommended order though it is both the most critical and the most challenging level. Funding, for most systems, comes from state and local agencies that have oversight responsibilities. Demonstrating the value of EBP and effective interventions is crucial at this level, as is adherence to a coherent strategy for EBP. Another distinction in applying the principles at the system level is the need for greater abstraction and policy integration. The principles for EBP must be understood and supported by policy makers so that appropriate policy development coincides effectively with implementation (National Institute of Justice, 2005).

Research Evaluation for Effectiveness of Evidence-Based Practices

Reference Link 19.1
Read about the issues of using experimental design in corrections.

In this chapter, eight separate principles have been identified that are related to reduced recidivism outcomes in the research literature. Though we know that these are evidence-based practices, at this point, we do not know how well supported each is by the evidence. Thus, students should understand that this research does not support each of these principles with equal volume and quality, and, even if it did, each principle would not necessarily have similar effects on outcomes. Too often programs or practices are promoted as having research support without any regard for either the quality or the research methods that were employed. Consequently, a research support pyramid (see Figure 19.2) has been included that shows how research support for each principle ranks.

The highest-quality research support depicted in this schema (gold level) reflects interventions and practices that have been evaluated with experimental/control design and with multiple site replications that concluded significant sustained reductions in recidivism were associated with the intervention. The criteria for the next levels of support progressively decrease in terms of research rigor requirements (silver and bronze), but all the top three levels require that a preponderance of all evidence supports effectiveness. The next rung lower in support (iron) is reserved for programs that have inconclusive support regarding their efficacy. Finally, the lowest-level designation (dirt) is reserved for those programs that have research (utilizing methods and criteria associated with gold and silver levels), but the findings were negative and the programs were determined not effective (National Institute of Justice, 2005).

THE FUTURE OF CORRECTIONS

Prison Tour Video Link 19.3
Watch the author discuss the future of corrections.

It is fitting that this chapter concludes with a section on future trends in corrections for two reasons. First and quite obviously, this is the last chapter of the text, and, as with most texts, this is the typical location for such a section. Second, this chapter addresses evaluation, research, and the connection between assessment and evaluation. This last point is most important because it is through the use of our evaluative research that we predict future trends in correctional agencies throughout the nation. It is on this note, and with much trepidation, that some speculative predictions regarding future trends in community corrections will be provided. Before doing so, it should be noted that many psychologists, particularly

FIGURE 19.2 Research Support Pyramid for Evidence-Based Practice Implementation

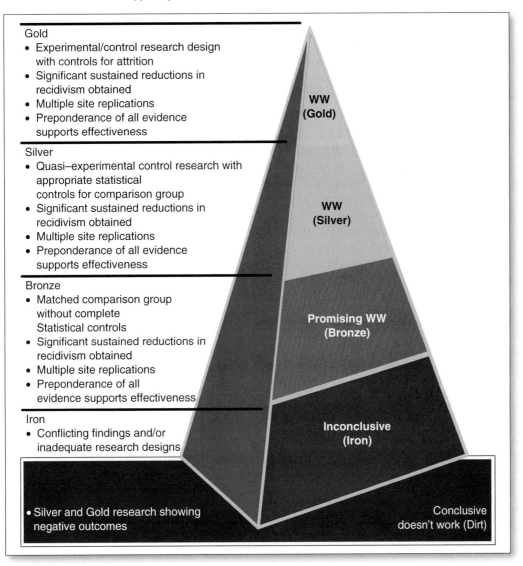

Gold
- Experimental/control research design with controls for attrition
- Significant sustained reductions in recidivism obtained
- Multiple site replications
- Preponderance of all evidence supports effectiveness

Silver
- Quasi–experimental control research with appropriate statistical controls for comparison group
- Significant sustained reductions in recidivism obtained
- Multiple site replications
- Preponderance of all evidence supports effectiveness

Bronze
- Matched comparison group without complete Statistical controls
- Significant sustained reductions in recidivism obtained
- Multiple site replications
- Preponderance of all evidence supports effectiveness

Iron
- Conflicting findings and/or inadequate research designs

WW (Gold)

WW (Silver)

Promising WW (Bronze)

Inconclusive (Iron)

- Silver and Gold research showing negative outcomes

Conclusive doesn't work (Dirt)

SOURCE: National Institute of Justice. (2005). *Implementing evidence based practice in corrections.* Washington, DC: U.S. Department of Justice.

behavioral psychologists, claim that the best predictor of future human behavior is past human behavior. In fact, empirical research has shown this to be generally true. It is with this in mind and with the inclusion of prior research from the field of corrections that some general observations and predictions will be made.

In providing some insight into future outcomes that we are likely to observe, it should be noted that this text has, in actuality, been addressing three key themes that are likely to continue throughout future years ahead. These three key themes are (1) the tendency for technology to have more impact on correctional agency operations, (2) the need for continued training of correctional staff, and (3) an increased emphasis on the reentry process for offenders. These three trends are likely to continue for a variety of practical rather than theoretical reasons. Evidence of this already exists throughout the correctional literature, and, as this text clearly demonstrates, agencies around the nation have already set a course for these three themes to be part of their future operations.

The use of technology is already commonplace within the correctional industry. However, it is the effectiveness of technology that will determine its usefulness as well as the cost-effectiveness that can be obtained. Increasingly, technology is becoming more reliable and is also becoming more affordable for state agencies. Technology can also save on the amount spent on human resources. Thus, technology will continue to be a driving force that will shape the landscape of correctional services in the future.

Video Link 19.2
Take a look at a high-tech prison.

Regardless of the role that technology will play in corrections, there will still be a need for trained and educated staff. In fact, the proliferation of technology will require that persons who work in corrections (both institutional and community-based) be competent enough to utilize high-tech tools of the trade. No longer will it be sufficient for these staff to act as mere turnkeys; rather they will be required to use equipment and tools that are more sophisticated than those of their predecessors. In addition, correctional populations are becoming more complicated in composition, in terms of mental and medical issues as well as cultural factors that must be considered. Due to legal requirements and concerns with liability, staff cannot be negligent and/or careless. Rather, they must act competently as trained professionals when working with the inmate population—a population that can be deceptive and dangerous.

Lastly, the correctional population will continue to grow, and, as it stands, prisons are full. Continuing along a "stuff 'em and cuff 'em" mentality will simply not work for a system that is already quite overstuffed. If something different cannot be introduced to alleviate the continued overcrowding of prisons and the already overloaded case management approaches that exist, then either correctional systems will need much larger budgets, or offenders will have to simply be set free without any form of supervision. Obviously, the latter possibility is simply too dangerous to consider, and the former will just result in more of the same problems that already face the criminal justice system. Thus, reentry initiatives will be used with much greater frequency in the future, both due to practicality and due to economics. With this in mind, a discussion of the likely trends in community supervision programs will follow.

Privatization in Corrections

The notion of privatized operations in corrections carries with it some degree of controversy. This is largely because some people have a moralistic opposition to the idea that money might be made off the misery of others. In other words, people in society may take exception to the idea that in order for one person to fulfill his or her sentence, the pockets of a private corporation are lined. However, it is probably a more realistic view to understand that, regardless of the circumstances, inmates must be housed somewhere when serving a stint of incarceration, and, so long as their constitutionally protected rights are upheld, the specific ownership of the physical facilities is irrelevant. In fact, if the private prison company can maintain security with less overhead to the taxpayers, then this is a good thing for everyone concerned.

The simple reality is that, like it or not, private corrections is here to stay, and the use of private facilities is growing steadily each year. Amongst everything else, private companies are forced to ensure that they stay within budget, and they are also forced to operate in an efficient and productive manner; to do otherwise results in a loss of revenue. For many business-minded administrators, this is superior to many state systems that are full of inherent waste, red tape, and civil service regulations that paralyze agencies from moving in an adaptive fashion. Private correctional systems, however, adhere to all of the legal requirements that state institutions must entertain, but they are able to adapt much more quickly and with little need for excessive staggering of new policies and procedures. For the most part, executive-level decision makers can simply generate a memo or set of protocols and disseminate them in a day, if they so desire; state systems do not have this flexibility.

Also, one must keep in mind that, when we refer to the civil rights of inmates, it is the state correctional systems that have had legal problems related to the constitutionality of their operations, not the private systems. Thus, it appears that state systems are not superior and, in some cases, may have been more lacking of legal integrity than privately run operations. Thus, state systems may provide worse services than private systems (in some cases) while still being more costly to taxpayers. With this in mind, also consider that we have seen that, in Florida and the Federal Bureau of Prisons, the vocational and/or industry operations of these prison systems that do produce revenue do so through private corporations (PRIDE in Florida, UNICOR for the Bureau of Prisons). The point in mentioning this is that it may well be that these types of operations are most appropriate for profit-generating endeavors, and, as it turns out, these income-generating programs are viewed as successful in operation.

In other situations where states may be reluctant to resort to complete privatization of industrial or security operations, the use of hybrid versions of privatization may also be seen more frequently in state systems. The author of this text works as a substance abuse counselor in a private prison (Richwood Correctional Center, owned and operated by LaSalle Corrections) that houses inmates from the Louisiana Department of Corrections. Further, counselors in the treatment program are hired by the state and, in other cases, are hired by LaSalle Corrections, depending on budgetary constraints and offender-client

Audio Link 19.2
Learn more about efforts to reduce overcrowding.

Video Link 19.3
Watch a clip on privatization in corrections.

Audio Link 19.3
Listen to a clip about the privatization of a prison.

population levels. This integration of state and private service delivery allows for services to continue at optimal levels but extends beyond what the state, all by itself, could afford to provide.

Lastly, the use of private correctional facilities has grown more in some states than in others, but, regardless of how common privatization becomes, it is doubtful that state systems will ever completely disappear. In all cases, states will maintain at least a fraction of their facilities since it is unlikely that private systems will be appropriate in housing the most incorrigible of inmates. But with state budgets being reduced throughout the nation, it is unlikely that many states will be able to fund their correctional systems to the level that is necessary; other alternatives must be considered. Thus, while private prisons will not completely replace state prisons, it is likely that private facilities will become much more common than they currently are.

PHOTO 19.2

This treatment group actively participates in a discussion of a controversial issue led by the group facilitator, Ms. Ashley Crockham.

Standards and Accreditation

From our readings in Chapters 14 and 15, it should be clear that an abundance of professional organizations and associations represent a wide variety of professions in the field of corrections. This is a good trend in corrections that will likely continue with increased enthusiasm. The desire to professionalize the workforce is strong since this can add legitimacy to a facility's operations. In addition, when employees meet the requirements of various governing bodies, it is presumed that, at a minimum, they are competent consistent with the nationally accepted standards within these associations.

PHOTO 19.3

Dr. Bonner trains correctional trainees on diversity and cultural competence at North Delta Regional Training Academy.

In addition, when employees meet the standards of external governing bodies, agencies are unlikely to be open to lawsuits for failure to train or other types of negligence. This is an effective incentive for most agencies, including private agencies. Further, many individual practitioners will seek to obtain credentials that may help them to receive promotions and/or extra levels of pay. Thus, the incentives to improve standards and credentials are strong, and this also translates to a desire among agencies to obtain accreditation. When agencies seek accreditation, they are making strides to enhance their reputation and to make a public statement that demonstrates their integrity.

Journal Article Link 19.3
Read about the accreditation panel of England and Wales.

Accreditation speaks volumes on behalf of the agency's professionalism and sense of ethical responsibility. The transparency of management to obtain and maintain accreditation means that administrators have nothing to hide. This is of benefit when one considers the closed nature of corrections from the broader community. The image within the community is likely to be enhanced when correctional agencies are accredited, and this, in turn, is likely to generate community support for correctional personnel from the outlying community. As we have seen in prior chapters, this can have benefits for administrators and staff who are the "face" of the agency for which they work. This can be a morale booster for employees and generates a culture of pride in the mission and work of the agency.

An Emphasis on Cultural Competence Will Continue to Be Important

Earlier chapters of this text addressed cultural competence and the increasing representation of minority offenders in the criminal justice system. It is clear that the United States is becoming more racially and culturally diverse. Indeed, multilingual skills and understanding differing religious beliefs, lifestyle orientations, and other matters of diversity will become mandatory for future employees in the area of corrections. The continued diversity among the offender population along with other challenges (such as mental health needs) means that offender populations are likely to become much more complicated in the future. Naturally, this can add to the already stressful conditions under which correctional staff work and means that agencies will need to find the means to mitigate these challenges and their associated stress.

An Emphasis on Employment Programs Will Be Most Viable

Research is showing that offenders simply need jobs if they are to be able to make ends meet while paying restitution, fines, and other obligations to society. Chapter 15 of this text has provided sufficient evidence to demonstrate that, if given the minimal educational and vocational skills necessary to function, recidivism among offenders will decline. Programs such as Project RIO in the state of Texas are finding that vocational programs that aid in job placement are quite effective in reducing recidivism. The results around the nation are quite clear, and it seems that, since employers are able to secure tax incentives for hiring offenders, these programs benefit society as a whole. These programs ensure that society is compensated for property crimes and, when used within a restorative justice or victim compensation framework, can heal damage done from nonviolent crimes. This is important because the victim, society, and the offender all benefit from such programs. Thus, vocational training will be critical, and the use of work-release and restitution programs will continue to be necessary.

Processing of Geriatric Offenders Will Be Shifted to Community Supervision Schemes

Audio Link 19.4
Listen to a clip about geriatric offenders.

The entire population is graying in the United States and in other industrialized countries. In addition, the prison population in the United States is graying at a faster rate than is the general society beyond prison walls. This issue has been given considerable attention in recent years, with Texas, California, Florida, New York, and Louisiana all experiencing a rise in per-capita elderly inmates who are incarcerated. The states just mentioned either have the largest prison population or have the highest rates of incarceration around the United States. In all cases, the costs associated with the elderly inmate are exponentially higher than those associated with the average inmate. This leads to other issues for administrators, such as the possibility of early release of inmates who are expected to die, the implementation of human caregiver programs such as hospice, as well as accountability to the public. It is this accountability that places prison administrators in a dilemma since public safety is the primary concern for all custodial programs. The sobering reality is that, like it or not, society will, one way or another, pay for the expense of keeping elderly inmates.

It is with this point in mind that state-level correctional systems will need to increase their use of community supervision programs with elderly offenders, including those who are chronically ill. This may seem to be an oversimplified recommendation, but it is one that has not truly been implemented by many states. Most states do have programs designed for the early release of elderly inmates, but these programs are not used extensively. The recommendation here is that community supervision be *automatically implemented* when an inmate reaches the age of 60 years old, unless he or she is a bona fide pedophile or child molester. In the case of pedophiles, the typical risk assessment methods should remain intact since these offenders have such poor prognoses for reform. However, all other elderly inmates should be automatically placed on community supervision since this would reduce costs of upkeep significantly.

Further, such inmates being automatically released should be given intensive supervision that uses the latest and greatest forms of human supervision and electronic gadgetry. Though this adds to the cost, the outcome is much cheaper than prison alternatives. With routine weekly contact by probation/parole officials, frequent electronic phone monitoring, the use of GPS tracking devices, house arrest, and other such innovations, the risk to public safety can be greatly minimized. Further, it is a simple fact that recidivism for these offenders is very low, and the crimes committed are seldom assaultive in nature. Thus public safety is not compromised one bit. In fact, this is the safest population to place on community supervision, as long as one excludes using such a policy for the pedophile population.

Media and Political Interest in Correctional Operations

The media can prove pivotal in the success and/or the failure of any prison's interface with the community. Prison facilities need to establish community-based partnerships to ensure community support. The local population can be very helpful to the prison since many local merchants may deal with the prison or staff employed at the prison and since the community sometimes acts as a source of volunteers. Further, it is just "good business" to have a good relationship with persons who live in the vicinity. Further, the media can also make the prison more visible so that community members will be apprised of developments within the facility.

However, certain groups of offenders, such as sex offenders, have drawn public attention and concern. This is of course understandable, but the public will tend to make erroneous conclusions regarding the offender population, if not presented in the appropriate light, and this can completely undermine a prison's ability to implement an effective reentry program and, in this case, can cast negative views on the prison that "lets them out just so they can do it again," as many local citizens may perceive the situation. **Media effects** are an important consideration in corrections and refer to the effect that the media have upon the public perception of prison or community supervision programs. How the media report specific incidents can affect this. Further, when programs are successful and/or innovative, the media can provide effective coverage of these as well to ensure that the public is getting the most accurate information possible regarding prison operations, staff, and/or inmate programs.

Garrett (2008) notes certain points to consider when deciding upon the involvement of the media in corrections:

- To what extent will the media representatives disrupt the day-to-day operations of the prison? Will schedules and routine activities be hindered?

- How are inmates likely to react to the media coverage, and how is this likely to impact their future behavior in the prison?

- How are people in the community likely to react to the coverage? Will this impair the operation of the prison?

- To what extent will any pictures that are taken provide the public or inmates with information that could help to form an escape plan or disruptive activities within the prison, such as a riot?

Garrett (2008) notes that there are no right or wrong answers to the previous questions, but they should serve as guides for administrators who must balance the pros and cons when dealing with the media. However, prison administrators who are attempting to build collaborative partnerships must foster good relations with the media and must always be aware that the media can be a double-edged sword when presenting coverage on prison operations.

CONCLUSION

Research and assessment of correctional programs are vital in this day and age. Through this process, we are able to identify program strengths and weaknesses that serve to inform the literature. The ultimate question that should guide research and assessment projects is "So what?" In other words, if we choose to conduct a research project, will the results provide a meaningful contribution to what is known about some phenomena? From another standpoint, if we did not conduct the research project, would there continue to be a significant gap in the literature, hindering our ability to make optimal decisions regarding community corrections programs? In essence, a quality research program is able to answer the question "So what?"

It is important to keep in mind that the assessment process is an integral component of the evaluation of any agency. This means that what agencies put into their program will be reflected in its final output. Thus, assessment can be seen as a measure of what goes into a program, and evaluation can be seen as a measure of what comes out of the program. The two work hand-in-hand. Because of this, students should be familiar with the assessment-evaluation cycle, since this is the primary means by which community supervision agencies measure their performance, and since this is what ultimately determines if an agency is meeting its goals and objectives. For agencies with unfavorable evaluations, an examination of the policies and activities of that agency may be in order, or, in some cases, a reassessment of the goals and objectives may take place.

Video Link 19.4
Watch a clip about the media and corrections.

Reference Link 19.2
Read about the role the media plays in the portrayal of crime and corrections.

Lastly, this chapter reflects on some of the themes that have emerged throughout this text. These themes are important to contemporary correctional practices and were also presented as the direction that corrections agencies will need to take in the future. A number of likely trends were noted, and recommendations were given for agencies that will face challenges that loom on the horizon. The field of corrections is both dynamic and demanding; practitioners who work in this field have their work cut out for them. However, the work of correctional personnel is critical, and warrants support from the various funding sources as well as the public at large. Without this support, the entire public is likely to pay dearly for such negligence.

END-OF-CHAPTER DISCUSSION QUESTIONS

1. Discuss how evaluative research is conducted and explain why it is important.

2. Compare process and outcome measures. Explain why each is important to evaluation projects.

3. Explain, in your own words, how the assessment-evaluative cycle works in correctional research.

4. What is meant by the term *evidence-based practices*? Provide at least two examples of how these practices might be used in a correctional agency.

5. Why does the author note that more emphasis on diversity and multiculturalism will be important in the field of corrections?

KEY TERMS

Assessment-evaluation cycle	Implementation evaluation	Outcome evaluation
Evaluative transparency	Learning organizations	Process evaluation
Evidence-based practice (EBP)	Media effects	Stakeholders

APPLIED EXERCISE 19.1

For this exercise, you will need to consider your readings in this chapter as they apply to prior readings in Chapter 15 on prison programming, with special consideration of life skills programs for offenders. Your assignment is as follows:

You are a researcher recently hired by the prison system of your state. You have been asked to design and evaluative a prison life skills program in your state. Specifically, you are asked to determine if the completion of the life skills program actually reduces recidivism among offenders who complete the course while in prison. You will need to provide a clear methodology for testing and evaluating your proposed program, including such factors as validity and reliability of your study as well as the validity and reliability of your instruments (if any), the use of control and experimental groups, distinctions between process and outcome measures, and any ethical issues that might be involved with conducting such research.

Each response to the questions below must consist of anywhere from 300 to 700 words of content being allowed per application. Students should complete this application exercise as a minipaper that explains the scenario and then addresses each question throughout the content of the discussion. The total word count should be 900 to 2,100 words.

GRADING RUBRIC

1. Identify the specific aspects of the life skills program that you would evaluate and explain why each would be important to your evaluation. Further, identify and distinguish between the process and the outcome measures within your study.

2. Identify and discuss the various research methods considerations that you might wish to employ. Be sure to discuss the likely validity and reliability of your study as well as the validity and reliability of the instruments that you might use. Also, determine if you will be able to use a control group and/or a comparison group within your study.

3. Be sure and explain how you would use your evaluative study to determine the effects of life skills, separate from educational or vocational programming. Note that the student has a wide degree of latitude with this aspect of the assignment.

4. Spelling, grammar, and writing style will be considered. In addition, the paper *must* be within the prescribed range in word count. Lastly, students *must* cite and reference their work, in APA format, or no credit will be given for this question.

"WHAT WOULD YOU DO?"

You are a correctional officer working the graveyard shift at a maximum-security prison. One night, during turnout, the Sergeants and the Lieutenant explain to you and the other staff on your shift (there are about 50 of you) that there will be a researcher who will be coming to each officer and giving you all a survey. This will be done intermittently throughout the week, and the "rank" officers make it clear that, while you are not required to fill out the survey, the study is quite beneficial, and they support any participation that you would be willing to give. They introduce to the group two persons dressed in semiformal attire, Dr. Smith and Dr. Wilson, both criminologists from the university located about 35 miles from your prison facility. Once they are introduced, Dr. Smith explains that "our study is in relation to inmate sexual assault in prisons. Basically, there is a tendency for inmates around the nation to underreport incidents, and this naturally makes it impossible to truly know how prevalent sexual assault may be in prisons," and then Dr. Smith points toward Dr. Wilson, who then adds, "So, we have decided that we should ask the custodial staff about their perceptions regarding this issue since you are the ones who spend the most time in proximity to the inmates who are involved in this behavior, when and if it occurs on your shift."

With that said, both Dr. Smith and Dr. Wilson begin passing out the surveys to the group and explain that, "while on your shift and when you have time, we are asking that you complete this survey. Later, during the late hours of the night, we will follow up and interview some of you, as time permits throughout the night. We know that you are busy and that you may not wish to participate. If you wish to decline participation, we will naturally honor your wishes without comment." After this, the supervisors let the shift personnel know that they will not be keeping track of whoever participates. Rather, they will be staying out of sight as much as possible throughout the night to ensure that they do not obstruct the data collection efforts of the researchers. At that point, the supervisors then assign work details to all staff members and dismiss them to relieve the prior shift and assume their duty posts.

As luck would have it, you are assigned to the "escort crew," which means that your assignment is to patrol the prison on foot, going from one cell block to another to relieve officers for their mealtime and/ or scheduled breaks; taking inmates to the infirmary or other areas of the prison, as may be required; and conducting security checks throughout the night. You will also escort inmates to early morning breakfast later in your shift. This is considered a good detail because the mobility keeps the shift from becoming monotonous, and you get to talk and visit with numerous people throughout the night. There are about seven of you assigned to the escort crew, and, at one point in the evening, you go to relieve an officer on one of the cell blocks so that he can go to the officer's dining quarters and have dinner. While there, three other members of the escort crew come on the cell block and say, "Hey, we are going to hang out in the dayroom since it is empty and fill out our surveys, watch some TV, and wait until the break relief is over. After that, Sarge says we gotta go to the laundry room and let some inmates get some supplies—we just wanted you to know." You say, "OK, no problem" and let them in while you make a security round on the cell block.

While making your rounds, you hear the officers laughing, and you go toward the dayroom to hear one say, "Man, this survey is whacked—those brainiacs are crazy if they think that I am gonna tell them shit about what goes on with those convicts," and then you hear another officer respond by saying, "Yeah, man, no shit, like I give a damn if some convict gets his booty stolen—serves 'em right. The assholes will stay out of here if they don't like it." Then you hear them laugh, and the other officer says, "Look, I got an idea—let's just fill them out real fast and put that nothing ever happens. Maybe we could put that they are all lying and making false allegations against inmates that they owe money to! That would really mess up the study and give them something to scratch their heads about, huh?"

The other two officers then say, "Hell, yeah, great idea, we can make this fun! After all, the surveys are anonymous, right?" You finish your security rounds while thinking about what you have just heard. You have not yet filled out your survey and have not even looked at it, but you begin to feel sorry for the researchers, just a little. You wonder to yourself, "Maybe this is why things never get better. No matter how much research they do, everybody is always lying to them," followed with "I wonder if they know how much lying is likely to be going on about these kinds of topics."

You enter the dayroom just in time to see the last of the officers place his survey in the sealed envelope that each officer was given to ensure that responses are anonymous. At this time, the other officer returns from break, and, as you are walking off the cell block so that the original officer can take over, you see the researchers walking toward you and the other escort officers who are stepping out of the cell block. They come to the other officers and offer to collect their sealed envelopes; each officer provides his survey and then heads off to the laundry room. Dr. Smith looks at you and says, "If possible, we would like to interview you since you are next on our list. It will not affect your survey results, and we have told the Sergeant that you might need to follow about 10 minutes behind everyone. Is that OK?"

Since the interview is really not optional (you know your supervisors would think that it would be rude to decline the polite request of the researchers) and since you really are not in a hurry to go to the laundry room, you tell them, "OK, sure." However, you know that they have no idea about the surveys that they just received, and, as of yet, you are a bit undecided as to what you think about all of this "research stuff," anyway. You contemplate what you may or may not say to them, and, at this point, you are not really sure what you do (or do not) want to do.

What would you do?

STUDENT STUDY SITE

Visit the Student Study Site at **www.sagepub.com/hanserintro** to access links to the videos, audio clips, SAGE journal articles, state rankings, and reference materials noted in this chapter, as well as additional study tools including eFlashcards, web quizzes, and more.

Glossary

Absolute immunity: Protection that exists for those persons who work in positions that require unimpaired decision-making functions.

Administrative segregation: A type of classification that is nonpunitive in nature but requires the separation of inmates from the general population due to the threat that they may pose to themselves, staff, other inmates, or institutional order.

Administrator: An individual in an agency who operates in a managerial role beyond immediate supervisory capacity, usually in some type of leadership role.

Adolescent-only offenders: Adolescents who typically commit acts of defiance or nonconformity simply as a means of expressing their developing sense of autonomy. However, these adolescents are not likely to continue their activities into late adulthood.

Age of responsibility: Roman civil law made distinctions between juveniles and adults based on the notion of age of responsibility.

Aggravating circumstances: Magnify the offensive nature of a crime and tend to result in longer sentences.

Alcatraz: A prison built on Alcatraz Island, California, that was first opened in 1934 and held a number of notorious offenders such as Al Capone and other Mafia leaders. Considered to be the first "supermax" facility in the United States.

Alexander Maconochie: Was in charge of the penal colony at Norfolk Island. Developed general scheme for parole.

American Correctional Chaplains Association (ACCA): A national organization that provides representation and networking opportunities for chaplains who work in various correctional environments.

American Correctional Food Service Association (ACFSA): Represents the correctional food service industry.

Americans with Disabilities Act (ADA): Requires correctional agencies to make reasonable modifications in their policies, practices, and procedures that are necessary to ensure accessibility for individuals with disabilities, unless making such modifications would fundamentally alter the program or service involved.

Anti-Drug Abuse Act of 1988: Three broad categories: (1) homicide offenses, (2) espionage and treason, and (3) nonhomicidal narcotics offenses.

Antisocial personality disorder: A pervasive pattern of disregard for, and violation of, the rights of others that begins in childhood or early adolescence and continues into adulthood.

Antiterrorism and Effective Death Penalty Act of 1996: Required that the inmate provide clear and convincing evidence (about an 80% likelihood) of a constitutional violation before a certificate of appeal would be granted.

Armed disturbance control team: Deals with disturbances that have escalated to matters of life and death.

Ashurst-Sumners Act: Required that all prison-manufactured products shipped out of a state be stamped with the prison name, and, with an amendment in 1940, prison products were banned from being shipped via interstate lines.

Assessment-evaluation cycle: The process whereby assessment data and evaluation data are compared, one with the other, to determine the effectiveness of programs and to find areas where improvement of agency services is required.

***Atkins v. Virginia* (2002):** Supreme Court ruling holding that the execution of the mentally retarded is unconstitutional.

Attica Prison Riot: A critical point in the reform of medical services in prisons due to the fact that among inmate grievances, complaints against insufficient medical services were pronounced.

Attorney General's Review Committee on Capital Cases: Makes an independent recommendation to the Attorney General. From January 27, 1995, to July 20, 2000, U.S. Attorneys submitted a total of 682 cases for review, and the Attorney General ultimately authorized seeking the death penalty for 159 of those defendants.

Auburn system: An alternative prison system located in New York.

Austin MacCormick: During the 1930s, wrote an influential book titled *The Education of Adult Prisoners* and conducted the most comprehensive survey ever undertaken of educational programs for adults in prison in the United States.

Authoritarian model: Strict control over staff and inmates with communication that flows from a top-to-bottom process.

Banishment: Exile from society.

Bastille: A fortification that was built in the city of Paris and was a symbol of tyranny and injustice for both commoners and political prisoners in France.

Baxter v. Palmigiano (1976): The distinction between prison disciplinary proceedings and genuine courtroom affairs was directly addressed. The Court noted that inmates do not have the right to either retained or appointed counsel for disciplinary hearings that are not part of an actual criminal prosecution.

Bell v. Wolfish (1979): Supreme Court case ruling that the use of body cavity searches of inmates after contact visits is permissible. Prison staff may search inmates' quarters in their absence. Double bunking does not deprive inmates of their liberty without due process of law.

Benjamin Rush: An American medical doctor and political activist who became influential in the push for prison reform.

"Big Four" in corrections: The four largest state correctional systems in the United States (California, Texas, Florida, and New York).

Big House prisons: Were typically large stone structures with brick walls, guard towers, and checkpoints throughout the facility.

Bipolar disorder: Characterized by one or more manic episodes, usually accompanied by major depressive episodes.

Black codes: Separate laws were required of slaves and free men who turned criminal.

Blind spots: In correctional facilities, these can occur when certain areas of the prison are obscured from easy view of security staff and/or surveillance equipment.

Blood feud: A cycle of back-and-forth warfare between mutually aggrieved parties.

Blood in, blood out: The idea that in order for inmates to be accepted within a prison gang, they must draw blood (usually through killing) in an altercation with an identified enemy of the gang.

Blood testing: Using blood samples to determine if an offender has been using drugs. This type of testing is seldom used due to the invasiveness of the process and potential health effects.

Blue Walters Substance Abuse Treatment Program: A substance abuse treatment program that has its origins in the state of Louisiana prison system.

Bounds v. Smith (1977): Supreme Court held that even when prison policies allow jailhouse lawyers to provide assistance to other inmates, prison systems must still provide inmates with either adequate law libraries or adequate legal assistance from persons trained in the law.

Branding: Usually on thumb with a letter denoting the offense.

Breed v. Jones (1975): Supreme Court held that trying a juvenile who had previously been adjudicated delinquent in juvenile court for the same crime as an adult in criminal court violates the double jeopardy clause of the Fifth Amendment when the adjudication involves violation of a criminal statute.

Bridle: An iron cage that fit over the head and included a metal plate in the front.

Bruscino v. Carlson (1988): Ruling that the high-security practices of USP Marion were constitutional.

Brutalization hypothesis: The contention that, rather than acting as a deterrent, the use of harsh punishments sensitizes people to violence and essentially *teaches* them to use violence.

Building tenders: Inmates who were chosen for their strength or intelligence to supervise the inmate population, particularly in dormitories and cell blocks.

Bureaucratic model: A formal organizational system that is not dependent upon the specific personnel or personalities assigned within it.

Capital punishment: Putting the offender to death amongst a public audience.

Case manager: Is directly responsible to the unit manager and has major responsibility for case management matters within the unit.

Centralized management: Tight forms of control in the communication process that ensure that decision-making power is reserved for only a small group of people.

Cesare Beccaria: Wrote treatise *An Essay on Crimes and Punishments*, was an anti–death penalty activist, and is the father of classical criminology.

Chancery courts: Were created to consider petitions of those in need of special aid or intervention, such as women and children left in need of protection and aid by reason of divorce, death of a spouse, or abandonment, and to grant relief to such persons.

Charles Montesquieu: French philosopher who wrote the *Persian Letters* on criminal law abuses in Europe.

Chief Justice Warren Burger: Famous and historical supporter of prison services and prison industries.

Child abuse: Occurs when a child (any youth under the age of 18 in most states) is maltreated by a parent, an immediate family member, or any person responsible for the child's welfare.

Child neglect: Occurs when a parent or caretaker of the child does not provide the proper or necessary support, education, medical, or other remedial care that is required by a given state's law, including food, shelter, and clothing.

Children of incarcerated: Children of parents who are incarcerated, particularly children who are born from mothers in prison.

Chivalry hypothesis: Contends that there is a bias in the criminal justice system against giving women harsh punishments.

Classical criminology: Emphasized that punishments must be useful, purposeful, and reasonable.

Code of Hammurabi: The earliest known written code of punishment.

Coker v. Georgia **(1977):** Supreme Court ruling that the death penalty was unconstitutional when used for the rape of an adult woman if she had not been killed during the offense. While other sentences such as life in prison are constitutional, the death penalty is not.

Collateral damage: Any damage incidental to an activity.

College Opportunity and Affordability Act: An act passed by the House of Representatives on February 7, 2008, including provisions that would make all age groups eligible for the Incarcerated Youth Offender grant and expand the spending cap from $1,800 per year to $3,300 for each offender.

Common fare: A diet that meets all nutritional requirements and reasonably accommodates recognized religious dietary restrictions.

Common law: Law based on custom or use.

Community service: The work that one is required to perform for repaying his or her debt to society after being found at fault for committing a criminal or deviant offense. In most cases community service is ordered by the sentencing judge and supervised by a community supervision officer.

Compensatory damages: Payments for the actual losses suffered by a plaintiff.

Comprehensive Crime Control Act of 1984: Created a U.S. Sentencing Commission to establish sentencing guidelines for the federal courts and established a regimen of determinate sentences.

Conflict theory: Concepts of inequality and power are the central issues underlying crime and its control.

Consent decree: An injunction against both individual defendants and their agency.

Contract labor system: Utilized inmate labor through state-negotiated contracts with private manufacturers, who provided the prison with raw materials so that prison labor could refine the materials for the manufacturer.

Contributing to the delinquency of a minor: A form of neglect where an adult specifically facilitates the ability of youth to commit delinquent or criminal acts and encourages these youth to engage in such acts.

Convict: Refers to an inmate who is respected for being self-reliant and independent of other inmates or the system.

Convict boss/officer: Denotes an identity where the correctional officer has developed a keen understanding of convict logic and socialization and uses that knowledge to maximize control over his assigned post.

Convict code: An inmate-driven set of beliefs that inmates aspired to live by, typically presented as the "gold standard" of behavior among inmates.

Co-occurring disorders: When an offender has two or more disorders.

Cooper v. Pate **(1964):** Supreme Court case ruling that state prison inmates could sue state officials in federal courts under the Civil Rights Act of 1871.

Correctional counselor: Develops and implements programs within the unit to meet the individual needs of the inmates confined, to include individual as well as group counseling.

Corrections: A process whereby practitioners from a variety of agencies and programs use tools, techniques, and facilities to engage in organized security and treatment functions intended to correct criminal tendencies among the offender population.

Crime control model: Emerged during a "get tough" era on crime. The use of longer sentences, more frequent use of the death penalty, and an increased use of intensive supervision probation all were indicative of this era's approach to crime.

Cruz v. Beto **(1972):** Supreme Court case ruling that inmates must be given reasonable opportunities to exercise their religious beliefs.

Custodial sexual misconduct: The use of force or the threat of force targeted toward female offenders in multiple state correctional systems.

Custody level: Related to the degree of staff supervision that is needed for a given inmate.

Cutter v. Wilkinson **(2005):** Supreme Court ruling holding that the Religious Land Use and Institutionalized Persons Act of 2000 does not afford more legal rights to religious inmates than nonreligious inmates.

Day reporting centers: Treatment facilities to which offenders are required to report, usually on a daily basis.

Death row: Refers to persons who have been convicted and sentenced to be executed but are awaiting the time at which their execution will take place.

Decentralized management: Where the authority and responsibility of management personnel are divided and distributed amongst various levels of the supervisory chain so that each level of supervision may make decisions that correspond to the problems that confront that particular level of management.

Declaratory judgment: A judicial determination of the legal rights of the person bringing suit.

Defamation: An invasion of a person's interest through his or her reputation. In order for this to occur, some form of slander or libel must have occurred against the aggrieved individual.

Detention: Secure confinement of juvenile offenders.

Determinate discretionary sentence: Type of sentence with a range of time to be served, with the specific sentence to be served within that range decided by the judge at the point of initial sentencing.

Determinate presumptive sentence: This type of sentence specifies the exact length of the sentence to be served by the inmate.

Determinate sentencing: Consists of fixed periods of incarceration with no later flexibility in the term that is served.

Detoxification: The use of medical drugs to ease the process of overcoming the physical symptoms of dependence that make the detoxification process so painful for the addicted substance abuser.

***Diagnostic and Statistical Manual of Mental Disorders* (DSM-IV-TR):** A reference tome formed by gatherings of psychiatrists and psychologists from around the world, this manual sets forth the specific guidelines in applying a specific diagnosis to a person presenting with a mental disorder.

Direct supervision design: Under this design cells are organized on the outside of the square space, with shower facilities and recreation cells interspersed among the typical inmate living quarters.

Discrimination: Focuses on attributes of offenders when providing a given sentence. This usually results in a differential response toward a group without providing any legally legitimate reference to reasons for that differential response.

Disparity: Refers to inconsistencies in sentencing and/or sanctions that result from the decision-making process.

Disturbance control team: Specialized teams trained to respond to, contain, and neutralize inmate disturbances in prisons.

Domestic violence: Behaviors used by one person in a relationship to control the other. Partners may be married or not married.

Ducking stool: Punishment that used a chair suspended over a body of water.

Dysthymic disorder: Characterized by at least two years of depressed mood for more days than not, accompanied by additional depressive symptoms that do not meet the criteria for a major depressive disorder.

Eastern Penitentiary: Part of the Pennsylvania system located near Philadelphia.

Education adviser: The unit team's (normally permanent) consultant in all education matters.

Educational neglect: Occurs when a parent or even a teacher permits chronic truancy or simply ignores the educational and/or special needs of a child.

Elam Lynds: Warden at Auburn and the primary organizer behind the development of the Auburn system.

Elderly first-time offenders: Those who commit their offense later in life. For those who commit violent crimes, these are usually crimes of passion rather than premeditated crimes.

Electronic monitoring: The use of any mechanism worn by the offender for the means of tracking his or her whereabouts through electronic detection.

Elizabeth Fry: A Quaker prison reform activist and an advocate for women who were incarcerated during these early years.

Elmira Reformatory: First reformatory.

Emergency preparedness: Consists of the planning, training, and budgeting process involved prior to the occurrence of an emergency.

Emergency response: Consists of the actual intervention used, the management of that intervention, containment of the emergency, and the successful resolution of the emergency event.

Emotional distress: Refers to acts (either intentional or negligent) that lead to emotional distress of the client.

Emotional intelligence: Describes how adept a person is at noticing and responding to the emotional cues and information exhibited by others with whom they interact.

Emotional neglect: Includes inadequate nurturing or affection, allowing a child to engage in inappropriate or illegal behavior such as drug or alcohol use, as well as ignoring a child's basic emotional needs.

English as a Second Language (ESL): Program enables inmates with limited English proficiency to improve their English language skills.

English Penal Servitude Act: Successfully lobbied by Maconochie in 1853, this act established several rehabilitation programs for convicts.

Establishment Clause: Clause of the First Amendment that holds that Congress will make no law to prohibit the free exercise of religion.

***Estelle v. Gamble* (1976):** Deliberate indifference to inmate medical needs constitutes cruel and unusual punishment and is therefore unconstitutional.

Evaluative transparency: When an agency's evaluative process allows for an outside person (whether an auditor, an evaluator, or the public at large) to have full view of the agency's operations, budgeting, policies, procedures, and outcomes.

Evidence-based practice (EBP): A significant trend throughout all human services that emphasize outcomes.

Ex parte Hull (1941): Supreme Court case ruling that marked the beginning of the end for the hands-off doctrine.

Farmer v. Brennan (1994): Supreme Court case ruling holding that a prison official is not liable under the Eighth Amendment for injury inflicted on an inmate by another inmate unless it can be determined that the prison official knew of the excessive risk of harm to that inmate and that the official chose to disregard that harm.

Federal Death Penalty Act of 1994: This act established constitutional procedures for imposition of the death penalty for 60 offenses under 13 existing and 28 newly created federal capital statutes.

Federal Prison Industries Inc. (FPI): Organization for federal prison labor.

Fine: A monetary penalty imposed by a judge or magistrate as a punishment for having committed an offense.

Ford v. Wainwright (1986): Supreme Court ruling that defendants who could successfully invoke the insanity defense could avoid the death penalty.

Four standards of mental health care: Legal requirement for adequate health care also extends to mental health care.

Francois Voltaire: Wrote critically of the French government and was imprisoned in the Bastille.

Free Exercise Clause: Requires government respect for, and noninterference with, the religious beliefs and practices of our nation's people.

Fulwood v. Clemmer (1962): U.S. District Court for the District of Columbia ruled that correctional officials must recognize the Muslim faith as a legitimate religion and not restrict those inmates who wish to hold services.

Furman v. Georgia (1972): Supreme Court ruling that the death penalty, as applied in 1972, was arbitrary and capricious and therefore violated the Eighth Amendment prohibition against cruel and unusual punishment.

Gag: A device that would constrain persons who were known to constantly scold others.

Gagnon v. Scarpelli (1971): Supreme Court ruling holding that a probationer's sentence can only be revoked after a preliminary revocation hearing and a final revocation hearing have been provided.

Gang cross-pollination: Occurs when a gang has developed such power and influence as to be equally effective regardless of whether its leadership is inside or outside of prison walls.

Gaols: A term used in England during the Middle Ages that was synonymous with today's jail.

Gates v. Collier (1972): One of a series of federal cases that declared a state prison system unconstitutional.

General deterrence: Punishing an offender in public so other observers will refrain from criminal behavior. Intended to cause vicarious learning whereby observers see that offenders are punished for a given crime and thus are discouraged from committing a like-mannered crime due to fear of punishment.

General educational development (GED): The *process* of earning the equivalent of your high school diploma.

Generalized anxiety disorder: Characterized by excessive anxiety and worry (apprehensive expectation), occurring more days than not for at least six months, about a number of events or activities.

Glass ceiling: A term for official or unofficial barriers to promotion that exist for women within the workforce.

Global positioning system (GPS): A receiver that uses 24 military satellites to determine the exact location of a coordinate. Through the use of satellite monitoring and remote tracking, offenders can be tracked to their exact location.

Good faith defense: In state tort cases, the person acted in the honest belief that the action taken was appropriate under the circumstances. In Section 1983 cases, the officer did not violate a clearly established constitutional or federal right of which a reasonable person should have known.

Graham v. Florida (2010): Supreme Court ruling that juveniles who commit crimes in which no one is killed may not be sentenced to life in prison without the possibility of parole.

Great Law: Correctional thinking and reform in Pennsylvania that occurred due to the work of William Penn and the Quakers.

Gregg v. Georgia (1976): Supreme Court case ruling holding that death penalty statutes that contain sufficient safeguards against arbitrary and capricious imposition are constitutional.

Greyhounds: Older inmates who have acquired respect within the offender subculture due to their track record and criminal history, both inside and outside the prison; they are career criminals who have earned status through years of hard-won adherence to prison and criminogenic ideals.

Habitual elderly offenders: Have a long history of crime and also have a prior record of imprisonment throughout their lifetime.

Hair testing: Using hair samples to determine if an offender has been using drugs.

Hands-off doctrine: A period of time during which the Supreme Court and the lower courts avoided intervening in prison operations.

Hawes-Cooper Act: Required that prison products be subject to the laws of states to which those products are shipped.

Head building tenders: High-ranking inmates who are given control of cell blocks and/or dormitories, and who are held responsible for behavior that occurs within those facilities.

Hearing stage: Stage of a revocation proceeding that allows the probation agency to present evidence of the violation while the offender is given the opportunity to refute the evidence provided.

Hedonistic calculus: A term first coined by Jeremy Bentham to describe how humans seem to weigh out pleasure and pain outcomes when deciding to engage in criminal behavior.

Health Insurance Portability and Accountability Act (HIPAA): Well known among medical personnel and mental health personnel, this act, for the most part, guides professionals on matters regarding the confidentiality of medical information.

HIV/AIDS: A chronic, potentially life-threatening condition caused by the human immunodeficiency virus (HIV).

Hogging: A term used to imply that a person is using others for some type of gain or benefit, such as by manipulating others into doing his or her work or fulfilling obligations on his or her behalf.

Holding pattern management: Where the system continues to operate but in a pattern of stasis where there is no true growth, nor is there a blockage in the systemic flow.

***Holt v. Sarver I* (1969):** As the civil rights movement began to take hold in the United States, this case represented the official turning point in which the hands-off doctrine began to eclipse in prison system operations. This Supreme Court case ruled that prison farms in the state of Arkansas were operated in a manner that violated the Eighth Amendment prohibition against cruel and unusual punishments.

***Holt v. Sarver II* (1970):** Second part of the initial federal ruling on prison farm operations in the state of Arkansas. The fact that the *Holt v. Sarver* rulings required two separate cases shows how tenuous and difficult it was to get change in the Arkansas prison system.

Home detention: The mandated action that forces an offender to stay within the confines of his or her home or on the property until a time specified by the sentencing judge.

Houses of refuge: Institutions that were oriented toward education and treatment for juveniles.

***Hudson v. Palmer* (1984):** Supreme Court case ruling holding that prison cells may be searched without the need of a warrant and without probable cause. Prison cells are not protected by the Fourth Amendment.

Hulks Act: A temporary measure to house offenders on large men-o-war naval troop transporters.

Hustle: Any action that is designed to deceive, manipulate, or take advantage of another person.

***Hutto v. Finney* (1978):** Supreme Court ruling holding that courts can set time limits on prison use of solitary confinement.

Implementation evaluation: Identifying problems and accomplishments during the early phases of program development for feedback to clinical and administrative staff.

Importation theory: Subculture within prisons is brought in from outside the walls by offenders who have developed their beliefs and norms while on the streets.

***In re Gault* (1967):** Supreme Court ruled that in hearings that may result in institutional commitment, juveniles have all of the constitutional rights afforded to adults.

***In re Holmes* (1955):** Supreme Court opinion that because juvenile courts are not criminal courts, the constitutional rights guaranteed to accused adults do not apply to juveniles.

Incapacitation: Deprives offenders of their liberty and removes them from society with the intent of ensuring that society cannot be further victimized by these offenders during their term of incarceration.

Indeterminate sentencing: Sentencing that includes a range of years that will be potentially served by the offender.

Individual personality traits: Traits associated with criminal behavior, including defiance, self-assertiveness, extroversion, impulsivity, narcissism, mental instability, a tendency toward hostility, a lack of concern for others, resentment, and a distrust of authority.

Injunction: A court order that requires an agency to take some form of action(s) or to refrain from a particular action or set of actions.

In loco parentis: "In the place of parents."

Institutional parole officer: Works with the offender and a number of institutional personnel to aid the offender in making the transition from prison life to community supervision while on parole.

Intensive supervision probation: The extensive supervision of offenders who are deemed the greatest risk to society or are in need of the greatest amount of governmental services.

Intentional tort: The actor, whether expressed or implied, was judged to have possessed intent or purpose to cause an injury.

Intermediate sanctions: A range of sentencing options that fall between incarceration and probation, being designed to allow for the crafting of sentences that respond to the offender, the offense, or both, with the intended outcome of the case being a primary consideration.

Isolation zone: Designed to prevent undetected access to the outer fencing of the prison facility.

Jail: A confinement facility, usually operated and controlled by county-level law enforcement, that is designed to hold persons charged with a crime who are either awaiting adjudication or serving a short sentence of one year or less after the point of adjudication.

Jail reentry programs: Programs usually interlaced with probation and parole agencies as a means of integrating the supervisory functions of both the jail and community supervision agencies. The continued care of the offender's specific needs is addressed and can include everything from referral to counseling to drug treatment, depending on the needs of the offender.

Jeremy Bentham: Believed behavior could be determined through scientific principles, created pleasure-pain hypothesis (aka hedonistic calculus).

John Augustus: Recognized as the father of modern probation.

John Howard: Sheriff of Bedfordshire in England, advocated prison reform, wrote *State of Prisons* treatise for British Parliament.

Johnson v. Avery (1969): Case where the Supreme Court held that prison authorities cannot prohibit inmates from aiding other inmates in preparing legal documents unless they also provide alternatives by which inmates are provided access to the courts.

Judicial Improvements Act of 1990: Extended the life of the Parole Commission until November 1, 1997.

Juvenile waiver: A sentencing option that is presented to distinguish it from the use of detention. This occurs when the juvenile case is transferred to adult court.

Labeling theory: Contends that individuals become stabilized in criminal roles when they are labeled as criminals, are stigmatized, develop criminal identities, are sent to prison, and are excluded from conventional roles.

LaSalle Corrections: A private company that owns and operates prisons in Louisiana and Texas.

Leadership: Entails skills and talents that motivate and influence persons toward a common goal or idea.

Learning organizations: Have the inherent ability to adapt and change, improving performance through continual revision of goals, objectives, policies, and procedures.

LeMaire v. Maass (1993): A suit in which the plaintiff, inmate LeMaire, considered the conditions of the Oregon prison (particularly the use of food loaf) to be unconstitutional.

Level of security: The type of physical barriers that are utilized to prevent inmates' escape and are related to public safety concerns.

Lex talionis: Refers to the Babylonian law of equal retaliation.

Libel: Written or published communication intended to lower the reputation of the person who is discussed and where people in the community would find such facts to actually be damaging to that person's reputation.

Life development intervention: A comprehensive approach to linking sport and recreation to counseling psychology that emphasizes continuous growth and positive change.

Life Skills for State and Local Prisoners Program: Provides financial assistance for establishing and operating programs designed to reduce recidivism through the development and improvement of life skills necessary for reintegration of adult prisoners into society.

Life-course-persistent juvenile: Adolescents who lack many of the necessary social skills and opportunities possessed by the adolescent-limited delinquent.

Little Hoover Commission: An internal state "watchdog" agency that was tasked with providing recommendations to the state governor and legislature.

Madrid v. Gomez (1995): Case where the constitutionality of supermax facilities was questioned. This was a wide-ranging attack on operations at the Pelican Bay Special Housing Unit (SHU) in California.

Major depressive disorder: Characterized by one or more major depressive episodes (e.g., at least two weeks of depressed mood or loss of interest accompanied by at least four additional symptoms of depression).

Malicious prosecution: Occurs when a criminal accusation is made by someone who has no probable cause and who generates such actions for improper reasons.

Malingering: When inmates falsely claim and consciously fake symptoms of an illness.

Management: Refers to persons who have been vested with an official title by the agency and who tend to be focused on the process of completing functions of operation within the prison facility.

Mandatory minimum: A certain minimum amount of time or a minimum percentage of a sentence must be served with no good time or early-release modifications.

Mark system: A system where the duration of the sentence was determined by the inmate's work habits and righteous conduct.

Martinson Report: An examination of a number of various programs that included educational and vocational assistance, mental health treatment, medical treatment, early release, and so on.

Maximum-security facilities: Nowadays these facilities use corrugated chain-link fence. These fences will be lit by floodlights at night and may even have electric shock features for those who touch them. Chain-link fences, with razor wire atop them, tend to be just as effective at containing inmates as stone walls but eliminate "blind spots" in security where inmates can hide.

McKeiver v. Pennsylvania (1971): Supreme Court held that the due process clause of the Fourteenth Amendment did not require jury trials in juvenile court.

Media effects: Refer to the effect that the media has upon the public perception of prison or community supervision programs.

Medical model: An approach to correctional treatment that utilizes a type of mental health approach incorporating fields such as psychology and biology.

Medium-security facilities: Consist of dormitories that have bunk beds with lockers for inmates to store their possessions. These facilities tend to have communal showers, toilets, and sinks. Dormitories are locked at night with one or more security officers holding watch.

Megan's laws: An informal but popular term for legislation in most every state that mandates a public notification process when sex offenders are released into the community.

Mental illness: Any diagnosed disorder contained within the DSM-IV-TR, as published by the American Psychiatric Association.

Mental retardation: Refers to significantly subaverage general intellectual functioning existing concurrently with deficits in adaptive behavior and manifested during the developmental period.

Minimal services view: Contends that inmates are entitled to no more than the bare minimum that is required by law.

Minimum-security facilities: Typically designed to serve the needs of farming areas or public transportation works rather than being optimized for the offender's reform. Not like typical prisons as envisioned by the public.

Mitigating factors: Circumstances that make the commission of a crime more understandable and help to reduce the level of culpability that an offender might have had.

Mood disorders: Disorders such as major depressive disorder, bipolar disorder, and dysthymic disorder. Major depressive disorder is characterized by one or more major depressive episodes.

Morris v. Travisono (1970): Held that Rhode Island prison authorities violated the Eighth and Fourteenth Amendments of the Constitution in inmate placement. This case resulted in a detailed set of procedures for classifying inmates that was overseen by the federal court system.

Mothers and Infants Nurturing Together (MINT): A Federal Bureau of Prisons community residential program for women who are pregnant at the time of commitment. This residential reentry center-based program promotes bonding and parenting skills for low-risk female inmates who are pregnant.

Mule: A person who smuggles drugs into prison for another inmate, often using his or her own body cavities to hide the drugs from prison authorities.

National Commission on Correctional Health Care (NCCHC): Sets the tone for standards of care in correctional settings.

National Institute of Corrections: An agency within the Federal Bureau of Prisons that is headed by a director appointed by the U.S. Attorney General.

Negative punishment: The removal of a valued stimulus when the offender commits an undesired behavior.

Negligence: Doing what a reasonably prudent person would not do in similar circumstances or failing to do what a reasonably prudent person would do in similar circumstances.

O'Lone v. Estate of Shabazz (1987): Case in which the Supreme Court held that the free exercise rights of a Muslim inmate were not violated when prison officials would not adjust the time of his work schedule. In other words, the Supreme Court ruled that depriving an inmate of attending a religious service for "legitimate penological interests" was not a violation of an inmate's First Amendment rights.

Offender Accountability Plan: Addresses needs for restitution, the need to respect the rights and privacy of prior victims, any particular arrangements that have been made with the victim, and provisions that might be included to ensure the offender's responsibility to the community at large.

Offender reentry: Includes all activities and programming conducted to prepare ex-convicts to return safely to the community and to live as law-abiding citizens.

Offender with special needs: A specialized offender (1) who has some notable physical, mental, and/or emotional challenge; (2) for whom these challenges prevent either a subjective or an objective need from being fulfilled for that individual; and (3) for whom the lack of this subjective or objective need impairs his or her day-to-day ability to function within the confines of the criminal law.

Offender-turned-elderly-in-prison: Inmates who have grown old in prison have long histories in the system and are the least likely to be discipline problems.

Office of Correctional Education (OCE): Was created to provide national leadership on issues related to correctional education.

Old Newgate Prison: First prison structure in America.

One hand on, one hand off doctrine: More conservative rulings are handed down from the Court, and this reflects an eclipse of the hands-off doctrine in American corrections.

Outcome evaluation: Involves quantitative research aimed at assessing the impact of the program on long-term treatment outcomes.

Pains of imprisonment: The various inconveniences and deprivations that occur as a result of incarceration.

Palmigiano v. Garrahy (1977): Ruling that attested to the importance of effective and appropriate classification systems.

Panopticon: Designed to allow security personnel to clearly observe all inmates without the inmates themselves being able to tell whether they are being watched.

Parens patriae: "Parent of the country," "in the place of parents."

Parole: The early release of an offender from a secure facility upon completion of a certain portion of his or her sentence.

Parole Commission and Reorganization Act: This act retitled the Board of Parole as the U.S. Parole Commission and established it as an independent agency within the Department of Justice.

Parole Commission Phaseout Act of 1996: This act extended the life of the Parole Commission until November 1, 2002, but only in regard to supervising offenders who were still on parole from previous years.

Parole revocations officer: Primarily tasked with the routine holding of preliminary parole revocation hearings by reviewing allegations made by parole officers against parolees.

Participative method: A form of management that includes opinions and feedback offered from both inmates and staff when making decisions regarding the operations and governance of the prison facility.

Passive agent: Views his or her job as just that, a job. These individuals will tend to do as little as possible, and they do not have passion for their jobs.

Paternal officers: Use a great degree of both control and assistance techniques in supervising offenders.

Patriarchy: A broad structure that shapes gender-related experiences and power.

Pell grants: Need-based federal monies set aside for persons who pursue a college education.

Perimeter security system: A collection of components or elements that, when assembled in a carefully formulated plan, achieve the objective of confinement with a high degree of confidence.

Philadelphia Prison System (PPS): Offers a full range of services to offenders in its care.

Philadelphia Society for Alleviating the Miseries of Public Prisons: First official prison reform group.

Physical abuse: Abuse that consists of some type of physical battery and/or abuse that causes some type of physiological harm to a child.

Physical neglect: Includes abandonment, the expulsion of a child from the home (being kicked out of the house), a failure to seek or excessive delay in seeking medical care for a child, inadequate supervision, and inadequate food, clothing, and shelter.

Pillory: Similar to the stock except the pillory consisted of a single large bored hole where the offender's neck would rest.

Pod: Prefabricated sections in most modern prisons. Within these pods, inmates will usually have individual cells with ding doors controlled from a secure remote control station.

Podular jail: Includes rounded or "podular" architecture for living units and allows for direct, as opposed to indirect, supervision of inmates by security staff.

Positive punishment: Punishment where a stimulus is applied to the offender when the offender commits an undesired behavior.

Positive reinforcers: Rewards for a desired behavior.

Post-Release Employment Project (PREP): A 7-year study in the 1990s conducted by the Bureau's Office of Research and Evaluation that validated, conclusively, that UNICOR successfully achieved its mission of preparing inmates for release and therefore provided long-term benefits to society.

Preliminary hearing: Initial examination of the facts of the arrest to determine if probable cause does exist for a violation.

Presentence investigation (PSI) report: A thorough file that includes a wide range of background information on the offender.

PRIDE Re-Entry and Transition Program: Supports the primary statutory mission in Florida, which is "to provide a joint effort between the department, the correctional work programs, and other vocational education, training and post-release job placement and help reduce recommitment."

Prison complex: A design that consists of multiple prison facilities that are in the same vicinity and share resources, including medical, transportation, and food service, in an effort to coordinate services, consolidate security regions, reduce transportation needs, and make the housing process more efficient.

Prison food loaf: A food product that contains all the typical ingredients of a well-balanced meal that would be served to inmates who do not have disciplinary problems; these ingredients are mixed together and baked as a single loaf-like product that, while bland in flavor, is quite nutritious when considering vitamin, mineral, and caloric content.

Prison grapevine: Grounded in the informal organization of the prison subculture, this informal network consists of information passed through the personal communications of employees to employees, inmates to inmates, employees to inmates, and inmates to employees.

Prison Industry Enhancement (PIE) Certification Program: Partnership between the Texas Department of Criminal Justice and a private company, which allows the company to employ offenders who have volunteered to be a part of the program.

Prison Litigation Reform Act of 1995: Law that limits an inmates' ability to file lawsuits and the compensation that they can receive.

Prison Rehabilitative Industries and Diversified Enterprises Inc. (PRIDE): An independent company that aligns its job training initiatives to the needs of the correctional system in the state of Florida. PRIDE Enterprises is recognized throughout the nation as a premier company that operates general manufacturing and service facilities throughout Florida.

Prisonization: The process of being socialized into the prison culture.

Private wrongs: Resorting to private revenge, including such types of wrongs as physical injury, damage to a person's property, or theft.

Proactive styles of management: Seek to anticipate and correct problems before they develop.

Probation: A control valve mechanism that mitigates the flow of inmates sent directly to the jailhouse.

Process evaluation: Traditionally refers to assessment of the effects of the program on clients while they are in the program, making it possible to assess the institution's intermediary goals.

***Procunier v. Martinez* (1974):** Prison officials my censor inmate mail only to the extent necessary to ensure security of the institution.

Progressive Era: A period of extraordinary urban and industrial growth and unprecedented social problems.

Prosecutorial Death Discretion Outcome: Observes that prosecutors are overwhelmingly Caucasian and that, when determining whether to seek the death penalty, they tend to do so disproportionately more often when the victim is also Caucasian than when the victim is African American.

Protective custody: "Special provisions to provide for the safety and well-being for inmates who, based on findings of fact, would be in danger in the general population." A security-level status, typically determined by the official classification process given to inmates who are deemed to be at risk of serious violence that is predictable and likely to occur if the inmate is not afforded protection.

Psychological abuse: Includes actions or the omission of actions by parents and other caregivers that could cause a child to have serious behavioral, emotional, or mental impairments.

Psychology services representative: A member of the decision-making team who is expected to be involved in the admission and information-gathering process prior to classification.

Public wrongs: Crimes against society or a social group that tend to include sacrilege as well as other crimes against religion, treason, witchcraft, incest, sex offenses of any sort, and even violations of hunting rules.

Punitive damages: Monetary awards reserved for person harmed in a malicious or willful manner by the guilty party. These damages are often added to other damages due to the seriousness of the injury and/or to serve as a warning to others who might consider similar actions.

Punitive officers: See themselves as needing to use threats and punishment in order to get compliance from the offender.

Punk: Common prison vernacular for an inmate who engages in homosexual activity, but is a derogatory term that implies that the inmate is feminine, weak, and subservient to masculine inmates.

Qualified immunity: Requires that staff demonstrate three key aspects prior to invoking this form of defense against a suit: (1) The officer must show that he or she was performing a discretionary act, not one that was mandatory by agency policy; (2) the officer must have been acting in good faith—that is, holding the sincere belief that his or her action was correct under the circumstances; and (3) the officer must have acted within the scope of his or her designated authority.

Rank-and-file building tenders: Inmate assistants to the head building tenders who help to ensure that order is maintained.

Rational basis test: Consists of four elements: (1) There must be a rational and clear connection between the regulation and the reason that is given for that regulation's existence; (2) inmates must be given alternative means to practice a given right that has been restricted, when feasible; (e) the means by which prison staff and inmates are affected must be kept as minimal as is realistically possible; and (4) when less restrictive alternative means of impeding upon an inmate's rights are available, prison personnel must utilize those alternative means.

Reactive styles of management: When a supervisor waits until a problem develops and then, after it has emerged, responds to remedy the situation.

Ready to Work Program: Developed to ensure that Florida's workforce possesses the competencies necessary to succeed in the competitive marketplace.

Recreation program administrator: Responsible for a number of duties including the expectation that this individual will survey the recreational needs and interests of the offender population at least one time each year.

Reform school: An industrial school.

Reformatories for women: Developed due to the efforts of an early generation of women reformers who appeared between 1840 and 1900, but their use became more widespread as activists pressed for alternatives to the penitentiary's harsh conditions of enforced silence and hard labor.

Regional-level administrators: Managers who oversee a specific region of a state.

Rehabilitation: Offenders will be deterred from reoffending due to their having worthwhile stakes in legitimate society.

Reintegration: Focused on the reentry of the offender into society. The ultimate goal of reintegration programs is to connect offenders to legitimate areas of society in a manner that is gainful and productive.

Reintegration model: Used to identify programs that looked to the external environment for causes of crime and the means by which criminality could be reduced.

Release valve mechanism: Whenever correctional systems use parole with the intent to reduce correctional populations rather than facilitate reintegration of offenders.

Religious Land Use and Institutionalized Persons Act of 2000: This act prohibits the government from substantially burdening an inmate's religious exercise.

Respect: Represents an inmate's sense of masculine standing within the prison culture; if an inmate is disrespected, he is honor-bound to avenge that disrespect, or he is considered weak by other inmates.

Restorative justice: Interventions that focus on restoring the health of the community, repairing the harm done, meeting victim's needs, and emphasizing that the offender can and must contribute to those repairs.

Retribution: Often referred to as the "eye for an eye" mentality, and simply implies that offenders committing a crime should be punished in a like fashion or in a manner that is commensurate with the severity of the crime that they have committed.

Rogues and mavericks: Employees within a facility who tend to act as if they are independent of the broader institution.

***Roper v. Simmons* (2005):** Supreme Court ruled that the death penalty was unconstitutional when used with persons who were under 18 years of age at the time of their offense.

***Ruiz v. Estelle* (1980):** This Supreme Court case ruled that the Texas prison system was unconstitutional, in violation of the Eighth Amendment prohibition against cruel and unusual punishments. This case forever changed the prison culture of the state of Texas.

Rumor control: The active process of administrators to circumvent faulty information that is disseminated among staff or inmates and has the potential to cause unrest or disharmony throughout the facility.

Runners and strikers: Inmates who keep the cell block clean, dispense supplies, and provide the building tenders with additional muscle during times when the general inmate population becomes unruly.

Rural jail: Usually small jails in rural county jurisdictions that are often challenged with tight budgets and limited training for staff.

Saliva testing: Using samples of saliva to determine if an offender has been using drugs.

Sally port: Entry design that allows security staff to bring vehicles close to the admissions area in a secure fashion.

Sanctuary: A place of refuge or asylum.

Sanford Bates: First director of the Federal Bureau of Prisons who also served as a past president of the American Correctional Association.

Schizophrenic disorders: Disorders as evidenced by five characteristic symptoms, at least two of which must be present before the diagnosis can be given to an individual: (1) delusions, (2) hallucinations, (3) disorganized speech, (4) grossly disorganized behavior, and (5) inappropriate affect. Further, the social, self-care, and/or occupational life of the individual must show signs of being well below the level achieved prior to the onset of the illness. Lastly, these symptoms must have existed for six months or longer.

Security threat group (STG): A gang that possesses high-functioning group and organizational characteristics. The group's mission integrates an economic objective, and uses some form of illicit industry such as drug trafficking to fulfill the economic necessities to carry forward other stated objectives.

Selective incapacitation: Identifying inmates who are of particular concern to public safety and providing them with much longer sentences than would be given to other inmates.

Sentencing stage: When a judge requires either that the offender be incarcerated or, when the violation is minor, that the offender continue his or her probation sentence but under more restrictive terms.

SENTRY system: A comprehensive database used by the Federal Bureau of Prisons to classify and track inmates within the system.

Shock incarceration: A short period of incarceration followed by a specified term of community supervision in hopes of deterring the offender from recidivating.

Short-term jails: Facilities that hold sentenced inmates for no more than one year.

Sir Walter Crofton: Directed the prison system of Ireland.

Slander: Verbal communication intended to lower the reputation of the person who is discussed and where people in the community would find such facts to actually be damaging to that person's reputation.

Snitch: The label given to an inmate who reveals the activity of another inmate to authorities, usually in exchange for some type of benefit within the prison or legal system.

Social learning theory: Contends that offenders learn to engage in crime through exposure to and the adoption of definitions that are favorable to the commission of crime.

Span of control: Refers to the number of persons that an officer supervises.

Span of influence: The extended impact that a supervisor has upon employee behavior that may occur beyond his or her own actual observation but, through the effects of other organizational members, is carried forth as the desired means of operation.

Special housing unit syndrome: The negative mental health effects of extended isolation.

Special Operations Response Teams (SORT): Response teams designed to respond to serious crises within a prison facility where the security of the institution is seriously at risk, posing a threat to public safety.

Specific deterrence: The infliction of a punishment upon a specific offender in the hope that that particular offender will be discouraged from committing future crimes.

Stakeholders: Agency personnel, the community in which the agency is located, and even the offender population that is being supervised.

Stocks: Wooden frames that were built in the outdoors, usually in a village or town square.

Strain theory/institutional anomie: This theory denotes that when individuals cannot obtain success goals (money, status, etc.), they will tend to experience a sense of pressure often called *strain.*

Strategic plan: A document that articulates agency goals and objectives and provides a means by which those goals and objectives might be realized.

Strategic planning: Consists of the determination of long-term goals and objectives for an agency, usually spanning a period of one or more years in scope.

Successful Treatment of Addiction and Recovery (STAR) program: A program that emphasizes the people, places, and things that inmates encounter that can affect likely relapse into drug use and recidivism into criminal activity.

Supermax facility: A highly restrictive, high-custody housing unit within a secure facility, or an entire secure facility, that isolates inmates from the general population and from each other due to grievous crimes, repetitive assaultive behavior, or violent institutional behavior.

Supervised release: Postrelease supervision.

Sweat testing: Using samples of sweat excretion to determine if an offender has been using drugs.

Symbiotic prison relationship: Exists between correctional staff and inmates as a means of developing mutually compliant and informal negotiations in behavior that is acceptable within the bounds of institutional security yet, at the same time, allows inmates to meet many of their basic human needs.

System-wide administrators: Managers who are at the executive level and direct the entire system throughout the state.

Tactical planning: Ground-level planning that is narrow in focus, usually being structured around the resolution of particular issues or something that confronts the agency on a short-term basis.

Technical violations: Actions that do not comply with the conditions and requirements of a probationer's sentence, as articulated by the court that acted as the sentencing authority.

Test of Adult Basic Education (TABE): One of the most comprehensive and reliable assessment products in the education industry, providing a solid foundation for effectively assessing the skills and knowledge of adult learners.

Texas Correctional Industries (TCI): Provides offenders with marketable job skills to help reduce recidivism through a coordinated program.

The Summary: The first inmate-operated prison newspaper in the entire world.

Theory of disablement: Whereby the offender is either temporarily or permanently isolated or maimed as a means of preventing a type of crime in the future.

Therapeutic community: An environment that provides necessary behavior modifiers in the form of sanctions and privileges that allow offenders immediate feedback about their behavior and treatment progress. In this total treatment environment the primary clinical staff are typically former substance abusers—"recovering addicts"—who themselves were rehabilitated in therapeutic communities.

Therapeutic recreation (TR): Programs designed to meet the needs of individuals with a variety of disabilities, impairments, or illnesses by providing specific services such as recreational activities, leisure education, and skills training in the cognitive, physical, behavioral, social, and affective domains.

Theriault v. Carlson (1977): Ruling from the Fifth Circuit Court of Appeals that the First Amendment does not protect so-called religions that are obvious shams, that tend to mock established institutions, and whose members lack religious sincerity. Other precedents are in agreement with this ruling.

Thompson v. Oklahoma (1988): Supreme Court found that the Eighth and Fourteenth Amendments prohibited the execution of a person who is under 16 years of age at the time of his or her offense.

Ticket of leave: Basically a permit that was given to a convict in exchange for a certain period of good conduct.

Title IV of the Higher Education Act: Permitted inmates to apply for financial aid in the form of Pell Grants to attend college.

Tort: A legal injury in which the action of one person causes injury to the person or property of another as the result of a violation of one's duty that has been established by law.

Totality of conditions: A standard used to determine if conditions in an institution are in violation of the Eighth Amendment.

Tower of London: One of the earliest examples of a jail used for confinement purposes; was constructed after 1066 A.D. under the reign of King William I of England.

Treason: The aiding and abetting of the enemy during a time of war.

Trial by ordeal: Very dangerous and/or impossible tests to prove the guilt or innocence of the accused.

Trop v. Dulles (1958): Supreme Court developed a phrase that would be cited in future cases due to the meaning and the essence of this catch-phrase and because it fit so well with many compelling arguments in favor of reform within the correctional system.

Trusties: Inmates who are in charge of other inmates.

Turnkeys: Inmates who are tasked with opening and closing interior locked gates and doors of the prison.

***Turner v. Safley* (1987):** A prison regulation that impinges on inmate's constitutional rights is valid if it is reasonably related to legitimate penological interests.

UNICOR Inc.: An organization for federal prison labor that was originally named Federal Prison Industries Inc.

Unit-level administrators: The third level of administrator in state agencies, which includes personnel who manage the individual prison facility.

Unit manager: Directs the housing unit activities and is responsible for the unit's operation and quality control of all correspondence and programs.

United States Parole Commission Extension Act of 2008: Provided for the continued performance of the U.S. Parole Commission.

United States Penitentiary (USP) Terre Haute: The physical location for federal death row.

***United States v. Booker* (2005):** A Supreme Court case holding that federal judges no longer were required to follow the sentencing guidelines that had been in effect since 1987.

Universal design: Refers to prison construction design that complies with ADA requirements and that accommodates all inmate needs, in a universal fashion, regardless of how varied the needs may be from inmate to inmate.

Urine testing: Using urine samples to determine if an offender has been using drugs. This is the most common type of method used.

USP Florence ADMAX: A federal prison with a design that is nearly indestructible on the inside. The cell design consists of a concrete bed, desk, stool, and bookcase, which are all constructed from reinforced concrete and are immovable. Cell windows are designed so that all views of the outside are restricted and inmates can only see the sky above them. Cells are positioned in such a manner so that inmates cannot make eye contact with one another. Essentially, these offenders have no contact with humans.

USP Marion: A special closed-custody unit designed to house the Federal Bureau of Prisons' worst inmates. In operating this prison, the Bureau of Prisons created a new classification level known as Level 6, which was over and above the other five security classifications that the federal government had typically used to classify inmates.

Victorian Era: Viewed women from a lens of inflexible femininity where women were to be considered pious and naïve of the evils of the world.

***Vitek v. Jones* (1980):** Inmates are entitled to due process in involuntary transfers from prison to a mental hospital.

Walnut Street Jail: America's first attempt to actually incarcerate inmates with the purpose of reforming them.

Weekend confinement: Confinement that is restricted to the weekends or other times when the person in custody is off from work. This can be likened to serving a sentence on an installment plan, whereby other aspects of life that keep the person functional in society are not impaired but the offender is required to pay for his or her crime through a series of small stints in jail.

Welfare worker: Views the offender more as a client rather than a supervisee on his or her caseload.

Wergild: A form of payment that was made by the offender or his or her family for a wrongful death that had been inflicted by the offender.

Western Penitentiary: Part of the Pennsylvania system located outside of Pittsburgh.

Whipping: Lashing the body of criminal offenders amongst a public audience.

William Penn: Known for the Great Law and Quaker reform.

***Wilson v. Seiter* (1991):** Deliberate indifference is required for liability to be attached for condition of confinement cases.

Windham School District: Secondary education program in Texas prisons.

Witchcraft: Commonly thought to entail genuine magical powers that would be used by the witch for personal revenge or personal gain.

***Witherspoon v. Illinois* (1968):** Supreme Court held that it was not sufficient to strike a potential juror from serving if the juror had doubts or reservations about the use of the death penalty.

***Wolff v. McDonnell* (1974):** Inmates are entitled to due process in prison disciplinary proceedings that can result in the loss of good time credits or in punitive segregation.

Work Against Recidivism (WAR) Program: Specifically targeted to successfully reintegrate offenders into society.

Work/education reform view: View that is thought to save society untold millions due to the lack of recidivism that has been shown to follow for inmates who have obtained employment and/or education.

Zebulon Brockway: The warden of Elmira Reformatory.

Zimmer Amendment: Restricted the purchase of several types of weight lifting equipment within the Federal Bureau of Prisons.

References

Abadinsky, H., & Winfree, L. T., Jr. (1992). *Crime and justice* (2nd ed.). Chicago: Nelson-Hall.

ABC Primetime. (2004, November 4). *Inside a maximum security women's prison.* Retrieved from http://abc news.go.com/Primetime/story?id=227295&p age=1

Aday, R. H. (1994). Aging in prison: A case study of new elderly offenders. *International Journal of Offender Therapy and Comparative Criminology, 38*(1), 121.

Agnew, R. (1992). Foundation for a general strain theory of crime and delinquency. *Criminology, 30*(1), 47–87.

Akers, R. A. (2000). *Criminological theories: Introduction, evaluation, and application.* Los Angeles: Roxbury.

Allen, H. E., Simonsen, C. E., & Latessa, E. J. (2004). *Corrections in America* (10th ed.). Upper Saddle River, NJ: Prentice Hall.

Allen, J. M., & Sawhney, R. (2010). *Administration and management in criminal justice.* Thousand Oaks, CA: Sage.

Allen, R. L. (1974). *Reluctant reformers: Racism and social reform movements in the United States.* Washington, DC: Howard University Press.

American Correctional Association. (1998). *Causes, preventive measures, and methods of controlling riots and disturbances in correctional institutes.* Upper Marlboro, MD: Graphic Communications.

American Correctional Association. (2001). A short history of direct-supervision facility design. *Corrections Today.* Alexandria, VA: Author.

American Jail Association. (1993). *American Jail Association code of ethics.* Retrieved January 28, 2003, from http://www.corrections.com/aja/resolutions/index.html

American Probation and Parole Association. (1991). *Issue paper on caseload standards.* Washington, DC: American Probation and Parole Association.

American Probation and Parole Association. (2011). *Probation and parole FAQs.* Washington, DC: American Probation and Parole Association.

American Psychiatric Association. (2000). *Diagnostic and statistical manual of mental disorders* (4th ed., text rev.). Washington, DC: Author.

Anderson, J. C. (2008). Special needs offenders. In P. M. Carlson & J. S. Garrett (Eds.), *Prison and jail administration* (2nd ed., 361–372). Gaithersburg, MD: Aspen.

Anderson, J. F., Mangels, N. J., & Dyson, L. (2010). *Significant prisoner rights cases.* Durham, NC: Carolina Academic Press.

Anderson, T. (2003). Issues in the availability of health care for women prisoners. In S. F. Sharp (Ed.), *The incarcerated woman: Rehabilitative programming in women's prisons* (pp. 49–60). Englewood Cliffs, NJ: Prentice Hall.

Angelone, R. (1999). Protective custody inmates. In P. M. Carslon & J. S. Garrett (Eds.), *Prison and jail administration: Practice and theory* (pp. 236–231). Gaithersberg, MD: Aspen.

Anno, B. J., Graham, C., Lawrence, J. E., & Shansky, R. (2004). *Correctional health care: Addressing the needs of elderly, chronically ill, and terminally ill inmates.* Washington, DC: National Institute of Corrections.

Appel, A. (1999). Accommodating inmates with disabilities. In P. M. Carlson & J. S. Garrett (Ed.), *Prison and jail administration* (pp. 346–352). Gaithersburg, MD: Aspen.

Arkansas speeds parole to ease jam. (2001). *Corrections Digest,* November 30.

Armstrong, J. J. (2008). Causes of institutional unrest. In P. M. Carlson & J. S. Garrett (Eds.), *Prison and jail administration: Practice and theory* (pp. 461–468). Boston: Jones & Bartlett.

Ashford, J. B., Sales, B. D., & Reid, W. H. (2002). *Treating adult and juvenile offenders with special needs.* Washington, DC: American Psychological Association.

Associated Press. (2001). *Prison escape probe to focus on lax security.* Retrieved January 28, 2003, from http://www.clickonsa.com/ant/news/stories/news-20010108-085202.html

Atkins v. Virginia, 536 U.S. 304 (2002).

Augustus, J. (1852). *John Augustus' original report of his labors* [Reprinted in 1939]. Montclair, NJ: Patterson Smith, 1972.

Ayers, E. L. (1984). *Vengeance and justice: Crime and punishment in the nineteenth century American South.* Oxford University Press.

Baird, S. C., & Austin, J. (1985). *Current state of the art in prison classification models: A literature review for the California Department of Corrections.* Sacramento, CA: Carter Center.

Barnes, H. E. (1968). *The evolution of penology in Pennsylvania.* Montclair, NJ: Patterson Smith. (Original work published in 1927)

Barnes, H. E., & Teeters, N. K. (1959). *New horizons in criminology* (3rd ed.). Upper Saddle River, NJ: Prentice Hall.

Bartol, C. R., & Bartol, A. M. (2010). *Criminal behavior: A psychosocial approach* (9th ed.). Upper Saddle River, NJ: Prentice Hall.

Baxter v. Palmigiano, 425 U.S. 308 (1976).

Bazos, A., & Hausman, J. (2004). *Correctional education as a crime control program.* Los Angeles: UCLA School of Public Policy and Social Research. Retrieved June 28, 2010, from http://www.ceanational.net/PDFs/ed-as-crime-control.pdf

BBC News. (1999). *Many elderly offenders "are mentally ill."* Retrieved from http://news.bbc.co.uk/1/hi/health/294252.stm

Becker, H. S. (1963). *Outsiders: Studies in the sociology of deviance.* New York: Free Press.

Becker, H. S. (1999). Career deviance. In S. H. Traub & C. B. Little (Eds.), *Theories of deviance* (pp. 390–397). Itasca, IL: Peacock.

Belenko, S. (2001). *Research on drug courts: A critical review. 2001 update.* New York: National Center on Addiction and Substance Abuse. Retrieved from www.drugpolicy.org/docUploads/2001drugcourts.pdf

Belknap, J. (2001). *The invisible woman: Gender, crime, and justice.* Belmont, CA: Wadsworth.

Bell v. Wolfish, 441 U.S. 520 (1979).

Bellamy, J. (1973). *Crime and public order in England in the later Middle Ages.* London: Routledge & Kegan Paul.

Benestante, J. (1996, April 19). Presentation before the Texas Board of Criminal Justice Special Committee on Prison Industries. Austin, TX: Texas Department of Criminal Justice.

Bernard, T. J. (1992). *The cycle of juvenile justice.* New York: Oxford University Press.

Bernard, T. J., McCleary, R., & Wright, R. A. (1999). *Life without parole: Living in prison today* (2nd ed.). Los Angeles: Roxbury.

Blackstone, W. (1803). *Commentaries on the laws of England* (12th ed., Vol. 4). London: Strahan.

Bloom, B., Brown, M., & Chesney-Lind, M. (1996). Women on probation and parole. In A. J. Lurigio (Ed.), *Community corrections in America: New directions and sounder investments for persons with mental illness and co-disorders* (pp. 51–76). Washington, DC: National Institute of Corrections.

Bloom, B., Owen, B., & Covington, S. (2003). *Gender responsive strategies: Research, practice, and guiding principles for women offenders.* Washington, DC: National Institute of Corrections. Retrieved from http://www.nicic.org/Library/018017

Bohm, R. (1999). *Deathquest: An introduction to the theory and practice of capital punishment in the United States.* city, state: Anderson Publishing.

Bosworth, M. (2010). *Explaining U.S. imprisonment.* Thousand Oaks, CA: Sage.

Bounds v. Smith, 430 U.S. 817 (1977).

Bowers, W. J., & Pierce, G. L. (1980). Deterrence or brutalization: What is the effect of executions? *Crime & Delinquency, 26*(4), 453–484.

Bowker, L. H. (1980). *Prison victimization.* New York: Elsevier.

Bradley, C. M. (2006, March/April). The right decision on the juvenile death penalty. *Judicature, 89,* 302–305.

Braithwaite, J. (1989). *Crime, shame, and reintegration.* Cambridge, UK: Cambridge University Press.

Branch-Johnson, W. (1957). *The English prison hulks.* Publisher unknown.

Branham, L. S., & Hamden, M. S. (2009). *Cases and materials on the law and policy of sentencing and corrections* (8th ed.). St. Paul, MN: West.

Breed v. Jones, 421 U.S. 519 (1975).

Brennan, P. K., & Vandenberg, A. L. (2009). Depictions of female offenders in front-page newspaper stories: The importance of race/ethnicity. *International Journal of Social Inquiry, 2*(2), 141–175.

Brennan, T. (1987a). Classification: An overview of selected methodological issues. In D. M. Gottfredson & M. Tonry (Eds.), *Prediction and classification: Criminal justice decision making.* Chicago: University of Chicago Press.

Brennan, T. (1987b). Classification for control in jails and prisons. In D. M. Gottfredson & M. Tonry (Eds.), *Prediction and classification: Criminal justice decision making.* Chicago: University of Chicago Press.

Brennan, T., Wells, D., & Alexander, J. (2004). *Enhancing prison classification systems: The emerging role of management information systems.* Washington, DC: National Institute of Corrections.

Brockway, Z. R. (1912). *Fifty years of prison service: An autobiography.* New York State Reformatory at Elmira. Annual report reprinted, Montclair, NJ: Patterson Smith, 1969.

Brown, J. W. (2003). The female inmate. *International Encyclopedia of Justice Studies.* Retrieved from http://www.eijs.com/Corrections/female_inmate.htm

Browne, J. (2010). Rooted in slavery: Prison labor exploitation. *Race, Poverty, & the Environment, 14*(2), 78–81.

Bruscino v. Carlson, 854 F. 2d 162 (7th Cir. 1988).

Bureau of Justice Assistance Center for Program Evaluation (BJA). (2007). *Reporting and using evaluation results.* Washington, DC: Author. Retrieved from http://www.ojp.usdoj.gov/BJA/evaluation/sitemap.htm

Bureau of Justice Statistics. (1998). *Substance abuse and treatment, state and federal prisoners, 1997.* Washington, DC: U.S Department of Justice.

Bureau of Justice Statistics. (2008). *Capital punishment statistical tables.* Retrieved from http://bjs.ojp.usdoj.gov/index.cfm?ty=tp&tid=181

Bureau of Justice Statistics. (2010). *Prisoners in 2009.* Washington, DC: U.S. Department of Justice.

Bureau of Labor Statistics. (2011). *Occupational outlook handbook 2010–2011: Probation officers and correctional treatment specialists.* Washington, DC: U.S. Department of Labor.

Bureau of Labor Statistics. (2012). *Occupational outlook handbook* (2012–13 edition). Retrieved from http://www.bls.gov/ooh

Burger, W. E. (1983). Commencement address: Warren E. Burger. *Pace Law Review, 4*(1), 1–9.

Burke, P. B. (1997). *Policy-driven responses to probation and parole violations.* Washington, DC: National Institute of Corrections.

Burrell, B. (2006). *Caseload standards for probation and parole.* Washington, DC: National Institute of Corrections.

Butterfield, F. (2003). Prison policy put priest in unit with his killer, experts say. *New York Times.* Retrieved from: http://www.nytimes.com/2003/08/29/us/prison-policy-put-priest-in-unit-with-his-killer-experts-say.html?pagewanted=1

Bynam, J. E., & Thompson, W. E. (1992). *Juvenile delinquency* (2nd ed.). Boston: Allyn & Bacon.

Cahill, A. J. (2001). *Rethinking rape.* Ithaca, NY: Cornell University Press.

Camp, C., & Camp, G. (2003). *The 2002 corrections yearbook: Adult corrections.* Middletown, CT: Criminal Justice Institute.

Campbell, D. T., & Stanley, J. C. (1963). *Experimental and quasi-experimental designs for research.* Boston: Houghton Mifflin.

Carlson, P. M., & DiIulio, J. J. (2008). Organizational management. In P. M. Carlson & J. S. Garrett (Eds.),

Prison and jail administration: Practice and theory (pp. 193–212). Boston: Jones & Bartlett.

Carlson, P. M., & Garrett, J. S. (Eds.). (1999). *Prison and jail administration: Practice and theory*. Gaithersburg, MD: Aspen.

Carlson, P. M., & Garrett, J. S. (Eds.). (2008). *Prison and jail administration* (2nd ed.). Gaithersburg, MD: Aspen.

Carlson, P. M., Roth, T., & Travisono, A. P. (2008). History of corrections. In P. M. Carlson & J. S. Garrett (Eds.), *Prison and jail administration* (2nd ed.). Gaithersburg, MD: Aspen.

Carp, R., & Stidham, R. (1990). *Judicial process in America*. Washington, DC: Congressional Quarterly Press.

Carroll, L. (1996). Lease system. In M. D. McShane & F. P. Williams (Eds.), *Encyclopedia of American prisons* (pp. 446–452). London: Taylor & Francis.

Carter, R. (1996). Determinate sentences. In M. D. McShane & F. P. Williams (Eds.), *Encyclopedia of American prisons* (pp. 237–240). Taylor & Francis.

Cavan, R. S. (1969). *Juvenile delinquency: Development, treatment, control* (2nd ed.). Philadelphia: J. B. Lippincott.

Center for Sex Offender Management. (2008). *An overview of sex offender treatment for a non-clinical audience*. Washington, DC: Office of Justice Programs, U.S. Department of Justice.

Center for Substance Abuse Treatment. (2005). *Substance abuse treatment for adults in the criminal justice system*. Treatment Improvement Protocol (TIP) Series 44. DHHS Publication No. (SMA) 05-4056. Rockville, MD: Substance Abuse and Mental Health Services Administration.

Centers for Disease Control and Prevention. (2003). *Prevention and control of infections with hepatitis viruses in correctional settings*. Atlanta, GA: U.S. Department of Health and Human Services.

Champion, D. (2002). *Probation, parole and community corrections* (4th ed.). Upper Saddle River, NJ: Prentice Hall.

Chen, M. K., & Shapiro, J. M. (2002). *Does prison harden inmates? A discontinuity-based approach*. Retrieved from http://129.3.20.41/eps/le/papers/0304/0304003.pdf

Clear, T. R., & Cole, G. F. (2002). *American corrections* (6th ed.). Belmont, CA: Wadsworth.

Clear, T. R., Cole, G. F., & Reisig, M. D. (2005). *American corrections* (7th ed.). Belmont, CA: Wadsworth.

Clear, T. R., Cole, G. F., & Reisig, M. D. (2008). *American corrections* (8th ed.). Belmont, CA: Wadsworth.

Cochran, J. K., Chamlin, M. B., & Seth, M. (1994). Deterrence or brutalization: An impact assessment of Oklahoma's return to capital punishment. *Criminology, 32,* 107–133.

Cohen, L., & Felson, M. (1979). Social change and crime rate trends: A routine activity approach. *American Sociological Review, 44*(4), 588–608.

Coker v. Georgia, 433 U.S. 584 (1977).

Coley, R. J., & Barton, P. E. (2006). *Locked up and locked out: An educational perspective on the U.S. prison population*. Princeton, NJ: Educational Testing Service. Retrieved June 28, 2010, from http://www.ets.org/Media/Research/pdf/PICLOCKEDUP.pdf

Collins, W. C. (2004). *Supermax prisons and the Constitution: Liability concerns in the extended control unit*. Washington, DC: National Institute of Corrections.

Colorado Division of Criminal Justice. (2007). *Evidence based correctional practices*. Denver, CO: Office of Research and Statistics.

Connecticut Department of Correction. (2010). *Administrative directive 10.18: Nutrition and food services*. Wethersfield, CT: Author.

Contardo, J., & Tolbert, M. (2010). *Prison postsecondary education: Bridging learning from incarceration to the community*. Retrieved June 19, 2012, from http://www.urban.org/projects/reentry-roundtable/upload/Contardo.pdf

Cooper v. Pate, 378 U.S. 546 (1964).

Cox, S. D. (2009). *The big house: Image and reality of the American prison*. New Haven, CT: Yale University Press.

Cox, S., Allen, J., Hanser, R., & Conrad, C. (2011). *Juvenile justice: A guide to theory, policy, and practice* (8th ed.). Thousand Oaks, CA: Sage.

Crawford, J. (2003). Alternative sentencing necessary for female inmates with children. *Corrections Today*. Retrieved from http://www.aca.org/publications/ctarchivespdf/june03/commentary_june.pdf

Cressey, D. R., & Irwin, J. (1962). Thieves, convicts and the inmate culture. *Social Problems, 10*(3), 142–155.

Crist, D., & Spencer, D. (1991). *Perimeter security for Minnesota correctional facilities*. St. Paul: Minnesota Department of Corrections.

Cromwell, P., Carmen, R., & Alarid, L. (2002). *Community-based corrections* (5th ed.). Belmont, CA: Wadsworth.

Crouch, B. M., & Marquart, J. W. (1989). *An appeal to justice: Litigated reform of Texas prisons*. Austin: University of Texas Press.

Cruz v. Beto, 405 U.S. 319 (1972).

Cullen, F. T., & Agnew, R. (2006). *Criminological theory: Past to present* (3rd ed.). Los Angeles: Roxbury.

Cutter v. Wilkinson, 544 U.S. 709 (2005).

Dammer, H. R. (2002). Religion in corrections. In D. Levinson (Ed.), *The encyclopedia of crime and punishment* (Vol. 3, p. 1375). Thousand Oaks, CA: Sage. Retrieved from http://academic.scranton.edu/faculty/DAMMERH2/ency-religion.html

Davis, A. J. (1982). Sexual assaults in the Philadelphia prison system and sheriff's vans. In A. M. Scacco Jr. (Ed.), *Male rape: A casebook of sexual aggressions*. New York: AMS Press.

Davis, S. F., & Palladino, J. J. (2002). *Psychology* (3rd ed.). Upper Saddle River, NJ: Prentice Hall.

Debro, J. (2007). The future of sentencing. In P. M. Carlson & J. S. Garrett (Eds.), *Prison and jail administration: Practice and theory* (pp. 503–510). Boston: Jones & Bartlett.

Death Penalty Information Center. (2004). *Constitutionality of the death penalty in America*. Retrieved from http://deathpenaltycurriculum.org/student/c/about/history/history-5.htm

Death Penalty Information Center. (2010). *Facts about the death penalty*. Washington, DC: Author.

DeJong, C., & Jackson, K. (1998). Putting race into context: Race, juvenile justice processing and urbanization. *Justice Quarterly, 15,* 487–504.

Del Carmen, R. V., Barnhill, M. B., Bonham, G., Hignite, L., & Jermstad, T. (2001). *Civil liabilities and other legal issues for probation/parole officers and supervisors*. Washington, DC: National Institute of Corrections.

Del Carmen, R. V., Ritter, S. E., & Witt, B. A. (2005). *Briefs of leading cases in corrections* (4th ed.). Anderson Publishing.

Department of Education. (1995). *Pell grants for prisoners.* Washington, DC: Author.

Dinitz, S. (2008). *The transformation of corrections: 50 years of silent revolutions.* Washington, DC: National Institute of Corrections.

Directorium Inquisitorum, edition of 1578, Book 3, page 137, column 1. Online in the Cornell University Collection. Retrieved May 16, 2008.

Dolan, L., Kolthoff, K., Schreck, M., Smilanch, P., & Todd, R. (2003). Gender-specific treatment for clients with co-occurring disorders. *Corrections Today, 65*(6), 100–107.

Dorne, C., & Gewerth, K. (1998). *American juvenile justice: Cases, legislation, and comments,* San Francisco: Austin & Winfield.

Drowns, R., & Hess, K. M. (1990). *Juvenile justice.* St. Paul, MN: West.

Duncan, M. G. (1999). *Romantic outlaws, beloved prisons: The unconscious meanings of crime and punishment.* New York: New York University Press.

Dressler, D. (1962). *Practice and theory of probation and parole.* New York: Columbia University Press.

Ecenbarger, W. (1994). Perfecting death: When the state kills it must do so humanely: Is that possible? *The Philadelphia Inquirer,* January 23.

Engelbert, P. (2001, July/August). Women in prison. *Agenda.* Retrieved from http://www-personal.umich.edu/~lormand/agenda/0107/womenprison.htm

English, D. J., Widom, C. S., & Brandford, C. (2002). *Childhood victimization and delinquency, adult criminality, and violent criminal behavior: A replication and extension.* Final report presented to the National Institute of Justice, Grant No. 97-IJ-CX-0017.

Estelle v. Gamble, 429 U.S. 97 (1976).

Etter, S. (2005). *Technology redefined: 2005 in review.* Quincy, MA: Corrections.com. Retrieved from http://www.corrections.com/news/article/6274

Fabelo, T. (1999). *Elderly offenders in Texas prisons.* Austin: Texas Department of Criminal Justice.

Farmer v. Brennan, 511 U.S. 825 (1994).

Faust, F. L., & Brantingham, P. J. (1974). *Juvenile justice philosophy.* St. Paul, MN : West.

Federal Bureau of Investigation. (2006). *Uniform crime reporting program data: Arrests by age, sex, and race, 2004* [Computer file] (ICPSR04460-v2). Washington, DC: Author.

Federal Bureau of Prisons. (2001). *CFR Title 28, Part 524.* Washington, DC: Author. Retrieved from http://www.access.gpo.gov/nara/cfr/waisidx_01/28cfr524_01.html

Federal Bureau of Prisons. (2006). Program statement: Bureau of Prisons inmate classification system. Washington, DC: Author.

Federal Bureau of Prisons. (2010a). *The Bureau celebrates 80th anniversary.* Washington, DC: U.S. Department of Justice. Retrieved from http://www.bop.gov/about/history/first_years.jsp

Federal Bureau of Prisons. (2010b). *Quick facts about the Bureau of Prisons.* Washington, DC: U.S. Department of Justice.

Feeley, M. M., & Little, D. L. (1991). The vanishing female: The decline of women in the criminal process, 1687–1912. *Law & Society Review, 24,* 719–757.

Festinger, L. (1958). The motivating effect of cognitive dissonance. In L. Gardner (Ed.), *Assessment of human motives* (pp. 69–85). New York: Holt.

Fleisher, M. S. (2008). Gang management in corrections. In P. M. Carlson & J. S. Garrett (Eds.), *Prison and jail administration: Practice and theory* (2nd ed.). Gaithersburg, MD: Aspen.

Fleisher, M. S., & Rison, R. H. (1999). Inmate work and consensual management in the Federal Bureau of Prisons. In D. Van Zyl Smit & F. Dunkel, (Eds.), *Prison labour—Salvation or slavery?* In *International Perspectives.* London: Dartmouth Onati International Series in Law and Society.

Fletcher, M. A. (1999, July 22). Putting more people in prison can increase crime: Study says communities suffer when too many men gone. *Washington Post.* Retrieved from http://www.sfgate.com/cgi-bin/article.cgi?f=/c/a/1999/07/22/MN90235.DTL&ao=all

Flores, A. W., Travis, L. F., & Latessa, E. J. (2003). *Case classification for juvenile corrections: An assessment of the Youth Level of Service/Case Management Inventory (YLS/CMI).* Cincinnati, OH: Center for Criminal Justice Research.

Ford v. Wainwright, 477 U.S. 399 (1986).

Franklin, C. A., Fearn, N. E., & Franklin, T. W. (2005). *Californian Journal of Health Promotion, 3*(2), 99–112.

Freedman, E. B. (1981). *Their sisters' keepers: Women's prison reform in America, 1830–1930.* Ann Arbor: University of Michigan Press.

Friel, C. M. (2008). *Advanced research design.* Retrieved from www.shsu.edu/~icc_cmf

Fulwood v. Clemmer, 206 F. Supp. 370—Dist. Court, Dist. of Columbia (1962).

Furman v. Georgia, 408 U.S. 238 (1972).

Gacono, C. B., Nieberding, R. J., Owen, A., Rubel, J. Bodholdt, R. (2001). Treating conduct disorder, antisocial, and psychopathic personalities. In J. B. Ashford, B. D. Sales, & W. H. Reid (Eds.), *Treating adults and juvenile offenders with special needs.* Washington, DC: American Psychological Association.

Gagnon v. Scarpelli 411 U.S. 778 (1973).

Garrett, J. S. (2008). Working with the media. In P. M. Carlson & J. S. Garrett (Eds.), *Prison and jail administration: Practice and theory.* Sudbury, MA: Jones & Bartlett.

Gates v. Collier, 501 F.2d 1291 (5th cir. 1974).

General Accounting Office. (1990). *Death penalty sentencing: Research indicates pattern of racial disparities.* Washington, DC: Author.

George, R. S. (2008). Prison architecture. In P. M. Carlson & J. S. Garrett (Ed.), *Prison and jail administration* (2nd ed., pp. 39–50). Gaithersburg, MD: Aspen.

Giever, D. (2006). Jails. In J. M. Pollock (Ed.), *Prisons today and tomorrow* (2nd ed.). Sudbury, MA: Jones & Bartlett.

Gillespie, W. (2002). *Prisonization: Individual and institutional factors affecting inmate conduct.* city, state LFB Scholarly.

Glaser, D. (1964). *The effectiveness of a prison and parole system.* New York: Macmillan.

Glaze, L. E., & Bonzcar, T. P. (2006). *Probation and parole in the United States, 2005.* Washington, DC: U.S. Department of Justice.

Glaze, L. E., & Bonczar, T. P. (2009). *Probation and Parole in the United States, 2008*. Washington, DC: U.S. Department of Justice.

Glaze, L. E., & Bonczar, T. P. (2011). *Probation and parole in the United States, 2010*. Washington, DC: U.S. Department of Justice.

Glaze, L. E., & Palla, S. (2005). *Probation and parole in the United States, 2004*. Washington, DC: U.S. Department of Justice, Bureau of Justice Statistics.

Gluck, S. (1997, June). Wayward youth, super predator: An evolutionary tale of juvenile delinquency from the 1950s to the present. *Corrections Today, 59*, 62–64.

Goldberg, R. (2003). *Drugs across the spectrum* (4th ed.). Belmont, CA: Wadsworth.

Golub, A. (1990). *The termination rate of adult criminal careers*. Pittsburgh, PA: Carnegie Mellon University Press.

Gordon, M., & Glaser, D. (1991). The use and effects of financial penalties in municipal courts. *Criminology, 29*, 651–676.

GovTrack.us. (2010). *110th Congress 2007–2008*. Washington, DC: Author. Retrieved from http://www.govtrack.us/congress/bill.xpd?bill=s110-3294

General Accounting Office. (1990a). *Death penalty sentencing: Research indicates pattern of racial disparities*. Washington, DC: General Accounting Office.

Government Accounting Office. (1990b). *Intermediate sanctions*. Washington, DC: Author.

Graham v. Florida, 08-7412, 560 U. S. _____ (2010).

Gramsci, A. (1996). *Prison notebooks* (J. Buttigieg, trans.). New York: Columbia University Press.

Greek, C. (2002). The cutting edge: Tracking probationers in space and time: The convergence of GIS and GPS systems. *Federal Probation, 66,* 51–53.

Greenwood, A. (2008). Taste-testing Nutraloaf: The prison food that just might be unconstitutionally bad. *Slate*. Retrieved from http://www.slate.com/id/2193538/

Gregg v. Georgia. 428 U.S. 153 (1976).

Griffin, B. S., & Griffin, C. T. (1978). *Juvenile delinquency in perspective*. New York: Harper & Row.

Guccione, J. (2002). Doing their time in the working world: Restitution center is for women who stole. They pay their debts, avoid prison. *Los Angeles Times*, April 15. Retrieved from http://articles.latimes.com/2002/apr/15/local/me-debt15

Haas, S. M., Hamilton, C. A., & Hanley, D. (2006, July). Implementation of the West Virginia Offender Reentry Initiative: An examination of staff attitudes and the application of the LSI-R. Charleston, WV: Mountain State Criminal Justice Research Services.

Hagan, F. (2000). *Research methods in criminal justice and criminology* (5th ed.). Needham Heights, MA: Allyn & Bacon.

Hanser, R. D. (2002). Inmate suicide in prisons: An analysis of legal liability under Section 1983. *The Prison Journal, 82*(4), 459–477.

Hanser, R. D. (2007). *Special needs offenders in the community*. Upper Saddle River, NJ: Prentice Hall.

Hanser, R. D. (2010a). Adrian Raine: Crime as a disorder. In F. T. Cullen & P. Wilcox (Eds.), *Encyclopedia of criminological theory*. Thousand Oaks, CA: Sage.

Hanser, R. D. (2010b). *Community corrections*. Thousand Oaks, CA: Sage.

Hanser, R. D., & Mire, S. (2010). *Correctional counseling*. Upper Saddle River, NJ: Pearson/Prentice Hall.

Hanser, R. D., & Moran, N. R. (2004). Labeling theory as an etiological paradigm for prison rape. In F. P. Reddington & B. W. Kreisel (Eds.), *Sexual assault: The victims, the perpetrators and the criminal justice system*. Durham, NC: Carolina Academic Press.

Hanson, G.R., Venturelli, P. J., & Fleckenstein, A. E. (2006). *Drugs and society* (9th ed.). Burlington, MA: Jones & Bartlett.

Hanson, G, Venturelli, P. J., & Fleckenstein, A. E. (2011). *Drugs and society* (11th ed.). Burlington, MA: Jones & Bartlett.

Harer, M. D. (1995, May). *Prison education program participation and recidivism: A test of the normalization hypothesis*. Washington, DC: Federal Bureau of Prisons.

Harer, M. D., & Steffensmeier, D. J. (1996). Rates of prison violence. *Criminology, 34*(3), 323–351.

Harlow, C. W. (1999). *Prior abuse reported by inmates and probationers*. Washington, DC: Bureau of Justice Statistics.

Harrison, P. M., & Beck, A. J. (2003). *Prisoners in 2002*. Washington, DC: Bureau of Justice Statistics.

Harrison, P., & Beck, A. (2005). *Prisoners in 2004*. Washington, DC: Bureau of Justice Statistics.

Harrison, P. M., & Beck, A. J. (2006a, May). *Prison and jail inmates at midyear 2005* (NCJ 213133). Washington, DC: U.S. Department of Justice, Office of Justice Programs, Bureau of Justice Statistics. Retrieved May 7, 2007, from http://www.ojp.usdoj.gov/bjs/abstract/pjim05.htm

Harrison, P. M., & Beck, A. J. (2006b, November). *Prisoners in 2005* (NCJ 215092). Washington, DC: U.S. Department of Justice, Office of Justice Programs, Bureau of Justice Statistics. Retrieved May 7, 2007, from http://www.ojp.usdoj.gov/bjs/abstract/p05.htm

Harrison, P. M., & Karberg, J. C. (2004). *Prison and jail inmates at midyear 2003*. Washington, DC: Bureau of Justice Statistics.

Hartney, C. (2007). *The nation's most punitive states for women*. Oakland, CA: National Council on Crime and Delinquency.

Hatton, J. (2006). *Betsy: The dramatic biography of prison reformer Elizabeth Fry*. city, state Kregel.

Hercik, J. M. (2007). *Prisoner reentry, religion, and research*. Washington, DC: U.S. Department of Health and Human Services.

Hochstellar, A., & DeLisa, M. (2005). Importation, deprivation, and varieties of serving time: An integrated-lifestyle-exposure model of prison offending. *Journal of Criminal Justice, 33*(3), 257–266.

Hoffman, P. B. (2003). *History of the federal parole system*. Washington, DC: U.S. Parole Commission.

Holsinger, A. M., Lowenkamp, C. T., & Latessa, E. J. (2004). Validating the LSI-R on a sample of jail inmates. *Journal of Offender Monitoring*, Winter/Spring, 8–9.

Holt v. Sarver I, 300 F. Supp. 825 (1969).

Holt v. Sarver II, 309 F. Supp. 362 (1970).

Hsia, H. M. (2004). *Disproportionate minority confinement 2002 update*. Washington, DC: Office of Juvenile Justice and Delinquency Prevention.

Hudson v. Palmer, 468 U.S. 517 (1984).

Hughes, E. C. (1945). Dilemmas and contradictions of status. *American Journal of Sociology*, March, 353–359.

Huizinga, D., Thornberry, T., Knight, K., & Lovegrove, P. (2007). *Disproportionate minority contact in the juvenile justice system: A study of differential minority arrest/referral to court in three cities*. Washington, DC: U.S. Department of Justice.

Human Rights Watch. (1996). *All too familiar, sexual abuse of women in U.S. state prisons*. New Haven, CT: Yale University Press.

Human Rights Watch. (1999). *Nowhere to hide: Retaliation against women in Michigan state prisons*. Retrieved from http://www.hrw.org/reports98/women/Mich.htm

Human Rights Watch. (2001). *No escape: Male rape in U.S. prisons*. Retrieved April 10, 2002, from http://www.hrw.org/reports/2001/prison/report.html

Hutto v. Finney, 437 U.S. 678 (1978).

Inciardi, J. A., Rivers, J. E., & McBride, D. C. (2008). *Drug treatment*. In P. M. Carslon & J. S. Garrett (Eds.), *Prison and jail administration: Practice and theory* (2nd ed.). Gaithersberg, MD: Aspen.

Ingram, G. L., & Carlson, P. M. (2008). Sex offenders. In P. M. Carlson & J. S. Garrett (Eds.), *Prison and jail administration* (2nd ed.). Gaithersburg, MD: Aspen.

International Association for Chiefs of Police. (2008). *Tracking sex offenders with modern technology: Implications and practical uses with law enforcement*. Alexandria, VA: Author.

In re Gault, 387 U.S. 1 (1967).

Ireland, T. O., Smith, C. A., & Thornberry, T. P. (2002). Developmental issues in the impact of child maltreatment on later delinquency and drug use. *Criminology, 40*(2), 359–399.

Jail Equipment World. (2010). *Security convection ovens*. Orlando, FL: Author. Retrieved from http://www.jailequipmentworld.com/

James, D. J., & Glaze, L. E. (2001). *Mental health problems of prison and jail inmates*. Washington, DC: Bureau of Justice Statistics.

James, D. J., & Glaze, L. E. (2006). *Mental health problems of prison and jail inmates*. Washington, DC: Bureau of Justice Statistics.

Johnson, B. R., & Larson, D. B. (2003). *The InnerChange Freedom Initiative: A preliminary evaluation of America's first faith based prison*. University of Pennsylvania, CRRUCS.

Johnson, B. R., Larson, D. B., & Pitts, T. C. (1997). Religious programs, institutional adjustment, and recidivism among former inmates in prison fellowship programs. *Justice Quarterly, 14*(1), 10–24.

Johnson, H. A., Wolfe, N., & Jones, M. (2008). *History of criminal justice* (4th ed.). Southington, CT: Anderson.

Johnson, L. B. (2008). Food service. In P. M. Carlson & J. S. Garrett (Eds.), *Prison and jail administration: Practice and theory* (pp. 149–158). Sudbury, MA: Jones & Bartlett.

Johnson, R., & Dobrzanska, A. (2005). *Life with the possibility of life: Mature coping among life-sentence prisoners*. Paper presented at the annual meeting of the American Society of Criminology, Royal York, Toronto. Retrieved October 26, 2009, from http://www.allacademic.com/meta/p31858_index.html

Johnston, N. (2009). *Prison reform in Pennsylvania*. Philadelphia: Pennsylvania Prison Society. Retrieved from http://www.prisonsociety.org/about/history.shtml

Johnson, S. C. (1999). Mental health services in a correctional setting. In P. M. Carlson & J. S. Garrett (Eds.), *Prison and jail administration* (2nd ed., pp. 107–116). Gaithersburg, MD: Aspen.

Johnson v. Avery, 393 U.S. 483 (1969).

Jones, J. (2007). *Pre-release planning and re-entry process: Addendum 02*. Tulsa: Oklahoma Department of Corrections.

Josi, D. A., & Sechrest, D. K. (1998). *The changing career of the correctional officer: Policy implications for the 21st century*. Boston: Butterworth-Heinemann.

Justice Policy Institute. (2008). *Substance abuse treatment and public safety*. Washington, DC: Author.

Kaftan, S. D. (2007). Management is not leadership. In P. K. Withrow (Ed.), *A view from the trenches: A manual for wardens by wardens* (2nd ed., pp. 1–7). Alexandria, VA: American Correctional Association.

Karberg, J. C., & James, D. J. (2005). *Substance dependence, abuse, and treatment of jail inmates, 2002*. Washington, DC: U.S. Department of Justice.

Karpowitz, D., & Kenner, M. (2001). *Education as crime prevention: The case for reinstating Pell Grant eligibility for the incarcerated*. Annandale-on-Hudson, NY: Bard College.

Kauffman, K. (1988). *Prison officers and their world*. Cambridge, MA: Harvard University Press.

Keel, R. O. (2005). *Rational choice and deterrence theory*. Retrieved May 14, 2012, from http://www.umsl.edu/~keelr/200/ratchoc.html

Kent v. United States, 383 U.S. 541 (1966).

Kerle, K. (1999). Short term institutions at the local level. In P. M. Carlson & J. S. Garrett (Eds.), *Prison and jail administration: Practice and theory*. Gaithersburg, MD: Aspen.

Kerle, K. (1982). Rural jail: Its people, problems and solutions. In D. Shanler (Ed.), *Criminal justice in rural America* (pp. 189–204). Washington, DC: National Institute of Justice.

Knowles, G. J. (1999). Male prison rape: A search for causation and prevention. *Howard Journal of Criminal Justice, 38*(3), 267–283.

Kohen, A., & Jolly, S. K. (2006). *Deterrence reconsidered: A theoretical and empirical case against the death penalty*. Paper presented at the annual meeting of the Midwest Political Science Association, Palmer House Hilton, Chicago. Retrieved from http://www.allacademic.com/meta/p140213_index.html

Kupers, T. (1999). *Prison madness: The mental health crisis behind bars and what we must do about it*. San Francisco: Jossey-Bass.

Kurshan, N. (1996). *Women and imprisonment in the U.S. History and current reality*. Retrieved August 12, 2006, from http://www.prisonactivist.org/archive/women/women-and-imprisonment.html

Labecki, L. S. (1994). Monitoring hostility: Avoiding prison disturbances through environmental scanning. *Corrections Today, 56*(5), 104, 106, 108–111.

Latessa, E. J., & Allen, H. E. (1999). *Corrections in the community* (2nd ed.). Cincinnati, OH: Anderson.

LeMaire v. Maass, 12 F. 3d 1444—9th Circuit (1993).

Lemert, E. M. (1999). Primary and secondary deviance. In S. H. Traub & C. B. Little (Eds.), *Theories of deviance* (pp. 385–390). Itasca, IL: Peacock.

Lempert, R. O., & Visher, C. A. (Eds.). (1987). *Randomized field experiments in criminal justice agencies:*

Workshop proceedings. Washington, DC: National Research Council.

Levinson, D. (Ed.). (2002). *The encyclopedia of crime and punishment* (Vol. 3). Thousand Oaks, CA: Sage.

Lilly, J. R., Cullen, F. T., & Ball, R. A. (2007). *Criminological theory: Context and consequences* (4th ed.). Thousand Oaks, CA: Sage.

Lindemuth, A. L. (2007). Designing therapeutic environments for inmates and prison staff in the United States: Precedents and contemporary applications. *Journal of Mediterranean Ecology, 8,* 87–97.

Linder, D. (2005). *A history of witchcraft persecutions before Salem.* Retrieved from http://law2.umkc.edu/faculty/projects/Ftrials/salem/witchhistory.html

Lindner, C. (2006). John Augustus, father of probation, and the anonymous letter. *Federal Probation, 70*(1), 150–165.

Lindquist, C. H., & Lindquist, C. A. (1999). Health behind bards: Utilization and evaluation of medical care among jail inmates. *Journal of Community Health, 24,* 285–303.

Little Hoover Commission. (2004). *Breaking the barriers for women on parole.* Sacramento, CA. Retrieved from http://www.lhc.ca.gov/lhcdir/177/execsum177.pdf

Ludwig, F. J. (1955). *Youth and the law: Handbook on laws affecting youth.* Brooklyn, NY: Foundation Press.

MacCormick, A. (1931). *The education of adult prisoners: A survey and a program* [Reprint 1976]. New York: AMS Press.

Madrid v. Gomez, 889 F. Supp. 1146 (1995).

Males, M., & Macallair, D. (2000). *The color of justice: An analysis of juvenile adult court transfer in California.* Washington, DC: Youth Law Center.

Martinson, R. (1974). What works? Questions and answers about prison reform. *Public Interest, 35.*

Maruschak, L. M. (2006). *Medical problems of jail inmates.* Washington, DC: U.S. Department of Justice, Office of Justice Programs.

Mays, G. L., & Winfree, L. T., Jr. (2002). *Contemporary corrections* (2nd ed.). Belmont, CA: Wadsworth/Thomson Learning.

McCollister, K. E., & French, M. T. (2001). *The economic cost of substance abuse treatment in criminal justice settings.* Miami, FL: University of Miami.

McGarry, P. (1990). *NIC focus: Intermediate sanctions.* Washington, DC: National Institute of Corrections.

McGraw-Hill. (2010). *Test of Adult Basic Education TABE.* Columbus, OH: CTB Research.

McKeiver v. Pennsylvania, 403 U.S. 528 (1971).

McNeece, C. A., Springer, D. W., & Arnold, E. M. (2002). Treating substance abuse disorders. In J. B. Ashford, B. D. Sales, & W. H. Reid (Eds.), *Treating adult and juvenile offenders with special needs* (pp. 131–170). Washington, DC: American Psychological Association.

McNeil, D. E., Binder, R. L., & Robinson, J. C. (2005). Incarceration associated with homelessness, mental disorder, and co-occurring substance abuse. *Psychiatric Services, 56,* 840–846.

McShane, M. D. (1996a). Chain gangs. In M. D. McShane & F. P. Williams (Eds.), *Encyclopedia of American prisons* (pp. 144–117). London: Taylor & Francis.

McShane, M. D. (1996b). Historical background. In M. D. McShane & F. P. Williams (Eds.), *Encyclopedia of American prisons* (pp. 455–457). London: Taylor & Francis.

Mears, B. (2003). *Supreme Court upholds sex offender registration laws.* Retrieved from http://www.cnn.com/2003/LAW/03/05/scotus.sex.offenders/index.html

Meko, J. A. (2008). A day in the life of a warden. In P. M. Carlson & J. S. Garrett (Eds.), *Prison and jail administration* (2nd ed.). Gaithersburg, MD: Aspen.

Merton, R. K. (1938). Social structure and anomie. *American Sociological Review, 3,* 672–682.

Messerschmidt, J. A. (1999). Masculinities and crime. In F. T. Cullen & R. Agnew (Eds.), *Criminological theory: Past to present.* Los Angeles: Roxbury.

Messner, S. F., & Rosenfeld, R. (2001). *Crime and the American dream* (3rd ed.). Belmont, CA: Wadsworth.

Michigan Department of Corrections. (2003). *Michigan presentence investigation.* Lansing, MI: Author. Retrieved from http://courts.michigan.gov/scao/resources/publications/manuals/prbofc/prb_sec4.pdf

Middle Tennessee State University. (2007). *Monitoring Tennessee's sex offenders using global positioning systems: A project evaluation.* Nashville: Author.

Miller, B. A., Nochajski, T. H., Leonard, K. E., Blane, H. T., Gondoii, D. M., & Bowers, P. M. (1990). Spousal violence and alcohol/drug problems among parolees and their spouses. *Women and Criminal Justice, 2,* 55–72.

Miller, W. (1958). Lower class culture as a generating milieu of gang delinquency. *Journal of Social Issues, 14,* 5–19.

Minton, T. D. (2011). *Jail inmates at midyear 2010.* Washington, DC: Bureau of Justice Statistics.

Mire, S. M., Forsyth, C., & Hanser, R. D. (2007). Jail diversion: Addressing the needs of offenders with mental illness and co-occurring disorders. *Journal of Offender Rehabiliation, 45(1/2),* 19–31.

Mitchell, M. (2011). Texas prison boom going bust. *Star-Telegram.* Retrieved from http://www.star-telegram.com/2011/09/03/3335901/texas-prison-boom-going-bust.html

Mobley, A. (2011). Garbage in, garbage out? Convict criminology, the convict code, and participatory prison reform. In M. Maquire & D. Okada (Eds.), *Critical issues in crime and justice: Thought, policy, and practice.* Los Angeles: Sage.

Moffitt, T. E. (1990). The neuropsychology of juvenile delinquency: A critical review. In M. Troney & N. Morris (Eds.), *Crime and justice: A review of research.* Chicago: University of Chicago Press.

Moffitt, T. E. (1993). Adolescence-limited and life-course persistent antisocial behavior: A developmental taxonomy. *Psychological Review, 100,* 674–701.

Montana Department of Corrections. (2010). *Recreation Programs DOC 5.5.3.* Helena: Author.

Morgan, D. W. (2004). *Whips and whipmaking.* Centreville, MD: Cornell Maritime Press.

Morris, N., & Rothman, D. J. (2000). *The Oxford history of prison.* New York: Oxford University Press.

Morris v. Travisono, 310 F.Supp. 857 (1970).

Morrissey v. Brewer 408 U.S. 471 (1972).

Morton, J. B. (1992). *An administrative overview of the older inmate.* Washington, DC: National Institute of Corrections.

Mumola, C. J. (2000, August). *Incarcerated parents and their children* (NCJ 182335). Washington, DC: U.S. Department of Justice, Office of Justice Programs, Bureau of Justice Statistics. Retrieved May 8, 2007, from http://www.ojp.usdoj.gov/bjs/abstract/iptc.htm

Murphy, J. F. (2008). Medellin v. Texas: Implications of the supreme court's decision for the United States and the rule of law in international affairs. Suffolk University: *Suffolk Transnational Law Review, 31*, 247–663.

Myers, P. L., & Salt, N. R. (2000). *Becoming an addictions counselor: A comprehensive text*. Burlington, MA: Jones & Bartlett.

Nacci, P. (2000). *Telemedicine can reduce correctional healthcare costs: An evaluation of a prison telemedicine network*. Washington, DC: National Institute of Justice.

Nacci, P. L., Turner, C. A., Waldron, R. J., & Broyles, E. (2002). *Implementing telemedicine in correctional facilities*. Washington, DC: U.S. Department of Justice.

National Advisory Commission on Criminal Justice Standards and Goals. (1973). *Corrections*. Washington, DC: Government Printing Office.

National Center for Women and Policing. (2003). *Hiring and retaining more women: The advantages to law enforcement agencies*. Beverly Hills, CA: Author.

National Commission on Correctional Health Care (NCCHC). (2002). *The health status of soon-to-be-released inmates: A report to Congress*. Chicago: Author

National Gang Intelligence Center. (2009). *National gang threat assessment 2009: Prison gangs*. *Washington, DC*: Retrieved January 22, 2010, from http://www.justice.gov/ndic/pubs32/32146/appc.htm#start

National Institute of Corrections. (1986). *Protective custody: Data update and intervention considerations*. Washington, DC: Author.

National Institute of Corrections. (1993). *The intermediate sanctions handbook: Experiences and tools for policymakers*. Washington, DC: Author.

National Institute of Corrections. (1995). *Corrections information series: Unit management*. Washington, DC: Author. Retrieved from http://www.nicic.org/pubs/pre/000159.pdf

National Institute of Corrections. (2001). *NIC research on small jail issues: Summary findings*. Washington, DC: U.S. Department of Justice.

National Institute of Justice. (1992). *Evaluating drug control and system improvement projects: Guidelines for projects supported by the Bureau of Justice Assistance*. Washington, DC: U.S. Department of Justice.

National Institute of Justice. (1998). *Restorative justice: An interview with visiting fellow Thomas Quinn*. Washington, DC: U.S. Department of Justice.

National Institute of Justice. (2005). *Implementing evidence based practice in corrections*. Washington, DC: U.S. Department of Justice.

National Law Enforcement and Corrections Technology Center. (2005). *Technology primer: Radio frequency identification*. Washington, DC: National Institute of Justice.

Nelson, K. E., Ohmart, H., & Harlow, N. (1978). *Promising strategies in probation and parole*. Washington, DC: U.S. Government Printing Office.

Neubauer, D. W. (2002). *Courts and the criminal justice system* (8th ed.). Belmont, CA: Wadsworth.

Neubauer, D. W. (2007). *America's courts and the criminal justice system* (9th ed.). Belmont, CA: Wadsworth/Thomson Learning.

New York Correction History Society. (2008). *The nation's first reformatory: Elmira*. New York. Retrieved from http://www.correctionhistory.org/index.html.

Nink, C., Olding, R., Jorgenson, J., & Gilbert, M. (2009). Expanding distance learning access in prisons: A growing need. *Corrections Today, 71*(4), 40-43.

Norman, B. (1991). *Health and safety in the prison environment*. Washington, DC: National Institute of Corrections, National Academy of Corrections, Health Services Division.

Nunez-Neto, B. (2008). *Offender reentry: Correctional statistics, reintegration into the community, and recidivism*. Washington, DC: Congressional Research Service.

Nyquist, O. (1960). *Juvenile justice: A comparative study with special reference to the Swedish Welfare Board and the California juvenile court system*. London: Macmillan.

Office of Justice Programs Drug Court Clearinghouse. (2003). *Drug testing in a drug court environment: Common issues to address*. Washington, DC: U.S. Department of Justice.

Office of National Drug Control Policy. (2001). *Fact sheet: Drug treatment in the criminal justice system*. Washington, DC: Author.

Office of Program Policy Analysis and Governmental Accountability. (2010). *Intermediate sanctions for non-violent offenders could produce savings*. Tallahassee, FL: Author.

O'Lone v. Estate of Shabazz, 482 U.S. 342 (1987).

Olson, L. (2004). An exploration of therapeutic recreation in adult federal medical centers and Wisconsin correctional facilities. *UW-L Journal of Undergraduate Research, VII*, 1–3.

Palmigiano v. Garrahy, 443 F.Supp. 956 (1977).

Patterson, O. (1982). *Slavery and social death: A comparative study*. Cambridge, MA: Harvard University Press.

Peak, K. J. (1995). *Justice administration: Police, courts, and corrections management*. Upper Saddle River, NJ: Prentice Hall.

Philadelphia Prison System. (2010). *About PPS: History of the Philadelphia Prison System*. Retrieved from http://www.phila.gov/prisons/history.htm

Philips, D. E. (2001). *Legendary Connecticut*. Willimantic, CT: Curbstone Press. Retrieved from http://www.curbstone.org/index.cfm?webpage=91

Poe-Yamagata, E., & Jones, M. (2000). *And justice for some: Differential treatment of minority youth in the justice system*. Washington, DC: Youth Law Center.

Pollak, O. (1950). *The criminality of women*. Philadelphia: University of Pennsylvania Press.

Pollock, J. (1986). *Sex and supervision: Guarding male and female inmates*. New York: Greenwood Press.

Pollock, J. (2006). *Prisons today and tomorrow* (2nd ed.). Boston: Jones & Bartlett.

Poore, D. (1994). *Understanding protective management*. Wewahitchka: Florida Department of Corrections.

Retrieved from http://www.fdle.state.fl.us/Content/getdoc/52ffc7a7-6d0f-4340-9419-e9c200c377be/Poore.aspx

Pope, C. E., Lovell, R., & Hsia, H. M. (2003). *Disproportionate minority confinement: A review of the research literature from 1989 through 2001.* Washington, DC: Office of Juvenile Justice and Delinquency Prevention.

PRIDE Enterprises. (2009). *Pride in our mission: 2008 annual report.* St. Petersburg, FL: Prison Rehabilitative Industries and Diversified Enterprises, Inc.

Procunier v. Martinez, 416 U.S. 396 (1974).

Quinney, R. (1991). *Criminology as peacemaking.* city: Indiana University Press.

Rafter, N. H. (1985). *Partial justice: Women in state prisons 1800–1935.* Boston: New England University Press.

Raine, A. (2004). Biological key to unlocking crime. *BBC News.* Retrieved from http://news.bbc.co.uk/2/hi/programmes/if/4102371.stm

Redding, H. (2004). *The components of prison security.* Naples, FL: International Foundation for Protection Officers. Retrieved from http://www.ifpo.org/articlebank/components_prison_security.html

Reiman, J. (2007). *The rich get richer and the poor get prison* (8th ed.). Boston: Allyn & Bacon.

Rice, J. S. (1993). *Self-development and horticultural therapy in a jail setting.* Dissertation, Philosophy, the Professional School of Psychology, San Francisco.

Rideau, W., & Wikberg, R. (1992). *Life sentences: Rage and survival behind bars.* New York: Time Books, Random House.

Riveland, C. (1999). *Supermax prisons: Overview and general considerations.* Washington, DC: National Institute of Corrections.

Robbins, S. P. (2005). *Organizational behavior* (12 ed.). Upper Saddle River, NJ: Prentice Hall.

Robinson, J. J., & Jones, J. W. (2000). *Drug testing in a drug court environment: Common issues to address.* Washington, DC: Office of Justice Programs, Drug Courts Program Office. Retrieved from http://www.ncjrs.gov/pdf.files1/ojp/181103.pdf

Roper v. Simmons. 543 U.S. 551 (2005).

Ross, P. H., & Lawrence, J. E. (2002). Healthcare for women offenders: Challenge for the new century. In R. L. Gido & T. Alleman (Eds.), *Turnstile justice: Issues in American corrections* (pp. 73–88). city, state: Prentice Hall.

Roth, M. P. (2006). Chain gangs. In *Prisons and prison systems: A global encyclopedia* (pp. 56–57). Westport, CT: Greenwood Press.

Roth, M. P. (2011). *Crime and punishment: A history of the criminal justice system.* Belmont, CA: Cengage Learning.

Rowe, D. (2002). *Biology and crime.* Los Angeles: Roxbury.

Ruiz v. Estelle, 503 F. Supp. 1265 (S.D. Tex. 1980).

Sabol, W. J., & Minton, T. D. (2008). *Jail inmates at midyear 2007.* Washington, DC: Bureau of Justice Statistics.

Sabol, W. J., Minton, T. D., & Harrison, P. M. (2008). *Prison and jail inmates at midyear 2006.* Washington, DC: Bureau of Justice Statistics.

Sacks, S., Sacks, J. Y., & Stommel, J. (2003). Modified therapeutic community programs: For inmates with mental illness and chemical abuse disorders. *Corrections Today, 65*(6), 90–100.

Sahagun, L. (2007). A mother's plight revives sanctuary movement. *Los Angeles Times,* June 2.

Samuel, B. (2001). Elizabeth Gurney Fry (1780–1845): Quaker prison reformer. *Quakerinfo.com.* Retrieved from http://www.quakerinfo.com/fry.shtml

Sanders, W. B. (1974). Some early beginnings of the children's court movement in England. In F. L. Faust & P. J. Brantingham (Eds.), *Juvenile justice philosophy* (pp. 46–51). St. Paul, MN: West.

Scacco, A. M., Jr. (1975). *Rape in prison.* Springfield, IL: Charles C. Thomas.

Scacco, A. M. (1982). *Male rape: A case book of sexual aggressions.* New York: AMS Press.

Schlossman, S., & Spillane, J. (1995). *Bright hopes, dim realities: Vocational innovation in American correctional education.* Berkeley, CA: National Center for Research in Vocational Education.

Schur, E. M. (1973). *Radical nonintervention: Rethinking the delinquency problem.* Englewood Cliffs, NJ: Prentice Hall.

Scillia, A. (1994). *Electronic monitoring: A new approach to work release.* Washington, DC: National Institute of Corrections.

Schutt, R. K. (2006). *Investigating the social world: The process and practice of research* (5th ed.). Thousand Oaks, CA: Pine Forge Press.

Scott, E., & Grisso, T. (1997). The evolution of adolescence: A developmental perspective on juvenile justice reform. *Journal of Criminal Law and Criminology, 88,* 137–189.

Sedlak, A. J., & McPherson, K. S. (2010). *Youth's needs and services: Findings from the survey of youth in residential placement.* Washington, DC: Office of Juvenile Justice and Delinquency Prevention.

Seiden, A. M. (1989). Psychological issues affecting women throughout the life cycle. In B. L. Parry (Ed.), *The psychiatric clinics of North America* (pp. 1–24). Philadelphia: W. B. Saunders.

Sellin, T. (1953). Philadelphia prisons of the eighteenth century. *Transactions of the American Philosophical Society, New Series, 43*(Part I), 326–330.

Sellin, T. (1970). The origin of the Pennsylvania system of prison discipline. *Prison Journal, 50*(Spring–Summer), 15–17.

Shusta, R. M., Levine, D. R., Wong, H. Z., & Harris, P. R. (2005). *Multicultural law enforcement: Strategies for peacekeeping in a diverse society* (3rd ed.). Upper Saddle River, NJ: Prentice Hall.

Sieh, E. W. (2006). *Community corrections and human dignity.* Sudbury, Mass.: Jones & Bartlett.

Silverman, I. J. (2001). *Corrections: A comprehensive view* (2nd ed.). Belmont, CA: Wadsworth.

Simms, B. E., Farley, J., & Littlefield, J. F. (1987). *Colleges with fences: A handbook for improving corrections education programs.* Columbus, OH: National Center for Research in Vocational Education.

Simonsen, C. E., & Gordon, M. S. (1982). *Juvenile justice in America* (2nd ed.). New York: Macmillan.

Singh, D., & White, C. (2000). *Rapua te huarahi tika: Searching for solutions: A review of research about effective interventions for reducing offending by indigenous and ethnic minority youth.* New Zealand: Ministry of Youth Affairs.

Smith, P., Goggin, C., & Gendreau, P. (2002). *The effects of prison sentences on recidivism: General effects and individual differences.* Saint John, Canada: Centre for Criminal Justice Studies, University of New Brunswick.

Smith v. Doe 538 U.S. 84 (2003).

Snyder, H. N., & Sickmund, M. (1999, November). *Juvenile offenders and victims: 1999 national report.* Washington, DC: U.S. Department of Justice.

Solomon, L., & Baird, S. C. (1982). Classification: Past failures, future potential. In *Classification as a management tool: Theories and model for decision-makers.* College Park, MD: American Correctional Association.

Spriggs, V. (2003). Identifying and providing services to Texas: Juvenile offenders with mental health needs. *Corrections Today, 65*(1), 64–66.

Stanko, S., Gillespie, W., & Crews, G. (2004). *Living in prison: A history of the correctional system with an insider's view.* Westport, CT: Greenwood Press.

Steadman, H. J. (1987). Mental health law and the criminal offender: Research directions for the 1990s. *Rutgers Law Review, 39,* 323–337.

Stepp, E. A. (2008). Emergency management. In P. M. Carlson & J. S. Garrett (Eds.), *Prison and jail administration: Practice and theory* (pp. 469–478). Boston: Jones & Bartlett.

Steurer, S., Smith, L., & Tracy, A. (2001). *Three state recidivism study.* Washington, DC: Office of Correctional Education, U.S. Department of Education.

Stohr, M., Walsh, A., & Hemmens, C. (Eds.). (2009). *Corrections: A text/reader.* Thousand Oaks, CA: Sage.

Stojkovic, S. (1996). Subculture: Historical background. In M. D. McShane & F. P. Williams (Eds.), *Encyclopedia of American prisons* (pp. 455–457). London: Taylor & Francis.

Surgeon General Executive Summary. (2002). *Youth violence: A report of the Surgeon General.* Washington, DC: Office of the Surgeon General.

Sykes, G. M. (1958). *The pain of imprisonment.* Princeton, NJ: Princeton University Press.

Tannenbaum, F. (1938). *Crime and the community.* Boston: Ginn.

Tartaro, C., & Ruddell, R. (2006). Trouble in Mayberry: A national analysis of suicides and attempts in small jails. *American Journal of Criminal Justice, 31*(1), 81–101.

Tekagi, P. (n.d.). *The Walnut Street Jail: A penal reform to centralize the powers of the state.* Retrieved from http://www.socialjusticejournal.org/pdf_free/Takagi-Walnut_Street_Jail.pdf

Tennessee Board of Probation and Parole. (2007). *Monitoring Tennessee's sex offenders using global positioning systems: An evaluative report.* Nashville, TN: Author.

Theriault v. Carlson, 495 F. 2d 390—Court of Appeals, 5th Circuit (1974).

Thompson v. Oklahoma, 487 U.S. 815 (1988).

Torres, S. (2005). Parole. In R. A. Wright & J. M. Mitchell (Eds.), *Encyclopedia of criminology.* New York: Routledge.

Townsend, C. K. (2003). Juvenile justice practitioners add value to communities. *Corrections Today, 65*(1), 40–43.

Trop v. Dulles, 356 U.S. 86 (1958).

Tucker, D. (1981). *A punk's song: View from the inside.* Fort Bragg, CA: AMS Press Inc.

Turner v. Safley, 482 U.S. 78 (1987).

United States v. Booker, 543 U.S. 220 (2005).

U.S. Census Bureau. (2000). Census 2000 redistricting data (P.L. 94-171). *Summary File for states, Tables PL1, PL2, PL3, and PL4.* Washington, DC: Author.

U.S. Census Bureau. (2006). State population estimates by demographic characteristics with 5 race groups (race alone or in combination groups): April 1, 2000 to July 1, 2005. Population Division. Retrieved May 8, 2007, from http://www.census.gov/popest/datasets.html

U.S. Congress. (2008). *United States Parole Commission Extension Act of 2008.* Washington, DC: Author. Retrieved from http://frwebgate.access.gpo.gov/cgi-bin/getdoc.cgi?dbname=110_cong_bills&docid=f:s3294enr.txt.pdf

U.S. Department of Justice. (1994). *Topics in community corrections: Mentally ill offenders in the community.* Washington, DC: National Institute of Corrections.

U.S. Department of Justice. (2001a). *Attorney general's remarks regarding the federal death penalty study.* Press conference with Attorney General Reno and Deputy Attorney General Holder, Topic: The Death Penalty (September 12).

U.S. Department of Justice. (2001b). *The federal death penalty system: Supplementary data, analysis and revised protocols for capital case review.* Washington, DC: Author.

U.S. Department of Justice. (2001c). *Survey of the federal death penalty system (1988–2000).* Washington, DC: Author.

U.S. Department of Justice. (2006). *Commonly asked questions about the American with Disabilities Act and law enforcement.* Washington, DC: Disability Rights Section. Retrieved from http://www.ada.gov/q&a_law.htm

U.S. Department of Justice, Bureau of Justice Statistics. (1994). *Special report: Women in prison.* Washington, DC.

U.S. Department of Justice, Civil Rights Division, Disability Rights Section. (2010). *Justice Department's 2010 ADA standards for accessible design go into effect.* Washington, DC: Author.

U.S. Sentencing Commission. (2007). *2007 federal guidelines manual.* Washington, DC: Author. Retrieved from http://www.ussc.gov/2007guid/CHAP5.html

Uzoaba, J. H. E. (1998). *Managing older offenders, where do we stand?* Montreal: Research Branch of Correctional Service of Canada.

Valdez, A. (2009). *Gangs: A guide to understanding street gangs* (5th ed.). San Clemente, CA: LawTech.

Van Baalen, S. M. (2008). Religious programming. In P. M. Carlson & J. S. Garrett (Eds.), *Prison and jail administration: Practice and theory* (pp. 127–138). Sudbury, MA: Jones & Bartlett.

Van Keulen, C. (1988). *Colorado alternative sentencing programs: Program guidelines.* Washington, DC: National Institute of Corrections. Retrieved from http://www.nicic.org/pubs/pre/007064.pdf

Vesely, R. (2004). California rebuked on female inmates. *Women's E-News.* Retrieved from http://www.womensenews.org/article.cfm/dyn/aid/2122/context/archive

Vitek v. Jones, 445 U.S. 480 (1980).

Vito, G. F., & Allen, H. E. (1981). Shock probation in Ohio: A comparison of outcomes. *International Journal of Offender Therapy and Comparative Criminology, 25,* 70–76.

Vold, G. B., Bernard, T. J., & Snipes, J. B. (1998). *Theoretical criminology* (4th ed.). New York: Oxford University Press.

Volkow, N. D. (2006). Treat the addict, cut the crime rate [Editorial]. *Washington Post*, August 19, p. A17.

Wallenstein, A. (1999). Intake and release in evolving jail practice. In P. M. Carlson & J. S. Garrett (Eds.), *Prison and jail administration: Practice and theory.* Gaithersburg, MD: Aspen.

Wallenstein, A., & Kerle, K. (2008). American jails. In P. M. Carlson & J. S. Garrett (Eds.), *Prison and jail administration* (2nd ed.), pp. 19–38. Gaithersburg, MD: Aspen.

Ward, D. A. (1994). Alcatraz and Marion: Confinement in super-maximum custody. In J. W. Roberts (Ed.), *Escaping prison myths: Selected topics in the history of federal corrections* (pp. 81–94). Washington, DC: American University Press.

Washington Department of Corrections. (2012). *Recreation program for offenders* (DOC 540.105). Olympia: Author.

Weisberg, J. (1991). This is your death. *The New Republic*, July 1.

Weisburd, D., & Chayet, E. F. (1996). Good time credit. In M. D. McShane & F. P. Williams (Eds.), *Encyclopedia of American prisons* (pp. 358–363). Taylor & Francis.

Weiss, C., & Friar, D. J. (1974). *Terror in prisons: Homosexual rape and why society condones it.* Indianapolis, IN: Bobbs-Merril, Inc.

West, H. C. (2010). *Prison inmates at midyear 2009—Statistical tables.* Washington, DC: Bureau of Justice Statistics.

Williams, D. J. (2003). The inclusion of strength training to offender substance abuse treatment: A pilot experiment conducted at a day reporting centre. *Empirical and Applied Criminal Justice Research Journal, 3*, 1–11.

Williams, D. J., & Strean, W. B. (2004). Physical activity as a helpful adjunct to substance abuse treatment. *Journal of Social Work Practice in the Addictions, 4*, 83–100.

Williams, D. J., Strean W. B., & Bengoechea, E. G. (2002). Understanding recreation and sport as a rehabilitative tool within juvenile justice programs. *Juvenile and Family Court Journal, 53*(2), 31–41.

Wilson, D. B., & MacKenzie, D. L. (2006). Boot camps. In B. C. Welsh & D. P. Farrington (Eds.), *Preventing crime: What works for children, offenders, victims and places* (pp. 73–86). Dordrecht, Netherlands: Springer.

Wilson, S. J., & Lipsey, M. W. (2000). Wilderness challenge programs for delinquent youth: A meta-analysis of outcome evaluations. *Evaluation and Program Planning, 23,* 1–12.

Wilson v. Seiter, 501 U.S. 294 (1991).

Winter, M. M. (2003). County jail suicides in a Midwestern state: Moving beyond the use of profiles. *The Prison Journal, 83*, 130–148.

Wintersteen, M. B., Diamond, G. S., & Fein, J. A. (2007). Screening for suicide risk in the pediatric emergency and acute care setting. *Current Opinion in Pediatrics, 19*(4), 398–404.

Witherspoon v. Illinois, 391 U.S. 510 (1968).

Wolff v. McDonnell, 418 U.S. 539 (1974).

Wolfgang, M. E. & Ferracuti, F. (1967). *The subculture of violence: Towards an integrated theory in criminology.* London: Tavistock.

Women's Prison Association. (2003). *A portrait of women in prison.* New York: Author.

Wooldredge, J. (1996). American Correctional Association. In M. D. McShane & F. P. Williams (Eds.), *Encyclopedia of American prisons* (pp. 45–52). London: Taylor & Francis.

Wright, R. A. (1994). *In defense of prisons.* Westport, CT: Greenwood Press.

Wright, R. L. (2008). A day in the life of a warden. In P. M. Carlson & J. S. Garrett (Eds.), *Prison and jail administration: Practice and theory* (pp. 235–242). Boston: Jones & Bartlett.

Young, V. D., & Reviere, R. (2001). Meeting the health care needs of the new woman inmate: A national survey of prison practices. *Journal of Offender Rehabilitation, 34,* 31–48.

Zupan, L. (1991). *Jails: Reform and the new generation philosophy.* Cincinnati, OH: Anderson.

Photo Credits

1: ©iStockphoto.com/ZU_09; **3:** ©iStockphoto.com/jsp; **6:** ©iStockphoto.com/Gene Chutka; **9:** © Bettman/CORBIS; **10:** © CORBIS; **12:** © Getty Images/Photos.com/Thinkstock; **15:** © Getty Images/Photos.com/Thinkstock (top), Original engraving done by Giuseppe Bossi, photo reproduction provided on Wikimedia commons by Jootsvandeputte (bottom); **18:** Artist Henry William Pickersgill (died 1879)/ Source via Wikimedia Commons/Dcoetzee; **19:** I. N. Phelps Stokes. Collection of American Historical Prints; **24:** AP Photo/Matt Rourke; **26:** Wikimedia Commons; **28:** Wikimedia Commons; **31:** New York State Archives. Education Dept. Division of Visual Instruction; **32:** Walter Bibikow/age footstock/Getty Images; **35:** Library of Congress, Prints & Photographs Division, Lomax Collection, [reproduction number LC-DIG-ppmsc-00346] (top), Arizona Leisure Vacation Guide, http://www.arizona-leisure.com/yuma-territorial-prison.html (bottom); **42:** Thesab/Wikimedia Commons; **44:** Federal Bureau of Prisons; **52:** ©iStockphoto.com/Francesco Carucci; **55:** © Larry Mulvehill/Corbis; **56:** © Scott Houston/Corbis; **58:** Robert Hanser; **62:** Per-Anders Pettersson/Edit/Getty Images; **63:** iStockphoto© Alina Solovyova-Vincent; **64:** Kevin Horan/Stone/Getty Images; **70:** AP Photo/*Corpus Christi Caller-Times*, Paul Iverson; **76:** ©iStockphoto.com/Frances Twitty; **78:** Steve Petteway, Collection of the Supreme Court of the United States; **80:** Robert Hanser: **83:** © Andrew Lichtenstein/Corbis; **87:** Robert Hanser; **88:** Thomas Northcut/Photodisk/Thinkstock; **90:** ©Tim Pannell/Corbis; **94:** iStockphoto© Moodboard_Images: **103:** Katie Orr/KPBS; **110:** Robert Hanser; **112:** Wikimedia Commons; **115:** © Andrew Lichtenstein/Corbis; **118:** Thinkstock Images/Comstock; **119:** Robert Hanser; **120:** Robert Hanser (top), © Jay LaPrete/AP/Corbis (bottom); **132:** Katie Orr/KPBS; **135:** NYC Department of Probation; **136:** Bulloch County, Georgia; **137:** iStockphoto© Ben Blankenburg; **138:** © Edmund D. Fountain/ZUMA Press/Corbis; **140:** © Joan Barnett Lee/ZUMA Press/Corbis; **142:** © Andri Tambunan/ZUMA Press/Corbis; **144:** Robert Hanser; **156:** © Brant Ward/*San Francisco Chronicle*/Corbis; **158:** iStockphoto© Deborah Cheramie; **164:** Robert Hanser; **165:** ©Gaetam Bally/Keystone/Corbis; **166:** Robert Hanser; **169:** Robert Hanser; **171:** AP Photo/Ann Heisenfelt; **180:** Comstock/Thinkstock Images; **183:** Wikimedia Commons (top and bottom); **184:** Wikimedia Commons (top and bottom); **187:** © Lizzie Himmel/Sygma/Corbis; **199:** Robert Hanser (top, middle, and bottom); **206:** AP Photo/Steve Ruark; **208:** Wikimedia Commons; **211:** iStockphoto/©Chris Schmidt; **212:** Robert Hanser; **217:** Robert Hanser (top and bottom); **219:** Robert Hanser; **222:** Robert Hanser; **228:** Robert Hanser; **234:** © Andrew Lichtenstein/Corbis; **238:** Baileys at http://www.baileysonline.com/blog/post/Prison-Blues-Clothing-Made-in-the-USA-with-an-Honorable-Mission.aspx (top), © Andrew Lichtenstein/Corbis (bottom); **239:** Robert Hanser; **246:** Robert Hanser; **250:** Robert Hanser; **256:** Comstock/Thinkstock; **258:** Orlando-Morningstar, D. (1997). Prison gangs. Special Needs Offenders Bulletin. Washington, DC: Federal Judicial Center. (top and bottom); **261:** AP Photo/Dirceu Portugal; **268:** Comstock/Thinkstock Images; **274:** Department of Education, Arts & Libraries London Borough of Barking & Dagenham. http://www.gac.culture.gov.uk/work.aspx?obj=29760; **278:** © Getty Images/Thinkstock Images/Comstock; **290:** Robert Hanser; **291:** AP Photo/*Columbus Dispatch*, Renee Sauer; **296:** AP Photo/Rich Pedroncelli; **303:** Getty Images Photographer Stephen Ferry; **305:** AP Photo/Steve Pope; **309:** AP Photo/Mick Groll; **316:** © F. Carter Smith/Sygma/Corbis; **320:** © Mark Peterson/CORBIS; **326:** © Bill Gentile/Corbis; **330:** Library of Congress; **331:** AP Photo/Suchat Pederson; **337:** AP Photo/David Branch; **338:** AP Photo/Mark Hertzberg; **339:** David Young-Wolff/Stone/Getty Images; **340:** © I Love Images/Corbis; **343:** © Reuters/CORBIS; **345:** © Michael Ainsworth/*Dallas Morning News*/Corbis; **348:** © Ed Kashi/Corbis; **354:** AP Photo/Wilfredo Lee; **360:** Robert Hanser (top and bottom); **363:** Per-Anders Pettersson/Edit/Getty Images; **373:** Robert Hanser; **376:** AP Photo/Michael Conroy; **382:** ©iStockphoto.com/Chris Johnson; **384:** Wikimedia Commons; **387:** © James Leynse/CORBIS; **392:** © Mike Groll/AP/CORBIS; **394:** © J.L. Sousa/ZUMA Press/CORBIS; **395:** *Sacramento Bee*/McClatchy-Tribune/Getty Images; **396:** © Mike Groll/AP/CORBIS; **404:** AP Photo/Andy Duback; **410:** AP Photo/*Watertown Daily Times*/John Hart; **416:** Robert Hanser; **420:** Kevork Djansezian/Getty Images; **424:** *New York Daily News* Archive/Getty Images (top), © Hilda Krus Photographer. Used with permission from Rikers Island (bottom); **425:** © Hilda Krus Photographer. Used with permission from Rikers Island (top and bottom); **428:** Robert Hanser; **429:** © Robin Nelson/ ZUMA/CORBIS; **430:** Robert Hanser; **436:** © Erin Tracy/ZUMA Press/CORBIS; **438:** Robert Hanser; **443:** AP Photo/Matt Gouras; **453:** Robert Hanser; **455:** Robert Hanser; **457:** Robert Hanser; **462:** AP Photo/Eric Risberg; **464:** © Greg Smith/CORBIS; **466:** © Mona Reeder/*Dallas Morning News*/CORBIS; **479:** © Reuters/CORBIS; **480:** © Mark Jenkinson/CORBIS; **481:** © Mark Jenkinson/CORBIS; **482:** Wikimedia Commons; **490:** ©iStockphoto.com/mediaphotos; **494:** Robert Hanser; **503:** Robert Hanser (top and bottom)

Index

B

Babylonian codes of law, 3
Baird, S.C., 210
Balanced justice, 88
Ball, R.A., 405
Banishment, 9, 11-12, 439
Bar-coding technology, 202
Barfield, Velma, 475
Barnes, H.E., 440
Barrio Azteca, 254, 259
Barton, B., 451
Bastille, 15, 50, 182-183
Bates, Sanford, 44
Batson v. Kentucky, 465
Battered woman's syndrome, 275
Baxter v. Palmigiano, 86
Bazos, Audrey, 386
Beard v. Banks, 82
Beaumont, Gustave de, 208
Beccaria, Cesare, 14-16, 68, 81, 389, 485
Beck, A.J., 278, 281
Bedford Hills Correctional Facility, 425
Beets, Betty Lou, 475
Behavior management, 418
Behavioral psychology, 17, 68
Bell v. Wolfish, 83, 88
Bentham, Jeremy, 14, 17-18, 26, 68, 184, 485
Bernard, T.J., 237
"Big Four" in corrections, 46-47, 470
Big House prisons, 42-43
Binder, R.L., 125
Bipolar disorder, 307
Birth control, 401
Black Codes, 32
Black Guerilla Family, 254, 257
Blind spots, 198
Block, Lynda, 475
Blood feud, 8, 10
"Blood in–blood out," 238, 255
Blood testing, for drugs, 169
Bloods, 254, 258
"Bloody Code," 11
Bloom, B., 287
Body cavity search, 84
Boiling water, ordeal of, 4
Booking
    of female inmates, 113
    information technology and integration for, 114
Booking area, 112-113
Booth v. Churner, 87
BOP. *See* Federal Bureau of Prisons
Bounds v. Smith, 80
Bowers, W.J., 485
Bradley, John, 483
Braille factory, 395
Braithwaite, John, 70, 440
Brandford, C., 335
Branding, 9-10
Breathalyzers, 170
Breed v. Jones, 331-332
Brennan, T., 213
Breyer, Stephen G., 78, 344
Bridle, 8
Brockway, Zebulon, 37, 385, 419

Brown, J.W., 281
Bruscino v. Carlson, 187
Brutalization hypothesis, 2, 485-487
"Bug juice," 244
Building tenders, 40, 252
Bulman, P., 257
Bureau of Prisons. *See* Federal Bureau of Prisons
Bureaucratic model, of prison management, 365-366
Burger, Warren F., 384
Butterfield, F., 221

C

Cafeteria, 199
Cage imprisonment, 4
California
    death penalty system in, 470-471
    drug treatment effects on violent crime and
        incarceration in, 417
    modern-day prison population in, 46
    San Quentin State Prison, 255, 257
California Youth Authority, 258-259
Camp Kourou, 50-51
Canada, 129-130, 461, 482
Capital punishment
    banishment, 11-12
    early history of, 9, 11
    examples of, 11
    in federal criminal cases, 478-479
    of juveniles, 328
Capitoline Hill, 5
Capone, Al, 186
Carcer, 5
Carl D. Perkins Vocational and Applied Technology
        Education Act Amendments of 1990, 387
Carlson, P.M., 35, 87, 201, 366, 372
Carmen, R., 441, 457
CARS. *See* Custody Assessment and Reclassification System
Case law implementation, of evidence-based practices,
        499-500
Case management software, 454
Case managers, 218, 451-453
Cat-o'-nine-tails, 11, 13
Caucasians
    female offenders, 277-278
    killing of, by African Americans, 475-478
    on death row, 474
CCTV systems. *See* Closed-circuit television systems
Cell blocks
    dome technology design of, 189
    inmate tracking around, 202
    prison guard's responsibilities for controlling, 43
Center for Sex Offender Management, 171
Central East Correctional Centre, 129-130
Centralized management, 367-368
Chain gangs, 34
Chamlin, M.B., 485
Chancery courts, 329
Chandler, David Ronald, 478
Chapin, Charles, 423
Chaplains, 429-430
Chemical detoxification, 412
Cherry Hill facility. *See* Eastern Penitentiary
Chicago Reform School Act, 330
Child abuse, 337-338

⑤SAGE researchmethods

The essential online tool for researchers from the world's leading methods publisher

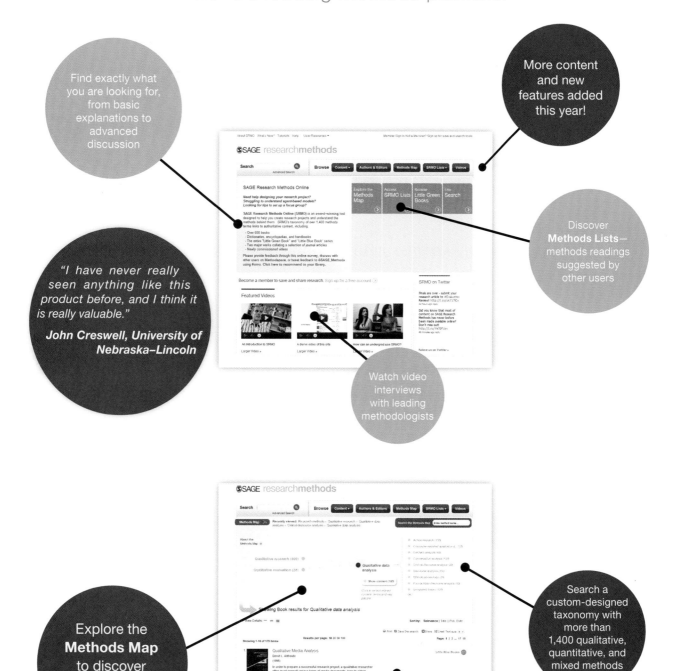

Find exactly what you are looking for, from basic explanations to advanced discussion

More content and new features added this year!

"I have never really seen anything like this product before, and I think it is really valuable."

John Creswell, University of Nebraska–Lincoln

Discover **Methods Lists**— methods readings suggested by other users

Watch video interviews with leading methodologists

Explore the **Methods Map** to discover links between methods

Search a custom-designed taxonomy with more than 1,400 qualitative, quantitative, and mixed methods terms

Uncover more than 120,000 pages of book, journal, and reference content to support your learning

Find out more at
www.sageresearchmethods.com